PRETRIAL

ASPEN COURSEBOOK SERIES

PRETRIAL

Ninth Edition

THOMAS A. MAUET
Director of Trial Advocacy
and Riepe Professor of Law
University of Arizona
Rogers College of Law

DAVID MARCUS
Professor of Law
University of Arizona
Rogers College of Law

Wolters Kluwer

Published by Wolters Kluwer in New York.

Wolters Kluwer serves customers worldwide with CCH, Aspen Publishers, and Kluwer Law International products. (www.wolterskluwerlb.com)

To contact Customer Service, e-mail customer.service@wolterskluwer.com, call 1-800-234-1660, fax 1-800-901-9075, or mail correspondence to:

> Wolters Kluwer
> Attn: Order Department
> PO Box 990
> Frederick, MD 21705

Printed in the United States of America.

1 2 3 4 5 6 7 8 9 0

ISBN 978-1-4548-5633-7

Library of Congress Cataloging-in-Publication Data

Mauet, Thomas A., author.
Pretrial / Thomas A. Mauet, Director of Trial Advocacy and Riepe Professor of Law, University of Arizona; David Marcus, Professor of Law, University of Arizona, Rogers College of Law. — Ninth Edition.
      pages cm
   Includes bibliographical references and index.
   ISBN 978-1-4548-5633-7 (alk. paper)
1. Pre-trial procedure — United States. I. Marcus, David Wright, 1976- author. II. Title. III. Title: Pre-trial.
KF8900.M386 2015
347.73'72 — dc23
                                                                            2014042655

Certified Chain of Custody
Product Line Contains At Least
20% Certified Forest Content
www.sfiprogram.org
SFI-00756

About Wolters Kluwer Law & Business

Wolters Kluwer Law & Business is a leading global provider of intelligent information and digital solutions for legal and business professionals in key specialty areas, and respected educational resources for professors and law students. Wolters Kluwer Law & Business connects legal and business professionals as well as those in the education market with timely, specialized authoritative content and information-enabled solutions to support success through productivity, accuracy and mobility.

Serving customers worldwide, Wolters Kluwer Law & Business products include those under the Aspen Publishers, CCH, Kluwer Law International, Loislaw, ftwilliam.com and MediRegs family of products.

CCH products have been a trusted resource since 1913, and are highly regarded resources for legal, securities, antitrust and trade regulation, government contracting, banking, pension, payroll, employment and labor, and healthcare reimbursement and compliance professionals.

Aspen Publishers products provide essential information to attorneys, business professionals and law students. Written by preeminent authorities, the product line offers analytical and practical information in a range of specialty practice areas from securities law and intellectual property to mergers and acquisitions and pension/benefits. Aspen's trusted legal education resources provide professors and students with high-quality, up-to-date and effective resources for successful instruction and study in all areas of the law.

Kluwer Law International products provide the global business community with reliable international legal information in English. Legal practitioners, corporate counsel and business executives around the world rely on Kluwer Law journals, looseleafs, books, and electronic products for comprehensive information in many areas of international legal practice.

Loislaw is a comprehensive online legal research product providing legal content to law firm practitioners of various specializations. Loislaw provides attorneys with the ability to quickly and efficiently find the necessary legal information they need, when and where they need it, by facilitating access to primary law as well as state-specific law, records, forms and treatises.

ftwilliam.com offers employee benefits professionals the highest quality plan documents (retirement, welfare and non-qualified) and government forms (5500/PBGC, 1099 and IRS) software at highly competitive prices.

MediRegs products provide integrated health care compliance content and software solutions for professionals in healthcare, higher education and life sciences, including professionals in accounting, law and consulting.

Wolters Kluwer Law & Business, a division of Wolters Kluwer, is headquartered in New York. Wolters Kluwer is a market-leading global information services company focused on professionals.

To my father, Rudolf B. Mauet
(T.M.)

To my father, Howard Marcus, who would
have been a great lawyer
(D.M.)

SUMMARY OF CONTENTS

CONTENTS

IV. CASE EVALUATION AND STRATEGY

PART B
CONDUCTING THE LITIGATION   121

V. PLEADINGS

VI. DISCOVERY

VII. MOTIONS

PREFACE

New lawyers quickly encounter an uncomfortable reality: A civil procedure course in law school only begins to prepare them for the twists and turns of civil litigation. For civil litigators, rules of procedure are not abstract subjects for academic study, but functional tools that regulate the pretrial stage of the litigation process. The new litigator's primary worry is that he or she might misunderstand or botch a step in pretrial litigation and thereby "miss the boat."

This book aims to ensure that new litigators do not miss the boat. Whether a third-year law student in a clinical program or a litigator in the first years of practice, you must approach every lawsuit systematically to make sure that you think through all important considerations and take all timely steps during the investigation, pleading, discovery, and motion practice stages of the pre-trial process. Only by doing so can you adequately prepare for settlement or trial. This text approaches pretrial litigation in just this systematic way. It reviews the procedural rules and thought processes a litigator should utilize before and during each stage of a civil case. In addition, this text discusses and gives examples of how an understanding of the various stages of civil litigation translates into pleadings, discovery, and motions.

There is no one "right way" to litigate. Consequently, while this book presents standard approaches to pleadings, motions, and discovery, lawyers litigate effectively in a myriad of ways. The examples presented here offer only one approach and simply illustrate how a lawyer can successfully proceed step-by-step through the litigation process.

This text is of necessity an overview of the basic steps in the civil litigation process. Because any single-volume work must limit the space it can devote to any specific topic, compromises and hard choices were inevitable. In making them, we followed a basic rule: Provide an overview that gives inexperienced litigators the basic information they need to handle routine civil cases. To determine what we believe new litigators *need* to know, we reflected on our beginning years as litigators, and we discussed the book's scope with a number of inexperienced lawyers. Sometimes their suggestions were surprising. For example, almost all recommended an overview of joinder, jurisdiction, and venue, since these are complex, technical areas. These new lawyers did not mean to suggest that some topics were more important than others; rather, they felt they were weak in some areas and stronger in others. In many ways their suggestions corresponded with our experiences and account in large measure for the text's coverage.

The text focuses on federal district court practice and the Federal Rules of Civil Procedure. Many states have adopted the Federal Rules, and most of the states that have not have modern code pleading rules that resemble federal practice. Also, legal details do not matter for much of the book's contents. Solid planning, investigation, and drafting are essential skills regardless of the particular jurisdiction involved, and the text's emphasis is on those skills. Hence, we have designed the book to be a basic resource regardless of the jurisdiction where a case will be litigated.

This book is not intended as a reference manual for nuanced legal research. We cite lightly, certainly as compared to standard treatises, since our goals do not include a detailed, technical discussion of doctrine. We have provided basic citations for most topics, with an emphasis on treatises that litigators commonly use. These are Wright; Hazard et al.; Moore's Manual; the Manual of Federal Practice; Moore's Federal Practice; and Wright & Miller. Most topics discussed in this text begin with a footnote that provides citations to the relevant portions of these treatises.

This edition comes with an authorization to download *Materials in Pretrial Litigation*, which include six tort and contract case files that can be used in a course on pretrial litigation. These materials contain the plaintiff's and the defendant's initial case files. The Teacher's Manual includes the witness materials for these case files. Course instructors may obtain this manual from Wolters Kluwer.

Thomas A. Mauet and David Marcus

What's New in the Ninth Edition

Tom Mauet published the first edition of *Pretrial* in 1987, and he remained the book's sole author for the next seven editions. During this time, experiential courses on pretrial litigation have spread like wildfire in American law schools. This phenomenon surely reflects the gravitational shift from trial to pretrial as the center of the civil litigation process. But the proliferation of these courses also indicates the influence of Tom's book. Not only is *Pretrial* required reading at many law schools, it also offers a model for how to teach essential lawyering skills in an intellectually sophisticated, yet relentlessly grounded, way. Even courses that use other materials bear the hallmarks of Tom's influence. For all that it offers law students and lawyers, *Pretrial* has won a coveted spot on many litigators' bookshelves, next to Tom's texts on evidence and trial practice.

For these reasons and others, I am excited and humbled to join Tom as his co-author on the ninth edition of *Pretrial.* I bring to the book a decade of experience teaching and writing on civil procedure, as well as lessons learned from my several years in practice as a civil litigator. Tom continues to provide ideas, suggest edits, offer advice, and contribute research. But he has turned primary responsibility for revisions over to me.

I have taken a "first do no harm" approach to this edition. Thousands of lawyers around the United States would agree that no one teaches how to litigate as well as Tom. I have left the book's organization, its overall themes, its flow, and its style mostly untouched. Tom is also a masterful strategist, so I have only lightly edited those sections that focus on litigation strategy.

The changes I have made for this edition fit into one of three categories. The first are minor stylistic edits, mostly to reflect my authorial voice. These edits appear throughout the text.

Second, in several places I have adjusted the way prior editions have presented applicable doctrine. These places include, for example, sections on choice of law in the federal courts, federal pleading doctrine, and class action doctrine. The revisions are to topics about which I have written at length. In a couple of instances I view the law somewhat differently than Tom does, but most of my changes are in the vein of modest refinements or clarifications.

Third, I have revised the text to account for a number of recent changes to the law of federal civil procedure. Among others, these include:

- Significant developments in the law of personal jurisdiction. Since the eighth edition, the Supreme Court has issued a number of important decisions on personal jurisdiction issues. I have rewritten relevant sections of *Pretrial* to account for the new clarity the Court has given to general jurisdiction, and to indicate where this law remains in flux.

- Adjustments to venue and removal jurisdiction law. In 2011 Congress made a number of changes to the federal venue and removal jurisdiction statutes. This edition accounts for these changes.

- Changes to class action practice. The Supreme Court has paid close attention to the class action in recent years. The ninth edition includes more commentary on class action doctrine than previous editions, and this commentary reflects the alterations the Supreme Court has made to practice under Rule 23 of the Federal Rules of Civil Procedure.

- The continuing evolution of federal pleading doctrine. The eighth edition discussed the Supreme Court's well-known *Twombly* and *Iqbal* decisions on the federal pleading standard. These decisions caused a good deal of ferment in federal procedural law, which had not died down before the eighth edition's date of publication. This edition presents an emerging consensus on the two decisions and their implications for pleading.

- Amendments and proposed amendments to the Federal Rules of Civil Procedure. The Supreme Court has approved minor changes to the Federal Rules since the eighth edition's publication, mostly to the rule regarding subpoenas issued to non-parties. As this edition went to press, however, fairly significant proposed amendments were pending, with a good chance of getting promulgated. I have tried to note in the text each instance where a proposed amendment would alter the law.

As Tom has before, I welcome any suggestions for how we might improve *Pretrial* in the future. Comments from practitioners are particularly welcome. Please do not hesitate to contact me by e-mail (dmarcus@email.arizona.edu) if you have any suggestions for future editions.

David Marcus

Tucson, Arizona
November 2014

CITATIONS

For ease in citing, the text uses the following abbreviated citations:

Wright
  Law of Federal Courts, Charles Alan Wright & Mary Kay Kane (6th ed. 2002)

James & Hazard
  Civil Procedure, Fleming James, Jr., Geoffrey C. Hazard, Jr. & John Leubsdorf (5th ed. 2001)

Friedenthal
  Civil Procedure, Jack H. Friedenthal, Mary Kay Kane & Arthur R. Miller (4th ed. 2005)

Moore's Manual
  Moore's Manual — Federal Practice and Procedure, James W. Moore, Allan D. Vestal & Philip B. Kurland (supplemented semi-annually)

Manual of Federal Practice
  Manual of Federal Practice, Richard A. Givens (5th ed.), which is part of Trial Practice Series (supplemented annually)

Moore's Federal Practice
  Moore's Federal Practice, James W. Moore, et al. (3d ed.) (updated quarterly)

Wright & Miller
  Federal Practice and Procedure: Civil, Charles Alan Wright, Arthur R. Miller, and E.H. Cooper (updated annually)

PRETRIAL

Part A
INVESTIGATING AND PLANNING THE LITIGATION

I
INTRODUCTION TO LITIGATION PLANNING

§1.1. Introduction

A partner in the firm that recently hired you has just called you into her office. She tells you that a prospective client who has a "problem" that might lead to litigation will be coming into the office soon. This problem, the partner says, appears to be just right for you to manage. With a smile, she hands you a note containing the prospective client's name and appointment time. Apprehensively you walk out of her office, thinking, "My God. What do I do now?"

What you do, when you do it, how you do it, and why you do it is what this book on civil pretrial litigation is all about. This first chapter offers an overview of the litigation process and discusses how to organize a coordinated litigation plan. The other chapters discuss each step in the plan in detail.

§1.2. Organizing litigation planning

Litigation planning addresses two basic questions. First, what overall litigation strategy will best serve the client's realistically attainable goals? Second, how does each part of the litigation plan contribute toward achieving those goals? Addressing these two questions early, and constantly keeping the answers to them in mind, will do much to develop and implement an intelligent, realistic, and cost-effective litigation plan.

An effective litigation plan obviously requires structure. This structure should trigger the sort of analysis you should undertake at key moments in the case, so that you will not "miss the boat" during any step in the litigation process. The basic steps in this plan are listed here, followed by a discussion of each step.

1. Establish the terms of the attorney-client relationship
2. Determine the client's needs and priorities

3. Determine the elements of potential claims, remedies, defenses, and counterclaims
4. Identify likely sources of proof
5. Determine what informal fact investigation is necessary
6. Determine what formal discovery is necessary
7. Identify solutions
8. Develop a litigation strategy
9. Make litigation cost and timetable estimates
10. Use a litigation file system

1.   Establish the terms of the attorney-client relationship

The first step in any litigation plan is to formally establish the attorney-client relationship. You must do so in writing, unless the client is a regular client with whom you have an established business relationship. An attorney-client agreement is a contract between the attorney and client, and general contract principles apply.

The agreement should spell out who the client is, who will do the work for the client, what work will be done, how you will be compensated, and when the client will be billed for costs and legal work. All too often either lawyers do not reach clear understandings with clients, or the agreement does not cover all likely issues, causing serious problems later. Representing a client in litigation is hard enough without client relationship problems adding to the difficulties.

Before entering into an agreement, of course, you must first decide if you should take the case. In a simple case you can frequently make an intelligent decision after interviewing the potential client and reviewing available records. For example, in a personal injury case arising out of an automobile accident, you can probably determine whether the client's case has merit by interviewing the client and by reviewing available records, such as police reports and medical records. More complicated cases may require substantial factual and legal investigation. For example, in a medical malpractice or product liability case, the common practice is to send all the records about the patient or product to an appropriate expert for evaluation before deciding whether to take the case.

Establishing the attorney-client agreement is discussed in §4.3.

2.   Determine the client's needs and priorities

People seek out lawyers when they have problems that need to be managed and solved. The lawyer, therefore, should first identify the client's problems and needs, viewing them broadly. The client's needs, seen from his perspective, may well conflict with possible solutions. But finding out what the client wants to have happen is the beginning step in dealing with the problems that brought him to a lawyer in the first place.

You should always keep in mind the client's immediate and long-term needs and interests. Clients often demand a lawsuit against every imagined wrongdoer, when any lawsuit may be against the client's best interests. You should assess what can be gained from a lawsuit and then see how a lawsuit would affect the client in the long term. For example, consider the frequently encountered situation of a client who wishes to sue another party with whom the client has an ongoing business relationship. While the particular matter may have merit, a lawsuit may jeopardize that valuable relationship and adversely affect current deals with that party. A lawsuit may vindicate the client on one deal but not make sense for their overall relationship.

You will also need to assess the client's priorities. Clients rarely get everything they want, so they must develop a scale of priorities that will help you fashion the litigation strategy. For example, suppose your client wants to sue another party over a contract dispute. Does she want a quick, inexpensive resolution to preserve an ongoing relationship? Does she simply want the other party to live up to the agreement, or does she want money damages because she considers the relationship destroyed? These possibilities must be arranged to reflect their relative importance to the client before you can sensibly decide how best to help that client.

Determining the client's needs and priorities is discussed in §2.3.

3. Determine the elements of potential claims, remedies, defenses, and counterclaims

The initial client interview will often identify the legal areas that the potential case involves. At this early stage, think expansively and consider all legal theories that might apply to the case. For example, while a "contract case" will obviously involve contract claims, it might also involve UCC claims; state and federal statutory claims, such as securities and product safety statutes; and business torts. Your initial thinking should include all of them.

After you have identified the possible applicable legal theories, determine what the legal requirements are for each theory. The applicable jurisdiction's jury instructions are particularly helpful here. Most jurisdictions have approved pattern jury instructions for commonly asserted claims and defenses. These instructions will tell you what the required elements are for a particular claim or defense. If pattern instructions are unavailable, you should consult practice manuals that cover the particular field or research the cases and statutes to learn the elements for the applicable law.

Remedies require the same type of analysis. The availability of remedies relates to the choice of claims, and some remedies are broader than others. For example, contract damages are available in contract disputes. If the dispute has fraud aspects, however, you may be able to bring a business tort claim and have broader damages rules apply. Statutory claims may permit the prevailing party to recover attorney's fees and costs. In litigation, particularly complex litigation, the nature of the remedies frequently influences whether the pleadings include a particular claim.

Consider potential counterclaims as well. Before bringing a lawsuit, always determine what the other side has against your client. This is particularly important in commercial litigation, where the parties have dealt with each other many times over a period of time. There is little point in starting a lawsuit if it provokes a large, previously dormant counterclaim.

Evaluating potential claims, remedies, defenses, and counterclaims is discussed in §3.3.

After you have identified the possible applicable legal theories and the elements for each of them, it is best to set up some type of litigation chart, or diagram, to list the theories and elements. For experienced litigators planning routine cases, this chart may be unnecessary. New litigators, however, should develop a chart system to analyze cases systematically from the beginning, by correlating the elements of claims, defenses and counterclaims with sources of proof, informal fact investigation, and formal discovery. A fully developed litigation chart will form the basis for your trial chart, should the case eventually go to trial.[1] For now, the chart guides your strategic litigation planning. Litigation charts are commonly organized like the one below.

Example:

You represent the plaintiff in an automobile negligence case.[2]

LITIGATION CHART

Elements of Claims, Defenses, and Counterclaims	Sources of Proof	Informal Fact Investigation	Formal Discovery
1. Negligence			
(a) negligence			
(b) causation			
(c) damages			
(1) lost income			
(2) med. expenses			
(3) disability			
(4) pain and suffering			

1. See Thomas A. Mauet, Trial Techniques and Trials §11.4 (9th ed. 2013).
2. The elements of a negligence claim are duty, breach of duty, proximate cause, injury, and damages. Duty is a legal question, however, so the terminology used here better fits the trial proof.

The chart should be continued for each potential claim, defense, and counterclaim. Developing a litigation chart is discussed in §2.2.

4. Identify likely sources of proof

Most litigation involves events or transactions that have occurred in the past. The likely sources of proof will particularly include those witnesses who have some knowledge of, and exhibits that contain information about, past events or transactions.

The usual witness sources include your client, other witnesses to the events or transactions, the opposing parties, witnesses who have no direct knowledge of the events or transactions but may have useful circumstantial information, and experts. Exhibit sources include physical objects, photographs, police reports, business records, transaction documents, and any other paperwork that has a bearing on the events or transactions involved. At this stage it is best to think expansively. Develop a long, thorough list early and refine it over time.

Finally, list the likely sources of proof of the elements of each possible legal theory on your developing litigation chart.

LITIGATION CHART

Elements of Claims, Defenses, and Counterclaims	Sources of Proof	Informal Fact Investigation	Formal Discovery
1. Negligence			
(a) negligence	plaintiff police officers bystanders defendant		
(b) causation	plaintiff defendant treating doctors police officers police reports		
(c) damages			
(1) lost income	plaintiff employer employment records		

(2) med. expenses	med. bills treating doctors pharmacy bills		
(3) disability	plaintiff treating doctors employment records		
(4) pain and suffering	plaintiff treating doctors		

Identifying the likely sources of proof is discussed in §2.2.4.

5. Determine what informal fact investigation is necessary

Once you have identified the likely sources of proof, you then need to decide how to acquire information from those sources. Your choices are twofold: informal fact investigation and formal discovery.

Inexperienced litigators frequently use formal discovery as the principal fact-gathering method. This approach is often a serious mistake. A lawyer should always acquire as much information as possible *before* filing suit, when formal discovery methods usually are unavailable. As a defendant, you will most likely begin the investigation after the suit has begun, but you should still consider informal sources of proof. Rule 11 of the Federal Rules of Civil Procedure requires that a lawyer make "an inquiry reasonable under the circumstances" to determine if a pleading has a basis in fact before signing the pleading.

Informal fact investigations are principally conducted by interviewing witnesses; by obtaining documents, records, and other data from willing sources; and by getting expert reviews of the case. These investigations have advantages and disadvantages. On one hand, they are relatively quick and inexpensive and can be done without the presence of other parties. This efficiency is important because evidence can become lost unless identified and obtained quickly. On the other hand, while such investigations can yield important information, this information does not usually come in a form that makes it directly admissible at trial. For example, a written statement from a witness during an interview is not normally admissible. At best, the statement is useful at trial for impeachment.

When you have identified the witnesses and exhibits that are best reached through informal investigations, note on your litigation chart how you plan to get the necessary information from those sources.

LITIGATION CHART

Elements of Claims, Defenses, and Counterclaims	Sources of Proof	Informal Fact Investigation	Formal Discovery
1. Negligence			
(a) negligence	plaintiff police officers bystanders defendant	interview interview interview	
(b) causation	plaintiff defendant treating doctors police officers police reports	Interview interview interview request letter	
(c) damages			
(1) lost income	plaintiff employer employment records	interview interview request letter	
(2) med. expenses	med. bills treating doctors pharmacy bills	pl. possession interview pl. possession	
(3) disability	plaintiff treating doctors employment records	interview interview request letter	
(4) pain and suffering	plaintiff treating doctors	interview interview	

Informal fact investigations are discussed in Chapter 2.

6. Determine what formal discovery is necessary

Formal discovery can ordinarily begin only after suit has been filed. For that reason, it is the last stage of the fact-gathering process. Formal discovery also has benefits and risks. On the upside, it is usually the only way to get information from the opposing party and other hostile or uncooperative witnesses. In addition, information obtained in discovery is often in a form that makes it admissible at trial. For example, obtaining business records from an opposing party or a nonparty will generate an admissible exhibit. On the downside, formal discovery is time-consuming and expensive. In a case with a modest litigation budget, formal discovery may be substantially limited because of its cost.

Once you have decided which witnesses and exhibits require formal discovery to access, you have to decide which discovery method to use to obtain the necessary information. Each of the formal discovery methods — initial disclosures, interrogatories, document requests, depositions, physical and mental examinations, and requests to admit facts — is particularly suited for gathering certain types of information. Cost efficiency and effectiveness require that you carefully select and use the methods in the proper sequence.

Formal discovery serves two purposes: to obtain information you need to get but don't have, and to pin down your opponent and other witnesses on facts you already have. You will need to use formal discovery to obtain missing information from your opponent and uncooperative witnesses and other sources. You will want to pin down your opponent to learn where the key factual disputes in the case will be and to meet your burden of proof more easily if the case goes to trial. Although they overlap, each discovery method is particularly suited for certain kinds of information.

The Federal Rules of Civil Procedure recognize six discovery methods:

1. Initial disclosures — Rule 26
2. Interrogatories — Rule 33
3. Requests to produce documents, electronically stored information, and tangible things — Rule 34
4. Depositions — Rule 30
5. Physical and mental examinations — Rule 35
6. Requests to admit facts and genuineness of documents — Rule 36

Initial disclosures include four categories of information: the identity of persons likely to have discoverable information; copies or descriptions of documents, data compilations, and tangible things; a computation of claimed damages; and insurance agreements. Initial disclosures are automatic and do not require a request or any action from the other side.

Interrogatories most effectively obtain basic factual data from other parties, such as the identity of proper parties, agents, employees, witnesses, and experts, and the identity, description, and location of documents, records, and tangible evidence. They may usefully seek other parties' positions on disputed facts. On the other hand, interrogatories are not usually effective instruments for getting detailed impressions and versions of events.

A request to produce documents, electronically stored information, and tangible things is the discovery method by which one obtains from another party copies of records, documents, data, and other tangible things for inspection, copying, and testing. Such a request also permits an entry on another person's land or property to inspect, photograph, and analyze things on it.

Depositions can be used for nonparty witnesses as well as parties. They are most effective in obtaining details, tying down parties and witnesses to details, and discovering everything they know pertinent to the case. A deposition is the only discovery vehicle that permits you to assess how good a witness a person is likely to be at trial. It is an excellent vehicle to secure admissions or other evidence favorable to your side. Further, a deposition is the only method that preserves testimony if a witness becomes unavailable for trial.

A physical or mental examination of a party can be obtained by court order when the physical or mental condition of that party is in controversy, a situation most common in personal injury cases. While other discovery methods can be used to get records of past examinations, this is the only means to force a party to be examined and tested prospectively. For that reason a physical or mental examination is the best method to evaluate such damages elements as permanence, extent of injury, medical prognosis.

Finally, a request to admit facts forces a party to admit or deny facts or a document's genuineness. Requests to admit are used principally to pin down the other party to specific facts, and thereby to learn what facts the other party will concede or dispute at trial. An admitted fact is deemed conclusively admitted for the purpose of the pending trial. This method is effective if limited to simple factual data, such as the dates of someone's employment or the genuineness of signatures on a contract. It is not useful for opinions or evaluative information.

When you have identified the witnesses and exhibits you will target with formal discovery methods, note on your litigation chart what discovery methods you plan to use to obtain the missing information. You might also annotate your litigation chart by putting question marks next to topics that you are unsure of or by writing in numbers to reflect your planned discovery sequence.

LITIGATION CHART

Elements of Claims, Defenses, and Counterclaims	Sources of Proof	Informal Fact Investigation	Formal Discovery
1. Negligence			
(a) negligence	plaintiff police officers bystanders defendant	interview interview interview	deposition? deposition & interrogatories
(b) causation	plaintiff defendant treating doctors police officers police reports	interview interview interview request letter	deposition deposition?
(c) damages			
(1) lost income	plaintiff employer employment records	interview interview request letter	request to admit
(2) med. expenses	med. bills treating doctors pharmacy bills	pl. possession interview pl. possession	deposition? request to admit

(3) disability	plaintiff treating doctors employment records	interview interview request letter	deposition?
(4) pain and suffering	plaintiff treating doctors	interview interview	deposition?

Formal discovery is discussed in Chapter 6.

7. Identify solutions

Litigation is only one of many ways to deal with conflict. Before deciding to litigate, you should consider your client's problems in broad terms to determine what approach will best serve the client's immediate and long-term interests. Discuss various approaches with your client, who ultimately gets to decide what to do. There are several basic possibilities:

1. Do nothing
2. Seek an informal resolution
3. Seek formal dispute resolution
4. Litigate

Doing nothing is always an option. The case may simply be too high-risk. The amount realistically recoverable may not be enough to justify the cost of seeking it. In addition, the noneconomic costs should always be assessed. Your client may not have the resolve for a lengthy fight. He may not want to take his time and that of others away from other pressing concerns. He may have more important ongoing business, professional, or personal relationships with the adversary. Finally, negative publicity surrounding the disputed matter may make litigation prohibitive. If you decide that doing nothing is the best course, let the client know and get his agreement in writing so you can formally end the case and your representation.

If your client decides to push ahead, you should always consider an attempt to resolve the dispute informally. Your adversary may also wish to avoid a lengthy, expensive battle. He may admit liability and only dispute damages. Always consider informal solutions before battle lines are drawn. Often a concise, respectful, but firm letter to the adversary, explaining why your client feels aggrieved, can produce a quick and satisfying solution. The fact that your client has gone to the trouble of getting a lawyer to help can signal powerfully to the adversary that your client is serious about the problem. The adversary may prove particularly receptive to an informal resolution.

If informal solutions are impossible, think next about alternative dispute resolution, such as mediation, arbitration, and summary trials. These can be relatively quick and inexpensive. Commercial contracts frequently require them. Many consumer form contracts also include provisions that require parties to arbitrate their disputes. By getting an impartial, experienced outside party involved, the adversaries can frequently get advisory opinions or binding decisions on both liability and damages.

The last possibility is formal litigation. Keep in mind that litigation is expensive and time-consuming and that even the winning litigant is rarely made whole. The client must understand these realities. The worst thing that can happen is for a lawyer to yield quickly to a client's insistence to sue, only to have that client become disinterested, then uncooperative, as the realities of litigation set in. The only safe way to protect against this outcome is to develop a litigation strategy, litigation budget, and litigation timetable and have your client approve them before starting the lawsuit.

Identifying solutions is discussed in §4.5.

8. Develop a litigation strategy

Up to now you have been thinking expansively, to ensure you are not "missing the boat" on anything that might influence the case. If you and the client have decided that litigation is the only solution, it is time to focus your thinking and begin making choices.

Assume that your client has valid claims, that attempts to resolve them informally have failed, and that the client agrees to pursue litigation. What do you do now?

Everything you do in litigation must have a purpose. A common mistake inexperienced litigators make is to conduct litigation mechanically so that it becomes an end unto itself, rather than becoming a means to an end. Always ask yourself two questions. What are my client's goals in this lawsuit? How does each decision I make help achieve those goals? Only if you constantly focus on the desired result will the individual steps in the process help achieve it. Perhaps the easiest way to think of litigation strategy is to consider its principal parts:

1. Where can I file the lawsuit?
2. What claims, defenses, or counterclaims should I plead?
3. How extensive should discovery be?
4. What motions should I plan?
5. When should I explore settlement?

First, where can you bring the lawsuit? Can you bring the case in federal court, state court, or both? Some types of claims can only be brought in federal court, some can only be brought in state court, and still others can be brought in both federal and state courts. Where geographically should you file suit? There are advantages and disadvantages that you must consider when you have a choice. While this choice is mainly the plaintiff's, the defendant may have some say in the matter as well by. He can remove the case from state to federal court, for example, or move to have the case transferred to a different forum.

Second, how "big" a lawsuit do you want? You will make this decision at the pleading stage. A world of difference divides a simple contract case involving two parties and a complex commercial case involving multiple parties. You have to keep in mind the consequences of your pleadings. Multiple claims frequently require multiple parties, which in turn usually generate extensive pleadings, discovery, and motions. Just because the claims are there does not necessarily require that you assert them. Also, litigation must be cost conscious. Inexperienced litigators sometimes allege every conceivable claim. Expensive, time-consuming litigation can result, which may not be in the client's best interests. As you think about the pleadings, review your litigation chart, see which claims and remedies are the most meritorious, and structure a lawsuit that will serve the client's objectives and that is feasible in light of the client's economic resources.

These pre-filing considerations boil down to several basic questions:

1. What parties must or can I join?
2. Will my preferred court have subject matter jurisdiction over the claims?
3. Will my preferred court have personal jurisdiction over the parties?
4. Where will proper venue lie?

Asking and answering these questions is critical because they determine what actions can properly be brought in a particular court. The questions are interrelated. For example, limits on the subject matter jurisdiction of the court you choose can affect the claims and parties you can join. The choice of parties necessarily relates to whether you can get personal jurisdiction over them. These decisions in turn influence the determination of where venue is proper.

Second, once you have decided on the pleadings, you need to select the discovery that is appropriate for your case and your purposes. What do you need to know that you don't already know or can't find out through informal fact investigation? What witnesses do you need to pin down with depositions? What are your cost constraints? In what order, and when, should you engage in formal discovery? How extensive should each discovery method be? Again, many inexperienced litigators mechanically begin a standard discovery sequence—initial disclosures, interrogatories, document production, depositions, physical examination, and requests to admit—without a clear idea of what information is needed and how best to get it. Without a consistent overall litigation strategy, the case then bogs down as discovery assumes a life of its own.

Third, what motions should you plan? Your motions strategy must be part of, and coordinated with, your overall litigation plan. For instance, if you plan on moving for summary judgment on some counts or some issues, your discovery must be focused on getting the facts that will support your motion. Now is the time to plan on making those dispositive motions and to make sure that you have thought through your litigation plan, principally parts addressing the pleadings and discovery, so you can support those motions.

Finally, when should you explore settlement, if your opposing party doesn't? Since the vast majority of civil cases that survive dispositive motions settle before trial, you need to consider what your position on settlement should be at the points when settlement is likely to come up. This task includes assessing the value of the case at various times, as well as the financial and emotional benefits of settlement. The likelihood of a settlement, particularly an early one, will also affect your handling of the litigation and the relationship with your adversary.

Devising a litigation strategy is discussed in §4.5.

9. Make litigation cost and timetable estimates

A litigation cost estimate is something every litigator should make in every case. Most clients, except perhaps those whose cases are on a contingency fee basis, will ask how much litigation will cost. You should give your client an estimate of likely costs *before* starting the litigation and get the client's approval. You should stress that you are making an estimate, not a guarantee, and that you do not have complete control over costs.

Creating a litigation budget forces you to develop a realistic litigation plan and determine which tasks are required at the case's outset. Over time, you will be able to estimate more accurately how much time and resources various parts of the process will likely require in a particular type of case. Many law firms use task-based litigation software that makes this calculation systematically, and many sophisticated clients will expect such an analysis when they send out requests for proposals to law firms interested in handling a substantial matter. The amount of detail these clients will expect in the litigation budget depends on the complexity of the lawsuit.

The cost estimate should be broken down by basic litigation categories. For example, in a simple personal injury case your estimate may be as follows:

Litigation Cost Estimate

Fact and legal investigation	15 hrs.
Pleadings	5 hrs.
Discovery	50 hrs.
Motions	20 hrs.
Pretrial memorandum and settlement	20 hrs.
Trial preparation and trial	60 hrs.

The total estimated time before trial amounts to 110 hours; trial preparation and trial will add another 60 hours. As defense counsel, if you are billing at $100 per hour, the likely cost if the case settles after the pretrial conference is $11,000; a trial will add another $6,000. Expenses, such as for experts, depositions, and travel costs, might add a few thousand dollars.

The client may not like the estimated litigation costs. But you should discuss what they are and whether your client wants you to limit costs (for example, by restricting formal discovery or limiting the number of experts) before plowing ahead. Explain the assumptions on which you base your cost estimate, and emphasize that it is only an estimate based on facts presently known.

You should prepare a cost estimate even if you are a plaintiff's lawyer and usually handle personal injury cases on a contingency fee basis. Doing so will help you determine if taking the case makes economic sense to you.

The last step in the litigation plan is to create a realistic timetable for the litigation. As plaintiff, you have substantial flexibility. Unless you face a statute of limitations problem or a short notice of claim period, or unless you have another particular reason to file suit quickly, you can take the time to think through your litigation plan before filing the complaint. Once the complaint is filed, procedural rules and judges' practices largely control the litigation timeline. Judges will usually hold a scheduling conference after the pleadings are filed to establish a timetable for discovery, motions, and the final pretrial conference. For example, a judge may order that all discovery be concluded within 6 months, that any dispositive motions be filed within 30 days of the discovery cut-off date, and that a final pretrial conference will occur 60 days after the discovery cut-off date. Even where the judge does not establish a timetable, every jurisdiction has an informal set of expectations in routine cases that you should usually follow.

When you have structured a realistic timetable for your litigation plan, it is best to plot it out on a calendar to ensure that you don't omit any steps or lose track of when particular steps should be taken.

Litigation Timetable

1/1 (today)	Client interview
by 2/1	Interview bystander witnesses Get pl.'s medical records Get pl.'s employment records Get police reports Interview police officers
by 3/1	File complaint
by 4/1	Interrogatories to def. Documents request to def. Deposition notice to def.
by 6/1	Depose def.
by 7/1	Depose other witnesses? Depose physicians?
by 8/1	Requests to admit to def.
by 10/1	Prepare pretrial memorandum
11/1	Pretrial conference
12/1	Anticipated initial trial date

Every client will ask: "How long is my case going to take?" You should give the client your best estimate, revising it later if necessary, while emphasizing that it is an estimate and that you cannot completely control the litigation's trajectory.

Devising a litigation timetable is discussed in §4.5.

10.   Use a litigation file system

The last step is to develop and use a system for organizing your litigation files. There is no magic way to do this. All law firms have systems for the types of cases they routinely handle. Those systems include both litigation software systems that organize all electronic data in a case as well as manual file systems that organize all hard copies. The important point is that your system must be logical and clearly indexed to reflect the kinds of materials your cases will generate. The system should be in place when litigation starts. A good file system grows in importance as more and more lawyers and paralegals work on a case.

Litigation files are usually divided into several categories. The files should have tabbed dividers for each category, and categories may be further divided. For example, discovery is frequently divided into initial disclosures, interrogatories, documents requests, depositions, mental and physical examinations, experts, and requests to admit facts.

The following file organization and categories are commonly used in routine civil cases:

1.   Court documents
   a.   pleadings
   b.   discovery
   c.   motions
   d.   orders
   e.   subpoenas
   f.   pretrial memoranda
2.   Attorney's records
   a.   chronological litigation history
   b.   case summary
   c.   client agreement, time sheets, bills, costs, billings
   d.   correspondence with client and lawyers
   e.   legal research
   f.   miscellaneous notes and memos
3.   Evidence
   a.   bills, invoices, statements, receipts
   b.   correspondence between parties and with nonparties
   c.   business records and public records
   d.   photographs, diagrams, maps, charts
   e.   physical evidence (needs to be safeguarded in secure location)

Certain paperwork, such as pleadings, orders, and correspondence, should be clipped together in chronological order with the most recent on top. Original evidence, such as bills and correspondence, should be put in clear plastic sheet protectors so that the originals will not be marked during the litigation process.

§1.3.   *Conclusion*

This overview chapter has discussed the basic sequential steps in litigation planning. The critical concept is that every step of that plan is connected to every other. Each step you take influences what happens later, and the various steps you take will make sense only if they are part of an overall plan. When you are immersed in the technical details of any particular step in the process, it is easy to lose sight of that overall plan. Consequently, before doing anything, always ask yourself two questions. Why am I doing this? How does this step fit into my overall litigation plan? If you never lose sight of the big picture and keep your long-term objectives in mind, you will have a much better chance to conclude your litigation with satisfactory results.

II
INFORMAL FACT INVESTIGATION

§2.1.   Introduction

Preparation and planning for litigation are the critical initial components of the litigation process. Too many lawyers rush to court and file a complaint to get the process started without a thorough investigation of the facts and the law or a thoughtful litigation strategy. Small wonder, then, that the results frequently disappoint.

Litigation outcomes usually depend on facts, not law. Hence, litigators spend much of their time identifying and acquiring admissible evidence that supports their contentions and evidence that refutes the other side's contentions. The evidence at trial will include witness testimony and exhibits. Hence, the fact investigation principally involves finding and acquiring "people and paper," which means following the people trail and the paper trail. The party that discharges this task more successfully will more likely convince the fact finder that its version of the facts reflects what really happened.

§2.2.   Structuring fact investigations

There are two ways to get the facts: through informal investigation or through formal discovery. Inexperienced litigators commonly err when they use informal investigation, such as an initial client interview and the review of an accident report, only to decide whether to take the case, and rely on formal discovery methods as the principal fact-gathering method. This mistake is serious. First, information is power, and the party that has a better grasp of the favorable and unfavorable facts is in a stronger position to evaluate the case accurately. Second, information obtained early on, particularly from witnesses, is more likely to be accurate and complete. Third, information sought before the action formally begins may come more easily, since a lawsuit often makes people cautious or uncooperative. Fourth, information obtained before suit has been filed is less expensive to acquire. Formal discovery is the most expensive way to get information. It is usually more effective and less expensive to investigate matters informally before filing suit, then use formal discovery methods to obtain missing information, pin down witnesses, and obtain specific information and records from the opposing party. Fifth, Rule 11 of the Federal Rules of Civil Procedure requires that a lawyer conduct a reasonable inquiry into the facts to ensure that a pleading is well grounded. Finally, you can get information informally without the opposing parties participating, or even being aware that you are conducting an investigation. For all these reasons, you should pursue informal channels for investigation as much as possible.

1. When do I start?

The best time to start is immediately, particularly in cases based primarily on eyewitness testimony. For example, a personal injury case should be investigated as soon after the accident as possible. Witnesses forget or have second thoughts about being interviewed; witnesses move away and disappear; and physical evidence can be lost, altered, or destroyed.

But an immediate investigation is not always required. For example, a prompt fact investigation may not be essential in contract and commercial cases, where the evidence will primarily consist of documents, correspondence, and other business records, and the danger that records will be lost or disappear mysteriously is low. Contract and commercial cases may have complex legal questions that you must research and answer before you can start an intelligently structured fact investigation. Moreover, delay sometimes helps. If you start an investigation of a prospective defendant who expects to be sued, you may spur the defendant into beginning its own investigation. Unless the defendant needs to investigate an affirmative defense or counterclaim, a sound approach may be simply to wait for the other side to do something.

2. What facts do I need to get?

Your job as a litigator is to obtain enough admissible evidence to prove your claims and disprove the other side's claims. Therefore, you need to identify what you must prove or disprove, as determined by the substantive law underlying the claims, remedies, defenses, and counterclaims in the case. How do you research this law, however, if you do not yet know what the pleadings will allege? What do you research first, the facts or the law?

This question has no easy answer, as the facts and law are intertwined. The investigation of one affects the investigation of the other. You will usually go back and forth periodically as you develop your theory of the case.

Example:

> You have what appears to be a routine personal injury case. From your initial interview of the client it appears to be a simple negligence case against the other driver. You do preliminary research on the negligence claim to see if the damages are sufficient to warrant litigation. You then continue your fact investigation and discover that the defendant is uninsured. To find another possible source of recovery, you wonder if there may be a claim against the municipality for not maintaining intersection markings and safe road conditions. Of course you need to research the law here. If a legal theory supports such a claim, you then need to go back to see if the facts support this theory. Back and forth you go between getting the facts and researching the law until you have identified those legal theories that have factual support. This process is ongoing and is how you will develop your "theory of the case," or what really happened from your side's point of view.

3.   How do I structure my fact investigation?

The easiest way to give structure to your investigation is to use a system that organizes the law and facts based on what you will need to prove if your case goes to trial. In short, this is a good time to start a "litigation chart."[1] A litigation chart is simply a diagram that sets out what you need to prove or disprove in a case and how you will do it. The chart is a graphic way of identifying four major components of the litigation plan:

1. Elements of claims, remedies, defenses, and counterclaims
2. Sources of proof
3. Informal fact investigation
4. Formal discovery

Start with the elements of each potential claim and remedy in the case. Most jurisdictions have pattern jury instructions for commonly tried claims, such as negligence, products liability, and contract claims. The elements instructions will itemize what must be proved for each claim, remedy, or defense. If pattern jury instructions don't exist, more basic research will be necessary. If the claim is based on a statute, read the statute and look at the case annotations that deal with elements and jury instructions. If the claim is based on common law, consult treatises covering the claim and research recent case law in the applicable jurisdiction. Regardless of where the applicable law is, you must find it and determine what the specific elements are. When you have done this, you will have completed the first step on your litigation chart.

---

1. The litigation chart will become a trial chart if the case is ultimately tried. See Thomas A. Mauet, Trial Techniques and Trials §11.4 (9th ed. 2013); Michael R. Fontham, Trial Technique and Evidence §§1-8 (3d ed. 2008).

Example:

> You represent the plaintiff in a potential contract case. Your client says she obtained goods from a seller and paid for them, but the goods were defective. From your initial client interview, and from reviewing the documents and records she provided, you decide to bring a contract claim against the defendant. Your jurisdiction's pattern jury instructions for contract claims list the elements you must prove to establish liability and damages.

LITIGATION CHART

Elements of Claims	Sources of Proof	Informal Fact Investigation	Formal Discovery
1. Contract			
(a) contract executed			
(b) pl.'s performance			
(c) def.'s breach			
(d) pl.'s damages			

You should use this approach for every other possible claim. For example, since the contract is for the sale of goods, a claim based on UCC warranties may be appropriate. If so, you should put the elements of this claim on your litigation chart. Most lawyers also use the chart for potential defenses and counterclaims.

The litigation chart has two principal benefits. First, it helps you identify what you have to prove or disprove so that you can focus your fact investigation on getting admissible evidence for each required element. Second, a litigation chart helps you pinpoint the strengths and weaknesses of your case as well as your opponent's case. In most trials the side that wins is the one that convinces the fact finder to resolve disputed issues in its favor. The litigation chart will help you identify the disputed matters on which you will need to develop additional admissible evidence to strengthen your version and rebut the other party's version.

Notice that the grid structure of your chart is just a simple spreadsheet. Commercially available case management software exists that allows you to create and use customized fields. In addition to the four fields in the litigation chart, you can add fields for questions, favorable/unfavorable facts, lawyer assigned, and so on. You can create hyperlinks to exhibits and witness testimony. You can export facts to create chronologies. Extending the fields using a case management program allows you to use the database for evidence analysis, discovery planning, and trial preparation. Some of these programs are powerful and flexible and can be extremely useful, particularly in large or complex litigation.

4. What are the likely sources of proof?

Facts come from five basic sources: the client, exhibits, witnesses, experts, and the opposing party. Informal investigation can reach most of these sources. The client, of course, must be interviewed. Whenever possible, obtain exhibits in your client's possession and other evidence, such as physical objects, photographs, documents, and records in the possession of third parties. You can frequently interview witnesses and hire consulting experts to help analyze and prepare your case.

Formal discovery may sometimes be the only way to get some essential information. You will have to depose uncooperative witnesses, for example, and use subpoenas to obtain exhibits in the possession of uncooperative third parties. Information from the opposing party can usually be obtained only through initial disclosures, interrogatories, depositions, and other discovery methods. Still, always try the informal approach first, since it is quicker, less expensive, and possibly more accurate and complete.

You can interview any person willing to be interviewed, unless you know that this person has legal representation. Ethics rules prevent you from interviewing a represented person unless her lawyer gives you consent. The rule applies to employees of corporations and other organizations known to be represented by counsel. Some courts have also held that the rule prevents ex parte contacts with former employees of the represented organization. This is a minority view, however, and the majority view allows such contacts. Jurisdiction-specific research is necessary.[2]

While you should always conduct informal fact investigations, their usefulness depends significantly on the particular case at hand. Some cases can be almost completely investigated through informal means, while others depend more on formal discovery. For example, you should be able to get all the basic information in an automobile negligence case informally, since the principal sources will be your client, police officers, police reports, medical reports, and disinterested nonparty witnesses. By contrast, in a products liability case brought against the manufacturer of a consumer product, most of the information about the product's design, manufacture, distribution, and safety history will be in the possession of the defendant manufacturer and can be obtained only through formal discovery methods.

Regardless of the type of case, you must first identify the likely sources of proof, then decide how to obtain that proof. The second step for developing your litigation chart is to list the likely sources of proof and match them with the required elements of the claims.

---

2. See Model Rules of Professional Conduct, Rule 4.2, and comment to the rule; see also §2.5.

Example:

> In a contract case, determine the witnesses and exhibits that will pro-
> vide the facts about the case. Your client, the plaintiff, is an obvious
> witness, and the contract is a central exhibit. Other than these obvious
> sources, where else can you go for proof? For example, what proof
> establishes that the plaintiff performed his obligations under the con-
> tract? The plaintiff is again a source of proof. In addition, the plaintiff
> may have business records showing his performance. The defendant
> may have written letters acknowledging the plaintiff's performance.
> The defendant may have business records proving performance. A
> nonparty witness may have knowledge of the plaintiff's performance.
>
> Continue this type of analysis for each element of every claim
> you are considering, and put those sources on your developing lit-
> igation chart.

LITIGATION CHART

Elements of Claims	Sources of Proof	Informal Fact Investigation	Formal Discovery
1. Contract			
(a) contract executed	Plaintiff defendant contract pl.'s secretary		
(b) pl. performed	Plaintiff pl.'s records def.'s records		

(c) def. breached	plaintiff
	pl.'s
	   correspondence
	def.'s
	   correspondence
	pl.'s records
	def.'s records
	experts		

(d) pl.'s damages	plaintiff
	pl.'s records
	replacement
	   vendor
	replacement
	   vendor's records
	experts		

The third step is to determine whether informal fact investigation can
reach sources of proof and, if so, what method can best yield the necessary

information. Witnesses can be interviewed, exhibits in your client's possession should be obtained and reviewed, and exhibits possessed by friendly or neutral nonparties can frequently be obtained simply by requesting them. Experts can be interviewed, and you can sometimes obtain their reports. Once again, think expansively here, since obtaining information informally is quicker and less expensive. Also, informally gathered information is frequently more candid and accurate, and you can obtain it without the opposing party participating or even knowing of your investigation. Put the methods by which you plan to obtain the information on the litigation chart.

LITIGATION CHART

Elements of Claims	Sources of Proof	Informal Fact Investigation	Formal Discovery
1. Contract			
(a) contract executed	plaintiff defendant contract pl.'s secretary	interview obtained from pl. interview	
(b) pl. performed	plaintiff pl.'s records def.'s records	interview obtained from pl.	

(c) def. breached	plaintiff
	pl.'s
	  correspondence
	def.'s
	  correspondence
	pl.'s records
	def.'s records
	experts
		interview
		
		obtained from pl.
		
		obtained from pl.
		interview	

(d) pl.'s damages	plaintiff
	pl.'s records
	replacement
	  vendor
	replacement
	  vendor's
	records
	experts
		interview
		obtained from pl.
		interview
		request letter
		interview	

The last step is to decide which information to seek with formal discovery methods, and how and when to use them. These considerations are discussed in Chapters 4 and 6.

5.   What is my litigation budget?

You can't buy a Cadillac on a Ford budget, and the same holds true for litigation. The client's financial resources are an important consideration. The value of the case, or the amount you can reasonably expect in a jury verdict, is another. The amount of work the case requires for adequate preparation is a third consideration. Consequently, you need to estimate how much work the case will require, and to determine whether you can feasibly accomplish the work given the resources involved. You need to prepare a litigation budget.

How do you do so? First, you need to estimate how much time you can devote to the case and whether you can adequately handle it within this time. If a client has a limit on what she can spend, that is the outside limit. If you are billing by the hour, simply divide your hourly rate into the fee limit, and you will know the total number of hours you can devote to this case. If your fee is a contingency fee, you should still make this type of calculation. Start with the dollar amount of a reasonably expected verdict after a successful trial. Reduce that amount by the likelihood that liability will not be proved. For instance, if you have a 50 percent likelihood of proving liability, reduce the expected verdict by that percentage. Next, divide this dollar amount by your usual hourly rate, and you will again determine the total hours you can devote to the case and still reasonably compensate yourself. Once you determine the total hours, estimate the time you will need to spend on each part of the litigation process: preliminary investigation, pleadings, discovery, motions, and trial.

Think you can't do it? You'd better start. Insurance companies and businesses regularly require lawyers to prepare detailed litigation budgets, knowing that litigation makes sense only if it is cost-effective. Keep in mind that your time *estimates* are only that, and it is sometimes appropriate to have a range for your estimates.

Example:

> You represent the plaintiff in an automobile accident case. Your fee is one-third of any recovery. Assume that if you win at trial, your client can realistically expect a verdict of about $90,000. However, you estimate your chances of proving liability at 50 percent. This risk reduces the value of the case to about $45,000, of which you will earn $15,000. Your time is presently billed at $100 per hour. This means you can devote up to 150 hours on the case and still be paid a fee equal to your hourly rate.
>
> The case will take approximately two days to try and require about four days of trial preparations, for an estimated total of 48 hours. How do you allocate the remaining 102 hours? Your prefiling investigation — client interviews, witness interviews, exhibits acquisition, legal research, and just plain thinking about the case — may require about 25 hours. Preparing and responding to pleadings may take about 10 hours. Preparing and responding to discovery will

require the largest amount of time, approximately 50 hours.[3] Making and responding to motions may take another 15 hours. Preparing pretrial memoranda and attending pretrial conferences may require 15 hours. How does your budget add up?

Investigation	25 hrs.
Pleadings	10 hrs.
Discovery	50 hrs.
Motions	15 hrs.
Pretrials	15 hrs.
	115 hrs.

You didn't come within the allocated 102 hours, but your initial time estimates are reasonably within range. With experience, you will be able to estimate time requirements of particular cases and the likelihood and amounts of a recovery more accurately. This ability will help you determine if you should take a case to begin with, and, if you do, how much time you can realistically expect to devote to the various stages of its preparation and trial.

Always keep in mind that your ethical obligations to the client must ultimately control your handling of the client's case. You have an obligation to handle the case competently; the requirements of the case, not the anticipated fee, should determine your performance.[4]

6.   What sources should I investigate?

The basic sources for informal investigations are fourfold: the client, exhibits, witnesses, and experts. Your litigation chart will provide directions for your informal fact investigation. That investigation should focus on obtaining basic facts, favorable and unfavorable, about the case and identifying credible, admissible evidence for each claim you consider filing.

Your fact investigation needs to be thorough enough to fill out your litigation chart, to the extent that you can do so through informal fact investigation, while meeting the cost constraints you have established. Practically, this means several things. First, the client must be interviewed as often as necessary to learn everything she knows about the case. You will also need to interview her periodically as you gather additional information from other sources.

Second, you should try to obtain all key documents, records, and other exhibits. In a personal injury case, this evidence includes the police accident reports, hospital and doctor's records, insurance claims records, and

---

3. Determining how to allocate these 50 hours among the various discovery methods is discussed in detail in §6.3.

4. See Model Rules of Professional Conduct, Rule 1.1.

employment history. These items can often be obtained informally, and many jurisdictions have statutes that require their release to the client on request. In a contract case, this evidence includes the contract, correspondence, invoices, shipping records, and related business records. Where physical evidence is important, it should be safeguarded or photographed before such evidence is altered or possibly lost.

Third, witnesses usually need to be identified, located, and interviewed, although what you do will depend on the particular case. In most cases, what witnesses say is critical. For example, in a personal injury case, where the plaintiff and defendant are likely to have contradictory versions of how the accident happened, the testimony of neutral witnesses will frequently determine the liability issue. You need to identify, locate, and interview them whenever possible. On the other hand, witness testimony is not invariably critical at trial. For example, in a contract or commercial case, documents, records, or the substantive law frequently decide the issues. In such a case there may be no advantage in interviewing witnesses quickly.

Finally, in some cases you will need to consult appropriate experts early in your investigation. For example, in medical malpractice and products liability cases, plaintiff's lawyers usually ask a physician or technical expert to review the case before filing suit. You might as well see what a qualified expert thinks of the strengths and weaknesses of your case early on.

§2.3.   *Client interviews*[5]

The initial meeting between client and lawyer may be the most important meeting in the client's life. How it goes will largely determine the nature of that relationship during the course of the litigation. Understanding what is involved in this meeting is critically important.

Client interviewing has two components: what information to get, and how to get it. Your litigation chart will determine what to get. How to get it depends on interviewing techniques that you should understand fully.

1.   Client attitudes and disclosure

The typical client is unsure of his rights and obligations, and a lawyer's office is an unfamiliar, imposing environment. The lawyer who empathizes with the client's psychological needs and knows the factors that promote and inhibit client disclosure will more successfully glean an accurate picture of the problems that brought the client to a lawyer in the first place.

---

5. For sources on interviewing, see, e.g., S. Krieger & R. Neumann, Essential Lawyering Skills: Interviewing, Counseling, Negotiation, and Persuasive Fact Analysis (4th ed. 2011); G. Herman & J. Cary, A Practical Approach to Client Interviewing, Counseling, and Decision-Making (2009); R. Cochran, The Counselor-at-Law: A Collaborative Approach to Client Interviewing and Counseling (2d ed. 2006); D. Binder et al., Lawyers as Counselors: A Client Centered Approach (2d ed. 2004).

A client comes to a lawyer to determine if his problems involve legal issues and, if so, how to deal with them. The lawyer needs to interview the client so she can identify the legal issues, get all relevant available information, and discuss with the client how best to handle the problems. How does a lawyer go about getting this information from the client?

Several factors can inhibit a client from a full disclosure of information. First, a client may feel that the interviewer is judging him. If so, the client might withhold or distort facts that may create negative impressions about him or his case. Second, a client often tries to satisfy what he feels are the lawyer's expectations. The client may tell the lawyer what he thinks will be a pleasing story and may withhold negative and contradictory facts. Third, a client may have a variety of internal reasons, such as embarrassment, modesty, and fear, that prevent him from disclosing all information.

On the other side, several positive factors promote full disclosure. First, a client is more likely to disclose fully if he feels that the lawyer has a personal interest in him. A friendly, sympathetic lawyer can get "all the facts" more readily from a client. Second, a client is more likely to disclose fully if he senses that the lawyer identifies with him. The lawyer who lets the client know that "she's been there too," or is familiar with and understands the client's situation, can better draw out all the facts. Third, some clients enjoy being the center of attention. The client may feel important when he supplies critical information, a sense that may stimulate him to provide even more information. Fourth, a client enjoys feeling that he is doing the right thing. The lawyer who can entrench the message that full disclosure is proper and decent is more likely to prompt the client to disclose fully.

Lawyers will obtain the fullest possible disclosure by stressing these positive psychological influences and by understanding and minimizing the negative ones. Lawyers who create a comfortable physical environment and show an understanding and appreciation of the client will be more successful in obtaining "all the facts," both good and bad. This sensitivity will establish a positive context for client relations during the course of the litigation process.

2. Interview environment

Creating a positive interview environment has several components. What kind of physical setting should you have? How will you record what the client says? What should the client do to prepare for the interview? What topics will you cover during the actual interview?

Many clients will be uncertain and insecure during the interview. After all, it may be the first time they have ever been to a lawyer's office. A physical setting that is informal, friendly, and private will help make a client feel relaxed and comfortable. A lawyer's private office is a good place to conduct an interview; a small conference room is another.

Strive for informality. Sit in a place other than behind your desk and have coffee and soft drinks available. Avoid interruptions. Leave the telephone alone, and close the door to keep others out. Schedule the interview so that you will have enough time to accomplish what you have planned. An interview with a client can easily take one or two hours, but perhaps much more. If possible, schedule client interviews as the last appointment for the day, provided you are still mentally sharp at that time. You can thereby continue the interview without running out of time because of other appointments. Remember that, as you are sizing up the client, the client is sizing you up as a lawyer.

A principal function of a client interview is to obtain information, in addition to establishing rapport and gaining the client's trust. This information needs to be recorded. There are several ways to do this. First, you can take notes yourself. Your own note taking has the advantage of privacy, but it can interfere with your interview. Second, you can have someone else — a secretary, clerk, or paralegal — take notes. This method relieves you of note taking, but it puts a third person into the interview environment. Doing so may inhibit the client's openness, particularly during the first interview. Third, you can make an audio recording of the interview with the client's permission. The advantage is completeness, but you will still need to make a summary of the interview, and many clients are uncomfortable having their statements recorded. Fourth, you can avoid taking notes altogether and dictate notes immediately following the interview. You can conduct the interview without distractions, but your notes of the interview may not be as complete as they otherwise would be.

The paramount consideration is to create an atmosphere in which the client feels comfortable and tells everything she knows about the problems that brought her to you. Most lawyers conduct the initial part of the interview without note taking. After the client becomes comfortable with you and the interview environment, and after you begin to get the details of her story, you can discuss the need to record what she says and then ask her if she will feel comfortable with the method you suggest. Once you explain why it is so important for you to have an accurate record of what she says and how the attorney-client privilege will prevent anyone else from getting it, the client will usually agree.

To prepare for the first interview, tell the client to collect all available paperwork, such as letters, documents, bills, and other records. Also, many lawyers ask the client to write down everything she can remember about the legal problems, particularly if they involve a recent event; to list the names of all persons involved; and to create a chronology of events. If the client directs her memo to the lawyer, and if no one outside the lawyer's staff is permitted to see it, the attorney-client privilege should protect it, even though the attorney-client relationship may not yet formally exist.[6] The client should bring the records and memo to the initial interview.

Some lawyers, particularly plaintiff's personal injury lawyers, frequently use paralegals to screen prospective clients by conducting the intake interviews. The interviewing techniques discussed here obviously have equal applicability regardless of who does the initial client interview.

---

6. See Wright & Miller §2017; McCormick on Evidence §§88–89 (7th ed. 2013); Fed. R. Civ. P. 26.

3. Initial client interview

The initial client interview should have several objectives, although accomplishing all of them may require more than one session. First, conduct yourself in a manner that establishes a good working relationship. When the client arrives at your office, don't make him wait. Greet him personally. Have the client make himself comfortable in your office or conference room, and spend a little time making small talk — about traffic or the weather, for instance. Offer him coffee or a soft drink. Remember that the client is sizing you up both as a lawyer and as a person. Second, spend a few minutes learning about the client's background to show him that you see him as a human being and not just as another case. This initial conversation also helps you evaluate the client as a witness, and it provides important biographical and financial information. Third, let the client know what is going to happen during the interview, what you need to accomplish, and the reasons for it. Explain that you need to get all the important facts in order to identify and analyze his legal problems intelligently. Stress the importance of candor and completeness. Give the client an overview of the litigation process and why this interview is an important part of it. Tell the client that his conversations with you and your staff are private and protected (privileged), so long as the client does not tell anyone else about the conversations (which would waive the privilege).

Fourth, have the client identify the general nature of his problems. You will usually have a general idea — a "car accident," or a "contract problem" — when the client makes the appointment. However, it is always useful to have the client initially tell his story his own way, without interruptions. You can size the client up as a trial witness, and you may discover facts you might never otherwise have stumbled upon. The prospective client can get the matter off his chest in his own words. These considerations are well worth "wasting time" on, even if the client talks about seemingly irrelevant things. The usual way to get the client to tell the story his way is to ask open-ended, non-leading questions. For example, the client will usually get started if you simply ask, "I know you were in an accident. Why don't you tell me what happened in your own words?" While the client tells his story, listen not only to what he says but also note things he omits, things that would usually be mentioned. After the client finishes, you can paraphrase what he has said. Telling the story back to the client serves as a check on accuracy and shows the client that you have been listening carefully.

Fifth, after the client has told his story, you need to get a detailed chronological history of the events and other background facts. An outline or checklist can often help to ensure that you do not overlook important topics. Your litigation chart, setting out the elements of the claims you are considering, should provide a start. Get a set of your jurisdiction's uniform or pattern interrogatories for this kind of case. (Your adversary will likely send these interrogatories to your client to answer after the lawsuit is filed, so you might as well get the information you will need to answer them now.) Deposition checklists for this type of case and witness can help you develop ideas for topics and necessary details as you go through the history of the case.[7] Don't use a checklist as a questionnaire, however, since your interview will quickly lose the personal touch. The standard method is to use the chronological storytelling approach, since most people think chronologically. While your checklist should be tailored to fit the particular case involved, you will usually cover the same basic topics regardless.

Sixth, you need to ask follow-up questions on potential problem areas. Specific, focused questions that bear on potential claims, remedies, defenses, and counterclaims are best (although most lawyers avoid aggressively cross-examining clients during the first meeting). A client naturally wants to impress his lawyer and convince her that the case is a good one, so he will often give only his version of what are disputed facts and omit altogether the unfavorable ones. It is always better to get the bad news early. Remind the client that your job is to get all the facts, both good and bad, so you can accurately assess the case and represent him effectively.[8] Remind him that the opposing lawyers will discover the bad facts soon enough, and he is better off dealing with them now. This sort of advice will usually keep the client from adopting an "I thought the lawyer was on my side" attitude.

Where do you probe? Look for information that might adversely affect the client's credibility. Are there problems with the client's background? Does he have a spotty work history or criminal convictions or other such trouble with the law? Clients frequently omit negative facts in their background. Therefore, you should look for the gaps and ask what the client has left out of the story. For example, in an automobile accident case, has the client omitted the fact that he was given a traffic citation? Was driving with a suspended license? Was drinking? Had just left a bar before the accident happened? Was using a car without permission? A useful technique for eliciting these kinds of facts is to get the client to be a kind of devil's advocate, without directly suggesting to the client that you don't believe his story. Ask him what the other side is probably going to say to his lawyer about the event. This will frequently draw out the other side's version of the disputed facts. Keep in mind that under Rule 11 you accept your client's version of the facts at your peril. The client needs to be pushed, probed, even cross-examined to test the facts he gives you. You may need to verify his version of the facts with an independent investigation.

The usual topics you will need to discuss with the client during the initial interview include the following.

a.   Statute of limitations

Determine when the statute of limitations begins to run on all potential claims, and when it ends. If the time to file a lawsuit is about

---

7. See, e.g., D. Danner & L. Varn, Pattern Deposition Checklists (4th ed. 1998); 2-3 D. Danner & L. Varn, Pattern Deposition Checklists (4th ed. Supp. 2013).

8. This assessment is required in any event by Rule 11's reasonable inquiry duty.

to end, you will need to file a complaint quickly to protect the client's rights.

b. Liability

Facts bearing on the liability of all parties must be developed fully. Details are critical. For example, in an automobile accident case, you will need to explore how the accident happened step by step. You need to get a detailed description of the scene of the collision. Diagrams and charts are very helpful. You need to establish the location of each car involved before the collision occurred, at the point of impact, and after the accident had run its course. You need to get details on speed, distance, time, and relationship to road markings. In a contract case, you will need to get a detailed chronology of all contacts between the parties before the contract was executed, when it was executed, and all events that have happened since it was executed.

c. Damages

You should obtain damages information for both your client and all other parties, for each possible claim. For example, in an automobile collision case, damages should include out-of-pocket expenses, lost income, future expenses, and future lost income, as well as intangible damages, such as pain and suffering. Find out if the client suffered an injury, the extent of it, how she was treated, how she felt then and feels now, and how the injury has affected her life. Find out if she had a preexisting condition that could affect damages. You should also explore insurance coverage for all parties, as well as collateral sources, such as health insurance, employer benefits, and government entitlements (e.g., Social Security and Veterans Administration benefits). In contract and commercial cases, and cases in which equitable relief is sought, you need to determine if the injuries to the client can be measured in monetary terms.

You must determine if the defendant has the ability to pay a judgment. Find out if the defendant has insurance and the amount of the policy's coverage, and determine if the policy covers the event or transaction. Identify the defendant's income sources and assets, particularly those that can easily be attached to collect a judgment. When representing a defendant, determine if the defendant has any insurance policies that may cover some or all of the claims against the defendant, and notify the insurance companies of the claims. Failure to do so in a timely manner may affect the insurance coverage and the insurance company's duty to defend.

d. Client background

Your client's background is important for several reasons. The client's personal background — education, employment, family history — helps you assess the client's credibility as a trial witness. His financial background — income and assets — may help determine damages. Finally, the client's financial picture bears on a mundane but obviously important question:

Does he have the ability to pay you? You need to get this background information from the client early on, but be sure you let the client know why this personal information is important for your evaluation of the case.

After you have obtained your client's background information, consider corroborating it. Obtain a claims check on the client to see if he has sued or been sued previously. Obtain a credit check to evaluate the client's financial condition. Do a background check for any criminal convictions and bankruptcies. The Internet can be a useful source for information, particularly about corporate clients.

e. Parties

It is frequently difficult to ascertain who all the parties to an event or transaction are and, if businesses are involved, their proper legal identities. Often the client does not know and has given little thought to this aspect of the case. Now you should begin to obtain the facts that will help you identify those parties. In an automobile accident case, for example, you will need to know not only who the other driver was, but also who owns the other vehicle, whether it is a business or rental vehicle, and whether it was loaned or stolen. You will also need to know where the accident occurred and who owns, or is in control of, the accident location. That entity may be responsible for designing, building, and maintaining the roadways. If the case involves a workplace accident and the applicable state law of workers' compensation bars an action against the employer, look for other potential defendants, such as manufacturers of equipment or independent contractors. Once again, keep Rule 11 in mind.

Your fact investigation will usually enable you to identify the parties you will want to name in your lawsuit. You also need to learn these parties' technical identities. For example, just because the truck that ran into your client had the name "Johnson Gas" on its side does not necessarily mean that the Johnson Gas Company is a properly named party. The potentially liable party may be a sole proprietorship or a corporation with a different name entirely.

For individuals, learn their correct full names. For corporations, partnerships, unincorporated businesses, and other artificial entities, you must not only learn their proper names, but also whether they are subsidiaries of other entities that you should name as parties. Each state's Secretary of State or Corporation Commission usually has a list of domestic and foreign corporations licensed to do business within that state. Such lists usually show a corporation's state of incorporation and principal place of business, information that can help you determine if diversity jurisdiction exists. These lists also identify the resident agent for service of process. If the party is an unincorporated business operating under an assumed name, you may be able to determine the true owners and properly named parties by consulting an assumed-name index, which many jurisdictions require.[9]

---

9. Rule 17 governs the capacity of individuals, corporations, and unincorporated associations to sue. It refers to state law. Hence, you must always check state law to determine whether a party has capacity to sue or be sued, and who or what the technically proper party is.

f. Defenses, counterclaims, and third-party claims

Plaintiffs and defendants alike must answer frequently overlooked questions: What do they have on us? And who else can be brought into the case? Cases are legion where a plaintiff has filed an action, only to be hit with a much larger, previously dormant, counterclaim. Think expansively, particularly in the commercial area, since the parties usually will have had previous dealings that could give rise to counterclaims or third-party claims. You should look at all possibly relevant transactions, since liberal joinder rules offer a lot of leeway for the joinder of claims.

g. Witnesses

You should question the client on all possible information sources, whether eyewitnesses, experts, or anyone else who possibly has useful information. Get names and information that will help to identify and locate people who might know something useful. Think expansively here, and don't be concerned with the admissibility of testimony at this point. Find out to whom your client has already talked about the case, what he has said, and whether he has signed any written statements, reports, or claim forms.

h. Records

The client should bring to the interview all paperwork in her possession, such as accident reports, insurance claims and policies, bills, checks, personal records, medical records, tax records, business records, and correspondence. If the client does not bring them, have her do so as soon as possible. You should keep these records; if the client needs them, make photocopies for her. Learn what other records may exist and who has them, so that you can obtain them now or later through discovery.

i. Physical evidence

Does the case involve objects like vehicles, machinery, or consumer products? While most common in negligence and products liability cases, such evidence can exist in other cases as well. How to locate, obtain, and preserve physical evidence is discussed in §2.4.

j. Other lawyers

Clients often shop around for lawyers. While a client has a perfect right to talk to more than one lawyer about taking a case, there are always clients who go from door to door until they find a lawyer willing to take it. Try to find out if the client has seen other lawyers about the case. On the theory that lawyers turn down cases because the cases lack merit, you should be appropriately cautious.

k.   Client goals

What does the client really want? In some cases, such as those involving personal injuries, the answer is often simple. The plaintiff basically
wants money damages and the defendant wants to avoid paying them. But
even in these straightforward situations a deeper probe is important.
What does the client view as a favorable outcome? Does he want the
case to go to trial, or is he willing to settle? Is he looking for vindication,
revenge, or other satisfaction not related to money damages? In other
cases, such as contract and commercial disputes involving businesses, the
question, "What does the client want?" may prove even harder to answer.
The client might want or need something other than money damages.
The dispute may be with another business with which the client has an
ongoing relationship, and that relationship may be more important than
compensation. Perhaps relief such as specific performance is more
important. Now is the time to find out what the client thinks he wants
and begin assessing whether his expectations are realistic or need to be
modified.

Avoid predicting what the case is worth or when the client will get any
money. These are questions that all clients ask sooner or later, usually
sooner. Explain that you cannot make any such predictions at this early
stage. It would be foolish to do so before you have gathered more information and researched the applicable law. Only after doing so are you in a
position to make an informed analysis of the strengths and weaknesses of
the case. Consider putting this disclaimer in writing in a follow-up letter to
the client. When the case reaches the settlement stage, some disappointed
clients think that the settlement amount is much less than what the lawyer
earlier said the case was worth.

l.   Conflicts

Obtain enough information from the client to enable you to determine if you or your firm has a conflict that will preclude your representation. Advise the client of this possibility. Conflicts of interest are discussed
in §4.2.

m.   Next steps

Following a client interview, write a short memo evaluating the client
and her story. You can easily forget your specific impressions of a client, yet
her credibility as a trial witness will often be critical to her case's success. A
written evaluation is particularly important where more than one lawyer
will work on the file.

If you conclude from the initial client interview that you will take the
case, you will need to discuss the details of a contractual relationship,
including fees. You should let the client know what steps you will take
concerning her problem and what she will need to do to help you.
These are discussed in §4.3.

4.   Follow-up client interviews

An initial interview of a client has many goals. Some cases are relatively simple, and interviewing a well-prepared client can take less than an hour. Many cases, however, will require more than one session to collect the basic information. Accordingly, you might use the first session just to build rapport with the client, get the client's story out, and compile a chronology of events. You could then use a second session to review the client's records and ask focused follow-up questions about problem areas. More complicated cases may require several client interviews to acquire the necessary information.

Periodic follow-up interviews will also be necessary during the litigation process. Whenever you receive additional information, through informal fact investigation or during formal discovery, you should review it with the client. The new information may differ from what the client previously told you. Obviously you must evaluate the contradictory information and discuss it with the client. In some cases the client may admit that what he previously told you was not entirely true and change his story. In others, he may deny the new information and stick to his version of the facts. Whatever the client's position, you must deal with the new information if it is at odds with the client's story. Is it true? Is it more accurate? What does the new information do to the client's story? This is an ongoing process, but the key point to remember is that the client must be kept informed as the fact-gathering process progresses.

§2.4.   Exhibits acquisition

Your interviews with the client should also suggest future exhibits. These include the scene, physical evidence, documents, and records. In addition, interviews with witnesses and your review of exhibits when you get them, particularly documents and business records, may disclose additional exhibits.

You need to acquire these exhibits, get copies of them, or protect them from being lost or altered. The order in which you do so will depend on how important it is to obtain the particular exhibits. For example, you should acquire physical evidence, such as the condition of a vehicle, machine, or consumer product, quickly, before it is repaired, altered, destroyed, or lost. Some records, such as a police accident report, are essential for you to begin your investigation.

The basic types of exhibits are the following.

1.   Scene

If a lawsuit involves an event, such as an automobile accident, an investigation of the scene is vital. Whenever possible, the lawyer should visit the scene, even if someone else will do the technical investigation. The investigation should include taking photographs of all locations from a variety of perspectives and making all necessary measurements so that you can make scale diagrams. Photographs should be in black and white and in color and be enlarged to 8 inches × 10 inches. Diagrams for courtroom use should be at least 30 inches × 40 inches. While photographic enlargements and courtroom diagrams need not be made until shortly before trial, the necessary preparations should be made now. You should visit the scene at the same time and day of week on which the event occurred, so your photographs will accurately show lighting, traffic, and other relevant conditions. You also might find additional witnesses to the event, namely people who are there each day at that time.

You can take photographs yourself if you are a reasonably proficient photographer, and if you have the equipment to take photographs that can be processed and enlarged with sufficient quality to make effective courtroom exhibits. This will not create a problem for you, a lawyer in the case, in terms of becoming a witness. Any person familiar with how the scene looked at the relevant time is a competent qualifying witness. However, if you would otherwise be the only person who can qualify the admission of the photographs, someone else must come along, because the lawyer cannot usually be a witness in a case she is trying. If you are not a proficient photographer, hire a commercial photographer to accompany you. You must tell the photographer specifically what pictures you will need.

Numerous photographs should be taken from a variety of perspectives. For example, in an intersection collision case, you will normally want pictures of how the intersection looked to each of the drivers as they approached it. Pictures should be taken in the road from the appropriate lane, with the camera held the same distance above the road as the driver's head. Several pictures should be taken, starting from perhaps 300 feet away, then moving to 150 feet, and so on. The photographs will then show what each driver saw as he approached the intersection. In addition, photographs should be taken from where other eyewitnesses, such as other drivers and pedestrians, were when the crash occurred. Finally, if there are nearby buildings, have overhead, bird's-eye-view pictures taken that will show lane markings, pedestrian walkways, traffic signs, and signals in the intersection. You must review witness statements beforehand to know where the witnesses were and what they saw and did before you can know what photographs you will need.

Diagrams present a different problem. Since the person who took the measurements and made a scale diagram is often the only witness who can qualify the diagram for admission in evidence, have someone other than the lawyer make one.

2. Physical evidence

You should obtain physical evidence, such as vehicles, machinery, and consumer products, if it is not already in the possession of police, other investigative agencies, or your client. The evidence must also be preserved for possible use at trial. This task includes not only locating the evidence, but also keeping it in the same condition and establishing chains of custody. Doing so is particularly important if experts will test the evidence before trial. When you cannot take or move evidence for safekeeping, take a thorough series of photographs and sufficient measurements so that you can make accurate diagrams and models for trial.

Preserving physical evidence often requires that you act quickly. In an automobile accident case, for example, skid marks and the condition of the vehicles involved will disappear as the skid marks wear off and the vehicles are repaired. In these situations you must take immediate steps to prevent the loss, destruction, or alteration of the evidence and ensure a chain of custody when such a chain will be an admissibility requirement.[10] Have someone such as an investigator do this, since he may be a necessary witness at trial.

How do you actually "preserve" physical evidence? First, you must gain actual physical possession of the objects to keep them in the same condition until the trial. Second, you must either label the objects or, if they cannot readily be labeled, put them in a container that can be sealed and labeled. These two steps ensure admissibility at trial by establishing the two basic requirements: identity and same condition. The usual way to accomplish this is to have someone like an investigator, who can serve as a trial witness, get the objects from wherever they are, label or put them in a container that is sealed and labeled, and have them taken to your office for safekeeping. This label should describe the object, show where it came from, note who obtained it, record when it was taken, and identify who received it at your office.

Nonparties, such as police departments and repair shops, frequently possess evidence. If the evidence does not belong to your client, the nonparties are probably under no legal obligation to preserve the evidence for you. However, most will be cooperative when they learn that they have important evidence. They will usually keep the evidence in an unaltered condition until you have had an opportunity to photograph and measure it. You should check if someone else, such as an investigator from the police department or insurance company, has already taken these steps. Finally, a nonparty will sometimes agree to preserve evidence until you can serve him with a subpoena or have the court issue a protective order.

Many times, of course, a client comes to a lawyer too late to take these steps and protect against the loss of evidence. If the client comes to you shortly after the event, however, you should always act quickly to preserve the evidence. Many cases, particularly in the personal injury and products liability areas, are won or lost on this type of evidence.

3.   Records

You should obtain all available documents and records from your client. You may as well obtain everything your client has; once suit is filed the

---

10. See McCormick on Evidence §213 (7th ed. 2013); Thomas A. Mauet, Trial Techniques and Trials §7.4 (9th ed. 2013).

opposing party will be able to discover from your client anything that is relevant and not privileged. If important documents and records are in the hands of other persons, see if those persons will voluntarily turn them over or provide copies. Public records are usually available on request. In many jurisdictions persons have a statutory right to obtain certain records on demand, such as their own medical reports. A written demand on behalf of the client, coupled with her written authorization, will usually suffice. If not, contact the sources to learn the required procedure for obtaining the records. These records are, of course, usually available by subpoena after suit is filed, but it is better to get them as soon as possible, since the records may be essential to a prefiling evaluation of the case. For example, in a personal injury case, you will need to review police accident reports, doctor's reports, hospital records, employment records, and perhaps others.[11] In a contract action, you will need to get the contract itself, as well as records that bear on the performance and nonperformance of the parties. These might include orders, shipping documents, invoices, and payment records.

If you can get these kinds of records from others, maintain them properly. Keep the records you receive together and in order, and do not mark them. Keep a record of how, from whom, and when you got them, since these persons may be necessary foundation witnesses if the case later goes to trial. Make additional copies that you can mark up and use during client and witness interviews.

4. Internet research

The Internet is an obvious and exceedingly important source of information, both before suit is filed and while the litigation is moving forward. Indeed, if you fail to conduct basic Google searches and thereby overlook important information, you risk Rule 11 sanctions. The Internet can yield significant information about parties, witnesses, experts, jurors, products, medical devices, and drugs, and most of it is free. In a simple case, such as a small personal injury case, you may only need one or two hours on the Internet to research your case. In a complex case, such as a wrongful death products liability case, you and your paralegal may spend scores of hours on the Internet investigating various aspects of the case.

For example, before you accept a new client or case, you can research your client to discover matters that may affect his credibility, his ability to pay your legal fees, and his litigation history. (These are frequently things the client did not tell you during your initial interview.) You can research the opposing parties to discover matters affecting their credibility and ability to pay a judgment. If the case involves corporations or other entities, you can obtain much useful information about them on the Internet. Before suit is filed, and as discovery progresses, you can research the

11. Since some records, such as hospital reports, will be technical, at the very least get a good dictionary or encyclopedia or use medical websites to help you understand them. Better yet, use a consulting expert to evaluate them for you.

known witnesses to discover matters affecting their credibility, such as prior criminal cases, civil judgments, bankruptcies, and current lawsuits.

If the case involves products, medical devices, or drugs, the Internet contains a wealth of information that you should explore before you file suit. The Internet is also useful for investigating experts you are considering hiring or the opposing party is using. Such investigations can disclose information that can affect the expert's suitability in a particular case and his credibility as a testifying expert.

If your court system creates prospective juror lists that are available before trial, or the judge allows written juror questionnaires before trial, you can use the Internet to investigate the backgrounds of the prospective jurors. This information will support challenges for cause and help you use your preemptory challenges more effectively.

A note of caution: A lawyer's ethical obligations do not change because the Internet is involved. In particular, the ethical obligations in Model Rules 4.1-4.4 and 8.4 apply whenever you are communicating with third parties through social networks such as Facebook. (See §2.5.1) And don't overlook the Fair Credit Reporting Act, 15 U.S.C. §1681 et seq., which imposes certain disclosure duties on users of information for background checks.

a.   People

Investigate your party, opposing parties, and known witnesses. You will want to gather information affecting their credibility, litigation history, and finances.

For information about parties affecting credibility, start with search engines like Google, Yahoo, and Bing.[12] Thesearchenginelist.com has a useful list of all-purpose and special search engines. Use more than one, since their databases and search methods may differ. For common names, search the name with a location or other personal information that will narrow the search. Check local newspapers over the past 10 years. Sites like Facebook, Twitter, and Instagram frequently contain revealing personal facts.[13] Check if the person has a blog. Check federal and state court records for any prior convictions that can be used for impeachment.

For information about parties' litigation history, check PACER, the federal court records site, and state counterparts. Most court records are now computerized and, as public records, can be searched. Check Westlaw Peoplemap and Lexis for the same information. In many cases you will also need to examine the actual court files.

For information about parties' finances, check the county assessor's and county recorder's records for judgments, liens, and taxes. Sites like Zillow contain records of real estate transactions.

---

12. For a discussion of search techniques for social media, see Thomas Roe Frazer III, Social Media: From Discovery to Marketing—A Primer for Lawyers, 36 Am. J. Trial Advoc. 539, 559-562 (2013).

13. A lawyer cannot "friend" a third party under false pretenses in order to gain access to private information on Facebook. See Model Rule 8.4.

b.   Corporations

A wealth of information is usually available when a party is a corporation. Always check the corporation's website. Search the Secretary of State or Corporation Commission's sites whenever the corporation is incorporated in or licensed to do business in a state. If a corporation is a public company, check the SEC site and other federal and state regulatory agency sites. Don't overlook the Freedom of Information Act and state Open Records Acts as ways of getting additional information. (Make the request as specific and focused as possible, or else you may not get a response for several months.)

Check newspapers and financial magazines over the past 10 years. Westlaw and Lexis contain business information and news. Dunn & Bradstreet rates business financial strength. Property records will disclose real estate holdings. Consider using a paid site such as Hoover's to obtain additional information.

c.   Products, medical devices, and drugs

When a case involves a product, medical device, or drug, always check the manufacturer's website for product information and claims. Use Westlaw terms and phrases functions to find other cases involving the same or similar products. Check newspaper sites. Check federal and state court sites. Check the sites of federal regulatory agencies, such as the Securities and Exchange Commission and the Food and Drug Administration. If the case involves a patent or trademark, check the U.S. Patent and Trademark Office. If a foreign patent is involved, check the European and Japanese Patent Offices. If the case involves common carriers, check the National Transportation Safety Board; if the case involves consumer products, check the Consumer Products Safety Commission. Check parallel state regulatory and licensing agencies. If the case involves a motor vehicle, check sites such as Carfax for the vehicle's history.

d.   Experts

Almost every case today involves experts, and Internet searches will reveal a great deal of information about your and your opponent's experts.

Check the expert's website. Use Google, Yahoo, and Bing to get general information. Check newspapers. If the expert is a university professor, check the university news and department sites. Use Westlaw expert witness databases to obtain profiles of experts and their litigation history. Use Westlaw and Lexis to find similar cases, and identify the lawyers and experts involved in those cases. You should then call the appropriate lawyer to find out who the best experts were. Plaintiff and defendant associations such as the American Association for Justice and Defense Research Institute maintain databases available to their members that include information about experts.

Check the expert's publication history, and use it to verify the expert's resume and deposition testimony. Always check state licensing boards for doctors, lawyers, engineers, and other professionals to learn if they are currently licensed, in good standing, and have ever been disciplined.

e. Jurors

In jurisdictions where juror lists are available before trial, or the judge has permitted written juror questionnaires before trial, you have an opportunity to research the jurors' backgrounds for relevant information. Check court and newspaper sites for involvement in litigation. Use Google, Yahoo, and Bing for general information, and Facebook, Twitter, YouTube, Instagram, LinkedIn, Google+, and other social network sites for information revealing experiences, interests, and attitudes relevant to the trial issues. Find out if any juror maintains a blog. Monitor them during the trial.

The Internet is constantly evolving, so popular sites common today may disappear tomorrow, and new sites may appear. Everyone has her favorite sites and search strategies. The important thing is not just to collect a list of useful sites. Rather, have a solid understanding of the kind of available information that will help you during the litigation process, a sense of when you should gather that information, and a search strategy for obtaining that information in a timely and cost-effective manner.

§2.5. Witness interviews

After you have interviewed your client and obtained the available exhibits, the next stage of your informal fact investigation involves interviewing witnesses. Here a great deal of flexibility is possible, and planning ahead is particularly important.

1. Whom to interview and when

The more you know, the more accurately you can assess the strengths and weaknesses of your case. An interview of every witness, favorable, neutral, and unfavorable, to find out what each knows seems to make sense. Economic realities, however, temper the benefits of interviewing everyone. In few cases can you simply interview everyone regardless of expense. On the other hand, every case has critical witnesses whom you must try to interview regardless of the cost. In addition, once you take the case, you must handle it competently regardless of cost constraints. Between these two extremes, you need to decide whether you should try to interview a particular known witness and attempt to identify and interview others. For example, suppose you represent a party in an automobile collision case. From your client and the accident reports, you learn who else was present. If a police report identifies an eyewitness, you need to interview him. What else should you do? Should you interview the police officer who wrote the report and other officers present who did not write reports? Should you try to locate bystanders who were present but have not been identified?

Three basic considerations determine how far you should go. First, you need to interview all critical witnesses regardless of cost. A competent lawyer simply must always do this. The critical witnesses are the eyewitnesses to an event, the participants to a business transaction, and other persons such as the principal investigating officers. Such witnesses will probably be witnesses at trial. For the hypothetical automobile collision case, the list would include the known eyewitness, the police officer who prepared the accident report, and other eyewitnesses whom you can identify. Second, cost considerations will influence your choice to interview witnesses who are not critical. For example, canvassing homes and stores near the accident scene may turn up someone else who saw the accident; however, doing this is expensive and may produce nothing useful. Attempting to identify and interview such possible witnesses may be worthwhile in a $200,000 lawsuit in which liability is unclear, but cannot be done in a $20,000 case where liability is clear. Third, how far you go in locating and interviewing witnesses depends on what you have developed so far. For example, if your client and two solid eyewitnesses clearly establish liability, other eyewitnesses who can corroborate the client are unnecessary. On the other hand, if one eyewitness contradicts your client's version, you should locate and interview other witnesses to see which version they support.

When you have decided on the witnesses you need to interview, you must decide the order in which to interview them. Here again flexibility is required. Interviews of favorable and neutral witnesses should proceed before you interview the unfavorable ones, since you will have better success in pinpointing the differences in their stories. Identifying and interviewing the favorable and neutral witnesses first will give you the basis for your side's version of any disputed events and will help you identify the areas of disagreement when you interview the unfavorable witnesses. You can then explore these areas in detail when you interview the unfavorable witnesses. Frequently, however, you won't know for sure whether a given witness will be favorable.

On the other hand, early interviews of unfavorable witnesses, before their attitudes and recall have solidified, have advantages. You might know, for example, that a witness in an accident case will be unfavorable because a police accident report quotes him. You may want to interview that witness quickly. He may change his mind, or tell you that he "didn't really see it happen," or "isn't sure" about important facts. You can thereby minimize the impact of this witness.

Are there limits on whom you can interview?[14] Ethical rules control here. Under Model Rules 4.2 and 4.3, you can interview any person *not* known to be represented by counsel. (This person, of course, has a right not to talk to you.) You *cannot* interview any person *known* to be

---

14. See Model Rules of Professional Conduct, Rule 4.2; Restatement (Third) of the Law: The Law Governing Lawyers §§99-100 (2000); J. Grenig & J. Kinsler, Handbook of Federal Civil Discovery & Disclosure §§14.8-14.9 (3d ed. 2010); J. Berch & M. Berch, May I Have a Word With You: Oops, Have I Already Violated the No-Contact Rule?, 6 Phoenix L. Rev. 433 (2013).

represented by counsel in the matter, unless the counsel gives you consent or you are authorized by law. Obviously, you cannot communicate with the opposing party if you know counsel represents the opposing party in the matter. (Such prohibited communications include, for example, a "friend" request on Facebook.) This rule applies even before the lawsuit commences.

Difficult questions arise when the opposing party is a corporation or other artificial entity. The only persons who can "speak" for the corporation are its employees and agents. The Comment to Rule 4.2 sets out three categories of employees of an organization with whom you may *not* communicate: (1) any person having managerial responsibility on behalf of the organization; (2) any person whose act or omission may be imputed to the organization; and (3) any person whose statement may constitute an admission on behalf of the organization.

Most states have adopted some version of Model Rule 4.2. However, while all states apply it to current employees, they differ over its application to former employees. Are former employees now nonparties, so that the rule does not apply, or are they still employees for purposes of the rule? Case law in the various jurisdictions differs, so jurisdiction-specific research will be necessary.

Under Model Rule 4.1, you cannot knowingly misrepresent material facts or applicable law when you interview a witness. You must disclose that you are a lawyer representing a party, that you do not represent the witness's interests, that you are trying to gather information to help your party in a particular matter, and that the witness has the right not to talk to you.

2. Who should do the interviewing?

Either the lawyer or an investigator should conduct the actual interviews. There are advantages and disadvantages with each approach. If the lawyer interviews, no additional investigator costs are incurred, and he can get a first-hand impression of the person as a trial witness. This is particularly important with key witnesses. On the other hand, lawyer interviews can create impeachment problems. If at trial the witness denies making a statement to the lawyer that is inconsistent with his testimony, the lawyer will have to be a prove-up witness. This situation puts the lawyer at odds with ethical rules that generally prevent a lawyer from being a witness in a trial in which the lawyer represents a party.[15] A common approach is to have the lawyer personally interview witnesses known to be favorable, but have another person present when interviewing neutral or unfavorable witnesses. That person can then prove up impeachment at trial if necessary.

Investigator interviews have economic and practical advantages. An investigator's time will usually be less expensive than the lawyer's, creating cost savings for the client. However, the time saved may be minimal, since the lawyer must spend time educating the investigator about the known

15. See Model Rules of Professional Conduct, Rule 3.7.

facts and the issues, and about what direction the interviews should take. An experienced investigator will probably locate witnesses better and will be an available impeachment prove-up witness at trial.

When hiring an appropriate investigator, you should establish a contractual relationship and give her specific instructions. A contract with the investigator will prevent misunderstandings about what work will be required, what the cost limitations of the case are, and how the investigator will be paid. The contract should expressly state that the investigator will be an employee of the lawyer, and that everything the investigator learns and obtains during the investigation will be reported only to the lawyer and will otherwise be kept confidential. Chances that the attorney's work-product doctrine will protect the investigative reports from disclosure will improve.[16] As always, you are well-advised to put the agreement in writing, either in a simple contract or in a letter to the investigator.

3.   Locating witnesses

Lawyers are perfectly capable of locating many witnesses. The client frequently knows the important ones. Records, such as business records and accident reports, will usually identify others. When their names are known, many witnesses can be easily located over the telephone, on the Internet, or by checking basic, available sources. Telephone listings, websites, neighbors at a previous address, workers at a former job, friends, and relatives are all good sources to help locate a known witness. A witness may have merely changed a telephone number, moved to a different apartment, or changed jobs, and tracking her down is relatively simple. If these leads do not work, check with the post office, voter registration and motor vehicle departments, utility companies, and other government agencies, such as the Veterans Administration, Social Security office, and unemployment and welfare agencies. Check paid Internet sites that search for missing persons under "locating people," "people search," and "people finder." If the witness is important to you, and you cannot locate her, you may need an experienced investigator.

4.   Purposes of the interview

You should try to accomplish several tasks during a witness interview, in the following order. First, learn everything the witness knows and does not know that is relevant to the case. Have the witness tell what he knows by using open-ended questions. You can follow up later with specific, focused questions; early on, though, you want details only of the critical events and transactions, not everything the witness knows that may possibly be relevant. When learning what the witness knows, make sure you pinpoint the admissible facts based on firsthand knowledge and separate them from

---

16. See Rule 26(b)(3). A lawyer's notes summarizing a witness interview are usually not discoverable under Rule 26(b)(3).

opinion, speculation, and hearsay. With witnesses who have unfavorable information, you should try to limit the damage by limiting the witness' testimony. Find out what the witness does not know, is not sure of, is only guessing about, or has only secondhand information about.

Second, pin the witness down. Go beyond generalizations and obtain specific, admissible facts. For example, "driving fast" should be changed to an approximation of speed in miles per hour. "He looked drunk" should be pursued to get the details underlying the conclusion, such as "staggering, glassy eyed, and smelling of alcohol." If you get only generalizations and conclusions, the witness can easily change his testimony later.

Third, get admissions. Admissions from an unfavorable witness that he "isn't sure," "didn't really see it," "was only guessing," or "was told" all serve to prevent the witness from changing or expanding his testimony at trial.

Fourth, get information that might be used for impeachment. If an unfavorable witness says something that later may be useful to impeach him, pin him down. For example, if an unfavorable witness to an accident says he was 200 feet away when it happened, make sure you commit him to that fact. Use "200 feet" in other questions, and recommit him to that fact, since at trial he may claim that the distance was shorter.

Fifth, get leads to other witnesses and information. A witness will often name other witnesses or divulge information not previously mentioned in any report. For example, asking a witness if anyone else was present at an accident scene will sometimes get a response like: "Sure, my sister Ellen was standing right next to me and saw the whole thing."

Finally, try to record the interview or get some type of written statement. How to do so is discussed later in this section.

5. Arranging the interview

Often the most difficult part of witness interviews is getting witnesses to agree to be interviewed in the first place. With favorable witnesses this is not usually a problem, and selecting a convenient time and place for the interview is a routine matter. Unfavorable witnesses, however, are frequently reluctant. Here you can take either of two approaches. You can attempt to arrange an interview, or you can try a surprise interview. A reluctant witness may agree to be interviewed at a convenient time and place, where privacy is assured, and if the interview won't take too long. Let such a witness know that cooperating now may eliminate the need to be deposed later, and suggest that an interview at home would be both convenient and private. Tell the witness that you need and appreciate her help in understanding what really happened, and that her information may help resolve the case more quickly.

If a witness will not agree to an arranged interview, an unannounced interview is the only alternative. Frequently, a witness who doesn't want to be bothered or "get involved" will nevertheless agree to talk when an investigator "pops into" the witness's office or "stops by" the house. Again, reassurance that the questions won't take long and may eliminate the need for the witness's further involvement might help. However, a witness has a perfect right to refuse to be interviewed, and you cannot harass or badger the witness hoping to change her mind. The only alternative in such situations is to depose the witness after the lawsuit commences.

Whenever you interview a witness, you must tell her that you are a lawyer, that you represent one of the parties in a dispute, and that you represent only that party. Tell the witness what you want to talk to her about. Model Rules 4.1 and 4.3 clearly require these disclosures.

6. Structuring the interview

How do you go about structuring a witness interview? First, review the case file, which should contain client interviews, exhibits such as police reports, perhaps other witness interviews, and the developing litigation chart. Second, get copies of any diagrams, photographs, and records you may use during the interview. Third, decide if and how you will record the interview. Finally, prepare an outline for the interview. A frequently followed order for witness interviews is the following:

1.   Witness background
2.   Story in witness's own words
3.   Detailed chronological story
4.   Questions focused on your theory of the case

First, witness background is important for assessing witness credibility and determining if there is any bias, interest, or other facts that affect credibility. Most witnesses don't mind talking about their work, family, and home. Asking these background questions usually puts witnesses at ease. Some witnesses, however, may resent what they consider to be intrusions into their private lives. In such cases you may want to slip the background information later into the interview, or simply touch on it at the end. Second, let the witness tell her story in her own words, even at the price of hearing irrelevant facts. It gives you a good picture of the kind of witness she will be at trial, and you may discover important facts that would never have come to light. Third, go over the story in chronological order and in detail. Get specifics on what the witness saw, heard, and did at all important times, and what she saw others do and say. Find out what exhibits the witness knows of and other witnesses she is aware of. Find out what the witness personally knows and what is only opinion, speculation, or hearsay. Find out to whom the witness has talked or given statements. Finally, ask focused questions based on your theory of the case. For example, if the witness gives information that contradicts your version of the events, see how you can minimize its effect. If the witness is "not sure," "guessing," "didn't see it myself," or says other things that lessen the damage, make sure you note it. In addition, see if the witness can corroborate something useful to your side. Witnesses are rarely completely unfavorable; a little searching will often turn up something positive.

7.   Recording the interview

Regardless of the witness, you should make a record of the interview. There are several possibilities:

1.   Use a court reporter
2.   Make a tape recording, with the witness' consent
3.   Obtain a written, signed statement
4.   Take notes during the interview
5.   Have another person take notes during the interview
6.   Make notes after the interview

The approach you use depends on what will best serve your interests and what the witness will permit. A short, written, and signed statement is often best for cooperative, favorable witnesses. After interviewing the witness, simply type a summary of his story and ask him to sign it. The statement should be from the witness's point of view (e.g., "I was standing on the corner of Main and Elm when I saw . . ."). Have the witness draw and label a diagram showing where he was and what he saw. Another method is to send the witness a confirming letter summarizing what he said, and ask the witness to sign and return a copy acknowledging its accuracy. The letter will lock a favorable witness into his basic story, and no damage results if the opposing side obtains the statement during discovery.[17]

You should get a detailed statement from unfavorable witnesses. Your chances of getting contradictions, admissions, and impeachment that may be valuable at trial will improve. Using a court reporter or a tape recorder is probably the most reliable method. Get the witness' permission if you plan to tape record, since surreptitious recordings are illegal in some jurisdictions. Avoid later criticism that the recording does not include everything the witness said by being mindful of when a conversation is off the record.

What is best and what a witness is willing to do often differ. Many witnesses are reluctant to talk, and they are usually under no legal obligation to talk to anyone. Of those willing to talk, many are understandably reluctant to give a signed statement or to have their statements recorded or reduced to writing. Hence, your priority should be to get the witness to tell what he knows, to learn what his trial testimony is likely to be, and to get leads on other witnesses and evidence. Only then should you try to get the most reliable type of statement the witness agrees to give. In short, an interview without any recording is better than no interview at all. You can always dictate immediately afterwards what the witness has said.

Whether a record of a witness interview is discoverable depends on the kind of record involved. Under Rule 26(b)(3), a "statement" is

---

17. While a lawyer's notes summarizing a witness interview are usually not discoverable, under Rule 26(b)(3) even trial preparation materials are not absolutely protected from discovery. Upon a showing of substantial need and undue hardship, such materials are discoverable, except that "mental impressions, conclusions, opinions, or legal theories of a party's attorney or other representative concerning the litigation" are always protected from disclosure.

discoverable if it is "a written statement that the person has signed or otherwise adopted or approved; or a contemporaneous stenographic, mechanical, electrical, or other recording—or a transcription of it— that recites substantially verbatim the person's oral statement." If the witness has helpful things to say, taking a discoverable statement usually creates no problems if the other side obtains it later, and the statement can be used to refresh memory or impeach if the witness testifies inconsistently at trial. If, however, what the witness says is unfavorable, there is usually no point in creating a discoverable statement that will only educate the other side to the fact that a good witness for them exists.

8. Interviewing techniques

Every witness is influenced by both positive and negative factors that affect her willingness to be interviewed and disclose what she knows.[18] An interviewer, therefore, should understand these factors and use them to accomplish his primary purpose of finding out what the witness knows. These factors bear on both friendly and hostile witnesses. Hostile witnesses may be unwilling to talk at all; friendly witnesses, although willing to talk, may be influenced by a variety of negative and positive factors.

Negative factors inhibit witness disclosure. Some witnesses feel that the interviewer is judging them. Others tell the interviewer what he apparently wants to hear. Still others become inhibited by emotions such as fear or embarrassment. The interviewer must learn to recognize situations in which these factors exist and use interviewing techniques that reduce their effect.

Positive factors promote disclosure. Witnesses usually respond favorably when the interviewer shows a personal interest in them. Witnesses like to feel that they are doing the decent thing by talking to the interviewer. They tend to identify with the side that values their testimony. Witnesses enjoy feeling important and may be more likely to help if they feel that the information they can provide is important to resolve a dispute fairly. Positive reinforcement is a strong motivator.

You can best get witnesses to disclose information fully and accurately by minimizing the negative factors and reinforcing the positive ones. Accordingly, pick a convenient time and place for the interview. When scheduling the interview, remind the witness that it is always better to talk when the events are fresh in her mind. Remind her that it is natural to want to help others, and that her disclosure of information will help ensure a just and accurate result. Point out what other witnesses have said about the case so as to give her an opportunity to correct inaccuracies. Finally, show interest in the witness. Empathy is also a strong motivator; a witness naturally will want to please someone who appears interested in her.

An interviewer can use either open- or closed-ended questions to achieve desired results. Use open-ended, direct-examination questions

18. See S. Krieger & R. Neumann, Essential Lawyering Skills: Interviewing, Counseling, Negotiation, and Persuasive Fact Analysis (4th ed. 2011).

to get the witness talking, to obtain the basic story, and to pursue leads. For example, questions in a "describe how" and "tell me" format will force the witness to give descriptive answers. But use closed, leading cross-examination questions to pin the witness down and develop potential impeachment. This question form can focus on specific, isolated facts. For example, ask: "You're sure the car was going 40 mph?" and "She couldn't have been going faster than that, could she?"

The content of questions can also effectively influence responses. Let the witness know your attitude on the matter being discussed, since she has a psychological interest in satisfying her listener's expectations. For example, telling a witness that you feel bad about the defendant cheating your client may get a more sympathetic story from the witness. Second, word choices can influence responses. For example, it is well known that using the phrase "how fast" rather than "how slowly" will increase estimations of speed. Third, leading questions are more likely to get the kind of answer you want. For example, asking a witness, "That car was going faster than the speed limit, wasn't it?" is more likely to elicit a "yes" response. Fourth, knowing what other people have said or what other evidence has already shown can influence witnesses, since witnesses prefer consistency and disdain conflict. For example, telling a witness that another eyewitness has already stated that the car was speeding will often influence the witness.

9. Evaluating witnesses

Following a witness interview, write a short memo evaluating the witness and her information. You can easily forget your impressions of the witness, yet witness credibility is frequently the critical component in case evaluation. The memo is particularly important if more than one lawyer will work on the file. The memo should evaluate the witness' credibility and effectiveness as a trial witness, note the witness' attitude toward the case, and summarize where the witness' anticipated testimony will help and hurt your case.[19] When evaluating witnesses, it is also a good idea to do a computer search to learn more about witnesses' backgrounds. Web sites such as Facebook can reveal things witnesses have written about themselves that reflect on their credibility.

§2.6. *Expert reviews*

Wrongful death, medical malpractice, product liability, major negligence, and commercial cases almost always use expert witnesses at trial. The plaintiff's case will probably require expert testimony to establish a prima facie case on liability and causation and to make out a solid case on damages. The defense case will probably have opposing experts. Accordingly, your

---

19. Such a memo should also be absolutely privileged as work product and therefore not discoverable. See Rule 26(b)(3).

investigation is frequently incomplete unless you have appropriate experts review the file.

You may need two experts: one to review the file and consult with you in order to develop facts and theories for trial, the other to be a trial witness. Of course, one expert can and sometimes does perform both roles. Remember, however, that under Rule 26(b)(4)(D) the facts and opinions of a consulting expert are usually protected from discovery, absent exceptional circumstances, but the identity and substance of facts and opinions of trial experts are discoverable. Hence, having a separate consulting expert will usually limit what is discoverable by other parties and should be valuable in developing theories and evidence for trial. Make sure that your agreement with the consulting expert clearly shows her status and requires that she communicate only with you, so that her work comes under the Rule 26 protection. Have your agreement with the consulting expert confirm that she will not share any material regarding the case with anyone else. Some lawyers require in the agreement that the client is responsible for paying the expert's fees. Doing this should not change the protection of the work-product doctrine.

If a case is complex and will involve substantial work, you might insist that an expert review the case before you agree to take it. The client should pay for the cost of the review. While the lawyer can usually advance the cost of the review, requiring the client to pay for the review in advance is often an effective way of weeding out clients who already know they have a weak case. Such clients will often refuse to pay for the review, which should make you think carefully about taking the case in the first place, particularly where the client has the ability to pay. This is a sensible approach whenever you have a case that will require expert witnesses. You and your client will benefit regardless of the review's results. If the case is complex and will require expert witnesses, Rule 11 may require an expert's review before filing suit. Some jurisdictions require in certain types of cases, such as medical malpractice, that you have an expert who has reviewed the case and is of the opinion that it has merit before you can file suit.

Do not send out a file for expert review until you have collected the reports and records the expert will inevitably need. Make sure the written materials you send her give a complete and neutral picture of the case.[20] In addition, have the expert review the file generally, and direct the expert to specific areas where you see potential problems. Do so in conversations with the expert, after you have sent her the necessary materials. For example, in a medical malpractice case you might ask the expert to evaluate whether the defendant physician improperly administered the anesthetic, and whether the physician breached the standard of care. A focused review is usually more productive. Keep in mind that Rule

20. Before 2010, courts split on the question of whether attorneys waived work product protection for documents given to experts asked to prepare reports. Compare Synthes Spine Co. L.P. v. Walden, 232 F.R.D. 460 (E.D. Pa. 2005), with Pritchard v. Dow Agro Sciences, 263 F.R.D. 277 (W.D. Pa. 2009). A 2010 amendment to Rule 26 clarifies that communications between an attorney and an expert retain work product protection, with several exceptions. See §6.5.

26(b)(4) protects from disclosure drafts of expert reports and communications between the attorney and the testifying expert, except for communications that relate to the expert's compensation, the facts or data that the attorney provided to the expert that the expert considered in forming the opinions, and the assumptions the lawyer provided and the expert relied on in forming the opinions.

While Rule 26 makes important discovery distinctions between consulting and testifying experts, hiring an expert as a consultant does not prevent you from using her as an expert at trial. You may need to make this decision at the discovery stage, however, since the required disclosures require that you identify all experts expected to testify at trial.

Because an expert is so important, and because a consulting expert may later be the testifying expert at trial, you must take care in selecting one. Perhaps the best way to select an expert is simply to ask litigators you know to recommend one who is knowledgeable in the subject area of your case, is willing to work with and educate you, and will be an effective trial witness. If this tack fails, or you need an expert in an extremely specialized area, some lawyers' groups, such as the American Association for Justice and Defense Research Institute, maintain expert directories, and law libraries sometimes have directories for various specialties.[21]

§2.7.   The "small" case

This book discusses how to organize and investigate a case using the litigation chart method. This approach integrates the legal and fact investigations so that you can intelligently plan the litigation before filing suit or when first responding to one. These are steps that every litigator should take when handling any litigation matter.

When a case is sufficiently large, the expenditure of substantial legal resources to achieve the best possible result makes sense. In such cases, the lawyers representing the parties will usually be able to do all the things a conscientious litigator should do, without serious cost constraints. What about the client with a "small" case, involving less than $10,000? His case, although possibly meritorious, involves so little money that it is not economically possible for you to handle it competently and receive adequate compensation for the work involved. What do you do?

This is hardly a theoretical question. The median federal civil case today has somewhere in the neighborhood of $170,000 at stake, so many cases in state and federal courts involve smaller amounts.[22] Automobile accidents involving a few hundred dollars in direct losses, and consumer

---

21. See, e.g., H. Philo et al., Lawyers Desk Reference, which lists experts by category and is revised periodically. The TASA Group, the Technical Advisory Service for Attorneys, is one of several organizations that refer experts in numerous fields. Many legal newspapers and journals also contain listings and information about experts. Local universities are a good source as well.

22. E. Lee & T. Willging, National Judicial Center, National, Case-Based Civil Rules Survey, Oct. 2009, at 2.

contract matters involving similarly small sums, are common disputes, and some are litigated.

The lawyer faces a simple dilemma. On the one hand, every lawyer has a professional obligation to represent each client competently. On the other hand, a lawyer needs to be compensated to stay in business. How do you resolve this conflict?

The very small cases present less difficulty. Most jurisdictions have small claims courts in which the litigants can represent themselves at trial. Many jurisdictions do not allow lawyers in small claims courts, and judges hear the cases informally without adhering to strict rules of procedure or evidence. These courts frequently have brochures that explain how to bring a claim and how the case will be heard. In addition, some jurisdictions have special procedures for other small cases, including limits on (or the outright elimination of) discovery. The intent of both types of procedures is to bring down the cost of trying a case so that it makes economic sense to bring a lawsuit to enforce a claim in the first place. The cases that are too large to be brought as small claims, yet too small to make normal litigation cost-effective, cause the greatest problems. What can you do when presented with such cases? They are particularly problematic; a case that is worth little may pose just as many legal and factual complexities as a larger one. However, several strategies can at least reduce the concerns.[23]

First, screening small cases is particularly important. You should carefully assess liability, damages, and the other party's ability to pay a judgment. There is nothing more unproductive than taking a small case with questionable liability or filing an action against a party who is effectively judgment proof. Small cases must be screened quickly before any substantial investment in time is made.

Second, the client must understand what you can realistically do given the size of the case, and she must agree to your approach. For example, if the case is not worth the filing of a suit, perhaps you can attempt to get a settlement or resolve it through an alternative dispute resolution method. If the case is large enough to bring suit, but formal litigation would be prohibitively expensive, perhaps you can make do without formal discovery or with limited discovery. Whatever your approach, make sure the client knows what it will be and the reasons for it, and also agrees to it in writing.

Third, make sure you get your costs covered in advance, and let the client know the overall anticipated costs. A client who has paid the anticipated costs in advance has a direct financial interest in the litigation and will usually be more cooperative and realistic. A client who understands how costs, such as a medical expert's fee, can devour any recovery will have a better grasp of what can realistically be done.

Fourth, get the client to do as much work as possible, such as obtaining documents and records and locating witnesses. Client assistance can substantially reduce costs. You can also tell the client that you will not take the

23. See S. Adelman & G. Haldeman, The Dog Case, 10 Litig. 11 (1984).

case until he has done this kind of preliminary work. Again, the client gets involved in the litigation this way.

Fifth, you can sometimes economize without seriously compromising the preparation of the case. The largest savings can be made in the area of formal discovery, particularly depositions. Sometimes depositions need not be transcribed. Sometimes you can avoid depositions of witnesses entirely and rely on witness statements. Sometimes the opposing lawyer will agree to reciprocal informal interviews of parties in place of depositions. You must discuss these savings with your client, of course, and he must agree to the procedures you take.

Sixth, the paramount rule, regardless of the size of the lawsuit, is always the same: you must competently handle the client's case.[24] You must do whatever is necessary to uncover the important facts and witnesses, even if it is not cost-effective. If the opposing lawyer will not agree to informal interviews of the parties and you do not know what the opposing party will say at trial, you simply must depose that party. If the case cannot be settled short of trial, you simply must try the case. Lawyers, wittingly or not, sometimes take cases that prove to be uneconomic. Once taken, however, the lawyer has the same professional obligation to prepare that case competently as he has for any other case.

Finally, keep in mind that when lawyers take cases, they frequently do so for reasons other than the compensation they will directly receive from that particular case. In small cases, accept the fact that you will not be paid at your usual rate. However, that fact alone should not prevent you from taking certain cases. The case may involve a regular client, who you want to ensure remains satisfied with your overall representation. The case may come from a new client who may become a regular client if your work impresses her. The case may be legally or factually challenging. A high profile case may enhance your reputation among lawyers and in the community. The case may be a new type of case and involve an area you have become interested in. Finally, you may decide to take a case to meet your pro bono obligations as a lawyer.

The high cost of litigation is a serious concern in our society and has sparked considerable discussion among the public, government, and the organized bar. Litigation procedures have become more streamlined in small cases; reformers frequently offer proposals to curtail formal discovery or to eliminate it altogether in certain types of cases; alternative dispute resolution is common; and judges take a more active role in litigation management and settlement discussions. If a lawyer decides to take a case, however, the cardinal rule is that he always has a professional obligation to represent a client competently. That the client's matter is a small case cannot excuse neglect of the lawyer's professional obligations. Adequate planning and preparation are necessary for any matter, regardless of size. The basic steps this book outlines can help ensure that your representation succeeds.

24. See Model Rules of Professional Conduct, Model Rule 1.1.

III

LEGAL INVESTIGATION

§3.1.   Introduction

As you conduct your informal fact investigation, you must also evaluate the various legal issues that every lawsuit involves. You will need to determine what jurisdiction's law applies; what claims, remedies, or defenses to pursue; what parties must or can be joined; whether the court has subject matter jurisdiction over the claims; whether the court has personal jurisdiction over the parties; and where venue is proper. This chapter discusses the legal choices a plaintiff must make before filing a lawsuit and a defendant must make before responding to one, and how these considerations relate to each other. While this discussion is based on federal district court litigation, the basic analytical sequence fits state court lawsuits as well.

A note of caution is in order. Choice of law, legal theories of claims and remedies, joinder, subject matter jurisdiction, personal jurisdiction, and venue can pose complex problems. The literature about them is extensive. A single volume can hardly deal with these issues in depth, much less one chapter in a general text on pretrial techniques. The discussion that follows is intended to get the new litigator to think intelligently about these legal considerations in broad terms. A serious legal issue must always be researched thoroughly before filing suit. As always, remember that Rule 11 requires that a lawyer conduct a reasonable inquiry into the law and determine that the pleading has evidentiary support and is not frivolous before filing. The rule, in short, requires that you do your homework.

§3.2.   Choice of law[1]

Before you can determine what claims, remedies, or defenses you can raise in your case, you need to know which jurisdiction's law applies. When a

---

1. Hazard et al. §§2.15–2.17; Moore's Manual §§3.01–3.05; Moore's Federal Practice §§124.30–124.32; Wright & Miller §§4501 et seq.

plaintiff brings a claim in federal court based exclusively on federal question jurisdiction, the resolution is simple: federal law applies.[2] However, if the complaint invokes diversity jurisdiction, state law will apply in one way or another. This situation prompts two types of choice-of-law questions.

1. When will state law apply in federal court?

Cases proceed in federal court based on diversity jurisdiction when the cause of action the plaintiff alleges does not include any federal legal element. These diversity cases pose complex choice-of-law conundrums. A civil case may trigger a lot of legal problems, some having to do with the substance of the dispute, others having to do with the process itself, others addressing remedies issues, and others implicating evidentiary questions. When does state law apply in federal court to govern one or more of these issues, and when does federal law apply? This question is often referred to (somewhat inexactly) as the so-called *Erie* problem, based on the landmark case of Erie R.R. Co. v. Tompkins, 304 U.S. 64 (1938).

Crudely put, the U.S. Supreme Court in *Erie* held that a federal court sitting in diversity must apply state substantive law to determine the parties' rights, duties, obligations, and defenses. Federal law, in contrast, governs procedural issues. Unfortunately, this seemingly simple distinction between procedure and substance is not always clear. For example, a state's basic negligence law is clearly substantive, while its discovery rules, contained in civil procedure acts, are clearly procedural. But matters like statutes of limitations, privileges, and burdens of proof fall into a confounding gray zone.

The Supreme Court has periodically grappled with the substance/procedure divide since deciding *Erie*. Leading cases include: Guaranty Trust Co. v. York, 326 U.S. 99 (1945), in which the Court held that state statutes of limitations apply, not federal ones; Byrd v. Blue Ridge Rural Elec. Coop., 356 U.S. 525 (1958), in which the Court held that the federal right to a jury trial on a claim prevailed over a contrary state rule that made the judge the trier of fact; Hanna v. Plumer, 380 U.S. 460 (1965), in which the Court applied the federal service-of-process rules over a conflicting state rule; Walker v. Armco Steel Corp., 446 U.S. 740 (1980), in which the Court applied a state rule defining how an action is to be commenced for statute of limitations purposes over the conflicting Rule 3 of the Federal Rules of Civil Procedure; Gasperini v. Center for Humanities, 518 U.S. 415 (1996), in which the Court held that a state law would apply to determine how a federal court should review the size of a jury verdict; and Shady Grove Orthopedic Assocs., P.A. v. Allstate Insurance Co., 559 U.S. 393 (2010), in which the Court held that Rule 23 of the Federal Rules of Civil Procedure preempted a state law that otherwise would have limited the availability of the class action device.

2. In some instances, as with the Federal Tort Claims Act, the federal substantive law refers to the forum state's substantive law.

As this list suggests, the Supreme Court continues to grapple with the complex question of whether a federal court will apply state law in a diversity case. Accordingly, any lawyer faced with an *Erie*-type question must thoroughly research the decided cases to determine how the issue is likely to be resolved in a particular case. The following is an introduction to how to approach an *Erie* problem, a step-by-step approach derived from the Court's opinion from Hanna v. Plumer.

The first step is easy. Determine if the state law at issue is clearly substantive or arguably procedural. If it is clearly substantive — unconscionability doctrine in a contract case, for instance, or the duty of care in a negligence dispute — then the state law applies in federal court.

If, however, the state law is arguably procedural — for instance, a state law prohibiting class actions in insurance disputes — then the analysis gets more complicated. Ask yourself whether there is a Federal Rule of Civil Procedure that arguably governs the legal issue involved. If the issue involves whether a particular claim can be litigated in a class action, for example, Rule 23 arguably applies. You should next determine if the state law and the Federal Rule necessarily conflict, or if you can interpret the Federal Rule to "make room" for the state law. This question is challenging. The Court in *Shady Grove* held that Rule 23 necessarily conflicts with any state law limitation on the availability of the class action device, and thus that Rule 23 preempts the state law and applies in federal court. Hence a state law prohibiting class actions in insurance disputes would yield to Rule 23 in diversity cases. In contrast, the Court in *Walker* held that a state law applies to determine when a case commences for statute of limitations purposes, even though Rule 3 states when a case commences, and even though Rule 3 and the state law identified different times of commencement.

If you cannot find any Federal Rule that arguably applies to the issue at hand, or if the Federal Rule that seems to apply does not necessarily conflict with the state law, then you should ask a couple more questions before applying the state law. The first involves a "modified outcome-determinative test." If, at the moment of filing, a lawyer thought that the state law would not apply in federal court, would she be tempted to forum-shop between federal court and state court as a result? In other words, would the application of the state law in state court, and its non-application in federal court, guide her choice as between the two? If so, *Hanna* counsels in favor of the application of state law in federal court, to negate this invitation to forum-shop. For instance, many states require plaintiffs in medical malpractice cases to attach affidavits from physicians to their complaints to attest to the validity of the claims. Some courts hold that these state laws apply to malpractice cases brought in federal court based on diversity jurisdiction.[3] If these laws did not apply, a lawyer representing a plaintiff would be more likely to choose to file in federal court, to get away from this burdensome requirement. In contrast, in *Hanna*, the Court held that a technical service-of-process requirement in

---

3. E.g., Chamberlain v. Giampapa, 210 F.3d 154, 160 (3d Cir. 2000); Williams v. United States, 754 F. Supp. 2d 942 (W.D. Tenn. 2010).

Massachusetts law did not apply in federal court. The lawyer considering where to file would simply comply with whatever service-of-process requirement applied, state or federal, and the difference between the two would not affect forum choice.

Many *Erie* problems are recurring, and you can often find precedent on the specific *Erie* problem you face. You may not need to go through these steps if the appellate court in your circuit has already decided the issue. Either way, careful research is a must if your case presents an *Erie* problem.

2.   Which state's substantive law applies?

The second choice-of-law issue deals with multistate events and transactions. If, for example, an Arizona driver sues a California driver over an automobile accident in Nevada and brings a diversity action in federal court, which state's tort law applies? Does it matter where the action is filed?

The Supreme Court in Klaxon Co. v. Stentor Elec. Mfg., 313 U.S. 487 (1941), held that in a federal diversity action the forum state's conflict-of-law rules govern to determine which state's substantive law will apply. In the above example, if plaintiff brings suit in federal district court in Arizona, then Arizona's conflicts-of-law rules govern. A plaintiff who can bring an action in more than one venue may therefore be able to acquire a more advantageous forum. For example, if the Arizona plaintiff can file suit in Arizona, the Arizona conflicts rules govern. Arizona substantive law may apply, since Arizona has an interest in applying its own law to its own citizens. If the Arizona plaintiff can file suit in Nevada, the Nevada conflicts rules govern and Nevada substantive law may apply. Nevada has an interest in applying its law to a lawsuit arising out of an accident that occurred within its borders. If Arizona and Nevada tort law differ and the plaintiff has a choice of forums in which to bring suit, he will obviously pick the one whose choice of law rules point to a more favorable body of applicable law.

A state court case that involves multistate transactions poses the same choice-of-law problems. An Arizona state court, in other words, would not automatically apply Arizona substantive law if the parties hail from different states, or if the lawsuit arises out of activity or conduct that took place in another state.

Even when the choice-of-law issue has been resolved, a determination of what the applicable state's substantive law actually is may be difficult. State law, of course, is what a particular state's legislature and supreme court have declared it to be. What happens, however, if there is no controlling statute and the state's high court has not spoken on a particular question of law? How should a federal district court decide what the applicable state law is? In such cases a state appellate court decision will be highly persuasive, although not binding.[4] If there is no appellate court

---

4. Cmm'r v. Estate of Bosch, 387 U.S. 456 (1967).

decision, the district court can certify the question to the state supreme court. If there is no such procedure, the district court can look at any available sources to determine what the state law is likely to be were the state courts presented with the question. Finally, if the district court feels that an antiquated state law would no longer be followed, the court may determine that it is not bound by precedent and can instead fashion a rule that the state courts would likely create if again faced with the issue.[5]

Lawyers often neglect to work through choice-of-law issues before filing a case, much to their detriment. You must do so anytime your case has interstate elements, both to take advantage of favorable choice-of-law rules when jurisdictional and venue doctrine permit suits in multiple fora, and to ensure that you do not unwittingly saddle your case with unfavorable law.

§3.3.   Legal theories for claims, remedies, and defenses

One or two theories for claims or defenses probably provided the initial direction for your fact investigation. Before filing suit or responding to one, however, you should always explore whether the presently available facts will support other legal claims or defenses. Prematurely labeling a client's legal problems poses dangers. Think expansively and consider all reasonably assertable claims before deciding which ones to raise in your initial pleading. Keep in mind, however, that Rule 11 provides sanctions for improper pleadings when the attorney has not conducted a reasonable inquiry into the facts and law.[6] Also, more claims usually create a more complex and costly lawsuit, something that may not be appropriate in a particular case.

This discussion obviously cannot review the numerous legal theories on which claims and defenses can be brought. It is always useful to review checklists of potential theories for claims and defenses before filing the initial pleading. Doing so will at least get you to consider other similar theories, both statutory and common law; to review the required elements of each theory; and to analyze the advantages and disadvantages of each in light of the existing facts. This review must be broad. Research to see if any federal and state statutes create a basis for claims and defenses, even if the lawsuit has a common law basis. For example, a claim against a railroad arising out of a collision at a grade crossing will obviously involve a common law negligence theory. However, since railroads are a heavily regulated industry, check if any statutes, such as the federal Grade Crossing Safety Act of 1994, or state laws requiring quadrant gates at certain crossings, apply. In short, always do a broad common law and statutory search as part of the overall legal research of the case. Your litigation chart should include each of these theories, with its required elements.

5. Bernhardt v. Polygraphic Co. of Am., 350 U.S. 198 (1956).
6. See discussion of Rule 11 in §5.2.4.

When you have identified all possible theories of claims or defenses, how do you find the "elements" for each of them? Lawyers raised on an exclusive diet of Lexis and Westlaw may begin a search of a database of applicable case law immediately. This method is inefficient and possibly misleading. A judicial opinion may contain only a partial list of elements, or an inaccurate one at that. The pattern jury instructions used in the applicable jurisdiction are the best place to start. These usually exist for common claims and defenses, with the required elements of a prima facie case itemized. Additional research will usually be necessary, particularly if the claims or defenses are not based on routine tort or contract theories. For common law claims and defenses, the best starting point is usually a hornbook or treatise on the substantive area involved. For statutory claims, you should obviously start with the statute involved and check the case annotations for elements and jury instructions. After checking these basic sources, always search for recent cases interpreting and applying the substantive law. Treatises and jury instructions are updated frequently, but they sometimes fall out of date. Here is where Lexis or Westlaw comes in handy. Finally, many states have practice manuals that cover types of litigation common to the jurisdiction; frequently these prove to be excellent practical reviews. With this type of research, you should have enough to mull over the pros and cons of the various legal theories that the available facts might support.

For example, assume you represent the plaintiff in a personal injury case arising out of an automobile accident. You begin, of course, with a negligence claim against the other driver. In addition, does a claim based on negligent maintenance of the defendant's vehicle lie? If the defendant had been drinking, can the drinking support a negligence or statutory claim? Again, the point is to think expansively so that you consider every theory of recovery that can be supported by provable facts.

What claims you decide to bring in a lawsuit are influenced not only by theories of recovery, but also by the remedies permitted under each legal theory. Your choice of remedies will significantly influence what proof is relevant at trial and the scope of discovery.[7]

The Federal Rules of Civil Procedure do not usually limit a party to the relief requested, and they provide for the liberal amendment of pleadings. Nevertheless, you should always frame your pleadings so that they accurately reflect all the types of relief to which your client may be entitled. In addition, the remedies you seek will determine what will be relevant for discovery purposes, as do all the allegations in the pleadings. The distinction between legal and equitable actions no longer controls what remedies are permissible, since federal courts, like most jurisdictions, have merged courts of law and equity and have power to order any appropriate relief. Hence, it is important to review all potentially available remedies, legal and equitable, and request all that are proper. The simplest way to look at remedies is to review first the general types of legal and equitable relief,

7. The leading treatise on remedies is D. Dobbs, Law of Remedies (2d ed. 1993). A more recent source is W. Tabb & R. Janutis, Remedies in a Nutshell (2d ed. 2013).

then relate that relief to the specific claims you are considering, and finally review any statutes and court rules that permit additional relief.

You should keep several considerations in mind as you analyze potential remedies. First, legal remedies (historically, those remedies permitted for actions in a court of law) include money damages and (sometimes) restitution. Money damages, the most frequently sought relief, can be compensatory, consequential, or punitive. While compensatory damages are always permitted, consequential or punitive damages are usually allowed in a more narrow range of instances. Equitable remedies (historically, those remedies granted by a court of chancery when legal remedies were inadequate or inflexible) include injunctions, recission, specific performance, reformation, unjust enrichment, accounting, constructive trust, equitable lien, and reclamation. Any of these remedies should be requested if appropriate to the circumstances, regardless of the kind of claims brought.

Second, the precise measure of the allowable money damages depends on the type of claim being asserted and is frequently controlled by both statute and case law. For example, damages for breach of contract depend on whether the contract involves land, personal property, construction, or employment. Tort damages also vary considerably, depending on whether the claim is based on personal injury, survival, wrongful death, undue influence, fraud, defamation, intentional tort, or statutory actions. Where a claim is statutory, the statute frequently specifies the allowable damages. Statutes also may cap or prohibit certain damages. Some states, for example, limit damages for noneconomic losses in medical malpractice cases.

Third, you must check to see if there are any statutory provisions that allow for recoveries for other damages, court costs, and attorney's fees. Check not only the statutes providing for specific causes of action, but also more general federal and state procedural rules.[8] State civil practice rules often have provisions for costs and fees that, if viewed as substantive, may be applied in federal diversity actions.

For example, assume you represent the plaintiff in a contract dispute over the sale of goods. The plaintiff delivered the goods but has not been paid. Certainly the plaintiff can receive compensatory damages, but are other remedies possibly available? Can the plaintiff support a claim for consequential damages? Is the defendant guilty of bad faith, or is there some other basis for a punitive damages claim? Are there any statutory means by which you can recover the plaintiff's attorney's fees and other costs? Once again, the point is to think expansively so that you consider every remedy that the law provides in your case.

---

8. Scores of federal statutes permit awards of attorney's fees and other costs to the successful litigant. Common examples of cases that involve these fee-shifting provisions include §1983 civil rights actions, employment discrimination actions under Title VII of the 1964 Civil Rights Act, consumer products warranty actions under the Magnuson-Moss Warranty Act, and actions under the Freedom of Information Act. See generally A. Conte, Attorney Fee Awards (3d ed. 2013).

Remedies issues should always be researched carefully to learn the full measure of damages permitted for the claims involved. A good place to start is with the damages instructions in those jurisdictions that have pattern jury instructions.

§3.4. Joinder of parties and claims

You can best resolve joinder-of-parties issues by asking the following series of questions:

1. Who is the real party in interest?
2. Does that party have capacity to sue?
3. Is joinder of parties required?
4. Is joinder of parties permitted?
5. Do any special pleading rules apply?
6. Is joinder of claims permitted?

1. Real party in interest

Rule 17(a) requires that an action be brought "in the name of the real party in interest."[9] This party is the one who, under applicable substantive law, has the right that the lawsuit seeks to enforce. The purpose of the rule is to ensure that the parties with the real interests actually prosecute cases. Potential issues arise when personal representatives are named parties. For diversity jurisdiction purposes, the citizenship of the real party in interest controls.

Rule 17(a) also specifies exceptions to the general rule by providing that "an executor," "an administrator," "a guardian," "a bailee," "a trustee of an express trust," "a party with whom or in whose name a contract has been made for another's benefit," or "a party authorized by statute" may sue in his own name. While the plaintiff has the burden to show that he is the proper real party in interest, the exceptions to Rule 17(a) have largely eliminated controversy in this area. The only areas where disputes still arise involve assignments and subrogation. While a complete assignment makes the assignee the real party in interest, 28 U.S.C. §1359 expressly provides that such an assignment cannot be used to create diversity where it would otherwise not exist. If an assignment or subrogation is only partial, both parties to the assignment or subrogation are usually considered real parties in interest.[10]

---

9. Wright §70; Hazard et al. §7.3; Moore's Manual §13.01; Manual of Federal Practice §§3.106–3.110; Moore's Federal Practice §§17.10–17.13; Wright & Miller §§1543–1558.

10. Wright §70; Hazard et al. §7.5; Moore's Manual §13.01; Manual of Federal Practice §3.109; Moore's Federal Practice §17.11; Wright & Miller §§1545, 1546.

If the wrong party is sued, Rule 17(a) provides that no dismissal should be entered unless after a reasonable time following an objection a proper substitution of parties is not made or the real party in interest ratifies the action.

2. Capacity to sue

A lawsuit must be brought by and against parties that have a legal capacity to sue.[11] Rule 17(b) governs capacity to sue, and it in turn refers to state law. For individuals, the state law of the individual's domicile determines capacity to sue. For corporations, the law of the state of incorporation controls. In other cases, including those involving representatives, the law of the forum state determines capacity to sue. The forum state's laws control partnerships and unincorporated associations, except that, regardless of the forum law, partnerships and unincorporated associations always have capacity to sue to protect substantive federal rights. Finally, under Rule 17(a) an infant or incompetent can sue or be sued in the name of a representative. If no representative has been appointed, a guardian ad litem can bring suit or be appointed for the sued party.

If a defendant wishes to challenge the plaintiff's claim of capacity to sue, Rule 9 requires the defendant to deny the claim "with particularity." Failing to make the denial in a responsive pleading will usually result in the waiver of any error.

3. Required joinder of parties

Rules governing the joinder of parties address a basic set of questions. What parties must, should, or may be brought into the lawsuit so that the plaintiff's claims can be properly decided? Rule 19 governs required party joinder,[12] while Rule 20 regulates the ordinary permissive joinder of parties.

Rule 19, dealing with required joinder, is divided into two basic rules. Rule 19(a) determines what parties must be joined; Rule 19(b) tells the court what it should do if all required parties cannot be joined.

Until recently, required party joinder analysis used a somewhat cumbersome vocabulary, and older cases distinguish confusingly between "necessary" and "indispensable" parties. This terminology has changed. Now the analysis of when a party is required, and what to do if she cannot

---

11. Wright §70; Hazard et al. §7.7; Moore's Manual §§13.10–13.17; Manual of Federal Practice §§3.111–3.117; Moore's Federal Practice §§17.20–17.29; Wright & Miller §§1559–1573.

12. Wright §71; Hazard et al. §§7.11–7.13; Moore's Manual §§14.01–14.06; Manual of Federal Practice §§3.120–3.124; Moore's Federal Practice §§19.01–19.09; Wright & Miller §§1601–1626.

be joined, proceeds in three straightforward steps. The first step determines when a party must be joined. Rule 19(a) requires joinder if a party's presence is (1) required to grant "complete relief," or (2) the party has an interest in the action so that the party's presence is, practically speaking, necessary to protect his interest, or the party's absence may expose other parties to double or inconsistent obligations. These requirements are interpreted narrowly. If, for example, a plaintiff sues only one of several possible defendants involved in an accident, the other potential tortfeasors the plaintiff leaves out are not required parties.[13] When the remedy sought involves money damages, Rule 19 rarely applies.

Second, if a party is required under Rule 19, the party must be joined if "feasible." Ordinarily, joinder is infeasible only when the party cannot be lawfully served with process, or when the party's joinder would destroy federal subject matter jurisdiction.

Rule 19(b) determines what happens when the joinder of a required party is infeasible — the third step in the analysis. The court must decide whether to proceed without the party or dismiss the action. It must balance four factors: (1) whether parties who are not joined or existing parties will be prejudiced, (2) whether an order can minimize any potential prejudice, (3) whether any judgment without the absent party can be adequate, and (4) whether the plaintiff will have an adequate remedy if the action is dismissed.[14]

These practical concerns frequently compete with each other, but certain results are likely. First, if the plaintiff would be left without any forum in which to pursue claims against all parties as a result of a dismissal, the court is unlikely to dismiss the action. Second, if an absent party can be brought in as a third-party defendant, a present defendant's claim of potential prejudice absent joinder will be unconvincing. The possibility of intervention also offers a strong ground for rejecting the claim of prejudice to an absent party. Third, the court will likely reject the possibility of incomplete relief to the plaintiff as a reason for dismissal, since that result alone prejudices no one.

In community property states, additional joinder issues arise. Spouses may be liable as joint obligors since a spouse's activities that form the basis for the lawsuit are frequently viewed as benefiting the marital community. For example, a spouse who causes an automobile collision on the way to work is usually viewed as causing an injury while engaging in an activity that benefits the marital community. Driving to work is part of earning money for the marital community. In such situations, the plaintiff should join the other spouse as an additional defendant.

13. Temple v. Synthes Corp., 498 U.S. 5 (1990).
14. See Republic of the Philippines v. Pimentel, 553 U.S. 851 (2008).

4.   Permissive joinder of parties

Permissive joinder, governed by Rule 20, determines who may be joined as a proper party.[15] The test under Rule 20 has two elements that the proposed joinder of a party must satisfy. First, a question of law or fact common to all parties arising out of the action must exist. Second, each plaintiff must have a claim that arises out of the same occurrences or transactions, or series of transactions or occurrences, as the other plaintiffs' claims.

Rule 20 is broad and permits joinder whenever a legal or factual relationship exists among the parties that makes a single proceeding involving all of them sensible. On the other hand, permissive joinder can operate to delay the litigation and make it unfairly expensive and burdensome. For that reason, Rule 20(b) gives the court broad regulatory powers, including the power to order separate trials to prevent any unfairness.

If joinder is improper, Rule 21 provides that the case cannot be dismissed. Rather, the misjoined parties are dropped and nonjoined parties added by court order.

5.   Special joinder rules

Required and permissive joinder rules, set forth in Rules 19 and 20, are not the only rules that regulate whether parties can be joined in a lawsuit. Several other joinder rules apply in certain instances. These include:

Rule 13 — counterclaims
Rule 13(g) — cross-claims
Rule 14 — impleader
Rule 22 — interpleader
Rule 24 — intervention
Rule 23 — class actions
Rule 23.1 — shareholder derivative suits

These rules are discussed in Chapter 5.

6.   Joinder of claims

Joinder of claims, governed by Rule 18, is always permissive, except when the special joinder rules just mentioned provide otherwise.[16] Each party can bring as many claims as the party has against every other party.

---

15. Wright §71; Hazard et al. §6.8; Moore's Manual §14.20; Manual of Federal Practice §§3.118–3.119; Moore's Federal Practice §§20.01 et seq.; Wright & Miller §§1651–1660.

16. Wright §78; Hazard et al. §6.7; Moore's Manual §10.08; Manual of Federal Practice §§3.163–3.166; Moore's Federal Practice §§18.01–18.04, 18.10; Wright & Miller §§1581–1594.

These include both present and contingent claims. Practical considerations principally dictate what claims to bring against another party.[17]

§3.5. Subject matter jurisdiction in district courts

Subject matter jurisdiction refers to the power of a court to hear particular matters. Federal district courts are courts of limited jurisdiction and cannot hear a case unless it falls within their power, as provided for in Article III of the United States Constitution, and unless Congress has extended jurisdiction over the particular type of case.

Because federal district courts are courts of limited jurisdiction, a party seeking to invoke the court's jurisdiction must affirmatively plead and demonstrate proper subject matter jurisdiction.[18] The basis for jurisdiction must appear on the face of a well-pleaded complaint and cannot rest on counterclaims, defenses, or anticipated defenses.[19] Although defendants most commonly raise lack of subject matter jurisdiction in an answer or in a Rule 12 motion to dismiss, a party or the court can raise lack of subject matter jurisdiction at any time, even after judgment or on appeal. If the court has no jurisdiction over the subject matter, the case must be dismissed.

1. "Case or controversy" and standing

A federal court can only decide an actual "case or controversy" that is ripe for adjudication.[20] Put another way, the court will not hear moot or collusive cases, render advisory opinions, or hear controversies that are essentially political or administrative issues. This requirement limits cases to those involving real controversies in which parties have a direct stake in the outcome and will actively represent their interests.

A party must also have "standing" to sue. The standing doctrine is derived from the "case or controversy" requirement and limits the kinds of cases that federal courts can entertain. To have standing, a plaintiff must show that the challenged conduct of the defendant has caused an "injury in fact," and that the interest that the suit seeks to protect falls within the "zone of interests" guaranteed by the statute or constitutional provision in question. The Supreme Court has considered the standing issue many

---

17. See §4.5.
18. See §5.3.1.
19. There is one exception to this rule. When a plaintiff sues for a declaratory judgment, the federal court's subject matter can depend upon what the defendant might have alleged had the defendant brought a "coercive action" for damages or injunctive relief against the plaintiff in the first instance. For instance, if the plaintiff seeks a declaratory judgment that he did not infringe a patent, the court will ask whether subject matter jurisdiction would exist had the defendant brought the suit for patent infringement. See, e.g., Medtronic, Inc. v. Mirowsky Family Ventures, LLC, 134 S. Ct. 843 (2014.
20. Wright §12; Wright & Miller §3529.

times and has not yet articulated a test that will easily resolve standing challenges in particular circumstances.[21]

The question of whether there is an actual case or controversy, and the related issue of standing, arise frequently in public interest, constitutional, and administrative litigation. For example, a suit to enjoin enforcement of a city regulatory code provision, brought by a local resident, will raise both issues. Such complex standing problems must be researched thoroughly, particularly when the plaintiff is an organization or association bringing suit on behalf of its members or third parties. In private litigation, in contrast, an obvious controversy will ordinarily exist, and the parties' standing is usually straightforward.

2. Federal question jurisdiction

28 U.S.C. §1331 provides that "district courts shall have original jurisdiction of all civil actions arising under the Constitution, laws, or treaties of the United States."[22] Section 1331 is generally referred to as conferring "general" federal question jurisdiction, as distinguished from other "specific" grants of jurisdiction found in §§1333 et seq. and from other non-Title 28 grants.

The general-versus-specific distinction is important because of the requirement that a party invoking the court's jurisdiction must affirmatively show the basis for jurisdiction. Issues over jurisdiction seldom arise when the basis is a specific grant in a statutory provision. Problems arise more often when the general grant under §1331 provides the asserted jurisdictional basis.

a. *"Arising under"*[23]

Jurisdictional issues occur under §1331 because its "arising under" language is so general. Section 1331 creates jurisdiction over civil actions "arising under the Constitution, laws or treaties of the United States." The constitutional provisions are contained in Article III, §§1 and 2. However, §1331, which contains the same language as Article III, §2, has been interpreted much more narrowly than the parallel constitutional language.

The basic requirements for jurisdiction under §1331 are that the claim be based on federal law, which must be demonstrated in the complaint,

---

21. See Wright §13. See also Clapper v. Amnesty Int'l USA, 133 S. Ct. 1138 (2013); Summers v. Earth Island Institute, 555 U.S. 488 (2009); Massachusetts v. E.P.A., 549 U.S. 497 (2007); Sierra Club v. Morton, 405 U.S. 727 (1972).

22. Wright §§17–22A; Hazard et al. §2.4; Moore's Manual §§5.10–5.12; Manual of Federal Practice §§1.59–1.66; Moore's Federal Practice §103; Wright & Miller §§3561–3566.

23. Wright §17; Moore's Manual §5.12; Hazard et al. §2.4; Manual of Federal Practice §§1.60–1.66, §§1.80–1.108; Moore's Federal Practice §103.5; Wright & Miller §3562.

and that the federal claim be substantial rather than frivolous.[24] For example, a plaintiff brings an action for employment discrimination. Federal question jurisdiction exists because the case proceeds under Title VII of the 1964 Civil Rights Act, a federal statute. Another plaintiff brings an action for an unlawful search of his house. Federal question jurisdiction exists because the lawsuit is brought under the Fourth Amendment of the U.S. Constitution and 28 U.S.C. §1983. Where federal law expressly creates a right to sue, jurisdiction exists. However, where a federal statute, although declaring rights, does not expressly confer a right of action, complex issues exist. They center on whether an implied right of action exists that is recognizable under §1331. These issues are notoriously complicated and require thorough research.

In some instances, state law provides the cause of action, but the claim implicates a federal legal issue. A plaintiff, for example, might bring a negligence per se claim under Arizona law, but argue that a federal statute supplies the applicable standard of care. Whether this sort of claim gives rise to federal question jurisdiction is complicated. These state law causes of action meet the requirements for federal jurisdiction when the federal issue involved is "substantial," meaning that its resolution is important "to the federal system as a whole,"[25] and when the grant of federal jurisdiction will not unduly upset the balance of judicial power between the federal government and the states.[26]

Remember that subject matter jurisdiction depends upon the contents of the plaintiff's complaint. A federal defense to a state law claim can never create federal question jurisdiction.

b.   Specific grants of jurisdiction

There are several other sections of Title 28 that grant federal courts jurisdiction to hear particular matters. These include:

§1333 — admiralty
§1334 — bankruptcy
§1336 — ICC/commerce
§1337 — commerce/antitrust
§1338 — patent, copyright, trademark, unfair competition
§1339 — postal
§1340 — IRS/customs
§§1341–1364 — miscellaneous provisions

---

24. Since the complaint must affirmatively show that federal jurisdiction exists, a defense based on federal law cannot create jurisdiction. Nor can a counterclaim create federal jurisdiction. See Holmes Group v. Vornado Air Circulation Systems, 535 U.S. 826 (2002).

25. Gunn v. Minton, 133 S. Ct. 1059, 1066 (2013).

26. Grable & Sons Metal Products, Inc. v. Darue Engineering & Mfg., 545 U.S. 308, 318-319 (2005).

Finally, numerous statutory provisions outside of Title 28 also confer jurisdiction on district courts. The more important ones are:

Jones Act, 46 U.S.C. §688
Federal Employer's Liability Act, 45 U.S.C. §56
Securities Act, 15 U.S.C. §77a
Civil Rights Act, 42 U.S.C. §1983

Where jurisdiction is based on these specific grants, the same pleading requirements apply: A plaintiff wishing to invoke the court's jurisdiction must always affirmatively plead a proper jurisdictional basis.

Keep in mind that these federal grants of jurisdiction can be exclusive or concurrent with state courts.[27] In several areas, notably admiralty, bankruptcy, and patent and copyright cases, the district courts have exclusive jurisdiction.

c. The United States as a party[28]

When the United States is a plaintiff, no special jurisdictional problems arise. However, the United States cannot be sued unless it has waived its sovereign immunity and has consented to be sued. A plaintiff suing the United States, therefore, must expressly demonstrate the statutory basis under which the government has consented to be sued. The most frequently used grounds are the Court of Claims Act,[29] the Tucker Act,[30] and the Federal Tort Claims Act.[31]

Frequently, a plaintiff may wish or need to sue a federal official or federal administrative agency, rather than the United States directly. Such a case can proceed if a specific statute permits suit against the agency or a named federal official. Such statutes frequently permit suits brought to challenge administrative agency decisions. For example, suit is frequently brought against the Commissioner of Social Security for denial of claimed Social Security benefits.[32] Where no statute permits a suit against a federal official or agency, a plaintiff can still sometimes sue an official individually for an alleged improper act. The plaintiff's ability to sue can also depend upon what sort of remedy she seeks, whether legal or equitable. Finally, there are a number of federal entities, which may be incorporated or unincorporated, of which the United States is whole or part owner. Examples include the Federal Deposit Insurance Corporation and Federal Housing Authority. Statutes and sometimes case law regulate whether such quasi-governmental entities can be sued in federal court.

---

27. For a recent decision on concurrent jurisdiction, see Mims v. Arrow Financial Services, LLC, 132 S. Ct. 740 (2012).

28. Wright §22; Hazard et al. §2.4; Moore's Manual §§13.01; Manual of Federal Practice §§1.128–1.135; Moore's Federal Practice §17.27; Wright & Miller §§3651–3660.

29. 28 U.S.C. §1491.

30. 28 U.S.C. §1346(a).

31. 28 U.S.C. §1346(b).

32. 42 U.S.C. §405.

3. Diversity jurisdiction

Section 1332 provides for the jurisdiction of federal courts in civil actions involving diversity of citizenship. It parallels the constitutional grant of power found in Article III, §2 of the Constitution.[33] Section 1332 allows federal courts to decide cases involving state law claims. It sets out four categories of actions for which diversity jurisdiction is proper:

1. Between citizens of different states
2. Between citizens of a state and citizens or subjects of a foreign state
3. Between citizens of different states and in which citizens or subjects of a foreign state are additional parties
4. Between a foreign state as plaintiff and citizens of a state or of different states

Of these four categories, plaintiffs most often invoke the first. The other three are usually referred to as the alienage sections. Diversity jurisdiction does not apply to domestic relations and probate matters, which are considered local matters properly raised only in state courts.

Diversity jurisdiction has two basic requirements. First, each plaintiff must be completely diverse from each defendant, meaning that no plaintiff can have the same state citizenship as any defendant. Second, the amount in controversy in the case must exceed a certain amount.

a. "Citizenship" requirement

Section 1332 is based on "citizenship," an imprecise term.[34] A natural person's citizenship is the state of domicile, and no person can have more than one domicile at a time. A person's domicile, in turn, is the state in which the person has her residence and where she intends to remain. If a person is in the process of moving from one state to another but has not yet acquired a new residence, or if a person has a new residence in a new state but is not sure that she intends to stay there, her citizenship defaults back to the state where she last had both a residence and an intent to remain.

The citizenship of corporations is both the state of incorporation and the state where it has its principal place of business. For the purpose of determining diversity jurisdiction, the principal place of business of a corporation is its "nerve center." This state is where the corporation's directors and officers control and coordinate the corporation's activities, normally its corporate headquarters.[35]

---

33. Wright §§23–31; Hazard et al. §2.3; Moore's Manual §§5.31-5.59; Manual of Federal Practice §§1.19–1.58; Moore's Federal Practice §102; Wright & Miller §§3601–3610.

34. Wright §§24, 26-27; Hazard et al. §2.3; Moore's Manual §§5.54-5.59; Manual of Federal Practice §§1.24–1.33; Moore's Federal Practice §§1.02.3-102.79; Wright & Miller §§3601–3642.

35. Hertz Corp. v. Friend, 559 U.S. 77 (2010).

The citizenship of the legal representative of a decedent, infant, or incompetent is deemed to be the same state as the decedent's, infant's, or incompetent's citizenship. Where the legal representative is nominal, such as with a guardian ad litem, the citizenship of the represented party is determinative for diversity purposes. (Other legal representatives, not mentioned in §1332, presumably retain their own citizenship for diversity purposes.) In direct actions against liability insurers, the insurer is considered a citizen of the state where the insured is domiciled,[36] as well as the state where incorporated and where its principal place of business is located. Unincorporated associations present particular difficulties. If the association is not an entity entitled by state law to sue or be sued in its own name, its citizenship is that of each of its members. If the association is an entity entitled to sue or be sued, the prevailing rule is that here also the association is considered to be a citizen of each state of which a member is a citizen.

Citizens or subjects of a foreign state pose an additional complexity. Until recently, §1332 deemed noncitizens who were lawfully admitted to reside in the United States to be citizens of the states in which they were domiciled. A green card holder living in Texas, therefore, could not bring a state law cause of action against a Texas citizen in federal court for lack of complete diversity. Based on this provision, however, some courts allowed diversity suits between noncitizens to proceed in federal court, so long as they were domiciled in different states. This result was inconsistent both with other parts of §1332 and with language in Article III. A 2011 statute revised §1332 to provide that a lawfully admitted noncitizen is not deemed a citizen of any state, and that diversity jurisdiction does not exist in a suit between a citizen of a state and a noncitizen domiciled in the same state. The Texas green card holder still cannot sue the Texas citizen based on diversity jurisdiction, but now the asserted statutory basis for diversity jurisdiction over suits between two foreign citizens is gone.

b.   Complete diversity requirement[37]

The requirement that diversity must be "complete" in order for the federal district courts to have jurisdiction means that each plaintiff must have a different state citizenship from each defendant. Stated another way, if any plaintiff and any defendant are citizens of the same state, diversity will not be complete and federal subject matter jurisdiction will not lie. For example, if citizens of Illinois and California sue citizens of Maine and Vermont, complete diversity exists. If citizens of Illinois and California sue citizens of Maine, Vermont, Connecticut, and California, complete diversity does not exist.

---

36. Some states have so-called direct action statutes that permit suits to be brought directly against an insurance company. The typical situation is an automobile accident involving the insured.

37. Wright §24; Hazard et al. §2.3; Moore's Manual §5.32; Manual of Federal Practice §1.34; Wright & Miller §3605.

The complete diversity requirement applies to every party that is actually joined, regardless of whether that party is required or permissive. To ensure complete diversity, a plaintiff can dismiss all but required parties from the action. In addition, a plaintiff may manipulate the parties to create complete diversity. Because of this, a party's characterization as a plaintiff or defendant in the complaint is not controlling. Parties will be realigned as plaintiffs or defendants, and nominal or formal parties will be ignored, to determine if complete diversity actually exists. Collusive assignments, made solely to create diversity, are also ignored.[38]

The complete diversity rule is somewhat misleading because it applies to the original plaintiffs' claims against original defendants and does not apply to many other situations. The concept of supplemental jurisdiction, which applies to counterclaims, cross-claims, impleader, and interventions as of right, significantly modifies the complete diversity requirement.

The citizenship of parties at the time the initial complaint was filed determines whether complete diversity exists. Later changes in citizenship by a party will not defeat jurisdiction.

The complete diversity requirement is based on an interpretation of the diversity jurisdiction statute. Article III of the U.S. Constitution allows for the existence of federal subject matter jurisdiction upon a lesser showing of diversity. Congress can expand the federal courts' jurisdiction to include cases that involve minimal diversity, or situations where only a single plaintiff is diverse from a single defendant. Congress has done something along these lines for class actions, which are governed by a complex array of requirements set forth in §1332 and elsewhere.[39]

c. Jurisdictional amount requirement[40]

Section 1332(a) requires that the "matter in controversy exceeds the sum or value of $75,000, exclusive of interest and costs." The plaintiff's complaint is the sole basis for determining if the requirement has been met. The allegations are controlling unless there is a "legal certainty" that the jurisdictional amount cannot be obtained. Only if the plaintiff requests damages, such as punitive damages, to which he is not entitled under the applicable substantive law, and if these prohibited damages are necessary to reach the jurisdictional amount, will the allegations fail to meet the amount-in-controversy requirement.

The principal issue in this area involves the problem of valuation, particularly for cases involving equitable relief. With injunctions, the measure of damages is the value of the right sought to be enforced or the value of the avoided injury. The value may be different, depending on whether it is measured from the plaintiff's or the defendant's perspective. Courts disagree as to which measure of damages is

---

38. See 28 U.S.C. §1359.

39. See Wright & Miller §1756.2.

40. Wright §§32–37; Hazard et al. §2.3; Moore's Manual §§5.70–5.76; Manual of Federal Practice §§1.72–1.79; Moore's Federal Practice §§102.100–102.109; Wright & Miller §§3701–3712.

appropriate, although the majority use the plaintiff's loss approach. For example, suppose the plaintiff brings suit to enjoin the enforcement of certain statutes, such as zoning ordinances or health regulations, and to have them declared unconstitutional. The court must determine what the amount of the loss to the plaintiff would be if the statutes continue to be enforced.

Another issue involves aggregation of claims to meet the jurisdictional amount. Four basic situations arise. First, when one plaintiff sues one defendant, the plaintiff can aggregate all claims against the defendant to meet the jurisdictional amount requirement. For example, a plaintiff has two claims against one defendant involving two separate, unrelated contracts, each worth $40,000. The plaintiff can properly aggregate the claims. Second, when one plaintiff sues multiple defendants, the plaintiff can aggregate claims only if the claims are joint rather than several and distinct. A version of the same example illustrates. A plaintiff has two claims, each involving $40,000, against two defendants, and the claims involve two separate, unrelated contracts. The plaintiff cannot aggregate these claims. However, if the liability is joint, as would be the case if the defendants are partners jointly liable on a partnership obligation, aggregation is proper. Third, when multiple plaintiffs sue one defendant, the plaintiffs cannot aggregate separate and distinct claims. The plaintiffs can aggregate only if the claims are undivided and involve a single title or right. For example, two plaintiffs each have a $40,000 claim against one defendant; the claims involve two separate, unrelated contracts. The plaintiffs cannot aggregate these claims. If the two plaintiffs are partners suing to recover a debt owed to the partnership, however, aggregation is proper. Finally, where there are multiple plaintiffs and multiple defendants, the above analysis applies to the individual claims.

Interest and costs raise fewer questions. Costs include attorneys' fees only if a contract or statute permits them. Interest, which is ordinarily incidental to the action, counts for the jurisdictional amount only if the interest itself is the basis of the action.

4. Supplemental jurisdiction

Because federal courts are courts of limited jurisdiction, a question often arises as to whether a federal court can exercise jurisdiction over claims for which no independent basis for federal subject matter jurisdiction exists.[41] The doctrine of supplemental jurisdiction governs here. As traditionally described, this doctrine includes two concepts. The first, "pendent jurisdiction," principally addresses the question of what happens when a plaintiff wants to join to a claim properly in federal court another one that on its own does not satisfy jurisdictional requirements. The closely related concept of "ancillary jurisdiction" principally addresses the question of what

41. Wright §9; Hazard et al. §2.5; Moore's Manual §5.90; Manual of Federal Practice §§1.109–1.112; Moore's Federal Practice §106; Wright & Miller §§3523, 3567.

happens when a plaintiff's claim has a proper federal jurisdictional basis, and another party wishes to bring a counterclaim, cross-claim, or third-party complaint that lacks an independent federal jurisdictional basis.

Both situations present similar concerns. On the one hand, both the litigants and the court have an interest in avoiding piecemeal litigation. Inefficiencies and unfairness result if the parties must bring some claims in federal court and others in state court. On the other hand, Article III of the U.S Constitution and federal legislation must permit state claims to be brought in federal court.

The concepts of pendent and ancillary jurisdiction were judicial creations, elaborated in leading cases like United Mine Workers of America v. Gibbs, 383 U.S. 715 (1966), and Owen Equipment & Erection Co. v. Kroger, 437 U.S. 365 (1978). Congress in 1990 codified pendent and ancillary jurisdiction as "supplemental jurisdiction." While retaining most of the former concepts, the statute modifies them in certain respects.

28 U.S.C. §1367, has three principal provisions:

(a) Except as provided in subsections (b) and (c) or as expressly provided otherwise by Federal statute, in any civil action of which the district courts have original jurisdiction, the district courts shall have supplemental jurisdiction over all other claims that are so related to claims in the action within such original jurisdiction that they form part of the same case or controversy under Article III of the United States Constitution. Such supplemental jurisdiction shall include claims that involve the joinder or intervention of additional parties.

(b) In any civil action of which the district courts have original jurisdiction founded solely on section 1332 of this title, the district courts shall not have supplemental jurisdiction under subsection (a) over claims by plaintiffs against persons made parties under Rules 14, 19, 20, or 24 of the Federal Rules of Civil Procedure, or over claims by persons proposed to be joined as plaintiffs under Rule 19 of such rules, or seeking to intervene as plaintiffs under Rule 24 of such rules, when exercising supplemental jurisdiction over such claims would be inconsistent with the jurisdictional requirements of section 1332.

(c) The district courts may decline to exercise supplemental jurisdiction over a claim under subsection (a) if —
(1) the claim raises a novel or complex issue of State law,
(2) the claim substantially predominates over the claim or claims over which the district court has original jurisdiction,
(3) the district court has dismissed all claims over which it has original jurisdiction, or
(4) in exceptional circumstances, there are other compelling reasons for declining jurisdiction.

Under the statute, subsection (a) confers on the district court supplemental jurisdiction over all other claims that are so related to the original claim that they form part of the same case or controversy. Generally, all claims that arise out of the same transaction or occurrence qualify by this standard.[42] Subsection (b) creates several exceptions to deal with situations in which a plaintiff in a diversity case might try to use supplemental jurisdiction as an end-run around the requirements for diversity jurisdiction. This section does not restrict the use of supplemental jurisdiction by defendants in recognized and accepted circumstances, such as those involving compulsory counterclaims, cross-claims, interpleader, intervention of right, and impleader. Such pleadings commonly involve indemnity. For example, consider a plaintiff who properly brings a claim in federal court for which subject matter jurisdiction exists. The defendant wishes to bring in a third-party defendant on an indemnification theory. Indemnification raises no federal question, however, and since the defendant and third-party defendant are citizens of the same state, diversity is lacking. In this situation, however, the statute grants supplemental jurisdiction over the third-party claim.

In Exxon Mobil Corp. v. Allapattah Services, 545 U.S. 546 (2005), the Court held that where complete diversity exists and at least one named plaintiff alleges a claim that satisfies the amount-in-controversy requirement, the district court has supplemental jurisdiction over the claims of an additional plaintiff that do not meet the amount-in-controversy requirement, so long as all claims arise out of the same case or controversy. In contrast, the supplemental jurisdiction statute does not permit the joinder of a plaintiff whose addition would destroy complete diversity.

5. Removal jurisdiction

The right to remove cases from state to federal courts protects nonresident parties from perceived local prejudices.[43] 28 U.S.C. §§1441-1453 govern the removal jurisdiction of the federal courts. Since it is a jurisdictional statute, it is strictly construed and its requirements must be followed closely.

Removal is the procedure in which a case, already filed in a state court, is transferred to the federal district court for the same district in which the state action is pending. The first requirement is that the case filed in state court satisfy subject matter jurisdiction requirements to proceed in federal court. The complaint at the time the removal petition is filed determines whether these requirements are met and thus whether removal jurisdiction exists.[44] Removal cannot be based on defenses or counterclaims.[45]

---

42. See Wright & Miller §3567.1.

43. Wright §§38–41; Hazard et al. §2.8; Moore's Manual §§8.01–8.47; Manual of Federal Practice §§1.149–1.173; Moore's Federal Practice §107; Wright & Miller §§3721–3740. The mechanics of the removal procedure are discussed in §7.6.

44. The notice of removal may assert an amount in controversy that differs from what the complaint states if the defendants show by a preponderance of the evidence, based on information unearthed during litigation, that the real amount in controversy exceeds what the plaintiff has alleged. 28 U.S.C. §1446(c)(2).

45. See Rivet v. Regions Bank, 522 U.S. 470 (1999); Beneficial National Bank v. Anderson, 539 U.S. 1 (2003).

Second, all defendants — except nominal, unknown, or fraudulently joined ones or ones who were not served with process prior to the filing of the notice — must join in the notice of removal. Since removal is for the benefit of defendants, each must agree to the removal. A "defendant" for removal purposes is each party against whom the original plaintiff brought a claim in state court.

Third, under §1446(b), the notice of removal must be filed within 30 days of the time the defendant receives formal service of plaintiff's initial pleading in state court, or within 30 days of receiving summons if state law does not require the initial pleading to be served on the defendant, whichever is shorter.[46] If a case is not initially removable but later becomes so (if the plaintiff drops a nondiverse defendant, for instance), the defendant may file a notice of removal within 30 days of receiving a court paper that first reveals that removal is now proper. A defendant, however, may not remove a case based on diversity jurisdiction more than a year after it began.[47] Once the notice of removal is filed, it operates as a stay on any state court proceedings.

There are three basic grounds for removal: diversity, federal question, and special removal statutes. Under §1441, removal jurisdiction can be based on diversity.[48] The complete diversity rule for removal has one important exception. Section 1441(b) prevents removal if any proper defendant is a citizen of the state where the action was brought. (The citizenship of defendants sued under fictitious names is disregarded.) A principal reason for permitting removal in diversity of citizenship cases is the possibility of local prejudice against noncitizen defendants. This worry disappears if a defendant is a citizen of the forum state. Accordingly, diversity jurisdiction for removal is narrower than diversity jurisdiction for cases initially filed in federal court.

Section 1441 also limits removal in federal question cases. A defendant can remove only claims for which an independent basis for federal subject matter jurisdiction exists and claims that meet the requirements of supplemental jurisdiction. If the defendant tries to remove a case that includes claims that fit in neither of these categories, the court must sever these problematic claims and remand them to state court.

The removal sections provide for removal in certain special circumstances. These include:

§1441(d) — civil actions against foreign states
§1442 — federal officers or agencies sued or prosecuted
§1442a — members of armed forces
§1443 — civil rights actions
§1444 — foreclosure against the United States

---

46. See Murphy Bros. v. Michette Pipestringing, 526 U.S. 344 (1999).
47. An exception to this rule applies when the plaintiff has deliberately concealed the amount in controversy to defeat removal. 28 U.S.C. §1446(c)(3)(B).
48. See Lincoln Property Co. v. Roche, 546 U.S. 81 (2005), regarding the diversity of citizenship basis for removal.

Specially tailored removal requirements also apply to class actions.

Section 1445 makes certain actions nonremovable. These include, for example, actions under state workers' compensation acts and actions against a common carrier, its receivers, or trustees, arising under specific federal statutes.

A case removed to federal court may be remanded back to the original state court under §1447. A motion to remand based on defects in the removal procedure must be made within 30 days of the filing of the notice of removal. A remand based on lack of subject matter jurisdiction may be made at any time before final judgment. While a court in a contested removal case will usually decide issues of subject matter jurisdiction before issues of personal jurisdiction, there is no requirement that it always proceed in this order.[49]

A plaintiff who wishes to file and keep a lawsuit in state court can use certain strategies to defeat removal. First, where diversity would otherwise permit removal, the plaintiff can add a defendant who either is not diverse from the plaintiff or is a citizen of the forum state. So long as such a joinder is not fraudulent, in the sense that plaintiff does not really wish to prosecute a claim against that party, the joinder will defeat removal. Second, where diversity does not exist, the plaintiff can draft the complaint to avoid pleading a claim that would permit removal based on federal question jurisdiction.

The mechanics of removal procedure are discussed in §7.6.

§3.6. *Personal jurisdiction*[50]

Personal jurisdiction refers to the power of a court to bring a party before it and usually has to do with the extent of the court's geographic reach. A judgment is not enforceable against a party unless that party can lawfully be brought into court and has received notice of the lawsuit. Personal jurisdiction doctrine flows from constitutional concepts of due process.

Jurisdiction to adjudicate can be in personam, in rem, or quasi in rem. In personam jurisdiction over a party is necessary for the full enforcement of a judgment against a party, and thus for res judicata and collateral estoppel, or claim preclusion and issue preclusion, to operate. An in rem action is one that involves disputes over interests in real or personal property; jurisdiction over the party exists by virtue of the party's ownership of the property. A typical in rem action is an eminent domain lawsuit. Finally, a quasi in rem action refers to an action brought to subject only certain property to the claims asserted. The defendant's property is garnished or attached, but only to the extent necessary to satisfy the judgment. These distinctions have less significance today at the federal court level, where the critical concerns involve the constitutional limits of personal

---

49. See Ruhrgas v. Marathon Gas, 526 U.S. 574 (1999).

50. Wright §§64–65; Hazard et al. §§3.1-3.8; Moore's Manual §§6.01–6.05; Wright & Miller §§1061–1075.

jurisdiction and the issue of whether service was properly made. Hence, issues surrounding personal jurisdiction involve two separate questions:

1. May the court constitutionally exercise jurisdiction over the defendant?
2. Was service of process on the defendant proper?

The first question involves the due process limitations on personal jurisdiction, and the second involves the service-of-process requirements of Rule 4.

1. Due process requirements

Due process issues do not arise for plaintiffs. By initiating a lawsuit a plaintiff voluntarily submits to the court's jurisdiction for all purposes, including responding to counterclaims and other claims brought in that action.

When a defendant (a person, corporation, or other entity) is a resident of or physically present in the forum state at the time of service of process, has consented to be sued in the forum state, or has engaged in continuous and systematic activity in the forum state, the court has "general jurisdiction" over the defendant. The plaintiff can sue the defendant for any claim, including those unrelated to the defendant's activities in the forum state. The Supreme Court has recently held that general jurisdiction only exists in the state where the defendant is "at home."[51] For an individual defendant, this is the state of the defendant's domicile. A corporate defendant is "at home" in its place of incorporation and where it has its principal place of business. General jurisdiction does not exist in a state just because the defendant engages in substantial business there. Thus, for example, significant sales in a state, or even the presence of stores or branch offices in a state, will unlikely suffice on their own to subject a defendant to the general jurisdiction of that state's courts.

If general jurisdiction does not exist, a court can entertain a case against a defendant only if it has "specific jurisdiction." Specific jurisdiction requires that the defendant have sufficient minimum contacts with the forum state such that the defendant can reasonably anticipate having to defend a lawsuit brought in the forum state that arises out of these contacts.

The question of whether a court has specific jurisdiction over a nonresident defendant arises often, particularly with businesses that engage in interstate and international transactions and in e-commerce on the Internet. Whether specific jurisdiction exists or not can be a fact-intensive inquiry and require research into a rich body of case law.

Leading Supreme Court cases include International Shoe Co. v. State of Washington, 326 U.S. 310 (1945); McGee v. International Life Ins. Co., 355 U.S. 220 (1957); Hanson v. Denckla, 357 U.S. 235 (1958); World-Wide

---

51. Daimler AG v. Bauman, 134 S. Ct. 746 (2014); Goodyear Dunlop Tires Operations, S.A. v. Brown, 131 S. Ct. 2846 (2011).

Volkswagen Corp. v. Woodson, 444 U.S. 286 (1980); Burger King Corp. v. Rudzewicz, 471 U.S. 462 (1985); Asahi Metal Industry Co. v. Superior Court, 480 U.S. 102 (1987); Burnham v. Superior Court, 495 U.S. 604 (1990); J. McIntyre Machinery Ltd. v. Nicastro, 131 S. Ct. 2780 (2011; and Walden v. Fiore, 134 S. Ct. 1115 (2014). The discussions in these cases are often fact intensive, but one common thread runs through the more recent of them. For specific jurisdiction to exist, the defendant must purposefully connect itself with the state where the case proceeds. Someone else cannot forge this connection for the defendant.[52]

In *International Shoe* the Court addressed the question of what activities by a corporation within a particular state will subject it to suit within that state consistent with due process. The Court held that jurisdiction exists when a corporation has such "minimum contacts" in the forum state such that a suit there would not offend "traditional notions of fair play and substantial justice." Subsequent decisions have expounded in particular on how substantial these contacts need to be. In *World-Wide Volkswagen*, the Court rejected the argument that a New York dealership should be subjected to suit in Oklahoma simply because the New York dealership could have foreseen that the vehicle it had sold might be involved in a collision in Oklahoma. The Court stressed that the minimum contacts requirement protects a defendant from being sued in a remote or inconvenient forum unless the defendant purposefully connected itself to the state. Requiring a defendant to defend in the forum state, the Court held, must be fair and not impose unreasonable burdens on the defendant.[53]

In *Asahi Metal* a plurality held that the mere placement of a product into the stream of commerce does not subject a party to the forum state's jurisdiction, even if the party was aware that the stream of commerce would carry the product into the forum state. The minimum contacts test requires that the defendant itself direct some action purposely toward the forum state. Designing the product for the forum state, or advertising the product in the state, might qualify. The Court revisited the "stream of commerce" scenario in *Nicastro*. There, a foreign manufacturer had targeted the American market as a whole for its products but had not singled out the forum state specifically. A plurality agreed that the defendant's actions had not met the minimum contacts threshold, even though the defendant knew that the stream of commerce would most likely carry its product to the forum state. The defendant must connect itself with the forum state. As these cases and others suggest, the Court has looked with particular skepticism upon the exercise of personal jurisdiction over foreign defendants.

The most recent personal jurisdiction issues center on e-commerce activities on the Internet. Businesses often use their web sites for a range of activities, from advertising and informational purposes to conducting commercial sales and transmitting products. When litigation, whether based on contract or tort claims, springs from such uses, the question also arises whether these kinds of activities can subject a nonresident

---

52. Walden v. Fiore, 134 S. Ct. 1115, 1122-1123 (2014).

53. In Burnham v. Superior Court, 495 U.S. 604, 628 (1990), the Court held that personal service within a forum state satisfies due process requirements.

defendant to in personam jurisdiction in the state to which its web site activities reach. In due process terms, are these business uses of the Internet adequate "minimum contacts," did the defendant "purposely avail" itself of the privilege of conducting business in the state, or did the defendant "purposely direct" its activities to residents of the state, so that the nonresident defendant can "reasonably" be required to defend itself in the forum state? Case law, not surprisingly, is hardly uniform, as courts grapple with applying the Supreme Court's personal jurisdiction jurisprudence to Internet commerce.[54]

Other unsettled personal jurisdiction issues include the extent to which contacts of a corporate subsidiary or agent will be attributed to the corporate parent for jurisdictional purposes. The mere fact that a subsidiary's actions are "important" to the parent are probably not sufficient.[55] Also, the application of general jurisdiction principles to unincorporated entities is unclear. The law on these issues is in flux and requires careful and up-to-date research.

The minimum-contacts analysis applies with equal force to in rem and quasi in rem actions.[56] Accordingly, distinctions such as in rem or quasi in rem have no direct bearing on the due process question of a defendant's amenability to suit in a particular forum. However, the distinctions are still important for determining the enforceability of judgments.

Personal jurisdiction doctrine protects a defendant against a place of suit that imposes unreasonable burdens on it. For this reason, a defendant must challenge the court's personal jurisdiction at the earliest possible time. Typically, a defendant will enter a special appearance upon service of process and make its jurisdictional objection. If it fails to do so, the defendant waives its personal jurisdiction challenge and is deemed to consent to litigation in the forum.

2. Service-of-process requirements

Amenability to process is different from, and independent of, the adequacy of service of process. If a party is not constitutionally amenable to process, any service on that party will have no effect unless the party waives objections to the service. If a party is amenable to process, the plaintiff must still serve process on that party properly.

Due process considerations require that service be made in a manner that is reasonably calculated to put a defendant on notice that he has been

---

54. See, e.g., Erin F. Norris, Note, Why the Internet Isn't Special: Restoring Predictability to Personal Jurisdiction, 53 Ariz. L. Rev. 1013 (2011); Daniel J. Kiley, Minimum E-Contacts: Personal Jurisdiction in the Internet Age, 47 Ariz. Att'y 58 (Nov. 2010).

55. See Daimler AG v. Bauman, 134 S. Ct. 746 (2014).

56. The Supreme Court made this determination in Shaffer v. Heitner, 433 U.S. 186 (1977). It held that a defendant's ownership of property by itself did not establish such contacts as would create proper personal jurisdiction over the defendant, where the claims were not related to the property.

sued.[57] Since Rule 4(e) permits service by any method allowed by the state law in which the district court is sitting, this means, in practical terms, that an out-of-state defendant can be served under the forum state's long-arm statutes. Alternatively, a defendant can be served pursuant to the law of the state in which service is effected.

Service of process under Rule 4 is discussed in §5.3.

§3.7. Venue[58]

Personal jurisdiction doctrine limits the states in which cases can proceed. Venue statutes further determine the place of suit. These statutes direct cases to proper geographic districts.

Since venue provisions are designed in part to protect a defendant from being forced to litigate in an "unfair" forum, a defendant can waive the benefits of the venue rules. Hence, a defendant must raise improper venue in a timely manner, either by a Rule 12 motion or in the answer. Otherwise objections will be deemed waived.

More than one venue may be open to the plaintiff's suit, so the question of which venue to choose may arise. This question involves both practical and legal considerations. On the practical side, convenience and the cost to the plaintiff, the plaintiff's lawyer, and witnesses will frequently dominate the decision. The plaintiff will often prefer her own district, if it is proper. If the plaintiff's principal witnesses are in another district, she should take their convenience into consideration. On the legal side, venue choice may have choice-of-law implications, since applicable substantive law may differ for such matters as statutes of limitations, elements of claims, and allowable damages. Finally, considerations such as the choice of judges, the desirability of prospective jury pools, and length of time until trial also matter.

1. Determining venue

The general venue statute for federal district courts is §1391. Under §1391(b), if jurisdiction is based on diversity or federal question, venue is proper in

> (1) a judicial district in which any defendant resides, if all defendants are residents of the State in which the district is located; (2) a judicial district in which a substantial part of the events or omissions giving rise to the claim occurred, or a substantial part of property that is the subject of the action is situated; or (3) if there is no district in which an action may

---

57. See Mullane v. Central Hanover Bank, 339 U.S. 306 (1950); Dusenberry v. United States, 534 U.S. 161 (2002).

58. Wright §§42–44; Hazard et al. §§3.13-3.15; Moore's Manual §§7.01 et seq.; Manual of Federal Practice §§2.1–2.78; Moore's Federal Practice §§110-111; Wright & Miller §§3801–3868.

otherwise be brought as provided in this section, any judicial district in which any defendant is subject to the court's personal jurisdiction with respect to such action.

There are also numerous special venue statutes, both in the Title 28 venue section and elsewhere, that control venue in special kinds of cases. The special provisions begin with §1394. Other venue provisions are scattered throughout the United States Code, usually as part of the substantive statute that creates a cause of action.[59] Consequently, you must always check whether a special venue statute exists that overrides the general provisions of §1391.

Congress thoroughly revised the federal venue statutes in 2011, as part of the Federal Courts Jurisdiction and Venue Clarification Act. Be particularly careful when relying on older treatises or sources for information about venue, as much of the law has changed.

Once you have identified the applicable statutes, the question of a party's residence arises, since §1391 is based on residence. An individual's residence is where the individual is domiciled. Entity defendants with capacity to sue or be sued are deemed to reside in any judicial district in which the defendant is subject to the personal jurisdiction of the court. An entity plaintiff, in contrast, resides "only in the judicial district in which it maintains its principal place of business," as §1391(c)(2) provides. Corporations that reside in states with multiple districts are deemed to reside in the district in which the defendant would be subject to personal jurisdiction, were that district a state. Noncitizens who are also not residents can be sued in any district pursuant to §1391(c)(3). Finally, when a defendant is the United States, its agencies, officers, or employees, §1391(e) controls and provides that venue is generally proper — unless law provides otherwise — in a district where the defendant resides, where a substantial part of the events or omissions giving rise to the claim occurred, where a substantial part of property involved in the action is located, or where the plaintiff resides if no property is involved.

The venue provisions control where a plaintiff files the initial complaint against the original defendants. They do not apply to counterclaims, cross-claims, or third-party claims, since these are seen as ancillary to the initial suit and hence raise no additional venue issues.

2. Change of venue

A change of venue can be based on three grounds: improper venue, governed by 28 U.S.C. §1406; inconvenient venue, governed by 28 U.S.C. §1404; and the doctrine of forum non conveniens.[60] Under §1406, the court has discretion either to dismiss or to transfer to a proper venue any case that has been filed in an improper venue. Since the statute encourages transfers "if it be in the interest of justice," transfers are the

---

59. For a list of such venue statutes, see Moore's Federal Practice §110.60.

60. Wright §44; Hazard et al. §§3.14-3.15; Moore's Manual §7.70-7.74; Manual of Federal Practice §§2.48–2.74; Moore's Federal Practice §111; Wright & Miller §§3841–3855.

usual remedy for suit in an improper venue. Keep in mind that proper venue is a personal right. By filing an action in an improper venue, a plaintiff waives the right to object to it. A defendant must raise any venue objection either by a Rule 12 motion or in the defendant's answer, lest objections be waived.

Under §1404(a), the court may transfer a case from a proper venue to another venue "for the convenience of parties and witnesses, in the interest of justice." The transferee venue must be one where the action "might have been brought" — meaning a court that would have had personal jurisdiction and would have been a proper venue had the case been filed there initially — or one "to which all parties have consented." Section 1404(a) recognizes that a plaintiff frequently has venue choices, and that the plaintiff's choice, while proper, may not be the most convenient forum for the case as a whole. If this situation exists, the court can transfer the case to a more convenient federal forum.

When a case is transferred from one venue to another, the substantive law follows the case.[61] This is important in diversity cases, where the forum state's substantive law, including its conflicts of law rules, is applied. When a case is transferred to another district, in another state, the transferee court still applies the substantive law that would have applied in the transferor court. This rule negates a defendant's incentive to forum-shop for a more favorable body of law to apply to the case.

The doctrine of forum non conveniens recognizes that there may be instances in which a court may dismiss an action because the selected forum, while proper, is inconvenient. The leading cases are Gulf Oil Corp. v. Gilbert, 330 U.S. 501 (1947), and Piper Aircraft Co. v. Reyno, 454 U.S. 235 (1981). Today the venue transfer rule, §1404(a), resolves most problems of inconvenient venue. However, the forum non conveniens doctrine is still used, particularly in cases in which the events on which the action is based occurred in a foreign country, and for which the more convenient venue is abroad.[62]

Not infrequently a contract will include a forum selection clause. If a party to the contract brings suit in a forum other than the one specified in the contract, the other contracting party, now a defendant, can move to enforce the clause. The forum selection clause cannot render venue in the non-contracted-for forum wrong. Thus, a Rule 12(b)(3) motion to dismiss, or a motion to dismiss based on 28 U.S.C. §1406(a), is improper. If the plaintiff sues in federal court, and the designated forum is another federal forum, the proper motion to make is a motion to transfer pursuant to §1404(a). If the designated forum is a state or foreign court, the defendant can enforce the clause through a forum non conveniens motion.[63] Courts will generally enforce these clauses, absent extraordinary circumstances.

---

61. This rule does not apply when the court enforces a forum selection clause pursuant to §1404(a). See Atlantic Marine Constr. Co. v. U.S. Dist. Ct., 134 S. Ct. 568, 582-583 (2013).

62. See, e.g., DiFederico v. Marriott Int'l, Inc., 714 F.3d 796 (4th Cir. 2013).

63. Atlantic Marine Constr. Co. v. U.S. Dist. Ct., 134 S. Ct. 568, 579-580 (2013).

IV

CASE EVALUATION AND STRATEGY

§4.1.   Introduction

Case evaluation requires that you gather enough facts and consider suffi-ciently the legal issues to decide intelligently whether to take the case. Then, if you decide to take it, the evaluation requires that you devise a realistic, cost-effective litigation plan. This chapter discusses making the initial decision to take a case, establishing the attorney-client relationship, developing a litigation strategy, and completing prefiling requirements.

§4.2.   Taking the case

You should take those cases that have factual and legal merit and are eco-nomically feasible, and you should usually decline the others. But just how and when do you decide whether to take a case?

1.   Conflicts check

Always check for conflicts of interest with existing and former clients. A lawyer's relationship with a client is based on two key duties: loyalty and confidentiality. A lawyer who represents multiple clients on the same matter may breach these duties if the interests of the clients are directly adverse. The lawyer may do so as well if she represents a client against a former client on a substantially related matter in which the client's inter-ests are materially adverse to the interests of the former client. A law firm and its lawyers are generally viewed as a single entity, and for conflicts purposes lawyers generally carry their former clients from former firms and government offices to their present firms. Hence, a conflict of interest may disqualify an entire firm, not just a lawyer within the firm. The bigger the firm, the more likely conflicts of interest will arise with present and former clients. The time to determine if a conflict of interest exists, and whether it bars representation of the client, is now, not when an opposing party moves to disqualify you or your firm.[1]

Law firms must have procedures to screen new matters for potential conflicts. These procedures include circulating a new client or new matter memorandum to all lawyers in the firm, using a docket or conflicts clerk to check for potential conflicts with existing or former clients in the firm's client data base, and having new lawyers list all former clients and matters they worked on at previous firms or government offices so that these can be entered into the conflicts data base. Developing a conflicts search procedure and following it carefully for every new client and matter will identify possible problems so that they can be analyzed and resolved before litigation is underway.

A conflict of interest situation in litigation arises when, simply stated, a law firm (1) represents a new client against another current client in the same or an unrelated matter, (2) represents a new client against a former client in the same or a substantially related matter, or (3) represents two clients in the same matter. When such a situation arises, it must be resolved under the applicable ethics rules.

Under Model Rule 1.7(a), a law firm cannot undertake the representation of a client if doing so would be "directly adverse" to another client, or if firm's representation of the first client "may be materially limited" by responsibilities to a second client, a third person, or the lawyer's own interests. As Model Rule 1.7(b) provides, this restriction does not apply if

> the lawyer reasonably believes the lawyer will be able to provide competent and diligent representation to each affected client; (2) the representation is not prohibited by law; (3) the representation does not involve the assertion of a claim by one client against another client represented by the lawyer in the same litigation or proceeding before a tribunal; and (4) each affected client gives informed consent, confirmed in writing.

The usual way to raise conflicts issues with clients is to send a "conflict waiver" letter both to the existing client and the potential client. The letter should set out the requirements of Model Rule 1.7; state your belief, based on the presently known facts, that joint representation is not precluded by the rule because the two parties do not have interests that are directly adverse to each other within the meaning of the rule; explain the advantages of joint representation (primarily cost savings and a united stance during the litigation); explain the risks of joint representation (primarily that a settlement offer to one party may create a conflict, a judgment against one party may create indemnification and contribution claims, and the attorney-client privilege may be affected); explain what may happen if claims do arise between the two parties (which usually means that you must drop the new party and continue representing only the original

1. The controlling conflicts rules are Rules 1.7 through 1.12 of the Model Rules of Professional Conduct.

party); and remind the party that he has the right to consult with independent counsel on these matters. Finally, the letter should provide that, if the party consents to the joint representation, he should sign the original of the letter, indicating his consent and opportunity to consult with independent counsel, and return it to you. Once you receive the signed consents from both parties, you can then begin to represent them jointly.

The questions of whether a conflict exists and, if so, whether and how it can be resolved can be complicated and require knowledge of all the applicable ethics rules, opinions, and case law for that jurisdiction. Accordingly, most law firms, as part of their conflicts-check procedures, have an experienced partner available to review all new matters in which a possible conflict of interest may exist. In difficult situations, outside counsel may be necessary to review the question of whether a conflict exists and whether it can be waived.

Consider, for example, the common situation in which a driver and passenger in a car, involved in a collision with another car, seek a lawyer to sue the driver of the other car. Since the passenger could potentially sue the driver of the car in which she was riding (if there is any evidence of that driver's negligence), as well as the driver of the other car, a conflict of interest may exist between the passenger and her driver. In this situation, the passenger must be fully informed of her right to sue her own driver and the consequences if she decides not to sue, and must have the opportunity to consult further about the situation. If the passenger waives her right to sue her driver, the conflict disappears, and the lawyer can represent both the passenger and her driver in a lawsuit against the driver of the other car. (Note, however, that other conflicts may arise, such as whether to accept a proposed aggregate settlement. Other ethics rules — Model Rule 1.8, in the case of the aggregate settlement — may apply.)

Always document the steps you took to check for conflicts. Also, you need to repeat your check for conflicts whenever something happens during the representation of your client that might give rise to new conflicts. Such events might include, for example, the addition of a new party.

2.   Feasibility analysis

Your litigation chart, which sets out the potential legal claims and required elements of proof for each claim, provided the direction for your factual and legal investigation. This investigation in turn provides the framework from which to analyze the case. In addition, keep in mind Rule 11, which provides that an attorney's signature on a pleading constitutes a verification that the attorney has conducted a reasonable inquiry into the facts and law.[2] Hence, you cannot plead claims, remedies, or defenses that you have not adequately investigated to determine whether they are well grounded.

2. See discussion of Rule 11 in §5.2.4.

As the lawyer for a prospective plaintiff, you should take a case only if you can realistically expect to prove a prima facie case on at least one theory of recovery. You should already have some admissible proof for each element of each asserted claim or have a reasonable basis for believing you will get such missing proof during formal discovery. In addition, the potential recovery must be large enough to justify the work and risks of litigation. Many lawyers, for example, refuse even a simple case on a contingency fee basis unless a realistic recovery is at least in the $20,000 range. The fee, usually one-third of any recovery, will simply not provide reasonable compensation for the work and risks involved. In a complex case, such as a medical malpractice claim, the realistic damages may have to be at least in the $500,000 range to make representation economically feasible.

For a plaintiff's lawyer, whether to accept or decline a case depends on the type of case and the factual and legal issues involved. For example, you might accept a simple automobile collision case not involving a serious injury after interviewing the client and reviewing the police accident report. Sometimes such a limited investigation will be enough to assess whether the client "has a case," whether the damages are substantial enough to make it worth pursuing, and whether a judgment can actually be collected. In more complex matters, however, such as serious personal injury, medical malpractice, products liability, or commercial cases, you may need to do substantial legal research and extensive factual investigation, and you may need to have an expert review the case before you can make this decision. The basic question is always the same: Do I know enough from my fact investigation and legal research to conclude that the client has a provable case with substantial damages that can be collected? If the case appears weak on liability or damages, involves a great deal of work, and would be taken on a contingency fee basis, the best time to turn it down is now. Cases rarely look better than when they first walk in the door. Every lawyer has taken cases and later regretted it. You can best avoid this outcome by rejecting marginal cases early.

There are exceptions. First, where a plaintiff is in imminent danger of having an applicable statute of limitations run, your first obligation is to file a claim to prevent the statute from running, even though you have not had an opportunity to investigate the facts and research the law. Protecting the plaintiff's claim from a limitations bar must take precedence over other considerations.[3] Second, lawyers frequently take cases for reasons other than the income that the case will produce.[4]

If you decide to take a case, you need to enter into an agreement with the client. If you turn down the case, you need to send the client a letter declining representation. These steps are discussed in the following sections.

As a defendant's lawyer, the decision whether to take a case is in one way easier and in another way more difficult. It is easier from the economic

---

3. Protecting the plaintiff's claim under these circumstances should not constitute a Rule 11 violation. See Cooter & Gell v. Hartmarx Corp., 496 U.S. 384, 401-402 (1990); Garr v. U.S. Healthcare, Inc., 22 F.3d 1274, 1279 (3d Cir. 1994).

4. See §2.7.

point of view, since defendant's cases are not taken on a contingency basis. So long as the defendant agrees on how to pay the lawyer for the legal services, and the defendant is able and willing to pay, a weak case poses no economic risk. However, the decision is more difficult in the sense that the lawyer and the defendant must agree on how best to defend the case. If the client realizes the case is not defensible on the merits, the client may try to pressure the lawyer to drag out the case or file unfounded defenses, counterclaims, or third-party claims. But a defense lawyer has the same obligations, under ethics rules as well as under Rule 11, as the plaintiff's lawyer. Such conflicts are best handled at the outset by letting the client know what you can and cannot do in defending the case and by reaching agreement on how you plan to defend.

§4.3.   Establishing the terms of the attorney-client agreement

The attorney-client relationship should be formally established with a written agreement, for several reasons. First, a written instrument is manifestly prudent for any contractual relationship. Second, the agreement will prove the existence of an attorney-client relationship for privilege purposes. Third, the agreement will establish the work to be done, what will not be done, and the basis for compensation, all of which are necessary for a good working relationship with the client. Fourth, Model Rule 1.5 requires that a client be informed, "preferably in writing," of how the fee is set and of all the material facts concerning the representation. Although a written agreement signed by the client is required only in contingency and referral cases, good practice dictates its use in all cases. For all these reasons, you need a written agreement with the client.

Unless your client is sophisticated and has experience working with lawyers, the client will have little understanding of the legal work involved in litigation and the various fee arrangements that can be made. Educating the client on these matters is in everyone's interest. You should discuss how you set your fees and the expected costs with the client.

Lawyers most commonly incorporate the terms of the representation in a letter from the lawyer to the client, usually called an engagement letter. The letter and a copy are sent to the client, who signs the copy to show approval of the terms and returns it to the lawyer. Lawyers sometimes use more formal contracts, particularly with contingency fee and institutional clients. Regardless of which method is used, the agreement, memorialized in writing, should be sufficiently detailed to cover all aspects of the relationship. Unfortunately, disputes between lawyers and clients are common. But an agreement drafted in clear, simple English that covers all likely issues and specifies what is not covered can help to avoid them. In disputes between lawyers and their clients, ambiguities and omissions in attorney-client agreements will usually be strictly construed against the lawyer.[5] The agreement should cover the following basic subjects.

5. See J. Toothman & W. Ross, Legal Fees: Law and Management 285 (2003).

1. Work covered

The agreement should specify the scope of the engagement, that is, what work will and will not be performed. For example, you might agree to prosecute a negligence claim arising out of a car accident through settlement or trial. If you will not handle any appeal or postjudgment proceedings to collect a judgment, or if there will be an additional charge for any such work, the agreement should specify this. If you will not handle a workers' compensation claim, insurance claim, or other related matters, the agreement should say so. In general, you must guard against a client thinking that you would do more than you agreed to do by spelling out what is not covered. You should also state explicitly that you have not guaranteed any particular outcome, especially when you represent the plaintiff in a personal injury case.

When representing a corporation or other entity, make clear that you represent the corporation only, not its employees. Make this limitation clear to the employees, since you are required by Model Rule 4.3 to "make reasonable efforts to correct [any] misunderstanding." Such confusion arises frequently when a lawyer represents a corporation and the corporation's officers erroneously believe that the lawyer also represents them. The safe approach is to warn the employees that you represent the corporation only in every case, even if the employee's interests appear to be aligned with the corporation.

2. Who will do the work?

The agreement should specify clearly who will do the work, unless the lawyer is a solo practitioner or it is clear that the entire law firm will collectively do the work. Clients usually think that they are hiring a particular lawyer to do all the necessary work on their problem. They may not tolerate a bill that shows several other lawyers in a firm working on their problem, when the clients have never met these lawyers and were never told they would be involved. Consequently, particularly when the client is sophisticated and the matter complex, the agreement should specify who the supervising lawyer will be and how the matter will be staffed with other partners, associates, paralegals, and support staff.

3. Lawyer's fee

A lawyer's fee is the compensation the lawyer will receive for professional services rendered on behalf of the client.[6] The agreement must spell out the amount of the lawyer's fee, how it will be determined, and when it will be paid. The total fee must be reasonable in light of the work to be done,

---

6. See Model Rules of Professional Conduct, Rule 1.5.

the difficulty of the work, the amount of time it will involve, and the customary range of fees for similar work in your locality.

The agreement should specify clearly how the fee will be determined. Three approaches are commonly employed: an hourly rate (common in corporate, commercial, and insurance defense cases), a fixed flat fee (common in criminal defense and family law cases), and a contingency fee (common in plaintiff's personal injury cases). Obviously the agreement can specify any number of combinations or modifications of these basic approaches, unless a rule or statute regulates the fee. For example, agreements frequently specify a minimum retainer fee, paid up front, that is credited against an hourly billing rate. The agreement might use alternate fee arrangements, such as capped fees, or incentive billing and defense contingency fees, which base the fee in part on obtaining favorable results. When the fee is based on an hourly rate, the client must understand that what is being paid for is the lawyer's expertise and time. Hence, any time expended on a client's case will be billed to the client, regardless of whether the time is spent on court appearances, conferences, research, document drafting, or telephone calls.

The agreement should define how the fee amount is determined and when it should be paid. For instance, in personal injury cases where the plaintiff's attorney's fees are usually a percentage of any recovery, the agreement must specify whether the percentage is computed before or after expenses are deducted and that the fee is due when any judgment is actually collected. If the fee is on an hourly basis, you should provide an estimate of the overall fee range, since a common misunderstanding with clients is what the total fee is likely to be.

If you will share a fee with another lawyer outside your firm, you must disclose this fact to the client and obtain his consent. The division of fees must be proportionate to the work done by each lawyer, or each lawyer assumes joint responsibility for the representation and the client agrees in writing.[7]

A lawyer has an ethical duty to make the fee reasonable. The lawyer may need to review the fee at the end of the representation, even in a contingent fee situation, to make sure it is in fact reasonable before submitting it to or collecting it from the client.[8] A fee agreement that was reasonable when made may no longer be reasonable at the end of the representation.

Many statutes and rules regulate and limit attorney's fees. For example, statutory causes of action frequently either limit attorney's fees or subject them to court approval.[9] Make sure that your agreement complies with any applicable statutes and rules.

---

7. See Model Rules of Professional Conduct, Rule 1.5(e).

8. See, e.g., In re Connelly, 55 P.3d 756, 761 (Ariz. 2002); In re Schwartz, 686 P.2d 1236, 1243 (Ariz. 1984).

9. See, e.g., Federal Tort Claims Act, 28 U.S.C. §2678; Awards of Attorneys Fees by Federal Courts, Federal Agencies and Selected Foreign Countries 62-63 (M. Capisio & H. Cohen eds., 2002).

An attorney's lien — the right of a lawyer to hold or retain money or property until all proper charges have been paid or adjusted — can usually be imposed on a judgment to ensure payment of the fee. This practice is common in contingent fee situations. In some jurisdictions an attorney's lien is only enforceable if the client expressly agrees to it. Hence, it is good practice to discuss the lien with the client and have the written agreement state that the client agrees to it.

4. Retainers

In some situations a lawyer should insist on a retainer to ensure payment of the fee and other costs. A retainer is simply a cash payment of a sum of money to the lawyer before work begins on the client's case. It ensures that the lawyer will get paid for the work and that costs the lawyer advances will be reimbursed. Lawyers commonly insist on a retainer, and then periodically deduct fees and costs as they are incurred. Regardless of the precise arrangement, the agreement must specify the amount of the retainer, when it must be remitted, and what fees and costs will be deducted from it.

Whenever a lawyer receives advanced funds from a client, the lawyer must put these funds in the lawyer's trust account.[10] Under only the rarest of circumstances — only to pay bank service charges — may a lawyer commingle her own funds with the client's. Otherwise always avoid commingling.[11] Funds of all of a lawyer's clients can be held in one trust account; however, a separate ledger must be kept for each client showing receipts and disbursements. Most states have adopted the Interest on Lawyer's Trust Accounts (IOLTA) system, which requires lawyers to hold client funds in interest-bearing accounts.[12]

5. Costs

The agreement should distinguish between fees due the lawyer for professional representation and the costs and expenses incurred during the course of that representation. The agreement should note anticipated costs, such as filing fees and other court costs; expert witness fees and expenses; court reporter fees; travel expenses; research costs; and photocopying, mailing, and telephone costs. It should state how those costs will be computed. An estimate of the usual costs for the type of case involved is sometimes a good idea. In some cases, such as commercial, medical malpractice, and products liability cases, the costs of paralegals, experts, travel,

---

10. See Model Rules of Professional Conduct, Rule 1.15.
11. Model Rules of Professional Conduct, Rule 1.15(b).
12. In Brown v. Legal Foundation of Washington, 538 U.S. 216 (2003), the Supreme Court held that interest earned on IOLTA funds was not a compensable regulatory taking for Fifth Amendment purposes since the client suffered no financial loss. The client's funds, if deposited in an individual account, would have earned no interest.

and other expenses can exceed the lawyer's fee. The agreement should also specify when the costs will be paid; customarily a lawyer bills her client at regular intervals, such as monthly or quarterly. The agreement should emphasize that costs are the client's obligation, even if no recovery is obtained.

Plaintiff's personal injury cases present a special situation. The justification for a contingency fee arrangement—the client is otherwise unable to pay for legal representation—also bears on the propriety of advancing costs. A lawyer may advance costs, such as court costs, deposition expenses, investigator fees, and expert witness fees. But the client ultimately is still responsible for paying those costs. The most common approach is to reimburse costs to the lawyer when a judgment is actually paid. If there is no recovery, the client is still responsible for paying the costs, although a client without money will probably not be able to reimburse the lawyer. For this reason, some lawyers accept contingency fee arrangements for cases that will have substantial costs only if the client advances a sum of money sufficient to cover the expected costs. Requiring a client to advance expected costs has another benefit: It tends to weed out weak cases. A prospective client who knows his case is weak often will refuse to advance costs for an expert review before filing suit or will refuse to pay a retainer. Clients who, though able, refuse to invest in their lawsuits are usually clients to avoid.

6.   Liens

Plaintiffs' lawyers frequently must deal with liens in personal injury cases. As Model Rule 1.15(d) provides, a lawyer has an ethical obligation to pay lienholders directly from any settlement or recovery. For example, the hospital that treated the plaintiff following his injury may have a bill that the plaintiff has not yet paid, and state statutes usually create a lien on the settlement or recovery in the amount of the unpaid bill.

You should tell your client that valid liens must be paid when any recovery is obtained, you have an ethical obligation to do so, and that the liens will automatically reduce the client's net recovery. Medicare, Medicaid, ERISA, the Veterans Administration, worker's compensation statutes, health and casualty insurance policies, and statutes establishing liens for healthcare providers are common sources of liens. Before taking the case, you should determine what liens exist and their total amount. If significant, they may make your representation economically infeasible. If you decide to take the case, you should contact potential lienholders and advise them of the litigation.

Plaintiffs' lawyers frequently include language in the attorney-client agreement that states expressly that the client has an obligation to pay any valid lien out of his share of any settlement or recovery. You should apprise the client that you have an obligation to contact potential lien-holders, that you will pay valid liens directly from the client's recovery, and that you cannot ethically release proceeds from the litigation to the client until liens are resolved.

The ethical and legal questions that liens pose are complicated. If you are considering whether to represent a plaintiff in a personal injury case, consider checking with a lawyer who specializes in liens first.

7.   Billings

The agreement should specify when fees and costs will be billed. While monthly billing is normally best for both lawyer and client, less frequent billings are sometimes appropriate, particularly for regular business clients, or if little work is done in any given month.

If the client is new or has a spotty payment history, consider advising the client of your intent to stop work on the case if your bills are not paid and to charge interest on late payments. You should also obtain the client's consent to withdraw in the event of non-payment, regardless of the status of the case.

8.   Authorization to file suit and withdraw

The agreement should contain a statement that authorizes the lawyer to file suit on behalf of the client or, if a defendant, authorizes the lawyer to defend the suit. The client should also be told that you have a right to withdraw from the case in case of non-payment of fees, or if later developments show that the matter has no merit. However, keep in mind that you must receive permission to withdraw from the court before which the case is pending, and your withdrawal cannot prejudice the client except under narrow circumstances.[13]

The terms of the agreement should then be put in writing, either in a letter to the client or in a written agreement. If a contingency fee agreement, it must be in writing and signed by the client. As with any legal document, the agreement should be written in plain English, not legalese.

Example (hourly fee agreement letter):

> Dear Mr. Jones:
>
> As we discussed in my office yesterday, I have agreed to represent you in the divorce proceedings recently started by your wife Joan. I will handle all negotiations necessary to attempt a property settlement before trial. If a trial becomes necessary, I will represent you to the conclusion of the trial and until the court enters a final divorce decree.
>
> Fees for representing you will be based on the time expended on your case. My present hourly rate is $100 per hour. You have

---

13. See Model Rules of Professional Conduct, Rule 1.16(c). Rule 1.16(b) provides for several instances when a lawyer can withdraw, notwithstanding prejudice to the client. These include, for example, when the client insists upon activity that the lawyer believes is criminal or fraudulent.

agreed to provide a retainer of $1,500 within one week. Based on what you have told me, I estimate the fee in your matter will be in the $3,000 to $5,000 range, although circumstances may change this estimate. The total fee will depend on the particular facts and circumstances of your situation and the time necessary to represent you to the conclusion of your divorce.

In addition to my fee, there will also be certain costs expended on your case, such as court filing fees, court reporter fees, and long distance telephone and photocopying charges. You will be responsible for paying all such costs. Costs in divorce cases vary but usually fall in the $200 to $400 range.

I will send you an itemized statement each month showing the time I have spent on your case and the other costs that have been incurred. I will subtract the amount reflected in each monthly statement from the $1,500 retainer until the retainer has been exhausted. I will then bill you directly, and you have agreed to pay those monthly statements in full when you receive them. In the event that you do not pay my bills promptly, you agree that I may withdraw from representing you in this matter.

Please confirm that this letter correctly reflects the terms of our agreement by signing and dating the enclosed copy of this letter on the spaces provided and returning the copy to me. If any of these terms is unclear, or you have other questions about this agreement, please call me as soon as possible.

Upon receipt of the signed letter and a check for the $1,500 retainer, I will begin to represent you and work on your case. No attorney-client relationship will arise until this letter is jointly signed and you return a signed copy of this letter to me. If I do not receive the signed letter and check within ten days, I will assume that you have decided to retain another lawyer to represent you in this matter.

Sincerely,

/s/ *John Smith*

Agreed: _____
       John Jones
Dated: _____

Example (contingency fee agreement):

AGREEMENT

Date: _____

I agree to employ the law firm of Smith & Smith as my attorneys to investigate and, if warranted, prosecute all claims for damages against Frank Johnson and all other persons or entities that may be liable on account of an automobile collision that occurred on June 1, 2013, at approximately 3:00 P.M., near the intersection of Maple and Elm Streets in Tucson, Arizona. I authorize you to file suit on my behalf.

I agree to pay Smith & Smith a fee that will be one-third (33 1/3 percent) of any sum recovered in this case, regardless of whether received through a settlement, lawsuit, or any other way. The fee will be calculated on the sum recovered, after costs and expenses have been deducted, except as otherwise provided for in this agreement. The fee will be paid when any moneys are actually received in this case. I agree that Smith & Smith has an express attorney's lien on any recovery to ensure that its fee is paid. I agree that no representations or guarantees of a recovery, or amount of any recovery, have been made.

I agree to pay all necessary costs and expenses, such as court filing fees, court reporter fees, expert witness fees and expenses, travel expenses, long distance telephone costs, and photocopying charges. These costs and expenses will not be due until a recovery is actually received in this case. I understand that I am also responsible for paying these costs and expenses, even if no recovery is received.

I understand that any liens on any recovery obtained in this case must be paid directly to lienholders before the recovery is disbursed to me. I understand that Smith & Smith has an obligation to contact potential lienholders and advise them about a recovery in this case, and to pay valid liens before disbursing the recovery to me.

I agree that this agreement does *not* cover matters other than those described above. It does not cover an appeal from any judgment entered, any efforts necessary to collect money due because of a judgment entered, or any efforts necessary to obtain other benefits, such as insurance, employment, Social Security and Veteran's Administration benefits.

I understand that I have the right to discharge Smith & Smith at any time. In that event, I agree to pay Smith & Smith for the reasonable value of its services up to the date of the discharge. The reasonable value of its services shall be made on the basis of a professional evaluation of its services to the ultimate recovery or results in the case.

If in the opinion of Smith & Smith the claims no longer appear to have merit, or a change in circumstances occurs, so that reasonable prospects for receipt or collection of a judgment no longer exist, Smith & Smith has the right to cancel this agreement and withdraw from representing me. In that event, Smith & Smith agrees to turn over to me all papers relating to this claim, and Smith & Smith is still entitled to reimbursement for reasonable costs and expenses it has incurred.

Agreed: _____
        John Jones

I agree to represent John Jones in the matter described above. Except as otherwise provided for in this agreement, I will receive no fee unless a recovery is obtained. If a recovery is actually received, I will receive a fee as described above.

I agree to notify John Jones of all developments in this matter promptly, and will make no settlement of this matter without his consent.

Agreed: _____

   John Smith for
    Smith & Smith

9. Next steps

Once you have decided to take the case and have reached an agreement with the client, you should take several steps to get the new relationship started on the right track and keep it there. First, if your agreement includes an express attorney's lien, send a notice of your attorney's lien to the opposing party's lawyer and any insurance companies. Some jurisdictions have standard attorney's lien forms used in litigation. Sending out the notices will ensure that your fee is paid when any judgment is paid.

Second, you should have the client sign authorization forms that will allow you to obtain certain records before filing suit. Depending on your jurisdiction's laws and practice, you may need signed authorizations to get police reports and motor vehicle records; hospital, doctor, employment, and insurance records; and Social Security, Veterans Administration, and other governmental records. Find out what type of authorization is necessary, and become familiar with the statutes requiring that such documents be made available to the client or his lawyer on request. You can also call the particular agency to learn its requirements and procedures. Some agencies have standard authorization forms.

Third, your client needs advice on what he should and should not do. He should be told not to talk to anyone other than you about the matter. Explain that persons may try to interview him or get him to make or sign statements. He should tell such persons that he is represented by a lawyer and cannot talk to them, and he should notify you of all such attempts. Explain that he is generally not required to talk to anyone unless required through the formal discovery process; he should direct all requests for information to you. He should not sign anything without first discussing it with you. Other persons may try to give him money. He should refuse any such attempts and report them to you. He should be told to save and collect all relevant records, documents, bills, checks, and paperwork of any kind in his possession and deliver them to you; he should send records and documents that subsequently come into his possession to you as well. Your client should also be circumspect about his online activity. Blog posts, Facebook posts, YouTube videos, and the like — even seemingly private, password-protected content — may all be discoverable. Your client should not alter content already on a social media site he maintains, lest he face a spoliation claim later. But he should take great care in adding information that his adversary might be able to use against him.

Fourth, your client needs a blueprint for the future, since he may have little idea how civil litigation actually proceeds. He should be told what needs to be done before suit is filed; what happens during the pleadings, discovery, and motion practice stages of the litigation process; and what his role in this process will be. He should have some idea of how much time each of these stages takes and how far in the future any trial is likely to be; at the same time he should be aware that most cases are settled before trial. He also needs to be reminded of the risks and costs of any lawsuit, including the risk of an adverse verdict after trial. A well-informed client will understand the process he is a part of and will be likely to assist you throughout. Many lawyers wisely use a follow-up letter or brochure that repeats this advice and contains a chronology of likely events, a document you can easily tailor to your litigation practice.

Discuss the client's obligations to pay fees and costs promptly, cooperate in discovery, make witnesses available, and pay for experts. Remind the client that the consequences for such failure include your asking the court for permission to withdraw from the representation.

This is a good time, particularly for the defense side, to have a serious talk with the client about who likely will (and probably ought to) lose. The client needs a dose of reality early, before he develops an unrealistic set of expectations about what you can do and about how the case will probably turn out. The client needs to be told clearly and regularly what you can do, as well as what you cannot do, to defend the case. Defending a weak case is hard enough; a difficult client, with unrealistic hopes and expectations about litigation, only compounds the problems.

Finally, maintain communication with your client. Litigation goes in spurts, with a period of activity often followed by weeks of inactivity. If your client has not heard from you recently, he may erroneously conclude that you don't care about him or have lost interest in his case. Accordingly, make sure you maintain contact. Send him copies of all pleadings, discovery, motions, and other court papers. Write him periodically to let him know what is going on in the case. If nothing is happening, let him know and explain why. A well-informed client will usually be a cooperative, satisfied client.

§4.4. *Declining representation*

A lawyer may not always be able to take a case. The matter may not be within the lawyer's expertise. It may not have merit or be large enough to justify a suit, or the defendant may not be able to pay a judgment. The lawyer may be too busy or have a conflict of interest. Or the lawyer may be unable to agree with the client on a fee. Whatever the reason, when a lawyer declines a potential case, she should do so in writing, usually in a letter to the prospective client.

Where a lawyer represents one party but cannot represent a related party because of a potential conflict of interest, the lawyer declining employment should send a letter to this effect to the related party, who may be expecting representation. Also, if a lawyer withdraws from representing a client, the lawyer should send the client an appropriate nonengagement letter. It is important to make a decision and send the letter promptly, since a person's rights may be affected by any delay.

The letter declining the case ensures that the party clearly understands that you will not be representing her, and can help resolve any question about whether you had a duty to protect her interests even though she was never a client.[14] If you decide not to represent a party, you nevertheless have an obligation to warn her if a statute of limitations or other notice statute may run shortly, so that she can get another lawyer in time.[15]

Example (letter):

Dear Mr. Jones:

As I explained in my office yesterday, I will not be able to represent you for any claims you may have based on an automobile collision that occurred near the intersection of Maple and Elm Streets in this city on June 1, 2013, at approximately 3:00 P.M. I want to emphasize that I have not researched your claims and have no opinion on the merits of your claims.

Since I cannot take your case, you may wish to see another lawyer about handling this matter for you. As we discussed yesterday, if you wish to have another lawyer represent you, you should do so promptly. If you do not, there may be legal problems, such as a statute of limitations bar, that might prevent you from pursuing your claims. Since your accident happened on June 1, 2013, and the statute of limitations for tort claims in this state is two years, if you wish to file a lawsuit you must do so *before* June 1, 2015. To avoid such problems, I recommend that you find another lawyer promptly, so you can protect any rights you might have.

Enclosed are the originals of the police reports and insurance claim forms you brought to my office.

Sincerely yours,

/s/John Smith

Make sure that the statute of limitations computation is correct and, if there is a shorter statutory or contractual notice requirement that applies, that you state this requirement and compute it correctly as well. If you are not sure of the computation period, do not state the date, since an incorrect statement could subject you to liability.

---

14. See, e.g., S. Fortney & V. Johnson, Legal Malpractice Law: Problems and Prevention 389-390 (2008).

15. See, e.g., Togstad v. Vesely, 291 N.W.2d 686 694-695 (Minn. 1980).

You should send this letter by registered mail, with return receipt by addressee only requested. When you get the signed return receipt, staple it to the copy of your letter. Send another copy by e-mail, with an acknowledgment of receipt requested. These documents will provide persuasive evidence to rebut any later claim that you never actually declined the case.

§4.5.   Planning the litigation

Assume you have accumulated the facts available through informal discovery; researched the possible legal claims, remedies, defenses, and counterclaims; put them on your litigation chart; researched other procedural questions; reached an agreement with the client to represent him; and have no timing problems. Now is the time to structure a litigation plan, before you file your initial pleading.

A litigation plan consists of defining the client's objectives and developing a strategy to achieve those objectives. Once you develop a strategy in broad terms, you can then divide the strategy into its component, chronological parts.

Even if you think you cannot develop a litigation plan, your client will think otherwise, and he is right. Sophisticated commercial clients, such as insurance companies and corporations, usually require a litigation plan before authorizing a lawsuit or, if a defendant, after receiving the complaint. The litigation plan usually includes an explanation of what claims, remedies, or defenses you will raise; a description of the basic facts, including the anticipated factual issues; an explanation of the planned discovery; a description of anticipated legal issues; an assessment of settlement possibilities; an assessment of the likely trial outcome; and cost projections for each stage of litigation. If sophisticated users of legal services have found that a detailed litigation plan promotes cost-effective representation, doesn't it make sense to make such a plan in every kind of case?

After you have completed your informal investigation, the basic steps in developing a litigation plan are the following:

1. Reevaluate the client's objectives, priorities, and cost constraints
2. Define the client's litigation objectives
3. Develop a "theory of the case"
4. Plan the pleadings and jury demand
5. Plan the discovery
6. Plan the dispositive motions
7. Plan the settlement approach
8. Develop a litigation timetable

1.   Reevaluate the client's objectives, priorities, and cost constraints

When the client first came to you for legal advice, he had one or more "problems" he told you about. One of your first steps was to identify his legal problems and objectives, and to develop a scale of priorities for those objectives. Now is the time to reassess those problems and objectives. You will have the benefit of your partially completed litigation chart showing the fruits of your research and informal fact investigation. You will also know the client's cost constraints. Finally, time has passed. All of these factors may influence what the client's current objectives and priorities are. You need to sit down with the client, review what you have done to date, determine if the client's thinking is the same or has changed, and analyze those objectives and priorities to see if they still make sense in light of what you now know about the case.[16]

2.   Define the client's litigation objectives

If the client's thinking is unchanged and the dispute cannot be resolved short of litigation, you next need to decide on broad litigation objectives that serve the client's overall objectives and priorities. Always remember that the client controls the objectives of the litigation, and the lawyer decides on the means to achieve those objectives. For example, suppose that your plaintiff-client wants to settle early in the case and to keep expenses at a minimum. Your strategy may be to keep the pleadings simple, to push for focused discovery, and then to start early settlement discussions. On the other hand, suppose that you anticipate that a trial will be necessary. Your strategy may be to use broad pleadings with alternative theories of recovery, to engage in extensive discovery, and to prepare thoroughly for trial. Your litigation objectives will then form the basis for the remainder of your litigation plan.

3.   Develop a "theory of the case"

Your side's story is a critical part of the litigation plan. You need to review what you presently know about the uncontested and contested facts and ask some basic questions. Is your side's story complete or are there significant missing pieces? Are your client and witnesses reliable? Do their stories make sense? Is your side's story one that has jury appeal? Where do your side's version and the other side's version of the facts clash? How do you plan to win the credibility battle over the disputed facts?

Trial lawyers frequently call their side's position the "theory of the case."[17] Those with experience know that, within broad limits, facts, not law, win most trials. Find the winning story that shows how the other side acted unfairly and that an injustice must be fixed. The winning side usually organizes credible witnesses and exhibits into a believable story, and it wins the war over the disputed facts by presenting more persuasive evidence for

16. Rule 1.2(a) of the Model Rules of Professional Conduct provides that the client decides the objectives of the representation, subject to certain limitations.

17. Thomas A. Mauet, Trial Techniques and Trials §2.3 (9th ed. 2013); 2 J. McElhaney, McElhaney's Litigation 13-15 (2013).

its side of the dispute. Your story will prevail only if you take the time to develop a coherent, persuasive theory of the case before drafting the pleadings.

4.   Plan the pleadings and jury demand

Pleadings are the vehicle by which you bring your theory of the case to court. If you understand the pleadings in this light, you should not err (and violate Rule 11) by raising a number of allegations in your pleadings and then wondering how you can find facts that fit into the theories of recovery.

What claims, remedies, or defenses should you assert? Inexperienced litigators often "throw the book at them" and plead every conceivable claim, remedy, or defense that meets Rule 11 requirements. This approach offers an illusion of safety and can come at a high price. By adding claims, a case becomes more complex, with additional costs and time investment. Adding claims frequently results in adding parties, again making the litigation more involved. Adding claims also broadens the scope of discovery, with the danger that discovery, always expensive and time consuming, may escalate out of control. While you must protect the client's legal interests by advancing essential claims, you should also consider the costs and disadvantages of pursuing every supportable claim against every proper party.

The better approach is to begin with your theory of the case. You have already gathered facts through informal investigation, and you should have a reasonable expectation as to what more you might uncover through formal discovery. What claims, remedies, or defenses does this information reasonably support? Beyond this question, do you have a realistic ability to prevail on each legal theory?

Once you have determined which legal theories have support, decide which ones to raise in a pleading. You again need to reflect on your overall litigation objectives. For example, if an objective is to hold down litigation costs, raising numerous legal theories may make little sense. Simplicity in the pleadings will better serve your objective.

What do your proposed pleadings do to your discovery plan? The range of permissible discovery will grow more expansive and more expensive as the pleadings increase in complexity. The scope of the pleadings controls the scope of discovery and often its costs, because anything relevant that is not privileged is discoverable. Pleading a variety of legal theories, just to be safe, may cause litigation to spin out of control. For example, consider a plaintiff who wishes to bring a negligence claim against a trucking company because of a vehicle collision. The plaintiff is considering whether to plead a claim for punitive damages. Doing so, however, will greatly expand the relevant scope of discovery, since the defendant's financial and safety history will now be discoverable. If the likelihood of getting punitive damages is small, does it really make sense to push such a claim? You may well be undertaking substantial additional work without a corresponding benefit to your client. On the other hand, plaintiffs frequently want broad discovery, at least compared to defendants. By adding peripheral parties, consistent with Rule 11 requirements, you make discovery easier, since discovery of parties is broader than that of nonparties.

One concern weighs against pleadings that omit valuable claims. A party who fails to bring all claims that arise out of a particular transaction may be precluded from doing so later. Before filing your pleading, research the relevant law of claim preclusion and think through the consequences of leaving claims out. Especially if you are tempted to leave certain claims out, talk to your client about her desire to pursue subsequent litigation if your first attempt fails. Get your client's consent in writing if you will indeed forgo potential claims.

When you have decided which of the possible legal theories to raise in the initial pleading, you will still need to consider the related legal issues. The plaintiff must appreciate how the choice of claims will affect various issues, such as the choice of parties that must be brought into the suit, whether subject matter jurisdiction exists for each claim, whether personal jurisdiction exists for each defendant, where venue is proper, and, if more than one venue, where the best place to file suit is. These questions are all interrelated, and substantial legal research will be necessary when the issues are complex. The time to research is now, not when you face a motion to dismiss for lack of subject matter jurisdiction or for failure to join an indispensable party.

A plaintiff must always balance the pros and cons of adding additional parties as defendants. This is particularly true when the potential additional party is an employee of a named defendant. A prototypical situation arises when a plaintiff, suing a trucking company or other commercial entity, must decide whether to name the company's driver as an additional defendant. The advantages are that discovery is easier if an employee is a named defendant and an employee is usually happy to testify to agency and scope of employment issues favorable to the plaintiff. The disadvantages are that the case becomes more complex, with more parties, sometimes more lawyers, and more work. Also, the idea of driving a wedge between the driver and company will usually fail because the same lawyer will probably represent both (unless a conflict arises). Plaintiffs sometimes name the driver as an additional defendant to obtain discovery advantages, then dismiss the driver as a named party before trial. But in many cases, naming the driver as an additional defendant is pointless, particularly where employment and scope of employment are not in dispute. On the other hand, if there is an issue as to whether the driver is an employee or an independent contractor, or was acting outside the scope of his employ, the driver must be named as a defendant.

Finally, decide if you want a jury trial.[18] If so, a party's first pleading, either the complaint or answer, must make a jury demand. Otherwise, under federal practice the right to a jury trial will be deemed waived. No hard and fast rules for this choice exist. Decisions must be made on a case-by-case basis, in consultation with the client. On the plus side, cases that have emotionally compelling witnesses and stories, where the client is sympathetic or the underdog, where the jury will want to do what's fair

---

18. See Thomas A. Mauet, Trial Techniques and Trials §12.4 (9th ed. 2013).

despite the law, and where the jury pool is favorable for your side, should be tried to a jury. On the other hand, a bench trial will usually be cheaper, faster, simpler, and often get an earlier trial date. It will be preferable if your side involves dry, technical evidence and has a client and witnesses with little jury appeal. If you advise your client to waive her right to a jury trial, and if your client agrees, get her informed consent in writing.

5.   Plan the discovery

The discovery stage is usually the largest part of the litigation process, the one that consumes the most time and money. Hence, it is particularly important to plan discovery to serve your client's overall objectives and cost considerations. Without planning, discovery usually becomes unfocused and expensive, two disasters you should avoid.

Planning discovery involves seven steps:

1. What facts do I need to establish a winning case on my claims (or to defeat the opponent's claims)?
2. What facts have I already obtained through informal fact investigation?
3. What "missing" facts do I still need to obtain through formal discovery?

Your litigation chart should already include the answers to the above questions. You must consider four other questions:

4. What discovery methods are the most effective to obtain the missing facts?
5. What facts and witnesses, about whom you already know through informal investigation, do you need to "pin down" with formal discovery methods?
6. What restrictions does your litigation budget place on your discovery plan?
7. Finally, in what order should you execute your discovery plan?

These questions obviously require some time to think through. When you have decided on what discovery methods to use for particular information, exhibits, and witnesses, put them on your litigation chart and your litigation timetable.[19]

6.   Plan the dispositive motions

What dispositive motions, such as summary judgment, should you plan? Will your planned discovery provide the basis for succeeding on those

---

19. This process is discussed in detail in §§6.3 and 6.4.

motions? On the other hand, if the other side will be making the motions, what discovery have you planned that will defeat them? The motions stage of the litigation process will only be successful if you have coordinated your discovery with your motions plan. You must look down the road before filing the pleadings to see what motions will be realistic and use discovery to obtain the facts necessary to prevail when the motions are later made.

7.   Plan the settlement approach

Your sense of when to discuss the possibility of settlement with the opposing party must be part of your overall litigation plan. When the client's objective is to settle quickly and keep costs down, you might consider discussing settlement early, such as before filing suit, after the pleadings have been closed, or after a critical witness's deposition. Otherwise, you will probably want to consider settlement after discovery closes, after dispositive motions have been decided, or when you are preparing for the final pretrial conference. At these later stages you will have a better grasp of the case's strengths and weaknesses, but you will have incurred substantial litigation expenses.

8.   Develop a litigation timetable

After thinking through each of the preceding steps in your litigation plan, you should draw up a realistic timetable. To do so, you need to consider the case's complexity, the opposing party's likely responses, and the usual time between the filing of a complaint and trial date in the jurisdiction where the case will proceed. You can then put the steps into a chronological sequence, and include them on your master calendar to remind yourself of the due date for each step in this particular case. Keep in mind that the court under Rule 16(b) will usually enter a scheduling order that will control the timetable.

The master calendar for this case, and all other open cases, becomes the firm's docket control system. Although a few lawyers still use a paper calendar system, nearly all firms today use docket-control software. The software system contains each date for each case in which some activity is scheduled or planned, such as court hearings, depositions, trial dates, and filing deadlines. It also contains reminders of important deadlines, such as the due date for serving interrogatory answers or expert witness reports. The system generates a daily schedule of events for all open cases, noting the time, location, and assigned lawyer for each scheduled event. For example, the daily activity printout would show that Smith v. Jones, Case No. 13 C 4332, office file number 13-121, assigned to John Burns, has a deposition of the defendant scheduled in Burns's office at 2:00 P.M. When court, deposition, or other dates change, you must make sure that the docket system reflects the changes. Keep in mind that such a system is only as good as the information provided to it. Such a docket control system is also essential for conflicts of interest checks, quality control, and malpractice prevention.

Litigation planning must be an integrated, creative, and flexible and continuing process. The plan needs to be integrated because each step should be tailored to achieving your client's litigation objectives, and because each step influences the other steps. It should be creative because every case is different and must be planned out to account for the conditions of the particular case. No standard formula can act as a substitute. Finally, the plan must be flexible and continuing because developments invariably occur during litigation that require changes.

§4.6.   *Example of litigation planning: Novelty Products, Inc. v. Gift Ideas, Inc.*

The following example illustrates the thought process that each step of a coordinated litigation plan involves.

Facts

Novelty Products, Inc. ("Novelty") is a New York corporation that manufactures novelty items that are sold to gift shops throughout the United States. Its corporate headquarters and manufacturing plant are in Buffalo, New York. Gift Ideas, Inc. ("Gift") is a California corporation that owns a chain of gift shops located throughout California. Its corporate headquarters are in Los Angeles.

Over the past five years Gift has periodically ordered products from Novelty under an established procedure. Gift's purchasing department places orders over the telephone, and Novelty sends a written confirmation of the order before delivering it. Gift then pays for each shipment within 30 days of receipt.

One of the items Gift has ordered from Novelty during that time is a patented tabletop electric cigarette lighter called the "Magic Lite." Gift has ordered the lighter, in increasingly large shipments, approximately every six months. The lighter now accounts for about half of all sales from Novelty to Gift. The latest lighter order, for $80,000, was made the usual way, and was shipped last month.

A few days ago Gift notified Novelty that the latest shipment of lighters would be returned unpaid. Gift has just decided to make and market a table-top electric cigarette lighter itself, and from now on its shops will only carry its own lighter. The Gift lighter, called the "Magic Flame," is almost identical in appearance and design to the Novelty lighter. A few months ago Novelty's design chief left the company and began working for Gift.

The shipment of lighters has been returned to Novelty, but Novelty has been unable to find another buyer for the lighters. Since Novelty will soon be marketing an improved version of the lighter, finding a buyer seems unlikely.

The president of Novelty now comes to you for help.

Assume you have researched potential claims against Gift, determined the elements of those claims, identified the sources of proof, and completed an informal fact investigation. You have interviewed your client and appropriate employees, and have reviewed your client's records and correspondence along with what you could obtain from other nonparty sources. You have also checked on the historical relationship between Novelty and Gift, and have concluded that there is no likelihood that Gift can file any counterclaims against Novelty. At this time your litigation chart (for the contract claim) appears as follows:

LITIGATION CHART

Elements of Claims	Sources of Proof	Informal Fact Investigation	Formal Discovery
1. Contract			
(a) contract executed	pl.'s records pl.'s witness def.'s records def.'s witnesses	obtained from client interviews	request to produce, depositions, interrogatories, request to admit
(b) pl.'s performance	pl.'s records pl.'s witness def.'s records def.'s witnesses	obtained from client interviews	initial disclosures, request to produce, depositions, interrogatories, request to admit
(c) def.'s breach (nonpayment & return of goods)	pl.'s records pl.'s witness def.'s records def.'s witnesses shippers	obtained from client interviews	initial disclosures, request to produce, depositions, request to admit, subpoenas
(d) pl.'s damages	pl.'s records pl.'s witness 3d parties who rejected lighters	obtained from client interviews	subpoenas

The litigation chart would be continued for every other potential claim you have been considering. In Novelty's case, these would include:

1. Bad faith
2. Theft of trade secret
3. Trademark infringement
4. Patent infringement
5. Unfair competition

Now is the time to develop the litigation plan. The steps are:

1. Reevaluate the client's objectives, priorities, and cost constraints
2. Define the client's litigation objectives
3. Develop a "theory of the case"
4. Plan the pleadings
5. Plan the discovery
6. Plan the dispositive motions
7. Plan the settlement approach
8. Develop a litigation timetable

1.   Reevaluate the client's objectives, priorities, and cost constraints

From your interviews with Novelty's president, the company's objectives have become clear: Novelty wants to be paid the $80,000 due under the contract, yet it also wants to maintain its other ongoing business with Gift. It wants to accomplish these dual objectives quickly at a minimum cost. After Gift rejects your demand that it pay the contract amount, Novelty's president agrees that litigation will be necessary. The president still hopes that litigation, if kept simple, will not destroy Novelty's ongoing business relationship with Gift. These client objectives remain unchanged.

2.   Define the client's litigation objectives

Since Novelty's president has authorized litigation, you need to decide on the basic litigation objectives and then get the client's approval. In this case Novelty has three possible approaches. It can keep the case simple and bring only a contract claim against Gift; it can bring the former design chief in as a defendant by alleging theft of a trade secret; or it can expand the case against Gift by alleging bad faith, copyright, trademark, and unfair competition claims. Which one of these litigation objectives will best serve Novelty's overall objectives?

You first recommend that Novelty not pursue a case against the former design chief, since he was not under contract with Novelty, and you have no proof that he helped Gift design its new lighter. Pressing a theft-of-trade-secrets claim against him has Rule 11 problems and runs counter to the client's preference for handling the case simply, quickly, and cheaply.

You next recommend that Novelty not pursue the complex case involving the patent, trademark, and unfair competition claims. You have doubts that Novelty will prevail on these claims on both legal and factual grounds. In addition, such claims would undoubtedly destroy the continuing business dealings between Novelty and Gift, which remain important to Novelty. The claims would also create lengthy, expensive, and publicity-generating litigation, all things Novelty needs to avoid. If permitted by applicable law of preclusion and claim-splitting, Novelty could always decide to bring a separate suit on these claims if circumstances require it. Joinder of claims is always permissive and there are no statutes of limitations that are about to run.

This leaves the basic contract claim against Gift, based on common law and the UCC sales provisions. This approach has advantages: you have an excellent chance of winning on the merits, and the case can be handled relatively quickly and inexpensively. The disadvantages are that damages may be low since a party has a duty to mitigate damages. However, to date Novelty has been unable to resell the returned lighters, so damages near the contract price may be appropriate. You also consider adding a bad faith claim, which, if permitted under the applicable jurisdiction's substantive tort law, might permit compensatory or punitive damages. You think that Gift is more likely to settle the case for the contract price if faced with a bad faith claim. However, your research of current bad faith law, under both New York and California law, reveals that such a claim probably cannot be brought in a contract case with your facts. If you brought such a claim, you would probably violate Rule 11 and destroy Novelty's hopes of preserving its business relationship with Gift.

You then develop a litigation budget for the proposed contract claim against Gift. You project the following amounts of time will be necessary:

Fact and legal investigation	15 hrs.
Pleadings	5 hrs.
Discovery	50 hrs.
Motions	15 hrs.
Pretrial conference	15 hrs.
Trial and trial preparation	50 hrs.

The total projected time remaining, without a trial, is about 100 hours; with a trial, the total time will be about 150 hours. Your hourly rate is presently $100. Accordingly, the legal fee to the client for resolving the dispute through a trial should be around $15,000. Since the contract case will not require experts, and the only significant costs will be deposition expenses, litigation costs should be in the $2,000 to $3,000 range. Since you feel the contract claim is strong and that under the circumstances getting $80,000 in damages is realistic, bringing the case and trying it if necessary still make economic sense to the client. This is so even though Novelty will have to bear its own legal expenses, based on your determination after research that no applicable law permits the recovery of attorney's fees in this situation.

While not part of this budget, every litigated case will require client time. In commercial cases, this means the time of the company's management and those employees involved in the transaction that the litigation addresses. This time comes at a real cost to the company. Estimate how much time will be required from the company during the litigation, and make sure the client understands and commits to spending the necessary hours on the case.

You meet with Novelty's president and present the above analysis and litigation budget to him. You remind him that this is your projected budget based on the facts presently known, and that unforeseen circumstances often arise that can increase the budget. He agrees with your analysis and budget and authorizes you to file suit against Gift on the contract claim. He again reminds you of his wish to settle quickly if possible and to keep the tone of the litigation as a simple dispute between two businesses over which one will bear the loss for an improperly canceled order.

3.   Develop a "theory of the case"

Before dealing with the pleadings, you need to consider what Novelty's theory of the case should be. You decide to portray Novelty as a small company that had ongoing business dealings with Gift, a larger corporate chain. The specific transaction was a routine one where Gift made an oral order and Novelty sent a confirming letter, shipped the lighters, and sent a bill. Gift refused to pay for the lighters, but had no valid reason to do so. Gift simply changed its mind after agreeing to buy because it was going to market its own lighter. When the lighters were returned, Novelty could not resell them because it was preparing to market an improved version of the original lighter. In short, according to your theory, Gift reneged on the deal and therefore owes Novelty the full $80,000. You feel that this theory will both be simple and have jury appeal.

4.   Plan the pleadings

So far, you have decided to bring a contract action against Gift, but many important questions still need answers. First, what substantive law will apply? Novelty, the plaintiff, is in Buffalo, New York; Gift is based in Los Angeles, California. The offer was made from Los Angeles and accepted in Buffalo. Since the contract was completed in New York and the place of contracting under the standard interests analysis usually controls the choice of the applicable substantive law, New York law will probably apply, regardless of whether the action is filed in New York or California. Filing the action in New York will also help, since it is the plaintiff's home state.

Since you have decided to sue only Gift, proper parties are not a concern. However, if you file in federal district court, will the court have subject matter jurisdiction over the claims? In this case, diversity jurisdiction under 28 U.S.C. §1332 exists. Since the plaintiff is a citizen of New York and the defendant is a citizen of California, complete diversity exists. Also, the claim exceeds the required jurisdictional amount of $75,000.

Can you get personal jurisdiction over Gift? If suit is filed in California, service of process on Gift will be easy, since Gift's corporate headquarters is in Los Angeles. If suit is filed in New York, can Gift be forced to defend a lawsuit there and can Gift be properly served with process? Your research indicates that Gift's dealings with Novelty are adequate "minimum con-tracts" such that Gift can be required to defend in New York. Moreover, since provisions of Rule 4 of the Federal Rule of Civil Procedure allow for service under the forum state's long-arm statute, you should be able to properly serve Gift if suit is filed in New York.

Finally, where is venue proper? Under 28 U.S.C. §1391, New York (the Western District) is a proper place to bring suit. Since the Western District of New York has such obvious advantages to Novelty, suit, if brought in federal court, should be brought there.

The other possibility, of course, is to file the complaint in state court. New York (Buffalo) is the obvious choice, and you should be able to serve Gift under the state long-arm statute. However, because the federal court will get the case to trial sooner, and because federal judges are more actively involved in the settlement process, you decide to file in federal court.

5.   Plan the discovery

The client has two basic objectives: keep the case simple and inexpensive, and try to settle it quickly. Keeping the pleadings simple serves the first objective. You should remember the second one when planning the dis-covery, as well as the later steps of your litigation plan, since your litigation budget allocates just 50 hours to discovery.

Consult your litigation chart. At this stage the facts you have gathered came principally from Novelty's employees and business records. In a con-tract case, this is to be expected. The untapped sources — Gift's employees and records — require formal discovery.

Since a basic objective is an early settlement, you don't want to get mired in lengthy discovery. You decide to ask for limited and accelerated discovery at the planning meeting and the Rule 16 pretrial conference. In addition, you have decided to move for partial summary judgment on liability as soon as possible. A carefully designed discovery plan can serve these objectives of getting the missing information, getting evidence for your summary judgment motion, and pushing for early settlement.

For example, you decide to use discovery only to get Gift's records and witness testimony that deal with the specific transaction involved. You decide that Novelty's records and witnesses can provide evidence of an established course of dealings between Novelty and Gift, which would be necessary at trial to prove the contract terms. Second, you decide to focus on the contract and its breach, not contract damages, which you can again prove through Novelty's records and witnesses. This limited discovery will give you the information necessary for your motion for partial summary judgment on liability.

You still need to decide which discovery methods to use to execute the plan and what order to use them in. Initial disclosures are automatic and required. You decide to send a set of interrogatories to Gift dealing with the basic chronological events involved in the transaction. You also decide to send Gift a request to produce all records dealing with the specific transaction. These records should, among other things, identify the Gift employees who handled the transaction and were involved in the decision to return the lighters. Finally, you decide to depose those same essential Gift employees in succession, during one or two days, to minimize their contact with each other. Afterwards, you will send a request to admit facts that covers the liability facts of the case.

The last decision is when to take these steps. Ordinarily you will want to move quickly to stay ahead of the other side. Here you decide to send out the interrogatories and requests to produce records at the earliest permitted time, and to send out the deposition notices for the necessary depositions as soon as you receive adequate answers to your interrogatories and documents requests. The request to admit facts can then follow shortly after the depositions.

6. Plan the dispositive motions

Your overall litigation objective is to seek an early settlement, preferably after pleadings are filed or discovery has begun. If the case does not settle at this time, you plan to move for partial summary judgment on liability as soon as discovery ends. You will then have the information necessary to support your motion and to create additional pressure for a settlement.

7. Plan the settlement approach

Early settlement has always been a priority in your case. Accordingly, if Gift does not initiate settlement overtures, you plan to do so repeatedly. You will suggest settlement after the pleadings are filed, after discovery is well under way and also when completed, after the motion for partial summary judgment is heard, and at the final pretrial conference.

Your approach has been to use focused discovery, particularly the request to admit facts, and the partial summary judgment motion to eliminate liability from the settlement discussions and put pressure on Gift. Since Novelty has been unable to resell the lighters, there is no mitigation of damages problem and damages are likely to be the full contract price. You decide that, with Novelty's consent, you will agree to settle for an amount close to the contract price, minus your total litigation expenses. This puts the settlement "value" of the case in the range of $65,000 to $80,000, depending on how early the case is settled.

8. Develop a litigation timetable

Now that you have developed a litigation plan that will realistically serve the client's objectives and priorities, you need to put the basic components on a timetable. Your basic timetable for Novelty is:

Litigation Timetable

1/1 (today)	Complete litigation plan
by 2/1	File complaint
by 3/1	Initial disclosure
by 4/1	Interrogatories, production requests to def.
by 5/1	Deposition notices to def. witnesses
by 6/1	Depose def. witnesses (same day if possible)
by 7/1	Requests to admit facts to def.
by 9/1	Motion for partial summary judgment on liability
by 10/1	Prepare pretrial memorandum
by 11/1	Pretrial conference
12/1	Initial trial date

You plan to recommend this schedule to the lawyer for Gift when you meet and confer to develop a discovery plan under Rule 26(f) and propose it to the trial judge when you meet for the pretrial conference under Rule 16. These dates can then be put on your general docket calendar to remind you when the basic steps in this case should be completed.

§4.7.   Prefiling requirements

Are you finally ready to begin drafting the pleadings? Not quite. There are still a few matters you need to consider before plunging ahead.

1.   Statutory notice requirements

Some actions, primarily claims against governmental bodies such as municipalities, often have statutory notice requirements that must be complied with or else suit will be barred. These statutes usually have time limitations substantially shorter than the applicable statute of limitations, often as short as six months or less, and usually have detailed fact requirements. These statutes are usually strictly construed, so each statutory requirement must be closely followed.

2.   Contract requirements

Many contracts, particularly insurance and employment contracts and contracts with governmental bodies, have notice and claims provisions that are drafted as conditions precedent. These provisions usually require notice of intent to sue, or presentation of claims before filing suit, and require that notice be given within a short period of time, usually much shorter than the applicable statute of limitations period. Make sure you comply with the conditions precedent required by the contract before filing suit.

3. Mediation, arbitration, and expert review requirements

By statute or contract, many disputes must be submitted to binding or nonbinding mediation or arbitration before suit can be brought. For example, construction contracts frequently have arbitration clauses. Many states require by statute that medical malpractice claims must first be presented to a medical review panel or that plaintiff must have an appropriately qualified expert who will testify that the defendant breached the applicable standard of care.

4. Administrative procedure requirements

Claims against governmental bodies usually cannot be brought in court until administrative procedures have been followed and exhausted. Sometimes this exhaustion requirement is statutory; sometimes it is judicially created. For example, claims for benefits from the Social Security and Veterans Administrations must ordinarily be pursued through the administrative process before resort to the judicial system is permitted.[20] Accordingly, determine what applicable administrative procedure statutes and case law apply to your claim, and make sure that they have been followed and exhausted before filing suit.

5. Appointment of legal guardian

Some individuals are incompetent to sue in their own name and must have a legal representative or specially appointed guardian litigate for them. Rule 17 governs capacity to sue. It generally defers to state law in determining both capacity to sue and the appropriate representative party.[21] Minors and incompetents, for example, can only sue through their legal guardians or conservators. Appropriate state court appointments of guardians, or other legal representatives, must be obtained before suit can properly be brought. Such appointments are a serious concern when statutes of limitations are about to run, because obtaining them may take some time.

6. Lis pendens

Some jurisdictions require the filing of a lis pendens notice and service on all interested parties whenever a suit involves an interest in real property or tangible personal property. The notice is filed in the public records, usually property and title records. This gives notice of the pending litigation to parties having an interest in the property. Once notified, any interest in the property they acquire is subject to any judgment that may be entered in

---

20. See 42 U.S.C. §421(d); Administrative Procedure Act, 5 U.S.C. §§551 et seq.
21. See §3.4.

that particular litigation. Where your suit involves real or personal property, you should always check to see if any lis pendens rules apply; if so, follow them so that a judgment will be valid and enforceable against such parties. State lis pendens notice requirements are applicable to federal cases involving real estate.[22]

7.   Attachment

Attachment is the legal process in which someone's property is seized to satisfy a judgment not yet rendered. While there are no federal attachment statutes, Rule 64 makes available the attachment procedures allowed under the forum state's law. State statutes often provide for attachment of a debtor's property interest under certain defined circumstances and usually specify the procedures, including service of process and bonds, that must be followed. Some jurisdictions also provide for prefiling attachment or garnishment procedures that may be used to freeze assets that may satisfy any future judgment. There are remedies for wrongful attachment, however, so caution is obviously in order.

8.   Temporary restraining orders

If you are seeking injunctive relief, you may be able to obtain a temporary restraining order (TRO) to prevent immediate irreparable injury to your client's interests. A TRO may be obtained under specified conditions for a strictly limited period of time, until a hearing for a preliminary injunction can be scheduled.[23] While a TRO is hard to obtain, there will be times when seeking a TRO is essential to preserve a client's rights.[24]

9.   Discovery before suit

Upon filing a verified petition that complies with Rule 27's requirements, you may depose a person before suit is filed to perpetuate that person's testimony. You should consider doing so in two situations. First, if you cannot get enough pre-filing factual information to comply with the Rule 11 requirements, Rule 27 may be your only recourse. Second, Rule 27 is useful if an important witness is old, sick, or is about to leave the jurisdiction.

10.   Demand letters

While not legally required to do so, lawyers frequently use demand letters, particularly in tort, contract, and commercial cases, to state a party's claim

22. See Rule 64; 28 U.S.C. §1964.
23. See Rule 65.
24. Obtaining a TRO or preliminary injunction is discussed in §7.5.

against another party and indicate an intent to litigate. For instance, in anticipatory breach situations it is advantageous to send a demand letter asserting that the other side appears to be in breach and requesting assurances of performance. Such letters, if not responded to, may constitute admissions by silence.

Demand letters also serve practical purposes. In small disputes, where a compromise is possible, a demand letter that notifies the other side of your intent to sue absent an acceptable settlement can often trigger settlement discussions. By including a draft of your proposed complaint, you show the other side that you are serious. A demand letter will often generate a denial letter stating the basis for rejecting your claim, possibly foreshadowing the defenses your adversary will raise if suit proceeds.

In some cases, where your opponent's possession of the important records limits your ability to get the facts, you might consider sending a draft of your complaint to your opponent and await a response. The opponent may respond by giving you information that will affect your decision to file the lawsuit or will affect the claims that you ultimately bring.

An effective demand letter details the event, shows why the other party is culpable, shows what injuries your client sustained and the impact those injuries had on the client's life, identifies the economic and non-economic damages your client sustained, and ends with a demand for a certain sum. Draft the letter to tell a persuasive story of what happened to your client and how he has been damaged.

Example:

Re: Martha Wilde construction contract dated January 15, 2013

Dear Mr. Johnson:

We represent Martha Wilde, the owner of the home at 1822 Forest Lane. On January 15, 2013, your company, Johnson Construction, Inc., entered into a contract with Ms. Wilde to do certain renovations in her home. Under the contract, the work was to have begun on or before March 1, 2013, and completed on or before May 1, 2013. As you knew, the completion date was an important and material provision of the contract. Ms. Wilde hired you to do the renovations because she planned to put her home up for sale on May 1, the beginning of the summer selling season, and the renovations were essential for that purpose. Ms. Wilde entered into the contract with your company relying on your assurances that the work would be completed by May 1.

The present date is June 15, 2013, and your company has yet to begin work under the contract. This delay constitutes a breach of a material term of the contract. Since you have breached the contract, it is hereby terminated, and Ms. Wilde is no longer required to perform any obligations under the contract. Furthermore, your breach of the contract has caused damages to Ms. Wilde that you knew she would incur if the contract were not performed in a timely fashion.

Because of your breach of the contract, Ms. Wilde has been unable to sell her home and has suffered other losses.

Accordingly, demand is hereby made upon Johnson Construction, Inc., to pay the sum of $25,000 for damages caused to Ms. Wilde because of your breach of the contract. Unless Johnson Construction, Inc., pays that amount by certified check to Ms. Wilde on or before July 1, 2013, she has authorized us to file suit on her behalf to recover all damages, expenses, attorneys' fees, and court costs incurred by Ms. Wilde as a result of your breach. We are prepared to file the attached complaint in Superior Court without further notice in the event you do not make the payment demanded and resolve this matter by that date.

Since we represent Ms. Wilde, please direct all future communications in this matter to me rather than to Ms. Wilde. I await a call from you or your legal representative.

11.   Preservation letters and litigation holds

When litigation is pending or reasonably anticipated, a party has a duty to preserve evidence in the party's possession, custody, or control when the party has notice or knowledge that the information may be relevant to the litigation. A danger always exists that a party will destroy documents, records, and data to keep the opposing party from obtaining them. This concern is even greater if that evidence is stored electronically. As plaintiff, if you are concerned that the defendant may alter or destroy evidence, you should put the defendant on notice, before filing the lawsuit, that you will seek both paper and electronic evidence and that the defendant has a duty to preserve all such evidence. You do so by sending a "preservation letter" to the party or, if you know that the party has legal representation, to the lawyer. Preservation letters are discussed in §6.8.

Your client has the same preservation obligations as the opposing party: to preserve documents, electronically stored information, and things relevant to the pending or reasonably anticipated lawsuit that are in your client's possession, custody, or control. Hence, you need to advise your client of the preservation obligation when the obligation first arises and to make sure that the obligation is in fact implemented. Send your client a "litigation hold letter," which spells out the preservation obligations, and then follow up to ensure compliance. Litigation holds are discussed in §6.8.

12.   Physical examinations

As plaintiff in a personal injury case, consider offering to have your client examined by a defense doctor before filing suit. There are several reasons to consider this. First, Rule 35 entitles the defense to such an examination after suit is filed. Second, the plaintiff's injuries will be more apparent at this time. Third, such an offer lets the defense know you're prepared and confident about your case. Fourth, the offer may pave the way to an earlier settlement of the case.

Part B
CONDUCTING THE LITIGATION

V

PLEADINGS

§5.1. Introduction

Pleadings get the lawsuit started, usually stop the running of the statute of limitations, and frame the issues involved in the lawsuit. Pleadings put the parties on notice of the legal claims and defenses, and, to some extent, the underlying factual bases for those claims and defenses.

The Federal Rules of Civil Procedure contain general pleading rules, although other sources exist and must always be kept in mind. Under Rule 83 district courts can create local rules governing litigation in that district. Most have done so. Local rules generally do not affect the substance of pleadings, but they do ordinarily control other pleadings-related issues, such as the number of copies filed, size of paper, format, bindings, and electronic filing. Particular federal statutory actions, such as bankruptcy and copyright, may also have special procedure rules. Finally, specialized federal courts, such as bankruptcy and claims courts, may have special statutory and local procedural rules. Hence, you should always check procedural statutes and local rules in addition to the Federal Rules of Civil Procedure to determine what rules apply to your particular case.

Good pleadings practice is a combination of two things: a solid litigation plan and technically precise drafting. The litigation plan, which you have already developed, will control the claims and remedies (if a plaintiff), or the defenses, counterclaims, cross-claims, and third-party claims (if a defendant). The drafting of pleadings then becomes the primary concern, since pleadings that are technically precise will avoid attacks by motions and eliminate the need to file amended pleadings to cure defects that should have been avoided in the first place.

§5.2.   General pleading requirements

The Federal Rules of Civil Procedure have made simplicity and limited purpose the touchstones of the pleadings stage of the litigation process. Under Rule 2, all actions are "civil actions," and under Rule 7(a) the only basic pleadings allowed are complaints, answers, and replies.

1.   General requirements for claims

Rule 8(a) provides the standard that a claim must meet. It applies to all claims, whether asserted in a complaint, as a cross-claim or counterclaim, or in a third-party complaint, unless a specific rule or statute provides otherwise.[1] In addition to a statement of the grounds for the court's jurisdiction and a demand for the relief sought, Rule 8(a) requires a "short and plain statement of the claim showing the pleader is entitled to relief."

For decades Rule 8 was commonly characterized as establishing a "notice pleading" rule. The pleader needed to include only enough information to notify the opposing party of the basis of the claims. Upon the promulgation of the Federal Rules in 1938, confusing distinctions about whether a statement was an allegation of fact, law, or conclusions of law lost significance. For the most part, the Federal Rules eschewed a requirement that specific facts substantiating the claims be pleaded. Pleaders could look to the form complaint in the Appendix of Forms as a blueprint, since Rule 84 deemed these complaint forms legally sufficient. The Supreme Court embraced this "notice pleading" interpretation of Rule 8 in Conley v. Gibson, 355 U.S. 41 (1957). It held that no complaint would be dismissed for failure to state a claim "unless it appears beyond doubt that a plaintiff can prove no set of facts in support of his claim which would entitle him to relief." Motions to dismiss rarely succeeded, as courts were instructed to bend over backwards to find some legally sufficient theory embedded within even the most cursory and vague of complaints.[2]

Starting in the 1960s, lower federal courts began to chafe at what some believed to be an overly permissive pleading standard. Although the Supreme Court rebuffed attempts to raise the pleading standard multiple times,[3] this view finally prevailed in Bell Atlantic v. Twombly, 550 U.S. 544

---

1. Wright §68; Moore's Manual §901; Manual of Federal Practice §3.5; Wright & Miller §§1202-1205; Moore's Federal Practice §§8.02–8.06. Rule 9, for example, governs claims for fraud or mistake. The Private Securities Litigation Reform Act, another example, includes a special pleading standard for securities fraud claims. See 15 U.S.C. §78u-4(b).

2. The emblematic case from this era is Dioguardi v. Durning, 139 F.2d 774 (2d Cir. 1944).

3. See Swierkiewicz v. Sorema N.A., 534 U.S. 506 (2002); Leatherman v. Tarrant County Narcotics Intelligence and Control Unit, 507 U.S. 163 (1993).

(2007), and Ashcroft v. Iqbal, 556 U.S. 662 (2009). *Twombly*, an antitrust case, and *Iqbal*, a civil rights case against government officials, adopted an interpretation of Rule 8 that differed from the "notice pleading" understanding. In *Twombly*, the Court rejected the Conley v. Gibson "no set of facts" standard and concluded that this language had "earned its retirement." The Court interpreted Rule 8 to require that complaints must allege enough facts to "plausibly suggest" liability and not merely allege facts consistent with liability. The Court clearly was concerned that under the old standard a party could file a "bare bones" complaint, which simply recited the elements of a claim in conclusory fashion, then subject the other party to significant litigation costs, particularly in complex litigation like antitrust.

The Court in *Iqbal* attempted to clarify how trial courts should apply the new plausibility standard. A judge determining whether a complaint meets the standard first has to disregard any "threadbare legal conclusions." Then the judge has to look at the remaining factual allegations in the complaint to determine whether they meet the plausibility standard.

Although there is some question as to exactly what this new pleading standard requires, the Court clearly has breathed new life into Rule 12(b)(6) motions to dismiss, which attack the sufficiency of the complaint under Rule 8. Judges now will dismiss complaints that contain only bare legal conclusions since they do not meet Rule 8's "short and plain statement" requirement. They will examine complaints more closely to determine if the factual allegations in them meet the plausibility standard. If the plaintiff pleads legal assertions but does not back them up with nonconclusory factual allegations, the court must be able to infer that discovery will plausibly unearth evidence to buttress these presently bare legal assertions. Under such circumstances, the complaint may fall short of the *Twombly/Iqbal* plausibility threshold. Anytime the court can readily imagine an innocent explanation for the occurrences described in the complaint, the complaint risks dismissal. Defendants have made aggressive use of the new pleading standard, and in any case of factual uncertainty or complexity, plaintiffs should expect a Rule 12(b)(6) motion to dismiss.

In light of *Twombly* and *Iqbal*, lawyers should do several things. First, draft complaints with an eye to the judge, not just the opposing party, since motions to dismiss are now much more common and the likelihood that they will succeed has increased. Second, make complaints factual; allege specific facts that plausibly establish each element of each claim whenever possible. A motion to dismiss is most likely to succeed when a complaint lacks a specific, nonconclusory fact for an element of a claim. Under these circumstances, a pleader must ask the court to infer from the facts alleged that specific facts to support this element will emerge in discovery. The court will be obliged to consider whether the contrary inference, that discovery will establish an innocent explanation for the complained-of incident or behavior, is more plausible. For this reason, plead facts to exclude alternative innocent explanations for allegedly wrongful conduct. Doing so will discourage a court from drawing an inference from the facts alleged in your adversary's favor.

Pleading specific facts creates an additional benefit: It may trigger more automatic discovery disclosures. Rule 26(a) provides for automatic initial disclosure of basic information that "the disclosing party may use to support its claims or defenses," and Rule 26(b) permits discovery of "any nonprivileged matter that is relevant to any party's claim or defense." A party may create discovery benefits by alleging specific facts in the pleadings, to make it harder for the opposing party to avoid making the required initial disclosures, or to argue that discovery seeks irrelevant matter. This is discussed in §§5.3 and 6.5.

Do not model your complaint on the one included in the Appendix of Forms. In September 2014, the Judicial Conference of the United States approved proposed amendments that will remove it altogether. The proposed amendment will likely become final. Whether it does or not, the proposed amendment confirms a perception that the form complaint no longer exemplifies what Rule 8 requires after *Twombly* and *Iqbal*. Also, if you think your complaint comes close to the line, and if you believe that further prefiling investigation might help turn up helpful facts, do not simply file and hope for the best. A 12(b)(6) dismissal is presumptively with prejudice.

The law of pleading remains in flux. What you must plead may depend upon the substantive nature of the claims you want to allege. Do substance-specific research into pleading standards within your jurisdiction before filing, to make sure that you know how courts have applied *Twombly* and *Iqbal* to your type of case.

2. Alternative and inconsistent pleadings

Rule 8(e)(2) allows a party to plead multiple claims or defenses in alternative or hypothetical form, either in one or in separate counts or defenses.[4] In practice, each claim is usually put in a separate count and each defense is designated separately. Keep in mind, however, that since pleadings can be used during trial, alternative or inconsistent pleadings may cast the party in a poor light. Hence, drafting must also be done with an eye toward the impression the pleading will have on the jurors.

3. Format requirements

Rules 10 and 11 set forth format requirements. There are several that must be followed for every pleading. Local rules may also specify additional requirements.

---

4. Moore's Manual §§9.10; Manual of Federal Practice §3.72.

a. Caption

The caption of a case refers to the names of the parties, the court in which the case is being filed, and the case number. Every pleading must have a caption containing this information.

b. File number

The file number is the case number that is stamped on the complaint when it is first filed with the clerk of the court. It must appear on all successive pleadings and other court papers. Although not required, the designation "Civil Action" is usually placed below the file number.

c. Parties to action

The complaint caption must list all the parties to the action. Subsequent pleadings need only list the first plaintiff and first defendant, with an appropriate reference to additional parties, such as "et al."

Make sure that your caption correctly states the proper name and legal description of each party. Under Rule 17, every action must be brought in the name of the real party in interest; according to this rule, the capacity to sue or be sued is controlled by the law of domicile, incorporation, or forum.[5] You must always check Rule 17(b) and (c) to see if a party has capacity to sue or be sued and that the correct person or entity is designated as a party. Common designations include the following:

- John Smith
- Sharon Jones, as guardian of the Estate of Robert Jones, a minor
- Robert Smith, as conservator of the Estate of Ellen Smith, an incompetent
- Frank Watson, as executor of the Estate of James Morley, deceased
- Barbara Myers, as trustee in bankruptcy of the Estate of Robert Jackson, bankrupt
- R. J. Smith Company, a corporation
- Johnson Hospital, a not-for-profit corporation
- Robert Smith, d/b/a Smith Cleaners
- Barnett and Lynch, a partnership
- Western Ranches Association, an unincorporated association

Where a party is being sued both individually and in a representative capacity, the caption should say so.

5. See §3.4.

Example:

John Smith, individually and as administrator of the Estate of Franklin Smith, deceased

The caption, then, simply lists each party and what side of the action each is on.

Example:

UNITED STATES DISTRICT COURT
FOR THE NORTHERN DISTRICT OF NEW YORK

Rebecca Smith, and J. W. Smith Company, a corporation, Plaintiffs v. Randolph Construction, a corporation, and William Johnson, d/b/a Solar Consultants, Defendants	No. _____ Civil Action

Sometimes you will be unable to identify a proper party by name before filing. In many state courts you can designate a party as "John Doe, the true name being presently unknown," and pursue the identity of the party through formal discovery. Plaintiffs sometimes do so when they have been able to identify some but not all liable parties. The advantage of doing this is that the plaintiff can get the case started against the known defendants and amend the complaint to add the additional parties when their identities are discovered (and the statute of limitations has not yet run as to the additional parties). However, in federal court the use of fictitious parties is prohibited, although some local rules provide for the use of fictitious parties if ordered by the court.

Keep in mind, however, that naming John or Jane Doe defendants, where permitted, to attempt to toll the applicable statute of limitations under the relation back doctrine will probably be ineffective, unless the person properly named later as a defendant had actual notice of the suit within the time period that Rule 15(c) specifies.[6]

d. Designation

Each pleading should be labeled to show what type it is, i.e., a complaint, counterclaim, cross-claim, third-party complaint, answer, or reply. Where multiple parties are involved, it is useful to show against whom the pleading is directed.

6. See §5.13.

Examples:

COMPLAINT
DEFENDANT SMITH COMPANY'S ANSWER TO CROSS-CLAIM OF
DEFENDANT FRANKLIN CORPORATION

THIRD-PARTY COMPLAINT AGAINST JONES CONSTRUCTION
COMPANY

e. Signing pleadings

Rule 11 requires that one of the party's lawyers sign every pleading or other court paper. An individual, not a law firm, must sign, although in practice the lawyer's firm is frequently shown as "of counsel." The pleading must also contain the lawyer's address, e-mail address, and telephone number.

Under the Federal Rules pleadings are not "verified" — that is, signed under oath by the parties and notarized — although this procedure remains proper in many state jurisdictions. Verification is still appropriate in a few special circumstances, most commonly in applications for a TRO under Rule 65(b).

f. Disclosure statement

Under Rule 7.1, a nongovernmental corporate party must file a disclosure statement that "identifies any parent corporation and any publically held corporation that owns 10% or more of its stock or states that there is no such corporation." This disclosure statement helps the judge to whom the case is assigned determine if she has a financial interest, usually stock ownership, in any party, and thus if she will need to recuse herself.

4. Rule 11

Under Rule 11, a lawyer's presentation to the court of a pleading, written motion, or other court paper[7] (except discovery disclosures, requests, responses, objections, and motions, which are covered under the certification sanctions of Rule 26(g) and Rule 37) automatically constitutes a certification as to the following: the pleading has evidentiary support or is likely to have evidentiary support after reasonable investigation, to the best of the lawyer's "knowledge, information, and belief"; the pleading is supported by existing law or can be supported by a "nonfrivolous argument" for a change in law; and it is not being filed for delay, harassment, or some other improper purpose.[8] A presentation to the court means signing,

---

7. Moore's Manual §9.20-9.22; Moore's Federal Practice §11.02; Wright & Miller §§1331 et seq.

8. Rule 11 parallels the applicable ethics considerations. See Model Rules of Professional Conduct, Rule 3.1.

filing, submitting, or later advocating a paper. Under Rule 11(b), "later advocating" a position in a previously presented paper is considered a presentation to the court.

Rule 11(a) requires that "every pleading, written motion, and other paper must be signed" by an attorney of record or by the unrepresented party filing it. Each paper must provide the address, e-mail address, and telephone number of the signer. If not signed, the paper "shall" be stricken unless corrected promptly after the signer learns of the omission.

Rule 11(b) imposes significant obligations on the lawyer. A subjective good faith belief that the pleading is well founded is not sufficient. A lawyer must make a reasonable inquiry into the law and facts, and have concluded that there is a sound basis in law and fact for each allegation against each party in the pleading. The rule applies to every lawyer signing any pleading, written motion, or other court paper, even if another lawyer does the actual research and drafting. Local counsel, for example, cannot assume that work done by other lawyers meets the rule's requirements. Rule 11(b) also imposes the same obligations on the client. A party, even if represented by counsel, can incur penalties if the party presents a paper to the court by signing, filing, submitting, or later advocating in violation of the rule's standards.

What amounts to a reasonable inquiry depends on the facts and circumstances that existed at the time the pleading was made.[9] The factors to be considered include the amount of time available to investigate the law and facts, the reliability of the client as a source of facts, and the extent to which an investigation could corroborate or alter those facts.

You can rely on your client as the sole source for critical facts if such reliance is reasonable under the circumstances. You must consider whether information from other sources can corroborate the client's story, what the cost of seeking such corroboration might be, whether the client has actual firsthand knowledge of the critical facts, how well you know the client, how reliable the client has been in the past, and whether the client's story is inherently plausible.[10] The reasonableness of the pleading or other court paper is measured at the time of its filing; Rule 11(b) does not impose a requirement to amend on discovering errors, although other practice rules do. However, if evidentiary support for a claim or defense is not obtained after a reasonable opportunity for investigation, Rule 11(b) calls upon the litigant not to advocate such claims or defenses.

Rule 11 does not prohibit filing a pleading or other court paper simply because the information you have may not yet be in admissible form. On the other hand, a mere hunch that the client may have a good claim is inadequate. You must have some reasonably reliable information that suggests that the client has a proper claim. The court can also consider whether you were on notice that your investigation, both legal and factual, was inadequate or incorrect. Arguments for the extension, modification,

---

9. See Charles Yablon, Hindsight, Regret, and Safe Harbors in Rule 11 Litigation, 37 Loy. L.A. L. Rev. 599 (2004).

10. See Chien v. Skystar Bio Pharm. Co., 246 F.R.D. 67 (D. Conn. 2009).

or reversal of existing law, or for the establishment of new law, are not violations of the rule so long as the arguments are "nonfrivolous."

If a pleading is signed in violation of Rule 11(b), the court "may" impose sanctions against the lawyer who signed the pleading, the law firm for whom the lawyer works, the party, or all three. A law firm is generally jointly responsible for the conduct of its partners, associates, and employees. Rule 11(c) does not provide factors a court should consider when deciding to impose sanctions, but rather gives considerable discretion to the court. Sanctions can include costs and attorney's fees that are directly incurred as a result of the violation, as well as nonmonetary sanctions. The court might strike the challenged paper, or it might require participation in educational programs. Sanctions are limited to what is sufficient to deter repetition of the conduct or similar conduct by others in the same situation, and are proper even though there was no subjective bad faith or harassment.[11] Their purpose is not to compensate the other side for expense incurred because of the flawed pleading. Factors the court will consider when deciding how to sanction include whether the misconduct was willful or repeated, the misconduct's effect on the pleadings and the litigation, and what amount will serve to deter this person, as well as other litigants, in the future. The court can impose sanctions without holding a hearing in every instance.

The court can impose sanctions in response to a formal motion for sanctions.[12] Such a motion is to be served separately from other motions and must describe the specific conduct alleged to violate the rule. However, under Rule 11(c) a motion for sanctions cannot be filed or presented to the court until the party threatening to seek sanctions has given its adversary 21 days to withdraw or correct the challenged paper, claim, defense, contention, allegation, or denial. This so-called safe harbor provision protects the party against a motion for sanctions by giving it a chance to withdraw or correct. The court can shorten or alter the 21-day rule.

The court can also impose sanctions on its own, but only after notice and an opportunity to respond. The court will issue an "order to show cause" specifically describing the conduct in question and directing an attorney, law firm, or party to show why it has not violated Rule 11(b). When the court acts on its own, there is no "safe harbor"; there is no opportunity for the litigant to withdraw or correct a challenged paper, but such a withdrawal or correction is a factor that the court may consider in determining whether to impose sanctions. In addition, monetary sanctions against a represented party for frivolous legal positions may not be awarded on the court's own initiative, and monetary sanctions generally may not be awarded unless the order to show cause is issued before a voluntary dismissal or settlement of the claims made by or against the

---

11. See Ideal Instruments, Inc. v. Rivard Instruments, Inc., 245 F.R.D. 381 (N.D. Iowa 2007) (sufficient to deter); Young v. City of Providence ex rel. Napolitano, 404 F.3d 33 (1st Cir. 2005) (no subjective bad faith required).

12. See Intravaia ex rel. Intravaia v. Rocky Point Union Free Sch. Dist., 919 F. Supp. 2d 285 (E.D.N.Y. 2013).

litigant. When awarded, a monetary sanction will usually be limited to a penalty payable to the court; a monetary award to an injured party will be allowed only in unusual circumstances.

Rule 11 is not self-enforcing. The bench and bar have responsibility to ensure that sanctions are imposed where appropriate. Rule 11 is not to be used as a tactical weapon or a vehicle for fee-shifting. In fact, a motion for sanctions improperly brought itself can trigger Rule 11 sanctions.

To avoid Rule 11 problems, conduct an adequate prefiling factual and legal investigation. Personally interview the client, critically analyze the client's information, interview corroborating witnesses, obtain and review relevant documents, and research the applicable law. Undertake basic online research. If the court can find relevant information on Google that you have overlooked, you may face sanctions. Make sure that each allegation, against each defendant, meets the "reasonable inquiry" standard. In short, do your homework first, think, reflect, get second opinions when in doubt, and then file.

Rule 11's reasonable inquiry requirement has teeth, and judges impose significant sanctions for violations.[13] The "good heart, empty head" excuse will not protect a lawyer against sanctions. A lawyer who means well but does not undertake sufficient investigation will run into trouble. Nor will courts excuse subpar filings on account of a lawyer's inexperience with a certain type of litigation.

Rule 11 has spawned substantial satellite litigation. Supreme Court opinions on Rule 11 include Pavelic & LeFlore v. Marvel Entertainment Group, 493 U.S. 120 (1989); Cooter & Gell v. Hartmarx Corp., 496 U.S. 384 (1990); Business Guides, Inc. v. Chromatic Communications Enterprises, Inc., 498 U.S. 533 (1991); Chambers v. NASCO, Inc., 501 U.S. 32 (1991); and Willy v. Coastal Corp., 503 U.S. 131 (1992).

In *Pavelic*, the Court held that because Rule 11 requires that pleadings and other papers shall be signed in the individual attorney's name, sanctions for violations of the rule could only be imposed on the individual lawyer signing, not on the lawyer's law firm. The 1993 amendments to Rule 11 modified this holding. Rule 11(c)(1)(A) establishes that a law firm is held jointly responsible when one of its partners, associates, or employees is determined to have violated the rule, absent exceptional circumstances. Because the 21-day safe harbor provision gives the law firm notice of an alleged violation, sanctions may be appropriate. The court may consider whether other attorneys in the firm, co-counsel, or other law firms should be held accountable for their part in causing a violation. In *Cooter & Gell*, the Supreme Court ruled that a voluntary dismissal of an action does not deprive the court of jurisdiction over a Rule 11 motion, since a Rule 11 violation is complete once the improper court paper is filed. In *Business Guides*, the Court held that Rule 11 applies to parties who sign pleadings, even if they are represented by counsel. In *Chambers*, the trial court imposed sanctions on the defendant for bad faith conduct under the court's "inherent power" to control the conduct of parties who appear

13. See Eon-Net LP v. Flagstar Bancorp, 653 F.3d 1314 (Fed. Cir. 2011), where the court upheld an award of $141,984.70 in Rule 11 sanctions.

before it. The Court upheld the trial court, noting that the availability of Rule 11 or other sanctions does not preclude the imposition of sanctions under the court's inherent powers. Finally, in *Willy*, the Court held that the court can impose Rule 11 sanctions on lawyers and their clients even if the trial court is later found not to have had proper subject matter jurisdiction over the case when the offensive conduct was committed.

5. Service and filing

Whenever a lawyer creates a pleading whether a complaint, answer, or reply two things must happen. First, the pleading must be properly served on the other parties. Second, it must be filed with the court. How service is accomplished depends on which pleading is being served.

a. Service of original complaint and summons on defendant

Rule 4 governs the service of an original complaint and summons on a defendant. If a served defendant decides to bring a third-party complaint against a new defendant, the new defendant also must be served with the third-party complaint in accordance with the provisions of Rule 4. The formality of service under Rule 4 is necessary to put the new defendant on notice that he has been sued, so that he can obtain a lawyer and defend against the lawsuit. Service under Rule 4 is discussed further in §5.3.

b. Service of all other pleadings on existing parties

After the original complaint and summons have been served on the defendant, service of any subsequent pleadings — an answer, reply, and amended pleadings — on existing parties must be done in accordance with the provisions of Rule 5. Fairness requires that all parties presently in the case receive notice of all events in the case, beginning with the pleadings. When a party is represented by a lawyer, service is made on the lawyer. Service is made on the party when she lacks representation. Rule 5 permits several methods of service, but the common ones are personal delivery, mail delivery, or delivery at the lawyer's office to a person in charge. Rule 5(b) also permits service by electronic means if consented to in writing.

c. Filing and proof of service

Pleadings must be filed with the clerk of the court as well as served on the parties. The original complaint must be filed with the clerk before service of the complaint and summons can be made. Other pleadings must be filed with the clerk either before service on the parties or within a reasonable time after service. Filing of other pleadings is usually done at the same time the pleading is being served on the other lawyers or parties. The usual practice is to take the original and an appropriate number of copies of the pleading to the clerk's office for filing. Make sure you get a copy stamped "filed" and dated as proof of filing for your own files. Under Rule 5(d) filing can also be made by electronic means if permitted by local rules.

Whenever service is made, you should attach a "proof of service" to the pleading. Proof of service of the complaint is made on the summons form. Local rules usually specify how proof of service of other pleadings is made. The usual practice is to have a certificate or affidavit of service attached to the end of the answer, reply, or amended pleading that shows when and how service was made, which includes the signature of the lawyer or the notarized signature of a member of the lawyer's staff.

§5.3.   Complaints

The complaint is the plaintiff's initial pleading that, when filed with the clerk of the court, starts the litigation. Rule 8(a) requires that the complaint contain the following information:

1.   A statement showing subject matter jurisdiction
2.   A statement of claims
3.   A statement of relief requested

In addition, the complaint should contain a jury demand, if the plaintiff wants a jury trial. A lawyer must sign it, the complaint must be filed with the clerk of the court, and it must be served with summons on the defendant. Beyond these requirements, the complaint's content and organization largely depend on logic and clarity. Many lawyers organize a complaint by using introductory headings, such as "jurisdictional allegation," "parties," "facts common to all counts," "demand for relief," and "jury demand."

1.   Subject matter jurisdiction

Since federal courts are courts of limited jurisdiction, the complaint must allege jurisdiction. Since jurisdiction cannot be assumed, the complaint must demonstrate it affirmatively.[14] This task requires care and detail. The jurisdictional allegation is usually the first part of a complaint and is customarily labeled as such. There are two principal heads of federal subject matter jurisdiction.

a.   Federal question jurisdiction[15]

Federal jurisdiction can be based on a federal statute, constitutional provision, or treaty. The general federal question statute is 28 U.S.C. §1331.

---

14. Wright §69; Hazard et al. §4.8; Moore's Manual §10.05; Manual of Federal Practice §3.6; Moore's Federal Practice §8.03; Wright & Miller §§1206, 1208–1209.
   15. See §3.5.

To establish this head of jurisdiction, the complaint should cite the particular statute, constitutional provision, or treaty, and perhaps quote the operative wording or paraphrase it. Failure to do so is not fatal, since jurisdictional allegations can be amended.[16] Conversely, citing a federal statute, constitutional provision, or treaty will not conclusively confer jurisdiction, since facts alleged in the complaint can contradict and disprove the jurisdictional allegation.

Example:

[Caption]

COMPLAINT

Plaintiff Ralph Johnson complains against Defendant Wilbur Jackson as follows:

Statement of Jurisdiction

1. Jurisdiction in this case is based on the existence of a federal question. This action arises under [the Constitution of the United States, Amendment _____, §____] [or the Act of _____, _____ Stat. _____, _____ U.S.C. §_____] [or the Treaty of the United States _____], as is shown more fully in this complaint.

b. *Diversity jurisdiction*[17]

Federal jurisdiction can also be based on diversity of citizenship. The diversity statute is 18 U.S.C. §1332. The jurisdictional allegation must affirmatively show that each plaintiff is diverse from each defendant and that the case meets the required amount in controversy. The essential requirement is citizenship, not residence. An individual has only one state of citizenship. A corporation, for jurisdictional purposes, is deemed a citizen of both the state where incorporated and the state where it has its principal place of business.[18]

---

16. See 28 U.S.C. §1653. The example in this text is drawn from Form 7 appended to the Federal Rules. A proposed amendment to the Federal Rules, pending at the time of publication, would abrogate the forms. Whether jurisdictional allegations along the lines of what this example suggests will remain sufficient depends to a certain extent upon how the federal courts apply the new *Twombly/Iqbal* plausibility pleading threshold to jurisdictional allegations. This issue is unsettled. For an example of a court applying the plausibility pleading threshold to jurisdictional allegations, see, Collazo-Rosado v. University of Puerto Rico, 775 F. Supp. 2d 376 (D.P.R. 2011).

17. See §3.5.

18. Hertz Corp. v. Friend, 559 U.S. 77 (2010).

Example (individuals):

<u>Statement of Jurisdiction</u>

Jurisdiction in this case is based on diversity of citizenship of the parties and the amount in controversy. Plaintiff is a citizen of the State of California. Defendant is a citizen of the State of Oregon.

Example (corporations):

<u>Statement of Jurisdiction</u>

Jurisdiction in this case is based on diversity of citizenship of the parties and the amount in controversy. Plaintiff is a corporation incorporated under the laws of the State of Delaware having its principal place of business in the State of New York. Defendant is a corporation incorporated under the laws of the State of Georgia having its principal place of business in the State of Florida.

Where the party is a legally recognized unincorporated association, such as a labor union or service organization, it is a citizen of every state of which any of its members is a citizen. Partnerships are considered citizens of each state where a general partner is a citizen. For legal representatives — such as a guardian of a minor, executor or administrator of an estate, and representative of an incompetent — the minor's, deceased's, or incompetent's citizenship controls for diversity purposes, although exceptions in special circumstances may exist.[19]

Diversity jurisdiction under 28 U.S.C. §1332 also requires that the "matter in controversy exceeds the sum or value of $75,000, exclusive of interest and costs. . . ." Since the jurisdictional amount must be alleged in the pleadings, customarily complaints simply paraphrase the statute at the end of the jurisdictional allegation.

Example:

<u>Jurisdictional Allegation</u>

. . . The amount in controversy exceeds the sum of seventy-five thousand dollars ($75,000), exclusive of interest and costs.

Where a statute makes notice of a claim a prerequisite to suit, some courts have held that the fact that notice was given is a jurisdictional requirement that must be alleged in the complaint.[20]

---

19. See Wright §29; Wright & Miller §3606.
20. See Manual of Federal Practice §3.6.

Because state trial courts are usually courts of general jurisdiction, a specific jurisdictional allegation in complaints brought in state courts may be unnecessary. However, some states require these allegations.

2. Statement of claims

Rule 8(a) requires that a pleading contain a "short and plain statement of the claim showing that the pleader is entitled to relief."[21] Rule 8(d) states that each allegation in the pleading shall be "simple, concise and direct." However, keep in mind that the Supreme Court's decisions in Bell Atlantic v. Twombly, 550 U.S. 544 (2007), and Ashcroft v. Iqbal, 556 U.S. 662 (2009), now require that the complaint must allege enough facts to "plausibly suggest" liability, and reject the allegation of "threadbare legal conclusions" as insufficient.

In light of Rule 8, as interpreted by *Twombly* and *Iqbal,* what is the most effective way to draft a complaint? Are there any general drafting "rules" that apply?

a.   Use plain English

Good legal drafting should always avoid legalese in favor of plain English. Pleadings are no different. Commonly used words, short sentences of simple construction, active verbs, and a preference for nouns and verbs over adjectives and adverbs create clear and forceful language. A style consistent with this advice benefits everyone in litigation — parties, lawyers, and judge.

The preference for simple English should also apply to naming parties. Use names rather than the pleading's designations (for example, "plaintiff," "defendant," "cross-claimant," "third-party defendant," "trustee," "obligor," and so forth) unless a local pleading rule requires the designation of the party. The use of names keeps things clear, particularly when the case involves multiple parties.

A common practice is to set out the full name of each party the first time it is used, then show in parentheses how you will refer to that party from then on.

Example:

> Defendant William B. Jones (hereafter "Jones") . . .
> The International Business Machines Corporation ("IBM") . . .

b.   Make it factual

Some believe that the Supreme Court's decisions in *Twombly* and *Iqbal* have breathed life back into "fact pleading." Under *Twombly* a complaint

---

21. Wright §68; Hazard et al. §§4.11-4.15; Moore's Manual §10.06; Manual of Federal Practice §§3.9-3.27; Moore's Federal Practice §§8.03–8.05; Wright & Miller §§1215–1254.

must contain factual "allegations plausibly suggesting," and not merely consistent with, an entitlement to relief. Mere "labels and conclusions," or "a formulaic recitation of the elements of a cause of action," will not do. The complaint must allege enough facts to "nudge a claim across the line from conceivable to plausible." Under *Iqbal*, judges deciding Rule 12(b)(6) motions to dismiss for failure to state a claim must disregard "threadbare" legal conclusions or "recitals of the elements of a cause of action" and then look at the remaining factual allegations to determine whether the complaint meets the plausibility standard.

If the complaint contains any bare legal assertions that are unsupported by non-conclusory factual allegations, the complaint risks violating the plausibility requirement. Accordingly, allege specific facts that plausibly establish each element of each claim and resist alternative innocent explanations for allegedly wrongful conduct.

Example (negligence):

> 1. On August 1, 2013, at approximately 3:00 P.M., plaintiff Jones and defendant Smith were driving automobiles on Elm Street, near Maple Avenue, in Chicago, Illinois. Jones was driving northbound on Elm Street. Smith was driving southbound on Elm Street.
> 2. Smith negligently crossed the center lane of Elm Street with his automobile, striking Jones's automobile.
> 3. As a result Jones received facial injuries, a broken arm, and other injuries. He experienced pain and suffering, incurred medical expenses, lost substantial income, and will incur more medical expenses and lost income in the future.

Example (contract):

> 1. On August 1, 2013, plaintiff Jones and defendant Smith entered into a contract. A copy of the contract is attached to this complaint as Exhibit A.
> 2. Jones paid Smith $80,000 and has performed all of her obligations under the contract.
> 3. Smith failed to repair Jones' house as he was required to do under the contract.

Sometimes making more detailed or specific factual allegations than required under Rule 8(a), as interpreted by *Twombly* and *Iqbal*, can be effective. First, specific factual allegations are harder for the defendant to deny. Second, a specific allegation can be used to support a later specific discovery request, as Rule 26 suggests. If the defendant denies the allegation in the complaint, she can hardly object to discovery methods that are directed to uncovering the denied fact. Rule 26(a) requires automatic initial disclosure of facts and documents "the disclosing party may use to support its claims or defenses," and Rule 26(b) provides that parties "may obtain discovery regarding any nonprivileged matter that is relevant to any party's claim or defense." Hence, alleging specific events, such as meetings, conversations, and transactions, and referring to specific records and documents in a pleading will make it more difficult for the responding party to deny those allegations and to avoid disclosing facts and documents relevant to the pleading. Seen in this light, the complaint can be plaintiff's first discovery device, since detailed allegations will trigger the automatic disclosure requirements and support later discovery requests. Third, if the plaintiff has a compelling story to tell, setting that story out in the complaint for both the judge and later the jury to read can be an effective approach, particularly if you hope for an early settlement of the case.

c. Plead "special matters" with particularity

Under Rule 9, certain allegations must be pleaded "specifically" and "with particularity." These include fraud, mistake, and special damages.[22] While capacity and authority to sue and conditions precedent can be pleaded generally, denials must be made specifically and with particularity.

What constitutes appropriate specificity and particularity in pleading these special matters is unclear.[23] It is safer as well as proper to set forth the specific elements of the special matter being pleaded and the facts that support them. Doing so will ensure that your pleading will include the requisite particularity.

Rule 9 is not the only special pleading rule. Legislatures may establish particular pleading requirements that require more of the pleader, even after *Twombly* and *Iqbal.* Congress has done so for securities fraud claims and prisoner civil rights litigation. Many state legislatures have done so for medical malpractice litigation.

Example (fraud):

> 1. On August 1, 2013, plaintiff Jones and defendant Smith entered into a contract. A copy of the contract is attached to this complaint as Exhibit A.
>
> 2. Under the contract, Jones agreed to pay Smith $80,000, and Smith agreed to sell Jones a parcel of land in Atlanta, Georgia. The precise location and description of the parcel are set out in the contract, attached as Exhibit A.
>
> 3. Before executing this contract on August 1, 2013, Smith represented that he had legal title to the parcel, that the parcel had no encumbrances of any kind, such as mortgages, tax liens, or judgment liens, and that Smith would be able to have the property rezoned to a B-2 zoning.
>
> 4. Those representations were false and fraudulent, Smith knew they were false and fraudulent when made, and Smith made them to induce Jones to enter into the contract.
>
> 5. Jones relied on Smith's representations and was damaged.

---

22. Subject matter jurisdiction must also be pleaded specifically. See §3.5.
23. See Moore's Manual §9.11.

d.   Use separate paragraphs

The rules require a separate paragraph for a "single set of circum-stances," admittedly an imprecise standard, whenever practicable. When in doubt, divide your allegations into paragraphs liberally, since this practice usually makes the pleadings simpler to follow. Keep each paragraph to a simple point, and avoid colorful characterizations. The complaint will be easier to answer, and you will minimize the likelihood that an answer will admit part and deny part of a single paragraph. As a result the positions of the parties will be clearer, benefiting everyone.

Example:

> 1. On June 1, 2013, plaintiff Jones and defendant Smith entered into a contract, a copy of which is attached as Exhibit A.
> 2. On June 15, 2013, Jones paid Smith $80,000 as required by the contract.
> 3. Jones has performed each of her obligations under the contract.
> 4. Smith failed to deliver 1,000 folding chairs to Jones by June 30, 2013, and has failed to perform his obligations under the contract.

In some jurisdictions the practice is to number the paragraphs with Arabic numbers; others use Roman numerals.

e.   Use separate counts

Although not required by the rules, pleadings customarily state each claim involving a separate theory of recovery in a separate count, even if all are based on the same occurrence or transaction. This practice has the advantage of setting out clearly each legal theory that forms a basis for recovery.

Since setting out different theories of recovery in different counts usually requires restating some allegations, Rule 10(c) permits a complaint to incorporate into the later count by reference those allegations made in earlier counts.

Example:

<u>Count II</u>

> 1-15. Plaintiff adopts Par. 1-15 of Count I as Par. 1-15 of this Count.
> 16. . . .
> 17. . . .

It is better to number all the paragraphs in all the counts of the complaint sequentially, rather than to begin each count with a Par. 1. This avoids confusion and makes it easier for the defendant to respond to each paragraph in the defendant's answer.

It is also useful to label the legal theory for each count and, where different counts are against different parties, show which parties are involved in each count.

Example:

Count I — Contract

(against defendants Jones and Roberts)

1. . . .
2. . . .
3. . . .

Count II — Implied Warranties

(against defendant Roberts only)

7. . . .
8. . . .
9. . . .

If the complaint alleges several theories of recovery, but the facts are common to all the counts, lawyers frequently set out the common facts separately and label them appropriately.

Example:

Factual Allegations

1. . . .
2. . . .
3. . . .

Example:

Allegations Common to All Counts

1. . . .
2. . . .
3. . . .

When this approach is used, the common allegations will immediately follow the jurisdictional allegation section.

f.   Use exhibits

Rule 10(c) permits the attachment of exhibits to pleadings. Lawyers do so most commonly in contract cases. A copy of the contract that forms the basis for the claim is attached to the complaint. When attached to the pleading, the exhibit becomes an integral part of it. By attaching exhibits, a complaint may state a claim more efficiently than if the pleader sets out the exhibit's contents in the body of the complaint.

Example:

> 1. Plaintiff Jones and defendant Smith entered into a contract on June 1, 2013. A copy of this contract is attached as Exhibit A.

Example:

> 8. The employee manual sets forth some of the terms of the employment contract entered into by Jones and Smith. A copy of this employee manual is attached as Exhibit B.

If the exhibit is lengthy, however, it may be easier to set out the key language in the pleading, rather than attach the exhibit to the pleading. Courts dislike lengthy attachments to pleadings.

3.   Prayer for relief

Rule 8(a) requires a pleading to make a "demand for the relief sought, which may include relief in the alternative or different types of relief."[24] The rule makes no distinction between legal and equitable relief.

Care in pleading relief is important for two reasons. First, since under federal law the nature of the remedy sought determines the right to a jury trial,[25] the demand for relief should be drafted to ensure the right to a jury trial, or to avoid it, as the case may be. Second, where a default judgment is requested, the type of relief sought affects the method under which default can be obtained. Also, the relief requested in the pleadings affects the relief granted.[26] Since default is always a possibility, you should always draft the prayer carefully. Third, if jurisdiction is based on diversity, make sure the prayer for relief asks for a sum in excess of $75,000, exclusive of interest and costs, as required by 28 U.S.C. §1332.

The demand for relief should specify the types of relief sought, including legal and equitable remedies, interest, costs, attorney's fees, and any

---

24. Wright §68; Hazard et al. §4.8; Moore's Manual §10.06; Manual of Federal Practice §3.8; Moore's Federal Practice §§8.03-8.05; Wright & Miller §§1255–1260.
25. See §3.3.
26. See Rules 54 and 55; §7.9.

special damages, with sufficient detail. Where the pleader seeks several specific types of relief, the complaint should itemize and number them.

Example:

> WHEREFORE, plaintiff demands judgment against defendant for the sum of $80,000, with interest and costs.
>
> WHEREFORE, plaintiff demands a preliminary and permanent injunction, an accounting for all damages, and interest and costs.

Example:

DEMAND FOR RELIEF

> Plaintiff demands:
> 1. That defendant pay damages in excess of the sum of $80,000;
> 2. That defendant be specifically ordered to perform his obligations under the contract;
> 3. That defendant pay interest, costs, and reasonable attorney's fees incurred by plaintiff.

Do you need a prayer for relief for each claim, or only one prayer for the complaint as a whole? Rule 8 does not specify, and local practices vary, so practical concerns should determine the answer. If each claim raised has different allowable damages, you may want to have a prayer for relief after each count for clarity's sake. However, if your claims all have the same allowable damages—when all claims seek negligence damages, for example—have one prayer for relief at the end of the complaint.

Can you ask for a specific dollar amount in damages? In some jurisdictions, local rules bar asking for specific amounts. This rule prevents lawyers from asking for large amounts to generate publicity for the lawsuit and the lawyer. In such jurisdictions the usual allegation is that plaintiff seeks damages "in excess of the jurisdictional amount of $75,000." If specific dollar amounts can be alleged, you should still be careful not to exaggerate your damages claims. In some jurisdictions pleadings can be read to the jury, and exaggerated claims will make you look greedy and unrealistic. Finally, if you anticipate that the defendant may not defend the case, a specific dollar amount in a damages claim may make it easier to obtain a default judgment under Rule 41. (See §7.9.)

4. Jury demand

Under Rule 38, a party may demand a jury trial, on any claim triable as of right by a jury, in writing at any time after the complaint is filed and "not later than 14 days after the last pleading directed to the issue is served."[27] To be effective, the jury trial demand must be served on the other parties and filed with the court. The party may specify in the demand which claims he wants to try to a jury. The rule permits the jury demand to be placed on the pleading itself, and this is the customary method of making the demand. A common practice is to place "<u>JURY TRIAL DEMANDED</u>" below the case number, and "<u>PLAINTIFF DEMANDS TRIAL BY JURY</u>" at the end of the complaint. Another common practice is to use a separate heading for the jury demand.

Example:

JURY DEMAND

Plaintiff demands a trial by jury on all claims on which she has the right to trial by jury.

Local rules usually have additional requirements, such as the filing of jury demand forms and the payment of fees.

If one party makes a jury demand, the other parties are entitled to rely on it. However, if a party makes a jury demand on only some counts, the other parties must make a timely jury demand on other counts. Failure to make a timely demand for a jury trial constitutes a waiver of the right under Rule 38(d). Courts have taken a strict view on waiver and only rarely exercise their discretion and permit a belated demand.[28]

5. Signature

Under Rule 11, the lawyer preparing a complaint must sign it, and that lawyer must be authorized to appear in the court in which the case is being filed. Signing the complaint triggers the Rule 11(b) certification about the complaint. The rule also requires that the lawyer's address, e-mail address, and telephone number be shown. Since the rule requires the signature of an individual lawyer, a common practice is to show the lawyer's firm as "of counsel." Finally, a complaint in a federal court need not be verified or supported by affidavit. Verification is still a common requirement in some state jurisdictions for certain kinds of complaints.

---

27. Wright §92; Moore's Manual §§22.02-22.26; Manual of Federal Practice §§7.20–7.21; Moore's Federal Practice §§38.03; Wright & Miller §§2318–2322.
    28. See Wright §92.

Example:

Dated this 3rd day of June, 2013.

Jane Smith Johnson
Attorney for Plaintiff
Suite 1400
100 Madison Avenue
Chicago, IL 60601
johnson@gmail.com
(312) 807-9000

6. Common problems

The complaint is one of the most important documents in the litigation process. In addition to getting the litigation started, the complaint sends messages to the defense about you: how well you have researched the facts and law, how well you have analyzed and made decisions about them, and how much you know about litigation. A well-planned and drafted complaint sends a clear message that you are competent and prepared to move the litigation ahead. Accordingly, unless something like a statute of limitations deadline creates a pressing need to file quickly, you should draft the complaint with particular care, have others review it, and make revisions before filing.

Problems in preparing complaints usually fall into three categories. First, the complaint is not well conceived. Many lawyers make complaints unnecessarily complex, having too many parties and alternative theories of recovery. Remember that complex complaints usually generate complex, lengthy, and expensive litigation, which may not be in the client's best interest. Most plaintiffs want a speedy, inexpensive, and favorable outcome. A good general rule is to file the simplest complaint that will serve the client's litigation objectives.

Second, the complaint is not well organized. Remember that a complaint should be factually and legally clear. Use headings to break the complaint into its logical components, such as jurisdiction, parties, facts, counts, and relief. Make sure that the jurisdictional allegation properly alleges the basis for federal jurisdiction and that the facts demonstrate it. Make sure the allegations show that venue is proper. Keep the factual paragraphs simple, limited to a single point, and avoid unnecessary characterizations. Make sure that the counts clearly set forth the required elements of each of the legal claims. Make sure that the prayer for relief contains all the kinds of relief to which you may be entitled and avoids requesting unsupportable dollar amounts. Finally, if you want a jury trial, make sure that the complaint contains a jury demand.

Third, the complaint is not well drafted. Remember that under *Twombly* and *Iqbal* you must allege enough facts to "plausibly suggest" liability and not merely allege facts consistent with liability. Bare legal conclusions or a formulaic recitation of the elements of the claims, unsupported by adequate factual allegations, will no longer suffice.

7.   Filing and service of summons

Under Rule 3, a federal action is commenced when the complaint is filed with the clerk of the court. Commencement is significant for statute of limitations purposes.[29] In federal question cases, the filing of the complaint tolls the statute of limitations. In diversity cases, however, state law controls, and if state law requires something more than the mere filing of the complaint, such as actual service on the defendant, state law must be complied with fully before the statute of limitations is tolled.[30]

After the action is commenced, the complaint must be served on each defendant. Rule 4 includes detailed rules that control the service of the complaint and summons on the defendants. There are several steps involved, and you should check local rules for any additional filing and service of summons requirements. For example, most districts require designation or civil cover sheets and appearance forms to be filed with the complaint and summons.

a.   Issuing the summons

Under Rule 4(b), the plaintiff must prepare the summons and present it to the clerk "on or after" filing the complaint. If the summons is in proper form, the clerk is directed to issue it to the plaintiff. In practice, the summons form, which is available from the clerk's office, is usually filled out in advance and taken to the clerk's office when the complaint is filed. To assist in service it is useful to list on the form where and when service on each defendant can most likely be made. For example, if the service is to be made at the defendant's work address, put down the working hours and where on the premises the defendant actually works. The clerk then "issues" the summons by signing and stamping it with the court seal, the date, and the case file number. In the case of multiple defendants, the plaintiff has two options: he can secure issuance of a separate original summons for each defendant or he can serve copies of a single original that names all of the defendants. Make sure you have enough copies of the complaint and summons for the clerk's administrative needs, for service on each defendant, and for your own files.

---

29. Wright §§64–65; Manual of Federal Practice §§3.80–3.94; Moore's Federal Practice §§3.02-3.06; Wright & Miller §§1061–1153.
    30. See Wright §65A.

b.   Summons content

Rule 4(a) controls the summons content. The following example is Form 3 in the Appendix of Forms.[31]

Example:

SUMMONS

To:_____ *(defendant)* _____

A lawsuit has been filed against you.

Within 21 days after service of this summons on you (not counting the day you received it), you must serve on the plaintiff an answer to the attached complaint or a motion under Rule 12 of the Federal Rules of Civil Procedure. The answer or motion must be served on the plaintiff's attorney, _____, whose address is _____. If you fail to do so, judgment by default will be entered against you for the relief demanded in the complaint. You also must file your answer or motion with the court.

_____
Clerk of Court

[Seal of the U.S. District Court]

Dated: _____

If there is a technical defect in the summons, such as the misspelling of the defendant's name, the court in its discretion may allow an amendment of the summons.

The federal summons is used even if service is effected under state service rules.

c.   Persons who may serve the summons

As a general rule, any person who is not a party and is at least 18 years old may serve the complaint and summons. Service by the U.S. Marshal (or a deputy marshal, or other person specially appointed by the court) is now required only in limited circumstances specified in Rule 4(c)(3) — for actions brought in forma pauperis and for actions brought by a seaman. On motion of a plaintiff, the court may appoint a process server.

---

31. A proposed amendment to the Federal Rules, pending at the time of publication, would abrogate the forms. Even if it gets promulgated, the illustration provided here would still likely suffice under Rule 4. For changes to the Federal Rules, see www.uscourts.gov.

d.   Methods of service

Rule 4(e)-(j) governs how service of summons may be made. The method depends on the entity being served.

i.   Individuals

Rule 4(e) permits service on an individual in several ways. First, an individual can be given a copy of the complaint and summons in person. Second, service can be made by leaving a copy of the complaint and summons "at the individual's dwelling or usual place of abode" with a person of suitable age and discretion residing there. Third, service can be made on an agent authorized by appointment or law to receive process. Fourth, where the individual is out of state, service may be made when any federal statute authorizes out-of-state service, pursuant to the laws of the state in which service is effected, and when a statute of the state in which the district court sits permits out-of-state service. These are the state long-arm statutes. They provide for extraterritorial service on any defendant who has had constitutionally sufficient contacts with that state.[32]

Finally, Rule 4(d) allows the plaintiff to request that the defendant waive formal service of the summons. Individuals, corporations, and associations that receive such a request for waiver of service then have a duty to avoid unnecessary service costs. The rule contains an incentive for a defendant to comply with the request by signing and returning it in a timely manner: additional time to answer the complaint. If the defendant does not comply, he becomes responsible for the costs of formal service. This request and waiver, coupled with mail service, is the predominant method for service on individuals and domestic and foreign corporations, partnerships, and unincorporated associations.

Under Rule 4(d), valid service is accomplished by using first class mail or other reliable means, such as messenger or fax, to deliver to the defendant two copies of a notice of commencement of the action and request for waiver of service, a copy of the complaint, notice to the defendant of the duty to avoid unnecessary costs of service and the penalties for non-compliance, and two copies of a waiver form and prepaid means of compliance (such as a return envelope, postage prepaid). The request must state the date on which it was sent. The person served then completes and signs one copy of the notice and waiver and returns it to the sender, who is ordinarily the plaintiff's lawyer. Note that sending the summons and complaint by registered or certified mail does not eliminate the requirement that the sender receive a signed acknowledgment of service from the person served. This method of service can be used for those defendants who reside in the forum state, those who reside outside the forum state, and even those who reside in foreign countries.

If the completed waiver of service is not returned to the sender within 30 days (60 days in the case of service outside the United States) of the date

---

32. See §3.6.

the request is sent, service of the complaint and summons must be made under Rule 4(e) or (f). For individuals, service is effected by the means mentioned above. If this method of service becomes necessary, the court shall order that the person being served pay the costs incurred in effecting service, and the costs (including attorney's fees) of any motion to collect the cost of service.

Service by mail is easier, quicker, and less expensive, and the requirement that the person served return a signed waiver to the sender eliminates the need for the traditional proof of service. Only if the person served by mail refuses or fails to return the signed waiver within the 30-day period must the sender then use other methods of service and the person served bear the actual cost of service.

The waiver of formal service rules is attractive, but it has one important caveat. If the case is in federal court based on diversity jurisdiction, state law will control what needs to be done to toll the running of the statute of limitations. Some states require not only filing of the complaint, but also require actual proper service of the complaint and summons on the defendant. If the defendant refuses to sign the waiver of formal service and return it to the plaintiff, and the statute of limitations runs before the plaintiff properly serves the defendant through one of the other methods Rule 4 permits, the lawsuit will be time-barred. Accordingly, a plaintiff should always serve the defendant with the complaint and summons through another method if the statute of limitations is about to run.

ii. Minors and incompetents

Service on minors and incompetents is made in the same manner as service would be made under the law of the state in which service is to be made. While state laws vary, they usually require service on a parent or a legal guardian of the infant or incompetent.

Service can also be made upon minors and incompetents in foreign countries under Rule 4(g). In such a case, service would be made according to the law of the foreign country or as the court directs.

iii. Corporations, partnerships, and associations

Rule 4(h) provides several ways for service upon domestic and foreign corporations, partnerships, and unincorporated associations that can be sued in their own name. First, service can be made by personal delivery to an officer, manager, or general agent. Second, service can be made to an agent authorized to receive service of process; the list of domestic and foreign corporations, usually compiled by each state's Secretary of State or Corporation Commission, should identify the authorized agent for service of process. Third, service on an out-of-state corporation can be made under any federal statute providing for service or under any method permitted by a statute of the state in which the district court sits, usually the state's long-arm statute. Alternatively, service can be made pursuant to the law of the state in which service is effected. Finally, service can be made by mail using the procedure set forth by Rule 4(d)(2). This mail service procedure, which is the same as what Rule 4 permits for individuals, described above, is now the most common way parties serve corporations with a complaint and summons.

iv.   United States and its agencies, officers, and employees; foreign, state, and local governments

Rule 4(i) details the requirements for service on the United States and its federal agencies, officers and employees, and Rule 4(j) details the requirements for foreign, state, and local governments. The requirements are technical, and the rule should always be reviewed before attempting service.

e.   Territorial limits of service

Rule 4(k) governs the geographical scope of service. There are four basic precepts.

i.   Statewide service

Summons may be served anywhere within the state in which the district court sits.

ii.   The 100-mile "bulge" rule[33]

The 100-mile "bulge" provision provides for some service within 100 miles of the place where the original action is commenced, even if service crosses state lines. However, this rule applies only to parties brought in as third-party defendants under Rule 14, or as additional necessary parties to a counterclaim or cross-claim under Rules 13 and 19.

The purpose of the rule is to permit service of process on additional parties that are brought into the action after the original suit is filed and are necessary for a fair and complete disposition of the action. This rule is important for multi-party litigation in large metropolitan areas, such as New York, Chicago, and Washington, D.C., which cover several jurisdictions. Without the bulge rule service on every party in the suit would often be difficult.

iii.   State long-arm statutes

Rule 4(e)-(h) provides for service on parties outside the state in which the district court sits whenever that state permits out-of-state service. The

---

33. See Wright & Miller §§1127-1129.

rule refers to state long-arm statutes and attachment procedures that create quasi in rem jurisdiction.[34] It puts federal and state process on essentially the same footing as far as territorial limits are concerned.

iv. Federal statute

Whenever a federal statute authorizes service on a party outside the state in which the district court sits, service may be made in accordance with the statute or order.

If the Rule 4(k) requirements are met, proper service of summons or filing a waiver of service is deemed to establish personal jurisdiction over a defendant. Under Rule 4(k)(2), if the exercise of jurisdiction over the defendant is constitutionally proper, service of summons or filing a waiver of service is also effective to confer personal jurisdiction over a defendant as to any federal claims. This is so even if the defendant is not subject to personal jurisdiction in any state courts.

Finally, keep in mind that under Rule 4(d)(1) a waiver of service of summons does not constitute a waiver of objections to the personal jurisdiction of the court or to venue. A defendant can waive service of summons and thereafter contest personal jurisdiction and venue in a Rule 12(b) motion or in the answer.

f. Timeliness of service

Under Rule 4(m) service of the complaint and summons must occur within 120 days after filing of the complaint.[35] If service is not made in time, the court will dismiss the action without prejudice as to the unserved defendant, unless good cause for the delay can be shown.

The complaint, of course, may be refiled against that same party. However, the plaintiff must refile the complaint within the applicable statute of limitations period because the "relation back" doctrine does not apply here. When a state cause of action is asserted and state law requires more than the mere filing of the complaint to satisfy the state statute of limitations, such as actual service of summons, these additional requirements must be met within the limitations period.[36]

g. Proof of service

As discussed above, the complaint and summons are served most commonly by mail service under the waiver rules of Rule 4(d). The proof of service will be the Waiver of Service of Summons (Form 7 in the Appendix

---

34. See §3.6.

35. A proposed amendment to Rule 4(m), pending at the time of publication, would shorten this period to 90 days. Make sure to check revisions to the Federal Rules to ensure that the information in this text is accurate. See www.uscourts.gov.

36. See Wright §65A; Wright & Miller §§1056-1057. The leading case is Ragan v. Merchants Transfer & Warehouse Co., 337 U.S. 530 (1949).

of Forms)[37] that the served party signs and returns to the sender, who is usually the plaintiff's lawyer.

When a process server serves the complaint and summons, Rule 4(l) requires that the person serving process establish proof of service promptly and in any event within the time during which the party served has to respond to the process. If process is served by anyone other than the U.S. marshal, proof must be in affidavit form. In practice, the proof-of-service affidavit is usually found on the summons form.

Example:

AFFIDAVIT OF SERVICE

I, _____, having been first duly sworn, state that I served a copy of the summons and complaint on _____(defendant)_____ by _____(method of service)_____ at ___(address)___ on ___(date)___.

_____(signature)_____

Signed and sworn to before me
on: _____

_____
Notary Public

My commission expires on _____

h.   *Informal service*

Sometimes you will know the lawyer who will represent the defendant in the lawsuit. You may have already had contact with the defendant's lawyer before filing suit, or you may know the lawyer who regularly handles the defendant's legal matters. In such instances, a good practice is to call the lawyer and let her know you are about to file suit. Ask her if she will accept service of process on behalf of the defendant. If so, simply deliver or mail the complaint and summons to her. However, because Rule 4 requires that the defendant sign and return the notice and waiver of service of summons within 30 days of service (60 days for defendants served outside the United States), make sure that the defendant's lawyer gets the signed waiver from her client and delivers it to you within that time period. Mail service is not deemed effective unless the defendant signs and returns the waiver form.

If you think the defendant will try to avoid service of process, or will contest the validity of service, serve the defendant formally under one of

---

37. A proposed amendment to the Federal Rules, pending at the time of publication, would abrogate the Appendix of Forms. For updated changes to the Federal Rules, see www.uscourts.gov.

the methods Rule 4 permits. Otherwise, informal service can be a convenient approach. It is frequently used in commercial litigation with corporate parties.

§5.4.   Rule 12 responses[38]

When a complaint and summons have been properly served on a defendant, he can respond in two basic ways. First, he can answer the complaint. Ordinarily, the defendant must answer within 21 days of service. If the defendant waived formal service, he has 60 days from the date the request was mailed to serve an answer (90 days in the case of defendants served outside of the United States).

Second, before filing an answer the defendant can make any of three motions attacking claimed defects in the complaint.[39] These are a motion to strike, a motion for a more definite statement, and a motion to dismiss, all of which Rule 12 governs. When a defendant decides to attack the complaint with a Rule 12 motion, he must do so within the time permitted for his answer, ordinarily within 21 days of service of the complaint.[40]

1.   Motion to strike

Under Rule 12(f), if the complaint contains "any redundant, immaterial, impertinent or scandalous matter," it can be stricken upon motion.[41] While such motions are infrequent, one should be considered if the complaint might be read to the jury during trial.

Example:

[Caption]

MOTION TO STRIKE

Defendant Johnson Corporation moves under Rule 12(f) for an order striking certain immaterial and scandalous matters from the complaint. In support of its motion defendant states:
1. Par. 2 of the complaint alleges that the "Johnson Corporation had gross receipts of $102,436,000 for fiscal year 2013." This allegation is immaterial to a contract action and should be stricken.

---

38. Wright §66; Hazard et al. §§4.4, 4.17; Moore's Manual §§11.20–11.29; Manual of Federal Practice §§3.38–3.44, 4.2–4.34; Moore's Federal Practice §§12.02-12.38; Wright & Miller §§1341–1397.

39. See §5.3 for the requirements of a complaint.

40. If a Rule 12 motion is denied, a defendant generally has 14 days from the denial of the motion to answer the complaint. See Rule 6 for how time periods are computed.

41. Moore's Manual §11.28; Manual of Federal Practice §§4.20–4.22; Moore's Federal Practice §12.21; Wright & Miller §§1380–1383.

2. Par. 7 of the complaint alleges that the "Johnson Corporation is an international cartel that dominates the furniture polish industry." This allegation is impertinent and scandalous and should be stricken.

WHEREFORE, defendant Johnson Corporation requests that the court enter an order striking these parts of plaintiff's complaint and requiring plaintiff to file an amended complaint that deletes the stricken matter within 14 days.

2. Motion for a more definite statement

Under Rule 12(e), if the complaint is "so vague or ambiguous" that the defendant cannot respond to it, the defendant may move for a more definite statement.[42] The motion must point out the defects and specify the details that are needed. The complaint need only be a "short and plain statement," however, and pleadings generally should be "simple, concise and direct." Moreover, discovery is the preferred method for flushing out details. For these reasons, such motions are disfavored. A more commonly used approach is to move to dismiss under Rule 12(b)(6) for failure to state a claim on which relief can be granted.

On the other hand, since Rule 26(a) requires initial disclosures for facts and documents that "the disclosing party may use to support its claims or defenses," lawyers may use the motion to try to obtain more details about the pleadings before the initial disclosures are due.

Example:

[Caption]

MOTION FOR A MORE DEFINITE STATEMENT

Defendant Johnson Corporation moves under Rule 12(e) for an order requiring plaintiff to provide a more definite statement. In support of its motion defendant states:

1. Par. 3 of the complaint alleges that "plaintiff and defendant and others entered into an agreement in 2013 under which defendant was obligated to deliver such amounts of furniture polish as plaintiff may from time to time request."

2. Nowhere else in the complaint is greater detail provided, and no copy of any contract is attached to the complaint. Without additional details, defendant cannot respond to this allegation.

WHEREFORE, defendant Johnson Corporation requests that the court enter an order requiring defendant to serve and file a more definite statement within 14 days showing what date this

---

42. Moore's Manual §11.27; Manual of Federal Practice §§4.18–4.20; Moore's Federal Practice §§12.36; Wright & Miller §§1374–1379.

alleged contract was entered into, where it was entered into, every party to it, the requirements under the contract, and, if in writing, a copy of the alleged contract.

3. Motion to dismiss under Rule 12(b)

Under Rule 12(b), the defendant may raise certain defenses either in the answer or by a motion to dismiss.[43] A Rule 12(b) motion is the predominant way to attack the complaint. It has several important characteristics.

a. The one motion requirement

If you decide to respond to the complaint with a motion to dismiss on Rule 12(b) grounds, Rule 12(g) requires that you present all defenses that can be raised in one motion to dismiss. In other words, you must consolidate all available Rule 12(b) defenses into one motion. This requirement prevents piecemeal attacks on the complaint.

b. Rule 12(b) defenses

A motion to dismiss may raise the following defenses:

1. Lack of subject matter jurisdiction
2. Lack of jurisdiction over the person
3. Improper venue
4. Insufficient process
5. Insufficient service of process
6. Failure to state a claim upon which relief can be granted
7. Failure to join a party under Rule 19

In addition, some case law provides that a Rule 12(b) motion to dismiss may assert some affirmative defenses.[44]

Federal practice has eliminated the need for special appearances to contest personal jurisdiction, since under Rule 12(g) the joinder of defenses does not create a waiver of any of them. Hence, a defendant can raise any of the Rule 12(b) defenses by motion and is not held to have waived the right to assert lack of personal jurisdiction.[45]

c. Waiver

Under Rule 12(g) and (h), defenses not consolidated into one motion to dismiss may be waived, but the waiver rules depend on the defense

---

43. Wright §66; Hazard et al. §4.4; Moore's Manual §11.03; Manual of Federal Practice §§3.38–3.44, 4.23–4.30; Moore's Federal Practice §§12.07–12.38; Wright & Miller §§1349-1360.

44. See Moore's Manual §11.57; Manual of Federal Practice §3.41.

45. See Manual of Federal Practice §3.41.

involved. Lack of jurisdiction over the person, improper venue, insufficiency of process, and insufficiency of service of process are all waived if not included in a motion to dismiss, or if not included in the answer if no motion is made. Hence, if a motion to dismiss raises any of these grounds, it must raise the others as well. Failure to state a claim and failure to join an indispensable party, however, may be raised in the answer, in a motion for judgment on the pleadings, or at trial. Finally, lack of subject matter jurisdiction is never waived and can be raised at any time.

The waiver rules create two categories of defenses to a claim. The procedural irregularity defenses are waived unless timely presented, while substantive defenses to a valid judgment cannot be so waived.

d.   Practice approach

Keep the underlying theory of Rule 12 in mind when deciding whether to present Rule 12(b) defenses in a motion to dismiss or in the answer. The rule enables courts to hear certain defenses that may terminate the litigation early in the litigation process. A Rule 12(b) motion obviously offers an efficient way to deal with a defective or meritless complaint. If you decide to assert a defense in a motion to dismiss, be sure to raise the other Rule 12(b) defenses available or risk waiving them.

Second, consider the types of defenses a Rule 12(b) motion can raise. Three of them — lack of jurisdiction over the person, insufficient process, and insufficient service of process — are essentially procedural defects that the plaintiff can usually cure. Since the plaintiff can ordinarily do so by filing an amended complaint or serving process on the defendant again, litigating these defenses may be pointless. For example, when a defect in service of process means that the court lacks personal jurisdiction over the defendant, but it is obvious that the defendant can be properly served later, an improper service or a lack of personal jurisdiction defense has little point, even though it is technically available. On the other hand, when personal jurisdiction over the defendant does not properly exist, and probably cannot be obtained, the motion makes sense.

Although a full-dress motion to dismiss based on an easily cured defect may not make sense, you can still use the defect to your advantage. You may need an extension to file an answer or, say, a Rule 12(b)(6) motion to dismiss. You can use the easily cured defect as a bargaining chip with your adversary's lawyer to get her consent to an extension. Tell her, for instance, that you will overlook the defect if she agrees to your extension.

An improper venue defense is waived if not included in a motion to dismiss that raises other 12(b) defenses.[46] Hence, if venue is in fact improper under venue rules, and the present venue is a logistically inconvenient location for the defendant, you should make the motion. If your motion succeeds, the court likely will transfer the case to a proper venue, not dismiss it.[47]

46. See §3.7.
47. See §3.7; 28 U.S.C. §§1404, 1406.

Finally, when the defenses are lack of subject matter jurisdiction, failure to state a claim upon which relief can be granted, and failure to join an indispensable party, the defendant has more flexibility. The defendant may present these defenses either in the answer or by a motion for judgment on the pleadings, even if the defendant has already made a motion to dismiss based on other Rule 12(b) grounds. Hence, the defendant has the option of including these grounds in a motion to dismiss or raising them later. Raising them by motion to dismiss, of course, will get the issue resolved sooner than by including them in the answer. Regardless of which approach the defendant takes, however, the plaintiff is on notice of a possible defect in his pleading and can usually file an amended complaint correcting the defect.

A motion to dismiss based on Rule 12(b) should clearly set out the defenses being asserted in separate paragraphs.

Example:

[Caption]

MOTION TO DISMISS

Defendant Jones moves under Rule 12(b) for an order dismissing the complaint. In support of his motion defendant states:

1. The court lacks jurisdiction over the subject matter of this action because it appears from the complaint that the alleged claim does not arise under the Constitution of the United States, any Act of Congress, or treaties of the United States.

2. The court lacks jurisdiction over the subject matter of this action because the controversy is not between citizens of different states, and because the amount in controversy between the plaintiff and this defendant is less than $75,000, exclusive of interest and costs.

3. The court lacks jurisdiction over the defendant because the defendant is a corporation incorporated under the laws of the State of Delaware, has its principal place of business in Delaware, and is not subject to service in the State of Maryland where service was attempted.

4. This action has been brought in an improper district, since the complaint alleges that jurisdiction is based on diversity of citizenship, plaintiff is a citizen of the State of California, defendant is a citizen of the State of Nevada, and the claims arose in the State of Nevada. Venue in the district of Arizona is therefore improper.

5. Service of process on the defendant was insufficient because service was made on the defendant's business partner at his place of business, as shown by the proof of service for the summons.

6. The complaint fails to state a claim against this defendant on which relief can be granted.

7. The complaint fails to join all indispensable parties as required by Rule 19 because the Phillips Corporation is an indispensable party, has not been joined as a party, and if brought within this court's jurisdiction would destroy this court's jurisdiction since complete diversity would be lacking.

WHEREFORE, defendant Jones requests that the court enter an order dismissing the complaint.

Basic assertions of the grounds for Rule 12(b) defenses should be elaborated upon factually and legally. Where facts are necessary, statements in affidavit form and exhibits should be attached to the motion, although the court under the rule can then treat the motion as one for summary judgment. A memorandum of law accompanying the motion should discuss relevant case law.

The most common motion to dismiss is a Rule 12(b)(6) motion for failure to state a claim upon which relief can be granted. Such motions, which defendants make with increased frequency after *Twombly* and *Iqbal*, attack complaints on the grounds that the complaint contains only a bare recitation of the elements of the claims, contains only threadbare legal conclusions, and does not contain enough factual allegations to plausibly suggest liability.

The motion is conceptually limited to matters alleged in the complaint. If the motion or the lawyers at a hearing on it present facts outside the pleadings, the court should treat the motion as one for summary judgment and proceed in accordance with Rule 56.[48] If the motion is granted, the plaintiff will routinely be given leave to file an amended complaint. However, if the plaintiff is acting in bad faith, has repeatedly failed to amend properly, or obviously cannot amend properly, leave to amend should be denied.[49]

Service of the motion must be made in one of the ways permitted under Rule 5 on every other party presently in the case. The most common methods are service by mail, personal service, and, especially in the federal courts, service by electronic means. The motion with proof of service must be filed with the clerk of court or, if permitted by local rules, with the judge.

§5.5. Answers[50]

When the plaintiff's complaint has been properly served on a defendant, that defendant must respond, either by filing a Rule 12 motion, discussed

---

48. An exception to this rule applies when the facts not in the complaint come from a document that is "integral" to the complaint. An example is an allegedly libelous article in a libel action or a contract in a breach of contract dispute. A document is not "integral" merely because the complaint quotes from it.

49. See, e.g., Williams v. Citigroup Inc., 659 F.3d 208 (2d Cir. 2011).

50. Wright §66; Hazard et al. §§4.4, 5.4-5.8; Moore's Manual §9.03[3]; Manual of Federal Practice §§3.28–3.44; Moore's Federal Practice §§8.06-8.08; Wright & Miller §§1261–1279, 1347–1348.

in the preceding section, or by answering the complaint. The answer, like any other pleading and court paper, must comply with the requirements of Rule 11, under which a lawyer signing the answer thereby certifies that evidence warrants the denials of factual contentions and that the answer contains or reflects no frivolous legal arguments.

1. Timing

As a general rule, under Rule 12(a) the defendant must serve an answer within 21 days of service of the complaint and summons. Different deadlines may apply if the U.S. government is a defendant, or if a specific federal statute applies. In addition, if the defendant waived formal service, the defendant has 60 days from the date the request was mailed to serve an answer (90 days in the case of defendants served outside the United States). This additional time is an added inducement to defendants to waive service by following the waiver provisions of Rule 4(d). Where the defendant first responds with a Rule 12 motion, it must serve an answer within 14 days after the defendant receives notice of the court's action on the motion or within 14 days after service of a more definite statement.

2. General requirements

Several rules regulate the form and content of the answer. Rule 8(b) requires that an answer shall "state in short and plain terms" the defenses asserted. It must either admit or deny the allegations, or state that the defendant is without knowledge or information sufficient to form a belief as to their truth. Rule 8(c) requires affirmative defenses to be set out in the answer, and under Rule 12(b), the specified defenses may be set out as well. The defenses may be set out alternatively, inconsistently, and hypothetically. A hypothetical defense can be raised to an allegation in a complaint if it is found to be true, thus permitting a response that both denies the allegation and raises a hypothetical defense to it.

Since a complaint must be answered, a failure to answer will constitute an admission of all facts alleged in the complaint; this does not apply, however, to the prayer for relief. Answering with a simple "admit," "deny," or "no knowledge or belief" is usually sufficient. Under Rule 9(a), however, the answer must include a specific denial where it raises an issue as to "a party's capacity to sue or be sued; a party's authority to sue or be sued in a representative capacity; or the legal existence of an organized association of persons that is made a party."

To parallel the complaint, the answer must be organized in paragraphs and by counts, setting out separate defenses in separate paragraphs. Where there is only one defendant the answer is simply titled "<u>ANSWER</u>." If there are multiple defendants, however, the title should specify the party answering. A title might say, for example, "<u>ANSWER OF DEFENDANT ACME TOOL CORPORATION</u>." If a defendant demands a jury trial, the "<u>JURY TRIAL DEMANDED</u>" notice should appear in the caption of the answer, and the words "<u>DEFENDANT DEMANDS TRIAL BY JURY</u>" at the end of the answer. Finally, the lawyer must sign the answer, like every pleading. This signature constitutes a certification that the pleading is made in accordance with Rule 11.

The answer, therefore, may have three parts: responses to the complaint's allegations, affirmative defenses, and Rule 12(b) defenses. A well-drafted answer will set out each part clearly.

3.   Responses

Rule 8(b) permits three types of responses to the complaint's allegations. The answer may either admit or deny the allegations, or state that the party is without knowledge or information sufficient to form a belief as to their truth. The format, whether informally brief or more formal, is largely a matter of local custom, although the trend is toward brief responses. Instead of referring to the "defendant," use the defendant's name after the introductory statement to personalize the party in the answer.

In many jurisdictions the requirement or common practice is for the answer to repeat each paragraph of the complaint, then state the answer to that paragraph. While this practice makes the answer as long as the complaint, it makes admissions and denials very clear. Find out what the practice is in the court in which the case was filed.

Example:

[Caption]

ANSWER

Defendant Jones answers the complaint as follows:

Count I

   1. Admits.
   2. Jones admits the allegations in Par. 2.
   3. Denies.
   4. Jones denies the allegations in Par. 4.
   5. No knowledge or belief.
   6. Jones states that she is without knowledge or information sufficient to form a belief as to the truth of the allegations in Par. 6, and therefore denies them.

Any response of "no knowledge or belief" must be based on good faith. Such a response is inappropriate for matters that are common knowledge or that the defendant can easily learn.[51] For example, if the complaint

---

51. See Moore's Manual §11.42.

alleges that the defendant corporation had "gross receipts during 2013 in the amount of $6,450,000," the defendant's lawyer cannot answer "no knowledge or belief" since the lawyer can easily find out if the allegation is true or not.

The answer may admit only part of an allegation and deny the remainder, or assert a lack of knowledge or information as to the remainder, as the case may be. The defendant must respond to each paragraph of the complaint individually, unless the defendant can in good faith collectively deny every allegation of the complaint.

Example:

1. Jones admits he is a citizen of the State of California, but denies the remaining allegations in Par. 1.

2. Jones admits he entered into a written contract with plaintiff on June 1, 2013, but denies that the contract was modified by agreement on August 1, 2013, or on any other date.

3. Jones denies he owned and operated a business known as Jones Excavating in 2013 or any other year. Jones does not have sufficient knowledge or information to form a belief as to the truth of the other allegations in Par. 3, and therefore denies them.

Within these guidelines the rules permit considerable drafting flexibility. The modern trend is toward brevity and conciseness. The standard approach is to have counts and numbered paragraphs corresponding to the counts and paragraphs of the complaint. However, it is just as effective to set out admissions, denials, and no-knowledge-or-information responses collectively when the situation is appropriate.

Example:

Count I

1. Jones admits the allegations of Pars. 1, 2, 3, 4, 5, and 6 of the complaint.

2. Jones denies the allegations of Pars. 8, 9, and 10 of the complaint.

3. Jones states she does not have sufficient knowledge or information to form a belief as to the truth of the allegations in Par. 7, and therefore denies them.

4. Jones denies all other allegations of Count I not specifically admitted.

Count II

1. Jones incorporates her answers to Pars. 1-3 of Count I.

2. Jones denies all other allegations of Count II.

Denying all allegations not specifically admitted is a safe practice to prevent a typographical error in the answer from prejudicing the defendant.

Claims under Rule 9(a) of no capacity or authority and claims under Rule 9(c) that conditions precedent have not been performed are raised by denials but must be particularly specified.[52]

Example:

> 1. Jones denies that plaintiff is a legal entity that has capacity to sue in its own name, and specifically denies that plaintiff has any legal existence that permits it to pursue this action in the name of "John Smith Corporation."
> 2. Jones denies that plaintiff has performed all conditions precedent as required under the contract, and specifically denies that plaintiff delivered a copy of the contract to Jones within 30 days of execution, although plaintiff was required to do so before the contract would be in force.

The defendant does not need to respond to every allegation in the complaint, since not every count, or every paragraph in a count, will contain an allegation directed at him. Where you represent one defendant in a case that has multiple defendants, and some counts or paragraphs do not apply to your defendant, the usual practice is to point this out in your answer. Doing so avoids the possibility of "silence" in your answer being interpreted as an admission.

Example:

<u>Count II</u>

The allegations in this count are not directed to this defendant.

Example:

> 12. The allegations in Par. 12 of plaintiff's complaint are not directed toward this defendant, so this defendant makes no answer to the allegations.

4.   Rule 12(b) defenses

As discussed previously,[53] the defendant can raise Rule 12(b) defenses in a pre-answer motion to dismiss or can include them in the answer. If the

---

52. Wright & Miller §§1294, 1304.
53. See §5.4.

defendant raises them in the answer, each should be labeled separately to refer to the specific defense being asserted, preferably by tracking the language of Rule 12(b) and elaborating where necessary.

Example:

FIRST DEFENSE

The complaint fails to state a claim against the defendant on which relief can be granted.

SECOND DEFENSE

This court lacks jurisdiction over the subject matter of this action, since the complaint alleges that jurisdiction is based on diversity of citizenship and there is no allegation that the amount in controversy exceeds $75,000, exclusive of interest and costs.

What is a "defense"? The safe approach is to list as a defense anything that might defeat part or all of any claim or request for damages in the plaintiff's complaint. For example, in a contract case the answer might list as a defense that the plaintiff is not entitled to any damages other than consequential damages. There is no penalty for incorrectly characterizing something as a defense; there is a risk that something not raised as a defense in the answer will be deemed waived because it is a defense that should have been raised.

5.   Affirmative defenses

Rule 8(c) sets forth what it characterizes as affirmative defenses:

> accord and satisfaction, arbitration and award, assumption of risk, contributory negligence, duress, estoppel, failure of consideration, fraud, illegality, injury by fellow servant, laches, license, payment, release, res judicata, statute of frauds, statute of limitations, and waiver.

Other defenses have also been characterized as affirmative defenses.[54] An affirmative defense is generally one in which a defendant has a burden of raising in the answer, and on which a defendant has a burden of proving at trial, unless in diversity cases applicable state law holds otherwise. When answering the complaint, the usual practice is to label each affirmative defense separately, and to describe clearly the affirmative defense being asserted, preferably by using the language of Rule 8(c) and elaborating where necessary.

---

54. See Manual of Federal Practice §3.35.

Example:

FIRST AFFIRMATIVE DEFENSE

Plaintiff's claim set out in the complaint did not occur within two years before commencement of this action and is barred by the applicable statute of limitations.

SECOND AFFIRMATIVE DEFENSE

Plaintiff's claim is barred by res judicata.

Affirmative defenses are usually considered substantive. In diversity cases, therefore, the trial court will apply the substantive law of the state in which it is sitting.[55] That forum state's law must be researched for the substantive law that will apply under its conflict of law rules and for the recognized defenses. However, under state law an affirmative defense may not necessarily be one that the defendant has the burden of pleading. The danger in asserting such a defense as an affirmative defense in the answer is that the defendant may be held to have undertaken the burden of proof. On the other hand, failing to raise in the answer all affirmative defenses mentioned in Rule 8(c) runs the risk that the defenses will be waived.[56] The safer course is to raise the defense and make it clear that you do not intend to assume a burden of proof not existing under state law.

Example:

THIRD AFFIRMATIVE DEFENSE

Plaintiff was contributorily negligent in sustaining the injuries complained of in her complaint. By raising the defense of contributory negligence, however, defendant expressly does not assume any burden of proof that applicable substantive law may place on plaintiff.

6. Practice approach

Drafting answers to complaints involves two basic considerations. First, make sure you respond to every allegation in every paragraph of every count of the complaint, since any allegation not responded to is deemed admitted. A safe practice is to deny all allegations not specifically admitted or otherwise answered. Where the allegations are admitted in part and denied in part, make sure the answer clearly states which facts it admits and clearly denies all remaining allegations. Clear, simple language is critical here.

---

55. Moore's Manual §11.53.
56. See Manual of Federal Practice §3.37; Moore's Manual §11.51.

Sometimes you may wish to admit an allegation even though you are not required to admit it. Remember that pleadings and discovery are always interrelated. If a fact alleged is denied, a plaintiff will invariably focus some of his efforts in discovery on the denied fact. Admitting a fact may have the effect of preventing further discovery of information that would prove the fact. When that information contains harmful or embarrassing facts, you might simply admit the allegation in your answer, although you could have denied it consistent with Rule 11.

Second, set out all Rule 12(b) defenses and affirmative defenses that you can raise in good faith. List and label them separately. No penalty results from raising inconsistent, hypothetical, or alternative defenses. If you are in doubt whether a defense is considered an affirmative defense, the safer course is to raise it in the answer. If you fail to raise a defense, you risk waiving it. If you need additional time to study potential defenses, it is better to move for additional time to respond than to serve a hastily considered answer.

If the plaintiff has not made a jury demand in the complaint and you want a jury trial, you must make an appropriate jury demand in the answer. If the plaintiff has made a jury demand, you do not need to make one, although it is prudent to do so. If the plaintiff has made a jury demand on some counts of the complaint and you want a jury on any of the remaining counts, you must make the jury demand on those counts on the answer. A defendant usually makes the jury demand with the words "JURY TRIAL DEMANDED" below the case number and the words "DEFENDANT DEMANDS TRIAL BY JURY" at the end of the answer. Local rules usually have additional requirements, such as jury demand forms and fees.

Service of the answer must be made on every other party presently in the case in one of the ways that Rule 5 permits. The most common methods are service by mail, personal service on each party's lawyer, or service by electronic means. The answer with proof of service must be filed with the clerk of the court or, if permitted by local rules, with the judge.

The answer must have a proof of service showing that the answer was actually served on each party's lawyer. While local rules usually specify how proof of service should be made, the usual practice is to have a certificate from a lawyer or an affidavit from a nonlawyer state how and when service was actually made. The signed certificate or signed and notarized affidavit is then filed with the clerk of the court.

Example:

<u>CERTIFICATE OF SERVICE</u>

I, ____ *(attorney)* ____, state that I served the above by mailing a copy to the attorneys for _____ *(plaintiff/defendant)* _____, at ____ *(state address)* ____, on ____ *(date)* ____.

Dated: _____   _____

                                             Name of attorney
                                             Address
                                             e-mail address
                                             Tel. No.

AFFIDAVIT OF SERVICE

I,_____ *(name)*_____ having been first duly sworn, state that I served the above by mailing a copy to the attorneys for the other parties at their addresses of record in this case.

_____
Name

Signed and subscribed to before me on ___ *(date)*___ .

_____
Notary Public

My commission expires on ___ *(date)*___ .

§5.6.   *Counterclaims*[57]

In addition to Rule 12 motions and the answer, both of which are responses to the complaint, a defendant can also counterclaim. This is a pleading brought against a plaintiff within the time the defendant has to answer. Included in the answer, the counterclaim is functionally identical to a complaint. As such, the analytical approach and the pleading strategy for the counterclaim are the same as for a complaint. The plaintiff must respond to the counterclaim, either with Rule 12 motions or a reply, within the usual time limits. Counterclaims are either compulsory or permissive, and different rules apply to each.

1.   Compulsory counterclaims

Compulsory counterclaims, governed by Rule 13(a), are claims that a defendant must bring against the plaintiff or be barred from doing so in the future. The purpose of the compulsory counterclaim rule is clear: If the court already has jurisdiction over the plaintiff, the defendant, and the subject matter of the lawsuit, a single proceeding for all claims related to the occurrence or transaction involved makes sense.

A claim is compulsory if four requirements are met:

1.   the claim must already exist when the defendant is required to answer the complaint;
2.   the claim must arise out of the same transaction or occurrence on which the complaint is based;

---

57. Wright §79; Hazard et al. §5.8; Moore's Manual §11.60; Manual of Federal Practice §§3.45–3.50; Moore's Federal Practice §§13.10–13.50; Wright & Miller §§1401–1430.

3. the court must be able to obtain jurisdiction over any necessary additional parties; and
4. the counterclaim must not be the subject of a pending action.[58]

No jurisdictional dollar amount is necessary. The court has supplemental jurisdiction over the counterclaim even if the plaintiff voluntarily dismisses the complaint. However, if the complaint is dismissed for jurisdictional defects, the counterclaim will be dismissed unless it has an independent jurisdictional basis.

The principal difficulty with compulsory counterclaims is in determining if the defendant's claim involves the same transaction or occurrence that gave rise to the plaintiff's claim. While this determination is often easy for tort claims, such as those stemming from an automobile accident, it is often difficult for corporate and commercial disputes that involve numerous lengthy transactions. Courts have devised several approaches to determine whether the same "transaction or occurrence" is involved. Considerations include deciding whether the legal or factual issues are the same, whether the trial would involve the same proof, and whether the complaint and counterclaim are logically related. The purpose of Rule 13(a) is to promote fairness and efficiency by having related claims heard in one trial to achieve consistent results. Accordingly, the phrase in general has been broadly interpreted. The "logical relation" test, the most flexible approach, has the support of most of the treatises on the topic.[59]

Keep in mind that where there is proper jurisdiction over the plaintiff's complaint, the court will also have supplemental jurisdiction over the compulsory counterclaims. In addition, since the plaintiff selected the venue by filing the original complaint, the plaintiff cannot complain about the same venue for the defendant's counterclaim. Hence, there are no basic jurisdiction or venue problems associated with bringing compulsory counterclaims.[60]

2. Permissive counterclaims

Permissive counterclaims, governed by Rule 13(b), are claims that a defendant may but does not have to bring against a plaintiff in the pending lawsuit. A counterclaim is permissive if it does not arise out of the transaction or occurrence on which the plaintiff's complaint is based.

A permissive counterclaim must have a separate jurisdictional basis because it does not arise from the same transaction as the plaintiff's claim. A defendant cannot use a counterclaim to bring a claim into federal court that could not have been filed there as an original claim. A permissive counterclaim, in other words, cannot enlarge federal jurisdiction. Also, if the permissive counterclaim has an independent jurisdictional basis,

---

58. See Moore's Manual §11.61.
59. See Moore's Manual §11.619(2); Wright §79.
60. See Moore's Manual §11.64(1); Wright §79.

but no proper venue exists in the district where the plaintiff's complaint was filed, it cannot be brought.[61]

The concept behind the permissive counterclaim rule is fairness. Since a plaintiff has total freedom to bring unrelated claims against the defendant in one lawsuit, the defendant should have the same freedom, restricted only by jurisdiction and venue requirements. If the counterclaims make the case too complex, the court can order separate trials on the counterclaims.

3.   The United States as plaintiff

Rule 13(d) modifies the general counterclaim rule when the United States is the plaintiff. As a sovereign power, the United States has immunity from suit unless it has waived that immunity and has consented to be sued. No procedural rule can enlarge the types of suits that can be brought against the United States. Accordingly, a defendant cannot assert a counterclaim against the United States unless the government has expressly consented to be sued on that type of claim. The only exception is recoupment, which can be asserted as a counterclaim to reduce or defeat a claim.[62] This rule does not work the other way around. Nothing restricts the prerogative of the United States as a defendant to bring any counterclaim against the plaintiff.

4.   Statutes of limitations

Statutes of limitations are usually considered substantive law. Federal statutes of limitations apply to federal claims, and state statutes apply to state claims brought under diversity jurisdiction. A counterclaim, like a complaint, must be filed within the applicable statutory period, or it will usually be barred.[63]

5.   Waiver and amended pleadings

Failure to plead a compulsory counterclaim bars the defendant from asserting the claim later in another action. Rule 13(a) operates like a statutory bar in both federal and state courts.[64]

If a compulsory counterclaim was omitted from the answer, the court may permit an amended answer to include the omitted counterclaim

---

61. See Manual of Federal Practice §3.47; Moore's Manual §§11.64(1).

62. See Moore's Manual §11.63(2); Manual of Federal Practice §3.49.

63. See Moore's Manual §11.64(5); Wright §79. An exception is recoupment, which only diminishes or defeats the plaintiff's claim and is usually viewed as arising out of the same transaction.

64. See Wright §79. This bar is frequently characterized as res judicata, waiver, or estoppel.

"when justice so requires." The relation back doctrine applies to otherwise untimely compulsory counterclaims that arise out of the same transaction described in the timely filed answer.[65]

Under Rule 13(e), a counterclaim that matures or accrues after the defendant serves his answer may, in the court's discretion, be raised in a supplemental answer. If the court refuses to allow the defendant to file a supplemental answer, no prejudice should occur because such a counterclaim by definition cannot be compulsory. The defendant can always assert it later as an independent claim. Of course, where the defendant requests leave to file a supplemental pleading early in the litigation process, leave will usually be granted.

6. Practice approach

A counterclaim is simply a complaint brought by a defendant against a plaintiff in a pending suit. In format, content, and signing the counterclaim should be drafted like a complaint.[66] The only difference is that the defendant's answer contains the counterclaim, and the answer, with the counterclaim, is served on the plaintiff's attorney like any post-complaint pleading, motion, or discovery. It is usually titled "<u>ANSWER AND COUNTERCLAIM</u>," with separate headings and sections for each. If there are several plaintiffs against whom the defendant brings counter-claims, the titles should be specific.

A defendant who does not include a counterclaim in the answer might waive it. To set the counterclaim off from the answer, it should be clearly labeled a counterclaim. If you are unsure whether the claim is in fact a counterclaim, the safe course is to label it as such, since an incorrect designation does not trigger any penalties. If you are unsure whether your counterclaim is compulsory or permissive, the safe course again is to assert the counterclaim to avoid a possible waiver. Finally, since a counterclaim is analogous to a complaint, you should make a jury demand on those counter-claims that you want tried to a jury, since failure to do so may constitute a waiver. The plaintiff's demand for a jury trial will not extend to the defendant's counterclaims.

Example:

COUNTERCLAIM

Defendant Acme Manufacturing complains of plaintiff Wilbur Johnson as follows:

1. [If the counterclaim is permissive, you must allege the jurisdictional basis for bringing the claim in federal court.]

2. [Draft the pleading in the same manner as any complaint.]

---

65. See Moore's Manual §11.64(5).
66. See §5.3.

7. Plaintiff's responses

The plaintiff must consider how best to respond to the answer and counterclaim. If the answer merely admits or denies the complaint's allegations, the plaintiff ordinarily need do nothing. However, if the answer contains redundant, immaterial, impertinent, or scandalous matters, the plaintiff can move to strike. If the answer contains Rule 12(b) defenses or affirmative defenses, plaintiff may move to strike "any insufficient defense." In short, the plaintiff can make any of the Rule 12 motions available to the defendant when responding to a complaint. The next section discusses the plaintiff's responses to an answer that includes a counterclaim.

§5.7.   Answer to counterclaims and replies[67]

Under Rule 7(a) the plaintiff must answer a "counterclaim designated as a counterclaim." There must be a counterclaim in fact, and it must be labeled a counterclaim on the defendant's answer. Only if both requirements are met must plaintiff answer the counterclaim. These requirements relieve the plaintiff of the burden of correctly guessing if the defendant's pleading is a counterclaim or an affirmative defense, since the distinction as a matter of substantive law is not always clear. However, a careful plaintiff will answer any responsive pleading that may be a counterclaim, even those not so labeled, since pleadings may be read to the jury during trial.

Since a counterclaim is the functional equivalent of a complaint, the plaintiff assumes the position of a defendant responding to the original complaint. Hence, the plaintiff can respond to the counterclaim with any Rule 12 motions or may respond with an answer. The answer itself can answer the counterclaim, assert Rule 12 defenses, and raise Rule 8(c) affirmative defenses.[68]

The plaintiff should draft an answer to a counterclaim in the same manner as a defendant's answer.[69] It should be titled "<u>ANSWER TO COUNTERCLAIM</u>." When a plaintiff must respond to more than one counterclaim, the reply should show in the title which counterclaim is being responded to.

---

67. Hazard et al. §5.9; Moore's Manual §12.02; Manual of Federal Practice §3.55; Moore's Federal Practice §7.02; Wright & Miller §§1184, 1188.

68. There is some case law permitting a compulsory counterclaim in the reply as well. See Moore's Manual §12.04.

69. See §5.5.

Example:

[Caption]

<u>ANSWER TO COUNTERCLAIM</u>

Plaintiff Wilbur Johnson answers Defendant Acme Manufacturing's counterclaim as follows:
1. Johnson admits the allegations in Par. 1 of the counterclaim.
2. . . .
3. . . .
WHEREFORE. . . .

Under Rule 12(a), the plaintiff must answer a counterclaim within 21 days after service of the defendant's answer containing the counterclaim. Service of the reply must be made in one of the ways permitted by Rule 5 on every party presently in the case. The most common methods are service by mail, personal service, and service by electronic means. The reply with proof of service must be filed with the clerk of court or, if permitted by local rules, with the judge.

Under Rule 7(a), a reply to an answer is permitted only if the court orders one. Courts infrequently do so.

§5.8. *Cross-claims*[70]

A cross-claim is essentially a complaint brought by one party against a co-party, usually one defendant against another codefendant. Rule 13(g) permits a cross-claim if the claim arises out of the same transaction or occurrence that is the subject matter of the original complaint or relates to any property that is the subject matter of the original action. If a defendant brings a counterclaim against two or more plaintiffs, those plaintiffs may cross-claim against each other. Also, if a defendant has brought third-party complaints against additional parties, those third-party defendants may cross-claim against each other.

Several rules govern cross-claims.

1.   Discretionary pleading

Cross-claims are always permissive. A cross-claimant may but is not required to bring his claim in the pending action. The cross-claimant can always bring the claim as a separate action. Hence, the decision to cross-claim involves no danger of waiver.

---

70. Wright §80; Hazard et al. §5.8; Moore's Manual §14.140; Manual of Federal Practice §3.51; Moore's Federal Practice §§13.60-13.80; Wright & Miller §§1431–1433.

2. Subject matter

A cross-claim must be based on the subject matter of the original complaint, a counterclaim, or property involved in the original complaint. This restriction protects the original plaintiff from being unfairly forced into litigation that involves a matter totally different from the matters raised in the original complaint and one in which he may not have any interest. Whether the cross-claim arises out of the same transaction or occurrence as the complaint, a counterclaim, or the property involved in the complaint involves the same test and analysis used for compulsory counterclaims.[71]

The rule allows both matured and contingent cross-claims. Accordingly, claims that the codefendant "is or may be liable" for all or part of plaintiff's claim against him are properly raised in the cross-claim. In fact, most cross-claims raise just such issues, usually based on indemnity or contribution.

3. When made

Rule 13(g) requires that the cross-claim be made in a party's responsive pleading, usually the answer. Accordingly, just as a counterclaim must be made when answering a complaint, a cross-claim also must be made at that time.

4. Jurisdiction, venue, and joinder

Since cross-claims must involve the same subject matter as the original complaint or a counterclaim, they will satisfy the requirements for supplemental jurisdiction, and the original pleading establishes proper venue for them. Hence, proper cross-claims create no jurisdiction or venue problems. If the original complaint is dismissed, however, the cross-claim will also be dismissed, unless it has an independent jurisdictional basis.

Difficulties may arise in a related area, however. Rule 13(h) applies the joinder requirements of Rules 19 and 20 to cross-claims as well as to counterclaims. While Rule 13(g) requires that a cross-claim be brought against a co-party, usually a codefendant, additional parties that are indispensable to the cross-claim must be joined. Where a required party cannot be brought in due to a lack of jurisdiction over him, the cross-claim must be dismissed, although the dismissal will necessarily be without prejudice. The cross-claim can always be brought as an independent action later. Further, if the addition of cross-claims makes the trial too complex, the court can order separate trials under Rule 13(i).

71. See §5.6.1.

5. Cross-claims against the United States

Cross-claims against the United States cannot enlarge the scope of claims for which the United States as a sovereign power has consented to be sued. The cross-claim, like counterclaims, must be based on a claim that could have been independently brought against the United States. Sovereign immunity appears to require this result, although Rule 13 explicitly requires it only for counterclaims, not cross-claims.

6. Practice approach

The cross-claim, like a counterclaim, must be part of the defendant's answer. It must be served with the answer on existing parties in the same way any pleadings, motions, or discovery are served.

The cross-claim, like a complaint,[72] counterclaim, or third-party complaint, is a pleading that asks for relief. Hence, it should be drafted like a complaint. The prayer for relief will ordinarily reflect the contingent liability position of the cross-claiming party.

Example:

CROSS-CLAIM AGAINST DEFENDANT JONES

Defendant John Smith cross-claims against Defendant James Jones as follows:

    1. . . .
    2. . . .

WHEREFORE, in the event that Defendant Smith is liable to Plaintiff, Defendant Smith demands judgment against codefendant Jones in the same amount, plus interest and costs.

7. Responses to cross-claims

When a cross-claim has been served on a co-party, that party can respond with any of the responses permitted to a complaint. The party can make any of the Rule 12 motions or can answer the cross-claim and raise Rule 12(b) defenses and affirmative defenses. The party responding to the cross-claim must do so by motion or answer within the required time for answering, normally 21 days.

---

72. See §5.3.

§5.9.   Third-party practice[73]

Rule 14 governs third-party practice, also called impleader. It is a method for bringing into the action new parties who may be liable to a defendant for some or all of the judgment that the plaintiff may obtain against the defendant. The original defendant becomes a "third-party plaintiff" filing a complaint against a new party, the "third-party defendant."

The filing of counterclaims and cross-claims involves new claims between original parties to the action. Third-party practice, by contrast, is a procedure by which new parties, the third-party defendants, are added to the action. The process helps carry out one of the principal purposes of federal pleadings rules: Whenever possible, consistent with jurisdictional limitations, a court should hear all related claims in one action to resolve multiparty disputes efficiently and to obtain consistent results.

Several rules for third-party actions should be understood. The terms usually employed to identify the parties are the original plaintiff; the original defendant, who is now also a third-party plaintiff; and the third-party defendant, the new party.

1.   Discretionary pleading

Under Rule 14(a), an original defendant can serve a third-party complaint on a third-party defendant without leave of court so long as the original defendant does so within 14 days of serving the original answer to plaintiff's complaint. After that time the original defendant must obtain the court's permission to do so. The original plaintiff, if served with a counterclaim, may under Rule 14(b) also bring in a third-party defendant.

The court retains discretion to allow or deny third-party practice, and any party may move to strike a third-party claim.[74] In deciding whether to allow third-party practice, the court must balance the preference for complete resolution of all related issues against any possible prejudice to the plaintiff. Ordinarily the court should permit third-party practice. If the case then becomes too complex, it can simply order separate trials on the third-party claims. If the court denies the third-party claim, the claim can usually be brought as an independent action.

2.   Subject matter

An original defendant, as a third-party plaintiff, may include in his third-party complaint any claim that asserts that the third-party defendant "is or may be liable" to the original defendant "for all or part of the claim against it." However, the original defendant's right to bring third-party claims is

---

73. Wright §76; Hazard et al. §7.17; Moore's Manual §§14.50-14.59; Manual of Federal Practice §§3.125–3.134; Moore's Federal Practice §§14.02–14.42; Wright & Miller §§1441–1465.

74. See Wright §76.

broader than would first appear from Rule 14's text. Four types of claims can be brought under the impleader rule.

First, and most commonly, an original defendant can bring an action based on indemnity, contribution, subrogation, or any other theory that passes part or all of the defendant's liability to one or more new parties. Second, the original defendant can bring a contingent claim against the third-party defendant. The "is or may be liable" language in the Rule permits accelerated contingent liability claims. Third, the original defendant may be able to bring an independent claim against a third-party defendant, since under Rule 18(a) any party can join claims against another. So long as the defendant has one claim against a third-party defendant that is proper under Rule 14(a), any other independent claims proper under the joinder rules can be added. Finally, the original defendant can bring a claim against the third-party defendant that the original plaintiff could not bring directly against the third-party defendant.

3. Jurisdiction and venue

Third-party practice necessarily involves two related questions: whether the new action is proper under Rule 14 and whether there is proper jurisdiction and venue over the new action. Although an action may be proper under Rule 14, jurisdiction and venue may be problematic.

Where a third-party claim is based on an indemnity type of claim, for instance, supplemental jurisdiction exists and there will be no jurisdiction or venue problems. This situation is much like that for compulsory counterclaims. Where a third-party claim is based on a claim that is independent of the original plaintiff's claim against the original defendant, however, an independent basis for jurisdiction must exist.[75] This situation is much like that for permissive counterclaims.

4. Statutes of limitations

As with any complaint, a third-party complaint is subject to all applicable statutes of limitations. Also, if the original plaintiff files an amended complaint directly against a third-party defendant, and if the plaintiff does not file her amended complaint within the limitations period, courts have split as to whether the relation back doctrine applies.[76]

---

75. The leading case is Owens Equip. & Erection Co. v. Kroger, 437 U.S. 365 (1978). See Wright §76.

76. See Wright & Miller §1498.2; §5.13.

5.   Practice approach

A third-party complaint under Rule 14 is the fourth type of complaint permitted by the Federal Rules, in addition to complaints, counterclaims, and cross-claims. As such, the third-party complaint should include the three basic parts of any complaint: a jurisdictional allegation, a statement of claims, and a prayer for relief. In short, the approach to drafting a third-party complaint is essentially identical to that of the original complaint, although the former should recite the circumstances of the already pending original complaint. The document itself is titled "THIRD-PARTY COMPLAINT." The caption should clearly show the status of the various parties.

Since a third-party complaint brings new parties into the suit, each new third-party defendant must be served with the third-party complaint and summons, as required by Rule 4.

A third-party claim can be filed within 14 days after serving the answer; after that leave of court is required. The usual procedure is to attach the proposed pleading to the motion.

Example:

[Caption]

DEFENDANT JOHNSON'S MOTION TO BRING IN THIRD-PARTY DEFENDANT

Defendant Thomas Johnson requests permission to proceed as a third-party plaintiff against Frank Jones. A copy of the proposed third-party complaint is attached to this motion as Exhibit A. In support of his motion Defendant Johnson states:

1. . . .
2. . . .

WHEREFORE, Defendant Johnson requests that an order be entered permitting him to proceed as third-party plaintiff against Frank Jones, file the third-party complaint (Exhibit A), and to have that complaint and summons served upon Frank Jones as third-party defendant.

_____
Attorney for
Defendant Johnson

Example:

UNITED STATES DISTRICT COURT
FOR THE DISTRICT OF VERMONT

Rebecca Smith,
    Plaintiff
 	
    v.
 	
Thomas Johnson,
    Defendant and Third-
    Party Plaintiff
 	
    v.
 	
Frank Jones,
    Third-Party Defendant
	No. 13 C 100
	
	Civil Action

THIRD-PARTY COMPLAINT
    Defendant Johnson complains of Third-Party Defendant Frank Jones as follows:
        1. Plaintiff Smith has previously filed a complaint against defendant Johnson. A copy of that complaint is attached as Exhibit A.
        2. . . .
        3. . . .
    WHEREFORE, Defendant Johnson demands judgment against Third-Party Defendant Jones for all sums that Plaintiff may receive in judgment against Defendant Johnson.

6. Third-party defendant responses

A third-party defendant who has been served with a third-party complaint can choose any of the responses of any party served with a complaint. He may make Rule 12 motions, or he may answer the third-party complaint. He can also assert any defenses the original defendant may have against the original plaintiff. This latter practice protects the third-party defendant who might otherwise be prejudiced by the original defendant's failure to assert all available defenses against the original plaintiff.

    Further, a third-party defendant can counterclaim against the original plaintiff directly, so long as that counterclaim involves the same transaction or occurrence that is the basis for plaintiff's claim against the original defendant. The court will have supplemental jurisdiction over such a counterclaim. He can also assert cross-claims against other third-party defendants under Rule 13.

    Finally, a third-party defendant can also bring a third-party complaint against a new party who in turn may be liable to him for all or part of the original third-party complaint filed by the original defendant.

    The approach for drafting each of these responses is essentially identical to the approach for responses discussed earlier in this chapter. Make sure that the particular response chosen bears a title that makes clear what type of response it is and identifies the pleading to which it responds. Where supplemental jurisdiction does not attach to a third-party claim, an independent jurisdictional basis must exist, as must personal jurisdiction over the new parties.

While the pleading possibilities under Rule 14 appear complex, its underlying philosophy is simple: The Federal Rules broadly permit adding parties and claims so that all parties and all aspects of a dispute can be disposed of in one consolidated proceeding that produces consistent results. If the pleadings make the case too complex, the court can always order separate trials. The court will try the claims between the original plaintiff and original defendant first. The third-party claims can then be tried later if necessary. Ordering separate trials for the original claims and the subsequent third-party claims will also protect the original plaintiff from any unfairness that the addition of the third-party claims might cause.

7.   Original plaintiff responses

Under Rule 14(a), after a third-party complaint has been filed, the original plaintiff can file an amended complaint directly against a third-party defendant. The plaintiff can thereby do what she could have, and perhaps should have, done in the first place. However, there must be an independent jurisdictional basis for the amended complaint. If a third-party defendant has counterclaimed directly against the original plaintiff, that plaintiff must reply to the counterclaim within the usual time limits.

§5.10.   Interpleader[77]

Interpleader addresses situations when a party, called a "stakeholder," may be subjected to double liability because two or more claimants are making competing claims on a fund or property. The procedure enables the stakeholder to ask a court to determine proper ownership of or interest in the disputed fund or property. The standard situation involves multiple claims on the proceeds of an insurance policy. If the insurance company does not know who should get the proceeds, it may pay the wrong person and later be forced to pay a second time. In an interpleader action the stakeholder is the plaintiff, and the competing claimants become the defendants.

There are two types of federal interpleader: Rule 22 interpleader and so-called statutory interpleader under 28 U.S.C. §1335. The two differ substantially.

---

77. Wright §74; Hazard et al. §7.18; Moore's Manual §14.70-14.76; Manual of Federal Practice §§1.98, 3.135; Moore's Federal Practice §§22.02–22.08; Wright & Miller §§1701–1721.

1. Rule 22 interpleader

Rule 22 interpleader is in some respects broad, in others restrictive. It is broad because it allows interpleading claims that "lack a common origin or are adverse and independent rather than identical." It also allows the plaintiff-stakeholder to deny "liability in whole or in part to any or all of the claimants." Accordingly, the plaintiff need not deposit the fund at issue with the clerk of the court or post an equivalent bond. The rule allows a defendant in a pending suit to plead interpleader in a counterclaim or cross-claim.

On the other hand, Rule 22 interpleader is restrictive since the usual jurisdiction and venue rules apply. Where federal jurisdiction is based on diversity of citizenship under 28 U.S.C. §1332, there must be complete diversity between a plaintiff-stakeholder and each defendant-claimant, a situation that in interpleader cases will rarely exist. The amount in controversy must also exceed $75,000, a determination based on the amount of the fund or value of the property involved. The general venue statute, 28 U.S.C. §1391, determines proper venue.

2. 28 U.S.C. §1335 interpleader

Statutory interpleader under §1335, while conceptually identical to Rule 22 interpleader, has significant procedural advantages. First, §1335 relaxes the diversity requirement by requiring that only two of the defendant-claimants have diverse citizenship. The plaintiff's citizenship is not considered. This relaxed diversity requirement allows most interpleader actions to proceed in federal court. Venue under §1397 is proper in any district where one or more of the defendant-claimants resides. Second, the amount in controversy need only exceed $500. Third, under §2361 the court may issue an injunction against any defendant-claimant pursuing another action involving the same fund or property in state or federal courts. Finally, statutory interpleader under §2361 permits nationwide service of process.

Section 1335 requires that the claims be "adverse to and independent of one another," but the claims need not have a common origin or be identical in type. However, the plaintiff must deposit the fund or property with the clerk of the court or post a bond in the amount of the fund or property.

Further, while §1335 itself is silent on whether statutory interpleader can be asserted in a counterclaim or cross-claim, most courts permit it.[78]

3. Practice approach

An interpleader complaint based on either Rule 22 or §1335 should have all the components of an ordinary complaint: a jurisdictional statement, a

---

78. See Wright §74.

statement of claims, and a prayer for relief. Under §1335, the jurisdictional statement should state whether the fund has been deposited with the court or a bond has been posted in the appropriate amount payable to the clerk. The prayer for relief should ask for all relief that is appropriate, including a determination of the amount of liability, if any; a determination of which claimants are entitled to the fund or property and in what amounts; an injunction against any claimants pursuing other actions in state or federal courts based on this claim; and fees and costs, including attorney's fees where permitted.[79]

Example:

Whole Life Insurance Co., a
    corporation,
        Plaintiff
    v.
 	
Thomas Smith
        and
James Smith,
        Defendants
	No. _____
	
	Civil Action

Example:

COMPLAINT FOR INTERPLEADER

Plaintiff Whole Life Insurance Co. complains of defendants Thomas Smith and James Smith as follows:

Statement of Jurisdiction

1. Jurisdiction in this action is based on 28 U.S.C. §1335. Defendant Thomas Smith is a citizen of the State of Maine. Defendant James Smith is a citizen of the State of Vermont. The amount in controversy exceeds the sum of $500, exclusive of interest and costs.

or

1. Jurisdiction is based on Rule 22 of the Federal Rules of Civil Procedure and 28 U.S.C. §1332. Plaintiff is a citizen of the State of New York. Defendant Thomas Smith is a citizen of the State of Maine.

---

79. Attorney's fees are permitted where the plaintiff is a passive litigant who does not dispute that she owes a set amount to someone. See Moore's Manual §14.75(1).

Defendant James Smith is a citizen of the State of Vermont. The amount in controversy exceeds the sum of $75,000, exclusive of interest and costs.

2. On June 1, 2013, plaintiff issued a life insurance policy on the life of Franklin Smith. A copy of that policy is attached as Exhibit A.

3. . . . .

4. . . . .

5. By reason of the defendants' conflicting claims, plaintiff cannot determine with certainty which defendant [, if either,] is entitled to any proceeds of the policy [or, if either is entitled, in what amount].

6. Plaintiff has deposited the face amount of the policy, $80,000, with the clerk of the court. [Required only under §1335 interpleader.]

WHEREFORE, plaintiff requests that the court enter a judgment finding that:

(1) Neither defendant is entitled to recover any money from the policy [permitted only under Rule 22 interpleader];

(2) Each defendant is permanently enjoined from pursuing any other actions or claims on this policy [permitted only under §1335 interpleader];

(3) If this court finds the policy in force at the time of Franklin Smith's death, that the defendants be required to interplead and settle their claims on the policy between themselves, and that plaintiff be discharged from any liability except to any person in such amount as the court adjudges plaintiff is liable;

(4) Plaintiff is entitled to costs [and reasonable attorney's fees if a passive litigant].

Since an interpleader brings new parties into the lawsuit, each defendant must be served with the complaint and summons, as required by Rule 4.

§5.11. *Intervention*[80]

Intervention, governed by Rule 24, is the procedure by which a nonparty having an interest in a pending action can protect its rights by becoming an additional party and presenting a claim or defense. The rule closely parallels the joinder rules by allowing two types of intervention, intervention of right and permissive intervention.

1. Intervention of right

Rule 24(a) allows intervention of right under two circumstances. Anyone who "is given an unconditional right to intervene by a federal statute" may

---

80. Wright §75; Hazard et al. §7.16; Moore's Manual §14.90-14.124; Manual of Federal Practice §§3.148–3.155; Moore's Federal Practice §§24.02–24.24; Wright & Miller §§1901–1923.

intervene.[81] These instances are rare. Rule 24(a)(2) addresses the second set of circumstances, which arise more often. It sets forth three requirements for intervention of right.

First, the intervenor must claim "an interest relating to the property or transaction that is the subject of the action." What is a sufficient "interest" remains unsettled, since the case law is hardly uniform. Various courts have held that the intervenor's interest must be "direct," "substantial," or "significantly protectable."[82] An analysis of the intervenor's claimed interest, of the relief sought, and of the nature of the claims and defenses asserted in the pending action is required.

Second, the intervenor must be "so situated that disposing of the action may as a practical matter impair or impede the movant's ability to protect its interest." The rule includes the critical phrase "as a practical matter" to clarify that this determination should not be limited to legal bars such as res judicata, but should include any substantial functional difficulties that might adversely affect the intervenor's interests.

Third, existing parties do not "adequately represent" the movant's interests. This requirement compares the interests of the existing parties with the claimed interests of the intervenor to determine how closely they are related. If the intervenor's interests are essentially identical to those of an existing party, so that the existing party will necessarily assert the same positions as the intervenor would, intervention should be denied.

2. Permissive intervention

Rule 24(b)(1) permits permissive intervention when someone "is given a conditional right to intervene by a federal statute." This seldom-used basis for intervention applies when the federal or a state government wishes to get involved in a case involving the constitutionality or interpretation of a statute.[83]

Litigants more frequently use Rule 24(b)(2), which permits intervention if anyone "has a claim or defense that shares with the main action a common question of law or fact." This requirement involves an analysis similar to that made for the permissive joinder of parties under Rule 20(a). This request to intervene is addressed to the court's discretion, and the court may deny it where the intervenor's request would "unduly delay or prejudice" the adjudication of the rights of the pending parties or inject unimportant issues into the case. If a court denies intervention, no adverse legal consequences result, since res judicata will not apply to the unsuccessful intervenor. The common situation where intervention is permitted involves an intervenor's claim against the defendant that is factually and legally similar to the plaintiff's pending claim against the defendant.

---

81. A list of such statutes is found at Moore's Federal Practice §24.02.
82. See Wright & Miller §1908.1.
83. See Moore's Federal Practice §24.02.

3. Timing

A prospective intervenor must move to intervene in a timely fashion, regardless of whether the intervention sought is of right or is permissive. Both Rule 24(a) and (b) require a "timely motion," but where intervention of right is requested, it will ordinarily be permitted, regardless of when the application is made, since the intervenor's right might otherwise be adversely affected. Still, someone may seek intervention of right so late in the pending action that the attempt is considered untimely and is therefore denied.

When permissive intervention is sought, the court must consider "whether the intervention will unduly delay or prejudice the adjudication of the original parties' rights." This determination requires an analysis of the relief the intervenor wants, whether the intervenor will be an active or passive party, and particularly the stage that the pending action has reached. Obviously, courts will view efforts to intervene with more favor when intervention is sought early in the pleading stage, before the parties have already engaged in substantial discovery.

4. Jurisdiction

The intervenor's addition to the pending action must meet jurisdiction and venue requirements. If the original basis for subject matter jurisdiction is diversity, the intervenor's claim must have an independent jurisdictional basis; supplemental jurisdiction cannot be invoked for plaintiff-intervenors. In federal question cases, the intervenor's claim usually will qualify for supplemental jurisdiction.[84]

Venue should not be an issue. It is a personal right, and the intervenor is generally held to accept the venue that already exists.

5. Practice approach

Rule 24 requires that the intervenor make a timely motion to intervene. The motion should be made in the district in which the original action is pending. The intervenor must attach an appropriate pleading to the motion. The motion, which must be served on all existing parties, should state the reason why intervention is appropriate under the circumstances.

---

84. See Wright & Miller §1917.

Example:

Frank Johnson,
        Plaintiff

        v.   No. 13 C 100

Wilma Smith,   Civil Action
        Defendant,
Jacob Franklin,
        Intervenor

Example:

MOTION TO INTERVENE AS A DEFENDANT

Jacob Franklin moves for leave to intervene as a defendant in this action. A copy of his proposed answer is attached as Exhibit A. In support of his motion Franklin states:
    1. Intervention is appropriate because . . .
    2. . . .
WHEREFORE, Jacob Franklin requests that he be permitted to intervene as a defendant, file his answer to the complaint, and participate in this action as a party defendant.

ANSWER OF DEFENDANT-INTERVENOR FRANKLIN

Defendant Franklin answers the complaint as follows:
    1. . . .
    2. . . .

If the court grants the motion to intervene, the intervenor becomes a party and has all the rights that parties ordinarily have. The intervenor usually cannot contest past orders, but can counterclaim and cross-claim, present any appropriate motions, and fully participate in discovery. Keep in mind, however, that the court has power to limit intervention to certain matters if permissive intervention has been granted.

The denial of a motion to intervene raises the difficult issue of whether the ruling is final and appealable.[85] While there is a split in authority on this question, the traditional rule is that a motion for intervention of right is appealable if denied, but the denial of a motion to intervene permissively is appealable only where an abuse of discretion is shown. If the motion to intervene is granted, it is not an appealable order.[86]

85. See Moore's Manual §14.124(5)(a); Moore's Federal Practice §24.15.
86. Wright & Miller §1923.

§5.12. Class actions[87]

The topic of class actions by itself can fill volumes, and literature on the subject in treatises, cases, and journals is extensive. Class action litigation is obviously a complicated area, one in which the inexperienced litigator should tread cautiously if at all. Hence, this section is limited to a brief overview of the class action requirements and initial considerations and steps for such suits. The principal concern of the inexperienced litigator should be to determine whether a case can be pursued as a class action. (The initial fight is usually over class certification and the scope of discovery that will be permitted on the certification question.) Assistance from someone with experience in class action litigation should be sought.

1. Requirements for class certification

Rule 23 governs class actions, whether the underlying substantive law generating the plaintiffs' claims is state or federal.[88] Before the court will certify a class and thereby let the case proceed on a class-wide basis, the party moving for class certification must establish that the proposed class meets two sets of requirements. The first set, in Rule 23(a), ensures that the interests of all class members will be protected. The second set, in Rule 23(b), guarantees that the case can proceed efficiently and manageably as a class action.

The Rule 23(a) requirements include the following: numerosity, commonality, typicality, and adequate representation. First, the class must be so "numerous that joinder of all members is impracticable." The rule itself does not define what a class is or how its members should be determined. Impracticability depends on the type of claims asserted and the persons asserting those claims. Accordingly, the numbers necessary for class certification are quite flexible, and the ultimate decision whether a class action is the preferred method of dealing with a claim is left to the discretion of the trial court. While hundreds of potential plaintiffs or defendants will almost always make the action suitable for class-action treatment, and fewer than 30 ordinarily is not enough, the case law on class numbers in the middle range—perhaps 30 to 50 members—shows no particular pattern.[89] The outcome depends as much on other considerations as it does on the number of class members.

Second, there must be "questions of law or fact common to the class." This commonality requirement is more demanding than the text suggests. The plaintiff must show with evidence the existence of questions that could plausibly generate answers "apt to drive the resolution of the litigation"

---

87. Wright §72; Hazard et al. §§7.19-7.22; Manual of Federal Practice §§3.138–3.147; Moore's Manual §14A.01-14A.81; Moore's Federal Practice §§23.01–23.88; Wright & Miller §§1751–1803.

88. Shady Grove Orthopedic Assoc. v. Allstate Ins. Co., 559 U.S. 393 (2009).

89. See Moore's Manual §14.07(1); Wright & Miller §1762.

for all of the class members.[90] In other words, the proposed class representative must convince the court that a decisionmaker could resolve a question of law or fact that goes to an element of all the class members' claims "in one stroke."[91] In an employment discrimination class action, for example, the plaintiffs must show that the question, "Did the defendant single out women for discriminatory treatment?" is capable of generating a single answer for all of the class members.

Third, the "claims or defenses of the representative parties" must be "typical of the claims or defenses of the class." Each claim or defense encompassed by the proposed class must be represented, and the class representative cannot be subject to any unique defenses. If, for instance, the class representative's claim might fail on statute of limitations grounds, while other class members may have timely claims, the proposed class will run into typicality problems.

Finally, the representative parties must "fairly and adequately protect the interests of the class," a requirement directed to both the representative parties and their lawyers. The interests of the representatives must be scrutinized to determine if their interests conflict with those of some or all of the class members. If they do, a possible solution is to certify separate sub-classes. In addition, the lawyers must have sufficient ability and experience to represent the class competently. Rule 23(b), which addresses the efficiency and manageability of a class suit, allows for certification in three situations. First, Rule 23(b)(1) permits class certification when separate actions would "create a risk of inconsistent or varying adjudications" that would "establish incompatible standards of conduct for the party opposing the class," or where separate adjudications "as a practical matter would be dispositive of the interests of the other members" in the class who are not parties to that adjudication. The former applies in actions against governmental entities to declare actions invalid, such as expenditures and bond issues. The "limited fund" scenario triggers the latter. These are instances when the value of class members' claims exceeds the assets available to pay them. All possible claimants get joined as class members to ensure that one or several do not exhaust the defendant's assets, and that instead everyone gets a fair pro rata distribution.

Second, Rule 23(b)(2) provides for class treatment when the party opposing the class has "acted or refused to act on grounds that apply generally to the class." Many of the cases brought on this basis are civil rights actions in which a party seeks a single injunction that is uniform for the class as a whole. Claims for monetary compensation or another such individualized remedy are rarely allowed.

Third, under Rule 23(b)(3), a class action is appropriate where "questions of law or fact common to the class members predominate over any questions affecting only individual members" and a class action is the superior method for handling the entire controversy. This provision, generally thought to govern class suits for money damages, is the most

---

90. Wal-Mart Stores, Inc. v. Dukes, 131 S. Ct. 2541, 2551 (2011) (quoting Richard A. Nagareda, Class Certification in the Age of Aggregate Proof, 84 N.Y.U. L. Rev. 97, 132 (2009)).

91. *Id.*

common basis for class actions. Courts not infrequently certify classes under Rule 23(b)(3) in antitrust and securities fraud cases, where causation and damages may be susceptible to classwide determination. A proposed class rarely succeeds under Rule 23(b)(3) in mass tort cases because the plaintiffs' claims are usually seen as too diverse to justify class action treatment.[92]

Sometimes whether a proposed class meets the requirements of Rule 23(a) or (b) boils down to an evidentiary dispute that implicates the merits. Did something common to all class members cause their injuries, for instance, or did their injuries result from idiosyncratic causes specific to each plaintiff? While the court does not explicitly rule on the merits at the class certification stage, it may need to make an evidentiary finding to determine if the proposed class meets the commonality requirement, for example, or the predominance requirement. In such circumstances, the party moving for class certification will bear the burden to show with evidence that the class does in fact satisfy Rule 23(a) and (b).[93]

2. Jurisdiction

The Class Action Fairness Act (CAFA) of 2005, which amended 28 U.S.C. §1332 and added 28 U.S.C. §1453, established special, quite complex jurisdictional rules for class actions The basics are as follows. CAFA adopted a "minimum diversity" standard for federal jurisdiction. So long as a single class member is diverse from a single defendant, the case satisfies the diversity-of-citizenship requirement for diversity jurisdiction. A special amount-in-controversy requirement—the class as a whole must allege $5 million in damages, not $75,000 per class member—also applies. There are several exceptions, however, to this minimal diversity requirement. For example, if two-thirds or more of the class members come from the same state as a primary defendant, the district court must decline jurisdiction. Also, a district court may, in its discretion, decline jurisdiction if more than one-third but fewer than two-thirds of the class members come from the same state as a primary defendant. Other exceptions exist, and an inexperienced litigator should carefully consult the diversity jurisdiction statute to determine which diversity of citizenship requirement applies in a particular case.[94] These rules replaced the former requirement that each named class representative be diverse from each defendant, and that each class member's claim exceed the amount-in-controversy requirement.

---

92. In Amchem Products v. Windsor, 521 U.S. 591 (1997), the Supreme Court held that a class proposed to be certified for settlement purposes only was not appropriate in an asbestos exposure case brought under Rule 23(b)(3). In Ortiz v. Fiberboard, 527 U.S. 815 (1999), the Court held that a proposed settlement class in an asbestos exposure case was not appropriate for certification under Rule 23(b)(1).

93. Comcast Corp. v. Behrend, 133 S. Ct. 1426 (2013).

94. See generally Vance, A Primer on the Class Action Fairness Act of 2005, 80 Tul. L. Rev. 1617 (2006).

Congress left federal question jurisdiction untouched, so the same rules apply to these class actions as to any other case.

3. Procedure

A class action begins just as any other case does, with the filing of the complaint. The complaint's caption should indicate that the case is a class action. The proposed class representative should be listed by name as the plaintiff, but indicate that he brings the case "individually and on behalf of all others similarly situated." Also, the complaint should include a separate section entitled "Class Action Allegations." In separate paragraphs, the complaint should include the definition of the proposed class, emphasizing why all members have similar claims. It should also enumerate each requirement of Rule 23(a) and the requirements of the applicable part of Rule 23(b) and allege that the proposed class meets them.

The current trend is to delay class certification until after discovery is underway. A court may stagger discovery, to allow discovery on issues pertaining to class certification, while limiting merits discovery until after the class is certified. The motion for class certification is complex and may require substantial evidentiary support. A lawyer who has never prosecuted a class action before should considering working with an experienced co-counsel, given this motion's difficulty. As Rule 23(f) provides, the party that loses the class certification motion may seek the court of appeals's permission to file an interlocutory appeal, but it must do so within 14 days of the district court's class certification decision.

If the court certifies a class under Rule 23(b)(3), the "best notice that is practicable under the circumstances," which includes "individual notice to all members who can be identified through reasonable effort," must go out to all class members. Class notices must be written "in plain, easily understood language." Notice can be an expensive undertaking, sometimes prohibitively so. For class members whose identity can be ascertained with reasonable effort, courts used to invariably require notice by first class mail. Some federal courts have shed their earlier skepticism and have grown increasingly tolerant of notice by e-mail. For unknown class members, some form of notice by publication is required. Since each side must bear its costs of litigation, the expense of actually notifying the individual class members can effectively prevent a claim from being pursued as a class action.[95] Upon receipt of notice, Rule 23(b)(3) class members have an opportunity to opt out of the class and retain control over their claims.

Rule 23(g) governs the selection and appointment of class counsel. It authorizes the appointment of interim class counsel before certification

---

95. The Supreme Court has held that in class action suits brought under Rule 23(c)(2) the party seeking the class action must bear the costs of actual notice to the reasonably-identifiable class members. Eisen v. Carlisle & Jacquelin, et al., 417 U.S. 156 (1974).

and sets forth the standards the court must consider in selecting class counsel. Rule 23(h) authorizes the court to address the issue of fees in an action certified as a class action when class counsel is first appointed.

The settlement of class actions, which Rule 23(e) governs, not surprisingly presents a host of additional complexities. The court must give the proposed settlement its preliminary approval, notice must go out to class members again, and they must have an opportunity to object. Again, consult with an experienced class action practitioner to ensure that you handle this stage of the litigation correctly.

4. Class actions and arbitration

Increasingly, companies that sell consumer goods try to protect themselves against class action litigation by including arbitration clauses coupled with class action waivers in the form contracts issued to the purchaser at the time of sale. A clause might provide, for instance, that "the purchaser agrees to arbitrate any dispute arising out of the purchase of the product, and agrees not to join or initiate any class action or class arbitration." Such clauses are now common in cell phone service contracts, for example. The Supreme Court has repeatedly allowed the enforcement of these clauses.[96] If you plan to bring a class action but discover that one of these clauses might be applicable, you must inquire into whether some specific exception allows class suits to proceed notwithstanding the contract. Otherwise, the clause will be enforced, and your class will fail to win certification.

§5.13. Amendments of pleadings and supplemental pleadings[97]

The principal concepts behind the Federal Rules' pleading requirements are that pleadings should accurately notify the parties of the basis for the claims involved and that enough flexibility should be permitted so that substantial justice is achieved in every case. Rule 15, the amendments rule, reflects these concerns. Amended pleadings should be freely allowed when fairness requires it — that is, whenever an amendment would create a more accurate or complete pleading and would not substantially prejudice the opposing parties. The rule applies to all pleadings.

1. Amendments as a matter of course

Rule 15(a) provides: "A party may amend its pleading once as a matter of course: (A) 21 days after serving it, or (B) if the pleading is one to which a

---

96. American Express Co. v. Italian Colors Restaurant, 133 S. Ct. 2304 (2013); AT&T Mobility LLC v. Concepcion, 131 S. Ct. 1740 (2011).

97. Hazard et al. §§5.11–5.17; Moore's Manual §§9.50–9.52; Manual of Federal Practice §§3.58–3.65; Moore's Federal Practice §§15.02–15.20, 15.30; Wright & Miller §§1471–1510.

responsive pleading is required, 21 days after service of a responsive pleading or 21 days after service of a motion under Rule 12(b), (e), or (f), whichever is earlier."

When the amended pleading seeks to add new parties, Rule 15(a), which permits timely amendments as a matter of course, seems to conflict with Rule 21, which permits additions of parties only by leave of court. Courts have ruled both ways on this issue, some holding that leave is always required, others not.[98]

Rule 15(c) may also seem to conflict with some state statutes of limitations, which apply in diversity cases. In circumstances where the rule would permit an amended complaint but the applicable state statute would bar the complaint, courts have held that Rule 15 controls and permits the amendment.[99]

2. Amendments by leave of court

Rule 15(a) permits amendments by leave of court or the opposing party's written consent. The rule provides that "the court should freely give leave when justice so requires." The amended pleading can change the jurisdictional allegations, factual claims, legal theories of recovery, events and transactions involved, and even parties to the action.[100] Yet courts have permitted amendments liberally, and grounds such as oversight, error, or delay by themselves are generally held insufficient to deny leave to amend.[101]

Courts may exercise their discretion and deny leave to amend when, in addition to delay or neglect, amendment would cause actual prejudice to the opposing party. Alternatively, the court may grant leave to amend while restricting it to particular matters, to minimize prejudice to an opposing party. Obviously, the amending party should seek leave to amend as early in the litigation process as possible to minimize prejudice. A motion during the pleading stage will in all likelihood be granted. One made after discovery is underway, however, may encounter difficulties.[102]

When a motion for leave to amend is made after a motion to dismiss for failure to state a claim on which relief can be granted, some courts will not grant leave if it appears certain that plaintiff cannot, under the existing facts, state a proper claim.[103] Courts often look to see if the proposed amended complaint properly states a claim before granting leave to amend. If it does not, leave can properly be denied.

When an amended pleading is permitted, Rule 15(a)(3) provides: "Unless the court orders otherwise, any required response to an amended

---

98. See Moore's Manual §9.51.

99. See Wright §59.

100. 28 U.S.C. §1653 provides that "defective allegations of jurisdiction may be amended, upon terms, in the trial or appellate courts."

101. See Moore's Manual §9.51.

102. See Nelson v. Adams, 529 U.S. 460 (2000), holding that a postjudgment amendment of pleadings, while proper under Rule 15, violated due process.

103. See Manual of Federal Practice §3.60.

pleading must be made within the time remaining to respond to the original pleading, or within 14 days after service of the amended pleading, whichever is later."

3. Statutes of limitations and "relation back"

An important concern involves whether the statute of limitations applies to amended pleadings. This question arises only if the amended pleading is filed after the applicable statute of limitations has run on a particular claim. Whether the statute will bar the amended pleading depends on whether the doctrine of "relation back," set out in Rule 15(c), will apply. If the amended pleading meets the requirements of Rule 15(c), its filing is said to "relate back" to the date of the original pleading's filing. It becomes timely for that reason, and the expired statute of limitations no longer poses a problem. The two principal types of amendments — changing facts and legal theories, and changing parties — require different analyses.

a. *Changing facts and theories*

Rule 15(c) provides: "An amendment to a pleading relates back to the date of the original pleading when: (A) the law that provides the applicable statute of limitations allows relation back; (B) the amendment asserts a claim or defense that arose out of the conduct, transaction, or occurrence set out — or attempted to be set out — in the original pleading." The basic idea is that, if the defendant is already on notice that it is being sued regarding a particular incident, the precise claims the plaintiff brings or fails to bring do not matter.

When the amended pleading alleges an entirely new claim, the relation back doctrine will not apply. Whether the claims or defenses in the amended pleading arose out of the same conduct, transaction, or occurrence in the original pleading is an imprecise standard, but courts have been reasonably lenient in permitting amendments, particularly when the proposed amendment only changes the legal theory involved.

b. *Changing parties*

Rule 15(c) also provides: "An amendment to a pleading relates back to the date of the original pleading when: . . . (C) the amendment changes the party or the naming of the party against whom the claim is asserted, if Rule 15(c)(1)(B) is satisfied and if, within the period provided by Rule 4(m) for serving the summons and complaint, the party to be brought in by amendment: (i) received such notice of the action that it would not be prejudiced in defending on the merits; and (ii) knew or should have known that the action would have been brought against it, but for a mistake concerning the proper party's identity." Put differently, the new party must have acquired actual knowledge of the lawsuit within the time Rule 4 establishes for service, and it must have known that it would have been the defending party all along, but for the claimant's mistake. Such situations arise, for example, when corporate and other artificial and governmental entities are involved, and where determining the technically proper defendant is difficult and sometimes impossible prior to discovery.[104] In *Krupski v. Costa Crociere SpA*, 560 U.S. 538 (2010), the Supreme Court held that changing a party under Rule 15(c)(1)(C) "depends on what the party to be added knew or should have known, not on the amending party's knowledge or timeliness in seeking to amend the pleading." In short, the plaintiff's diligence is not a requirement under the rule.

4. Supplemental pleadings

Under Rule 15(d), a party may move to file a supplemental pleading alleging transactions, occurrences, and events that have occurred since the time the original pleading was served. Permitting the motion is discretionary with the court, which can impose any reasonable terms to protect the other parties.

Since a supplemental pleading by definition raises new matters that have arisen since the original pleading was filed, statute of limitations and relation back issues will rarely be concerns.

5. Practice approach

A motion for leave to amend, like any other motion, must meet the Rule 7(b) requirements. The motion must state with particularity the grounds for the motion and the relief sought. Timely notice must be sent to other parties. The better practice is to attach the amended pleading as an exhibit to the motion. In addition, it is both more convenient and a safer practice to have a complete amended pleading, rather than incorporate by reference parts of the original pleading. It is simply easier to deal with a complete pleading, and responses will likely be more accurate.

Example:

[Caption]

<u>MOTION FOR LEAVE TO FILE AMENDED COMPLAINT</u>

Plaintiff moves for an order permitting plaintiff to file an amended complaint. A copy of the amended complaint is attached to this motion as Exhibit A. In support of this motion plaintiff states:

---

104. See Manual of Federal Practice §3.61.

1. Plaintiff's original complaint was against one defendant, William Smith, and alleged one theory of liability based on negligence.

2. New information, based on both informal fact investigation and discovery, has revealed that another party, Acme Motors, may be liable to plaintiff and that a valid claim against Acme may exist, based on products liability and implied warranty.

WHEREFORE, plaintiff requests that an order be entered permitting plaintiff to file the amended complaint attached as Exhibit A, which adds Acme Motors as a defendant and alleges two additional counts, based on products liability and implied warranty, against Acme Motors.

_____

Attorney for Plaintiff

If the motion is allowed, or the amended pleading is of right, a party that is required to respond to the amended pleading must do so either within the time remaining to respond to the original pleading or within 14 days of service of the amended pleading, whichever is greater.

Many motions to permit an amended pleading are made after an opposing party has been granted a motion to dismiss under Rule 12. Here the dismissed party should move for leave to file an amended pleading within 14 days of dismissal.[105] The better and more common practice, however, is to move for leave to file an amended pleading and have the motion to amend granted at the hearing on the motion to dismiss, if that motion is granted. The order granting the motion to dismiss will therefore also contain an order permitting the amended pleading.

105. See Moore's Manual §9.51.

VI

DISCOVERY

§6.1. *Introduction*

Discovery is the principal fact-gathering method in the formal litigation process. An active discovery period is when parties fight most of their battles, when parties incur most of their litigation costs, and when the war is often won or lost. Consequently, every litigator must understand discovery so that she can effectively and efficiently use the various discovery methods as tactical and strategic tools.

Federal discovery has several principal characteristics. First, it is largely a self-executing process. For the most part, lawyers conduct discovery without prior judicial approval, although courts may actively supervise and even dictate the order and timing of discovery. Second, the discovery rules are flexible and usually permit any order, and sometimes the repeated use, of the various discovery methods subject only to the court's approved discovery plan and court protection against abuse. Third, orders regulating discovery are usually not appealable. Since discovery issues will often be moot by the time a final judgment is entered in the case, appeals are relatively infrequent. The trial court therefore resolves most discovery issues.

Recent years have seen numerous changes to the discovery rules, principally motivated by increasing pressure for discovery reform. Many judges, litigators, legislators, and the public see civil litigation as unnecessarily complicated, slow, and expensive. Reformers often identify Rules 26 through 37, the discovery rules, as the worst offenders. Hence, recent years have witnessed repeated efforts to simplify discovery, make the discovery rules reflect changes in technology, and impose effective sanctions for discovery abuse.

On this note, a word of caution is in order. The Judicial Conference of the United States has recently approved a number of amendments to the Federal Rules. At the time of this edition's printing, the proposed amendments are still pending and have not yet become final. If they do, they will affect the discovery process in a number of dramatic ways. Mostly they are devised to narrow the scope of discovery. For instance, a proposed amendment to Rule 26(b)(1) would emphasize that discovery requests are subject to a proportionality requirement. The discovery request would be improper if it is not "proportional to the needs of the case." *This chapter presents discovery as it is currently regulated under existing rules.* Make sure to check the most recent amendments to the Federal Rules and adjust the advice that this chapter provides with them in mind.[1]

Finally, ethics rules apply to discovery. Model Rule 3.4(d) commands that a "lawyer shall not . . . make a frivolous discovery request or fail to make a reasonably diligent effort to comply with a legally proper discovery request by an opposing party."

§6.2. *Scope of discovery*[2]

Rule 26 is the basic discovery rule that controls the scope of discovery. This section discusses what "relevance" means in the discovery context and reviews specialized issues that Rule 26 regulates. These issues involve insurance, statements, experts, privileges, and work product.

1. Relevance

Rule 26(b)(1), as it presently reads, provides that "[p]arties may obtain discovery regarding any non-privileged matter that is relevant to any party's claim or defense — including the existence, description, nature, custody, condition, and location of any documents or other tangible things and the identity and location of persons who know of any discoverable matter." In addition, "for good cause, the court may order discovery of any matter relevant to the subject matter involved in the action." Rule 26(b)(1) also provides that parties can request information within the scope of discovery, even if it is not admissible at trial.[3]

---

1. All amendments to the Federal Rules, proposed and otherwise, are available at the U.S. Courts' website: www.uscourts.gov.

2. Wright §81; Hazard et al. §§8.1, 8.5; Moore's Manual §§15.02-15.03; Manual of Federal Practice §5.1 et seq.; Moore's Federal Practice §26.41; Wright & Miller §2007.

3. Wright §81; Moore's Manual §15.03; Manual of Federal Practice §5.24; Moore's Federal Practice §26.41(4); Wright & Miller §2008. A proposed amendment to Rule 26(b)(1), pending at the time of publication, would change this scope-of-discovery provision by jettisoning the "relevant to the subject matter" provision. Make sure to check revisions to the Federal Rules to ensure that the information in this text is accurate. See www.uscourts.gov.

Rule 26 creates two levels of discoverable material: discovery by right, as to matters relevant to claims and defenses, and discretionary broader discovery, as to matters relevant to the subject matter of the litigation.[4]

Relevant matter may be obtained from other parties and sometimes non-parties through six discovery methods:

- Required disclosures — Rule 26(a)
- Interrogatories — Rule 33
- Requests to produce documents, electronically stored information, and things — Rule 34
- Depositions — Rules 27-32
- Physical and mental examinations — Rule 35
- Requests for admissions — Rule 36

This chapter discusses each of these methods in detail.

2. Insurance agreements

Rule 26(a)(1)(A) makes discoverable "any insurance agreement under which an insurance business may be liable to satisfy all or part of a possible judgment in the action or to indemnify or reimburse for payments made to satisfy the judgment."[5] This information is critical for assessing case value and the defendant's ability to pay a judgment.

3. Statements

A "statement" under Rule 26(b)(3)(C) is "(i) a written statement that the person has signed or otherwise adopted or approved; or (ii) a contemporaneous stenographic, mechanical, electrical, or other recording — or a transcription of it — that recites substantially verbatim the person's oral statement."[6] If a witness has been interviewed, but nothing tangible was produced, such as a written statement, recording, or transcript, no "statement" exists that can be discovered. It also means that if a lawyer, after interviewing a witness, later makes notes summarizing the interview, but the notes are not substantially verbatim, the lawyer's notes of the witness interview are not discoverable. They fall within the Rule 26(b)(3) work-product doctrine.

A party is entitled to obtain a copy of his prior statement in the possession of anyone else upon demand, without a court order or a showing of

---

4. Again, the proposed amendment would eliminate the "relevant to the subject matter" provision.

5. Wright §81; Moore's Manual §15.02(1)(b)(v); Manual of Federal Practice §5.37; Moore's Federal Practice §26.22; Wright & Miller §2010.

6. Moore's Manual §15.03(7)(b); Moore's Federal Practice §26.71; Wright & Miller §§2027, 2028.

need. A party is considered to have a right to his own written or recorded statements. Statements made by a party to his own lawyer are not discoverable, principally because the attorney-client privilege will apply to such communications.

A witness is also entitled to obtain a copy of his prior statement. Note that the rule does not expressly allow discovery of a witness's statement. Only the witness himself has a right to obtain a copy of his own statement. A lawyer, however, can always urge a witness to ask for a copy of his own statement and then obtain it from the witness. Because it is so easy to obtain the statement indirectly, many lawyers, and some courts, view witness statements as being discoverable directly.

4. Experts

There are three basic kinds of experts: testifying experts, consulting experts, and informally consulted experts.[7] Different rules govern the discoverability of their identity, opinions, reports, and background information. There are also experts who are employees of a party and were involved in the events on which the litigation is based. They are usually treated like any fact witness, unless their duties as employees regularly involve giving expert testimony.[8]

Rule 26(a)(2) governs the disclosures of expert witnesses expected to testify at trial. The "identity of any witness" the party "may use at trial to present evidence under Federal Rules of Evidence 702, 703, or 705" must be disclosed. Also required to be disclosed is "a written report — prepared and signed by the witness — if the witness is one retained or specially employed to provide expert testimony in the case or one whose duties as the party's employee regularly involve giving expert testimony." This written report must contain "a complete statement of all opinions the witness will express and the basis and reasons for them; the facts or data considered by the witness in forming them; any exhibits that will be used to summarize or support them; the witness's qualifications, including a list of all publications authored in the previous 10 years; a list of all other cases in which, during the previous 4 years, the witness testified as an expert at trial or by deposition; and a statement of the compensation to be paid for the study and testimony in the case."

Rule 26(a)(2)(C) requires that non-retained experts who are not required to provide a written report, such as treating physicians, must disclose "a summary of the facts and opinions to which the witness is expected to testify."

Rule 26(b)(4)(C) provides work-product protection to all communications between the party's attorney and any retained expert required to provide an expert report, except for communications which "relate to

---

7. Hazard et al. §§8.8, 8.13; Moore's Manual §15.02(2); Manual of Federal Practice §5.36; Moore's Federal Practice §26.86; Wright & Miller §§2029–2034.
8. Rule 26(a)(2)(B); Greenhaw v. City of Cedar Rapids, Iowa, 255 F.R.D. 484 (N.D. Iowa 2009).

compensation for the expert's study or testimony; identify facts or data that the party's attorney provided and that the expert considered in forming the opinions to be expressed; or identify assumptions that the party's attorney provided and that the expert relied on in forming the opinions to be expressed."[9]

Rule 26(b)(4)(B) provides work-product protection for "drafts of any report or disclosure required under Rule 26(a)(2), regardless of the form in which the draft is recorded."

Each of these provisions is a relatively new addition to the Federal Rules. They significantly restrict topics that previously had been subject to discovery, principally through depositions of the testifying experts. The Advisory Committee concluded that lawyers were spending too much time, with too little benefit, getting drafts of reports and probing every communication between the attorney and expert. The Committee concluded that lawyers should instead use expert depositions to focus on the experts' opinions and bases underlying them.

Rule 26(b)(4)(D) also governs consulting experts who have been retained or employed to help the lawyer during the litigation process, but who are not expected to be witnesses at trial. Such experts ordinarily cannot be subjected to the discovery process, unless a requesting party can show "exceptional circumstances under which it is impracticable . . . to obtain facts or opinions on the same subject by other means." The rule in effect establishes a qualified privilege for the work of a consulting expert, one akin to that for a lawyer's trial preparation materials. The only exception is Rule 35(b), which makes the reports of a suitably licensed or certified examiner's mental or physical examination of a party discoverable in certain circumstances.[10]

Informally consulted experts — those experts who have not been employed or retained by the lawyer but have provided information — are not governed by the discovery rules. The existence, identity, and opinions of such an expert are not discoverable. Experts with minimal or incidental contact with the lawyer thus cannot be drawn into the discovery process.

5. Privileges

Rule 26(b)(1) excludes privileged matter from discovery.[11] Federal Rules of Evidence 501 and 502 control federal privileges.

What privilege law will apply? Rule 501 provides that federal privileges, as developed by the courts, will ordinarily govern this aspect of discovery. In

---

9. For a summary of additional material that can be discovered from a testifying expert, see Gregory P. Joseph, The Temptation to Depose Every Expert, 40 Litig. 35, 38 (Winter 2014).

10. See §6.10.

11. Hazard et al. §§8.5, 8.7-8.8; Moore's Manual §15.03(6); Manual of Federal Practice §§5.30–5.34; Moore's Federal Practice §§26.90-26.91; Wright & Miller §§2016–2020; T. Mauet & W. Wolfson, Trial Evidence §§8.8–8.14 (5th ed. 2012).

civil cases for which state law "supplies the rule of decision" as to an element of a claim or defense, however, state privileges will apply. In sum, federal privilege law applies in federal civil cases based on federal question jurisdiction, and state privileges rules apply in federal civil cases based on diversity jurisdiction. The forum state's choice-of-law rules determine which state's privileges rules will apply. Where a privilege is based on the U.S. Constitution, such as the Fifth Amendment's self-incrimination clause, it applies regardless of the type of federal case involved.

Next, what is the applicable federal or state privilege law? When the Federal Rules of Evidence were enacted, Congress chose not to codify federal common law privileges, preferring to let federal privileges continue to develop in the courts. Therefore, care must always be taken to research the law of the appropriate jurisdiction, because privilege law can vary.

Both courts and legislatures, in contrast, develop state privileges, although in recent years the trend has been toward codification. State jurisdictions vary widely in their privilege law. While almost all states recognize frequently asserted privileges such as marital, attorney-client, and doctor-patient, they vary substantially in their recognition of others, such as the privilege for accountants, reporter's informants, and governmental secrets. The scope of any privilege and whether it applies in civil or criminal cases also vary significantly. Privileges is an area of evidence law that, when joined with choice of law issues, always requires substantial research.

Finally, what is the proper procedure for asserting a privilege claim? Under Rule 26(b)(5), a party who wishes to withhold discoverable materials based on a claim of privilege must make the claim expressly. Also, the party claiming the privilege must describe the nature of the documents, communications, or things "in a manner that, without revealing information itself privileged or protected, will enable other parties to assess the claim." Failure to comply with the notice requirement may be viewed as a waiver of the privilege.

This collection of descriptions and documents for which a privilege is claimed is commonly called a "privilege log." The documents themselves, of course, must be segregated from other discoverable documents and may later need to be presented to the court for an in camera inspection if the requesting party moves to compel their production.

6. Trial preparation materials

Ever since the Supreme Court decided *Hickman v. Taylor*, 329 U.S. 495 (1947), federal courts have recognized a two-tier privilege rule applicable to an attorney's work product. With some changes and added details, Rule 26(b)(3) codifies this rule.[12]

---

12. Wright §82; Hazard et al. §8.8; Moore's Manual §15.03(7); Manual of Federal Practice §§5.35, 5.175; Moore's Federal Practice §26.70; Wright & Miller §§2021–2028. For an expansive view of the "prepared in anticipation of litigation" requirement, see United States v. Roxworthy, 457 F.3d 590 (6th Cir. 2006).

A privilege protects the attorney's work product, now called "trial preparation materials." Trial preparation materials include "documents and tangible things" that were "prepared in anticipation of litigation or for trial" by another party or that party's "representative." A representative includes not only the lawyer but may include the lawyer's employees and agents, such as an investigator. The party must expressly claim the privilege under Rule 26(b)(5).

For "fact work product," the privilege is qualified. These are trial preparation materials that the party or her representative gathered, but that do not reflect an attorney's mental impressions or opinions. A photograph of the accident scene taken by the lawyer's investigator, for example, is considered fact work product. The rule permits a party seeking discovery to obtain protected documents and tangible things upon a showing of "substantial need" because the party cannot obtain the "substantial equivalent" by other means without "undue hardship." A party invoking this exception cannot show undue hardship simply by arguing added expense or inconvenience. With witness statements, the requesting party must give some demonstrable reason why he cannot get the substantial equivalent of the statement himself before the court will order production.

The work product privilege is absolute for "mental impressions, conclusions, opinions, or legal theories of a party's attorney or other representative concerning the litigation."[13]

§6.3.   Discovery strategy

The discovery rules in the Federal Rules of Civil Procedure are both broad and extensive, and in many cases they permit more discovery than either party will wish to make. Consequently, your overriding concern at the discovery stage is: What will be an effective discovery strategy for this particular case? As outlined previously, discovery planning is essentially a seven-step process.[14]

1.   What facts do I need to establish a winning case on my claims (or to defeat the opponent's claims)?

Remember that under Rule 26(b)(1), the claims and defenses raised in the pleadings determine the scope of relevant discovery. Before starting discovery, review your pleadings and amend them if necessary.

2.   What facts have I already obtained through informal fact investigation?

Your litigation chart should already answer this question.

---

13. Manual of Federal Practice §§5.35, 5.175; Moore's Manual §15.03(7); Moore's Federal Practice §26.70(2)(c); Wright & Miller §2026.
    14. See §4.5.5.

3. What "missing" facts do I still need to obtain through formal discovery?

Discovery is the vehicle you use to force other parties and nonparties to disclose information they have that is relevant to the litigation. Your first question, therefore, should be: What information do I need to know, that I do not already know from my informal investigation and has not been admitted in the pleadings, so that I can properly prepare the case for a possible trial? While the answer will vary with each case, it will usually include most of the following:

1. Identity of proper parties
2. Defendant's ability to pay a judgment (insurance coverage and financial condition)
3. Identity of agents and employees
4. Opponent's factual basis for legal claims
5. Opponent's position on factual issues
6. Identity and location of witnesses
7. Prospective testimony of adverse parties, agents, and employees
8. Prospective testimony of witnesses
9. Identity, opinions, reasoning, and backgrounds of experts
10. Prospective testimony of experts
11. Tangible evidence
12. Documents
13. Records
14. Electronic evidence
15. Statements of parties and witnesses
16. Deposition testimony of favorable witnesses that may become unavailable for trial

Not all of this information is necessarily discoverable. However, you should always compile a similar roster for each case, using your litigation chart, since it will control the information you will try to discover. Think in terms of evidence, not just in terms of information, and think how you can use the formal discovery rules to create evidence that later will be admissible at trial.

4. What discovery methods are most effective for obtaining the "missing" facts?

The Federal Rules provide for six methods of discovery: required disclosures, interrogatories, requests to produce documents, depositions, physical and mental examinations, and requests to admit facts. Although the methods overlap to a certain extent, each one is particularly well suited for certain kinds of information.

Initial disclosures, part of the required disclosures under Rule 26(a)(1), is the automatic discovery method by which parties must disclose, early in the litigation, basic information they have about the case. This information includes the identity of witnesses the party plans to rely upon to support her claims or defenses; copies of documents, electronically stored information, and tangible things that the party presently has that will support her claims or defenses; a computation of damages and the sources of those computations; and insurance agreements that may pay part or all of any judgment.

Interrogatories are most effective for obtaining basic factual data from other parties, such as the identity of proper parties, agents, employees, witnesses, and experts; the identity and location of documents, records, and tangible evidence; and sometimes financial and statistical data. They can helpfully elicit other parties' positions on disputed facts. On the other hand, interrogatories are not usually effective instruments for getting detailed facts, impressions, or versions of events.

A request to produce documents and tangible things is the discovery method by which one obtains from another party copies of records, documents, electronically stored information, and other tangible things for inspection, copying, and testing. Such a request also permits an entry on another person's land or property to inspect, photograph, and analyze things on it. This is the only discovery device that forces another party actually to produce records and things, and to permit entry onto someone else's property to gather evidence. A subpoena to a nonparty witness can obtain the same information.

Depositions are most effective for tying down parties, nonparty witnesses, and experts to details, and for discovering everything deponents know that is pertinent to the case. It is the only discovery vehicle that permits you to assess how good a witness a person is likely to be at trial. It is an excellent vehicle to secure admissions or other evidence favorable to your side. Further, a deposition is the only method to preserve testimony if a witness will become unavailable for trial.

A physical and mental examination of a party can be obtained by court order when the physical or mental condition of that party is in controversy, a situation most common in personal injury cases. While other discovery methods can be used to get records of past examinations, this method is the only means to force a party to be examined and tested contemporaneously with the litigation. For that reason it is the best method for evaluating a party on such damages elements as permanence and extent of injury and medical prognosis.

Finally, a request to admit facts is the method that forces a party to admit or deny facts or a document's genuineness. An admitted fact is deemed conclusively admitted for the purpose of the pending trial. This method is effective if limited to simple factual data, such as someone's employment on a specific date, or the genuineness of signatures on a contract. It is not a good method for dealing with opinions or evaluative information.

There are three more areas where, upon motion and court order, you may obtain additional discovery.

Under Rule 26(b)(1), you may be able to obtain discovery of "any matter relevant to the subject matter involved in the action" if the court orders it "for good cause." This is broader than the scope of discovery by right rule, which permits discovery of any matter "relevant to any party's claim or defense."[15]

Under Rule 26(b)(4)(D), you can obtain discovery of your opponent's consulting expert only on a showing of "exceptional circumstances under which it is impracticable for the party to obtain facts or opinions on the same subject by other means." While this is obviously a difficult standard, the rule contemplates those rare cases where relevant expert information is solely in the possession of one party's expert, such as where a consulting expert has engaged in destructive testing of a product.

Finally, under Rule 26(b)(3), trial preparation materials, which are protected from disclosure by a qualified privilege, can be obtained from an opponent only upon a showing of "substantial need." The party seeking production must also be unable "without undue hardship" to obtain the substantial equivalent of the materials by other means. This exception to the attorney's work-product rule arises most often in regard to non-verbatim memos of witness interviews, which are not usually discoverable. Where one side has interviewed a witness who now refuses to talk to other lawyers, who cannot be subpoenaed, or who has a lapse of memory, and the substantial equivalent of the statement cannot be obtained, the court may order the production of the memorandum.

5.   What facts and witnesses that I already know of through informal investigation do I need to "pin down" by using formal discovery?

There is little point in using formal discovery methods with your favorable witnesses, unless those witnesses are old, sick, or are likely to move away. If this is the case, you will want to take the witness' deposition to preserve the testimony for trial, since the transcript will usually qualify as former testimony.[16]

There is also little point in using formal discovery methods, such as a request to produce coupled with a subpoena, if someone is willing to provide information informally and voluntarily. If a nonparty, for instance, is willing to provide you with documents, you do not need to go through formal channels.

Good reasons exist to depose unfavorable, hostile, or adverse witnesses and parties, however, even if you already know from your informal fact investigation what they will say at trial. First, there are always benefits in learning in detail what those witnesses will say. Second, witnesses may testify inconsistently with their previous statements, or inconsistently with each other. Third, you may be able to limit the witnesses' trial testimony by getting the witnesses to admit to topics they have no firsthand knowledge of, are not sure of, or are only approximating or guessing at.

---

15. As mentioned, a proposed amendment, pending at the time of publication, would eliminate the "relevant to the subject matter" provision.

16. See Rule 32; FRE 804(b)(1).

6.   What restrictions does my litigation budget place on my discovery plan?

Information gathering, especially formal discovery, is expensive, and any discovery strategy must necessarily consider cost. Your litigation budget, which you have already prepared, will have analyzed the amount of time you will allocate to discovery. At this point, however, you should give the discovery portion a second look, for three reasons. First, the pleadings, now completed, may force changes in your discovery strategy. Second, since discovery will usually consume the majority of your pretrial time allotment, it is particularly important to review it. Third, discovery can easily escalate out of control, so staying with your game plan is essential.

Most formal discovery methods are expensive, and responding to discovery, particularly interrogatories and document requests, can take a lot of time and cost a lot of money. Depositions are pricey as well, so cost effectiveness is particularly important for them. Deposition costs include the lawyer's time, witness fees, the court reporter's attendance fees, and transcript costs. Assuming a one-hour deposition, the witness, reporter, and transcript costs will probably exceed $300. A lawyer may need two hours to prepare for the deposition and one hour after the deposition to make a summary of her impressions. Even a short deposition, then, will cost the client at least several hundred dollars.

Deposition costs, therefore, require that you use this discovery method cautiously. You will probably need to depose your adverse party and critical witnesses in every case. However, you can often postpone depositions of experts and rely on expert reports, initial disclosures, interrogatory answers and various records for settlement purposes, then depose your adversary's experts only when a trial becomes a realistic possibility. With some experts, such as the plaintiff's medical expert in a personal injury case, you may not always need to depose the witness if his written report sufficiently details his opinions, bases for the opinions, supporting records, and other background information. Similarly, consider moving for a physical examination of the opposing party only when a trial becomes likely. Also, use investigators to interview nonparty witnesses who are not central to the case. You can often get the essence of a witness's testimony without a deposition, and you must always balance the additional benefit of depositions with their cost in all cases where litigation costs are a concern.

Example:

> Consider a typical automobile accident case, in which you represent the plaintiff. You previously estimated the value of plaintiff's case at $90,000, of which you will earn about $30,000 if the case succeeds. You have made various estimates of time requirements, and have allocated 60 hours to preparing and responding to discovery. How do you estimate how much time you should plan spending on the various discovery methods?

Start by breaking down formal discovery into its component parts to consider what discovery is essential. First, you will need to confer with your opposing counsel to develop a proposed discovery plan, attend a pretrial conference with the judge, and prepare initial disclosures required under Rule 26(a)(1). You estimate these steps will take five hours.

Second, you will need to submit interrogatories to the defendant and answer the defendant's interrogatories. In automobile cases involving only negligence claims, many jurisdictions use standard interrogatories. Sending interrogatories to the defendant, answering the defendant's, and reviewing the defendant's answers for sufficiency will probably take only a few hours, particularly if you have done your informal fact investigation before filing suit. You estimate interrogatories will take five hours.

Third, you will need to depose the critical witnesses. These will include the parties and occurrence witnesses. You will need to depose the defendant and one bystander, and to prepare your plaintiff for deposition, since the defendant will certainly depose him. In a simple automobile case, the plaintiff's deposition will probably take two or three hours, and the defendant's and the bystander's will perhaps take one hour each. Preparation for each deposition will probably take at least as long as the deposition itself. In addition, you will need to prepare a summary of each deposition immediately afterward and review the transcript of the plaintiff's testimony for accuracy. Accordingly, you estimate that these depositions will take approximately 20 hours.

Fourth, you will need to send requests to produce documents to the defendant and nonparties, and answer the defendant's production requests. You will also need to organize and review all the documents and records you receive. These will include hospital records, physician records, employment records, vehicle repair records, police reports, and insurance reports. You estimate that this work will take 10 hours.

Fifth, the defendant may want to have the plaintiff medically examined, particularly if plaintiff is claiming any permanent physical injuries. You will need to review the information that this examination generates. It is usually disclosed through interrogatory answers and the report of the examining doctor. You estimate that this task will require five hours.

Sixth, the plaintiff and the defendant will probably depose each other's medical experts. The defendant will want to depose the plaintiff's treating physician and the plaintiff will want to depose the defendant's examining physician. Preparing, taking, and summarizing these medical-expert depositions will take substantial time. You estimate this will take 15 hours.

Finally, you may want to send a request to admit facts to the defendant, and you may have to respond to the defendant's. You estimate this will take four hours.

Notice that this time estimate already adds up to over 60 hours, and it does not yet take into account all possible variables. On the positive side, both parties may agree not to depose each other's experts, or the case may settle early. On the negative side, you may need to depose additional witnesses, and you may need to file motions to enforce or protect your discovery rights. The point, however, is to analyze the cost considerations as you develop your discovery strategy, because the two must be consistent with each other.

7.   In what order should I execute my discovery plan?

Formal discovery should be used as a progressive device in which each discovery method functions as a sequential building block. Rule 26(d) requires no particular sequence, except that, before any discovery requests can be made, you must first confer with the opposing lawyer to develop a proposed discovery plan and make the initial disclosures required by Rule 26(a). After this point, the parties can engage in discovery to the extent permitted by the rules, and consistent with the court's scheduling order setting forth the discovery plan. Under Rule 16, the judge may hold a scheduling conference with the parties to decide how to regulate and expedite the case, particularly the discovery phase. Many judges do just this. At the conference, the judge will have the report of the parties on their proposed discovery plan. After the conference, the judge will enter an order that will control the remainder of the litigation. For example, the court may order that any interrogatories and document requests be served within 60 days and answered within 30 days of service; that depositions of nonexperts be completed within six months; and that experts be deposed within nine months. The court will probably set a "discovery cutoff" date, when all discovery must be completed.

The only limitations on discovery should not be confining, and if the facts of the case make the limits imposed by the rules unrealistic, the court has discretion to modify them. In addition, the court has power under Rules 26(c) and 37 to issue orders to compel and impose sanctions for failure to comply with the required disclosure rules and for other abuse of discovery. Finally, under Rule 29 the parties may, and frequently do, stipulate to modify certain discovery procedures without court approval, unless the stipulation would interfere with other court-ordered time limits and schedules. In that event, court approval is necessary.

Because the discovery process is so flexible, the relevant questions are: When should I start discovery? In what order should I proceed?

The initial question can be answered simply. You should start discovery as soon as the rules permit and as soon as practical. If you have done your pre-filing investigation and preparation work, you should be able to begin discovery as soon as you have conferred with your opponent to develop a proposed discovery plan. Although the parties may agree to begin discovery prior to this meeting, or court or local rule may permit it, the meeting may help eliminate some unnecessary discovery and provide a clearer focus for the discovery plan.

The following is a common discovery sequence:

1. discovery planning conference and pretrial scheduling conference
2. required initial disclosures
3. interrogatories
4. requests to produce documents, electronically stored information, and things, and subpoenas
5. depositions of parties and witnesses
6. physical and mental examinations
7. expert disclosures and depositions
8. requests to admit facts
9. pretrial disclosures

This sequence utilizes the building block approach to discovery. Once the initial disclosures are received, you can serve interrogatories and requests to produce on parties and subpoenas on nonparty witnesses in order to obtain the additional information and documents, records, and other evidence identified in the interrogatory answers. After you have received this information you are ready to take depositions of parties, witnesses, and experts. In personal injury cases the physical and mental examinations of parties are ordinarily conducted later in the litigation process, since these examinations usually focus on such issues as permanence of injury, prognosis, and loss of earning capacity. Once these steps have been completed, requests to admit can further pinpoint areas of dispute and eliminate the need to prove uncontested facts at trial.

This sequence, of course, can be and often is modified. Amended, supplemental, or additional pleadings may be filed that will necessarily alter the course of discovery. In addition, changing the usual sequence, by serving more than one discovery device at the same time, might create tactical benefits. Keep in mind that the discovery process educates your opponents as well as yourself. Lawyers sometimes take the deposition of an adverse party early, before interrogatories or notices to produce have been sent out, on the theory that the adverse party will have neither the time nor the inclination to prepare thoroughly by collecting and reviewing all the pertinent records beforehand. Lawyers frequently couple interrogatories requesting the identification of documents with a request to produce the documents identified, and use early requests to admit facts in order to narrow the scope of discovery.

There is no magic formula for deciding on the best sequence for discovery. The specific needs and circumstances of each case should determine the order of discovery. An important point to remember, however, is that discovery should not be used simply because it is available. Each step must have a specific purpose and be part of an overall discovery strategy. In addition to this basic seven-step process, keep two additional considerations in mind.

8.   How can I conduct discovery informally?

The Federal Rules prescribe how discovery should be conducted, and a procedurally safe approach to discovery is to always do it "by the book." However, life doesn't always go by the book, nor does discovery in the litigation world. Litigators usually try to arrange things between themselves informally, as they do throughout the case, and as Rule 29 encourages.

What aspects of discovery can be handled informally? The simple task of scheduling depositions can be. Instead of simply serving notice on your party opponent for his deposition, why not contact the other party's lawyer and try to arrange a mutually agreeable date and time? Doing so will probably avoid any motions to reschedule the deposition, and will usually result in the same courtesy being extended to you in the future. Serve a notice of deposition after you have worked out the arrangement.

You can make informal accommodations for the deposition of non-party deponents, whom you must subpoena and usually depose in the location convenient to that deponent. Serve the subpoena first, then see if the deponent is willing to come to your office. Offering to pay the witness' reasonable, legitimately incurred expenses in coming to your office, rather than following the formal Rule 45 procedures, frequently benefits everyone.[17]

Informal arrangements to work out the mechanics of document production are also common. Why not call the other party's lawyer and work out how, when, where, and in what order each party will produce requested documents and electronic data, along with how they will be copied and who will pay for the charges? Lawyers also commonly reach informal agreements when arranging to depose each other's experts, and they stipulate that they will not seek discovery of communications between experts and attorneys.

There are many other instances when the informal resolution of problems makes sense. The point is the same: Whenever possible, try to work out the mechanics and details of discovery with the other side and with nonparties. Courtesy and reasonableness somehow make the world work better, and discovery is no different.

9.   How can I limit discovery against my party?

As the lawyer for a party, you often have an interest in limiting the discovery of your case, unless your case is so strong that you don't want to limit it, or unless early complete disclosure will force a favorable settlement. There are three basic ways to affect the discovery of information.

First, if your client is a business entity, take immediate steps to control the paperwork and e-mail and other electronic information generated in the business that has any bearing on the litigation. If information is not written down or recorded, it cannot be turned over in response to a request

---

17. See §6.9.1(c).

to produce. Have the business's employees communicate directly to you about the pending litigation rather than to supervisors, since communications may then come within the attorney-client privilege.[18] This advice applies as well to individual clients. Advise them against blog or Facebook posts about the case or the underlying events. Second, again, if your client is a business entity, make sure that employees notify you if anyone tries to interview any of them about the case. Since any statements employees make may be admissions that are admissible against the business employer under FRE 801, you are probably entitled to treat such an employee as a party. This means that no one can interview the employee without your permission, and you can represent the employee at his deposition.[19]

Third, obtain statements from witnesses in a manner that makes them protected work product. Verbatim, signed statements from adverse witnesses are useful, since they can be used to impeach. They may be dangerous, however, when taken from favorable witnesses, and so it is safer to have your investigator — or you yourself — interview the witness. You can then prepare a summary of the witness's information with observations on how strong or weak the witness is, what kind of witness she will make at trial, and how her testimony fits into the theory of the case, along with other pertinent mental impressions. You will then have a useful record of the witness, and one that will probably be protected from disclosure. Even if the other side does obtain the statement through a showing of substantial need, it will not include any verbatim statements usable to impeach. The observations about the witness, however, should be absolutely protected as the lawyer's work product.

Finally, consider ways in which you can protect your testifying expert during the discovery process.[20] Rule 26(a)(2) requires that each party disclose the identity of each expert "it may use at trial to present evidence under Federal Rule of Evidence 702, 703, or 705," and that the expert's report be a "complete statement of all opinions the witness will express and the basis and reasons for them" and the "facts or data considered by the witness in forming them." Under Rule 26(b)(4), however, drafts of reports are not discoverable. Neither are communications between the attorney and expert, except to the extent that these communications relate to compensation, facts or data that the attorney provided and the expert considered, or assumptions the attorney provided and the expert relied on.

How detailed should your disclosures be? While you may frequently want to minimize discovery, remember that the opposing party can always move to compel more detailed information. It is often a sound strategy to

---

18. See Upjohn Co. v. United States, 449 U.S. 383 (1981). *Upjohn* rejected the "control group" test for determining which corporate employees' communications with corporate counsel will be protected by the attorney-client privilege. Any employee who has information necessary for the corporate counsel to evaluate will have those communications to corporate counsel protected by the privilege. See Hazard et al. §8.10. However, state laws on the scope of the attorney-client privilege for corporate employees vary widely. Thorough research of the applicable jurisdiction's law is always necessary. T. Mauet & W. Wolfson, Trial Evidence §8.12 (5th ed. 2012).

19. See §2.5.

20. See §2.6.

provide broad disclosure to other parties, which can provide substantial benefits in the future. First, this strategy can forestall motions to compel full and complete disclosure. Second, it gives you a stronger position from which to resist motions for additional discretionary discovery. Third, providing complete responses puts you in a stronger position if you seek more expert discovery from other parties. Courts quite naturally look at scope-of-discovery issues as a two-way street. Fourth, providing detailed disclosures may sometimes cause your opponent to forgo the expert's deposition before trial.

Finally, maintain a professional relationship with your testifying expert to minimize the danger of disclosing matters that the attorney-client privilege and work-product doctrine otherwise might protect. Allowing your experts to communicate directly with your client is dangerous. Disclosing information to your expert that is work product runs the danger that it may end up being discovered. Indeed, Rule 26(b)(4)(C) exempts from protection against discovery information the lawyer gives the expert to help the expert develop her opinion. But since the expert must have sufficient information in order to evaluate the case and develop opinions, the question becomes how to best convey the necessary information to your expert. The safe approach is to give your expert only those materials that are discoverable by other parties anyway.

§6.4. Discovery planning meeting and pretrial scheduling conference

Before formal discovery can begin, the parties must complete three steps: confer to plan discovery, submit a written report to the court, and attend a pretrial scheduling conference with the judge. Rules 26(f) and 16(b) control here.

1. Law

Rule 26(f) requires that the parties that have appeared in the case confer to discuss the pleadings and the possibility of settlement, and to develop a proposed discovery plan.[21] They must do so "as soon as practicable," and in any event at least 21 days before a scheduling conference is held or a scheduling order due. This is the "meet and confer" requirement. The discovery plan should contain the parties' views on the following topics:

1. changes to and timing of initial disclosures;
2. the subjects of, timing for, and order of other discovery;
3. issues relating to disclosure or discovery of electronically stored information and the forms in which it should be produced;

---

21. Hazard et al. §8.12; Manual of Federal Practice §5.8; Moore's Federal Practice §26.143.

4. issues relating to claims of privilege or protection of trial-preparation materials;
5. whether discovery limits should be modified and imposed; and
6. need for protective orders or pretrial conference orders.

The parties are under an obligation to make good faith efforts to agree on a proposed discovery plan. Within 14 days after the conference, the parties must submit to the court a written report outlining the discovery plan.

As it reads at the time of printing, Rule 16(b) requires that the court enter a scheduling order after receiving the parties' written report of their planning conference. The order shall be issued "as soon as practicable," but in any event within the earlier of 120 days after any defendant has been served with the complaint or 90 days after any defendant has appeared.[22] The usual procedure is for the district judge or a magistrate judge to set a scheduling conference with the parties, then receive the parties' written report at least seven days before the conference. At the scheduling conference, the judge will discuss the case with the lawyers and fashion a sequence and timing for discovery and other matters, such as amending pleadings and scheduling expert disclosures, dispositive motions, pretrial disclosures, and settlement conferences.

2. Practice approach

a. Timing

When should the lawyers hold their discovery planning conference? Rule 26(f) merely provides that it be held "as soon as practicable" and at least 21 days before the pretrial scheduling conference or order. Hence, you need to know which date the judge has or will set for the scheduling conference and work backward from that date.

Most judges will hold the scheduling conference shortly after the defendants have appeared and answered the complaint. At this time, the judge and parties can get a general picture of the case, what is at issue, how "big" the case is, and accordingly what the discovery needs are.

Complications can arise. What happens if not all defendants named in the complaint have been served? What happens if defendants file Rule 12(b) motions? What if defendants bring in third-party defendants? In these situations, the "as soon as practicable" language controls. Since the principal purpose of the parties' planning meeting and the court's scheduling conference is to set a realistic discovery plan, this task cannot be accomplished when the pleadings are still substantially incomplete. Accordingly, most judges will wait until all parties have appeared and answered the complaint. On the other hand, if all but one defendant

---

22. A proposed amendment to Rule 16, pending at the time of publication, would shorten this period to 90 days after service or 60 days after the defendant's appearance. Make sure to check revisions to the Federal Rules to ensure that the information in this text is accurate. See www.uscourts.gov.

have appeared, and the unserved defendant is either not a critical party or may never be served, the judge will probably still set an early scheduling conference date. Every judge has her own preferences; many have standing orders that provide when the conference will be held. Check with the judge's clerk after the case has been assigned if you don't know the judge's practice.

Since you must confer with the other parties to develop a proposed discovery plan, contact the other lawyers after they have appeared in the case. Rule 26(f) holds each party responsible for arranging and participating in the planning conference and "attempting in good faith to agree on the proposed discovery plan." Hence, you must attempt to schedule the conference, even if the other side is uncooperative.

At the conference the parties should discuss amendments to the pleadings, the possibility of settlement, the details of the proposed discovery plan, and other matters, such as the preservation of physical evidence and electronic data from inadvertent or intentional destruction and the need for protective orders for trade secrets and other proprietary or confidential information. Aside from these matters, the conference, whether in person or by telephone, often accomplishes another intended purpose: getting the lawyers to meet in an informal setting. The reality is that if lawyers actually communicate directly, early in the litigation, to discuss their needs and concerns, the litigation process, particularly discovery, will proceed more efficiently and less contentiously.

Agreeing on a proposed discovery plan frequently creates conflict, particularly in larger cases. As a general rule, plaintiffs usually prefer quick and broad discovery, while defendants usually prefer more measured and focused discovery. For example, in a products liability case, the plaintiff will want broad discovery to get at the defendant manufacturer's records, which will detail the design, manufacturing, marketing, and safety history of the product; the defendant will want discovery to target the plaintiff's claimed damages and causation evidence but hope to defer discovery on other issues. After the parties meet, consider writing a letter summarizing what happened at the meeting. Make sure it accurately sets out what was agreed on and where the parties disagree. This letter can later form the basis of the written discovery plan. If another party sends you such a letter, make sure it is accurate and, if not, send a letter identifying the inaccuracies.

Absent the court entering a case management or discovery scheduling order under Rule 16, the parties are generally free to conduct the discovery they want when they want it. However, courts are increasingly willing to enter such orders and limit discovery to successive, focused issues, especially in large, complex cases. For example, the court may direct that the plaintiff designate an expert on causation and submit the expert's report. The expert's deposition will follow, and then the court will schedule a *Daubert* hearing on the admissibility of the expert's opinions. The parties can then pursue discovery directed to the defendant's design and manufacture of the product. Thereafter, discovery can be directed to punitive damages evidence. Be prepared at the pretrial conference to argue for a discovery plan that serves your client's interests.

b.   Written report of proposed discovery plan

Rule 26(f) requires that the parties submit a written report of their conference and proposed discovery plan to the court within 14 days of the conference. This requirement gives the judge at least seven days to review the report before meeting with the parties at the scheduling conference.

The report should itemize the decisions and disagreements of the parties on each of the major components of the litigation process: pleadings, discovery, dispositive motions, settlement, and trial. Keep in mind that the judge may have a standing order on how the written report should be organized and what it should contain.

Example:

[Caption]

REPORT OF PARTIES' PLANNING MEETING

The parties submit the following written report, pursuant to Rule 26(f):

1. Meeting. A meeting was held on June 1, 2013, at the offices of Johnson & Barnes, 100 Main Street, Boise, Idaho. Present were William Johnson, plaintiff's attorney, and Sarah Anton, defendant's attorney. The parties jointly propose to the court the following:

2. Scheduling conference. The parties request a scheduling conference before the entry of a scheduling order.

3. Pleadings. Plaintiff should have until July 1, 2013, to add additional parties and amend pleadings. Defendant should have until August 1, 2013, to add additional parties and amend pleadings.

4. Discovery.
      a. Initial disclosures under Rule 26(a)(1) will be exchanged by June 15, 2013.
      b. Discovery will be needed on the following subjects: plaintiff's and defendant's conduct before, during, and after the collision; plaintiff's medical treatment; plaintiff's future medical needs; plaintiff's present and future lost income; and other claimed damages.
      c. Interrogatories will be limited to 20 by each party to another party, and will be served by July 15, 2013. Responses are due 30 days after service.
      d. Documents requests will be limited to 20 by each party to another party, and will be served by September 15, 2013. Responses are due 30 days after service.
      e. Disclosure or discovery of electronically stored information should be handled in accordance with the proposal attached to this report.

f. The parties have agreed to an order regarding claims of privilege and protection as trial-preparation materials asserted after production. The proposed order is attached to this report.

g. Depositions of non-experts will be limited to 8 by each party, and will be taken by December 1, 2013. Each deposition will be limited to 3 hours, unless extended by agreement of the parties.

h. Written reports from plaintiff's retained experts under Rule 26(a)(2) are due December 15, 2013. Written reports from defendant's retained experts are due January 15, 2014.

i. Depositions of experts will be limited to 2 by each party, and will be taken between December 15, 2013, and February 15, 2014. Each deposition will be limited to 4 hours, unless extended by agreement of the parties.

j. Requests to admit will be limited to 15 by each party to another party, and will be served by March 1, 2014. Responses are due 30 days after service.

k. Supplementation under Rule 26(e) is due by April 1, 2014.

l. Discovery cut-off date is April 1, 2014.

5. Dispositive motions. Dispositive motions will be served and filed by April 15, 2014. Responses are due by May 15, 2014.

6. Settlement. Settlement cannot be evaluated until after the experts' reports have been received. The parties request that the court schedule a conference to discuss settlement after February 15, 2014.

7. Trial.

a. Witness and exhibits lists under Rule 26(b)(3) should be due from plaintiff by May 1, 2014, and from defendant by May 15, 2014.

b. Parties should have 15 days after service of witness and exhibits lists to specify objections under Rule 26(a)(3).

c. The case should be ready for trial by July 1, 2014. The trial is expected to take approximately 4 days.

Respectfully submitted,

_____

William Johnson, attorney
   for plaintiff

_____

Sarah Anton, attorney for
defendant

If the parties cannot agree on certain matters, the written report should state what the disagreements are and the basis for them.

Example:

> 6. Settlement. The parties cannot agree on when a conference to discuss settlement should be held. Plaintiff prefers a conference after initial disclosures have been served. Defendant prefers a date after experts have been deposed.

What happens if one of the parties does not participate in a Rule 26(f) conference? This sometimes happens when a defendant has not meaningfully responded to the lawsuit. The defendant may not defend against the lawsuit, and ultimately a default judgment will be entered. In such a situation, the plaintiff should recite those facts in a written discovery plan and present the plan in a timely fashion. Also, the party's refusal to participate in the planning meeting must be reported to the court, since the failure to meet can subject that party to sanctions under Rule 37(f).

c.   Scheduling conference

Rule 16(b) requires the court only to enter a scheduling order. A scheduling conference is optional, although many judges hold scheduling conferences in all cases or delegate them to magistrate judges. Some judges, however, will not hold a conference if the case appears routine, and if the parties' written report shows no serious disagreements and proposes a reasonable chronology of events. At the conference, the judge will have the parties' written report containing their proposed discovery plan.

Your purpose at the scheduling conference is twofold: convince the judge to accept the agreed parts of the written report and your side of the matters on which the parties disagree. Remember that the judge will have attitudes about how litigation should be handled and about the pace, sequence, and discovery complexity that is appropriate to certain kinds of cases. A diversity personal injury case or simple contract dispute differs from an antitrust or multiparty building construction case. Hence, the judge may routinely ratify the parties' written report without much discussion in routine cases, but go over the report in detail in large or complex cases. The more complicated the case, and the more contentious the parties, the more likely the judge will actively control the litigation, beginning with a Rule 16 scheduling conference. In some districts, cases are divided into routine and complex cases. If routine, the judge may put the case on a "fast track," and schedule discovery so that the parties complete it within a few months.

After the scheduling conference, the judge will enter a scheduling order, which will usually cover the same subjects as the parties' written report. The order controls what discovery will take place and when it will be completed, unless the judge later modifies the order.

Because the scheduling order is so important, make sure you get it right the first time. To succeed in this regard, your conference with other parties to make a discovery plan must be candid and realistic and achieve a compromise between the parties' preferences and the likely attitude of the judge. Lawyers must also "educate the judge" about the unusual circumstances that justify a discovery schedule different from what the judge would expect in this kind of case. Only when there is candid, open communication among the parties and judge will the result be mutually beneficial: a scheduling order that realistically and efficiently regulates the remainder of the litigation process.

§6.5. Required disclosures

Rule 26(a) creates three categories of required disclosures that parties must make without a discovery request: initial disclosures, expert disclosures, and pretrial disclosures. Disclosures are mandatory except in certain types of cases that Rule 26(a)(1)(B) exempts from the initial disclosures requirement.

All disclosures shall be made in writing, signed, and served on all other parties unless the court orders otherwise. The disclosures shall be made at the times provided by Rule 26. The times for initial disclosures can be modified by agreement of the parties or by court order. The times for expert disclosures and pretrial disclosures can be modified only by court order.

1. Initial disclosures

Under Rule 26(a)(1), each party must make initial disclosures to the other side of "core" information involving witnesses, documents, damages, and insurance:[23]

1. "the name and, if known, the address and telephone number of each individual likely to have discoverable information — along with the subjects of that information — that the disclosing party may use to support its claims or defenses, unless the use would be solely for impeachment;"
2. "a copy — or a description by category and location — of, all documents, electronically stored information, and tangible things that the disclosing party has in its possession, custody, or control and may use to support its claims or defenses, unless the use would be solely for impeachment;"
3. "a computation of each category of damages claimed by the disclosing party — who must also make available for inspection and copying as under Rule 34 the documents or other evidentiary material, unless privileged or protected from disclosure, on which each computation is based, including materials bearing on the nature and extent of injuries suffered; and"
4. "for inspection and copying as under Rule 34, any insurance agreement under which an insurance business may be liable to satisfy part or all of a possible judgment in the action or to indemnify or reimburse for payments made to satisfy the judgment."

23. See Wright §83A; Hazard et al. §8.11; Moore's Federal Practice §§26.22.

A party must make the disclosures based on the information "then reasonably available to it" and cannot fail to make disclosures because its investigation of the case is not complete or it is challenging the adequacy of the other party's disclosure. A party is under a duty to supplement and correct disclosures if it learns that the disclosure was in "some material respect incomplete or incorrect."

Rule 26(a) and (f) control the timing of the initial disclosures. The parties must confer to develop a discovery plan "as soon as practicable" and at least 21 days before the pretrial conference. No discovery can be done until after this conference. Initial disclosures are due within 14 days of the parties' conference, unless the parties stipulate or a court order provides otherwise.

Initial disclosures have three basic features. First, this discovery is automatic. It requires no triggering request or action from the other parties, and it will occur sooner than other discovery. Second, initial disclosures should partially replace what once were the first sets of interrogatories and document requests that invariably sought the same basic information. Third, under Rule 26(a)(1)(A), initial disclosures require the production of only those documents the disclosing party "may use to support its claims or defenses." To obtain the documents that *hurt* the disclosing party, you must serve a Rule 34 request on that party.

Since initial disclosures are automatic, they are a departure from traditional discovery, which required a party to produce information only when served with a specific request. Initial disclosures change how lawyers litigate. First, because Rule 26(a)(1)(A) requires the disclosure of "discoverable information . . . that the disclosing party may use to support its claims and defenses, unless the use would be solely for impeachment," the specificity of the allegations in the pleadings may influence the scope of the initial disclosures. Lawyers may make their complaints and answers more fact-specific as a result, even if not required to do so by the pleading rules. Second, lawyers may more frequently move for a more definite statement under Rule 12(e) to identify what the case is about and hence what is required to be disclosed in the initial disclosures. Third, Rule 26(a) requires a party to make initial disclosures "based on the information then reasonably available to it" and cannot avoid making disclosures because it has not completed its investigation of the case.

Finally, keep in mind that a party has a duty to supplement its disclosures. Rule 26(e) requires supplementation "in a timely manner if the party learns that in some material respect the disclosure or response is incomplete or incorrect, and if the additional or corrective information has not otherwise been made known to the other parties during the discovery process or in writing." The sanctions for violating Rule 26 are severe. Rule 37(c) requires the court to exclude from trial a witness or information not listed or produced in the initial disclosures, unless the failure to disclose was "substantially justified or is harmless."

2.   Expert disclosures

Under Rule 26(a)(2), each party must also make expert disclosures. The disclosure includes the "identity of any witness it may use at trial to present evidence under Federal Rule of Evidence 702, 703, or 705." Also required is disclosure of a written signed report of a witness who is "retained or specially employed to provide expert testimony in the case, or one whose duties as the party's employee regularly involve giving expert testimony." The report must contain a "complete statement" of all opinions and bases; the "facts or data considered" to reach the opinions; summary exhibits; witness qualifications; all publications within 10 years; compensation; and names of other cases in which the witness has testified at trial or deposition within four years. Rule 26(e) requires supplementation "in a timely manner" if the disclosure is in some material respect incomplete or incorrect and the other parties were not made aware of it.

Expert disclosures are due at least 90 days before trial, or 30 days after the other party's disclosure if the expert is solely a rebuttal witness, unless the court directs or the parties stipulate otherwise. The expert disclosures deadline is set at the Rule 16 scheduling conference.

Expert witness discovery is broad. Rule 26(a)(2) requires a "complete statement" of all opinions and bases for the opinions, the facts or data relied on, and the background of the expert. Rule 26(b)(4) provides for depositions of testifying experts as of right. However, keep in mind the 2010 amendments to the expert witness discovery rules that limit disclosure of certain things. Rule 26(b)(4)(C) gives work-product protection to the expert's drafts of his report and to communications between the attorney and expert (except for communications that relate to compensation, facts or data the attorney provided, and assumptions the attorney provided). Keep in mind that courts are not in agreement on whether the identity of non-testifying experts is discoverable.[24]

Note that an "expert" is someone who will give testimony under FRE 702, 703, and 705. Rules 701 and 702 make it clear that all testifying experts, regardless of what forms their testimony take, must be qualified under Rule 702.

3.   Pretrial disclosures

Under Rule 26(a)(3) each party must make pretrial disclosures in the following categories of evidence:

1.   witnesses who are expected to testify at trial
2.   witnesses who may be called "if the need arises"
3.   witnesses who are expected to be presented through depositions (and a transcript of pertinent portions of the testimony)
4.   each exhibit expected to be offered at trial
5.   each exhibit that may be offered "if the need arises"

---

24. See, e.g., Wright & Miller §2032.

Pretrial disclosures are due at least 30 days before trial unless the court directs otherwise. Objections to depositions and exhibits must be made within 14 days after the disclosures are made. Failure to object will be deemed a waiver of all objections except relevance.

Witnesses and exhibits expected to be called and offered at trial include rebuttal witnesses and exhibits. However, the rule specifically excludes evidence that will be used "solely for impeachment."

These pretrial disclosures are usually made as part of the more comprehensive joint pretrial memorandum. This is discussed in §8.2.

4. Practice approach to initial disclosures

A lawyer preparing initial disclosures should ask three questions: When must I serve initial disclosures on the other parties? What must I disclose? How should I organize and draft my initial disclosures?

a. Timing

Under Rule 26(f), the parties must confer to develop a discovery plan as soon as practicable, and in any event at least 21 days before the court holds a scheduling conference under Rule 16. The parties must submit a written report outlining their discovery plan within 14 days after they confer.

The logical time to have this conference is shortly after the defendant has answered the complaint or, if the answer contains counterclaims, cross-claims, or third-party complaints, when the plaintiff has replied or other parties have answered. At this time, the claims and defenses will be reasonably clear, and the parties should be able to confer and develop a realistic discovery plan and schedule they can present to the court. The court may, of course, schedule an early pretrial conference, and that will trigger the due dates of the lawyers' conference and submission of the discovery plan.

b. Drafting the initial disclosures

Drafting initial disclosures requires that you make disclosures based on the information "then reasonably available," as Rule 26(a)(1) provides. The rule also states that a party cannot avoid disclosures because it has not yet "fully investigated the case or because it challenges the sufficiency of another party's disclosures or because another party has not made its disclosures." A party must disclose the core evidence it may use to support the claims and defenses raised in its own pleading.

Keep in mind that a threadbare disclosure will probably result in motions to compel as well as follow-up interrogatories and document requests. Moreover, Rule 26(e) requires supplementation of initial disclosures "in a timely manner" when the party learns that its disclosures "in some material respect" are "incomplete or incorrect," and the additional and corrective information has not been made known to the other parties.

Draft the initial disclosures carefully and completely the first time. Doing so sends a message to the opposing party that you have done your homework, understand the issues and the facts, and are fully prepared to litigate. This message is important to send early in the litigation process.

i.   Heading

An initial disclosure, like any court document, must contain a caption showing the court, parties, and civil case number. It should contain a heading that identifies which party is making the initial disclosure.

Example:

[Caption]

PLAINTIFF'S INITIAL DISCLOSURES

Plaintiff Johnson makes the following initial disclosures pursuant to Rule 26(a)(1) of the Federal Rules of Civil Procedure:

ii.   Content

Rule 26(a)(1) requires the disclosure of four categories of information. Drafting the actual information is simply a matter of carefully following the rule so that you provide what is required.

(1) *Witnesses.* The first category includes the name and, if known, the address and telephone number of each individual "likely to have discoverable information that the disclosing party may use to support its claims or defenses, unless the use would be solely for impeachment." The disclosure must also identify "the subjects of that information."

Example:

A. The following individuals are likely to have discoverable information that the plaintiff may use to support its claims:

1.   William Dawes (occurrence witness)
     483 Bright Street
     Wilmington, NC
     677-4123
2.   Ellen Johnson (occurrence witness) address and telephone unknown
3.   Mary Wilson, RN (nurse at emergency room)
     Mercy General Hospital
     Wilmington, NC
     447-7000

(2) *Documents.* The second category of disclosures that Rule 26(a)(1)(A) provides for includes "a copy—or a description by category and location—of all documents, electronically stored information, and tangible things that the disclosing party has in its possession, custody, or control and may use to support its claims or defenses, unless the use would be solely for impeachment." While an itemized list of each document and all electronically stored information (ESI) is not required, enough of a description is necessary to enable the other parties to make informed decisions about which materials they want to inspect, and to thereby request the identified materials. An adequate description of the documents and ESI should probably include the type of document and ESI, its date, and the general subject matter of its contents. The disclosing party can always decide to provide actual copies of the documents and ESI with the initial disclosure.

Example:

The following records, electronically stored information, and tangible things are in the possession, custody, or control of the plaintiff and may be used to support the plaintiff's claims:

1. 2013 Honda Civic automobile, presently in possession of plaintiff at plaintiff's residence.
2. Mercy Hospital medical records, in the possession of both Mercy Hospital and plaintiff's attorney (electronic copy attached).
3. Wilmington Police Department accident report, in the possession of both the Wilmington Police Department and plaintiff's attorney (hard copy attached).

(3) *Damages.* The third category is a computation of any category of damages, making available for inspection and copying the documents on which the damages are computed. The disclosing party can always decide to provide copies of the documents with the initial disclosure.

Example:

Plaintiff's present damages are as follows and are based on the following records, which are in the possession of plaintiff's attorney and can be inspected and copied at any mutually convenient time:

1.	hospital expenses (Mercy Hospital)	$2,498.71
2.	doctor's expenses (Dr. Albert Rosen)	3,433.80
3.	drugs (Walgreen's Pharmacy)	126.00
4.	vehicle repair (Dobbs Honda)	2,135.00
5.	rental vehicle (Hertz Car Rental)	288.39
6.	lost wages (Macy's)	3,122.00
7.	past pain & suffering	50,000.00
8.	future pain & suffering	30,000.00

(4) *Insurance.* The fourth category is any insurance agreements that may be liable for all or part of any judgment. The disclosing party should make these agreements available for inspection and copying. The disclosing party can always decide to provide copies of the agreements with the initial disclosure.

Example:

> Defendant was insured under a general casualty insurance policy issued by Allstate Insurance, Policy No. 4522147. A copy of the policy is attached.

iii. Signing and serving

The party's lawyer must sign the initial disclosures and serve them on every other party. Service is made by any permitted method under Rule 5, most commonly by mailing a copy to the lawyers for the other parties. However, under Rule 5(d) initial disclosures are not filed with the court until they are used in the proceeding or the court orders filing.

Note that under Rule 26(g), signing a disclosure (and, for that matter, every discovery request, response, or objection) constitutes a certification that "to the best of the person's knowledge, information, and belief formed after reasonable inquiry" the disclosure "is complete and correct as of the time it is made." If you cannot in good faith certify that the disclosure is complete and correct, consider certifying what specific steps you have taken to achieve complete and correct disclosure.

c. *Effect of initial disclosures*

Initial disclosures affect how litigation proceeds in the federal courts. First, initial disclosures have partially replaced the boilerplate interrogatories and document requests that customarily sought the basic information of which Rule 26(a)(1) now requires automatic disclosure. This basic information will be available early in the discovery period. Accordingly, interrogatories and document requests can be used as supplemental methods to get missing information and to pin down the other party to specific facts and positions. Second, since Rule 26(a)(1)(A) refers to "discoverable information — along with the subjects of the information — that the disclosing party may use to support its claims or defenses," parties will draft their pleadings with more factual detail, since the claims and defenses control the scope of the initial disclosures. Third, since the rules contain limits on the number of depositions and interrogatories, parties are more likely to move to compel more complete responses to the initial disclosures before pursuing the information through other discovery methods. Fourth, parties may be able to depose witnesses and parties sooner, if the initial disclosures have provided an adequate factual and documentary setting. Finally, initial disclosures may result in more motions for sanctions and other relief for failing to make adequate timely disclosure of required information. Lawyers will undoubtedly ask that witnesses and exhibits be precluded from trial if they were not properly and timely disclosed.

5.   Practice approach to expert disclosures

A lawyer preparing expert disclosures should ask three basic questions: When must I make the disclosures? What must I disclose? How should I organize and draft the disclosures?

a.   Timing

Under Rule 26(a)(2), expert disclosures are due at least 90 days before trial, or 30 days after the other party's disclosure if the expert is solely a rebuttal witness, unless the court directs otherwise. The court may have entered a pretrial order under Rule 16 establishing shorter time limits for the expert disclosures.

b.   Topics

Under Rule 26(a)(2), each party must disclose "the identity of any witness it may use at trial to present evidence" under FRE 702, 703, or 705. It also requires a written signed report for a witness who is "retained or specially employed to provide expert testimony," or "whose duties as the party's employee regularly involve giving expert testimony." The latter category includes witnesses like design engineers for manufacturers and research chemists for pharmaceutical companies. The written report must contain:

1. a complete statement of all opinions to be expressed and the basis and reasons for them;
2. facts or other data considered by the witness in forming the opinions;
3. any exhibits to be used as a summary of or support for the opinions;
4. the qualifications of the witness, including a list of all publications authored by the witness within the preceding 10 years;
5. the compensation to be paid for the study and testimony;
6. a listing of any other cases in which the witness has testified as an expert at trial or by deposition within the preceding four years.

An expert witness can be deposed as of right under Rule 26(b)(4), but only after the expert has first provided his required written report.

c.   Drafting the expert disclosure

Drafting the expert disclosure is just a matter of following the language of the rule and making sure that you provide all the required information.

i.   Heading

The expert disclosure must contain a caption showing the court, parties, and civil case number. It should contain a heading that identifies which party is making the expert disclosure.

Example:

[Caption]

PLAINTIFF'S DISCLOSURE OF EXPERT TESTIMONY

Plaintiff Johnson makes the following disclosure of expert testimony pursuant to Rule 26(a)(2). The following experts are expected to testify on behalf of the plaintiff at trial:

ii.   Content

The required disclosure is best made by tracking the requirements of the rule.

Example:

1. Emily Lieberman, M.D.
   a. Dr. Lieberman's opinions, the bases for her opinions, and the data and information she considered to reach her opinions are contained in her signed written report dated June 1, 2013, a copy of which is attached.
   b. Dr. Lieberman will use no summary exhibits during her testimony.
   c. Dr. Lieberman's professional qualifications, including her publications within the last 10 years, are contained on her current curriculum vitae, a copy of which is attached.
   d. Dr. Lieberman is being compensated for her study and testimony at the rate of $300 per hour.
   e. Dr. Lieberman has testified as an expert at trial or deposition a total of 6 times within the last 4 years. A list of those 6 cases is attached.

iii.   Expert report

Rule 26(a)(2) requires disclosure of a signed written report from an expert who "is one retained or specially employed to provide expert testimony in the case." The report must include a "complete statement of all opinions the witness will express and the basis and reasons for them." How do you get such a report from the expert that meets the requirements of the rule?

It goes without saying that the report should be prepared and written by the expert, who must sign it and who is responsible for its content. On the other hand, the expert needs to know the requirements of the rule and the topics on which the expert will be asked to give opinions. The usual practice is for the lawyer and expert to meet to discuss the issues. The lawyer explains the issues on which he seeks expert opinions and what the rules require of the report. Sometimes the lawyer may ask the expert to assume certain facts as true and provide a factual summary with, preferably, the underlying source of the facts. The expert later drafts a written report of her evaluation of the issues and her opinions and the reasons for them. She then submits the report to the lawyer.

How the expert's report looks when complete varies according to the circumstances, but most are organized along the following lines:

Example:

EXPERT REPORT

by

Mary G. Smith, M.D.

Case: Williams v. Johnson
          No. 13 C 1287

1. Introduction
          I have been retained as an expert by counsel for the plaintiff in the above-captioned litigation.
          I have been asked to express opinions on . . .
          I am being compensated for my time spent studying this matter and any time spent testifying at the rate of $300 per hour.
2. Professional qualifications
          I am a medical doctor and have been licensed to practice medicine since 1990 . . .
          Attached is a curriculum vitae detailing my professional background.
3. Matters considered
          As part of my review I have requested, received, and reviewed the following materials:
          I have also conducted an examination of the plaintiff . . .
          I have ordered and received the following tests . . .
4. Factual background
          On June 1, 2013, . . .
5. Opinions
          I have reached the following opinions:
6. Bases for the opinions
          My opinions are based on the following:
7. Conclusion
          For the foregoing reasons . . .

Date: _____   _____
                                                        Mary G. Smith, M.D.

Keep in mind that drafts of the expert's report qualify as protected work product under Rule 26(b)(4). In addition, communications between the expert and the attorney who retained him are also protected (except for communications that relate to the expert's compensation, facts or data that the attorney provided and the expert considered, and assumptions the attorney provided and the expert relied on).[25]

d.   Effect of expert disclosure

Rule 26(a)(2), which controls expert disclosure, and Rule 26(b)(4), which permits expert depositions as of right, have substantially changed discovery practice directed to experts. First, expert discovery is often likely to be earlier, because expert disclosure is required at least 90 days before trial. This rule reduces the expert disclosure delaying games some lawyers played as the case moved closer to trial, with no disclosure until just before trial. However, expert disclosure may also come later, since no expert discovery is required until 90 days before trial. Most lawyers ask the court to accelerate the expert disclosure dates during the Rule 16 scheduling conference. Second, pre-deposition discovery of experts is significantly expanded and now requires a "complete statement" of the expert's opinions, basis, and data, as well as her complete biographical picture. Since expert disclosure must be made before the expert can be deposed, motion practice may address the completeness of the disclosed information. Third, not taking an expert's deposition may be a realistic option in some cases, saving the lawyers time and the client's money. For example, the defense may not always need to take the deposition of plaintiff's emergency room treating physician if expert disclosure is complete and the emergency room records have been obtained. The defense may forgo this discovery particularly since the party taking the deposition of an adversary's expert is required to reimburse the expert "a reasonable fee for time spent in responding to discovery." Even when the expert is deposed, the actual deposition may be significantly shorter because of the required expert disclosure.

6.   Practice approach to pretrial disclosures

Pretrial disclosures, governed by Rule 26(a)(3), are discussed in §8.2.

§6.6.   Interrogatories

The second step in the discovery process frequently involves interrogatories. They provide the best method for getting basic facts about the other side's case not already obtained from the other party's initial disclosures. In states that do not have initial disclosures, interrogatories are usually the

---

25. See Wright & Miller §2016.5.

first discovery method employed. Further discovery can develop the information received in the interrogatory answers.

1. Law

Although Rule 33 governs interrogatories, local rules often supplement it.[26] Some districts have approved pattern interrogatories for common cases, such as automobile personal injury suits. Hence, you should always check the local rules for the particular jurisdiction.

Interrogatories may be used to learn basic facts, identify witnesses and experts, and identify documents and other tangible things. They can obtain information that comes within the scope of discovery set by Rule 26(b). Interrogatories can ask for "an opinion or contention that relates to fact or the application of law to fact." The line between what is "opinion" and what is a question of "pure law" is admittedly imprecise and has generated substantial litigation.[27] Because such issues usually become either clearer or moot as discovery progresses, the court may order that such interrogatories remain unanswered until a later time.

Any party can propound interrogatories to any other party at any time after the parties have conferred to develop a Rule 26(f) discovery plan. In practice, interrogatories are frequently served after a review of the other party's initial disclosures.

Before initial disclosures were added to the Federal Rules, parties often used boilerplate pattern interrogatories to ask for basic information from their adversaries. Now, interrogatories in federal court are used in a more nuanced way. They seek information that the initial disclosures do not reveal, or attempt to clarify what the initial disclosures do reveal.

Any party can serve on any other party interrogatories "not exceeding 25 in number including all discrete subparts," unless the parties stipulate in writing or the court orders otherwise. The parties can ask for leave of court to serve more interrogatories. The question of whether an interrogatory is a single interrogatory or whether it is a compound interrogatory that attempts to get around interrogatory limits frequently arises.[28] The Committee Notes to Rule 33 provide that an interrogatory that requests information about discrete separate subjects counts as more than one interrogatory. On the other hand, an interrogatory that seeks information about one subject, but asks that information about the subject be broken down into categories, does count as a single interrogatory. As always, you need to know how your judge will count interrogatories, since her approach may affect how you draft them.

The answering party must state objections to interrogatories and answer any part of an interrogatory to which there is no objection.

---

26. Wright §86; Hazard et al. §8.17; Moore's Manual §15.09; Shepard's Manual §§5.10, 5.126–5.144; Moore's Federal Practice §33; Wright & Miller §§2161–2182.

27. Moore's Manual §15.09; Shepard's Manual §5.137; Moore's Federal Practice §33.17; Wright & Miller §2167.

28. See Wright & Miller §2168.1.

Objections must be stated "with specificity," and grounds not stated in a timely objection will generally be deemed waived. Boilerplate objections to interrogatories, as with boilerplate objections to all discovery, can subject the lawyer to sanctions under Rule 26(g).

Answers are due within 30 days of service of the interrogatories, unless either a court order or a written stipulation between the parties sets a different time. The answer must respond to each interrogatory separately with either an answer or an objection. An answer must be a "full" answer that fairly meets the substance of the interrogatory. The answering party has an obligation to find the information if it is within the party's possession, even if not within the personal knowledge of the actual person answering.[29]

Under Rule 33(d) the answering party may specify business records and electronically stored information (ESI) from which an answer may be derived or ascertained, instead of giving a direct answer, if the "burden of deriving or ascertaining the answer will be substantially the same for either party." Where this is the case, the answer need only specify the records and ESI in sufficient detail to allow the requesting party to locate and identify the records and ESI and to give the requesting party a reasonable opportunity to inspect and copy them.

The party responding to an interrogatory must sign the answer under oath. If a lawyer objects to any interrogatories, she must sign as well.

Finally, an answering party has a continuing obligation to supplement certain answers "in a timely manner." Rule 26(e) requires supplementation of responses, even though complete when made, if "the party learns that in some material respect the disclosure or response is incomplete or incorrect and if the additional or corrective information has not otherwise been made known to the other parties during the discovery process or in writing." Hence, unless the other parties have obtained the corrective information through other discovery or have been provided with that information in writing, the answering party must amend its answers within a reasonable time. Failing to do so will, on motion, subject the answering party to Rule 37 sanctions.

2. Practice approach

A lawyer preparing to propound interrogatories to another party must ask three basic questions: When should I send out interrogatories? What kind of information should I seek? How should I organize and draft interrogatories to get the desired information?

a. Timing

Interrogatories can be served on any other party once the parties have had the Rule 26(f) discovery planning conference. However, the better

---

29. Moore's Manual §15.25; Moore's Federal Practice §§33.101-33.102; Wright & Miller §2177.

approach is to wait until you have received the other party's initial disclosures and attended the Rule 16 pretrial conference. This wait will give you an opportunity to review the other party's initial disclosures and learn how the judge intends to schedule and regulate the discovery process in this case. Your interrogatories can be more focused, an important consideration since Rule 33 limits each party to 25 interrogatories without leave of court or its adversary's written stipulation.

In state courts that do not use initial disclosures, parties commonly send out interrogatories as soon as the initial pleadings have been made. For example, plaintiffs usually serve interrogatories on the defendant shortly after the defendant has answered the complaint; defendants frequently serve interrogatories on the plaintiff with their initial response to the complaint (an answer or a Rule 12 motion).

Sending interrogatories out quickly accomplishes two important things. First, the discovery process gets started, which is particularly important since the use of the other discovery methods often depends on the interrogatory answers. With court-imposed discovery cutoff dates increasingly a part of the litigation process, efficiency is important. Second, other parties learn that you intend to litigate actively, an important message to send to your adversaries early on.

b. Topics

Before drafting the interrogatories, ask yourself: What information do I want now so that I can use subsequent discovery methods to develop the information more fully? If you have thought through your discovery strategy,[30] you should know what information you need that you can readily obtain through interrogatories. If you have not gathered the following information through initial disclosures, you should seek it in interrogatories.

i.   Identity of parties, agents, and employees

You may not know the proper formal names of parties, parent corporations, or subsidiaries; where they are incorporated or licensed to do business; or the type of legal entities they are or their relationships to other parties. This is especially so in commercial litigation. You need to know this information for a variety of purposes that have to do with jurisdictional and joinder issues, for instance. You will also need to learn the identity of all agents and employees and their relationships to the party. Interrogatories are the best method for getting this information.

---

30. See §6.3.

ii.   Identity of witnesses

Almost every lawsuit will have witnesses to the events and transactions on which the parties base their claims. Interrogatories are a good method for obtaining the witnesses' identities, locations, and relationships to the parties.

iii.   Identity of documents and tangible things

Similarly, almost every lawsuit will have certain documents, records, and other tangible things on which the claims are based, or that are relevant to the claims. Interrogatories are the best method for identifying and locating these, for determining who has custody or control of them, and for determining if they are in paper or electronic form.

iv.   Identity of testifying experts, opinions, bases, and background

Under Rule 26(a)(2), the expert disclosure rule, the other parties must disclose the identity and written reports of their testifying experts. The reports must contain a "complete statement" of all the experts' opinions, bases and supporting data for the opinions, and information about the experts' professional backgrounds. In state courts not recognizing initial disclosures, interrogatories will be the usual method to obtain much of this information.

Keep in mind, however, that Rule 26 only requires expert disclosures 90 days before the trial date, and the court will probably have entered a pretrial order under Rule 16 that controls when the parties must make expert disclosures. At this early stage in the litigation process, the parties may not yet have selected the experts who will ultimately be the testifying experts at trial. If you seek this information through interrogatories, the response will frequently be "not yet known." Nevertheless, many lawyers ask for expert disclosure early, to make an early record of the request. Keep in mind that Rule 26(e) requires that a party amend a discovery answer "in a timely manner" if the party learns it is incomplete or incorrect and the requesting party has not been provided with the additional or corrective information during the discovery process or in writing. Some lawyers, however, ask for expert information in a later interrogatory, after a substantial amount of discovery, with the idea that a useful answer is more likely to be forthcoming at this time.

v.   Details and sequences of events and transactions

Interrogatories are a useful method for obtaining concrete facts underlying vague or generalized claims. For this reason they are particularly useful in commercial litigation, where lawsuits frequently arise from a series of events and transactions spread out over time that are not detailed in the pleadings.

vi.　Technical and statistical data

Interrogatories are a good method to identify and obtain technical and statistical data, such as financial statements, accounting information, and sales figures.

vii.　Damages information and insurance coverage

The plaintiff's complaint will often contain only a general request for damages "in excess of $75,000," the minimum jurisdictional amount in diversity cases. Damages interrogatories to the plaintiff are useful for drawing out the specific legal theories of recovery the plaintiff is asserting, the dollar amount claimed for each type of damages, and the basis for each claim.

Since it is vitally important for a plaintiff to determine the defendant's ability to pay a judgment, a standard interrogatory should ask about insurance policies that may cover the event or transactions on which the lawsuit is based, and for the details of the coverage. Rule 26(b)(2) makes this information discoverable. If the pleadings make the defendant's financial condition relevant by alleging a punitive damages claim, for instance, this information should also be requested. The defendant, however, will usually object to any discovery of its financial condition or ask that such discovery be stayed until the court has heard and ruled on a summary judgment motion attacking the punitive damages claim. If you suspect that the defendant's insurer may be defending under a reservation of rights, you should try to obtain this information through an interrogatory because this fact will influence how you and the defense conduct the litigation.

viii.　Identity of persons who prepared answers and of sources used

Where interrogatories are served on a corporate party, they should ask for the identity of each person who participated in preparing the answers, and ask for the identity of the documents used to prepare each answer. This information will be important in deciding whom to depose and what documents to request.

ix.　Positions on issues, opinions of fact, and contentions

Interrogatories that ask for an "opinion," a "contention that relates to facts," or the "application of law to fact" are proper. On the other hand, interrogatories that ask for matters of "pure law" are objectionable. The dividing line is unclear, and discovery motions often deal with this problem.[31] Where a pleading is vague, however, a proper interrogatory can help. For example, a defendant in a negligence action can properly ask what specific conduct the plaintiff claims constituted the negligence. Likewise, in a contract action the defendant can ask what conduct the plaintiff claims constituted a breach. Contention interrogatories also have the practical effect of forcing the opposing party to focus on its evidence and strategy.

The court has the power under Rule 33(a) to postpone answers to such interrogatories. Accordingly, many lawyers avoid these requests in initial interrogatories, since they may trigger objections and delay answers to the more basic interrogatories.

Interrogatories, while important, are frequently overused. They take time to prepare and answer but often produce little information. Therefore, interrogatories should often be used selectively — to target the "missing gaps" in the opposing party's initial disclosures, or to pin down the opposing party on specific facts that may be used at trial for impeachment if the party that signed the interrogatory testifies inconsistently at trial.

c.   Drafting the interrogatories

The drafting lawyer's principal task is to prepare a set of interrogatories that will successfully elicit the desired information. The questions must be drafted so as to force the answering party to respond to them squarely and to eliminate the possibility of evasive, though superficially responsive, answers. Always ask yourself: If I received this interrogatory, could I avoid giving a meaningful answer because of the interrogatory's wording? If so, redraft the interrogatory. Also, the questions must be organized sequentially to make sure that they cover all desired topics. Firms frequently store basic interrogatories for recurrent types of actions in databases, making these interrogatories easy to modify for a specific case. In addition, many jurisdictions have approved pattern or uniform interrogatories that, if appropriate for the case, should be submitted verbatim to the other side. Finally, make sure you do not exceed or violate the requirement that interrogatories served on any party not exceed "25 written interrogatories, including all discrete subparts."

i.   Headings

An interrogatory, like any court document, must contain a caption showing the court, parties, and civil case number. Further, the interrogatories should include a heading that identifies which party is submitting the interrogatories to which other party. It is also a good practice to label

---

31. Moore's Manual §15.25; Manual of Federal Practice §5.137; Moore's Federal Practice §§33.70-33.79, 33.173; Wright & Miller §2167.

them "First Set," "Second Set," and so on, and to number them sequentially with a later set picking up where the previous set left off. This practice avoids confusion when references are later made to interrogatories and answers.

Example:

[Caption]

PLAINTIFF JOHNSON'S INTERROGATORIES TO DEFENDANT ACME CORPORATION

(First Set)

Plaintiff Johnson requests that defendant Acme Corporation, through an officer or authorized agent of the corporation, answer the following interrogatories under oath and serve them upon plaintiff within 30 days, pursuant to Rule 33 of the Federal Rules of Civil Procedure:

1. . . .
2. . . .
3. . . .

Example:

[Caption]

PLAINTIFF JOHNSON'S INTERROGATORIES TO DEFENDANT ACME CORPORATION

(Second Set)

Plaintiff Johnson requests that. . . .

15. . . .
16. . . .
17. . . .

Consider using headings for related sections of the interrogatories, such as "parties," "collision," "medical history," "contract," and "damages," particularly in more complex cases. These make the interrogatories easier to understand and answer.

ii.   Definitions and instructions

A common practice in more complex interrogatories is to have the actual interrogatories preceded by a definitions and instructions section. Terms used repeatedly in the interrogatories can be defined, making the interrogatories easier to follow while deterring evasive answers. Terms commonly defined in interrogatories include "record," "agreement," "document," "electronically stored information," "communication," "witness," "participate," "transaction," "occurrence," "collision," "state," "knowledge," "describe," and "identify." Use broad descriptions of these basic terms so that the answering party cannot give a superficially accurate but effectively unresponsive answer. Make sure the definitions of records and documents include paper, handwritten, and electronic data.

Example:

DEFINITIONS

The following terms used in these interrogatories have the following meanings:

1. To "identify" means to (a) state a person's full name, home address, business address, and present and past relationship to any party; (b) state the title of any document, who prepared it, when it was prepared, where it is located, and who its custodian is.
2. A "document" means any legal documents, business records, letters, memoranda, notes, work papers, drafts, copies, interoffice and intraoffice communications and messages, drawings, and graphic material, whether created or stored in handwritten, printed, tangible, electronic, mechanical, or electrical form of any kind, including material on computer hard drives, tapes, disks, files, and other memories, backup copies and "deleted" files, whether located on-site or off-site.
3. A "communication" means all oral conversations, discussions, letters, telegrams, memoranda, e-mail, facsimile transmissions, and any other transmission of information in any form, both oral and written.

An instruction section detailing how interrogatories should be answered may prove useful. This section makes the particular interrogatories easier to understand.

Example:

INSTRUCTIONS

In answering each interrogatory:
    (a) state whether the answer is within the personal knowledge of the person answering the interrogatory and, if not, identify each person known to have personal knowledge of the answer;
    (b) identify each document that was used in any way to formulate the answer.

Finally, in cases where a series of events or transactions is involved, it may be useful to state the time frame the interrogatories are intended to cover.

Example:

Unless expressly stated otherwise, each interrogatory relates to the time period beginning June 1, 2013, through and including the date on which answers to these interrogatories are signed.

Keep in mind, however, that such preambles are useful only in more complex interrogatories, such as those used in commercial disputes. In other cases, such as simple contract or personal injury actions, they are usually unnecessary because they make the interrogatories more complex than they need to be. Definitions and instructions should be unnecessary for interrogatories drafted in clear, plain English. If the definitions and instructions are too lengthy and detailed, and the case is a relatively simple one, the answering party may object that the interrogatories are unduly burdensome and ask the court to strike the interrogatories and sanction the requesting party.

iii.   Interrogatory style

Clear, simple interrogatories are more likely to yield clear, simple answers that will provide useful information. Such questions and answers will be more effective if they are used during trial, either as admissions or for impeachment purposes. The more complex the interrogatories, the more complex and less useful the answers are likely to be. Accordingly, err on the side of simplicity.

Interrogatories must adequately cover the necessary subjects. They are usually drafted as imperatives, not as actual questions, since the imperative form affirmatively requires the answering party to supply information.

The first purpose of interrogatories is to identify parties, witnesses, documents, and experts.

Example (parties and agents):

1. State the full name of the defendant, where and when incorporated, where and when licensed to do business, where it has its principal place of business, and all names under which it does business.

2. Identify each officer and director of the defendant during the time period of June 1, 2013, through the date on which answers to these interrogatories are signed.

3. Identify each company, subdivision, and subsidiary in which the defendant has any ownership, control, or interest of any kind for the period referred to in Interrogatory #2 above.

Example (witnesses):

> 1. Identify each person who was present during the execution of the contract that forms the basis of Count I of plaintiff's complaint.
> 2. Identify each person who participated in or was present during any of the negotiations of the contract executed by plaintiff and defendant on June 1, 2013.
> 3. State the full name and address of each person who witnessed, or claims to have witnessed, the collision between vehicles driven by the plaintiff and defendant occurring on June 1, 2013.
> 4. State the full name and address of each person who was present, or claims to have been present, at the scene of the collision during and after the collision, other than the persons identified in Interrogatory #3 above.
> 5. State the full name and address of each person who has any knowledge of the facts of the collision, other than those persons already identified in Interrogatories #3 and 4 above.

Note that rather than ask for witnesses in a general way, the interrogatories first focus on witnesses to a particular transaction or event, then expand the scope in subsequent questions to ensure that all possible known witnesses are identified. This order organizes the information into useful categories.

Example (documents):

> 1. Identify each document that relates to the shipping of the machinery by plaintiff to defendant on or about June 1, 2013.
> 2. Identify each document in your possession and control that refers to the plaintiff's employment termination that is the basis for plaintiff's complaint.
> 3. Identify each document that you contend put the defendant on notice of a dangerous condition existing on the roadway at the intersection of Main and Elm Streets on or about June 1, 2013.

A common practice is to combine an interrogatory that asks for the identity of documents and electronically stored information (ESI) with a request to produce all documents and ESI identified in the interrogatory answer. Copies of the identified documents and ESI are produced more quickly this way.[32]

Interrogatories can also obtain information about experts expected to testify at trial. Use a basic imperative with subsections.

---

32. See §6.7 on drafting document requests and §6.8 on rules governing the production of electronically stored information.

Example (experts):

>   1. As to each expert expected to testify at trial, state:
>   a. the expert's full name, address, and professional qualifications;
>   b. the subject matter on which the expert is expected to testify;
>   c. the facts and opinions to which the expert is expected to testify; and
>   d. the grounds of each opinion.

Remember that Rule 26(a)(2) requires the disclosure of expert witness information. Hence, expert disclosures, not interrogatories, are the preferred method for obtaining information about the other party's testifying experts. However, in state courts not having expert disclosure rules, interrogatories are still the method for obtaining information about the other parties' experts.

The above interrogatories are all directed toward obtaining the identity of parties and agents, witnesses, documents, and experts, and are a part of almost every interrogatory set. These questions obtain the hard data that will provide the springboard for further investigation and discovery.

Interrogatories should also ask for the specific facts on which the pleadings are based. These requests are particularly important since the pleadings frequently contain general language that gives little detailed information about the facts on which claims, defenses, or damages are based. Interrogatories should develop the basic facts so that the parties can focus on specific facts underlying the legal claims.

Example (facts underlying complaint in personal injury action):

>   1.   Describe the personal injuries you received as a result of this occurrence.
>   2.   If you were hospitalized as a result of this occurrence, state the name and address of each such hospital or clinic, the dates of your hospitalization at each facility, and the amount of each facility's bill.

If a single interrogatory asks for several categories of information, set out those categories in lettered subsections. You make it clear what information you want, and you increase the chances that you will elicit complete answers. Since each subpart relates to the same subject, it should count as a single interrogatory under Rule 33, an important consideration given the presumptive 25-interrogatory limit.

Example:

>   3. If you were treated by any physicians as a result of this occurrence, state:
>   a.   the name and address of each such physician;

b.   each physician's areas of specialty;

c.   the dates of each examination, consultation, or appointment; and

d.   the amount of each physician's bill.

4. If you were unable to work as a result of this occurrence, state:

a.   the dates during which you were unable to work;

b.   your employers during those dates;

c.   the type of work you were unable to do; and

d.   the amount of lost wages or income.

5. State any other losses or expenses you claim resulted from this occurrence, other than those already stated above.

6. During the past 10 years, have you suffered any other personal injuries? If so, state:

a.   when, where, and how you were injured;

b.   the nature and extent of the injuries;

c. the name and address of each medical facility where you were treated; and

d. each physician by whom you were treated for those injuries.

7. During the past 10 years, have you been hospitalized, treated, examined, or tested at any hospital, clinic, or physician's office for any medical condition other than personal injuries? If so, state:

a.   the name and address of each such medical facility and physician;

b.   the dates such services were provided; and

c.   the medical conditions involved.

These kinds of questions serve to discover systematically the facts on which the plaintiff's case is based, and the answers will point to the areas that need to be explored in greater detail.

Finally, interrogatories should be used to identify the facts on which specific claims are based. Complaints commonly allege in general fashion that the defendant "breached the contract" or "negligently operated a motor vehicle." An interrogatory provides an effective means to develop the facts that the other party claims support the legal contentions. These are commonly called "contention interrogatories." Keep in mind, however, that such contention interrogatories are frequently objected to on the ground that they are overly broad. Particular care must be used in drafting them. In addition, the court may order that such contention interrogatories need not be answered until a later time, when the answering party knows more facts.

Examples:

1.   State the basis upon which you claim that defendant acted negligently.

2.   State the conduct by the plaintiff and any of its officers, employees, or agents that you claim constituted a breach of the contract.

3.   Do you contend that Samuel Jones lacked authority to enter into a contract on behalf of the defendant corporation? If so:

      (a)   state each fact on which this contention is based;

      (b)   identify each person having knowledge of each fact;

      (c)   identify each document containing information of each fact.

What are the common problems that arise when drafting interrogatories? Remember that the skill in drafting interrogatories is in finding a clear, simple way to elicit the information you need and are entitled to get without making the interrogatories unduly burdensome. Overly broad interrogatories are common. Examples include interrogatories that ask "Identify in detail each and every fact that relates to your claim in Count I," "Identify all documents that relate to your complaint," "State in detail everything you did on May 1, 2013," and "State every fact on which you base your denial that the defendant was negligent." The answering party will either object or provide a brief summary of the relevant facts. Remember that interrogatories are effective in obtaining basic information. They are not usually effective in obtaining details of events, descriptions, or mental impressions.

Another common problem are premature interrogatories. Examples include interrogatories that ask "Identify each witness that you expect to call at trial," and "Identify each exhibit you intend to introduce at trial." These request information that is probably not yet known or has not yet been decided. Parties disclose such information when the pretrial memorandum is due, which is at least 30 days before trial. The answering party will usually object or answer, "Not known at present; investigation continues," or give a partial answer to the extent it can, such as "Other than the plaintiff, plaintiff's employer, and treating physician, plaintiff has not yet determined who her trial witnesses will be."

A third common problem are interrogatories that ask for facts only, but do not also request the identity of documents that contain the facts and persons having knowledge of the facts. For example, an interrogatory that asks "Identify all persons who attended the May 1, 2013, meeting" is proper, but should also be combined with an interrogatory that asks "Identify each record, memorandum, and document of any kind that states the persons who attended the May 1, 2013, meeting." Asking for facts and documents is the better approach, since you later will want to send a request to produce the documents identified in the interrogatory answer.

Finally, interrogatories are problematic when they are drafted so that the answer can give literally true but misleading answers. For example, asking "Identify each eyewitness to the collision other than the plaintiff and defendant" may get a literally true answer that none is known. A broader interrogatory asking "Identify each person who was at or near the scene during or after the collision" or "Identify each person who has knowledge of the collision" may yield more useful information.

iv. Signing and serving

The interrogatories must be signed by a lawyer and served on every other party. Service is made by any permitted method under Rule 5, most commonly by mailing a copy to the lawyers for the other parties. However, under Rule 5(d) interrogatories are not to be filed with the court until they are used in the proceeding or the court orders otherwise.

d. *Responses to interrogatories*

A party must usually answer interrogatories within 30 days of their service. Since they frequently require a substantial amount of work, information necessary to prepare the answers must be obtained reasonably quickly. If the client is out of town and unavailable, or the interrogatories are lengthy, move for additional time to answer. Call the opposing lawyer, explain your problem, and ask the lawyer to agree not to oppose your motion for additional time.

i. Researching and preparing answers

A common procedure in answering interrogatories is to send the interrogatories to the client, ask her to respond to the request for information from her own records and from personal recall, and then return the information to you, her lawyer. You then draft the actual answers. After the client reviews the answers for accuracy and completeness, the client must sign the answer and notarize her signature and return it to you. This procedure works well with individual clients. When the interrogatories are complicated, the client and lawyer must work together on preparing the answers.

Corporate parties and other artificial entities present special challenges. First, the lawyer representing the corporation must decide who in the corporation should answer the interrogatories. Ordinarily a corporate officer who has personal knowledge of the transactions involved, or who has knowledge of the corporate record-keeping system, is an appropriate choice. The selection of the person is not as significant as might first appear, however, because although the answer binds whoever provides it, the answer will also be imputed to the corporate party.

Second, the corporate party has an obligation to investigate files, records, and computer systems that are in its possession or control, to collect the requested information, and to put that information in the answer. Records are considered in a party's possession or control if they are records that are kept at the company's offices or in its computer systems. They are also considered in the party's control if they are physically in the possession of another, like an accountant or a storage company, but the party has the power to get the records returned. The corporation's duty to investigate is limited only by the extent of its own records, but there is no duty to conduct an independent outside investigation.[33] A corporate party cannot avoid

---

33. Moore's Federal Practice §33.102; Wright & Miller §2174.

answering a proper interrogatory by selecting someone to answer the interrogatories who has no personal knowledge of any relevant facts.

Third, under Rule 33(d) a party can answer an interrogatory by specifying the business records and electronically stored information from which the requested information can be derived if the burden of obtaining the desired information from those sources is substantially the same for either party. A responding party should answer in this manner if possible, to avoid doing the requesting party's work, to provide a response more quickly, and to minimize the cost of responding.

ii.　Objections

A party on whom interrogatories have been served has two possible responses: an answer or an objection. If the response is an objection, simply state the objection as your answer to a particular interrogatory. All grounds for the objection "must be stated with specificity." If part of an interrogatory is objectionable, the part not objected to must still be answered. There are several bases for objecting.

First, a party may object on the basis that the information sought is irrelevant. Rule 26(b)(l)'s broad definition of relevance makes such an objection unlikely to succeed. Also, the court can impose sanctions for frivolous objections. Second, a party may object on the ground of privilege, relying on either the privilege for qualified trial preparation materials and absolute mental impressions under Rule 26(b) or on the privileges codified in FRE 501. Rule 26(b)(5) requires that a claim of privilege be made expressly and shall describe the nature of the matters claimed to be privileged in a manner that, "without revealing information itself privileged or protected, will enable other parties to assess the claim." Third, an objection can be made to interrogatories that ask for information that cannot be obtained by interrogatories, such as an interrogatory that demands the production of records. Fourth, an objection can be made on the basis that the interrogatory is annoying, embarrassing, oppressive, overly broad, unduly burdensome, and expensive. This frequently raised objection has generated a substantial body of case law. Along with such an objection, the answering party should also move for a protective order under Rule 26(c).[34] The claim that an interrogatory is unduly burdensome requires that the court apply Rule 26(b)(2) and balance the burden of collecting the information requested against the benefit to the requesting party. Where the work involved in obtaining the information is enormous and the benefit to the requesting party is small in light of the issues in the case, an objection to the interrogatory should be sustained.[35]

You should make your objection in the answer to the interrogatory. Draft the objection so that the opposing lawyer (and the judge, if a motion to compel follows) knows that you are serious and have a well-founded basis

---

34. See §6.13.1.
35. See Wright & Miller §2174.

for your objection. You may thereby discourage the opposing lawyer from filing a motion to compel answers.

The usual practice is to repeat the interrogatory and then state your answer.

Example:

Interrogatory No. 8: State which officers were involved in the sale of forklift trucks to the XYZ Corporation on August 1, 2013.

Answer: Defendant objects to Interrogatory No. 8 on the ground that it asks for information that is irrelevant because it pertains to a transaction with a nonparty, the XYZ Corporation, that has no relevance to the controversy between the plaintiff and defendant.

Interrogatory No. 9: Identify all conversations between defendant's employees and defendant's corporate counsel between August 1, 2013, and the present date.

Answer: Defendant objects to Interrogatory No. 9 on the ground that it asks for material that is privileged under the attorney-client privilege.

Interrogatory No. 10: Identify all witnesses you have interviewed or from whom you have taken statements.

Answer: Defendant objects to Interrogatory No. 10. While plaintiff has a right to ask for the identity of all witnesses to the collision, a request for the identity of witnesses interviewed, or from whom statements have been taken, seeks attorney work product that is protected from disclosure under Rule 26(b)(3).

If a proper objection exists, consider making the appropriate objection but also answering the interrogatory to the extent appropriate.

Example:

Interrogatory No. 10: Identify all witnesses you have interviewed or from whom you have taken statements.

Answer: Defendant objects to Interrogatory No. 10, since it seeks attorney work product and is protected from disclosure under Rule 26(b)(3). However, since an interrogatory asking for the identity of all witnesses to the collision would be proper, defendant in the spirit of cooperation answers as follows:

The only known witnesses to the collision, other than the plaintiff and defendant, are Jennifer Jones, 200 Elm St., Dallas, Texas, and Wilbur Johnson, 400 Maple St., Ft. Worth, Texas.

Answering in this way should not be deemed a waiver of an otherwise proper objection, and again often results in the party not moving to compel answers. If the answer contains any objections, Rule 33(b) requires that the lawyer making the objections must sign the answer.

iii.   Answers

The other possible response is to answer the interrogatory. There are three basic types of responses.

First, the party can answer the interrogatory by supplying the requested information if it is either known or ascertainable from the party's personal knowledge or records. The answer should be brief, since you ordinarily don't want to volunteer information that has not been requested. On the other hand, you must answer with the essential facts at your disposal, since failing to disclose can subject you to serious sanctions. In addition, if you have a strong case and hope for an early settlement, you may want to volunteer information. You need to ask yourself: What message do I want to send to the other side? Full answers convey the message that you have good evidence to support your claims or defenses and that you are confident in the merits of your case. Finally, keep in mind that the opposing party can use interrogatories and answers at trial, since a party's answers are admissions and can be used for impeachment. The lawyer's task in answering interrogatories is to strike an appropriate balance between the advantages of brevity and a full, detailed answer.

Example:

Interrogatory No. 2: Identify each person who was present during the execution of the contract that forms the basis of Count I of plaintiff's complaint.

Answer: John Marlowe and Phillip Johnson.

Interrogatory No. 3: Identify each physician who treated you as a result of this occurrence.

Answer: Dr. William Jackson, Mercy Hospital, Seattle, Washington; Dr. Erica Olson, 3420 Cascades Highway, Seattle, Washington; possibly other physicians at Mercy Hospital, whose names are unknown; investigation continues.

Interrogatory No. 4: State the name and address of each person who was present or claims to have been present during the collision.

Answer: Mary Jones, 2440 Congress St, Tucson, Arizona; Frank Wilson, 1831 N. Campbell Ave., Tucson, Arizona; Abby Jones, 2440 Congress St., Tucson, Arizona; Jennifer Jones, 2440 Congress St., Tucson, Arizona; in addition, there were several other pedestrians in the vicinity, but the names and addresses of such persons are presently unknown; investigation continues.

Sometimes an interrogatory asks for information about which the answering party has some personal knowledge, but not to the detail requested. Also, no records exist that can supply those details. The answer should accurately indicate that this is the situation.

Example:

> Interrogatory No. 6: Identify each communication between John Marlowe and Phillip Johnson that relates to the contract that forms the basis of Count I of plaintiff's complaint.

> Answer: There were several telephone conversations between Marlowe and Johnson during a period of approximately four weeks preceding the execution of the contract. The exact dates and substance of each of these conversations are unknown.

This type of answer is satisfactory when the answer cannot state facts that are not within the knowledge or recall of the answering party and no records exist to supply the details. The better practice is to follow up on this type of response through depositions, which allow the extent and details of the party's recall to be explored and developed.

Where an interrogatory asks for a party's contentions, a more complete answer is called for since the answering party does not wish to limit its proof or theories of liability.

Example:

> Interrogatory No. 4: State the basis on which you claim that defendant acted negligently at the time of the collision.

> Answer: Defendant (1) drove in excess of the posted speed limit; (2) drove in excess of a reasonable speed under the existing conditions and circumstances; (3) failed to keep a proper lookout to ensure the safety of others; (4) failed to keep his vehicle in the proper lane; (5) failed to yield the right of way; and (6) failed to obey traffic signals, markers, and "rules of the road." Investigation continues.

In this type of answer the "investigation continues" response is important because additional investigation and discovery may develop additional facts to support the negligence claim.

A second type of response is simply to state "no knowledge" where this is accurate. Keep in mind that an answering party must search his own records to determine if the information exists, and, if it does, use the information to answer the interrogatory.

Example:

> Interrogatory No. 4: State if any witnesses to the collision prepared written reports of any kind regarding the collision.

> Answer: No knowledge of any such reports.

Rule 26(e) imposes a continuing duty to amend interrogatory answers "in a timely manner" if the answering party learns that its response "in some material respect is incomplete or incorrect" and the "additional or corrective information has not otherwise been made known to the other parties during the discovery process or in writing." A common response in interrogatory answers is to answer based on present knowledge and acknowledge the continuing duty under the rule.

Example:

> Interrogatory No. 2: Identify each person who saw or heard the collision.
>
> Answer: Other than plaintiff and defendant, none presently known; investigation continues.
>
> Interrogatory No. 3: Identify each person who was present at or near the collision when it happened, other than the persons already identified in your answer to Interrogatory No. 2.
>
> Answer: None at present; plaintiff is aware of her continuing duty to supplement responses under Rule 26(e).

The third type of answer is to identify business records and electronically stored information (ESI) that provide the answers. Rule 33(d) requires only that the answer specify the records and give the requesting party a reasonable opportunity to examine and copy them. Actual production with the interrogatory answer is not required. But such records and ESI are always discoverable through a request to produce under Rule 34. For this reason, many lawyers simply attach copies of the pertinent documents and ESI as exhibits to the interrogatory answers.

Examples:

> Interrogatory No. 5: Identify each communication between Phillip Johnson and Jane East between June 1, 2013, and August 4, 2013, relating to the contract that forms the basis of Count I of plaintiff's complaint.
>
> Answer: Any such communications are kept in the defendant's telephone logbook, the pertinent dates of which may be examined and copied at a reasonable time at the defendant's place of business.
>
> Interrogatory No. 6: Identify each sales transaction entered into between plaintiff and defendant for the period of January 1, 2013, through August 4, 2013.
>
> Answer: These transactions are recorded on the defendant's Sales Records, which are computerized after sales transactions are completed. A printout of these transactions is attached as Exhibit A.

Interrogatories are frequently coupled with a document request directed to any records and ESI identified in the interrogatory answers.

Example:

> Interrogatory No. 4: If any witnesses to the collision prepared written accounts of any kind regarding the collision, identify each witness and the location of the written account. If your answer to this interrogatory identifies any such written accounts, you are hereby requested pursuant to Rule 34 to make available for copying, within 30 days of service of this interrogatory and documents request, any such written accounts within your possession, custody, and control.
>
> Answer: The only witness known to have prepared a written account of the collision is William Morris, 123 Elm Street, Boston, MA. A copy of his written account is in the possession of plaintiff's attorney, and a copy of which is attached as Exhibit A.

The standard approach in drafting interrogatory answers is to draft the shortest answer that fairly provides the information requested. Keep in mind, however, that, as with all court papers, your answers send messages to your opponent and the court. If your own answers to interrogatories are threadbare, the court will hardly be responsive if you complain that the other side's interrogatory answers are inadequate. Answering interrogatories more fully than expected sends positive signals about your case — that you are well prepared, know the facts, and have a winning case.

iv. Signing, serving, and filing

The format for interrogatory answers, like any other court document, should have the case caption and title of the document. The answers must be signed and sworn to by the party making them. The signature of the party's lawyer does *not* comply with the rule. If any interrogatories are objected to, the attorney must sign as to the objections.

The completed interrogatory answers must then be served on each party. Service is made by any proper method under Rule 5, most commonly by mailing a copy to the lawyers for the other parties. However, under Rule 5(d), interrogatory answers are not to be filed with the court until they are used in the proceeding or the court orders filing.

Example:

[Caption]

DEFENDANT ACME CORPORATION'S ANSWERS TO PLAINTIFF'S INTERROGATORIES

Defendant Acme Corporation answers the first set of interrogatories put forth by plaintiff as follows:

Interrogatory No. 1: . . .

Answer: . . .

Acme Corporation

By _____
William Phillips
    Vice President for Administration
    of Acme Corporation

As to the interrogatories to which objections have been made:

By _____
Attorney for defendant

State of Arizona   SS.
County of Pima.

    William Phillips, after being first duly sworn, states that he is an officer of Acme Corporation and is authorized to make the above interrogatory answers on behalf of Acme Corporation; that the above answers have been prepared with the assistance of counsel; that the answers are based either on his personal knowledge, the personal knowledge of Acme Corporation employees, or on information obtained from Acme Corporation records; and that the answers are true to the best of his knowledge, information and belief.

_____
          William Phillips

Signed and sworn to before me on this _____ day of _____, _____

_____
Notary Public

My commission expires on _____

§6.7. *Requests to produce and subpoenas*

After answers to interrogatories have been received you will usually have enough detailed information to ask for copies of identified documents and electronically stored information not already obtained as part of the other party's initial disclosures under Rule 26(a)(1). You will do so with a request to produce. Hence, requests to produce are usually the next step in the discovery process, although requests to produce are also frequently served with interrogatories.

This section discusses the production of documents and things. The next section (§6.8) discusses the rules that govern the production of electronically stored information, or ESI.

1.   Law

Rule 34 governs requests to produce documents, ESI, and things for inspection and copying and for entry upon land to inspect tangible things.[36] A request to produce can only be served upon parties. As it does for all discovery, Rule 26(b) controls the scope of the request. It permits the discovery of any "nonprivileged matter that is relevant to any claim or defense." The rule expressly requires that the items to be inspected must be described with "reasonable particularity."

Under Rule 34(c), a nonparty's books, documents, ESI, and tangible things can also be subpoenaed for production, inspection, and copying. This process, controlled by Rule 45(a), is discussed later in this section.

Rule 34 permits requests to produce for "any designated documents or electronically stored information . . . stored in any medium from which information can be obtained either directly or, if necessary, after translation by the responding party into a reasonably usable form." It also permits requests to produce for "any designated tangible things" or "to permit entry onto designated land or other property," in order to "inspect, measure, survey, photograph, test, or sample" the property.

Lawyers principally use Rule 34 requests for the production of documents. The rule requires a party to produce all documents that are in that party's "possession, custody or control." A party must produce all relevant documents, even those not in the party's actual possession, if the party has a lawful right to get them from another person or entity.[37] In short, a party cannot avoid production through the simple device of transferring the documents to another person or entity, such as the party's lawyer, accountant, insurer, or corporate subsidiary. When a party tries to use this avoidance device, he is deemed to have retained "control" of the documents and is required to get them returned in order to comply with the production request. On the other hand, the mere fact that a party *can* obtain documents from a third person or entity usually does not mean that the documents are in the party's control. Otherwise, a litigant could shift the cost and effort of investigation to the other side.

A request to produce may be served at any time after the parties hold the conference to develop a discovery plan required under Rule 26(f). It must describe each item or category to be produced with "reasonable particularity." In other words, a responding party must reasonably be able to determine what particular documents the request seeks, in light

---

36. Wright §87; Hazard et al. §8.18; Moore's Manual §15.26; Manual of Federal Practice §§5.161–5.194; Moore's Federal Practice §§34.01–34.16; Wright & Miller §§2201–2218.

37. Moore's Manual §15.26; Manual of Federal Practice §5.172; Moore's Federal Practice §34.14; Wright & Miller §2210.

of the context of the case and the overall nature of the documents involved.[38]

Rule 34 requires that the documents produced for inspection must be produced in either the same order as they are normally kept, or in the order, with labels, that corresponds with the categories of the request. The producing party cannot purposefully disorganize documents and records to make them more difficult to comprehend. The producing party must make the originals available for inspection and copying. Most courts take the view that the producing party has the choice of complying either by producing the records in the same order as they are ordinarily kept, or by producing them in the order that corresponds to the categories of the request. The requesting party cannot insist on the method of complying. Some courts, however, take the position that a producing party cannot produce a mass of jumbled documents, even if they were ordinarily kept in this manner. They must be organized in a useful way.[39] Further, the request to produce must specify a "reasonable time, place, and manner" for the inspection. The responding party must serve a written response for each category requested, usually within 30 days of service of the request, stating that he objects, with reasons for the objection, or that he will comply.

Note the broad language of Rule 34(a). It provides that a request to produce can be directed to "any designated documents or electronically stored information — including writings, drawings, graphs, charts, photographs, sound recordings, images, and other data or data compilations — stored in any medium from which information can be obtained." The terms "documents" and "electronically stored information" collectively encompass information of any kind stored in any medium. And courts usually consider "deleted" documents in computer databases as documents under the rule.[40]

2. Practice approach

a. Timing

Before serving a request to produce documents or a request for entry upon land to inspect, you need to know what documents you want produced and what things you want to inspect. If you have received the other party's initial disclosures under Rule 26(a)(1), you will probably already have copies of some of those documents or descriptions of them. If you have drafted your interrogatories carefully, and have asked for descriptions of relevant documents and for the identity of those persons whose custody those documents are in, answers to the interrogatories should provide sufficient detail to meet the particularity requirement for

38. Moore's Manual §15.26; Manual of Federal Practice §5.168; Moore's Federal Practice §34.11; Wright & Miller §2211.

39. See Moore's Federal Practice, §34.13[3]; Wright & Miller, §2213.

40. See R. Hardaway et al., E-Discovery's Threat to Civil Litigation: Reevaluating Rule 26 for the Digital Age, 63 Rutgers L. Rev. 521 (2011).

production requests. Hence, requests to produce should normally be served as soon as possible after the answers to interrogatories have been received.

This timetable presumes that the party has adequately, and in a timely fashion, made initial disclosures and answered your interrogatories. If the answering party has objected, failed to answer, or served evasive or incomplete answers, you must resolve the problems through appropriate discovery motions.[41] This motion practice, however, will necessarily delay the requests to produce. In this situation you should consider serving a request to produce anyway, since you can ordinarily determine in a general way what documents the other party is likely to have and describe them sufficiently by topic or subject matter to meet the particularity requirement. Discovery can easily get sidetracked or stall completely. You must weigh the benefits and liabilities of waiting or going ahead in light of your overall discovery strategy.

Of course, in some cases you will know what documents you want from the other side and can describe them with reasonable particularity when the parties make their initial disclosures. If so, most lawyers will then serve interrogatories and requests to produce on the opposing party at the same time. This frequently shortens the discovery process by several weeks.

A proposed amendment to Rule 34 would allow parties to serve "early" requests to produce 21 days after service of the complaint, even before the Rule 26(f) conference. The idea behind this proposal is to enable a more focused discussion at the conference, and possibly to tailor the request more narrowly. Check updates to the Federal Rules to see if this proposed amendment has been promulgated.

b. Organization

Before actually drafting the request to produce, you need to organize your thoughts on what you want from the other party. If you have intelligently thought through your discovery strategy, received initial disclosures, and obtained answers to your interrogatories, then the bulk of your work is already done. You will know in sufficient detail what documents you want, what documents the answering party admits having, how those documents are described or labeled, and who their custodian is. However, be careful when reviewing the other side's initial disclosures made under Rule 26 since that rule requires the disclosing party to provide a copy or description of only those documents that it "may use to support its claims or defenses." You will need to use the Rule 34 requests to obtain the other relevant documents in the disclosing party's possession, especially those documents that hurt the disclosing party. You should also review your client's records and documents, to help you identify what records and documents you will need from the other side.

If you have not yet received interrogatory answers but have decided to send out requests to produce anyway, you will have to evaluate what

---

41. See §6.13.

documents the other party is likely to have, how they are likely to be labeled and organized, and who their custodian is. If this task proves difficult or impossible, you should consider deposing that party at an early date in order to question the deponent about his records. In the case of a corporate party, you should also consider deposing the party's custodian of records. This deposition will help you determine what kind of records the corporation generates and maintains, how they are organized and stored, where they are stored, and who their custodian is. You can thereby draft a more focused document request.

Avoid overly broad requests. Copying, filing, numbering, and indexing documents can be expensive. If the case is a commercial or products liability case large enough to warrant using an electronic litigation support system that stores and cross-indexes the documents, the cost of such a system can be several dollars per document. If you are not sure of the volume of documents you are requesting, use interrogatories or depositions to find out before plunging ahead.

c. Drafting requests to produce

i.   Heading

A request to produce should be drafted like any other court document. It must have a caption showing the court, case title, and docket number, and it must be properly labeled. Where a case has several parties, a designation indicating which party is sending the request to which other party is useful. Otherwise, the simple title "<u>REQUEST TO PRODUCE DOCUMENTS</u>" will suffice.

Example:

[Caption]

<u>PLAINTIFF JOHNSON'S REQUEST TO PRODUCE DOCUMENTS
TO DEFENDANT ACME CORPORATION</u>

Plaintiff Johnson requests defendant Acme Corporation to produce the documents and things listed below, pursuant to Rule 34 of the Federal Rules of Civil Procedure:

       1. . . .
       2. . . .
       3. . . .

ii.   Definitions

Requests to produce present the same definitional problems as interrogatories. Accordingly, terms and phrases frequently used, such as "document," "record," "relating to," "transaction," "communication," and "occurrence," should be defined if the complexity of the case warrants doing so. Definitions should be identical to those used in the interrogatories.[42]

Example:

DEFINITIONS

The following terms used in this request to produce have the following meanings:

1. A "document" means all writings of any kind, including all handwritten, typed, printed, or otherwise visually produced or recorded materials, whether originals, copies, nonidentical copies, annotated copies, or drafts, in your possession, custody, or control. A "document" includes, but is not limited to, records, reports, studies, contracts, agreements, letters and other correspondence, memoranda, notes, diaries, minutes, notations, drawings, blueprints, sketches, charts, statistics, summaries, bills, invoices, statements, checks, receipts, emails, tweets, telegrams, other wire and wireless communications, telephone records, notes and notations of telephone calls, voice mail, instant and text messaging, conversations and other communications, photographs, slides, photographic negatives, microfilm records, movies, videotapes, and published material of any kind. A "document" includes anything which is encompassed by the term "document" as used in the Federal Rules of Civil Procedure.

2. "Electronically stored information" means . . .

Another method is to incorporate by reference definitions already used in interrogatories.

Example:

DEFINITIONS

Plaintiff incorporates by reference each of the definitions in plaintiff's interrogatories previously served on defendant.

Yet another method is to incorporate by reference your opponent's definitions previously used in the opponent's interrogatories or requests to produce. He will be hard pressed to object to your use of his definitions.

Finally, make sure your definitions of records, documents, and the like are sufficiently broad. They should always specifically include handwritten and electronically created and stored records.

42. See §6.6.

iii.   Drafting requests

Rule 34 permits three kinds of requests: to inspect and copy documents and electronically stored information, to inspect and examine tangible things, and to enter upon land to inspect and examine things.

The requests to produce must specify a reasonable date, time, and place for the production or entry. Rule 34 requires only that this be "reasonable," which must necessarily take into account the volume and complexity of the records sought. Since the rule requires a response within 30 days of service, the date set for the production should be a longer time period.

Example:

A. Plaintiff requests that defendant produce the following documents and electronically stored information for inspection and copying at the offices of Mary Anton, plaintiff's attorney, 200 Main Street, Suite 400, Tucson, Arizona, on August 21, 2013, at 2:00 P.M.:

1. . . .

B. Plaintiff requests that defendant produce the following things for inspection, copying, and testing at the offices of Independent Testing, 2000 Main Street, Tucson, Arizona, on August 22, 2013, at 9:00 A.M.:

1. . . .

C. Plaintiff requests that defendant permit plaintiff to enter defendant's lumber yard located at 4000 Monroe Street, Tucson, Arizona, for the purpose of inspecting, photographing, and measuring the premises on August 23, 2013, at 2:00 P.M.

Most requests to produce involve documents and electronically stored information. There are several ways to draft requests that will meet Rule 34's particularity requirement.

First, you can use the other party's initial disclosures and interrogatory answers. If those answers have listed and described a variety of documents, a reference to the descriptions should suffice. The responding party will be hard-pressed to claim that a description it furnished is now suddenly insufficient.

Example:

1. Each document and electronically stored information identified in defendant's answer to Interrogatory No. 6 in plaintiff's first set of interrogatories.

Second, ask for all documents and electronically stored information that relate to a specific transaction, event, or date. A specific request can help you to avoid a challenge on vagueness grounds.

Example:

> 2. All documents and electronically stored information relating to the sale of the property located at 4931 Sunrise St., Tucson, Arizona, entered into between plaintiff and defendant on July 31, 2013.

Third, you can ask for specific types of documents and electronically stored information that relate to a more general time frame or course of conduct.

Example:

> 3. All bills of lading, invoices, and shipping confirmation notices for all goods shipped from plaintiff to defendant during the period from January 1, 2013, through April 30, 2013.

In each of the above examples, the party responding to the request to produce should not have difficulty understanding the request or identifying the documents requested. In contrast, a request calling for the production of "all documents relating to the allegations in plaintiff's complaint," "all documents which support your claim in Count I," or similarly vague language is probably defective and unenforceable since it does not meet Rule 34's reasonable particularity requirement. A request calling for the production of "all documents you intend to introduce at trial" is improperly premature, since you are not required to disclose this information until the pretrial disclosures are due.

The responding party might not object to a general request, but, regardless, a general request is usually not an effective approach for discovery. Requests to produce should balance the safety of inclusiveness with the utility of a more focused request. A request that is too broad may result in a huge volume of paperwork deposited in your office. You may have neither the time nor assistance to review all of it in order to extract the few relevant documents.

Fourth, it is always useful to ask for the identity of any documents that existed at one time but have since been destroyed. This request prevents the literally true but misleading response that "no records" of the description requested exist.

Finally, consider sequencing your document requests to progress from the more specific to the more general. For example, requests might seek (1) all medical records relating to plaintiff's treatment of her knees and all other injuries following the collision; (2) all medical records relating to plaintiff's treatment for any knee conditions before the collision date; (3) all medical records relating to plaintiff's treatment for any orthopedic conditions for a period of five years preceding the collision date; and (4) all medical records relating to plaintiff's treatment for any medical condition for a period of five years preceding the collision date. This strategy often obtains more useful information than does one generally worded request.

iv.   Signing and serving

The request to produce should be signed by the lawyer and served on each party. Service is made by any permitted method under Rule 5, most commonly by mailing a copy to the lawyers for the other parties. However, under Rule 5(d), requests to produce are not to be filed with the court until they are used in the proceeding or the court orders otherwise.

d.   *Common problems*

What are the common problems that arise when drafting document requests? Remember that the skill in drafting document requests, like interrogatories, lies in finding a clear, simple way to get the documents you need, while meeting the rule's "reasonable particularity" requirement, without making the requests overly burdensome.

Overly broad document requests are common. For example, a document request that asks the responding party to produce "all records relating to plaintiff's allegation that defendant breached the contract" is overly broad. It does not meet the particularity requirement. The rule requires that the documents be identified, either individually or by category, with sufficient particularity that the responding party can reasonably identify which documents are being requested. A good technique is to use the responding party's answers to interrogatories to describe the documents.

Another common problem are document requests that do not adequately define what is being sought, so that the responding party can give literally true but evasive responses. For example, asking a party to produce "all documents relating to the board meeting on June 1, 2013" may not get a fruitful response, unless "documents" is broadly defined to include all paper records, handwritten records, handwritten notes, electronic records, correspondence, e-mail, voice mail, and so forth. Document requests should define commonly used terms such as "records," "documents," and "communications" expansively so that the responding party cannot evade the request.

Another common problem is the failure to couple a document request with an interrogatory asking about records that once existed but have been destroyed, discarded, lost, or sent to another party. Such an interrogatory should ask, "If your response to any document request is that none exists or none is presently in your possession, state whether such documents were ever in existence, where and in whose possession they are now, who prepared the documents, who was custodian of the documents, who made the decision to destroy or send away the documents, when that decision was made, and any other reasons and circumstances why such records no longer exist." Asking about destroyed records through a broadly worded interrogatory is a good way to begin tracking down possible "smoking guns."

Finally, document requests are sometimes premature. Asking a party to "produce all documents you intend to introduce as exhibits at trial" is premature, since such information is usually disclosed only when the pretrial disclosures are due. Asking for that information now will get either an objection or a response of "not known at present; investigation continues."

e.   *Responses to requests to produce*

A party served with a request to produce usually must respond in writing within 30 days of service of the request. Even though the lawyers for the requesting and responding parties frequently reach an informal agreement on how and when to produce documents and conduct inspections,[43] the responding party should serve and file a written response, since Rule 34 requires it.

i.   Researching and preparing responses

If the preliminary investigation has been done, and answers to interrogatories have been prepared and served, you already will have done most of the initial work involved in responding to requests to produce. In addition, you should always send the requests to your client and ask the client a couple of questions about them. First, does the client know what the requests actually call for? If not, you may want to object on grounds of vagueness. Second, how much effort will be required to collect the documents and ESI requested? If the time is substantial and the case is not complex, you may be able to object on the grounds that the requests are unduly burdensome and move for a protective order, or at least for additional time to respond.

When you receive a broadly worded request, particularly when directed to a business, you need to search not only the paper records but also the computer databases. You will probably need to work with employees who operate the business's computer systems to learn how records, e-mail, and the like are created, stored, and retrieved.

After your party has collected the documents and electronically stored information, review the material to determine if all of it is relevant. Make sure that those documents are in fact all the available documents your party has in his possession, custody, or control. You can be sure that your party and other witnesses will be questioned about the completeness of the tendered documents during their depositions. Now is the time to review the documents for completeness with your client.

Review the documents collected to see if any are privileged. Since privileges are usually deemed waived unless an objection to their production is timely asserted, object first. The most common privilege is the attorney-client privilege, which protects all confidential communications, relating to the providing of legal services, made between a client (its directors and officers, and certain employees, depending on the breadth of the applicable privilege) and its in-house and outside counsel.

---

43. See §6.3.8.

When thousands of documents are involved, a privileged document can easily be overlooked and inadvertently disclosed to the other party. Does inadvertent disclosure waive the privilege? Prior to the enactment of FRE 502 in 2008, courts took three approaches: (a) always yes; (b) usually no; and (c) it depends, considering the reasonableness of the precautions taken, the efforts necessary to undo the problem, the scope of the discovery involved, the extent of the disclosed information, and basic fairness. Most courts followed this case-by-case approach. Federal Rule of Evidence 502 adopted a version of it in 2008. The rule provides that a disclosure of materials protected by attorney-client privilege or work-product doctrine does not waive the privilege or doctrine if the "disclosure is inadvertent, the holder of the privilege or protection took reasonable steps to prevent disclosure, and the holder promptly took reasonable steps to rectify the error."[44] In addition, if a federal court orders that the "privilege or protection is not waived by disclosure connected with the litigation pending before the court," the disclosure is also not a waiver in any other federal or state proceeding. This means that if the parties enter into a non-waiver agreement, and the trial court makes that agreement part of a federal court order, the non-waiver agreement and order prevents third parties from claiming that the disclosure caused a waiver as to any third parties. Some states have adopted similar rules.

The purpose and impact of FRE 502 are clear. Discovery costs will be lower because privilege reviews need to be less thorough than before. So long as a disclosure was inadvertent and the other requirements of FRE 502 are met, the disclosure will not trigger a waiver of the attorney-client privilege or work-product doctrine. Nonetheless, despite FRE 502's protection for privileged information, you should avoid the problem of inadvertent disclosure by preventing it from arising in the first place — by carefully reviewing each document for privileges and then physically segregating the privileged documents from the properly discoverable documents. You can then create a "privilege log" that lists each document and describes it generically (e.g., "letter dated 6/1/13 by Tom Wolfe, CEO of Acme Manufacturing, to Jean Smith, attorney for Acme Manufacturing, regarding contract negotiations"). Such a privilege log will be necessary if disputes arise over whether particular documents are actually privileged and protected from disclosure.

Finally, review the documents collected to see if any contain confidential information. While these will be discoverable if relevant to the claims and defenses, a business has a legitimate interest in keeping certain information confidential, such as financial records, future plans, customer lists, production processes, patented information, and the like. In this situation, you will need to move for an appropriate protective order, or at least reach an agreement in writing with the opposing lawyer and party in advance of any disclosures. The need for such protective orders is usually addressed at the parties' initial pretrial conference and discussed in the written report of a discovery plan required under Rule 26(f).

44. See Wright & Miller §2016.3.

ii. Objections

As with interrogatories, a party on whom requests to produce have been served has two possible responses: an answer or an objection. An objection might have one (or more) of several bases. First, an objection might claim that the documents sought are irrelevant. Rule 26's broad definition of relevance for discovery purposes makes this objection less likely to succeed. Moreover, the court will have probably ruled upon this objection, if the party made a version of it to the interrogatory that asked for the identity of the documents. Second, an objection can be based on a privilege, either the protection for trial preparation materials and mental impressions under Rule 26(b), or the privileges recognized under FRE 501. Under Rule 26(b)(5), the privilege must be expressly asserted and "shall describe the nature of the documents, communications, or tangible things not produced or disclosed—and do so in a manner that, without revealing information itself privileged or protected, will enable other parties to assess the claim." In practice, lawyers usually prepare a "privilege log" containing a generic description of each document for which a privilege is claimed and the particular privilege being asserted for that document, and a copy of each document. If the requesting party later moves to compel production, the privilege log and accompanying documents can, if necessary, be tendered to the court for an in camera inspection. Third, a lawyer might object to the request as annoying, embarrassing, oppressive, or unduly burdensome and expensive. Here the answering party should seek a protective order under Rule 26(c), as well as make an objection to a request to produce on the response.

Example:

[Caption]

RESPONSE TO PLAINTIFF'S REQUEST TO PRODUCE

Defendant Acme Corporation responds to plaintiff's Request to Produce as follows:

1. Acme objects to plaintiff's Request No. 1 on the ground that it requests documents the disclosure of which would violate the attorney-client privilege, since the request on its face asks for the production of "all correspondence from corporate officers to corporate counsel regarding the contract dated July 1, 2013."

Frequently a request may be objectionable in part. Where this is so, the response should make clear to which part of the request the responding party objects and with which part it agrees to comply.[45] Such an objection is

---

45. A proposed amendment to Rule 34 would require the responding party to state whether it is withholding any responsive materials pursuant to the objection. Make sure to check revisions to the Federal Rules to ensure that the information in this text is accurate. See www.uscourts.gov.

a common response to a broad request asking for a variety of documents, some of which may be privileged.

Example:

> 2. Acme objects to plaintiff's Request No. 2 to the extent it asks for privileged communications protected by the attorney-client privilege. Plaintiff's Request No. 2 asks for the production of "all memoranda by defendant's subsidiary, Acme Productions, relating to a bid on U.S. Government Contract No. 13-3287, commonly known as the 'Tristar Contract.'" These memoranda include documents prepared by Acme Productions officers and employees. Some of these documents were prepared at the request of and sent to Acme Corporation's General Counsel. They relate to the pending litigation and are protected from disclosure by the attorney-client privilege. Acme will produce the nonprivileged memoranda at the requested time and place.

iii. Answers

If the responding party does not object to a request to produce, she must answer it. An answer involves two considerations: the formal response and the practical concerns involved in arranging for the actual production of the documents. There should be a formal answer even if, as is often the case, the production is worked out informally between the attorneys, since Rule 34 requires a written response. In some jurisdictions, the practice is to set out each request with your response (like interrogatory answers); in others the practice is to state only your responses (like the answer to a complaint).

Example:

[Caption]

RESPONSE TO PLAINTIFF'S REQUEST FOR PRODUCTION
AND INSPECTION

> Defendant Acme Corporation responds to plaintiff's Request for Production and Inspection as follows:
>
> 1–8. Acme agrees to produce the documents and electronically stored information requested in plaintiff's Request Nos. 1 through 8 at the offices of plaintiff's attorney on or before August 15, 2013.
>
> 9. Acme agrees to permit the inspection of the items described in plaintiff's Request No. 9 at its manufacturing plant

located at 9000 Main St., Tucson, Arizona, at a mutually agreed upon date and time, but not later than August 31, 2013.

Attorney for Defendant Acme Corporation

If the request is for documents that are already in the lawyer's possession, they can be attached to the response.

Example:

3. Acme agrees to produce the contract requested in plaintiff's Request No. 3. A copy is attached to this response.

If records requested do not exist, the response should clearly say so.

Example:

3. There are no documents in the possession, custody, or control of defendant Acme Corporation requested by plaintiff's Request No. 3.

Most requests to produce are worked out informally between the lawyers, who usually call each other and agree on the mechanics of delivering and copying the pertinent records. The lawyers will usually work out when and where the documents will be produced, how the documents will be organized, and who will perform and pay for the actual copying. The usual procedure is for the documents to be produced at, or delivered to, the requesting attorney's offices on an agreed-upon date. The responding party has the option of producing the records either in the order in which they are ordinarily kept, or in an order that corresponds to the categories of the request. Since most production requests overlap on particulars to ensure completeness, a common approach, and often the easier one, is for the responding party to produce the documents in their usual order.

The rule requires only production, not copying, of the records by the responding party. However, the responding party should make copies so as to retain possession of the original documents. For this reason the responding party will commonly make copies of the records that comply with the requests and number the pages. (Each page is given a "Bates" stamp, a stamped page number, named after the company that makes the devices that stamp consecutive numbers on documents.) The usual rule assigns the cost of copying to the responding party, unless the parties have reached an agreement to allocate copying costs or the court has entered an order allocating production costs. Make sure that the copies you receive are clear and show any handwritten notes legibly; if not, insist on examining the originals. As the lawyer for the answering party, make sure you keep a copy of everything submitted to the opposing side so that no issues arise later over what you actually delivered.

When the documents involved are so voluminous that copying all of them would be prohibitively expensive, a common solution is to have the lawyer for the requesting party review the documents at the offices of either the responding party or the responding party's lawyer. The requesting lawyer can then select the relevant documents for photocopying. The responding party or a commercial copy service then does the copying.

Always index, bind, and "Bates" stamp every document you send or receive to create a clear record of what, when, and to or from whom documents were sent or received. Make sure you keep a copy of what you have sent to the other parties in the litigation. Disputes frequently arise over whether certain documents were sent or received, and clear, complete records are necessary to resolve these disputes.

iv.   Signing and serving

The response to requests to produce must be signed and served on every other party. Service is made by any permitted method under Rule 5, most commonly by mailing a copy to the lawyers for the other parties. However, under Rule 5(d), responses to requests to produce are not to be filed with the court until they are used in the proceeding or the court orders otherwise.

3.   Document subpoenas to nonparties

Rule 34(c) provides that subpoenas can be issued to command a nonparty "to produce documents and tangible things or to permit an inspection." Rule 45 provides a vehicle for obtaining documents, electronically stored information, and things directly from nonparties, without also requiring the attendance of the nonparty at a deposition. Pursuant to 2013 amendments to Rule 45, the subpoena must be issued from the district court where the action is pending. The documents and things sought should be described with the same particularity required of requests to produce. If the subpoena is unreasonable or oppressive, the court can on motion quash it or require that the party issuing the subpoena pay in advance the reasonable cost of compliance. The subpoena can only command the production of documents within 100 miles of where the person commanded to produce resides, is employed, or regularly transacts business. The parties can always agree, however, to have documents produced electronically.

§6.8.   Electronically stored information

Perhaps nothing has changed the landscape of discovery over the past three decades more than the computer revolution. Once created only on paper, business records now routinely exist and are stored in electronic form. E-mail, voice mail, text messaging, and tweeting are primary methods of communication. They often reveal much more than what written letters once indicated. Smart phones record calling information, take photographs, contain appointment calendars, and record voice memos. Digital photographs can be stored and exchanged instantaneously. Digital information can be accumulated and stored with ease, in multiple places. Information erased from one hard drive may remain on laptops, in the "cloud," or in other backup and storage systems.

Electronic information is both fragile, because it can be modified and deleted easily, and durable, because it is usually sent to, copied, and stored in multiple locations and is difficult to erase completely. This explosion of electronic information has changed civil litigation. Consequently, a thorough discovery plan must include a plan to identify and obtain electronic information from the other parties, as well as a plan to respond to electronic information requests.

1.   Law

In 2006, the Federal Rules of Civil Procedure were significantly amended to provide a comprehensive set of procedural rules to govern the discovery of a new category: "electronically stored information" (ESI).[46] The principal changes were the following.

Rule 16 — Pretrial conferences; scheduling; management

Rule 16(b) now provides that the judge's pretrial scheduling order, which regulates the discovery process, may "provide for disclosure or discovery of electronically stored information," as well as "any agreements the parties reach for asserting claims of privilege or of protection as trial-preparation material after information is produced."

Rule 26 — General provisions governing discovery; duty of disclosure

As amended in 2006, Rule 26(f) provides that the parties' meet and confer conference must "discuss any issues about preserving discoverable information." In addition, the parties' proposed discovery plan shall include the parties' views and proposals concerning "any issues about disclosure or discovery of electronically stored information, including the form or forms in which it should be produced," and "any issues about claims of privilege or of protection as trial-preparation materials, including — if the parties agree on a procedure to assert such claims after production — whether to ask the court to include their agreement in an order." This amendment, coupled with the amendment to Rule 16(b),

---

46. Hazard et al. §8.19; A. Cohen & D. Lender, Electronic Discovery: Law and Practice (2d ed. 2012); S. Scheindlin & D. Capra, Electronic Discovery and Digital Evidence (2009).

effectively forces the parties to discuss ESI and privilege and work-product issues at their Rule 26(f) conference.

Rule 26(b)(2)(B) provides: "A party need not provide discovery of electronically stored information from sources that the party identifies as not reasonably accessible because of undue burden or cost. On motion to compel discovery or for a protective order, the party from whom discovery is sought must show that the information is not reasonably accessible because of undue burden or cost. If that showing is made, the court may nonetheless order discovery from such sources if the requesting party shows good cause, considering the limitations of Rule 26(b)(2)(C). The court may specify conditions for the discovery." This new subsection sets out the procedure to be followed when the responding party claims that the requested ESI is not reasonably accessible.

Rule 26(b)(5)(B) provides: "If information produced in discovery is subject to a claim of privilege or of protection as trial preparation material, the party making the claim may notify any party that received the information of the claim and the basis for it. After being notified, a party must promptly return, sequester, or destroy the specified information and any copies it has; must not use or disclose the information until the claim is resolved; must take reasonable steps to retrieve the information if the party disclosed it before being notified; and may promptly present the information to the court under seal for a determination of the claim. The producing party must preserve the information until the claim is resolved." This new subsection sets out the procedure to be followed when privileged information is inadvertently disclosed, provides for the disclosure of privileged materials without waiving the privilege, and provides for the return of such information under certain circumstances.

Rule 33 — Interrogatories to parties

Rule 33(d) presently provides that an interrogatory answer can specify ESI from which the answer can be derived in the same way that business records can be specified from which the answer can be derived.

Rule 34 — Production of documents, electronically stored information, and things and entry upon land for inspection and other purposes

Rule 34's title was amended expressly to include "Electronically Stored Information." Under the new version of Rule 34(a), a document request can include "electronically stored information" and other data compilations "stored in any medium." Also, Rule 34(b) now provides that a document request "may specify the form or forms in which electronically stored information is to be produced." The responding party can object to the request, including "an objection to a requested form for producing electronically stored information. If the responding party objects to a requested form — or if no form was specified in the request — the party must state the form or forms it intends to use." Finally, unless the parties otherwise agree, or the court otherwise orders, "if a request does not specify a form for producing electronically stored information, a party must produce it in a form or forms in which it is ordinarily maintained or in a reasonably usable form or forms. Also, a "party need not produce the same electronically stored information in more than one form." This amendment sets out the procedure for discovering ESI and the forms for the production of ESI.

Rule 37—Failure to make disclosure or cooperate in discovery; sanctions

Rule 37(e), a subsection added in 2006, provides: "Absent exceptional circumstances, a court may not impose sanctions under these rules on a party for failing to provide electronically stored information lost as a result of the routine, good-faith operation of an electronic information system." This language creates a "safe harbor" for a party losing ESI because of a reasonable ESI destruction program. A proposed amendment to Rule 37(e) would clarify the protection responding parties enjoy. If adopted, the amendment would require a showing of prejudice to the requesting party before the court could order measures to address any harm from a lack of production. The court could impose a severe sanction, such as an instruction to jurors that they could presume that the missing ESI contained information unfavorable to the responding party, but only upon a finding of the responding party's intent to deprive the requesting party of the information's use. Make sure to check Rule 37 for updates.

Rule 45—Subpoena

Under the amended Rule 45, a subpoena issued to a nonparty "may specify the form or forms in which electronically stored information is to be produced." The amendment makes it clear that nonparties can be compelled to provide ESI and parallels the changes in Rules 26 and 34.

2.   Practice

The discovery rules governing ESI were significant changes to the Federal Rules. Lawyers need to learn the rules, understand how courts will apply them, and use that knowledge in their litigation practices. A good way to understand the new rules is to consider the sequential steps the rules require.

a.   Initiate a "litigation hold" with your party and the opposing parties and learn about your party's ESI and key IT personnel.

Initiating a "litigation hold" on your party is now the first step in the litigation process. A litigant and her lawyer have a duty to preserve information relevant to the claims and defenses raised in the pending or contemplated lawsuit. This duty arises from statutes, ethics rules, and case law. Some statutes impose a duty on corporations to preserve certain records for certain periods of time. Model Rule 3.4 of the Model Rules of

Professional Conduct provides that "A lawyer shall not: (a) unlawfully obstruct another party's access to evidence or unlawfully alter, destroy or conceal a document or other material having potential evidentiary value." Modern case law recognizes the common law obligation to preserve evidence. When a party reasonably anticipates litigation, it has a duty to suspend its documents destruction policies and impose a litigation hold to preserve relevant documents and ESI. This duty to preserve may arise even before a complaint is filed and served. For example, a demand letter to a future defendant, a discrimination allegation filed with the employer or the EEOC, or notice that a company driver was involved in an accident that injured another person usually triggers the duty to preserve. In short, whenever a prospective party first learns of an event or issue that may lead to litigation, that knowledge triggers the obligation to initiate a litigation hold.

When you are first brought into the matter and become aware that litigation may follow, you need to impose a litigation hold on your party's relevant information to make sure it is neither altered nor destroyed. The duty to preserve falls first on the lawyer, who is held to know this duty, and then on the lawyer's party, whom the lawyer must educate about the duty. You should meet with your party — in the case of a company, its key officers — and inform the party of what a litigation hold is and why it needs to be imposed immediately. You must advise the company, and in particular its officers and information technology (IT) personnel, about the scope of the contemplated lawsuit and the scope of information relevant to the lawsuit, and ensure that no document retention policies destroy or alter any relevant information. And the duty to preserve means that you must make sure that key information relevant to the lawsuit is backed up and secured electronically.

When a client stores documents and information in "the cloud" — that is, with a third-party networked storage provider — control over this information can be a problem. To the extent that you have an ongoing relationship with a client that stores documents offsite with a third party, advise its personnel to have discussions early on with a cloud provider about document retention and accessibility practices.

Social media have made litigation holds ubiquitous. They are not just for corporate or commercial litigants with sophisticated electronic document retention systems, but for everyone with a Facebook page or a blog. An individual who alters her Facebook page upon learning about impending litigation may be subject to sanctions or a spoliation claim.

Document the steps you take to impose a litigation hold on your party's information. These steps include sending your party a "litigation hold letter" detailing the party's obligation to preserve information, and making sure that your office records in detail the steps you have taken to ensure that your party understands and follows the requirements of a litigation hold. Doing anything less may expose you, as well as your party, to spoliation claims and sanctions.

As plaintiff, consider sending the parties you contemplate suing a "preservation letter" that will notify these parties of the possible lawsuit. This step is particularly important with defendants who are not frequently involved in litigation, who may not be aware of the duty to preserve relevant information, and whose records are important for the plaintiff to obtain. If the defendants are corporations or other artificial entities, you should send the letter to the highest officers of the corporation, and especially the corporation's general counsel. Of course, if you know that a lawyer represents the corporation, ethics rules require that you send the letter to this lawyer.

A preservation letter will be much more explicit than a typical demand letter. It should set out the possible claims; the key dates, persons, and events involved; the time frame of relevant evidence; and the kinds of documentary and ESI involved. Make sure the letter is reasonable in its requests and tailored to the discovery needs of the lawsuit. A well-crafted preservation letter shows the opposing party that you are professional, knowledgeable, and focused, and a court later is more likely to find that your letter triggered a duty for the opposing party to preserve all relevant information. However, make sure that you do not demand more from the opposing party than you demand of your own party. A good way to do this is to have the preservation letter to the opposing party use the same language as your litigation hold letter to your own party, and use the same language you will later use in your Rule 34 requests.

Example:

> Please take notice that the ABC Company is considering bringing a lawsuit against the XYZ Company based on your failure to perform your obligations under a contract you entered into with the ABC Company on June 1, 2013. A copy of that contract is attached. The claims include breach of contract and fraud, and the time frame of the claims covers the period from approximately January 15, 2013, when the ABC Company first contacted the XYZ Company, to the present date. I represent the ABC Company. Please direct all your future communications about this matter to me.
>
> Federal and state case law both require that a "litigation hold" be put in place when any entity reasonably anticipates becoming involved in litigation. Accordingly, we request the following:
>
> (1) You immediately stop any destruction or alteration of documents or electronically stored information in your possession, custody, or control, including e-mail; text messages; voice mail; electronic calendars; telephone logs; social media and other online content; photographs; word processing documents; spreadsheets; and databases, including all underlying metadata and version control, that may be relevant to the above described lawsuit. You must immediately notify your directors, officers, and IT personnel of this legal obligation.
>
> (2) You immediately instruct all employees not to destroy or alter any documents or electronically stored information in their possession, custody, or control, including all notes, memoranda, calendars, e-mails, instant messages, and photographs, that may be contained on laptops, home computers, USB drives, CDs,

PDAs, cellular telephones, and other storage media, that may be relevant to the above described lawsuit.

(3) You immediately take steps to secure and preserve any backup tapes, hard drives, CDs, paper and other archival storage media in your possession, custody, or control, including those provided by third-party vendors, that may be relevant to the above described lawsuit.

If a lawyer will represent you in this matter, please have your lawyer contact me as soon as possible to make sure that you have complied with the requirements of this litigation hold. If you will be handling this matter yourself, please contact me as soon as possible.

If important information is in the possession of a nonparty, consider sending the nonparty an appropriate preservation letter.

Once the lawsuit is underway, and before the parties' Rule 26(f) conference, consider making a motion for a protective order. The order will be helpful if you later seek sanctions on grounds that the opposing party failed to preserve all relevant information.

As defendant, your duty to preserve information also arises when you reasonably anticipate litigation. Sometimes this will happen only when your client is served with a complaint and summons. However, a defendant frequently knows of a current dispute that may lead to future litigation, and the duty to preserve relevant information arises from the time of an event, such as the filing of a grievance against an employer, that triggers the duty.

Regardless of whether you represent the plaintiff or the defendant, you must learn from your party how it generates and stores its paper records and ESI; what computer hardware, software, storage, and backup systems it uses; what retention policies it has in place; how these retention policies work and whether they are followed; and who the key IT personnel are. You should also learn what ESI the party regularly uses, what ESI is and is not readily accessible, and how much time and expense the location, retrieval, and review of both categories of ESI will entail. You will need to meet with those officers and IT personnel to educate yourself about your party's systems and satisfy yourself that the party's personnel understand and follow the requirements of a litigation hold. You also should put the party's legal obligations and the legal consequences of failing to preserve information in a litigation hold letter and send it to the party's directors, officers, IT personnel, and other employees that have access to the information. Work with your client's general counsel, if it has one, as she may be particularly helpful with the implementation of a litigation hold. Make sure that your client's employees know about the need to preserve information, and take steps to secure information on thumb drives, laptops, external hard drives, and the like. Consider asking employees to sign a statement indicating that they are aware of the need to preserve information for litigation purposes.

You may have to obtain copies of the relevant documents and ESI and safeguard them in your office. Remember that you, the lawyer, are responsible for ensuring that your party understands and complies with the litigation hold. Some lawyers now include the requirements of a litigation hold in the client engagement letter and have the client specifically agree to follow those requirements.

Consider hiring an experienced technical expert early in the process if you anticipate that the case will involve substantial ESI and the party you represent does not have the appropriate expert. (A sizeable industry of ESI consultants has developed over the past decade.) This expert can help on several fronts. First, the expert can help you identify the likely sources of relevant information from the opposing party. If you need to depose the opposing party's IT manager to learn about its computer systems before serving a Rule 34 request, the expert can help you ask the proper questions to get the necessary technical information. Second, the expert can help you draft the technical language of the Rule 34 request that will most accurately describe the information you are trying to get and the systems in which that information typically is located. Third, the expert can help you organize, encode, and store the information after you receive it. Fourth, the expert can help you access and understand the metadata behind the information without altering the information during the process. Finally, the expert may become a witness in pretrial discovery hearings and a trial witness on chain of custody issues and other technical matters.

b. *"Meet and confer" under Rule 26(f) with opposing counsel about ESI discovery issues, including whether to enter into a "clawback" agreement to govern privileged and trial-preparation material.*

The time requirements in Rules 16 and 26 mean that the parties must meet and confer within a few weeks after a defendant has been formally brought into the lawsuit. The court's scheduling order issued under Rule 16 may "provide for disclosure or discovery of electronically stored information" and "any agreements the parties reach for asserting claims of privilege or of protection as trial-preparation material after information is produced."

You need to determine the scope of what you want to discover from your adversary. You should address the time frame for discoverable information; the kinds of ESI involved; the hardware, software, storage, and backup systems the parties use; and who the key IT personnel are. Remember that the most common dispute is over whether requested ESI discovery is overly broad in terms of time frame and the kinds of ESI sought, so that the time and expense of the requested discovery is unreasonable. If both sides during the meet and confer required by Rule 26 have a candid discussion of their ESI systems and cooperate in producing relevant ESI, they can streamline discovery and make it less contentious and costly. The meet and confer works best when both parties, such as businesses, have similar ESI and cost issues and mutual interests in focused and efficient discovery.

You need to discuss five additional subjects. First, determine if there will be disputes over whether your party's or the opposing party's ESI is "not reasonably accessible because of undue burden or cost." The ESI discovery rules create two categories of information. Electronically stored information that is reasonably accessible is discoverable (if relevant and not privileged). ESI that is not reasonably accessible is not discoverable unless the court rules otherwise. Which category ESI fits into, and whether relatively inaccessible ESI should nonetheless be produced, may be major issues in many cases. These determinations may require the participation of the parties' IT personnel.

Second, figure out if you want to enter into a "clawback" agreement to govern privileged and trial-preparation materials and whether you want the court to include such an agreement in the court's scheduling order. Because of the sheer volume of information stored electronically, you may inadvertently produce a privileged document.

Rule 26(b)(5) controls the procedure for dealing with privileged and trial-preparation materials that have been accidently turned over to the other side. Under the rule, a party making the claim of privilege must notify any party who received the privileged materials of the claim and the basis for it. The party who received the privileged materials must then "promptly return, sequester, or destroy the specified information and any copies it has" and "must not use or disclose the information until the claim is resolved." The receiving party may also present the materials to the court for resolution of the claim. In effect, the rule freezes the materials until the court can determine if the privilege claim has merit. However, Rule 26(b)(5) is procedural only; it does not control the question of whether the claim of privilege will be upheld. Substantive law determines whether a privilege exists, and the law varies depending on the jurisdiction.

To mitigate the risk that the inadvertent exchange of privileged documents will amount a waiver of the privilege, parties frequently enter into agreements on privilege and trial-preparation issues — "clawback" agreements — and ask the court to incorporate them into the pretrial discovery order. Clawback agreements between the parties can be of several types. A straightforward one provides simply that, if a party inadvertently turns over privileged or trial-preparation documents or ESI, the receiving party will notify the producing party of this fact and will return the documents or ESI promptly and not attempt to use them later as evidence. In addition, the parties agree that the inadvertent production will not be deemed a waiver of the privilege or trial-preparation protection. A more elaborate clawback agreement will include this provision. In addition, it will specify at the start of discovery how parties will search for and separate privileged material. If the parties abide by this agreed-upon method, and if they inadvertently exchange privileged material, the parties can take back the material without a lengthy fight over waiver. Pursuant to one of these agreements, a party sometimes will exchange documents without screening them for privilege. Once his adversary has selected the documents she wishes to rely upon, the party will go through them, find privileged documents, and reclaim them. These agreements work together with FRE 502, which provides that the inadvertent disclosure of privileged information does not amount to a waiver of the privilege if the party took reasonable steps to prevent the disclosure and respond to the error. Ask to make the clawback agreement part of the court order; under FRE 502, doing so makes the agreement binding and enforceable. Clawback agreements may make particular sense when both parties have equivalent litigation resources, or when both parties expect to exchange and receive equivalent amounts of information.

Third, determine the form or forms in which you want the opposing party to produce its ESI, and determine if the opposing party will object to those forms. Determine if you will object to the form or forms in which the opposing party wants you to produce your ESI.

Fourth, determine how long it will realistically take for you and the opposing party to accumulate, Bates stamp, review, copy, and actually turn over the discoverable ESI. Remember that in most cases discovery is a two-way street. A party that makes sweeping demands for ESI can expect the other side to do the same thing. Focused requests are usually in both sides' best interests.

Fifth, consider ways to streamline ESI discovery. A multitiered discovery plan offers one way to do so. You and your adversary might agree to limit discovery initially to those sources that are most readily accessible, then seek discovery from more inaccessible sources only upon a showing of necessity. Another way is to agree upon search terms, or to agree to a sampling method that obviates the need, at least initially, to look through entire databases for relevant documents.

After the parties meet and confer about discovery issues, they must present their proposed discovery plan, including those matters on which they agree and disagree, to the court. Courts usually require that the parties present their plan in writing sufficiently in advance of the Rule 16 conference so that the court has time to review it. The court may incorporate the parties' agreements as to how ESI discovery will proceed in its pretrial order.

c.   Attend the Rule 16 conference to discuss the parties' discovery plan with the court, and argue for your approach in disputed areas.

The Rule 16 conference with the court is a key event in the litigation because it will control the discovery process (and other matters set forth in Rule 16(b)). You must prepare seriously for the conference. Once the court enters the scheduling order, the order controls motions and discovery, and it cannot be modified without a showing of good cause and the court's agreement.

At the conference, be prepared to explain to the court why the agreed-on matters are reasonable and why the court should adopt the parties' plan. The court will usually accept discovery plans that the parties have agreed on. More importantly, where the parties disagree on discovery issues — most commonly, the time frame and breadth of the ESI search — be prepared to argue why your position is more reasonable. You can only do this if you are knowledgeable about your party and the opposing party's claims and defenses, what information will be relevant to those claims and defenses, and the parties' ESI and hardware and software systems that they will have to mine for relevant information.

    d.   Make sure your initial disclosures under Rule 26(a) include required ESI disclosures.

Amended Rule 26(a)(1)(A) now provides that initial disclosures must include "a copy—or description by category and location—of all documents, electronically stored information, and tangible things that the disclosing party has in its possession, custody, or control and may use to support its claims or defenses, unless the use would be solely for impeachment." In short, your initial disclosures now must include your party's ESI relevant to the lawsuit.

    e.   Consider using ESI to answer Rule 33 interrogatories.

Amended Rule 33(d) now provides that a party answering interrogatories can answer by designating ESI from which the answer can be ascertained, provided that the burden of ascertaining the answer is substantially the same for the party serving the interrogatory as for the party served.

    f.   As the requesting party for your Rule 34 requests to produce and Rule 45 subpoenas, determine the form or forms in which you want the requested ESI to be produced. Consider early interrogatories and depositions of opposing parties' IT personnel to learn details of their ESI systems.

Amended Rules 34 and 45 now expressly include ESI and provide that the request "may specify the form or forms in which electronically stored information is to be produced." This is important, because if you do not specify the form or forms, the "party must produce it in a form or forms in which it is ordinarily maintained or in a reasonably usable form or forms." Once the responding party has produced the information in accordance with the rule, a court will hardly be sympathetic to a belated request to have the information produced in another format.

    You cannot formulate a sensible Rule 34 request until you know the formats in which the opposing party generates and maintains its ESI. You should have received some useful information during the parties' Rule 26(f) meet and confer and from the opposing party's initial disclosures under Rule 26(a). In addition, your party's IT personnel and the opposing party's former employees (if they can be interviewed under Model Rule 4.2, which depends on how that rule is interpreted in the applicable jurisdiction; see §2.5.1) should be able to give you valuable advice on how the opposing party likely maintains its ESI. In many cases, these sources will be adequate for you to draft focused and technically precise Rule 34 requests that set out the form or forms in which you want the ESI produced.

    In other cases, you may need to submit interrogatories to the opposing party and depose the opposing party's key IT personnel to acquire detailed information about the opposing party's computer systems and how it organizes its ESI before you can draft effective Rule 34 requests. In still other cases, you may need to hire an experienced IT expert early in the litigation to help you draft focused, specific, and technically accurate requests. In short, you must learn how your opposing party generates and maintains each type of electronic information, both on its main computer systems and its backup systems.

What are the options you have for requesting ESI under Rule 34? First, you can still request that the opposing party produce documents in paper form, if they still exist as such. The advantage is that paper is easy to review and sequentially number using the common Bates stamp. The disadvantage is that paper is cumbersome if the volume is great, and paper gives you only the paper itself, not the underlying information (the metadata). In addition, paper records are much harder to search.

Second, you can request the information in "image format," as TIFF or PDF images. The advantages are that the images cannot be altered and they can easily be Bates numbered. The disadvantage is that images do not contain metadata, and problems can arise when searching through the data and accessing attachments.

Third, you can request ESI in "native format." Native format refers to the format in which the ESI was created and is maintained. For example, the native format of a business record created and stored in Word is Word. Most of the time you will want ESI produced in its native format. Make sure that you also specifically request the metadata, or the data underlying the creation of the record. For example, a business record in Word will have metadata that discloses when changes in the record were made, who made the changes, who received copies of the changes, and when these changes and exchanges took place.[47] Documents in their native format, however, are difficult to Bates stamp, and the data can easily be altered. Also, privileged information in such documents is hard to redact.

Example:

> Responsive documents that comprise electronically stored information (ESI) are to be produced in the native format in which such responsive documents are ordinarily maintained on an appropriate medium, such as CDs or DVDs.

Make sure you also request a copy of the software used to create the ESI if it is not commonly used. For example, if a party creates spreadsheets using proprietary software, you will need to get not only the data but also the software in order to access and analyze the data.

Finally, always ask for "deleted" and "erased" information, since information no longer on a computer's hard drive may still exist on backup systems or on paper. Always couple the Rule 34 requests with an

---

47. Web-based applications, such as Adobe.com and GoogleDocs, may rely on some form of external version control instead of embedded metadata for change tracking, perhaps requiring a specific request for all version control system-retained versions. Also consider that web-based applications will, by definition, be located offsite, likely with retention dates different than those enforced by the entity's main and backup computer systems. Data that would have been flagged as expired and discarded through best business practices may escape such destruction when hosted remotely. These data thus may be available for discovery perhaps indefinitely.

interrogatory that asks for all relevant information about any deleted or erased information, including when and by whom the information was first created, where it was stored before it was deleted or erased, why it was deleted or erased, who authorized or caused its deletion or erasure, what policies exist that apply to the deletion and erasure of the information, and whether the information or drafts of the information exist in any form.

Example (interrogatory):

> If any such document or electronically stored information (ESI) was, but is no longer, in your possession, custody, or control, state what disposition was made of it, explain the circumstances surrounding its disposition and the authorization for such disposition, and identify any person or entity now in possession of such document or ESI.

Follow up on the interrogatory answers when you depose the officers, IT personnel, and other employees of the party. The information you pursue and obtain may form the basis for a spoliation claim.

The common practice for Rule 34 requests is to define ESI broadly, the same way that "documents" is usually defined broadly.

Example:

> "Electronically stored information" (ESI) includes documents, records, files, memoranda, contracts, agreements, notes, work papers, diagrams, charts, preliminary material, drafts, summaries, calendars, drawings, graphics, e-mail, voice mail, text and instant messaging, and data compilations of any kind, whether in electronic, mechanical, electric, digital, or any other form, and any other information stored on computer systems, hard drives, tapes, disks, backup devices and systems, laptops, PDAs, cellular telephones and pagers, and any other electronic devices and systems, both on-site and off-site, that can store information. ESI includes all metadata and all deleted or erased files on a computer or any other storage device.

Another approach takes a more simple tack, because the term "ESI" in Rule 34 is intended to be all encompassing.

Example:

> The term "Electronically stored information" (ESI) includes all "documents," as defined above, and all data or data compilations of any kind stored in any medium from which information can be obtained and that are in your possession, custody, or control. The term ESI also includes active data (information readily available and accessible to users), replicate data (clone files created by automatic backup features), archival data (information copied to removable

media to provide access to data in the event of a system failure), residual data (information that has been deleted but is still recoverable from a computer system), metadata, and source code to software creating such information. The term ESI also includes anything else that is encompassed by the term "electronically stored information" as used in Rule 34 of the Federal Rules of Civil Procedure.

"Residual data" is particularly volatile since every minute a computer is on puts residual data at risk of destruction through normal system operation. User activity greatly increases this risk. For that reason, residual data should probably be secured first, at least where the costs of doing so are justifiable.

g.   *As the producing party, determine if you will object to a request or subpoena for ESI on the grounds that (a) the requested ESI is "not reasonably accessible," or (b) the requested form of production is improper. If (b), suggest another form.*

When there is no dispute over whether the requested ESI is reasonably accessible (and is relevant and not privileged), it must be produced. However, when you receive a Rule 34 request, you can object and move for a protective order on the ground that the ESI is "not reasonably accessible because of undue burden or cost." The analysis will necessarily focus in large measure on the formats and systems in which the ESI is stored. Active data, such as information stored on a computer hard drive, or data that can quickly and easily be retrieved from storage systems, are usually considered reasonably accessible. Erased and fragmented information, backup tapes, and data in obsolete systems are usually considered not reasonably accessible; current software cannot read such information, and it must be restored before it is usable. If requested information is not reasonably accessible, it may still be discoverable. If the requesting party insists that the information should nevertheless be produced, the producing party has the burden to demonstrate why production should not be compelled.

The producing party can also object to the form of the requested production of ESI and suggest an alternative. The usual basis for such an objection is that the ESI is reasonably accessible in a certain format, but that the requesting party wants the ESI produced in a different format without a sufficient justification for the request.

Rule 45, which governs subpoenas to a nonparty, mirrors Rule 34. You can send a preservation letter to a nonparty, which will trigger the duty to preserve relevant information. You can meet and confer with the nonparty over discovery issues. You can send the nonparty a subpoena that designates the form or forms in which ESI is to be produced. The nonparty can object to an ESI request on the same grounds that a party can object. The nonparty can ask the court to bar discovery because it is overly broad and ask the court to shift some or all of the cost of complying with an ESI request to the requesting party. Courts recognize that discovery of ESI from a nonparty sometimes involves considerable time and expense, and courts under these circumstances are more willing to shift those costs to the requesting party.

> h. *As the requesting party, if the court rules that the requested ESI is not reasonably accessible, be prepared to show that good cause exists to require that the ESI still be produced.*

The court will have to decide whether requested ESI is not reasonably accessible if either the requesting party moves to compel production or the producing party moves for a protective order to bar production. Either way, the court will first need to determine if the requested ESI is in fact not reasonably accessible and then, if so, whether the information should nevertheless be produced. This determination involves a cost-benefit analysis, with the producing party having the burden to show that the cost exceeds the benefit. On the benefit side, how much information does the ESI contain that is not obtainable from other sources, and how significant is this information to the litigation? On the cost side, what will be the cost, in terms of time and money, necessary to retrieve the requested information? This conflict frequently arises when a party seeks to obtain the opposing party's e-mails. Courts have sometimes ordered "sampling." The responding party searches through a subset of databases for responsive information, for instance, and documents the cost of doing so. The court then compares the quality of the information obtained through this modest search, compares it to the cost of obtaining the information, and determines whether to require the responding party to complete its search through remaining databases.

> i. *As the producing party, if the court orders discovery of ESI that is not reasonably accessible, be prepared to show that cost-shifting is warranted because the request creates an undue burden or cost.*

Traditionally the producing party bears the costs of producing the requested information. This is the general rule for paper discovery, and it remains the general rule for ESI. When documents, records, and data are on a computer system's hard drive, the producing party can usually copy these files quickly and inexpensively. The producing party ordinarily still bears the costs even when they are more substantial. Many courts take the position that a party cannot reap the benefits of computerization and at the same time use the technology to argue that it should be protected from the costs of searching its computers to comply with a discovery request. Put another way, a party cannot select a storage system and then complain about the costs associated with retrieving data from the storage system it selected.

What happens, however, if a Rule 34 request asks for electronic information not on a computer hard drive or in another easily accessible location? What if the information sought cannot be extracted from computerized storage systems without expending substantial time and incurring substantial expense? For example, retailers, banks, and other financial institutions generate vast amounts of transactions data that they warehouse in large storage facilities. Trying to find and copy only certain of this ESI can be a daunting technical task that will involve time, expense, and expertise. As another example, large businesses create large numbers of e-mails on a daily basis, and searching for specific e-mails by subjects, dates, and senders can require extensive effort. If the court determines that the transactions data or e-mails are not reasonably accessible but should nonetheless be produced, the producing party can ask the court to shift some or all of the costs of production onto the requesting party.[48]

In recent years courts have begun to soften the traditional rule that the responding party always bears the costs of complying with a reasonable request for electronic information. When the information sought is unique and not in an easily retrievable form, and the costs of obtaining the information are high, courts have begun to examine such requests more closely and shift the costs of production partly or entirely onto the requesting party. The analysis is essentially a balancing test, weighing the significance of the information sought against the cost of obtaining it.

The most cited case is Zubulake v. USB Warburg LLC, 217 F.R.D. 309, (S.D.N.Y. 2003), commonly called *Zubulake I*. *Zubulake I* involved a document request for e-mails in a gender discrimination and wrongful retaliation case. The court set forth a seven-part test on cost-shifting, with the most important factor at the top and the rest decreasing in importance:

1. The extent to which a discovery request is specifically tailored to discover relevant information;
2. The availability of such information from other sources;
3. The total cost of production compared to the amount in controversy;
4. The cost of production compared to the parties' available resources;
5. The relative ability of each party to control costs and its incentive to do so;
6. The importance of the issues at stake in the litigation; and
7. The relative benefits to the parties of obtaining the information.

Another case, Boeynaems v. LA Fitness Int'l, LLC, 285 F.R.D. 331 (E.D. Pa. 2012), includes a lengthy discussion of a number of decisions on cost-shifting and ESI.

Note that the cost to the responding party of screening the electronic information for privileged communications is *not* a factor. Courts generally reason that, whether the information is in paper or electronic form, the

---

48. A proposed amendment to Rule 26 would explicitly recognize the authority of the court to shift costs, codifying what case law already authorizes. Make sure to check revisions to the Federal Rules to ensure that the information in this text is accurate. See www.uscourts.gov.

responding party will still need to screen for privilege, a cost the respond-ing party should bear.

If the court rules that ESI must be produced even though it is not reasonably accessible, and the court shifts some or all of the cost of retrieval on the requesting party, that party must then decide whether to go ahead with the request and pay those costs. If the projected costs are high, and the likelihood of obtaining significant information is low, the requesting party may decide to forgo obtaining this information.

> j. *As the requesting party, if the responding party has altered or destroyed ESI after the time that party knew or should have known of its obligation to preserve ESI, determine if Rule 37 sanctions for spoliation are appropriate.*

"Spoliation" refers to the alteration or destruction of evidence by parties to the litigation. It is easy to delete vast quantities of ESI quickly, and recovering that information is usually costly, time-consuming, and not always possible. Spoliation does not occur if records are destroyed *before* the party had notice or should have known that particular information may be relevant to a dispute. However, once a party has notice, the party has a duty to preserve relevant information. Whenever a party intentionally destroys or alters such information *after* being on notice, it acts in bad faith. This constitutes spoliation.

The more common situation occurs when a party has notice and its records are destroyed or altered through inaction or negligence. Many businesses have document retention policies, which are in reality docu-ment destruction policies. What happens if relevant documents, records, or data are destroyed because of such a policy? For example, many busi-nesses have policies in which certain electronic records, such as e-mails, are routinely deleted or overwritten at regular intervals. The business saves money by reusing its storage capacity, but the policy results in the system-atic purge of information relevant to future litigation.

Courts appear willing to accept selective retention policies for elec-tronic documents to the same extent that such policies have been allowed for paper records. However, the policy must be made in good faith, must be reasonable, and must comply with applicable statutes and regulations. In addition, the policy should provide for an effective means of promptly stopping the destruction or alteration of relevant data when notice of a dispute is received. When a document retention policy is simply a thinly veiled attempt to purge a business of records and data that an opponent would want to discover whenever litigation arises, courts have not hesitated to find that spoliation has occurred.

Rule 37 (e) provides: "Absent exceptional circumstances, a court may not impose sanctions under these rules on a party for failing to provide electronically stored information lost as a result of the routine, good-faith operation of an electronic information system." This "safe harbor" provision is more limited than that label suggests. Sanctions cannot be imposed for the routine, good faith destruction of ESI. A party acts in bad faith when it lets ESI be deleted or altered by inaction if it knows or should have known that the ESI is relevant to actual or reasonably anticipated litigation. In such a situation, a party has an affirmative obligation to timely modify or suspend the routine destruction features of its computer systems.

When courts impose sanctions on a party for destroying or failing to prevent the destruction of ESI, they usually focus on three factors: (1) the nature and extent of the destruction, (2) whether the destruction was made in bad faith, and (3) whether the requesting party was significantly prejudiced. Sanctions should be commensurate with the degree of the violation. Courts have imposed fines, awarded attorney's fees, shifted costs, admitted evidence of spoliation during trial, given the jury an adverse inference instruction, precluded evidence, and entered judgment on a claim or even all claims against the violating party.

A proposed amendment to Rule 37(e), pending at the time of this edition's publication, would limit the court's power to sanction a party for failing to preserve ESI to those instances when the party acted intentionally. Otherwise, the court can only issue those orders necessary to address the prejudice the other side suffers as a result of the failure to preserve.

k.   As the responding party, if no prior agreement exists, screen your ESI for privileged and confidential information.

You need to screen all your party's documents and ESI for privileged and trial-preparation materials before turning them over to the requesting party, unless you have entered into a clawback agreement that allows you to review documents for privilege once your adversary has gone through them. Review each paper document or ESI and its underlying metadata. If the document includes a privileged communication or trial-preparation material, it must be segregated and recorded in a "privilege log." (Many lawyers and clients label their written communications "Privileged Communication" or "Attorney-client Privileged Materials" so that a word search of a database will quickly identify most of the privileged communications. In addition, e-discovery search software, using basic linguistic or more sophisticated sociological programs, can sift through extensive e-mails, correspondence, records, and other data with increasing speed and accuracy. Document review will soon be mostly an electronic activity.) The privilege log records the basic information of each document or ESI, such as the date, person who made the communication, the recipients of the communication, and the general nature of the communication (but not in such detail that a waiver occurs). Spreadsheet programs work well for this purpose. The opposing party gets the privilege log, but not the privileged materials. If a dispute arises as to whether a particular document or ESI is actually privileged, the court usually inspects the disputed material in camera.

Do the same review for confidential information like trade secrets, customer lists, and financial data. These should be put under a protective order early in the litigation to ensure that the opposing side does not misuse the information or disseminate it to other persons.

*l. The producing and requesting parties must work out the mechanics for
producing the discoverable ESI.*

Use your party's IT director to identify, locate, and copy the ESI called
for in the Rule 34 request. You must search for ESI in every location where
it may be stored. Determine whether no ESI exists that complies with a
request. If ESI once existed but now no longer exists, find out why it no
longer exists.

If the discovery request will require you to cull through an enormous
database, or a number of enormous databases, to find relevant material,
consider hiring an e-discovery vendor to assist with your production. While
outsourcing may be expensive, some of these vendors offer sophisticated
techniques to streamline production. These techniques include "predictive coding." The computer selects a statistically significant sample of ESI,
which lawyers then review. They feed their findings about what makes the
responsive documents responsive back into the computer. It then selects
another sample, using the information about relevance the lawyers have
provided. This process repeats several times, until the computer has
"learned" how to find responsive documents at an acceptable error rate.
Some studies indicate that predictive coding can better find responsive
materials than lawyers going document-by-document. Courts are
beginning to approve predictive coding as an appropriate method to
search through ESI to find documents that respond to a discovery
request.[49]

When you have gathered the ESI that is responsive to the request, you
need to work out the mechanics for its delivery to the requesting party. The
most common arrangement is to put the ESI in the form or forms
requested and deliver them to the opposing party by the required date.
Most lawyers will also create a TIFF or PDF version of the ESI that is Bates
numbered and give one copy to the opposing party and keep the other
copy. In this way there will be no question what was given to the opposing
party. A good practice is to have your written response to the Rule 34
request spell out exactly what you are producing and when and how you
are producing it. If the requesting party has requested ESI that does not
exist or no longer exists, your written response to the Rule 34 request
should spell this out as well.

The responding party can transfer ESI to the requesting party in a
number of ways, whether on CDs or a hard drive, or through a secure
online file transfer. Consider an agreement under which all the parties
agree to deposit all discovery materials into a central depository organized
and managed by a professional vendor that specializes in this work. All the
lawyers and parties can be given passwords and can then access the central
depository from remote locations at any time during the litigation.

---

49. See Moore v. Publicis Groupe, 287 F.R.D. 182 (S.D.N.Y. 2012).

§6.9. Depositions

Depositions are usually taken after both interrogatory answers and responses to documents requests have been received, since those answers and documents will usually be necessary to plan an intelligent deposition. Although depositions are both expensive and time consuming, they are essential for assessing witness credibility, learning what witnesses know and don't know, getting details, and pinning witnesses down. They can be used on parties and nonparties, and they are the only method in which the opposing counsel does not directly control the responses. For these reasons, depositions play a critical role in the discovery plan of virtually every case.

Rules 27 through 32 govern depositions. Rule 30, which regulates oral depositions, is the principal one, however, since oral depositions are the predominant way in which depositions are taken.[50] Rule 45 controls deposition subpoenas directed to nonparties.

1. Law

a. Timing

Oral depositions may be taken of any party or nonparty. They can be taken after the parties meet to develop a discovery plan under Rule 26(f).[51] Leave of court is not necessary to take a deposition before the meeting if the deposition notice certifies, with supporting facts, that the deponent is expected to leave the country and will thereafter be unavailable for examination. Court approval is required under Rule 30(a) if the person to be deposed is imprisoned.

b. Number and length of depositions

Each side — plaintiffs, defendants, or third-party defendants — has a presumptive limit of 10 depositions. Under Rule 30(a), this number can increase by court order or written stipulation of the parties. This means that when a case has multiple plaintiffs or defendants, the plaintiffs or defendants must get together and decide how to use their 10 depositions most effectively. It also means that the court, under Rule 26(b)(2), will be more actively involved in determining the number and order of depositions. While a deposition is normally considered to be of one person, Rule 30(b)(6) permits a deposition to be directed to corporations and other entities, and the corporation or other entity must designate one or more persons to testify on its behalf. Under these circumstances, a single

---

50. Lawyers rarely use depositions on written questions, governed by Rule 33.

51. Wright §§84-85; Hazard et al. §8.16; Moore's Manual §15.20; Manual of Federal Practice §§5.18–5.125; Moore's Federal Practice §§30.01–30.64; Wright & Miller §§2071–2157; D. Malone, The Effective Deposition: Techniques and Strategies That Work (4th ed. 2012); H. Hecht, Effective Depositions (ABA, 2d ed. 2010).

deposition may be taken of more than one person and still count as one deposition for purposes of the 10-deposition limit.

Under Rule 30(d), a deposition of a person is limited to one day of seven hours, unless the court orders otherwise or the parties otherwise stipulate. Lunch and other breaks do not count toward the seven hours. No person can be deposed more than once without court order or written stipulation of the parties. However, Rule 30(d)(1) also provides that "the court must allow additional time consistent with Rule 26(b)(2) if needed to fairly examine the deponent or if the deponent, another person, or any other circumstance, impedes or delays the examination." If you think you need more than seven hours (which should happen rarely), ask the other side in advance to agree to reasonable additional time, or get a court order. Don't assume that you can go past the seven-hour limit and then seek additional time.

c. Notice

Whenever a deposition will be taken, the party taking the deposition must give "reasonable" written notice to every party to the action. Rule 30(b) does not specify what is reasonable, although some local rules specify minimum requirements, frequently five days. Also, most of the courts to address the issue describe reasonable notice as a flexible standard that depends on the nature of the case and the deponent involved.[52]

The notice must state the name and address of each person to be deposed. If the name is not known, the notice must describe the person to be deposed in sufficient detail to identify that person individually or as part of a class or group. This is frequently the case with corporations and other artificial entities, where the actual name of the proper person to be deposed is unknown. In such a case, under Rule 30(b)(6), the corporation or other entity must designate an officer, director, managing agent, or other person to testify on its behalf. The notice must also state the time and place for the deposition.

A document request that complies with the requirements of Rule 34 can accompany notice to a party deponent. A subpoena to a nonparty can also command the nonparty deponent to produce designated materials at the deposition. In this situation, notice to the parties must include a designation of the materials the nonparty deponent has been directed to produce at the deposition. The easy way to provide this information is to attach a copy of the subpoena to the notices. You should, however, always have the necessary documents of the party or nonparty witness before taking the deposition, unless you plan to catch the party or witness unprepared, before he has had time to collect and review the relevant documents and records.

The notice of deposition must designate how the deposition will be recorded, whether by audio, audiovisual, or stenographic means. Any

---

52. Wright & Miller §2111.

other party can designate by notice other means of recording, with each party bearing the cost of its method.

In addition to the notice to other parties, of course, the person to be deposed must also be notified. Where the deponent is also a party, the notice of deposition is sufficient. Where the deponent is a nonparty, he must be subpoenaed in accordance with Rule 45.

Subpoenas can be issued directly by the attorneys as officers of the court. The attorney simply fills out a blank subpoena form issued by the clerk of the appropriate court, or the attorney as an officer of the court can also issue and sign a subpoena on behalf of the court, if authorized to practice law in the court in which the case is pending. As 2013 amendments to Rule 45 provide, the subpoena shall issue from the district court where the action is pending, and the subpoena can be served anywhere within the United States.

The witness attendance fee and transportation costs must accompany the subpoena. 28 U.S.C. §1821 sets these fees. Consistent with the requirements of Rule 45(b), the common practice is to attach a check to the subpoena for one day's witness attendance fee and the transportation costs incurred by the deponent traveling to and from the place where the deposition is to be held.

If the terms of the notice of deposition or subpoena are unreasonable or oppressive, make your objection known to the other parties. If the dispute cannot be worked out informally, file a motion for a protective order. Alternatively, if you represent a nonparty deponent, move to quash the subpoena in the district where compliance with the subpoena is required.

d.   Location

Rule 30 does not specify where a deposition may be conducted. Accordingly, the deposition of a party can be held anywhere. If for some reason the location is unreasonable, the deposed party must seek a protective order under Rule 26(c).[53] The deposition of a nonparty must meet the requirements of Rule 45. Usually, this location must be within 100 miles of where the person resides, is employed, or regularly transacts business.

e.   Persons present

The usual persons present at a deposition are the person being deposed, the parties' lawyers, and the court reporter. A videographer will also be present when the deposition is videotaped.

Parties usually have the right to be present at any deposition, although they infrequently appear. However, if a party's appearance is for an improper purpose, such as intimidation or harassment of a deponent, you must seek a protective order from the court. Nonparties and members of the media are usually held to have no right to attend depositions, since a deposition, unlike a trial, is not considered to proceed in a public forum.

---

53. See §6.13.1.

f. Recording

Under Rule 28, a deposition must be taken in the presence of someone authorized to administer oaths. Invariably, a certified court reporter who will stenographically record the testimony is also a notary public and therefore able to perform both functions. Rule 30(b)(3) allows the deposition to be recorded by audio, audiovisual, or stenographic means. Rule 30(b)(4) also authorizes depositions to be taken by telephone or "other remote means." While the predominant means of recording remains the court reporter, since he can create a written transcript, the other methods can reduce costs or more vividly memorialize the deponent's testimony. These other methods, particularly videotaping, have become a common way of recording experts' depositions when the experts are not expected to testify at trial and their depositions will be introduced in evidence during the trial. Video depositions are also a good idea if you believe that the opposing counsel will unduly interfere with your efforts to depose the witness, such as by repeatedly making objections that serve no proper purpose and are made only to coach the witness on a desirable response. There is no requirement that a deposition be transcribed.

g. Signing and correcting

Under Rule 30(e), the deponent or any party is entitled to a transcript of the deposition. The deponent has the right to review the transcript for accuracy and sign it. Any party may also request that the deponent review and sign, so long as the party makes the request before the deposition's completion. This is commonly called the "read and sign" right. The deponent has 30 days after receiving notice that the transcript is ready to review it and, if there are any changes, to make and sign a statement noting the changes and the reasons for them. That statement will then be appended to the deposition transcript.

The reporter must certify that the witness was sworn and that the transcript is accurate. The reporter should then seal the original, which should include any exhibits that were marked and used during the deposition, and promptly send it to the lawyer who arranged for the transcript to be made. Rule 30(f) imposes an obligation on the lawyer to store the transcript "under conditions that will protect it against loss, destruction, tampering, or deterioration." Under Rule 5(d), depositions are not to be filed with the court until they are used in the proceeding or the court orders otherwise.

h. Objections

Rule 30(c) provides that the reporter shall note on the deposition all objections to the qualifications of the reporter or other officer; those to the procedure, evidence, and conduct of parties; and any other objections. As the rule provides, testimony objected to shall be "taken subject to any objection," meaning that the witness should answer the questions asked with all objections being noted. A judge can then rule on the objections later, in the event that any party wishes to use the transcript at trial.

Rule 30(c)(2) governs the conduct of attorneys making objections during the deposition. Any objections must be "stated concisely and in a nonargumentative and nonsuggestive manner." Also, "a person may instruct a deponent not to answer only when necessary to preserve a privilege, to enforce a limitation directed by the court, or to present a motion" to limit or terminate the examination.

Rule 32(d) provides that objections to a witness' competency or the materiality or relevance of the testimony need not be made during the taking of the deposition, unless the ground for the objection could have been eliminated if made known at that time. However, objections to the form of questions, and other errors that might have been cured if the objection had been made, are waived unless timely made.

Rule 30 addresses the special problems concerning privilege objections. The usual procedure with objections — requiring answers "subject to the objection" — will not work. Therefore, a timely objection must be made, and if a lawyer represents the deponent, the deponent's lawyer can instruct the deponent not to answer pursuant to Rule 30(c)(2).[54] The party taking the deposition then has the option of moving for an order to compel discovery under Rule 37.

If the examination is conducted in bad faith to annoy, embarrass, or harass the deponent, then a party or the deponent can demand that the deposition be suspended, to enable the party or deponent to move for a protective order under Rule 30(d) to terminate or limit the examination.

i.   Conferring with counsel during the deposition

You can confer with your client during the deposition to determine whether to assert a privilege. However, in most jurisdictions you cannot confer with a client while a question is pending (unless a privilege issue is involved). Some courts bar any conferring during a deposition (except for privilege issues) and require that the atmosphere and conduct of the

---

54. The problem is more complicated with nonparty witnesses who are not represented by counsel. Can a lawyer for a party make an objection for the witness? Under Model Rule 3.4(f), the usual answer is no. Since a party's lawyer does not represent the witness, the lawyer ordinarily cannot give legal advice to the witness other than recommending that the witness get advice, particularly since the witness may have interests that are, or may be, adverse to the party's. However, there is nothing improper in objecting to a question on behalf of your client; state the basis of your objection, and suggest that the witness talk to a lawyer to get legal advice before answering the question.

The problem also arises with employees of business entities. The lawyer for the business will usually treat the employee as her client and represent the employee at the employee's deposition. The theory is that, since the employee's statements may be admissible at trial as admissions against the business, the lawyer for the business has a right to represent him (unless, of course, the employee is also a party or has his own lawyer). In some situations a former employee may be treated as a client, particularly where the former employee was a management level employee and was involved in acts that are the basis of the lawsuit. See §6.3.9.

lawyers during a deposition resemble that of a trial. Other courts expressly permit conferring during a deposition, particularly during breaks. Check the local rules, the informal practices of the lawyers, and whether the judge has any standing orders on how depositions are to be conducted.

2. Practice approach

Deposition rules are sufficiently broad that they rarely restrict the deposition process in any meaningful way. Since the rules permit such latitude, your overall discovery strategy should determine how you use depositions. There are several questions that you should always ask.

a. Should I take a deposition?

Depositions are probably both the most effective discovery vehicle when used properly and the most ineffective one when misused. You should consider the pros and cons of depositions in general and weigh these considerations when deciding if you should depose a particular witness.

On the plus side, depositions are by far the most effective discovery device for obtaining detailed information. The question-and-answer process permits follow-up questioning on promising topics. Depositions allow you to learn the information and where it is, and what this witness knows and doesn't know. Second, a deposition commits the deponent to the details of his story. You learn what the witness is going to say at trial, giving you an opportunity to look for contrary evidence that you can later use at trial to refute the testimony. Third, the deposition gives you an opportunity to develop specific facts that may be used as admissions and impeachment at trial. Fourth, a deposition is in many respects a trial simulation, so you can evaluate the deponent as a trial witness. Finally, opposing counsel has only limited objection rights, making depositions the only discovery method in which counsel does not prepare the responses.

On the minus side, depositions are expensive. Even a short deposition will cost hundreds of dollars in lawyer's fees, reporter's fees, video operator costs, transcript costs, and possibly the witness' lodging and mileage fees. Where the amount at issue in a dispute is modest, costs are usually the primary reason for limiting the use of depositions. Second, depositions can perpetuate unfavorable testimony. Taking a deposition simply to find out what a witness will say can come at a price, if that witness is unfavorable and later becomes unavailable for trial. Third, a deposition educates your opponents as much as it educates you. Where you believe your opponent will learn more from the deposition than you, or you can get the same information informally such as by having an investigator interview the witness, taking the deposition can be counterproductive. Fourth, taking depositions may motivate an inactive opponent to prepare and pursue discovery. Unless your opponent has been using delaying tactics, motivating an opponent rarely does you any good.

b. Whose deposition should I take?

The cost-benefit factors discussed above must be used to decide which witnesses to depose. In addition, keep in mind that Rule 30(a) limits each side to 10 depositions total and a single deposition of a particular person unless a court order or written stipulation of the parties provides otherwise. There are three basic categories of witnesses to consider.

First, you should always depose the opposing parties. You obviously will want to tie them down to the detailed facts and their versions of disputed events and transactions, and to evaluate them as potential witnesses. The only exception might be nominal parties, such as a guardian or administrator of an estate. When the party is an artificial entity like a corporation, the officers and employees directly involved in the transactions and events at issue should be deposed.

Second, consider deposing the principal nonparty witnesses you have identified. In personal injury cases, this category would include eyewitnesses to the event involved, as well as witnesses to the major damages elements. In contract and commercial cases, the list would include the witnesses to the conversations, agreements, and conduct that are relevant to the transactions involved, and witnesses to any breaches and resulting damages.

The nonparty witnesses category obviously has the potential to be the largest one. When deciding which witnesses to depose, you need to keep cost-effectiveness in mind. While you obviously need to learn what the testimony of important witnesses will be, there comes a point at which the information obtained from witnesses who are merely corroborative and peripheral is not worth pursuing through depositions.

A good rule of thumb for depositions is that you should depose your opponent's witnesses, not your own, since there is usually no benefit in deposing witnesses you know will be favorable. However, if such a witness is elderly or in poor health, or may leave the jurisdiction and be unavailable for trial, you should always consider taking the witness' deposition to preserve the testimony. Hence, at the beginning of the depositions stage, lawyers will usually depose a favorable witness who the lawyers know will provide strong testimony, in order to guard against disaster. If the witness becomes unavailable, a deposition will usually qualify as former testimony under FRE 804(b)(1). If you depose a witness for this purpose, make sure that you conduct the deposition so that the transcript is clear and complete. Consider taking a videotaped deposition, which you can present effectively to a jury.

Third, consider what experts you need to depose. Under Rule 26(b)(4), any party can depose any expert "identified as an expert whose opinions may be presented at trial." From the experts' written reports, you will have a substantial amount of information about the other party's experts, including their opinions, bases for the opinions, data relied upon, exhibits to be used, and biographical information. In some cases, you may not need to depose the other party's expert. For example, in a personal injury case the information you will have from the expert disclosure, medical records, and other information obtained through interrogatories, documents requests, and depositions of other witnesses will sometimes be adequate to know what the plaintiff's treating doctor will say at trial. If you do not depose your adversary's expert, you will not draw the expert's attention to weaknesses in her anticipated testimony, depriving her of a chance to strengthen her opinion before trial. An expert can also cure an omission from required disclosures with testimony at a deposition and thereby protect against the automatic preclusion sanction that Rule 37 provides for incomplete disclosures.

In most cases, however, an expert deposition will be essential. The amount of information you receive about the other party's experts may be inadequate to learn what the witness will say at trial. If the case depends in large part on the relative persuasiveness of the experts, you will need to depose the other party's expert to get a good feel for the kind of witness she will make at trial. The point is that you need not depose every expert in every case. Deposing experts is expensive and time-consuming, particularly since under Rule 26(b)(4)(E) the party deposing the expert must pay the expert's reasonable fees. You should take these depositions only when there is a clear need to do so.

Where the expert is outside the court's jurisdiction and the expert will not come forward voluntarily to testify at trial, the expert will usually be "unavailable" under FRE 804(a)(5). Since the expert cannot be compelled to testify at trial, the expert's deposition can be admitted at trial as former testimony under Rule 32 and FRE 804(b)(1). For this reason, the deposition of such an expert should be taken to ensure that the questions and answers will be available for admission at trial. It is particularly important that an "unavailable" expert's testimony be clear and complete, Also, you should particularly consider a videotaped deposition for an absent expert. It presents a vivid re-creation of the deponent's testimony to the jury, and it is particularly useful where the expert will use exhibits, visual aids, and demonstrations during her testimony. Taking the deposition and then editing out objectionable questions and answers is admittedly expensive. Nevertheless, a video deposition, if done carefully, is a vastly superior method of presenting the absent expert's testimony.

By taking a deposition, you can benefit your opponent as well as yourself. Once taken, if the witness later becomes unavailable, the deposition probably will qualify for admission at trial under FRE 804(b)(1). If you suspect this may happen, and if the witness is unfavorable, consider taking only a short deposition to learn the basics of what the witness has to say. If the witness is one of your opponent's expert witnesses, and you suspect the expert may be unavailable at trial, consider not asking background qualifications questions. (Of course, nothing will prevent your opponent from asking the qualifications questions.)

c.   When should I take depositions?

Rule 30(a) permits parties to take oral depositions at any time after they confer to plan discovery under Rule 26(f). Several tactical considerations primarily determine deposition timing.

First, depositions can be taken before an action has been commenced if Rule 27(a) requirements are met. These requirements are technical and detailed; you must draw up a verified petition that sets out the facts of the anticipated suit, the details expected from the witness, and the reasons a deposition is necessary. The petition must be served, with a notice of deposition, to each anticipated adverse party that can be found. The amount of work required under Rule 27(a) is at least as much as is required to prepare, file, and serve a complaint and summons. For that reason, Rule 27(a) is ordinarily used only in those circumstances where service on the adverse party cannot be made quickly.

Second, you may want to depose your opponent as soon as permitted after the suit's commencement. An early deposition may be necessary when you need facts to support a jurisdictional motion, or when you need to learn the identity of proper parties and officers and agents of such parties. Also, you might want to depose a custodian of records early on to learn about your opponent's records, so that you can prepare a more focused document request.

An early deposition may also catch your opponent unprepared, not yet having collected and reviewed records and documents. The witness may disclaim knowledge of certain facts, or assert facts that can be disproved. You can then use this testimony as admissions and for impeachment at trial.

On the other hand, an early deposition poses obvious risks. Without interrogatory answers and documents received through document requests, you cannot prepare as thoroughly as you should. Rule 30(a) bars a second deposition of a person without a court order or written stipulation of the parties. If any party objects, you may be prevented from taking a second deposition. In short, taking an early deposition with the idea of taking a second detailed one later is risky.

Third, the usual approach is to take depositions after initial disclosures, interrogatory answers, and documents have been received. Only then will you have the necessary facts and documents to prepare thoroughly and take a detailed, complete deposition. This timing is particularly well advised for depositions of adverse parties. You can pin down your adversary only if you have the preliminary discovery on hand.

Deciding when to take a deposition can only be done on a case-by-case basis. Your decision must balance the benefits of an early deposition against a later one based on the extent of your knowledge from your pre-filing investigation and existing discovery. The question of when to take a particular deposition should never be a routine matter, but should always be decided by weighing the benefits, disadvantages, and risks of a particular course of action.

d.   What order of depositions should I use?

There are several approaches to establishing the order of depositions, and the approach that will be effective in a given case depends on the issues, parties, and witnesses involved.

First, consistent with the idea that discovery should build upon itself, a common approach is to depose neutral and unfavorable witnesses first, then adverse employees, officers, and parties to the action, and finally, the adverse parties' experts. By arranging depositions in this manner, you can use information obtained from witnesses to prepare for depositions of parties to the action and, in turn, the experts. This approach, however, has built-in disadvantages, since every deposition educates both you and the other parties. Every witness deposition you take before taking the adverse party's deposition prepares that party for her own deposition.

The second approach reverses this order. The adverse parties' depositions go first, followed by those of nonparty witnesses. You can pin down the adverse parties to detailed testimony before hearing from other witnesses, who may offer conflicting testimony.

The third possibility is to schedule a series of depositions back to back so that later deponents do not have time to review the transcripts of the earlier depositions. This tactic works well with unfavorable witnesses and adverse parties, who might otherwise try to find out what an earlier witness said and then tell a consistent story. If you worry that witnesses might collaborate in this manner, simply schedule the first deposition for the morning, the second for early afternoon, and so on, allowing enough time so that you can realistically keep to the schedule. For example, when deposing corporate employees, you may get inconsistencies by scheduling them back-to-back, starting at the bottom and working up to management.

As with the decision on the timing of depositions, a decision on the order of depositions can only be made on a case-by-case basis. The decision should not be routine or rote, but should always involve weighing the advantages, disadvantages, and risks of a particular approach.

e.   What must I do to schedule a deposition?

Scheduling a deposition involves two decisions: when and where. When has been discussed above. Where depends on your personal preference and what the rules allow. Rule 30 does not deal with location, so it leaves the choice up to the party taking the deposition of another party. However, Rule 45 has specific location rules for deposing nonparty witnesses. Such witnesses can be deposed anywhere within 100 miles of where the person resides, is employed, or engages in business regularly. In addition, Rule 30(b)(4) permits the court to order that a deposition be taken by telephone or other remote electronic means. The parties can also stipulate to this effect.

The usual location for a deposition is in your own offices. You will be comfortable there, have your files with you, and have your deponent away from familiar surroundings. If you have previously obtained responses to your document requests, you should have no need to go to the deponent's place of business.

You will likely have to travel to a distant nonparty witness for the deposition, unless you can get the witness to come to you. While making the deposition convenient for nonparty witnesses, Rule 45 can inconvenience everyone else. Therefore, try to have the witness come to you. If, in addition to the mileage and witness fees, you offer to compensate the witness for actual travel expenses and lost wages, the witness may be more likely to come to your offices. (If you provide this compensation, which most jurisdictions permit, notify the other lawyers that you are compensating the witness for actual lost wages or time.)

Expert depositions proceed best at experts' offices. The deposition will be convenient for the expert, and you will have access to the expert's reports, records, and reference material. You will avoid what otherwise is a common problem: the expert who, for one reason or another, fails to bring all necessary paperwork, thereby making a thorough deposition impossible. Make sure, however, that you bring everything you need to the expert's office.

Regardless of where you depose the expert, make sure you have previously obtained all records you will need for the deposition from the opposing party or through subpoenas. Before deposing a doctor, for example, make sure you have the relevant hospital records as well as the doctor's own medical records. In addition, under Rule 26(b)(4) you must obtain the expert's report from the testifying expert before the deposition. A good deposition of an expert is impossible without a review of all relevant reports.

After you have selected a time and place for the depositions, you must do the following:

1. Send notices to parties.
2. Serve subpoenas and witness fees on nonparty witnesses.
3. Reserve a suitable room for the deposition.
4. Arrange for a court reporter and video operator.
5. Reconfirm deposition date and attendance.

The notices to parties and subpoenas to witnesses should be served with a reasonable lead time. Given the busy schedules of most people, 20 or 30 days' notice is usually appropriate. When deposing a party, good practice requires that you call that party's lawyer and select a mutually convenient time before preparing the notices. Doing so avoids delays, avoids motions to reset deposition dates, and generally helps create good working relationships between lawyers, to everyone's benefit. With nonparty witnesses, first serve a subpoena, and then try to arrange for the witness to travel to your office.

The notices must be sent to every party to the action. If the deposition is of a party, nothing else need be done. If the deposition is of a nonparty, you also must serve a subpoena on the witness that complies with Rule 45's requirements. Such subpoena forms are available from the clerk of the court. The notice must state how the deposition will be recorded. Other parties may choose to record the deposition by other means, at their expense.

Example:

[Caption]

<u>NOTICE OF DEPOSITION</u>

To:
(defendant's attorney) _____

Please take notice that I will take the deposition of Rudolf Watson, defendant, before a notary public, or any other authorized officer, on August 30, 2013, at 2:00 P.M., at Room 201, 400 Elm St., Chicago, Illinois, pursuant to Rule 30 of the Federal Rules of Civil Procedure. You are required to have the deponent present at that date, time, and place for oral examination. The deposition will also be recorded by videotape.

_____
Attorney for Plaintiff

If you wish to have the party deponent produce records and documents at the deposition, the notice can be accompanied by a statement directing that certain records and documents be produced at that time. The documents and records must be described with reasonable particularity, in compliance with Rule 34. However, the better practice is to get all the necessary records and documents from the party before noticing the party's deposition. You should also send a copy of the notice to the court reporter who will take the deposition.

The subpoena for a nonparty will be on a standard form issued by the appropriate clerk's office. It also can command the production of documents and things at the deposition. Make sure you attach a check for the necessary witness fees.[55]

Example:

[Caption]

<u>SUBPOENA</u>

To:
(name and address of deponent)
_____

YOU ARE COMMANDED to appear at the place, date, and time specified below to testify at the taking of a deposition in the above case.

Place of deposition _____   *Date and Time* _____

_____

55. 28 U.S.C. §§1821 provides for a daily attendance fee, actual expenses of travel or mileage fee, and a subsistence fee.

YOU ARE COMMANDED to produce and permit inspection and copying of the following documents or objects at the place, date, and time specified below (list documents or objects):

Place _____   Date and Time _____

_____   _____

Issuing officer signature and title   Date
(indicate if attorney for
plaintiff or defendant)

Issuing officer's signature and title:

_____

(See Rule 45, FRCP, Parts C & D on Reverse)

After you have served the notice and subpoena, arrange for a suitable room in which to take the deposition. Make sure you schedule a court reporter and tell him where and when the deposition will be held. Schedule a videographer if you plan to videotape the deposition. Those who should be present include the deponent, the court reporter, the lawyers for the parties, and perhaps the parties themselves. A conference room or private office in your law office suite is usually the best place to take the deposition. However, if you want to be particularly accommodating to a witness for tactical reasons, use a location convenient for the witness. If the deponent is required to produce documents and you are afraid she will not fully comply, depose her where the records are kept.

Finally, you should reconfirm the deposition with the parties, lawyers, witnesses, and court reporter involved shortly before its date. Rule 30 allows the court to order the deposing party to pay reasonable expenses, including attorney's fees, to the other parties and lawyers if the party giving notice fails to attend the scheduled deposition, or fails to serve a subpoena on a witness and fails to notify the other parties of this fact. Hence, if your conduct causes another party or lawyer to attend a scheduled deposition, and those parties or lawyers were not notified of your failure to subpoena a witness, they can recover reasonable expenses incurred by attending that deposition. Whenever you must cancel a scheduled deposition for any reason, notify everyone entitled to notice immediately.

f.   How should I prepare for taking a deposition?

Taking a good deposition obviously requires preparation. You must collect all the documentation that has any bearing on the witness' anticipated testimony, review it, and have copies available for use during the deposition. The witness can mark a copy during the deposition, in which case it should be given to the court reporter to attach as an exhibit to the deposition transcript.

This documentation includes all documents and records where the witness is "down on paper." These include any written or signed statements, oral interviews reduced to writing, police reports in which the witness is mentioned, and records created by or mentioning the witness.

If the deponent is a party, this documentation should include the party's pleadings, the party's initial disclosures, interrogatory answers, responses to documents requests, and any affidavits that accompanied motions. You will probably want to question the party about specific allegations and representations contained in the pleadings and discovery.

When you have reviewed the available material, you should begin to outline how you will take the particular deposition. Your plan depends on several considerations: Is the deponent an adverse party, unfavorable witness, or friendly witness? What information do you need to obtain? What foundations for exhibits do you want to establish? What admissions or impeachment should you try to obtain? Are you taking the deposition only to discover information, or should you take it with an eye toward preserving the witness' testimony for possible later use, such as for a motion to preclude expert testimony, a motion for summary judgment, or for trial? What are the risks involved in deposing this person? You must take these considerations into account so that you have good answers to the fundamental question you must ask yourself: Why am I taking this deposition?

These considerations affect how you will take a particular deposition. Regardless of your approach, your questioning should be thorough, because a basic purpose for depositions is to find out all that the deponent knows. Make an outline of your anticipated topics with suitable references to the exhibits you will want to use. While you obviously should tailor your outline to the facts of the case, you should usually explore certain general topics. A number of books contain checklists for various types of cases and witnesses. These are useful but should never be a substitute for an outline specific to the particular deponent.

Example (preliminary matters):

1. Background
   a. Name and address
   b. Personal and family history
   c. Education
   d. Job history
2. Preparation for deposition
   a. Documents witness has seen, at any time
   b. To whom witness has talked, at any time
   c. Any documents or papers witness has with him, other than subpoenaed documents
3. Documents, records, and ESI
   a. Notice to produce and subpoenas
   b. Record keeping
   c. Records search
   d. Identifying produced records
   e. Identifying any destroyed records
   f. Names and addresses of other persons and entities that may have records related to case
4. Identity of party
   a. Officers, directors, employees, agents
   b. Parent corporation and subsidiaries, licensees

   c. Incorporation and places of business
   d. Residence
   e. Place where licensed to do business
   f. Names used in business
  5. Witnesses
   a. Names and addresses of persons witnessing events and transactions
   b. Names and addresses of persons deponent has communicated with about case
   c. Names and addresses of persons who may know something about case

These background topics should usually be pursued regardless of the deponent. When the deponent is a party, the interrogatory answers should contain most of this information already, but you should have the deponent reconfirm the information and explain it in greater detail where necessary.

These background topics do not need to be the first matters covered in the deposition. An effective approach is to question the witness first about her personal knowledge, then ask about the background and documents later. In this way you will find out what the witness knows, then find out what the witness can say about the documents. This approach often works well if the case involves numerous documents. It also works well with experts, who can be questioned about their opinions first, then the bases for their opinions, and, last, about their professional backgrounds. Remember that depositions are limited to one day of seven hours, which means that you must make sure you get to the important matters quickly.

Once you have organized your preliminary matters, you should outline the substantive areas you want to cover. These areas depend on the type of case, legal and factual issues, and the witness' relationship to them. The key to the deposition here is detail. You need to make sure that the outline covers all the topics and is logically organized, usually chronologically, to ensure that you are thorough and avoid mistakes. Sometimes, however, it may be useful to vary your topics from a strictly chronological order so that the deponent cannot anticipate questions.

The deposition should extract from the witness what the witness knows that is pertinent to the case. You usually get only one opportunity to depose a person, so you must be prepared to get the most out of that opportunity. On the other hand, keep in mind that the basic purpose of any deposition is to learn what the witness knows and did, and what his trial testimony will be. Endless questioning, particularly if repetitive and argumentative, accomplishes nothing positive and only serves to educate the opposing lawyer and witness as to the likely content and tone of the cross-examination at trial. There is a difference between finding out what you need to know and finding out everything you can possibly know. Good trial lawyers know the difference.

Example (plaintiff in personal injury case):

1. Background questions
   a. (Preliminary matters as outlined previously)
   b. Health history before accident
2. Vehicles involved
   a. Make, year, registration
   b. Insurance
   c. Condition, inspection, repair records
3. Scene of collision
   a. Neighborhood
   b. Roads
   c. Traffic markings and controls
   d. Lighting
4. Weather and road conditions
5. Events before accident
   a. Activities earlier in day
   b. Food, alcohol, drugs, eyeglasses
   c. Physical condition at time
6. Events immediately before collision
   a. Location and direction of vehicles
   b. Passengers
   c. Traffic conditions
   d. Visibility
   e. Other distractions
   f. Where first saw defendant's car
   g. Marking diagrams and photographs
7. Collision
   a. Speed of cars before impact
   b. Traffic signals
   c. Braking and other conduct of plaintiff
   d. Braking and other conduct of defendant
   e. Point of impact
   f. Where cars ended up
   g. Marking diagrams and photographs
8. Events after collision
   a. Bystander activities
   b. Police activities
   c. What plaintiff and defendant did
   d. What plaintiff and defendant said
   e. Plaintiff's and defendant's condition after collision
   f. Ambulance
9. Medical treatment
   a. At hospital—diagnosis and treatment
   b. Doctor's visits after discharge—treatments
   c. Medication, therapy
10. Present physical condition
    a. Any physical limitations
    b. Any mental conditions
    c. Medication

11. Damages
    a. Vehicle
    b. Hospital expenses
    c. Doctor's bills
    d. Lost wages
    e. Insurance payments
    f. Other claimed losses

Example (corporate plaintiff in contract breach case):

1. Background questions
    a. (Preliminary matters as outlined previously)
2. First contact with defendant
    a. Reasons — how came about
    b. Persons involved
3. Course of dealing up to contract
    a. Types of business conducted
    b. Business practices
    c. Specific contracts entered into
    d. Performance history
4. Negotiations leading up to contract
    a. Dates, times, places, participants
    b. All communications
5. Contract execution
    a. Date, time, place, participants
6. Conduct following execution
    a. Performance by each party
7. Breach claimed
    a. When, what
    b. Witnesses
8. Conduct following breach
    a. Attempts to mitigate
9. Damages claimed
    a. Breach damages
    b. Consequential damages

Example (treating physician in personal injury case):

1. Professional background
    a. Education
    b. Internship and residency
    c. Licenses and specialty boards
    d. Description of practice
    e. Experience in type of injury involved here
2. Physician's medical records and reports
    a. Identify them
    b. Treatises he relies on
    c. Consultations

3. First contact with plaintiff at hospital
    a. Where and when
    b. History
    c. Symptoms
    d. Examination and findings
    e. Tests
    f. Diagnosis
    g. Treatment
4. Subsequent contacts with plaintiff
    a. Where and when
    b. Symptoms
    c. Examinations and findings
    d. Tests
    e. Prognosis
5. Opinions and conclusions
    a. Extent of injuries
    b. Permanence of injuries
    c. Effect on plaintiff
    d. Causation
    e. Why physician disagrees with other experts
6. Fees
    a. How much
    b. Future fees

g.   *How should I prepare to take the deposition of a testifying expert?*

Depositions of testifying experts require additional preparation. Rule 26(b) allows you to depose as of right any expert "whose opinions may be presented at trial." You may do so only after the expert is disclosed as a testifying expert and has submitted his signed, written report. The written report is due at least 90 days before trial, unless the court orders otherwise. Rule 26(e) requires that the report be supplemented "in a timely manner" if it is incomplete or incorrect in some material respect, and if the other parties have not been apprised of the additional or corrective information during the discovery process or in writing.

When you subpoena the expert for his deposition under Rule 45, have the subpoena direct the expert to produce his written report, all lab and field notes, all data the expert considered in reaching his opinions and conclusions, the expert's compensation agreement with the lawyer, and all payments received to date. This information should be properly obtained despite the limitations that the 2010 amendments to Rule 26(b)(4) placed on discovery. Since these materials may be voluminous, try to get them from the opposing lawyer before the deposition (but subpoena them for the deposition in any event). In practice, lawyers frequently work out reciprocal agreements, which are often incorporated into the court's pretrial scheduling order under Rule 16.

Talk to other lawyers who have deposed the expert or examined the expert at trial. Obtain transcripts of the expert's depositions and trial testimony. Talk to your own experts and client about the expert. This research will give you a better feel for how the expert testifies and conducts himself during a deposition.

Obtain the expert's published books, articles, and speeches. Make sure that the expert's resume accurately details his education, training, employment history, teaching positions and status, licenses, memberships, and honors. Look for gaps in the history that may hide negative events in the expert's past.

As with any witness, prepare an outline of your anticipated topics with suitable references to the exhibits you plan to use. Most expert depositions will explore the following topics:

Example (testifying expert):

1. Professional background
   a. Education
   b. Training
   c. Job history and experience
   d. Experience as expert
   e. Experience as testifying expert
   f. Any facts *not* on resume
2. Expert engagement
   a. Date hired
   b. Compensation communications with retaining lawyer
   c. Facts and data provided by lawyer
   d. Assumptions provided by lawyer
   e. History of relationship with lawyer
3. Compensation
   a. Basis of compensation, before and at trial
   b. Payments received to date
   c. Expected additional payments in future
4. Subpoena
   a. Received subpoena with document request
   b. Itemize all documents produced
   c. Any documents not yet produced
   d. Any documents expert has with him not covered by subpoena
5. What expert did and how he did it
   a. Tests and studies done — chronology of activities
   b. Methods used
   c. Equipment used
   d. Others who helped or were consulted
   e. All data considered
   f. All data actually relied on
   g. All assumptions made
   h. What other tests could have been done but were not, and why
   i. What reasoning did expert use to go from the facts to his conclusions?

       j. What experience does expert have in doing this analysis?
       k. Has expert written and published articles about this analysis?
       l. Do other experts do the same kind of analysis?
      m. Do the expert's peers generally accept this kind of analysis?

6. Opinions
    a. All opinions reached
    b. Considering additional opinions
    c. Considering changing or modifying opinions reached

7. Bases for opinions
    a. All bases for each opinion reached
    b. Assumptions made
    c. What facts accepted and rejected
    d. Review opinions and bases with others
    e. Certainty of opinions
    f. Exhibits used as summary or support for opinions

8. Other reasonable opinions
    a. Read other experts' reports
    b. Other experts have different opinions
    c. Any criticisms of other experts' opinions and reasons, and why
    d. If other experts' opinions wrong or inaccurate, how did he analyze and find errors

9. Authorities in field
    a. Literature
    b. Experts—who would you hire

Note that under Rule 26(b)(4)(E) a party taking an expert's deposition is usually required to pay the expert "a reasonable fee for time spent in responding to discovery." The rule expressly applies to any "expert whose opinions may be presented at trial," including experts retained as testifying experts; the rule might also apply to nonretained experts, such as treating physicians.

    h. How should I prepare for a Rule 30(b)(6) deposition?

Rule 30(b)(6) has special procedures that govern a deposition notice or subpoena directed to a corporation or other organization. This rule is important, particularly in commercial litigation, because frequently you will not know which specific employee of a corporate party has the information you need to obtain. Rule 30(b)(6) requires that a corporation or other entity noticed or subpoenaed under the rule must designate one or more persons to testify as to "information known or reasonably available to the organization." The persons can be employees or non-employees. The corporation cannot frustrate the deposition by designating a person who has no personal knowledge of the facts. Rather, if the designated person does not know the information requested, he must get the information by obtaining the relevant documents and records and interviewing the employees who have knowledge of the relevant facts. The designated person must collect the entirety of the corporation's knowledge and be prepared to communicate that knowledge. The deposition of the corporation under this rule counts as one deposition, even if the corporation designates more than one person, and the seven-hour time limit for depositions applies to each person designated. A person deposed as the representative of the corporation under this rule can also be deposed again in his individual capacity.

Any person deposed under Rule 30(b)(6) testifies in a representative capacity and makes admissions that will be imputed to the corporation under FRE 801(d)(2). Both the party taking the deposition and the responding corporation should therefore proceed carefully and plan thoroughly.

Rule 30(b)(6) is a good vehicle to learn who knows what, who did what and when, which former employees were involved, what documents and records exist, where these documents are and who made them, and what already obtained documents and records mean. It allows you to develop a blueprint of how the corporation is organized and of how records and ESI are generated and maintained, and to identify the key employees involved in the events and transactions underlying the lawsuit. Rule 30(b)(6) shifts the burden to the corporation to select and educate witnesses who must acquire the specific information called for in the deposition notice. Accordingly, a deposition under this rule should be taken early in the discovery process, since the whole point of the rule is to identify knowledgeable persons and documents early in the litigation. You can then serve more focused interrogatories and documents requests and consider follow-up depositions of key employees.

A Rule 30(b)(6) deposition has some advantages for the corporation. The corporation gets to select the representative witnesses who will appear at the deposition, so the corporation can pick witnesses who will make good impressions. Since the deposition notice must state with reasonable particularity the matters on which the deposition will be conducted, the corporation can learn in advance the topics that will be covered during the deposition and prepare for them. Some courts have held that the list of topics in the deposition notice limits the scope of the deposition. The majority view, however, is that Rule 26, not the deposition notice, governs the scope of a Rule 30(b)(6) deposition.[56]

The notice or subpoena for a Rule 30(b)(6) deposition must designate the subject matter with "reasonable particularity." The more focused and detailed the notice, the better. Consider limiting the number of topics and categories of information on the notice. The corporation will be less likely to object on the ground that the notice is unduly broad or burdensome, and more likely to designate a person who is actually knowledgeable on those topics. Couple a Rule 34 document request with the notice for the documents and records you will want at the deposition.

---

56. For a thorough discussion of case law on the scope of a Rule 30(b)(6) deposition, see American General Life Ins. Co. v. Billard, Civ. No. 10-1012, 2010 WL 4367052 (N.D. Iowa Oct. 28, 2010).

Example:

[Caption]

<u>NOTICE OF RULE 30(B)(6) DEPOSITION</u>

To: Blivitz Oil, Inc., plaintiff,
      and its attorney of record:
      Dominic Gianna
      201 St. Charles Avenue
      New Orleans, LA 70170

PLEASE TAKE NOTICE that defendant Luigi Oil Services, Inc., through its counsel, will take the deposition of Blivitz Oil, Inc., upon oral examination pursuant to Federal Rule of Civil Procedure 30(b)(6) as to the matters set forth below. Blivitz Oil, Inc. is required to designate one or more officers, directors, managing agents, or other persons to testify on its behalf who have knowledge of the matters specified below:

1. Blivitz Oil, Inc.'s calculations and substantiation of damages it claims it is due from defendant Luigi Oil Services, Inc., as set forth in Blivitz Oil, Inc.'s complaint.

2. The authenticity of the documents listed on and attached to Exhibit A, attached to this notice.

In accordance with Federal Rule of Civil Procedure 34, you are required to bring with you to the deposition:

1. All documents, records, writings, and calculations of any kind, both electronic and hard copy, evidencing the damages Blivitz Oil, Inc. claims it has sustained as set forth in its complaint.

The deposition will be held on June 1, 2013, at 9:00 A.M., at the offices of Gloria Torres, 123 Main Street, Tucson, AZ 85701, before an officer authorized to take depositions, and continuing until completed.

_____

Gloria Torres
123 Main Street
Tucson, AZ 85701
Attorney for defendant
Luigi Oil Services, Inc.

[Proof of service]

When the deposition notice (or subpoena to a nonparty) is served, the corporation must designate one or more appropriate persons to testify on its behalf. Rule 30(b)(6) requires only that the person designated be able to "testify about information known or reasonably available to the organization." That person must be knowledgeable as to the matters designated in the notice, but there is no requirement that the person designated is the most knowledgeable person. The corporation can designate an employee, the usual choice, or it can designate another person, such as a former employee, so long as that person consents to testify on the corporation's behalf.

The corporation then has the obligation to prepare the designated witness so he can testify as to the collective corporate knowledge on the designated topics. The witness must talk to the relevant employees and must review the relevant documents and records to acquire the necessary knowledge. A corporation risks sanctions if it designates a person who has little or no personal knowledge and makes no attempt to educate that person as to the collective corporate knowledge, so that the witness will simply say "I don't know" when questioned at the deposition. The corporation has the obligation to bring the designated person up to speed. When preparing that witness, make sure you show him documents and provide him with information that is not privileged, since showing the witness privileged communications will probably constitute a waiver of the privilege.

Representing the corporation at the deposition can put the lawyer in an awkward position. As the corporate lawyer, you represent the corporation, not employees of the corporation. Therefore, your duty is to the corporation, not the employee who appears as the designated witness. The employee is not your client, and you should treat the employee as an unrepresented person under Model Rule 4.3. You should explain this situation to the employee. Trying to accommodate the employee by "representing" him at the deposition is in essence agreeing to jointly represent both the corporation and the employee, which can create conflicts. If there are any concerns, the employee should have his own lawyer present at the deposition.

When the deposition starts, clarify that the witness appears in a representative, not individual, capacity. This is important because the corporation's collective knowledge is relevant at a Rule 30(b)(6) deposition, and the witness's statements of that corporate knowledge constitute admissions imputed to the corporation. If the witness testifies in his individual capacity, then he only has to draw upon his own individual recollection and is not responsible for corporate information.

Depositions under Rule 30(b)(6) raise common problems. First, is the subject matter of the questions asked within the scope of the notice? As noted earlier, the deposition notice should be focused and detailed, but each specific topic should be described in the notice broadly enough so that the corporation cannot complain that the deposition questions exceed the scope of the notice. (Although the deposition notice may not control the scope of the deposition by law, your adversary will likely object if your questions do exceed the notice's scope.) Second, did the designated witness reasonably prepare for the deposition and get the necessary information to adequately represent the corporate knowledge of the designated topics? Remember that the witness must testify as to "information known or reasonably available to the corporation." The witness need not be the most knowledgeable person available. These two issues arise commonly and, if counsel cannot resolve them, will require motion practice.

If the corporation fails to comply with the requirements of Rule 30(b)(6), you can ask for Rule 37 sanctions, and you can use the witness's deposition answers as party admissions at trial. These consequences ordinarily operate as significant deterrents.

i.   How should I prepare for a videotaped deposition?

Rule 30(b) permits videotaped depositions as of right, and depositions of lay and expert witnesses by videotape and video-conferencing are increasingly common. Videotaped depositions have benefits and costs. On the plus side, a video recording preserves deposition testimony much more vividly and has much more impact on a jury than a stenographic transcript. This consideration is important if you plan to introduce the recording during trial as former testimony under FRE 804(b)(1) or to use the videotape as impeachment with a prior inconsistent statement during trial. In addition, videotaping a deposition usually stops lawyer misconduct that is all too common — improperly coaching a witness, making improper objections, and the like. A recording will demonstrate this misconduct vividly. On the minus side, videotaping is expensive, although many lawyers now have their own equipment and trained personnel. However, hiring an experienced professional videographer is usually money well spent.

Preparation for the deposition involves two principal concerns: preparing the setting for the deposition and preparing your party for the deposition. The setting for the videotaping is important, particularly when you want the deponent to look and sound persuasive. The video and sound equipment must be of professional quality. Have a running time and date clock visible on the recording throughout the taping. Decide if you want one or two cameras. If you use only one camera, the usual procedure is to start with a wide-angle shot showing all the participants in the deposition ("orientation shot"). After the witness is sworn, the camera is brought closer and focuses on the head and upper body of the deponent, or the deponent and the examining lawyer. Be careful not to use only close-ups of the witness, which can get too intense if uninterrupted. This process is repeated after each break. If you use two cameras, one camera can be a close-up of the deponent, the other a close-up of the questioning lawyer or a wide angle of all the participants. The two different shots can then be combined later. You must also work out how the deponent will handle exhibits and conduct any demonstrations. Take close-ups of each exhibit so they can be edited later into the videotape.

The lighting, background, and setting are critical in creating an attractive visual image. The lighting must be adequate to illuminate the participants properly, and should be diffused to avoid harsh shadows, particularly on the deponent's face. The background should be a light, softly textured wall or curtain with warm colors that will highlight the deponent. Avoid visual distractions, such as plants, pictures, or windows. The setting should be a courtroom, a conference room, or their equivalent with a solid, stable chair and table. The deponent should have a wireless (lavaliere) microphone with excellent tone quality, and the lawyers should have a table microphone. An experienced videographer will be familiar with how to create a good visual and sound environment for a videotaped deposition and should be consulted in advance. You will probably also need to work out the logistics with opposing counsel in advance.

What do you do if your client is being deposed and the opposing lawyer seems to be setting the stage deliberately to make the recording of your client look bad? What if, for example, the visual background is distracting or jarring, or the lighting casts dark shadows on your client's face and makes him look sinister? First, ask the opposing lawyer to fix the problem so that the recording will be fair. Remind the opposing lawyer that Rule 30(b)(5) requires that "the deponent's and attorneys' appearance or demeanor must not be distorted through recording techniques." If that doesn't work, call the judge assigned to the case and explain the situation. If the staging is so unfair that you can credibly contend it is being done in bad faith or in such manner as unreasonably to annoy, embarrass, or oppress the deponent or party, you can suspend the deposition and move the court under Rule 26(c) for an appropriate protective order.

To prepare your client for a videotaped deposition, take all the steps involved in preparing a witness to testify at trial. The client must understand that in most cases the deposition *is* the trial, and he must look, act, and sound as if he is testifying at trial before a jury. Tell the client he's on stage, and his appearance and nonverbal behavior are key to projecting credibility and sincerity. He must be told how to dress, how to maintain eye contact with either the camera or the questioner, how to project his voice to sound confident, how to avoid long pauses that may suggest uncertainty, and how to control his body movements to develop reinforcing gestures and eliminate distracting mannerisms. This preparation will obviously take time, and rehearsing on videotape is essential.

A final note on videotaped depositions: You might be able to reduce the expense of a videographer and court reporter if you and your adversary agree at the outset of discovery on a single firm to provide these services. The firm may be willing to provide a discount if it will handle all depositions in the case.

j.   How do I start the deposition?

If all goes well, the parties' lawyers, the court reporter, video operator, and the deponent will all appear at the designated place, date, and time. You should also consider having your client attend, since she will learn by observing. Your client's attendance is particularly helpful when the deponent will testify to conversations and transactions with your client. The deponent is more likely to be truthful and candid when your client is listening to the testimony. The deposition can begin after routine introductions have been made, the participants have settled down in the deposition room, the court reporter has set up the stenographic equipment, and the video operator is ready. Start by giving the court reporter a copy of a pleading with a complete caption and your business card. Also, the reporter should be given the correct spelling for the names of all persons present. Then proceed.

First, ask the court reporter to swear in the witness. Have the transcript affirmatively show that the witness was sworn.

Second, make sure an introductory statement for the record identifies whose deposition it is, the date and place, and everyone present. Also, the statement should reflect that notice was given, that the deposition is being taken under the Federal Rules of Civil Procedure, and that the witness has been sworn. Rule 30(b)(5) requires that the court reporter put these matters on the record. In many jurisdictions the lawyer taking the deposition makes the introductory statement on the record.

Example:

> Q. This is the deposition of the plaintiff, Margaret Singer, being taken in the case of Margaret Singer v. Robert Johnson, Case No. 13 C 483 in the United States District Court for the Northern District of Ohio. It is being held at the law offices of Marlyn Anders, 200 Main Street, Suite 400, Cleveland, Ohio. Today's date is August 15, 2013. Present in addition to Ms. Singer are myself, Marlyn Anders, attorney for defendant Johnson, Sharon Witts, attorney for plaintiff Singer, and Darlene Winters, a certified court reporter and notary public. Ms. Singer, you were just sworn to tell the truth by the court reporter, correct?
> A. That's right.

When the deponent is a party, he will usually have been prepared for the deposition, will know what to expect, and will be familiar with the procedure. When the deponent is a nonparty, however, this may not be the case, and it is sometimes worthwhile to explain the deposition procedure and its importance. This explanation prevents a witness from later claiming, if impeached from the transcript, that the lawyer confused or pressured him.

Example:

> Q. Mr. Johnson, have you ever attended a deposition before?
> A. No.
> Q. Do you know how a deposition works?
> A. Not really.
> Q. Mr. Johnson, I'm going to ask you questions about this accident, and you'll have to answer them under oath. The other lawyers can also ask questions if they want to. Afterward the court reporter will

type up everything said here today. That's called a transcript. Do you understand?

A. Yes.

Q. It's important that you understand the questions and give accurate answers. If there's anything you don't understand, or anything you don't know or aren't sure of, you let us know, all right?

A. Yes.

When the deponent is a party who has also been served with a request to produce, or the deponent is a witness who has been served with a subpoena duces tecum, have the deponent produce the records or documents on the record, even if he voluntarily sent them to you in advance. Identify them for the record, make copies of them and give the court reporter a copy to attach to the transcript, and mark them as exhibits.

Example:

Q. Ms. Jones, you received a subpoena for certain records of your company along with the subpoena to appear, correct?

A. Yes.

Q. Did you comply and bring the records?

A. Yes.

Q. May I see them? (Lawyer obtains them from witness.) For the record, the witness has handed me photocopies totaling five pages. The court reporter will mark them Deposition Exhibit A. Page one is an invoice, page two is a bill of lading, page three is a shipping notice, and pages four and five are account ledgers. Each page bears the name of ABC Shipping Company. Ms. Jones, have I accurately described these five pages?

A. Yes.

Q. These are all business records of ABC Shipping?

A. Yes.

Q. Did you search the company records for all records relating to the transaction described on the subpoena served on you?

A. Yes.

Q. These five pages are the only ones that exist?

A. Yes.

Q. Other than these records, does your company make other records for a transaction of this kind?

A. No.

If you anticipate the need to introduce the records in evidence at trial, you should qualify the witness as a "custodian or other qualified witness" and establish a business records foundation under FRE 803(6). If the witness is a party or agent of the party, the testimony will qualify as an admission; if a nonparty, the testimony should qualify as former testimony if the witness is unavailable at trial. Whenever possible, establish multiple bases for admissibility of records and other exhibits.

If you will examine the witness about a number of documents, make sure that you have a good exhibit marking system. Practices vary. For example, the plaintiff may use numbers 1 to 300; the defendant may use numbers 301 to 600. In this way, all deposition documents will be marked "Deposition exhibit no.." In some jurisdictions, the practice is for each side to designate its own deposition exhibits. For example, plaintiff will call its exhibits "Plaintiff deposition exhibit no.," the defense "Defendant deposition exhibit no." Still others designate exhibits by the witness name. For example, if a Shirley Williams is being deposed, the exhibits will be called "Williams exhibit no.." In other jurisdictions, the exhibits are only marked as "Exhibit no.," so that the same exhibit number will be used when the case is tried. The basic idea is to have clarity in the marking system. You can then use the witness to establish the legal foundation for admissibility at trial for particular deposition exhibits. At the end of the deposition, make sure the court reporter has all the marked exhibits, to be attached to the deposition transcript.

Example:

Q. Ms. Williams, you work for the defendant, the ABC Corporation?
A. Yes.
Q. You're the secretary to ABC's president, Mr. Greenberg?
A. Yes.
Q. You've been working for ABC and Mr. Greenberg since 2005?
A. Yes.
Q. Ms. Williams, you've seen Mr. Greenberg write his signature before, right?
A. Of course.
Q. About how many times?
A. Certainly hundreds of times, maybe thousands.
Q. And you've seen him write things out in longhand, right?
A. Certainly.
Q. Ms. Williams, I'm showing you a check which has been marked "Plaintiff's deposition exhibit no. 7." It's dated June 1, 2013, and is filled out by hand. Take a look at it.
A. All right.
Q. Have you seen that check before?
A. I don't think so.
Q. But you recognize the signature in the lower right hand corner of the check, right?
A. Sure. That's Mr. Greenberg's signature.
Q. Any doubt about that?
A. No. I know Mr. Greenberg's signature. That's his.
Q. Look at the rest of the face of the check. Is that also Mr. Greenberg's handwriting?
A. Yes. It's all filled out by him.

Finally, good practice requires that you put any stipulations on the record and state expressly what they are. Parties frequently deal with the status of objections, sometimes stipulating that all objections are preserved or that all objections are preserved except those directed to the form of the question. These sorts of stipulations can be useful because they eliminate the need to make most objections during the deposition, allowing for a much clearer and shorter transcript. Objections can then be raised later if the transcript will be used during trial. However, agreeing to the "usual stipulations" is bad practice and should be avoided, particularly when you are outside your usual practice area. Find out what the usual stipulations are, and then decide whether to agree with them.

k.   What questioning styles should I use?

The questioning style you employ during the deposition must be consistent with your purposes. Are you taking the deposition primarily to gather information from a witness? Are you taking a party's deposition to pin the party down on details, to obtain admissions, and to develop impeachment? Are you deposing a favorable witness to preserve the witness' testimony in the event he becomes unavailable for trial? The different purposes will affect how you conduct the deposition.[57]

Regardless of your purposes, you should always keep two concerns uppermost in your mind: Have I clearly and unambiguously stated questions and received answers? How will this deposition sound if it is read to a jury during trial? Find out if the court reporter is using a real-time reporting system, where the questions and answers appear on a computer screen almost immediately. If you can tie into this system, you will be able to see your questions and the witness' answers and determine immediately if they are clear and usable as admissions or impeachment at trial. If not, you can rephrase and clarify as necessary.

i.   Getting information

Always ask yourself: What does the witness know? What does the witness not know? If he doesn't know, who knows? If he doesn't know, where is the information? In many depositions your goal is to gather information that will support your theory of the case, support your story of what really happened, and prove the elements of your claims or defenses. When your principal goal during the deposition is to gather information, let the witness ramble on rather than control the witness with narrow, focused questions. Pause after the witness answers, in case the witness wants to provide additional information. You are more likely to have the witness volunteer useful information if you ask broad questions in a friendly, informal way. The "who, what, where, when, how, and why" questions work well

57. Techniques for examining a deponent are much the same, and as varied, as techniques for direct and cross-examinations of witnesses at trial. For a discussion of these techniques, see, e.g., T. Mauet, Trial Techniques and Trials (9th ed. 2013); P. Bergman, Trial Advocacy in a Nutshell (5th ed. 2013); D. Gitchel & M. O'Brien, Trial Advocacy Basics (2006).

here. You can always steer the witness to the topics that need to be covered and use follow-up questions to tie down the details. What is sometimes called the "funnel" approach works well here: For each topic, begin with an introductory question, follow that with a series of open-ended questions that draw everything possible out of the witness, and then reca- pitulate and summarize what the witness has just told you. Then move to the next topic. Whether the questions and answers violate evidentiary rules, such as leading or hearsay, is unimportant, if your only goal is to get information.

Just as important as finding out what the witness knows is finding out what the witness does *not* know or has no firsthand knowledge about. This will prevent the witness from adding to his testimony at trial, since you will be able to impeach the witness on these new points. If the witness says he doesn't know or doesn't remember and you want the information, use follow-up questions. Ask: Has the witness forgotten? Does the witness not know? Who does know? Where is the information? What would help the witness remember? Who has the witness talked to about the informa- tion? Where would you look? Who would you ask?

Find out what materials the witness reviewed to prepare for his testi- mony. Under FRE 612, if a witness used records and documents to refresh his recollection "before testifying," the adverse party may be entitled to see those records and documents. Most courts have held that this right trumps the work product doctrine, and some courts have held that this right pre- vails over claims that a privilege protects the records and documents.[58]

ii.   Eliciting detail and pinning down specific facts

When deposing an adverse party, you usually have dual purposes: to find out what the party knows in detail, and to pin the party down to specific, useful facts. Ask open, nonleading questions to try to get the deponent to talk and to detail what he knows. Actively listen to the witness and use follow-up questions. Look and listen for verbal and nonverbal cues, especially when you are asking about sensitive topics. If the opposing law- yer has done his homework, the party will hesitate to volunteer information not specifically asked for. But even a well-prepared party may sometimes divulge something you would never have uncovered but for your attention to the party's demeanor and attitude.

You can accomplish the second purpose, pinning the party down, with leading, focused, cross-examination type questions. Your attitude and tone can be more forceful and adversarial. One of the most common mistakes is to let the witness give ambiguous or qualified answers that do not make for effective impeachment or admissions at trial. If the party hedges, ask follow-up questions that pin him down. If the party refuses, try to get him to admit that he is only "guessing," "approximating," or that he

---

58. See, e.g., Thomas v. Euro RSCG Lie, 264 F.R.D. 120, 122-123 (S.D.N.Y. 2010); Heron Interact, Inc. v. Guidelines, Inc., 244 F.R.D. 75, 78 (D. Mass. 2007).

simply "doesn't know." Parties have a predictable talent for improving their recall of facts and details at trial. Therefore, getting an "I don't know" or an "I can only approximate" response can be useful for impeachment purposes if the party at trial claims to know specifically. Make the key questions self-contained, so that the individual questions and answers will make sense when used for impeachment.

A common avoidance method is the "I don't know" answer. When a witness frequently responds, "I don't know," follow it up. If you don't know the information now, did you once know it? Who else would know it? What other employee should know it? Where would the information be recorded? Who would know if there is a record of that information? In short, let the witness realize that an "I don't know" answer will trigger a number of follow-up questions.

Avoid questions that give the witness an easy way to avoid answering the substance of a question, such as: "Do you recall?" "Do you remember?" "Can you tell me?" Rephrase the question to be a simple imperative. Avoid pronouns and other imprecise terms. Instead of asking, "What did he tell her at that time," ask, "What did John Smith say to Helen Johnson at the board meeting on June 1, 2013?"

Make sure to ask follow-up questions to make the witness's answers unambiguous and complete. This task is like building a box. Build the sides of the box with questions. But always ask questions to put a "lid on the box," to ensure that the testimony can be used with greatest effect at summary judgment or trial. Let's say, for instance, that you represent the plaintiff, Helen Johnson, in an employment discrimination lawsuit. Your client did not get promoted, and she believes it is because of her gender. The company defends on grounds that your client did not perform her job duties adequately. You depose her supervisor, Mr. John Smith. You have the following colloquy:

Example:

    Q. Mr. Smith, you were Helen Johnson's supervisor while she was employed at the company, right?
    A. Yes.
    Q. Ms. Johnson reported to you?
    A. Yes.
    Q. You were in a position to observe Ms. Johnson in the workplace?
    A. Yes.
    Q. You evaluated Ms. Johnson's performance?
    A. Yes.
    Q. How would you describe Ms. Johnson as an employee?
    A. Superb.
    Q. Did Ms. Johnson ever disappoint you as an employee?
    A. No.

The questions go on in this vein, and you establish that Mr. Smith was never dissatisfied with your client's performance. At summary judgment, however, the defendant includes an affidavit from another supervisor,

Ms. Frank, who describes a number of your client's failings at work. Your deposition of Mr. Smith failed to "put the lid on the box." You should have inquired with Mr. Smith as to whether anyone else was as well positioned as he to evaluate your client's performance.

Example:

> Q. Mr. Smith, you were Helen Johnson's supervisor while she was employed at the company, right?
> A. Yes.
> Q. Ms. Johnson reported to you?
> A. Yes.
> Q. You were in a position to observe Ms. Johnson in the workplace?
> A. Yes.
> Q. You evaluated Ms. Johnson's performance?
> A. Yes.
> Q. Did anyone else supervise Ms. Johnson?
> A. Yes, Ms. Frank.
> Q. Who is Ms. Frank?
> A. My supervisor. Ms. Johnson reported to me, and I reported to Ms. Frank.
> Q. Did Ms. Frank ever directly supervise Ms. Johnson?
> A. No. I passed along information about the employees I supervised to Ms. Frank. She did not have any direct connection to Ms. Johnson.
> Q. As far as you know, did Ms. Frank ever evaluate Ms. Johnson directly?
> A. No. As far as I know, everything she learned about Ms. Johnson she learned from me.
> Q. Did you ever report unfavorable information about Ms. Johnson to Ms. Frank?
> A. No.
> Q. As far as you know, would Ms. Frank have any reason to think poorly of Ms. Johnson's performance at work?
> Q. No.

These questions "put the lid on the box." They make the significance of Mr. Smith's testimony unambiguous and give your adversary little wiggle room to get out from under it.

iii.   Preserving testimony

When deposing someone to preserve testimony for later admission at trial as former testimony under FRE 804(b)(1), your principal concern is to create clear, progressive testimony that will not run afoul of evidentiary rules. Under Rule 32(d), absent any contrary stipulations, all objections are preserved except those directed to form or others that could have been cured had they been made promptly. Therefore, unless the witness is an adverse party or hostile witness, use nonleading questions. Have the witness paint verbal pictures of the events and transactions, the way you would at trial. Avoid objectionable forms of questions, such as those that can be considered leading, compound, argumentative, speculative, ambiguous, or narrative. Don't ask questions that call for hearsay or improper opinions.

Deposition purposes, of course, do not always separate out with such clear definition. For example, even when you are deposing a witness and are trying to pin the witness down with leading questions, you may want to use that witness to establish the foundations for records, documents, and other exhibits for possible use at trial.[59] If so, you must establish that the witness is a qualified witness, and state questions and get answers that meet the applicable evidentiary foundation requirements for each exhibit.

At the end of a deposition, some lawyers ask the deponent if he would like to correct anything he has said, or whether he has any additional information pertinent to the case that he has not been asked about. If the witness answers no, you can use this answer to impeach him at trial if he testifies inconsistently or testifies to new facts not previously disclosed, suggesting to the jury that the new or different testimony is a recent creation.

iv.   In what order should I cover my topics?

There are three basic approaches to ordering the topics you need to cover during a deposition: chronological, topical, and impact. The chronological approach is commonly used when you want to find out everything that a witness to an event knows. The witness is simply directed to the beginning of the time line, and the questions move steadily from beginning to end. The topical approach is commonly used with witnesses to discrete transactions and events, where you can cover each transaction and event separately, and you do not need to cover them in order. It is also sometimes used with experts. The impact approach immediately confronts the witness on difficult matters. It is commonly used with adverse parties, where the lawyer immediately wants to create an atmosphere of control or uncertainty.

Regardless of your approach, examine the witness first, then the documents. Find out what the witness actually knows and pin the witness down. Next explore the witness's opinions, beliefs, and other hearsay knowledge. Only then should you examine the witness about documents and records that may be relevant to his knowledge and to the issues in the case.

---

59. See T. Mauet, Trial Techniques and Trials ch. 7 (9th ed. 2013), on establishing foundations for various types of exhibits.

v.   Common problems

Inexperienced litigators frequently encounter problems while taking depositions. First, their time estimates are too short. Even a simple deposition will probably take half an hour; an eyewitness to a car crash may take an hour or more. If the deponent is a witness to a series of commercial transactions, or is an expert or a party in a medical or products liability case, the deposition may take a few hours. Keep in mind, however, that under Rule 30(d) the time limit on a deposition is one day of seven hours.

Second, inexperienced litigators have unclear purposes. Depositions can be taken for one or more of three basic reasons: discovering information (what the witness knows and doesn't know), pinning down for admissions and impeachment purposes, and preserving testimony. You need to determine which purpose each deposition involves and conduct yourself accordingly. If your purposes include pinning down and preserving testimony, you are creating a document — the transcript — that you will later use at trial. How it looks and reads is important. Follow your outline, and don't let the witness distract you from your goal.

Third, inexperienced litigators' forms of questions are unclear. How you ask questions has much to do with what your deposition purposes are. If discovering information, use non-leading questions that get the witness talking. If pinning down, use focused leading questions. If preserving testimony, use questions that you would use if you were conducting a direct examination of the witness at trial. Ambiguous, confusing, or complex questions serve no purpose well. Arguing with the witness, or letting your ego take over, never accomplishes anything positive. Arguing with the opposing lawyer is just as pointless. Listen to the lawyer's objections and adjust if necessary, but otherwise ignore the lawyer and focus on asking well-stated questions to the witness.

Fourth, inexperienced litigators come to the deposition without necessary documentation. You ordinarily cannot take a good deposition of a witness or represent your client at a deposition unless you have previously obtained all the documentation necessary for that deposition. If the party or witness was directed, by notice or subpoena, to bring such documentation to the deposition but doesn't, refuse to take the deposition under these circumstances and continue the deposition to another date.

Fifth, inexperienced litigators explore unnecessary topics and details. Since litigators with little trial experience don't know what will be important if the case is finally tried, they cover all the bases by asking everything they can think of about every conceivable topic. This overkill rarely accomplishes anything useful. The way to deal with this is to spend time beforehand planning the deposition and getting help from more experienced litigators who have trial experience.

l.   *How should I handle objections?*

You can expect three basic types of objections from the opposing lawyer at a deposition.

First, the opposing lawyer might object to the form of the questions or answers. Rule 32(d) requires that unless such an objection is made promptly, it is waived. Even after a timely objection is made, the witness must still answer the question "subject to the objection." If you are taking the deposition only to gather information, you can safely ignore the objection. After the lawyer has made the objection, simply tell the witness: "Please answer the question." If you may use the transcript later at trial, however, determine if the objection has possible validity. If it does, rephrase the question properly to overcome the objection. Remember that you can never be totally sure that you will not need to use the transcript during trial.

Second, your adversary can object on evidentiary grounds other than privilege. However, since it is not necessary to object if the grounds are relevance, hearsay, or if the objection is not based on form, the other parties can reserve objections until such time as the deposition is used at trial. That is, if such an objection is not made at the deposition, it can still be made at trial. Indeed, this is the customary procedure. If made at the deposition, the deponent must still answer. Simply tell the witness: "Please answer the question." Again, however, if you plan to use the deposition at trial, and a proper objection is made, you should rephrase the question to eliminate the problem.

Third, your adversary can object on grounds of privilege or harassment. If made on privilege grounds, the witness will probably refuse to answer, since the witness's lawyer will direct the witness not to answer the question.[60] If on harassment grounds, the lawyer might couple her objection with a demand under Rule 30(d) that the deposition be suspended in order to make a motion to limit or terminate the deposition. With either objection, the witness will probably refuse to answer, leaving you with two options. First, you can terminate the examination and move to compel answers. Second, you can ask other questions not objected to and finish the examination to the extent possible.

Regardless of how you react to the witness' refusal, you must decide whether to seek an order compelling an answer. You can discuss the legal issue with the lawyer making the objection to learn the reason for it, and then either rephrase the question or ask the lawyer to withdraw the objection. If the witness persists in refusing to answer, if the information you seek is important, and if you wish to force the issue, you must make a clear record. The question, the witness' refusal to answer, and the grounds for the refusal should be clearly spelled out, since the court reporter must provide a transcript of this portion of the deposition that you will attach to your motion to compel discovery.[61]

---

60. See discussion in §6.2.

61. Asking the court reporter to "certify the question," while not necessary to raise the matter in a motion to compel answers, lets the court reporter know that this question should be on a list of questions the witness refused to answer that will be appended to the end of the deposition transcript. This is a common practice in state court litigation.

Example:

> Q. Mr. Jones, you were the maintenance man at XYZ Leasing during this time, correct?
> A. Yes.
> Q. You talked to people about the problem, didn't you?
> A. Yes.
> Q. These included the company lawyer, Mr. Johnson?
> A. Yes.
> Q. Tell us what you told Mr. Johnson about the problem.
> Jones' Lawyer: Objection. Mr. Jones, don't answer that question. That question calls for the disclosure of attorney-client communications, which are privileged.
> Q. Mr. Jones, do you refuse to answer the question?
> A. Yes.
> Q. Your refusal is based on your assertion of the attorney-client privilege?
> A. Yes.

By following up with these questions, you will have made a clear record of the witness' refusal to answer and the reason for it. Ask the court reporter to mark this part of the deposition and transcribe it later so you can attach it to your motion to compel.

Finally, some lawyers misuse objections to coach the deponent into making more desirable responses. This conduct violates Rule 30(c)(2), which provides that "[a]n objection must be stated concisely and in a nonargumentative and nonsuggestive manner." The purpose of this rule is clear. Lawyers cannot use objections to frustrate an otherwise proper deposition, such as by using objections to coach the witness on a desired response or to frustrate and impede the examining lawyer. Lawyers cannot instruct deponents not to answer a question unless necessary to preserve a privilege, to enforce a previous court-ordered limitation, or to make a motion to terminate the deposition because it is being taken in bad faith or is unreasonably annoying or oppressive. Rule 30(c)(1) provides that the examination and cross-examination of the deponent "proceed as they would at trial under the Federal Rules of Evidence, except Rules 103 and 615," and many jurisdictions have local rules that go even further in prohibiting specific behavior during a deposition. Where bad behavior occurs repeatedly — such as when a lawyer makes constant "clarification" or "if he knows" objections — you should note your objection to the opposing lawyer, warn him to stop his improper conduct, and make sure the court reporter records it. If this conduct persists, you may want to recess the deposition and bring the matter to the court through a motion to compel discovery or for sanctions. Another avenue is to call the judge assigned to the case, provided that you have determined beforehand that the judge will take calls to resolve issues at a deposition. If past experience with a particular lawyer suggests a danger of bad behavior, a video deposition might be an effective response. It will graphically capture the lawyer's conduct and sometimes will even act as a deterrent to such conduct.

The videotape will show the misconduct more vividly than a written transcript. Many courts limit or forbid consultation between the witness and
her lawyer during questioning, requiring what amounts to a trial environment for the deposition. In some jurisdictions, conversations between the
witness and her lawyer during breaks are discoverable.[62] Make sure you
know your judge's guidelines for taking depositions.

   m.   How should I prepare and represent a deponent?

   When you receive a notice of deposition for your client, your client's
preparation may well be the most important single task for you in the litigation process. The opposing lawyers will use the deposition to determine
what your client knows, develop admissions and impeachment, pin your
client down to details, and generally size up your client as a trial witness.
If the deposition goes well, the settlement value of the case will rise. Hence,
preparation for the deposition is critical. Treat deposition preparation just
like trial preparation. If the deposition will be videotaped, you must receive
notice of the videotaping on the deposition notice as required under Rule
30(b)(2). If so, you must prepare the client not only on how to answer the
questions but also on his appearance and non-verbal demeanor.
   Shortly before the deposition date, have your client come to your
office with enough time allocated to prepare him thoroughly. Scheduling
this work for the early afternoon, as the last appointment for the day, is a
good idea. You do not want to be rushed by other obligations. On the other
hand, some lawyers prefer to schedule such interviews in the morning,
when they and the clients are fresh.
   Before you start preparing, create a positive atmosphere that relieves
the client's anxiety and concerns. Many persons, especially those who have
never been deposed before, are worried about how they will perform and
what the other lawyer is like and what she will do. Tell the client his job is to
give truthful, short answers to the questions, and you will take care of
everything else. Witnesses do not perform well under stress. Ask the client
directly about his concerns, then deal with them candidly.
   As for preparation, first have the pleadings, discovery, documents,
records, reports, photographs, diagrams, and sketches available for the
client to review. Show the client only his statements, however, and not
those of others. Letting your client read other persons' statements will
always create the impression, particularly at trial, that your client has
tailored his testimony to be consistent with other witnesses, or has used
the other statements to acquire information he himself does not personally
have. You might have to disclose these statements at trial, since under FRE
612 an adverse party may be able to obtain any documents used to refresh
the witness' recollection, even if used before trial. The adverse party may be
able to use them during the witness' cross-examination and to introduce in
evidence relevant portions of the documents. You can avoid this problem
by not showing your client other witnesses' statements. Always assume that

62. See, e.g., Hall v. Clifton Precision, 150 F.R.D. 525 (E.D. Pa. 1993).

the opposing lawyer will ask the deponent what she did to prepare for the deposition and what materials she reviewed. Although your communications with your client are privileged, your communications with nonparty deponents, and what you show your client and other deponents, are usually not. Tell the deponent she may be questioned about these things. If you represent an expert, make sure the expert has everything he considered in reaching his opinions and conclusions with him. Make sure you have a copy of everything he considered and that you have disclosed this material to the other side.

Second, review what a deposition is, what its purpose is, why it is so critical, and what the procedure will be. Explain to the client that once the deposition begins, you will be relatively inactive, except to make objections to preserve error when necessary, or to instruct him not to answer if necessary to do so.

Third, review verbal and nonverbal behavior, particularly if the deposition will be videotaped. The nonverbal impression the client makes is as important as the words he says. He should be told to dress appropriately. For most witnesses proper attire means a conservative suit or jacket and tie. If the witness usually wears a uniform, such as a police officer, he should wear the uniform if he is testifying in his capacity as a police officer. He should be told to maintain eye contact with the questioner, since looking down usually creates a negative impression. He should be instructed to sit comfortably in the chair, sit still, rest his hands comfortably and use them to gesture to emphasize his testimony when appropriate. Finally, he should be trained to use clear, simple, proper English and avoid speech forms that suggest hesitancy and uncertainty. This preparation takes time, but it is necessary; preparing a witness for the nonverbal aspects of a deposition, particularly a videotaped deposition, is as important as trial preparation.

Fourth, review how your client should answer questions in order to ensure accuracy. Impress upon him that even though the atmosphere will probably be informal, he must answer carefully. Standard advice includes the following:

- Listen, think, then answer.
- Make sure you understand the question. If you don't, say so.
- If you know the answer, give it. If you don't know, say so. If you know but can't remember just then, say so. If you can only estimate or approximate, say so. However, give positive, truthful answers whenever possible.
- Answer only what the question specifically calls for. Don't exaggerate or speculate. Give the best short, accurate, truthful answer possible. Do not say more than you need to in order to answer the question. Know that the deposition is not the time and place for someone to tell his story.
- Answer questions only with what you personally know, saw, heard, or did, unless the question asks otherwise.
- Be calm and serious at all times. Avoid arguing with the lawyers or getting upset over the questions. I will be there to protect you from unfair questions and procedures by making objections and instructing you on what to do and say.
- Bring nothing (notes, etc.) to the deposition.

Fifth, discuss how objections will be handled. Explain that most objections are made "for the record." Usually the witness must answer despite the objection, which is made for possible later use at trial. However, be sure the client knows not to answer when you object and tell the client not to answer. The client should stay silent if you object based on privilege or harassment grounds. Answering the question may waive any error.

Sixth, review with the client what questions the lawyers are likely to ask. Draw upon your short outline, as discussed previously. Make sure that the client can accurately respond to expected questions in a positive, convincing manner whenever possible. Prepare the client, but don't coach him on what to say, and make sure the client uses his vocabulary, not yours. Let the client know that other lawyers present may ask additional questions, but that you will probably not ask questions unless necessary to correct a mistake or clarify something ambiguous.

Finally, explain that the client has a right to review the deposition if it is transcribed, noting any corrections and the reasons for them, and then signing the error sheet. Explain why the client should not waive his right to "read and sign," stressing the importance of correcting any errors in the transcript. Rule 30(e) requires that, if the deponent or a party makes a request before the deposition ends, the deponent can make changes to his or her testimony as recorded in the transcript. If this request is made, the deponent or party has 30 days after being notified that the transcript is available for review to read, note corrections, and sign the transcript.

Lawyers use different methods to educate clients on what will happen during a deposition and on how important their depositions are. Many lawyers send the client a letter explaining the do's and don'ts of depositions, which the client can then review before coming to your office for further preparation. Another common method is to send the client an audio or visual recording that contains the same advice and includes an exemplar of a deposition. Some lawyers use commercially available recordings; others make their own recordings showing them representing a client at a deposition. This sort of preparation can all be helpful, but there is no substitute for spending the necessary amount of time with the client to deal with the client's anxiety and concerns and to prepare him to be an effective witness.

Above all, the client must understand that her deposition is a pivotal event in the litigation, one that will require time for preparation and practice. Many lawyers videotape the client's practice deposition, using another lawyer as the questioner, and play back the videotape for the client. This technique effectively demonstrates to the client the impression she is making and encourages further improvement.

Preparation sessions for a client take a few hours, but they can also take substantially more. For example, if your client is the CEO of a large corporation involved in a complex case, you may need several sessions. One session may be a get-acquainted meeting to discuss the deposition process and its relationship to the overall case. The next session may include an overview of the anticipated main topics, a review of documents, and some preliminary practice to see how the CEO answers questions. At a third session, you may take a videotaped practice deposition of the CEO, followed by a critique of the CEO's performance. Final preparation and fine-tuning just before the actual deposition will happen at a fourth session. The important point is that in most litigation, the deposition is the only time your client will testify, and how well she does will importantly influence the outcome of that case.

Finally, remember the limitations of Model Rules 3.3 and 3.4. A lawyer has an ethical duty not to offer evidence he knows to be false. The client's memory about past events, transactions, meetings, and conversations must control, not the lawyer's version what he wishes the client to say. A lawyer cannot, covertly or overtly, try to change the client's story.

n.   After the deposition

Four tasks follow after the deposition is over. First, decide if you want to order a transcript of the deposition. The party taking the deposition usually orders it; typically the other parties will want a copy as well. How long it takes to get the transcript depends on the court reporter, but it sometimes can take weeks. You do not need to order a transcript of every deposition in the case. Transcripts usually cost at least three dollars per page, often more, and typically run 40 to 50 pages for each hour of testimony. The cost can rise steeply if you need the transcript on an expedited basis. If the deposition provided nothing useful, or you are on a tight litigation budget, don't order the transcript until you know the case is going to be tried, or unless you think you will need deposition testimony for summary judgment.

Second, write a memo recording your impressions of the witness immediately afterwards, when your impressions are still fresh. Include a summary of the kind of witness she will make at trial and how she helps or hurts your case. This is important, since a transcript may not reflect the impression the witness made. Furthermore, the lawyer taking the deposition may not be the same lawyer who will later try the case.

Third, prepare a deposition summary when you get the transcript. A deposition summary, which paralegals frequently write, records in summary form the witness' testimony and correlates it to the transcript pages. It can also show subject matter and be cross-referenced, which is particularly useful if the summaries will be put into a computer database. Deposition summaries are organized in one of three ways: chronological, by page and line (see example); by topics (good for lawyers to review); and in narrative form based on the witness' answers (good for witnesses to review).

Example:

Ronald Smith	
v.	Case No. 13 C 1022
James Woods	File No. 13-153

Example:

<u>DEPOSITION SUMMARY OF MARIAN WELLS</u>
<u>JUNE 1, 2013</u>

Page/Line	Subject	Text	References
8: 7-22	Address	Wells lives at 231 Barton, Dallas, Texas with husband, 3 children	
9: 12-34	Job	Works at IBM as computer programmer in R & D Division	IBM
10: 6-18	School	Graduated from Southern Methodist University in 1990, B.S. degree, math major	

Deposition summaries enable lawyers to review the depositions of witnesses, evaluate the case for settlement purposes, and prepare for trial.

Fourth, if the deponent is your party, arrange to have the party review the transcript for errors, and consider noting any errors and the reasons for them on the correction page (sometimes called the "error sheet" or "change statement"). If the party makes any corrections, she must sign the correction page and return it to the court reporter. Under Rule 30(e), a witness has 30 days from the time the transcript is available in which to review the transcript and make any changes.

However, making corrections and signing the correction page has a downside: it commits the client to the corrected version and gives the other side additional impeachment material for use at trial. For that reason, some lawyers never have their clients sign the correction sheet (unless making a correction is essential to avoid summary judgment).

Under Rule 5(d), depositions are not to be filed with the court until they are used in the proceeding or the court orders otherwise. Under Rule 30(f), the lawyer ordering the transcript receives the transcript under seal from the court reporter, and the lawyer is responsible for storing the transcript and protecting it from loss, destruction, tampering, and deterioration.

§6.10.   *Physical and mental examinations*

In some cases, primarily personal injury cases, the physical and mental condition of a party is a critical fact affecting both liability and damages. Under these circumstances, the party should be examined to evaluate the authenticity of the condition and its extent and causes, and to develop a prognosis. Rule 35 governs this process.

1. Law

Rule 35 applies to physical and mental examinations of a party and of a person in the custody or under the legal control of a party.[63] The rule clearly includes minors and other legally incapacitated persons who are not the actual named parties, but are the real parties in interest.

A court order is required for such examinations, unless the person to be examined voluntarily agrees to the examination, as permitted under Rule 29 with a written stipulation. In other situations you must move for a court order and give notice to the person and all parties. For the court to order an examination, the physical or mental condition of a party or related person must be "in controversy," and you must show "good cause" for requesting it.[64]

The good-cause requirement has sometimes caused difficulty. In most cases, however — typically personal injury cases or paternity cases where the physical condition of a party is important — few problems arise and the parties often informally arrange for the necessary examinations. The pleadings make the need for examinations apparent for these types of cases. However, issues like testimonial competency will not be apparent from the pleadings. Therefore, the moving party must make a sufficient showing of need in the motion to satisfy the good cause requirement.[65]

The court's order must specify the date, time, place, manner, conditions, and scope of the examination, as well as the person or persons who will perform it. The nature of the claims, defenses, and facts and issues in controversy determine the scope of the examination. Rule 35 provides only that the physical or mental examination be done by a "suitably licensed or certified examiner." In practice the moving party usually suggests a physician and the court ordinarily approves the selection unless another party, or the person to be examined, has a serious objection. The court has discretion to approve or disapprove, and some districts have local rules that provide for the selection of "impartial experts" from approved lists.[66]

Upon request by the examined party, the party moving for the examination must deliver to the examined party a detailed written report of the examining physician setting out findings, results of tests, diagnoses, and conclusions, as well as reports of all earlier examinations for the same conditions. The party moving for the examination can then, upon request, get any previous or future reports about the same person for the same condition, unless, where a nonparty is examined, the party shows he cannot obtain the report. This procedure essentially provides for reciprocal discovery when one side requests a report from the examining physician. When the examined party asks for a copy of the report of the physician who

---

63. Wright §88; James & Hazard §8.20; Moore's Manual §15.27; Manual of Federal Practice §§5.195–5.198; Moore's Federal Practice §§35.01–35.12; Wright & Miller §§2231–2239.

64. See Schlagenhauf v. Holder, 379 U.S. 104, 118-119 (1964).

65. Moore's Manual §15.27(1); Manual of Federal Practice §5.196; Moore's Federal Practice §35.04; Wright & Miller §§2232, 2234.

66. Note that FRE 706 also gives the court authority to appoint and compensate experts.

examined him, this request operates as a waiver of the doctor-patient privilege not only as to that physician, but also as to any other physician who has or may later examine him as to the same conditions.

These disclosure requirements and waiver effects apply regardless of whether the examinations are made pursuant to a court order or through agreement of the parties, unless that agreement expressly provides otherwise. In addition, the discovery permitted under Rule 35 does not restrict other permissible discovery. However, Rule 35 is the only rule that can compel discovery where otherwise the doctor-patient privilege would prevent disclosure.

2.   Practice approach

Since the situations in which physical and mental examinations can be compelled are usually obvious, parties frequently arrange these examinations informally. If you reach an informal agreement with the opposing party, however, you should memorialize it in a letter or, even better, in a Rule 29 stipulation that you file with the court.

When you cannot work out an arrangement, you must move for a court order compelling the desired examination. To comply with Rule 35, the motion must (1) ask for the examination of a party or a person in the custody or control of the party; (2) allege a genuine controversy about that person's physical or mental condition; (3) demonstrate good cause for the examination; (4) request the date, time, place, manner, conditions, and scope of the examination; and (5) designate the examiner who should conduct it. In addition, the motion should indicate that the parties conferred and attempted to resolve their differences, since Rules 26(c) and 37(a) require such a certification whenever parties bring discovery motions.

Example:

[Caption]

MOTION FOR ORDER COMPELLING PLAINTIFF'S PHYSICAL EXAMINATION

Defendant moves under Rule 35 of the Federal Rules of Civil Procedure for an order compelling plaintiff to submit to a physical examination. In support of her motion defendant states:

1. Plaintiff's physical condition is genuinely in controversy, since plaintiff's complaint alleges that "as a result of this collision, plaintiff has suffered severe and permanent injuries to his back and legs."

2. Since plaintiff alleges that his physical limitations are compensable, good cause exists for a physical examination to evaluate the plaintiff's current physical condition, physical limitations, and prognosis.

3. William B. Rudolf, M.D., a board certified orthopedic surgeon, has agreed to examine the plaintiff at his offices at 200 Main Street, Suite 301, Washington, D.C., on August 15, 2013, at 4:00 P.M., or at another time if directed by this court.

4. The parties have conferred but are unable to agree on a physician to conduct the appropriate examination.

WHEREFORE, defendant requests that this court enter an order directing the plaintiff to be examined on the terms set forth above.

_____
Attorney for Defendant

If the court grants the motion, an order must be entered. In federal court the practice is for the court clerk to prepare orders, which the judge then signs. If permitted, however, draft an appropriate order in situations where a nonparty, here the physician, is involved. The physician will want a copy of the order before conducting the examination.

Example:

[Caption]

ORDER

This matter being heard on defendant's motion to compel the physical examination of plaintiff, all parties having been given notice, and the court having heard arguments, it is hereby ordered that:

1. Plaintiff John Williams be examined by William B. Rudolf, M.D., at 200 Main Street, Suite 301, Washington, D.C., on August 15, 2013, at 4:00 P.M., unless the plaintiff and Dr. Rudolf mutually agree to an earlier date and time.

2. Plaintiff shall submit to such orthopedic examinations and tests as are necessary to diagnose and evaluate the plaintiff's back and legs, so that Dr. Rudolf may reach opinions and conclusions about the extent of any injuries, their origin, and prognosis.

3. Dr. Rudolf shall prepare a written report detailing his findings, test results, diagnosis and opinions, along with any earlier similar reports on the same conditions, and deliver it to defendant's attorneys on or before September 15, 2013.

Entered:

Dated:_____   _____
                                      United States District Judge

Finally, keep in mind the reciprocal discovery provisions of Rule 35(b)(1). If the examined party requests a copy of the examiner's report, the party moving for the examination has the right to receive from the examined party other reports dealing with the same conditions, regardless of when made. You must, however, request those reports. Perhaps the safer approach is to send the examined party a document titled <u>"REQUEST FOR MEDICAL REPORTS,"</u> show that you make the request under the provisions of Rule 35(b)(1), and file the request with the court. If the other party fails to deliver, or later attempts to use such reports, you have made a record of your request. You can then object to the introduction of those reports at trial on grounds that the party did not comply with Rule 35 during discovery.

§6.11.   *Requests for admissions*

Requests to admit facts and the genuineness of documents are not designed to "discover." Up to now the parties have been acquiring information, through informal and formal discovery, and the information acquisition phase of the litigation process is essentially complete. The next step is to sift through all of this acquired information and begin planning what you will introduce at trial and how you will do it. A request to admit (along with the pretrial statement and motions in limine) is a basic tool that you can use to streamline your proof at trial.

1.   Law

Rule 36 governs requests to admit facts and the genuineness of documents.[67] These requests can only be propounded to parties. Admissions made in response to the requests are conclusive admissions for the pending action only and cannot be used for any other purposes. This limit encourages a party to admit facts without worrying about collateral consequences. Any matter admitted is deemed "conclusively established," which means that the admitting party cannot introduce evidence at trial contradicting its earlier admission (unless the court allows the admission's withdrawal or amendment).

Requests may be served on other parties at any time after the parties meet to develop a discovery plan under Rule 26(f). Like other discovery provisions, requests can be employed essentially at any time during the litigation process.

A request can be directed to four categories: the truth of facts, the application of law to fact, opinions about either, and the genuineness of documents. The basic scope of these requests is the same as for discovery more generally. They can seek anything that is relevant but not privileged. Each request must be separately stated.

After a request has been served on a party, that party must serve a response within 30 days or the matters requested will be deemed admitted,

---

67. Wright §89; Hazard et al. §8.21; Moore's Manual §15.28; Manual of Federal Practice §§5.199–5.215; Moore's Federal Practice §§36.01–36.13; Wright & Miller §§2251–2265.

unless a stipulation between the parties or a court order changes the dead-line. This automatic provision of Rule 36 makes it a formidable weapon, as inertia or inattentiveness can have automatic, often devastating, conse-quences. Hence, one cardinal rule governs practice under this provision: Make sure you respond and serve the response within the 30-day period. While under Rule 6(b) the court can extend time, asking the court to extend time to answer a request for admissions after the deadline to answer has passed requires a showing that the party "failed to act because of excusable neglect." Rule 36(b) also permits the withdrawal or amendment of admissions under certain circumstances. However, the message of the rule is clear: respond to the request for admissions within the 30-day period, and make sure your responses are complete and accurate.

Rule 36 permits four types of responses. First, you can object to a matter in the request. Second, you can admit the matter. Third, you can deny the matter. Fourth, you can neither admit nor deny because, after reasonable inquiry, you do not have sufficient information to determine if the matter is true or not.

How you respond, and whether your response is justified under the circumstances, determines whether Rule 37 sanctions can be imposed. Rule 37(c) provides that reasonable expenses — including attorney's fees — incurred in proving a denied matter can be taxed as costs against the losing party. However, if you neither admit nor deny because of genuinely insufficient knowledge, Rule 37 sanctions cannot be imposed.[68]

Once you have received a response, you can move the court to review the sufficiency of the objections and responses. The rule requires that a response must specifically deny the matter or set forth in detail why the answering party cannot admit or deny after making a reasonable inquiry. A denial must fairly meet the substance of the requested admission. The better practice is to make a motion under Rule 36(a) to determine the sufficiency of an answer and see if the court will deem the matter admitted. This tactic will protect against surprises at trial. The court can enter an order compelling an answer or amended answer if appropriate, order that the matter be deemed admitted, or continue the motion to the pretrial conference or to another date before trial.

2. Practice approach

Because Rule 36 has a broad scope, using and responding to requests for admissions involve strategic concerns that you must coordinate with your overall trial strategy. Note the emphasis on trial strategy, not on discovery. Requests to admit do not "discover" additional information; they are used to sharpen trial issues, streamline the presentation of evidence, and

68. See Wright §90; Hazard et al. §8.23; Moore's Manual §15.44; Manual of Federal Practice §§5.214-5.216; Moore's Federal Practice §§37.70; Wright & Miller §§2265, 2288, 2290.

eliminate the need to formally prove uncontroverted facts.[69] Hence, the question is not what you can get the other side to admit. The better question is: What do you want the other side to admit that ties in to your overall trial strategy?

a. Timing

Rule 36 permits requests to admit at any time after the parties meet to plan discovery, so practical considerations control the decision as to when to propound them. Requests are most frequently made at the end of the discovery stage. Discovery is essentially complete when you have received initial disclosures, interrogatory answers, and records pursuant to document requests; you have deposed the parties and necessary witnesses; and, where appropriate, you have completed physical and mental examinations. Requests to admit come into play at this point because the existing discovery will identify what still remains at issue. The requests should be served before the final pretrial conference is scheduled or summary judgment motions are made. Requests to admit served at that time will help determine what facts the other side will concede or contest if the case goes to trial.

Another approach is to serve requests to admit early in the discovery process, sometimes coupled with interrogatories and document requests, to bring potential Rule 37 sanctions into play. For example, if you have a strong case on liability and want to push for an early settlement, send the other side an early request to admit facts that prove liability. Your opponent will have to decide what facts and issues she intends to dispute, enabling later discovery to be more focused. If a party denies a fact in a request to admit without a substantial basis for the denial, and that fact is later proved at trial, the party proving the fact can receive as court costs the reasonable expense of proving the denied fact at trial, including attorney's fees. By making requests to admit early, you start the period for which you may be entitled to get Rule 37 costs. Where you think the opposing party will use dilatory tactics or avoid serious settlement discussions on a case that should be settled quickly, making a request to admit early raises the risks for the party using those tactics.

b. What to request

To determine what to request, look first at the elements of your claims and defenses. Second, analyze each "fact" you will need to prove to meet your burden of proof at trial on each element. Every trial lawyer must conduct this review when preparing for trial. Third, review the pleadings, to see what has been admitted, and your discovery results, to see what facts

---

69. Some courts have held that since requests to admit differ from other devices used for information-gathering, discovery cutoff dates do not apply to them. Compare Freeman v. City of Detroit, 274 F.R.D. 610 (E.D. Mich. 2011), with Kelly v. McGraw Hill Companies, Inc., 279 F.R.D. 470 (N.D. Ill. 2012).

are conceded. Reviewing the discovery is particularly critical, since a fact, when conceded in interrogatory answers or in a party deposition, is only an admission by a party opponent — *not* the same thing as a conclusive admission. The party admitting a fact can still present contrary evidence at trial. To avoid this result, focus on matters opposing parties have admitted in previous discovery. Those parties are likely to admit the facts in a request to admit if they have previously admitted them. The advantage is that when a party admits a fact under Rule 36, it is deemed conclusively established for purposes of that pending action. The admitting party cannot then introduce contrary evidence at trial, unless the court permits amendment or withdrawal.

Fourth, think through your trial strategy. What witnesses and exhibits do you need to prove your case at trial? Where are your strengths and weaknesses? Is some of your evidence technical and likely to bore the jury? Is some of it costly to present? Is some of your testimony dramatic or emotional? Do some of your exhibits have significant visual impact? In short, don't ask the other side to admit something just because it's there. Ask the other side to make an admission because it improves your case at trial. You will *not* ask the other side to admit your most compelling, emotional, or dramatic evidence. You want the jury to hear and see precisely this evidence. On the other hand, if the evidence is technical, boring but necessary, excessively expensive to present, or comes from a weak witness, you want it admitted through requests to admit.

c. Drafting the requests

The cardinal rule for drafting requests to admit is to keep them simple and clear. A lengthy, complicated request practically begs a denial, an objection, or a lengthy, equivocal response. Motions will ensue, and the request in the end will probably achieve nothing.

Simplicity requires that a request be short and contain a single statement of fact. Such requests are difficult to quibble with, and they stand the best chance of being admitted outright. They should also comply with admissibility rules, such as those concerning relevance, hearsay, and authentication.

Organize your requests into the four permitted categories:

1. truth of facts
2. application of law to fact
3. opinions of fact and application of law to facts
4. genuineness of documents

When drafting requests to admit facts, ask that the facts be admitted as true.

Example (facts):

[Caption]

REQUESTS TO ADMIT FACTS AND GENUINENESS OF DOCUMENTS

Plaintiff Ralph Johnson requests defendant Marion Smith to make the following admissions, within 30 days after service of this request, for the purposes of this action only:

Admit that each of the following facts is true:

1. On May 1, 2013, plaintiff had a valid driver's license issued by the state of Colorado.

2. On May 1, 2013, defendant was the registered owner of a Chevrolet sedan having a Colorado license no. BCD-437.

When drafting requests to admit the genuineness of documents, the usual request is to ask that attached documents are "genuine." Genuine means that the document is what it purports to be. In other words, the document was made by the person or entity it appears to be made by and, if signed, was signed by the person it appears to be signed by. Keep in mind, however, that a party admitting the genuineness of a document admits that and no more. That party may still raise other evidentiary objections, such as relevance or hearsay, to the document's admissibility at trial.

Example (genuineness of documents):

Admit that each of the following documents is genuine:

3. The contract, attached as Exhibit A.

4. The check, attached as Exhibit B.

You can do much better than merely ask that a document be admitted as genuine, however. Always think about the evidentiary foundation necessary to get a particular document or record admitted at trial, then get the opposing party to admit the foundation requirements.

Example (foundation for documents):

Admit that the following facts are true:

5. The contract, attached as Exhibit A, bears the signature of the defendant.

6. The defendant signed the original of Exhibit A on May 1, 2013.

7. The contract, attached as Exhibit A, is an accurate copy of the original contract signed by the defendant.

8. A bill of lading, attached as Exhibit B, is a business record of the XYZ Corporation under FRE 803(b).

9. The bill of lading, attached as Exhibit B, is an accurate copy (other than a possible change in size) of the original made by XYZ Corporation.

Keep in mind that a fact can be contained in a document, so you may want the other party to admit the fact, admit the genuineness of the document containing the fact, or both. Juries usually respond favorably to exhibits, so it's a sound idea to get the document before the jury at trial.

Requests to admit can also ask for "opinions of fact" and the "application of law to fact." These requests are problematic since questions of "pure law" cannot be asked. For instance, a request that asks a party to admit negligence or culpability is objectionable. The line between "opinions of fact" and "application of law to fact," on one hand, and "pure law," on the other, is fuzzy.[70] Treading close to the line will probably draw objections. Accordingly, err on the safe side and leave the legal disputes for resolution at summary judgment or trial. Common situations where the application of law to fact is raised involve issues of title, ownership, agency, and employment.

Example (application of law to fact):

> Admit that each of the following statements is true:
> 10. Defendant was the legal titleholder of a lot commonly known as 3401 Fifth Street, Tucson, Arizona, on August 1, 2013.
> 11. On August 1, 2013, William Oats was an employee of XYZ Corporation.
> 12. On August 1, 2013, William Oats was authorized to enter into sales contracts on behalf of XYZ Corporation.

Consider coupling requests to admit with interrogatories asking for the facts that support any response that does not admit a request. When the opposing party must answer an interrogatory asking why she did not make an admission in response to a request to admit, the party will have difficultly denying the request in the first place. If the request is not admitted and the follow-up interrogatory is answered, you may have a better understanding of how the opposing side will attempt to deal with this issue at trial.

Example:

REQUESTS FOR ADMISSIONS

> 1. Admit that the defendant's car crossed the center lane and was in the plaintiff's lane of traffic when the collision happened.
> 2. . . .

---

70. See Wright §89; Moore's Manual §15.28; Moore's Federal Practice §36.10(1); Wright & Miller §§2255, 2256.

INTERROGATORIES

1. If you fail to admit Request for Admissions No. 1:
    (a) State the facts on which you base your denial;
    (b) Identify all documents that support your denial;
    (c) Identify each person with information that supports your denial.
2. . . .

What are the common problems that arise when drafting requests to admit? Remember that the point of using requests to admit is to streamline the presentation of your case at trial by eliminating the need to present boring but necessary or expensive evidence. The most common problem, therefore, is the failure to coordinate requests to admit with overall trial strategy. Always ask: What are the interesting and exciting parts of my case that I want the jury to hear? What parts of my case have no jury appeal and consist of boring or technical proof, which I would prefer to prove through a request to admit? In addition, your overall strategy may include making a summary judgment motion. The requests to admit should be considered in light of what you need to prove to win the motion.

Another common problem is that the requests to admit contain characterizations that the other party does not want to admit. For example, asking "Admit that there was no reason to believe that ABC Corporation would not deliver the goods by June 1, 2013," or "Admit that defendant harbored doubts about its denying the claim for benefits" will usually generate a denial. Avoid characterizations—"quibble words"—in the requests. Simple requests, consisting of nouns and verbs and avoiding adjectives and adverbs, are more likely to be admitted.

Another common problem is a request that asks a party to admit a fact, rather than a request that asks the party to admit the foundation for the admissibility of a record or document containing the fact. Visual exhibits have persuasive power. Jurors would much rather look at a key record or document, blown up as a courtroom exhibit, than listen to the judge instruct them that a certain fact will be deemed conclusively admitted.

Finally, keep in mind that requests to admit are designed to streamline the trial. The request and response will be read to the jury during trial, and the judge will probably give a specific jury instruction based on the request and response. Always consider how the request will sound to the jurors. When using requests to provide the basis for admissibility of an exhibit at trial, always review what technical evidentiary foundation the particular exhibit requires to be admitted in evidence. Draft the request to admit accordingly.

The requests to admit should be signed by the lawyer and served on each party. Service is made by any permitted method under Rule 5, most commonly by mailing a copy to the lawyers of the other parties. However, under Rule 5(d) the requests to admit are not to be filed with the court until it is used in the proceeding or the court orders otherwise.

d.   Choosing a response

A party on whom requests to admit have been served must respond, usually within 30 days of receiving the requests. Otherwise, the matters in the requests will automatically be deemed conclusively admitted for purposes of the pending action. Therefore, you must respond within the time limit. There are four basic types of responses to a request.

First, you can object to the request. As with discovery generally, you can object that the matter requested is irrelevant or privileged. In addition, you can seek a protective order if the request is unduly burdensome or harassing.

Second, you can admit the request. When you do so, you conclusively admit the matter for the purpose of the pending action only. Such an admission prevents you from presenting contrary evidence at trial.

Third, you can deny the request. The denial must be based on good faith. If the requesting party later proves the denied matter at trial, Rule 37 provides that the party may get reasonable expenses, including attorney's fees, involved in proving the matter. The response can, of course, admit some parts of a request and deny others.

Fourth, under certain circumstances you can "state in detail why the answering party cannot truthfully admit or deny it." The answering party must have made a "reasonable inquiry" in an effort to acquire necessary information for responding to the request but still be unable to respond. In practice, lawyers deny such requests after detailing the reasons why the matter cannot be admitted or denied.

When you have decided what the appropriate response should be, draft the response as you might draft answers to interrogatories. Include the request, followed by your response.

Example:

[Caption]

RESPONSE TO REQUESTS FOR ADMISSIONS

Defendant Marian Smith responds to plaintiff Ralph Johnson's requests for admissions as follows:

Request No. 1: A contract, attached as Exhibit A, is a true and accurate copy of the contract signed by plaintiff on August 1, 2013.

Answer: Admit.

Request No. 2: Plaintiff performed all his obligations under the contract.

Answer: Deny.

Request No. 3: On August 1, 2013, William Oats was authorized to enter into sales contracts on behalf of XYZ Corporation.

Answer: Objection. Responding to this request would disclose the substance of conversations between William Oats, an attorney, and the XYZ Corporation, which are protected from disclosure by the attorney-client privilege.

Request No. 4: Mary Doyle is the sole titleholder of a lot commonly known as 3401 Fifth Street, Seattle, Washington.

Answer: Defendant cannot truthfully admit or deny this request and therefore denies it. Public records neither confirm nor deny, and defendant has no access to any documents that could confirm or deny it. Defendant has made reasonable inquiry and the information it has obtained or can readily obtain is insufficient to admit or deny.

The response to requests to admit should be signed by the party's lawyer and served on each party. Service is made by any permitted method under Rule 5, most commonly by mailing a copy to the lawyers for the other parties. However, under Rule 5(d) the response is not to be filed with the court until it is used in the proceeding or the court orders otherwise.

e. Requestor's responses

When a party has made and served responses to requests to admit on the requesting party, the requesting party can take two steps: move to review the sufficiency of an answer, and move to review the sufficiency and justification of an objection. The requesting party directs both to the court's discretion. The court can enter any appropriate order; it can deem a matter admitted, require an amended answer, or continue the issue to the pretrial conference or other time before trial.

When the answering party denies a request to admit facts, follow up with interrogatories that ask the answering party for the basis for the denial. Another approach is to send "contention interrogatories" along with the requests to admit, again asking for the basis for each denial. The answering party will often just admit the request, rather than attempt to justify the denial in the accompanying interrogatory answer.

§6.12. Supplementing discovery

Rule 26(e) imposes a duty to supplement and correct disclosures and discovery responses. This duty applies to required disclosures — initial, expert, and pretrial disclosures — and responses to discovery — interrogatories, document requests, and requests to admit. The duty to supplement expert disclosures extends both to the expert's report and the expert's deposition.

The time requirements are unclear. Required disclosures must be supplemented "in a timely manner." Responses to interrogatories, document requests, and requests to admit must be supplemented when a party "learns that in some material respect the disclosure or response is incomplete or incorrect," and that the "additional or corrective information has not otherwise been made known to the other parties during the discovery process or in writing." The intent of the rule is fairness: parties must supplement periodically so the opposing parties are not unfairly disadvantaged, and they cannot withhold information to gain strategic advantages. Being timely is particularly important as the trial date nears. Problems arise most frequently with experts. Experts develop additional opinions and bases for their opinions, but these new opinions and bases were neither in the expert's report nor the expert's deposition testimony.

Failure to supplement can have drastic consequences. Under Rule 37(c), failure to disclose or supplement disclosures or discovery responses will result in the exclusion of the undisclosed information at the trial, hearing, or motion, "unless the failure was substantially justified or is harmless." In addition, the court on motion and after a hearing may impose other sanctions, including reasonable expenses and attorney's fees.

The message of Rule 26(e) is clear: periodically review your disclosures and discovery responses, and if you have acquired material new information that has not been included in your disclosures and responses, and if it has not yet been made known to the other parties, disclose the information promptly. Either amend your disclosures and responses or notify the other parties of the new information in writing.

§6.13.   Discovery motions

Discovery under the Federal Rules largely proceeds without judicial intervention. The parties can conduct discovery without prior judicial approval, except for physical and mental examinations, discovery before the parties have conferred to develop a discovery plan, discovery that would exceed the numerical limits on interrogatories and depositions, and discovery that would violate a court order regulating discovery entered under Rule 16. Usually, the court needs to get involved only when a dispute over discovery arises.

Four points bear emphasizing. First, Rule 37(a) requires the moving party's lawyer to certify what good faith efforts have been made to confer with the other party to resolve a discovery dispute informally before the court will intervene. The lawyer must sign an appropriate certification and attach it to the motion. The certification can also be made part of the motion, probably the more common approach.

Second, discovery abuse has probably attracted more controversy and reform proposals than any other aspect of the litigation process. The past three decades have witnessed a trend toward more court involvement in discovery, as well as greater judicial willingness to impose stiffer sanctions.

Third, Rule 26 gives courts powers to regulate discovery. Rule 26(b)(2) allows the court the power to limit discovery where it is unnecessarily cumulative or duplicative, or is obtainable from other sources with less effort and expense. Rule 16 empowers courts to hold discovery conferences and impose a discovery plan. Rule 26(g) requires that a lawyer sign a certification that he has read the discovery document; that he has made a reasonable inquiry; and that the document is consistent with the rules and law, is not made for any improper purpose, and is not unreasonably burdensome or expensive.

Fourth, judges tend to find discovery disputes tedious and unpleasant. Before pulling the trigger on a discovery motion, try everything you can to resolve the problem informally. Request a more informal conference with the court before filing a motion. (In fact, a proposed amendment to Rule 16, pending as this edition went to press, would require just this request.) You can also bargain with your adversary rather than filing a motion to compel. Perhaps your adversary will agree to allow you additional interrogatories, for instance, in exchange for your forbearance.

There are two principal types of discovery motions, those for protective orders and those for orders compelling discovery.

1. Protective orders

Rule 26(c) and Rule 30(d) (for oral depositions) govern protective orders.[71] Whenever an entity or person from whom discovery is sought believes that the discovery requests are annoying, embarrassing, oppressive, unduly burdensome, or unduly expensive, that person or entity should move for a protective order. Both parties and nonparty deponents can seek protective orders.

The motion must usually be brought in the district where the action is pending. However, when a deposition has been terminated so that a witness can move for a protective order, the witness can bring the motion either in the district where the action is pending or the district where the deposition is being taken. A nonparty deponent may prefer the latter, since the deposition is often taken where the deponent resides or does business.

Under Rule 26(c), the moving party must show "good cause." While grounds for protection are numerous, the most common one is that the discovery requested is so lengthy and detailed that it is unduly oppressive and expensive. Examples include discovery involving lengthy or repetitive interrogatories and depositions, or overly detailed document requests and requests to admit. An attempt to take "apex" depositions on high corporate officers who have no firsthand knowledge of any relevant facts also may provide good cause. If the dominant purpose of the discovery is not to develop information reasonably necessary to prepare for trial or settlement, but to harass the corporate officer or force the opposition into submission, a protective order is appropriate. Interrogatories and document requests that ask for disclosure and production of income tax returns, corporate financial data, and other proprietary information are problematic. Unless this information is relevant to claims of lost income or punitive damages, a protective order barring, limiting, or delaying such discovery is appropriate. Other motions frequently seek to limit disclosure;

---

71. Wright §83; Hazard et al. §8.23; Moore's Manual §15.04; Manual of Federal Practice §§5.94–5.105; Moore's Federal Practice §§26.10-26.108; Wright & Miller §§2035–2044.

they ask the court to restrict the persons present at depositions and thereby prevent the disclosure of business secrets to persons outside the litigation, to limit the discovery methods that the parties may use, and to seal depositions and other discovery.

Attempts to discover electronically stored information frequently give rise to motions for protective orders. While relevant information in electronic form is clearly discoverable through a properly worded Rule 34 production request, motions commonly seek protection on the ground that the request imposes an undue burden in terms of time and cost.

These motions are directed to the sound discretion of the court. When a document request is broad, the likelihood of obtaining relevant information is low, and the burden on the disclosing party is high, the court may issue a protective order barring the request, limiting the request, ordering the requesting party to pay the cost of production, or ordering that the cost be shared. For example, a document request that asks for all e-mail between all company employees for a two-year period is exceptionally broad. The likelihood of finding relevant information (the "smoking gun") is low. The expense to the disclosing party to find and retrieve the requested information will be high (particularly when compared to the money in dispute in the case). The court usually will balance the competing concerns (the "proportionality" of potential discovery yield with anticipated discovery cost) and may consider any of these options. As the requesting party, make your e-discovery request as focused and specific as possible to reduce the likelihood of successful objections and court-ordered cost-shifting.

Rule 26(c) requires that the moving party's lawyer include with the motion a certification that he has made a good faith attempt to confer with the opposing party and resolve the dispute without court action.

Many discovery matters come up by motions to compel after a party has objected to discovery requests. Objections are permitted in answers to interrogatories, document requests, and requests to admit. The objection protects the responding party. The requesting party must move for an order to compel discovery, and the responding party does not first need to move for a protective order.

However, if you plan to move for a protective order, make the motion early. Do not wait until the other side moves to compel discovery. The judge will wonder how serious your motion for a protective order is if it follows on the heels of your opponent's motion to compel discovery. Hence, the better practice is to object to the discovery request and immediately file your motion for a protective order.

If a protective order is appropriate, Rule 26(c) provides a variety of remedies that can protect a party or person from embarrassment, oppression, and undue burden or expense. These include barring the requested discovery; regulating the terms, conditions, methods, and scope of discovery; limiting persons present at the discovery; requiring the sealing of depositions and documents; and regulating or barring disclosure of trade secrets and confidential information.

The motion for a protective order must be prepared like any other motion, and must include statements of the facts as well as a request for the relief sought.

Example:

[Caption]

MOTION FOR PROTECTIVE ORDER

Plaintiff Willard Johnson requests that this court enter a protective order pursuant to Rule 26(c) against defendant Clark Johnson, and in support of his motion states:

1. On March 8, 2013, defendant took plaintiff's first deposition. This deposition took approximately four hours and generated a transcript of 238 pages.

2. On April 15, 2013, defendant again took plaintiff's deposition without opposition by plaintiff. This deposition took approximately three hours and generated a transcript of 181 pages.

3. On July 2, 2013, plaintiff was served with a third notice of plaintiff's deposition.

4. This pending action involves a simple intersection collision. The two previous depositions have exhaustively covered what plaintiff knows about the collision, what happened afterwards, his medical treatment, and all claimed damages.

5. The notice for a third deposition, under these circumstances, violates Rule 30(a), constitutes an attempt to annoy, oppress, and place undue burdens on the plaintiff, and has no proper purpose. Since plaintiff lives out of state, another deposition will again impose significant financial and time expenses.

WHEREFORE, plaintiff Willard Johnson requests that this court enter a protective order barring defendant Clark Johnson from taking further depositions of the plaintiff.

_____

Attorney for Plaintiff

A certificate of compliance must accompany each discovery motion, either attached as a separate document or contained within the motion. If a separate document, it should look like the following:

Example:

CERTIFICATE OF COMPLIANCE WITH RULE 26

I, Allen Smith, attorney of record for Plaintiff Willard Johnson, certify that I have complied with the requirements of Rule 26(c) by doing the following:

1. On July 3, 2013, I sent a letter to defendant's counsel asking why a third deposition of the plaintiff was necessary. I received no written or oral reply to my letter.

2. On July 10, I called defendant's counsel and spoke with him. He stated that he noticed the plaintiff's deposition a third time to "make sure he'd covered all the bases," and gave no other reason for wanting a third deposition.

3. I requested that defendant's counsel withdraw the notice for the plaintiff's deposition, but he refused. Consequently this motion for a protective order is necessary.

Dated:_____   _____

                                    Attorney for Plaintiff

Example:

[Caption]

<u>MOTION FOR PROTECTIVE ORDER</u>

Plaintiff Nancy Jones moves pursuant to Rule 26(c) for a protective order against defendant XYZ Corporation, and in support of the motion states:

1. The pending case is a product liability case involving a rubber hose manufactured by defendant XYZ.

2. Plaintiff has previously served a motion to produce the rubber hose involved for the purposes of inspection and testing. Defendant's response stated that the rubber hose has already been shipped to ABC Laboratories for testing.

3. There is a substantial danger that any testing by ABC Laboratories will alter or destroy the rubber hose and forever prevent plaintiff from inspecting and testing it.

4. In compliance with Rule 26(c), I hereby certify that I telephonically conferred with the attorney for defendant XYZ Corporation. The attorney refused to delay the testing by ABC Laboratories, and specifically stated that the testing would go forward unless this court granted a protective order. Consequently, this motion for a protective order has become necessary.

WHEREFORE, plaintiff requests this court to enter a protective order against defendant as follows:

(a) prevent anything from being done with or to the rubber hose until plaintiff has had a reasonable opportunity to inspect and photograph it;

(b) prevent any tests that would destroy or affect the appearance and integrity of the rubber hose;

(c) if destructive testing is necessary, order that such testing be conducted at a time and place so that plaintiff's experts can be present, observe the testing procedure, and obtain a copy of all test results;

(d) award payment of reasonable expenses, including attorney's fees, to plaintiff incurred as a result of making this motion.

                                    _____
                                    Attorney for Plaintiff

A common practice is to prepare a proposed order and attach it to the motion. The proposed order should mirror the motion and set out what information needs to be protected and how it will be protected.

After the motion is prepared and signed, a copy along with a notice of motion must be served on every other party under Rule 5. The original of the motion and notice of motion, with a proof of service, must be filed with the clerk of the court. Remember that many federal district judges delegate discovery matters to magistrate judges, so make sure your notice of motion correctly specifies who will hear the motion.

2.   Compelling discovery

Rule 37(a) governs motions for orders compelling disclosure or discovery.[72] A party seeking to compel discovery must move for an appropriate order in the district where the action is pending, except if the matters relate to discovery from a nonparty. In this situation, the moving party must bring the motion in the district where she seeks discovery.

The attorney for the moving party must attach a certification to the motion describing her good faith attempts to meet and confer and to resolve the dispute.

A party can move for an order compelling discovery whenever her adversary fails to answer or gives evasive or incomplete answers to proper discovery. Frequently an issue arises when a party responds by objecting to an interrogatory, request to produce, or request to admit. A motion to compel must then be made to determine whether the objection is proper. An issue also frequently arises when a party fails to answer interrogatories; fails to produce documents after being served with a request to produce; refuses to designate a deponent on behalf of a corporate party; or, in the case of deponents, refuses to appear, be sworn, or answer questions. Another problem might involve inadequate initial disclosures.

Under Rule 37(a)(5), the court must award reasonable expenses, including attorney's fees, to the prevailing party when a motion to compel is granted and also when the discovery sought is provided after the motion's filing. Even if a motion is granted, however, the court may deny a request for fees and costs if it determines that the requesting party made no good faith effort to resolve the dispute before asking for the court's intervention. If the motion is denied, the court must award expenses to the prevailing party unless the circumstances make such an award unjust.

Rule 37(c)(1) provides a self-executing sanction for failure to make the Rule 26(a) required disclosures. Unless you have substantial justification for failing to make the required disclosures, you will not be permitted to use any witness or information that you did not disclose at trial, in a motion, or at a hearing, unless the failure to disclose was substantially justified or is harmless. In addition to or in lieu of the preclusion sanction,

72. Wright §90; Hazard §8.23; Moore's Manual §15.40; Manual of Federal Practice §§5.214–5.218; Moore's Federal Practice §37.02; Wright & Miller §§2281–2293.

the court may order other appropriate sanctions, including expenses or attorney's fees. The court may even inform the jury of the party's failure to make disclosure.

The most common motions to compel usually involve either a party's failure to respond to discovery at all, or a response with evasive or incomplete answers that do not fairly meet the substance of the request.

Example:

[Caption]

<u>MOTION TO COMPEL DISCOVERY</u>

Defendant Alfred Jenkens moves that this court enter an order compelling plaintiff Thomas Smith to answer interrogatories, and in support of his motion states:

1. On June 5, 2013, defendant served his first set of interrogatories on plaintiff.

2. On July 15, 2013, defendant by letter reminded plaintiff's lawyer that answers to interrogatories were overdue and had not yet been received. A copy of this letter is attached as Exhibit A. No response to this letter has been received.

3. Over 100 days have passed since defendant served interrogatories on plaintiff and to date no answers have been received.

4. Defendant's counsel has called plaintiff's counsel three times since July 15, 2013, each time reminding him that the answers had not been received. During the last call, defendant's counsel told plaintiff's counsel that a motion to compel would be filed unless answers were received immediately. That last call was made one week ago.

WHEREFORE, defendant requests the court to order plaintiff to serve interrogatory answers within five days and award reasonable expenses, including attorney's fees, to defendant incurred as a result of making this motion.

_____
Attorney for Defendant

After the motion is prepared and signed, a copy along with a notice of motion must be served on every other party under Rule 5. The originals of the motion and notice of motion, with a proof of service, must be filed with the clerk of the court. Keep in mind that many federal district judges delegate discovery matters to magistrate judges, so make sure your notice of motion correctly specifies who will hear the motion.

A good practice is to ask the court to set out in its order compelling discovery what the sanctions will be if the order is not obeyed. This detail improves the likelihood that the opposing party will comply with the order.

As a tactical matter, always consider *not* moving to compel discovery. Under Rule 37(c), a party that fails to disclose information or a witness required to be disclosed under Rule 26 shall not be allowed to use as evidence such information or witness at trial, at a hearing, or in a motion. This preclusion is required "unless the failure was substantially justified or is harmless." You may be better off not seeking to compel discovery and instead moving to preclude the undisclosed information or witness when the opposing party attempts to introduce it at trial.

3.   Sanctions for abuse

Several sources give the court power to impose sanctions for abuse.[73] Rule 11(c) authorizes the court to impose appropriate sanctions on any attorney, law firm, or party that has improperly signed, filed, submitted, or later advocated a pleading, written motion, or other paper. Rule 26(g) requires the court to impose sanctions on an improperly signed certification regarding a discovery request, response, or objection. Rule 30(d) gives the court power to impose sanctions, including reasonable expenses and attorney's fees, on a person who impedes, delays, or frustrates the fair examination of a deponent. Rule 37 deals with a party's failure to disclose, admit facts, attend depositions, answer interrogatories, or respond to a request for inspection. 28 U.S.C. §1927 gives the court broad power over any person who "multiplies the proceedings in any case unreasonably and vexatiously." That person can be required "to satisfy personally the excess costs, expenses, and attorney's fees reasonably incurred because of such conduct." Finally, case law supports the court's "inherent power" to impose sanctions for misconduct.[74]

You should always base your motion for sanctions on the correct rule, the one that allows sanctions against the person you want to sanction and permits the specific sanctions you want imposed. Keep the following considerations in mind. First, always describe the other party's bad faith whenever you can, even if the rule does not require it. Second, show actual prejudice to your party whenever you can, even if the rule does not require it. Third, make sure that your conduct during discovery is clean. You can be sure that the other party will attempt to show that you have been guilty of the same or other alleged misconduct. The court will undoubtedly take these considerations into account when deciding a motion for sanctions. The severity of the sanctions should be commensurate with the seriousness and impact of the abuse.[75]

Of these rules, Rule 37 is the most frequently used. It deals explicitly with failures to comply with discovery orders and failures to make discovery.

Rule 37(a) addresses sanctions permitted after a motion to compel disclosure or discovery. Under Rule 37(a)(5), sanctions "must" be

---

73. Wright §90; Hazard §8.23; Moore's Manual §§15.41-15.44; Manual of Federal Practice §§5.219–5.235; Moore's Federal Practice §§37.40–37.44; Wright & Miller §§2281–2293; G. Joseph, Rule Traps, 30 Litig. 6 (Winter 2003).

74. Chambers v. NASCO, Inc., 501 U.S. 32, 44 (1991); Isaacson v. Manty, 721 F.3d 533, 538 (8th Cir. 2013).

75. See, e.g., B.K.B. v. Maui Police Dep't, 276 F.3d 1091, 1108-1109 (9th Cir. 2002).

imposed, after a hearing, against the losing party or that party's lawyer, unless the moving party failed to make a good faith effort to resolve the dispute informally before bringing the motion, or other circumstances exist that would make the imposition of sanctions unjust. Sanctions against the losing party or lawyer can include the reasonable expenses incurred by the winning party in making or opposing the motion, including reasonable attorney's fees. If the discovery motion is denied, the court can also enter any appropriate protective order.

Under Rule 37(b), sanctions for discovery abuse can be imposed where a deponent or party fails to obey a previous court order regarding discovery. In this situation, the court can enter essentially any sanction appropriate to the level of misconduct involved.[76] Such sanctions can include an order deeming certain facts admitted, barring a party from presenting evidence, striking pleadings, dismissing all or part of the action, entering a default judgment, and treating a refusal to obey as a contempt of court. Sanctions can also include an award of reasonable expenses, including attorney's fees.

Rule 37(c) provides that a party failing to make disclosures required under Rules 26(a) or 26(e) will be barred from using the withheld information or witness at a trial or hearing, "unless the failure was substantially justified or is harmless." The court can also impose other appropriate sanctions, including reasonable expenses and attorney's fees. Think of Rule 37(c) as an evidence rule. If you don't disclose as required under the various provisions of Rule 26, the undisclosed evidence is excluded. The message is clear: disclose fully, disclose early, and supplement in a timely manner.

Motions to compel directed to parties must be filed in the district in which the action is pending. Motions directed to nonparties must be filed in the district in which discovery is sought to be conducted.

Rule 37(c) also permits the award of reasonable expenses, including attorney's fees, incurred as a result of proving matters that a party denied in response to a Rule 36 request to admit, unless the party had a good reason for its failure to admit. Reasonable expenses include the attorney's time and witness expenses, such as travel and lodging, that the requesting party incurred to prepare and prove the denied fact at trial.

Finally, Rule 26(g) gives the court power to impose sanctions against the lawyer or party who signs a Rule 26(a) disclosure that violates the requirements of that rule without substantial justification. The sanctions can be imposed after a party's motion or on the court's own initiative. They can include any appropriate sanction, including reasonable expenses and attorney's fees.

Rules 26 and 37 give the court the power and discretion to respond effectively to discovery abuse. The difficult decisions involve those situations where the discovery abuse was not caused by the party itself, but by the party's lawyer. Under these circumstances, a party who may have a meritorious claim or defense might unjustly suffer adverse consequences due to her lawyer's abuse. For that reason, Rule 37(b) also permits the imposition

---

76. National Hockey League v. Metropolitan Hockey Club, Inc., 427 U.S. 639 (1976). Note that an order imposing sanctions for discovery abuse under the rules is not a final appealable order. See Cunningham v. Hamilton, 527 U.S. 198 (1999).

of reasonable expenses, including attorney's fees, against the abusing party or his lawyer, or both, unless there was a substantial justification for the noncompliance. This alternative or additional sanction enables the court to fine the lawyer directly if the lawyer caused the failure to comply.

Conversely, a lawyer must protect himself from the possible imposition of sanctions when his client is to blame for a failure to comply with a discovery order. The common problem involves a client who fails to provide documents or information necessary to respond to discovery requests, or a client who fails repeatedly to submit to a deposition. When this occurs, the lawyer must make it clear to the judge and the other lawyers that his client is the cause of the problem. The lawyer can do so orally in conversations with the other lawyers, and perhaps through letters to them explaining what steps he has taken to try to comply with their discovery requests. If you follow this step, the other lawyers will probably ask for discovery abuse sanctions only against your client. If the other lawyers ask for sanctions directly against you, you must, both in a written response to the motion and at the hearing on the motion, detail the efforts you have made to comply with the discovery. If the client continues to refuse to cooperate with the lawyer, the lawyer may need to withdraw from the representation.

§6.14.   Discovery review

Under Rule 16, judges may enter scheduling orders for the completion of discovery, among other matters. Since most judges now actively participate in case management, they commonly set a discovery cutoff date at the scheduling conference. A cutoff date means that all formal discovery must be completed by that date. (Keep in mind that a request to admit facts is not usually considered discovery for this purpose.)

About three months before the cutoff date is a good time to review the status of discovery. Among the things you should consider are the following:

1. Required disclosures (Rule 26)
   a. Initial disclosures, expert disclosures, and pretrial disclosures received?
   b. Supplemental disclosures necessary?
   c. Motions pending?
2. Interrogatories (Rule 33)
   a. Answers to all interrogatories received?
   b. Supplemental answers necessary?
   c. Experts and opinions disclosed?
   d. Motions pending?
3. Documents requests (Rule 34)
   a. Responses to requests received?
   b. Documents and electronically stored information actually delivered?
   c. Supplemental responses necessary?
   d. Expert reports received?

      e. Motions pending?
  4. Mental and physical examinations (Rule 35)
      a. Plaintiff's examination done?
      b. Medical report requested and received?
  5. Depositions (Rule 30)
      a. All necessary witnesses deposed?
      b. Experts deposed?
      c. Ordered transcripts received?

Discovery in large part is making sure you get what you need and what you are entitled to. As the months pass, many loose ends appear. You never received all the documents and electronically stored information you were promised. You have yet to depose one of the experts. The other side never supplemented its interrogatory answers. The court has not yet ruled on a motion. These kinds of loose ends tend to get lost in the shuffle as more immediate matters capture your attention.

Hence, you should review the status of discovery well in advance of the discovery cutoff date. Mark this date on your litigation calendar and docket control system. Why three months? It takes time to tie up the loose ends. You need to remind your adversary, first by letter and then by follow-up calls, that you have not gotten all of your requested discovery. If informal efforts to resolve discovery disputes fail, you need to move to compel responses.

Taking these steps early makes good sense. The last thing a judge wants to receive on the eve of the discovery cutoff date is a motion to extend the time to complete discovery. The judge will naturally want to know what you have been doing during the preceding months. If you have not actively pursued discovery, don't expect the judge to help you now.

***

This chapter began with a word of caution, one that merits repeating here. As of the time this book went to press, proposed amendments to the Federal Rules were under consideration. These proposed amendments would change a number of the discovery rules, some in fairly dramatic ways. A number of the proposed amendments are straightforward but significant. One proposal would shorten the time the judge has to issue a scheduling order under Rule 16. Other proposed amendments would adjust the discovery rules in more fundamental ways. The proposals include a thorough revision of Rule 37(e), designed to create a uniform, national standard to govern possible sanctions when a party fails to preserve discoverable information. Perhaps most important, and most likely to generate litigation, is a proposed revision to Rule 26 that would impose an explicit "proportionality" limit on the scope of discovery.

Make sure to check the most recent amendments to the Federal Rules. If the proposed amendments go through, the discovery rules will change significantly.

VII

MOTIONS

§7.1.   Introduction

"Motion practice" is a significant part of the litigation process. Motions are used to regulate routine "housekeeping" matters in litigation, such as the rescheduling of discovery, hearings, and other deadlines. Motions are also used to reach dispositive results, such as motions to dismiss or motions for summary judgment. Every litigated matter will involve motions, so every litigator must know when and how to present appropriate, well-drafted motions.

A motion is simply an application to a court for an order. An effective motion, however, involves both technical requirements, such as format and service rules, and substantive requirements that control the motion's organization and construction to make it more persuasive. This chapter addresses both routine housekeeping and dispositive motions. It adds to the discussion of pleadings motions in §5.4 and the discussion of discovery motions in §6.13.

§7.2.   General requirements for motions

Rules 5 through 11, supplemented by local rules, govern how motions are made. They address filing requirements, page size, page limitations, format, organization, supporting memoranda and exhibits, special service times, and other matters. While motions may address numerous issues and seek a wide variety of relief, their basic requirements are generally the same.

1. Form

The format requirements for motions are identical to those for pleadings. A motion must have a caption showing the name of the court, the names of the parties to the action, and a designation of the motion involved. Where there are multiple parties, the name of the first party on each side, followed by an "et al." designation, is sufficient.

A lawyer representing the moving party must sign every motion. The signature also constitutes a certification that the written motion complies with the Rule 11 requirements. The motion must show the lawyer's name, address, e-mail address, and telephone number.

Example:

UNITED STATES DISTRICT COURT
FOR THE DISTRICT OF IOWA

John Smith, Plaintiff	
	No. 13 C 100
v.	
Johnson Corporation, et al., Defendants	

MOTION TO RESET HEARING DATE

Plaintiff John Smith moves this Court for an order continuing the hearing on defendant's motion for discovery sanctions, presently set for July 1, 2013, for ten days. In support of his motion, plaintiff states:

    1. . . .
    2. . . .
    3. . . .

WHEREFORE, plaintiff John Smith requests the Court to enter an order continuing the hearing, presently set for July 1, 2013, to July 11, 2013.

———————————————
Attorney for Plaintiff
Address
E-mail address
Telephone

In many jurisdictions the practice required by local rule is to state only the motion itself and put all supporting points, legal authority, and exhibits in an attached memorandum.

2. Notice, service, and filing

Rule 6(c) requires that a written motion, any supporting affidavits, and notice of the motion and hearing be served on every party at least 14 days before the hearing date, unless the Federal Rules or a court order alters the time requirement. As a practical matter, all documentation that accompanies a motion should be attached to and served with the motion. The motion with proof of service must be filed with the clerk of court or, if permitted by local rules, with the judge.

Example:

[Caption]

<u>NOTICE OF MOTION</u>

To: Alfred Jackson
      Attorney for Johnson Corporation
      100 Madison St., Suite 1400
      Chicago, Illinois 60602

Please take notice that on June 15, 2013, at 9:30 A.M., plaintiff will appear before the Hon. Prentice Marshall in Courtroom No. 2303, United States Court House, 219 S. Dearborn St., Chicago, Illinois, and present a motion to reset a hearing date. A copy of the motion, with supporting memorandum and exhibits, is attached to this notice.

_____
Attorney for Plaintiff
Address
E-mail address
Telephone

For the convenience of the court and other parties, it is good practice to give more notice than the minimum required by Rule 6 when possible under the circumstances. Also, call the other lawyers to select a mutually agreeable hearing date, if possible, before sending out the written notices. This practice gives the court time to read the motion, avoids disputes over whether notice was adequate, minimizes continuances, and fosters a good working relationship with the other lawyers in the case.

A motion can be served in any of the ways set out in Rule 5(b). The standard methods are to mail the motion and notice of motion to a lawyer for each party or have the motion and notice delivered to them or someone at their offices. Service by electronic means is proper if the person consents in writing. Following service, the originals of the notice and motion should be filed with the clerk of the court along with a proof of service. In many jurisdictions the motion and notice of motion are filed with the clerk of the judge who will actually hear the motion, as well as with the clerk's office. Filing must occur "within a reasonable time" after service, but obviously must be done before the date set for the hearing. The usual procedure is to file the originals immediately after service. Be sure you get a copy of the motion, notice, and proof of service stamped "filed" and dated by the clerk to keep in your files.

In the federal system, most lawyers file and serve motions through a district's electronic case filing (ECF) system. A district's local rules will govern its ECF system, so make sure to check them. Generally speaking, by signing up as an e-filer, a party agrees to accept service by electronic means. If all parties to the case are represented by counsel and are e-filers, then moving parties do not need to attach proof of service to their motions. Make sure to check your judge's individual rules. She may want you to send a courtesy hard copy to her chambers in addition to the e-filed motion.

Proof of service is merely a certificate, signed by a lawyer or a non-lawyer, that states that service on the other parties has been made in a proper way. The Federal Rules do not define the requirements for a certificate of service, but local rules usually do. You should check these, since some local rules provide for a certificate from an attorney, while a non-attorney may be required to make a declaration under penalties of perjury or a notarized affidavit of service. The certificate of service is usually attached to the end of the motion.

Example:

CERTIFICATE OF SERVICE

I, James Brown, served the above motion for a continuance by mailing a copy to Sharon Smith, the attorney for defendant Johnson Corporation, at 100 Madison St., Chicago, Illinois 60601 on June 7, 2013.

_____
Attorney for Plaintiff

To select the hearing day for the motion, check with the clerk of the judge to whom the case is assigned to determine on what days the judge hears motions. Some judges hold daily court hearings; others hear motions only on designated days. Find out what your judge's practice is so that the date you select will be one on which the judge can hear the motion. Finally, check with the clerk the day before the hearing to make sure the case will actually appear on the next day's motion calendar and to find out when you should be in the courtroom. Many judges arrange their court calendars to hear uncontested and routine cases first and contested matters afterwards.

3.   Content of the motion

Under Rule 7(b), a motion must be in writing, must "state with particularity the grounds for seeking the order," and must state the relief sought. Since the rule permits a great deal of flexibility, tactical considerations principally govern the motion's contents. What will be an effective way to present this motion?

The usual procedure, required by many local rules, is to draft a concise motion summarily setting out the matter and the relief requested, supplement it with a memorandum of law if appropriate, and attach any necessary exhibits and supporting documents. Some local rules also require that the motion state whether the other party opposes the motion. Call the other side's lawyer to find out her position. The judge can scan the motion quickly, then review the more detailed supporting materials.

The seriousness and complexity of the motion and local practice may alter this usual procedure. For example, if you move to reset a hearing date because you will be on trial in another case, file a brief motion. It need only point out when the hearing is presently scheduled, state where and when the conflicting trial is scheduled and how long that trial will last, and suggest a new date for the hearing. For this sort of motion the judge will want brevity, and the factual representations by counsel in the motion should be enough.

At the other extreme, a motion for summary judgment will usually require a thorough presentation of both law and facts. Your motion will probably need to set out the background of the case and the relief requested, and incorporate by reference a memorandum that thoroughly discusses the applicable law and existing facts. The memorandum should also contain exhibits, such as documents and records obtained in discovery, and witness statements in affidavit form. The motion and accompanying materials should be a self-contained package that has everything the judge will need to rule.

Learn what your judge's personal preferences on oral argument are and modify your written motion accordingly. Some judges dislike oral argument and prefer to get everything in writing; others at best skim the written motions and prefer that oral argument set out the details. While you must always comply with the Rule 7 and local rule requirements, and while you must always protect your record by having the essential matters in your motion, you should also respect your judge's preferences.

In short, drafting a motion requires a flexible approach. The relative complexity of the motion, local custom in presenting motions, and even the preferences of the judge all come into play. Motions specifically tailored to these considerations that do not mechanically follow a set blueprint have a much better chance of success.[1]

1. The motion should be drafted with precision the first time, since no rule expressly allows amendments of motions. Rule 15 applies only to pleadings.

4.   Responses to motions

Once served with a motion, the respondent has two choices: oppose or not oppose the motion. If the motion is a routine one and you do not oppose it, notify the opposing lawyer of your position. The lawyer will then tell the judge at the hearing that you have no objection to the motion. You will not have to come to court. However, you should file a statement that says you have no opposition to the motion, since a written record of your position is prudent. Also, a statement should eliminate the danger that the other lawyer will misrepresent your position.

Example:

[Caption]

<u>STATEMENT OF NONOPPOSITION TO DEFENDANT'S MOTION</u>
<u>FOR ADDITIONAL TIME TO ANSWER</u>

Plaintiff John Smith does not oppose defendant's motion for 10 additional days to answer plaintiff's complaint, presently set before the Hon. Prentice Marshall on June 15, 2013, at 9:30 A.M.

_____
Attorney for Plaintiff

Another approach is to agree to a "consent order," a proposed order that would dispose of the motion to which both parties agree. The judge will usually sign it, although obviously she does not have to.

If you decide to oppose the motion, serve and file your response in advance of the hearing. Rule 6(c) generally requires service at least 14 days before the hearing. Make sure you file your response with the judge's clerk before the hearing. The response should set out the reasons for your opposition and include case law and other authority you will want the judge to consider.

Example:

[Caption]

<u>DEFENDANT'S OPPOSITION TO PLAINTIFF'S MOTION FOR</u>
<u>LEAVE TO FILE A SECOND AMENDED ANSWER</u>

Defendant Wilbur Johnson opposes plaintiff's motion for leave to file a Second Amended Answer, presently set before the Hon.

Prentice Marshall on June 15, 2013, at 9:30 A.M., for the following reasons:

      1. . . .

      2. . . .

      3. . . .

    WHEREFORE, defendant Wilbur Johnson requests the Court to enter an order denying plaintiff's motion for leave to file a second amended answer.

_____

Attorney for Defendant

5. Hearing and argument

On the date set for the hearing, check whether an order has already been entered. Many judges will enter orders granting routine and uncontested motions in advance of the hearing day. They are particularly likely to do so when both parties jointly make the motion or the court has been notified in advance that the motion is unopposed. Check with the clerk before the motion calendar starts to determine if the judge has ruled on the motion. Some courts post a list of decided motions outside the courtroom. If yours has already been decided, make sure you get a copy of the order from the court clerk. Most clerks mail copies of the order to the lawyers in the case.

If your motion is still pending, the clerk will eventually call your case. The usual practice is for the lawyers to approach the bench when their case is called, state who they are, and which parties they represent. If the motion is a routine one, the judge will usually let the lawyers make brief comments, make a ruling from the bench, and immediately enter an appropriate order. If a significant motion is involved, the judge will probably permit lengthier arguments and take the motion "under advisement," meaning that the judge will research and consider the issues further before deciding.

To prepare for oral argument at the hearing, you must learn what your judge's practice is. Some judges disfavor oral argument and dispense with it altogether for routine motions or, for other motions, give the lawyers very little time to argue. In this situation you want to make sure your written motion omits nothing, and you want to prepare a very succinct presentation of your main argument. At the other extreme are judges who at best scan written motions and rely heavily if not exclusively on oral argument. If you don't know your judge's preferences, ask lawyers familiar with the judge, or watch a motion calendar in that judge's courtroom and see how the judge conducts hearings.

If the judge's practice is to allow substantial oral argument, you need to decide what will persuade the judge to rule in your favor. Sometimes the weight of prevailing law will be persuasive, at other times the facts. Whatever it is, don't repeat the contents of the motion unless the judge tells you he needs his memory refreshed. Many judges begin the hearing by telling the lawyers that they have read the motion and response, and then ask the lawyers if they have anything to add. Take heed of this request, since usually a motion has an important point that will persuade the judge. It may be the law, facts, basic fairness, or the result of a particular ruling. Basic fairness or the results of a ruling can frequently be argued more persuasively orally. Sometimes judges will issue a tentative order in advance of the hearing, indicating how the judge plans to rule. Obviously, you will want to tailor your argument to the judge's tentative order.

Regardless of what points you have selected to argue orally, act confident and professional. Address your comments to the judge, not opposing counsel. Above all, don't interrupt or argue with counsel. The judge will usually ask the movant to argue first, and then give the respondent an opportunity to argue. Nothing is as unprofessional and ineffective as two lawyers bickering with each other, yet unfortunately such squabbles are common during motion hearings.

As the movant, standard procedure is to approach the lectern positioned before the bench or to stand at counsel table, introduce yourself, state what party you represent, give the other lawyers a chance to identify themselves and their parties, state what your motion is for, and then go immediately to the points you have selected to emphasize. When you are finished, the other lawyers can respond. When they are through, you may, depending on the judge's practice, have a short opportunity to rebut. Always be prepared to answer any questions the judge may ask.

Example:

> Judge: Call the next case.
>
> Clerk: Williams v. Louisiana Chemical Company. Defendant's motion to reset the trial date. (Lawyers for plaintiff and defendant come to the podium.)
>
> Defense Lawyer: Good morning, your honor. Dominic Gianna for the defendant.
>
> Plaintiff Lawyer: Lorna Propes for plaintiff Williams, your honor.
>
> Defense Lawyer: This is our motion to reset the trial date for this case. We filed our motion, and plaintiff filed a written response.
>
> Judge: I've read the motion and response.
>
> Defense Lawyer: Your honor, our motion to reset the trial date should be granted for three reasons. First, . . .
>
> Judge: Thank you. Plaintiff, do you wish to respond?
>
> Plaintiff Lawyer: Yes, your honor. We oppose the motion because . . .
>
> Judge: Thank you, counsel. The trial date previously set will be vacated, and the trial will be rescheduled for April 1, 2013.

To repeat, always think through your oral argument in advance, coordinate it with the written motion, and use the argument to supplement the motion by emphasizing the important points that will present your side in its best light.

6. Order

Regardless of when the motion is decided, the court will enter an order.[2] In federal court, routine motions can be decided by a "minute order or docket entry," which is merely a form on which the clerk makes an entry reflecting the ruling. The minute order is then signed by the judge or stamped with his signature, and a copy is mailed to the lawyers. If the motion is important, the judge may prepare a written order explaining the reasons for the ruling.[3] In the federal system, most orders and rulings are posted on the court's electronic case management system (CM/ECF; if lawyers are not registered participants, they must be served by other means authorized by Rule 5). Make sure that every pending motion is ultimately decided by an order, that the order accurately reflects the court's ruling, and that you obtain a copy of the order.

The court may refer certain motions to a magistrate judge, since magistrate judges are empowered to hear routine civil pretrial matters.[4] Magistrate judges often supervise the discovery process in civil cases. The motion procedure before a magistrate judge is identical to that before the district judge.

§7.3. *Extensions of time and continuances*

The kinds of motions that can be presented to the court are limited only by the movant's imagination. Practically, however, routine housekeeping motions invariably deal with time and date modifications. These are the motions for extensions of time, continuances, and new hearing and trial dates.

Rule 6(b) governs extensions of time. If a motion to extend time is made before the expiration of the applicable time period, the court may grant the motion for "good cause." However, if the motion is made after the applicable time period had expired, the court may grant the motion only where "excusable neglect" caused the failure to act timely.

What constitutes "good cause" or "excusable neglect" depends upon the court's discretion, and must be evaluated in the context of the pending case. Courts are generally realistic and accommodating with respect to extensions of time when the applicable period has not yet run. Usually any reason other than one involving bad faith and actual prejudice to an opponent will result in the grant of a reasonable extension of time.[5]

Excusable neglect, on the other hand, is judged against a substantially stricter standard. Courts have usually denied extensions of time where the lawyer's inadvertence or ignorance of the applicable rule or a lawyer's busy case load and other work demands caused the failure to act within the required time limit.[6] Extensions usually require an extraordinary situation

---

2. See Rule 77(d).
3. This practice may differ from state practice. In some state courts, the prevailing lawyer sometimes prepares a draft order reflecting the court's ruling, which the judge then signs.
4. See Magistrate's Act, 28 U.S.C. §§631 et seq.
5. See Wright & Miller §1165.
6. See Wright & Miller §1165.

involving good faith, such as the death or serious illness of a lawyer or a member of her family, a delay by a client in forwarding a complaint and summons, or difficulties in substituting proper parties or different lawyers.

Some time periods for post-trial matters usually cannot be enlarged. These include a motion for judgment after trial, motion for new trial (Rule 50(b)), motion to amend findings and judgment (Rules 52(b) and 59(e)), motion for a new trial (Rule 59(b)), and motion to set aside a judgment for reasons such as mistake, fraud, or newly discovered evidence (Rule 60(b)).

Make the motion and have it decided within the applicable time period. Give the court solid reasons why an extension is necessary, and ask only for such additional time as is reasonably needed. Above all, do not miss a deadline. Creating, maintaining, and following a reliable docket control system is the best way to avoid these disasters. The system will remind you of all significant dates for each case you are handling. These systems vary from simple calendars to sophisticated computer programs, but they are critical for every litigator.

Routine motions for extensions of time or continuances should be structured simply. The body of the motion can ordinarily contain the information that forms the basis for the request.

Example:

[Caption]

MOTION FOR ADDITIONAL TIME TO ANSWER OR RESPOND

Defendant Robert Johnson moves this court for an order granting defendant an additional 10 days to answer or respond to plaintiff's complaint. In support of his motion defendant states:

1. Defendant was served with the summons and complaint on June 1, 2013. Under the rules defendant's answer is due on or before June 22, 2013.

2. Defendant's attorney received the complaint from the defendant on June 13, 2013.

3. Plaintiff's complaint has five counts and is based on an alleged series of contracts with the defendant.

4. To answer the complaint, defendant's attorney will have to evaluate numerous business records, which the defendant is presently locating, and review them with defendant.

5. Defendant's attorney believes he can prepare and serve an answer or otherwise respond if an additional 10 days to answer or respond is granted.

WHEREFORE, defendant requests that this court enter an order extending defendant's time to answer or respond to July 1, 2013.

_____
Attorney for Defendant

Note that the motion asserts facts in the body of the motion that are based on the lawyer's own knowledge, or on information already contained in the court file. In this situation the facts do not need to be stated in affidavit form. Where someone other than the attorney knows of the facts that are the basis of the motion, the facts must be in affidavit form and attached to the motion.

§7.4. Substitution of parties

During the pendency of an action, events may happen that will require the replacement of a named party by someone else. This substitution of parties can be required when a party dies, becomes incompetent, or loses all legal interest in the action. A public official named as a party can die, resign, or be voted out of office. In such situations, Rule 25 provides for substitution with a successor party. Unless death abates the action, the court will order a substitution upon notification and demonstration of the change. In the case of public officials, the substitution is automatic.

The usual procedure is to make a motion for substitution of parties, state the reason for the substitution in the body of the motion, and attach any necessary documents as exhibits. For example, if a party dies and will be substituted by the administrator of the estate, attach a copy of the death certificate and the probate court order appointing the administrator of the estate.

§7.5. Temporary restraining orders and preliminary injunctions

There are three types of injunctions: temporary restraining orders, preliminary injunctions, and permanent injunctions. A permanent injunction is a final remedy that can be ordered only after a trial on the merits of the case. Temporary restraining orders and preliminary injunctions, governed by Rule 65, are provisional remedies. A temporary restraining order can be granted without notice to the other side, and it can remain in force only until a hearing for a preliminary injunction can be held. Its purpose is to avoid an immediate irreparable injury to the petitioning party. A preliminary injunction, by contrast, can be issued only after an adversarial hearing. Its purpose is to maintain the status quo until the case is tried, or to protect a party against irreparable harm pending the outcome of the case.

As an equitable remedy, an injunction can only be granted if legal remedies are inadequate. Accordingly, make sure that the underlying complaint asks for injunctive relief and establishes that such relief would be proper upon proof of the complaint's allegations. While Rule 65 governs temporary restraining orders and preliminary injunctions, local rules often impose additional requirements.

1. Temporary restraining orders

a. Law

Rule 65(b) applies when a party seeks a temporary restraining order (TRO).[7] Since a TRO is an extraordinary remedy, the rule's requirements must be followed precisely.

First, a TRO can be granted without notice to the opposing party, but only if three requirements are met. These requirements reduce the risk that a TRO will be granted in error and cause an injustice to the other party. The motion must be supported by an affidavit or a verified complaint alleging specific facts that clearly show that "immediate and irreparable injury, loss or damage will result" unless the TRO is issued before the opposing side can be heard. In addition, the attorney representing the applicant must describe in writing any "efforts made to give notice," or the "reasons why [notice] should not be required." Finally, the applicant for a TRO must post security in an amount the court deems sufficient to cover the costs and damages that the other side may incur if the TRO is found to have been wrongfully issued. Although Rule 65(b) expressly requires only that an applicant for a TRO show an "immediate and irreparable injury," case law generally provides that the applicant must make the same showing, at least on a preliminary basis, as that required for a preliminary injunction.[8] In addition to an irreparable injury, the applicant must establish a likelihood of success on the merits of the case, that the threatened injury to the applicant exceeds any foreseeable injury to the adverse party if the order is granted, and that any order will not be against the public interest. As a practical matter, a court will not enter a TRO unless these considerations, taken as a whole, appear to weigh heavily in the applicant's favor. Keep in mind that jurisdictions differ on the relative weight to be put on these considerations.[9]

Second, if the court grants a TRO, its order must state why the TRO was issued, specify why the injury is irreparable, and describe in reasonable detail the enjoined acts. The TRO is limited to the duration set by the court. This duration cannot exceed 14 days, although the court can extend the TRO for another 14 days for good cause.

Third, the court must set a date for a hearing on a preliminary injunction at the earliest possible time whenever a TRO is granted without notice. The party against whom the TRO was issued can move to have the TRO dissolved or modified with two days' notice.

b. Practice approach

Apply for a TRO only under appropriate circumstances. The motion involves a great deal of work, and the court cannot properly issue a TRO

7. Hazard et al. §10.6; Moore's Manual §10A.21; Manual of Federal Practice §7.101; Moore's Federal Practice §§65.30-65.41; Wright & Miller §§2951–2953.

8. Moore's Manual §10A.21; Manual of Federal Practice §7.101; Moore's Federal Practice §65.36; Wright & Miller §2951.

9. See Wright & Miller §2951.

unless an immediate and irreparable injury will occur without it. Since a TRO is a powerful and extraordinary step, courts are necessarily reluctant to grant it except in the most compelling of circumstances.

An immediate and irreparable injury and an inadequate remedy at law are difficult to demonstrate. The threatened harm must be both imminent and serious. Common situations involve threatened damage to unique property and proprietary interests. A TRO may be appropriate, for example, if someone is about to cut down mature elm trees on another's property, if a magazine is about to release personal photographs of a private person without authorization, if a former employee is about to breach a covenant not to compete, or if a former employee is about to sell trade secrets to a foreign competitor. In these situations, money damages cannot make the wronged party whole, and any remedial delay pending further litigation can result in an injury without redress. Make sure you know and can accurately describe both the threatened conduct and the persons and entities you seek to enjoin.

Second, make sure that the court has both subject matter jurisdiction over the claim and personal jurisdiction over the defendant. Lack of subject matter jurisdiction will result in dismissal of the complaint. Lack of personal jurisdiction will make any injunctive relief ordered unenforceable. If you file in state court, the defendant may be able to remove to federal court if the requirements of 28 U.S.C. §1441 are met. If removal happens, you may lose valuable time in actually obtaining the TRO. You may simply file in federal court in the first place.

Third, moving for a TRO requires that you prepare, file, and ultimately serve several items at nearly the same time. These include:

- a verified complaint, or an unverified complaint with witness affidavits, and summons
- an application for a TRO and a preliminary injunction
- an attorney's affidavit of attempted notice
- witness affidavits
- security for costs and damages
- a draft of a proposed court order

i. Complaint and summons

When a TRO is sought, the allegations in the complaint will form the factual basis for the motion and must be coordinated with it. The relief requested in the complaint should include a TRO, a preliminary injunction, and a permanent injunction. The factual allegations should be specific enough to show that the pleader is entitled to the relief requested if the allegations are proved, as they must in any complaint. Finally, although not required, the party should verify the allegations, since a verified complaint has the same evidentiary effect as an affidavit. A complaint is verified when it contains a statement that the party has read the complaint and personally knows the facts, and that the alleged facts are true. The statement is sworn to before a notary public.

The complaint is usually filed at the same time as the application for the TRO. This means that the summons will not yet have been served. However, since the rules require that the attorney certify how she has attempted to notify the adverse party of the TRO application, you should always try to have service of the complaint and summons expedited.

The complaint, application, and supporting documents are usually filed with the emergency judge, an assignment that is usually rotated among the active judges. Find out who the present emergency judge is and notify the judge's secretary or clerk of the situation.

ii.   Application for TRO and preliminary injunction

The application for a TRO should be combined with a request for a preliminary injunction, since under Rule 65(b) a hearing on a preliminary injunction must be scheduled as soon as possible after a TRO without notice is granted.

The application must allege that an immediate and irreparable injury will occur unless the TRO and preliminary injunction are granted. Since the application must be supported by facts, it usually refers to the verified complaint and accompanying witness affidavits for factual support. As with motions generally, the application itself is usually drafted simply and refers to the supporting material for the substance.

Example:

[Caption]

APPLICATION FOR TEMPORARY RESTRAINING ORDER AND PRELIMINARY INJUNCTION

Pursuant to Rule 65, Plaintiff applies for a temporary restraining order and requests that the court set a hearing for a preliminary injunction.

1. In support of his application for a preliminary injunction, Plaintiff states that he will suffer an immediate and irreparable injury unless his application for a temporary restraining order is granted.

2. Plaintiff also states that

(a) defendant will perform the threatened acts, as more fully set out in the complaint, unless enjoined;

(b) defendant's threatened action, if carried out, will result in irreparable injury to plaintiff; and

(c) a preliminary injunction will not injure or inconvenience the defendant.

3. Plaintiff incorporates by reference the allegations of his verified complaint and the facts as set forth in the witness affidavits attached as Exhibits A through C.

4. Plaintiff's attorney's certificate showing her efforts to give notice to the adverse party, and why notice to the defendant should not be required, is attached as Exhibit D.

5. Plaintiff is ready to provide security in such amount as the court determines is necessary to cover the costs and expenses incurred by the defendant in the event that the defendant is erroneously restrained and enjoined.

WHEREFORE, Plaintiff requests that the court enter a temporary restraining order against defendant and set a hearing for a temporary injunction at the earliest possible time.

_____

Attorney for Plaintiff

iii. Attorney's certificate regarding notice

Rule 65(b) requires that the attorney for the moving party certify in writing "any efforts made to give notice and the reasons why it should not be required." Notice here includes informal as well as formal notice. Courts clearly prefer any notice over none at all, such as a telephone call to the adverse party, his lawyer if known, or an agent. Accordingly, the lawyer's certificate should show all the steps she took to give some advance notice to the adverse party. A sound approach is to notify the defendant by whatever means are available, unless any notice would create an even more immediate danger of irreparable injury.

Example:

CERTIFICATE OF ATTORNEY IN SUPPORT OF APPLICATION FOR TEMPORARY RESTRAINING ORDER WITHOUT NOTICE

I, Terry Anton, attorney for plaintiff, make this certificate, in accordance with Rule 65(b), to support plaintiff's application for a temporary restraining order without notice to the defendant.

1. On June 1, 2013, at approximately 1:00 P.M., I was first informed of defendant's imminent conduct as set forth in the complaint. I immediately began drafting the complaint, this application, and the supporting documents.

2. At the same time I telephoned defendant at his place of business to advise him of this application, but could not personally contact him. I left a message with his answering service, but have received no call from him.

3. I have attempted to locate the defendant's residence and present whereabouts without success.

4. I have no knowledge of any attorney who may presently represent the defendant, and have attempted to learn this without success.

_____
Attorney for Plaintiff

iv. Witness affidavits

Rule 65 requires that the applicant for a TRO establish specific facts through a verified complaint or witness affidavits that demonstrate the required "immediate and irreparable injury." Accordingly, you should review the verified complaint, determine what additional facts are not included but are necessary, and put them in affidavit form. The affidavit should describe who the witness is and demonstrate that the witness has firsthand knowledge of all the facts recited in the affidavit.

Example:

AFFIDAVIT

I, William Jones, having been first duly sworn, state:

1. I am the plaintiff in this action. I live at 123 Maple Lane, Denver, and am the owner of that property.

2. On June 1, 2013, at approximately 8:30 A.M. I saw the defendant . . .

3. . . .

4. . . .

I hereby declare, under penalties of perjury, that the facts stated in this affidavit are personally known to me, and that they are true.

_____
Name of Affiant

Signed and sworn to
before me on June 2, 2013.

_____
Notary Public

My commission expires on _____.

Note that 28 U.S.C. §1746 sets forth a procedure for making and using unsworn declarations under penalty of perjury. It can be used for witness affidavits.

v.   Security for costs

Rule 65(c) requires that a TRO cannot be issued unless the applicant provides adequate security to cover any costs and damages that the adverse party may incur if the TRO is wrongfully issued. (The language of the rule seems to permit no exceptions, although under extraordinary circumstances courts have the power to waive the bond.) Accordingly, the likely security requirement requires some thought. Ordinarily you will need to obtain a bond from a surety or post a cash bond with the clerk of the court, although the court can set any other security requirement. Since the court will not issue the TRO until the security has been set and met, you should always have the plaintiff prepared to deposit the likely cash bond immediately if the TRO is granted. Check with the clerk's office to determine its requirements for receiving bonds and other security. If you need a bond from a surety or fidelity company, call it immediately to find out what information and documentation the company will require before issuing a bond. The client is ultimately responsible for the cost of the bond, regardless of the outcome of the case.

vi.   Hearing, order, and service

The necessary papers need to be presented to the assigned judge or the emergency judge, who will review the papers to determine if the Rule 65 requirements and standards have been met. The judge will usually decide the motion in chambers on an ex parte basis, since the other side will probably not have received notice of the application for the TRO.

Federal judges usually write either minute or full written orders. However, since time is critical with a TRO, you should prepare a draft order for the judge in advance so that the judge can sign it immediately if she grants the application. Rule 65(b) requires that the order specify the date and hour issued, describe the injury, state why the injury is irreparable, state why the TRO was granted without notice, specify the terms and duration of the order, and set a hearing date for the preliminary injunction at the earliest possible time. The order must be promptly filed in the clerk's office.

Example:

[Caption]

<u>ORDER</u>

This cause being heard on the application of the plaintiff for a temporary restraining order and preliminary injunction, the plaintiff appearing ex parte without notice to the defendant, and the court having considered the verified complaint, witness affidavits, and the attorney's certificate attached as exhibits to plaintiff's application,

THE COURT FINDS:

1. Plaintiff's threatened injury as described in the verified complaint is irreparable because. . . .

2. This order is being granted without notice to defendant because. . . .

THE COURT ORDERS:

1. The defendant is hereby restrained from. . . .

2. This order shall remain in effect until June 4, 2013, at 5:00 P.M.

3. A hearing on plaintiff's motion for a preliminary injunction is set for June 4, 2013, at 2:00 P.M. and the defendant is hereby ordered to appear in this courtroom at that time.

4. A copy of this order, along with copies of the complaint, summons, motion, and supporting documentation, shall be served immediately on the defendant.

SO ORDERED:

_____
Judge

Date: _____

Time: _____

Since the court's order is not enforceable until the defendant receives actual notice of it, you should attempt to notify the defendant by telephone of the court's order and arrange for immediate proper service of a certified copy of the order under Rule 4.

2. Preliminary injunctions

a. Law

Rule 65(a) governs preliminary injunctions. It has several requirements.[10] The procedure is simpler than that for a TRO, because the TRO's crisis atmosphere has dissipated.

First, the rule requires notice to the adverse party. Although it does not specify the necessary time period, the 14-day notice period for motions under Rule 6(c) applies. Also, notice of the motion should include service of the complaint and summons.

Second, the movant must post security in an amount the court deems proper for the payment of costs and damages that may be incurred if the party is found to have been wrongly enjoined.

---

10. Moore's Manual §10A.22; Hazard et al. §10.6; Manual of Federal Practice §7.100; Moore's Federal Practice §§65.20-65.24; Wright & Miller §§2947–2950.

Third, the movant has the burden of showing, through verified pleadings or testimony and other evidence at the hearing, that: (1) if the injunction is not ordered, the movant will likely suffer an irreparable injury; (2) the movant will likely succeed on the merits of his claims at trial; (3) the threatened injury to movant exceeds any threatened injury to the adverse party; and (4) a preliminary injunction would not be against the public interest.[11]

Fourth, if the court orders a preliminary injunction, the order must be specific and describe the enjoined acts with reasonable detail. The order granting a preliminary injunction remains in effect until the court has a trial on the merits, although the court can modify or vacate the order if warranted.

The court can consolidate the hearing on the motion for a preliminary injunction with a trial on the merits. If consolidation is not ordered, evidence presented at the hearing on the motion for a preliminary injunction need not be repeated at the trial on the merits. Courts frequently order consolidation where injunctive relief is the principal remedy sought and the evidence at the hearing for the preliminary injunction would largely duplicate evidence at trial.

An order granting or denying either a preliminary injunction and or a permanent injunction is appealable. An order granting or denying a TRO is not appealable.[12] Since the issuance of injunctive orders is addressed to the court's discretion, the order will be reversed on appeal only if it was erroneous as a matter of law or improvidently granted.

b.   Practice approach

A preliminary injunction can come before the court in two ways. First, a hearing date can be set by the judge as part of an order granting an application for a TRO. Second, the plaintiff can move for a preliminary injunction.

The critical point to remember is that the hearing on the preliminary injunction is often the determinative proceeding in an injunction case as a practical matter. Proof presented at the hearing need not be duplicated at a later trial. Furthermore, where injunctive relief is the sole or principal remedy sought, the court will often accelerate and consolidate the trial and hearing. In practice, the hearing is the trial and is conducted essentially like a bench trial. The court will frequently order that discovery be expedited and state what discovery will be permitted under the circumstances. As the plaintiff's lawyer, you must be prepared to go to trial quickly and present your entire case on short notice. You must have live witnesses prepared to testify and essential documents that can be qualified for admission in evidence at the preliminary injunction hearing. When the hearing has been consolidated with the trial, the court will enter a permanent injunction, rather than only a preliminary injunction, if it rules in the plaintiff's favor.

Before moving for a preliminary injunction, assess the benefits and risks. On the plus side, moving for a preliminary injunction gets the court involved early and attracts the defendant's attention quickly. If you want the case resolved quickly, either through a settlement or an early trial, or

11. See Winter v. Natural Resources Defense Council, 555 U.S. 7 (2008).
12. See Wright §102.

you want to reach a "standstill agreement" with the other party that will maintain the status quo while the case is pending, the motion may help accomplish these objectives. On the minus side, moving for a preliminary injunction is expensive because you may end up with two hearings — the hearing on the motion and the later bench trial. It also requires that you be prepared to present all your evidence on short notice. If you need substantial discovery to prepare for the hearing and expedited discovery is not practical, the motion may do more harm than good. Finally, the required bond may be substantial, depending on the relief requested.

In many cases, it is simpler and cheaper for the plaintiff not to move for a preliminary injunction and instead ask for a prompt trial on the merits. The court may be receptive, especially if neither side has asked for a jury trial on any of the claims. You will have more time to prepare fully, avoid the bond requirement, avoid the possibility of two rounds of discovery, and avoid the additional cost of preparing for both a full hearing and a trial.

As defendant, decide if you want to resist the preliminary injunction, especially if the plaintiff's burden of proof is low. Consider asking for a high bond requirement, which the plaintiff may have trouble meeting or be unwilling to post. Consider a standstill agreement until a trial on the merits can be held.

If you decide to present a motion for a preliminary injunction, you should draft it both to allege the legal requirements for such relief and to specify precisely what acts you want the court to enjoin.

Example:

[Caption]

MOTION FOR PRELIMINARY INJUNCTION

Plaintiff moves for a preliminary injunction to enjoin defendant, his officers, employees, agents and any persons working with him, until a trial on the merits is held and a final order is entered in this action. In support of his motion plaintiff states:

1. Defendant will act in the manner alleged in the complaint unless enjoined.

2. Defendant's threatened action if carried out will result in irreparable injury, loss and damage, as more fully alleged in the complaint.

3. The injury to plaintiff, if defendant is not enjoined, will substantially exceed any foreseeable injury to the defendant.

4. A preliminary injunction will not be against the public interest.

WHEREFORE, plaintiff requests that the court enter a preliminary injunction enjoining defendant from [specify and describe conduct sought to be enjoined].

_____
Attorney for Plaintiff

§7.6.   Removal

1.   Law

The right of a defendant to remove a case from state to federal court is governed by 28 U.S.C. §§1441-1453. The applicable law is discussed in §3.5.

2.   Practice approach

A defendant considering removal must ask several questions before preparing a petition for removal.

a.   Can I remove?

Removal is a procedure by which a defendant can transfer a case from state court to federal court when the plaintiff's complaint alleges a claim over which a federal court would have had original jurisdiction. The propriety of removal depends solely on the plaintiff's claims. A defense or anticipated defense cannot support removal, even if the defense is based on federal law.[13]

b.   Should I remove?

Removal is nothing more than a change from a state to a federal forum. Consequently, removal makes sense only if the defendants will benefit from the change. The potential advantages include a quicker trial date, since federal courts frequently have less of a backlog than state courts. Federal districts, however, give priority to criminal cases and usually place diversity cases at the end of the line. Procedural differences that may exist between the state and federal courts offer another potential advantage. For example, discovery rights might be broader in federal court. Also, the Federal Rules of Evidence may be more relaxed on admissibility issues than state evidence rules. Removal may also get the case away from an unfavorable state judge. Finally, federal jury panels are usually drawn from a larger geographical pool and may have different characteristics than a state jury panel.

c.   Can I get codefendants to remove?

All defendants, except nominal or fraudulently joined ones, must agree to remove. Do not file a removal notice unless your codefendants agree to join in the removal. Defendants for this purpose include only those defendants who have been served with the complaint and summons. Defendants named in the complaint who have not been served with the complaint and summons need not agree to removal, since they are not yet in the lawsuit. This "unanimity rule," when coupled with the 30-day time

---

13. See Rivet v. Regions Bank, 522 U.S. 470 (1999).

limit, created problems for cases with multiple defendants who were not all served with the complaint at the same time. In 2011, Congress amended 28 U.S.C. §1446 to deal with this difficulty. If a plaintiff serves the complaint and summons on defendants at different times, and if a later-served defendant files a notice of removal within 30 days of service on it, the earlier-served defendants can consent to the removal even if their own efforts at removal would be untimely.

d.   Can I remove all claims?

A defendant can remove a case based on federal question jurisdiction regardless of its state citizenship. If the basis for removal is complete diversity, the defendant cannot remove the case if it is a citizen of the state in which the case is filed.

What happens if some but not all claims are removable? All claims pending in federal court must satisfy jurisdictional requirements. For this reason, section 1441(c) requires that all claims for which either original or supplemental jurisdiction does not exist must be severed and remanded back to state court.

When fewer than all claims are removable, you must decide whether removing some but not all claims is strategically advantageous and economically feasible. The advantages are the potential benefits of removal discussed above. The disadvantages include the time and costs expended in litigating in two different forums.

e.   What are the procedural requirements for removal?

If after considering the relevant issues you decide to remove the case, make sure you follow the procedure set out in 28 U.S.C. §§1446-1450. There are several basic steps.

i.   Timing

Section 1446(b) requires that the notice of removal be filed in the federal district court in the division in which the state action is pending within 30 days after the defendant receives formal service of the complaint and summons.[14] If an amended pleading is the first indication that the case is removable, the defendant must file the petition within 30 days of the receipt of such pleading. If the case as initially filed, for example, does not meet the complete diversity requirement, but the nondiverse defendant is then dropped, the remaining defendants have 30 days from this moment to remove. Section 1446(c) imposes an absolute time limit of one year for removals based on diversity, measured from the commencement of the action.

---

14. See Murphy Bros., Inc. v. Michetti Pipe Stringing, Inc., 526 U.S. 344, 347-348 (1999), holding that a defendant must remove the case within 30 days after being formally served.

ii. Notice of removal

Each defendant in the case who has been served, except nominal or fraudulently named defendants, must sign and file a "notice of removal." The notice must contain a "short and plain statement of the grounds for removal." In other words, the notice must allege the jurisdictional requirements for removal set out in §1441(a), since the plaintiff's state court complaint will not usually allege them. When diversity is the basis for removal, for instance, the notice must allege complete diversity and the jurisdictional amount, and it must allege that none of the defendants is a citizen of the state where the action proceeds. If multiple grounds for removal exist, the notice of removal should allege each.

Example:

[Federal Court Caption]

Mary Jones, 　　　Plaintiff	
	No. _____
v.	
John Smith, 　　　Defendant	

NOTICE OF REMOVAL

To: The United States District Court for the District of Arizona:

Defendant John Smith hereby gives notice that the above captioned case is being removed from the Superior Court of Pima County, Arizona, to the United States District Court for the District of Arizona. In support of this notice defendant states:

1. Plaintiff Mary Jones commenced this action against defendant John Smith in the Superior Court of Pima County under the caption of "Mary Jones, Plaintiff v. John Smith, Defendant," Docket No. 13 C 10478, by serving a copy of the complaint and summons on defendant on June 1, 2013.

2. The complaint alleges that [summarize each count]. A copy of the complaint and summons is attached. No other pleadings or other proceedings have been filed or taken to date.

3. This action is a civil action and is one over which this court has original jurisdiction under 28 U.S.C. §1331 [and/or §1332, etc.] and is an action that can be removed to this District Court pursuant to 28 U.S.C. §1441.

4. [If federal question:] This court has original jurisdiction over this action. It appears from plaintiff's complaint that this is a civil

action that arises under the _____ Act, _____ U.S.C. §_____, [or Constitution or treaty] because plaintiff claims that. . . .

5. [If diversity:] This court has original jurisdiction over this action. It appears from plaintiff's complaint that this is a civil action, and:

(a) Plaintiff, both when this action was commenced and now, was and is a citizen of the State of California;

(b) Defendant, both when this action was commenced and now, was and is a citizen of the State of Nevada. Defendant was not, when this action was commenced, nor is he now, a citizen of the State of Arizona.

(c) The amount in controversy, exclusive of interest and costs, exceeds $75,000.

6. [If multiple defendants:] Each defendant served consents to the removal of this case.

7. [If no jury demand was made in the complaint, and you want one, add a jury demand and immediately comply with all federal jury demand requirements.]

_____
Attorney for Defendant

If the case has more than one defendant, each defendant's lawyer should sign the notice of removal, since each defendant must agree to remove.

iii.   Notice to adverse parties

Section 1446(d) requires that each adverse party be notified promptly of the filing of the notice of removal. This is done in the same way that notice is customarily given.

Example:

[Federal Court Caption]

NOTICE OF FILING NOTICE OF REMOVAL

To: [*attorney for plaintiff*]

Please take notice that on June 10, 2013, defendant John Smith filed a Notice of Removal in the United States District Court for the District of Arizona. A copy of the Notice of Removal is attached to this notice.

_____
Attorney for Defendant

The original notice should be filed with the clerk of the court after copies of the notice have been sent to the attorneys of all adverse parties.

iv.   File notice of removal in state court

The final step in the removal process is filing a copy of the notice of removal with the clerk of the state court. This act terminates the state court's jurisdiction over the action.

v.   Further proceedings

Once the above steps are completed, removal is complete. No order is required to effect removal. The federal district court retains jurisdiction unless and until the case is remanded back to the state court. The federal court can proceed as with any other case.

The usual state of affairs after a case has been removed is that the defendant who has been served has not yet responded to the complaint, and other defendants have not been served. Under Rule 81(c), the served defendant must answer or otherwise plead within 21 days of receipt of the initial pleading or summons or within seven days of filing the notice of removal, whichever is longer. The answer or other response must comply with the federal pleading rules. If the plaintiff has not served all defendants before the notice of removal is filed, service must be made in compliance with Rule 4. In short, all action taken after removal must be taken under the Federal Rules.

vi.   Motion to remand

If removal is improper, the plaintiff should describe the defect in a timely motion to remand, brought pursuant to §1447(c). If the motion is based on a defect in the notice of removal, the plaintiff must move within 30 days of the notice of removal's filing. If the defect involves a lack of subject matter jurisdiction, the motion to remand can be made at any time. If the motion is granted, the order remanding the case may also require the payment of costs and actual expenses, including attorney's fees, incurred as a result of the improper removal.[15]

---

15. In Martin v. Franklin Capital Corp., 546 U.S. 132, 136 (2005), the Supreme Court held that under the removal statute attorney fees "should not be awarded when the removing party has an objectively reasonable basis for removal."

§7.7. *Judgment on the pleadings*[16]

Rule 12(c) governs motions for judgment on the pleadings. Any party can move for judgment on the pleadings after the pleadings are closed, but sufficiently before trial so that trial will not be delayed. The motion determines if the moving party is entitled to judgment based on the allegations in the complaint and the answer. For purposes of the motion, the movant's well-pleaded allegations that have been denied are deemed false, while the opponent's allegations are deemed true. In short, the pleadings are viewed in the light most favorable to the nonmoving party. The motion should be granted only when the undisputed facts as pleaded show that the movant is entitled to judgment.[17] If a party presents matters outside the pleadings and the court decides to receive them, the motion is treated as one for summary judgment.

A motion for judgment on the pleadings under Rule 12(c) is different from a motion to dismiss under Rule 12(b)(6). The motion to dismiss considers only if a complaint (or counterclaim, cross-claim, or third-party complaint) properly sets forth a claim upon which relief can be granted. The analysis is limited to the allegations supporting the claim. A defendant should make a Rule 12(b)(6) motion after receiving the complaint but before answering. By contrast, the motion for judgment on the pleadings considers not only the complaint but also the answer. It is filed after the pleadings are closed. The motion for judgment on the pleadings asks whether, in light of undisputed allegations in the pleadings, one party is entitled to judgment as a matter of law.

The motion for judgment on the pleadings is usually made only in cases where legal defenses, such as the statute of limitations, clearly exist. Since under the Federal Rules answers need not be responded to, a defendant cannot move for judgment on the pleadings on grounds that the plaintiff has not affirmatively denied allegations in the defendant's answer.

Example:

[Caption]

MOTION FOR JUDGMENT ON THE PLEADINGS

Defendant Johnson Corporation moves this Court to enter judgment on the pleadings in favor of the defendant. On the undisputed facts in the pleadings, defendant is entitled to judgment under Rule 12(c) as a matter of law.

---

16. Hazard et al. §5.10; Manual of Federal Practice §§4.31–4.34; Moore's Manual §§16.01-16.07; Wright & Miller §§1367–1372; Moore's Federal Practice §12.38.

17. See Moore's Manual §16.01.

In support of its motion defendant states:
    1. . . .
    2. . . .
    3. . . .
    WHEREFORE, defendant Johnson Corporation requests the Court to enter judgment on the pleadings in favor of the defendant.

_____
Attorney for Defendant

Rule 15 provides that the court should "freely give leave" to amend pleadings "when justice so requires." Therefore, if a motion for judgment on the pleadings will likely be granted, the plaintiff should move for leave to amend if the defect can be cured. Under these circumstances the motion for leave to amend should attach the proposed amended pleading. Where the motion for leave to amend is made before substantial discovery has occurred, it should ordinarily be granted, despite the pendency of a motion for judgment on the pleadings.[18]

§7.8.   *Summary judgment*[19]

Rule 56 governs summary judgment. It is designed to provide an efficient method for merits decisions before trial when there are no genuine disputes over any material facts. A motion for summary judgment can be made on any claim—complaint, counterclaim, cross-claim, or third-party claim—and on any defense. Partial summary judgment can be granted on fewer than all parties, on fewer than all claims, or on one of several issues within a claim, such as liability.

1.   When made

Under Rule 56(b), "a party may file a motion for summary judgment at any time until 30 days after the close of all discovery," unless local rules or court orders set a different time. A motion for summary judgment must be served on all other parties at least 14 days before the hearing date.

Since Rule 56(a) allows motions for summary judgment early in the litigation process, litigation strategy principally determines when to bring such a motion. As a practical matter, early motions have little chance of success, especially before the pleadings have been closed. Parties usually file summary judgment motions after substantial discovery has occurred,

18. See Manual of Federal Practice §4.33.
19. Wright §99; Hazard et al. §§9.1-9.7; Moore's Manual §§17.01–17.83; Wright & Miller §§2711–2742; Moore's Federal Practice §§56.02–56.131; Manual of Federal Practice §§4.35–4.42.

after the important facts have become known, and after it becomes apparent that no serious disputes over the essential facts exist.

2.   Standards and matters considered

A moving party is entitled to summary judgment only if "there is no genuine dispute as to any material fact" and "the movant is entitled to judgment as a matter of law." The motion asks the court to decide if there are any material facts in issue and whether the substantive law entitles the moving party to judgment. The court does not determine what facts are true. To decide if material facts are in dispute, the court can consider discovery, exhibits, witness affidavits, and other materials in the record.

The claim involved and the allegations in the pleadings determine which are the material facts. The court will resolve any doubts against the moving party, and it will draw all reasonable inferences from the evidence submitted in favor of the party opposing summary judgment. Keep in mind that the pleadings do not control. If the pleadings show a dispute, but the discovery and affidavits show that no dispute over any material fact exists, the motion should be granted.

To survive a summary judgment motion, a case must involve a "genuine" dispute, or one about which reasonable finders of fact could disagree. This requirement can open the door for some discretion to creep into summary judgment procedure. Scott v. Harris, 550 U.S. 372 (2007), involved a civil rights claim brought by a motorist against a police officer who had used force to stop him from fleeing. The force caused the motorist's car to flip over, resulting in severe injuries. A dashboard camera recorded everything. The question at summary judgment asked whether the police officer's force was unreasonable. Although juries often decide issues of reasonableness, and although the reasonableness of the force depended upon one's interpretation of the recording, the Supreme Court directed summary judgment in the officer's favor. Given the circumstances of the car chase, the Court held that no reasonable juror could watch the recording and conclude that the force was unreasonable.

Scott v. Harris seems to license judges to draw the inferences they prefer from the evidence submitted, rather than inferences that favor the nonmoving party. But *Scott* is probably best read as a singular case and not one through which the Court intended to expand the reach of summary judgment. In Tolan v. Cotton, 134 S.Ct. 1861 (2014), the Court reversed a decision by the lower courts to grant summary judgment in another excessive force case. Again the issue involved the reasonableness of force used by a police officer who had severely wounded the plaintiff during a nighttime encounter. The parties adduced conflicting evidence as to the circumstances leading up to the police officer's decision to discharge his firearm, including disputes about how aggressive the plaintiff had been, how dark the setting was, and so forth. The fact that the Court decided the case, which made no new doctrine and resolved no circuit split, suggests a message: lower courts should hesitate to resolve disputes of fact that might appropriately benefit from presentation at trial.

Moreover, the dispute must be "material." If the parties disagree about a factual issue of tangential importance, but all of the evidence bearing on an element of the plaintiff's claim is undisputed and favors the defendant, the court should grant the motion.

If the motion fails to demonstrate that summary judgment should be granted, in theory the nonmoving party can do nothing. The moving party bears the burden to show no genuine dispute of material fact, and the opposing party can defend against the motion simply by showing why the moving party has not met this burden. As a matter of practice, of course, the opposing party always responds to the motion with a memorandum and affidavits to show why the motion should not be granted. If the motion with accompanying materials shows that the motion should be granted, the opponent ordinarily must present a response, with evidence, to show that genuine disputes over material facts remain.[20]

3.   Hearing, order, and appealability

At the hearing on the motion for summary judgment the judge will usually allow oral argument, and then ordinarily will take the case under advisement and enter a written order at a later time. The order will set out whether the motion is granted or, if partial summary judgment is requested, on what claims or defenses the motion is granted or denied. It will also provide the findings and reasoning that support the order.

Appealability of the order depends on whether the order denies or grants the motion. When an order denies the motion, the order is usually not appealable. A party may not appeal a denial of summary judgment after the trial court has conducted a full trial on the merits.[21] When an order granting the motion disposes of the entire case, the order is final and appealable.[22] Where the order grants only partial summary judgment, either for some but not all parties or for some but not all claims, the order may be appealable. Rule 54(b) permits the judge to direct final judgment as to some of the claims or parties, and thereby make the order appealable, but "only if the court expressly determines that there is no just reason for delay."

When the motion is denied, the usual reason is that material facts are still in dispute. An order denying summary judgment on that basis is not final and cannot be appealed.[23]

---

20. In Celotex Corp. v. Catratt, 477 U.S. 317, 322-323 (1986), the Court rejected the notion that the moving party must always support the motion with affidavits showing the absence of a genuine dispute over a material fact. Where a party has the burden of proof on an essential element and fails to make a sufficient showing to establish that element after an adequate time for discovery, there is no genuine dispute over a material fact and the other party may be entitled to summary judgment without a further factual showing. *Celotex* was part of a trilogy of summary judgment decisions that included Matsushita Elec. Indus. Co. v. Zenith Radio Corp., 475 U.S. 574 (1986), and Anderson v. Liberty Lobby, Inc., 477 U.S. 242 (1986).

21. Ortiz v. Jordan, 131 S. Ct. 884, 888-889 (2011).
22. See Moore's Manual §17.80(1).
23. See Moore's Manual §17.19(2).

4. Practice approach

Summary judgment motions have three important characteristics. First, a summary judgment motion, if granted, will terminate part — and sometimes all — of the litigation. Second, a summary judgment motion is time consuming and expensive for the client. Third, the summary judgment motion frequently may not succeed. Even if the motion is successful, the losing party may successfully appeal. Therefore, the threshold question any lawyer contemplating bringing a summary judgment motion must ask is: Does the motion make legal, factual, and economic sense in this particular case?

a. Should I move for summary judgment?

Since summary judgment "shall" be granted under Rule 56 if "there is no genuine issue as to any material fact" and "the movant is entitled to judgment as a matter of law," the first step is to determine if the case is suitable for disposition through summary judgment. Small cases, those involving one or two issues, are suitable candidates. Contract cases, such as suits on promissory notes where the parties concede that signatures are either genuine or fraudulent, are also good candidates. So are cases involving affirmative legal defenses, such as a statute of limitations or res judicata. These cases present clear legal issues, they involve simple facts, and the motion, if successful, may terminate the entire litigation.

Certain kinds of cases may also be suitable for partial summary judgment motions. In a case having numerous parties or claims, a summary judgment motion may eliminate one or more parties or claims, thereby simplifying the case. A partial summary judgment motion can be directed at a specific part of the case. For example, the motion can attack punitive damages or consequential damages claims. Partial summary judgment may be sought on liability issues, to limit the trial to the issue of damages. Partial summary judgment motions may make sense only in larger cases, but they can be extremely beneficial in them.

What kinds of cases are usually not suitable for summary judgment motions? Poor candidates include cases involving mental state issues, such as fraud and intentional tort cases; cases involving circumstantial evidence; and those involving witness credibility issues. These cases invariably involve disputed facts and simply cannot be resolved by this motion.

There are other questionable reasons to pursue summary judgment. One reason frequently given is that the motion will expedite discovery. However, summary judgment is an expensive discovery vehicle, and motions to compel are generally more efficient and effective. Another reason given is that the motion will force an earlier disclosure of the other side's experts. But witness affidavits from experts presented at summary judgment are rarely from the experts who will testify if the case goes to trial. The other side may obtain an affidavit from its consulting expert and save its testifying experts for trial. Yet another reason given is that the motion will "educate the judge." There are usually easier ways to accomplish this, such as a good pretrial memorandum. Finally, some argue that a summary judgment motion increases the pressure on the other side to settle. While this may be true, a party reluctant to explore settlement will usually feel pressure only when the trial date draws near.

There are good reasons not to file a summary judgment motion. First, the motion educates your opponent, since the motion is essentially a condensed trial. An early motion educates your opponent earlier. Your opponent will learn the facts, witnesses, and exhibits you believe are essential to your case and how you will present them. Second, the costs associated in bringing a serious motion are substantial, since the time necessary to compile a persuasive motion will be significant. The cost of preparing exhibits and witness affidavits for the summary judgment motion also can be substantial. The client must be advised what the expected costs are to bring the motion before the decision can be made. Third, summary judgment motions often fail. The client must also be advised of the likelihood of success or failure before an intelligent decision can be made to make the motion. You need to consider what will happen if you win the motion in the trial court, but lose it on appeal. This is principally a concern for plaintiff, who might be better off simply trying the case than winning a motion that might be reversed on appeal. Fourth, you may decide not to present a motion for partial summary judgment because that part of the case has strong jury appeal, and it will improve your entire case if it goes to trial. Finally, keep in mind that on appeal the appellate court reviews the trial court decision de novo, while on appeal from a judgment after trial the trial judge's findings of fact are reviewed on a clearly erroneous standard.

b.   When should I bring a summary judgment motion?

One possibility is to bring the motion early in the litigation process, soon after the right to amend pleadings has passed but before substantial discovery has been taken. This strategy can succeed in simple cases involving simple issues, such as contract disputes where the parties disagree over whether payment was made or whether they executed the contract. The court, however, may delay its decision. The opposing party will likely ask that the motion be continued while it takes additional discovery before responding.

Most summary judgment motions are brought after substantial discovery has been done, but well in advance of the trial date. This timing is advantageous, because it enables the moving party to use the other side's discovery responses to demonstrate that no factual dispute over any material fact exists. Be sure to make the motion well before the trial date, or before the court even sets a trial date. Summary judgment motions must be filed within 30 days of the discovery cutoff date, unless the judge's scheduling order for the case sets a different time. Courts may view summary judgment motions filed on the latest possible date as an attempt to delay trial and treat them with skepticism for that reason.

If you decide to make a summary judgment motion, file and serve the motion well in advance of the hearing date. Rule 6(c) requires that the motion be served at least 14 days before the hearing date. The opposing party needs time to respond, and the court will need time to consider a serious motion. Filing and serving the motion well in advance of the hearing date will minimize continuances.

c. How should I organize a summary judgment motion?

Rule 56 states only that the movant show that she is "entitled to judgment as a matter of law" and that there is no "genuine dispute as to any material fact." Therefore, the movant must demonstrate that the material facts are undisputed, and that the legal significance of these undisputed facts requires judgment in her favor. Hence, the two essential components of a summary judgment motion are:

1. the memorandum of law, which discusses the applicable substantive law, and
2. the statement of facts, which, with supporting exhibits, discusses the applicable facts.

d. How do I prepare the memorandum of law?

A good place to start is to get the pattern jury instructions used in your jurisdiction for the claims or defenses involved in the motion. The elements instructions will tell you what specific proof is necessary for each of those claims or defenses on which you seek summary judgment. The instructions also provide a useful blueprint for the specific contents of the memorandum of law. If your jurisdiction does not use pattern jury instructions, you must research the substantive law (which you should have already done before filing or responding to the lawsuit). Once you have done so, you can then draft a memorandum of law. You tell the judge exactly what must be proven to establish a prima facie case on each claim or defense involved. You then explain how, given the applicable law, the undisputed facts require judgment in your client's favor.

e. How do I prepare the statement of facts?

Summary judgment is a fact-driven motion, so how you organize and present your facts is critical. Your statement of facts must show that there is no material fact over which there is a genuine dispute. The statement of facts will contain the material facts that are necessary to the motion and will cite to the evidentiary sources unearthed in discovery that support it. A good method is to use the elements instructions to determine which facts are material, then organize and state those material facts in paragraphs much like the factual allegations in a complaint. Under Rule 56(c), each material fact stated must then be cross-referenced to the admissible sources that prove that fact.

Keep in mind the hierarchy of factual sources necessary to demonstrate that no material facts are in dispute. There are three basic sources:

1. opponent's discovery responses
2. records and documents (yours and opponent's)
3. witness affidavits

Of these, your opponent's discovery responses will usually be the most persuasive, since the opponent will have difficulty contesting the facts that they contain. Particularly persuasive are your opponent's responses to your requests to admit under Rule 36, since the matters admitted are deemed conclusively established for purposes of this litigation. Least persuasive are witness affidavits, since your opponent can usually attach contrary witness affidavits in its response and thereby create a genuine dispute over a material fact.

Rule 56 used to include the pleadings in its list of items that courts could consider in connection with summary judgment. A 2010 amendment to the rule removed this reference, recognizing the general understanding that the pleadings are not really a source of proof. Some courts may treat a party's pleadings as a source of admissions. But any information in the complaint or answer that would be helpful to invoke at summary judgment should be memorialized elsewhere, such as in an affidavit, a response to a request for admissions, or deposition testimony. Certainly a party opposing summary judgment may not invoke his pleading as the sole support for a claim that a genuine dispute of material fact exists.[24]

Example:

DEFENDANT'S STATEMENT OF FACTS

Defendant Alice Smith, through her attorney, submits this Statement of Facts pursuant to Rule 56(c) and local rules in support of her Motion for Summary Judgment on Count I of plaintiff's complaint alleging breach of contract.

1. Alice Smith, defendant, is the president, chairperson of the board of directors, and majority shareholder of Smith Optical Company. (Exhibit #1, Smith Resp. to Request for Admissions, p. 3.)

2. James Woods, plaintiff, was hired as an employee of Smith Optical Company on June 1, 2011, and was terminated as an employee on December 1, 2013. (Exhibit #3, Woods deposition transcript, p. 14; Exhibit #4, Smith deposition transcript, p. 22; Exhibit #7, Termination letter dated December 1, 2013, attached as exhibit to Smith deposition)

---

24. Edward Brunet et al., Summary Judgment: Federal Law and Practice §8.5 (2014 ed.).

3. When James Woods was first hired, he was given a copy of Smith Optical Company's Employee Personnel Manual. (Exhibit #3, Woods deposition transcript, p. 26)

4. The Employee Personnel Manual that James Woods was given when first hired provided that "The three-step procedure for terminating employees for inadequate performance shall NOT be applicable if an employee engages in criminal conduct, acts of dishonesty, or acts which threaten the health or safety of other employees or customers." (Exhibit #5, Employee Personnel Manual, p. 7; Exhibit #6, Affidavit of Helen Griggs, custodian of records for Smith Optical Company)

5. The termination of James Woods was approved at the board meeting of Smith Optical Company held on December 15, 2013. (Exhibit #4, Smith deposition, p. 44; Exhibit #8, Board minutes of 12/15/13 meeting; Exhibit #6, Affidavit of Helen Griggs, custodian of records)

Each exhibit cited must be attached to the statement of facts. The usual practice is to bind and tab the exhibits so that the judge, when reading the statement of facts, can quickly find the exhibit. Check both the local rules and the judge's rules since many of them are quite specific on how exhibits must be organized, bound, and tabbed.

f.   How do I prepare exhibits?

The moving party needs to present these factual sources properly. Discovery materials present no problems, since they are part of the record. Copies of or excerpts from discovery responses can be appended to the statement of facts. Other evidence must be prepared carefully to meet the Rule 56(c) requirements. These include, for example, records, documents, electronically stored information, photographs, and other demonstrative aids presented as exhibits, as well as witness testimony presented by witness affidavits.

The principal concern with exhibits is that they be properly qualified, since Rule 56(c) requires that any facts presented in support of the motion must be admissible in evidence. For example, merely attaching a business record as an exhibit to the statement of facts will probably be deemed inadequate. The sounder practice is to determine what evidentiary foundation would be necessary to get this exhibit admitted at trial, then prepare an accompanying witness affidavit that establishes the proper foundation for that exhibit. For example, most documentary exhibits can be properly introduced as either business records or, if signed instruments, by authenticating the signatures of the persons signing the instruments. Finally, make sure that the exhibit contents do not violate other evidentiary rules. For instance, double hearsay problems are common in business records. The key point to remember is that the judge need not consider "evidence" that supports the summary judgment motion if that evidence would not be admitted at trial. Hence, it is your responsibility to demonstrate that each exhibit would be admissible at trial, through a carefully drafted affidavit from an appropriately qualified foundation witness.

Another useful approach is to send a request to admit facts under Rule 36 to the opposing party, asking it to admit the evidentiary foundations for the exhibits you will use to support your summary judgment motion. The opposing party's admissions make the motion's presentation much simpler.

Since brevity is important, consider using summaries under FRE 1006 to summarize voluminous records. Sometimes such information can be presented in graphs and charts and still meet FRE 1006's requirements.

g. How do I prepare witness affidavits?

Drafting witness affidavits must also be done carefully. Rule 56(c) requires that affidavits be based on "personal knowledge," state only "facts that would be admissible in evidence," and "show that the affiant or declarant is competent to testify" on the matters contained in the affidavits. The standard practice is for the lawyer to draft the witness affidavit in consultation with the witness. Hence, you need to plan what the witness would testify about if she were testifying at the trial of the case and prepare the witness affidavit to recite that testimony. Have the affidavit read like a direct examination, using the witness's vocabulary, not legalese, so the affidavit contains the witness's own "testimony." Accordingly, the affidavit should first show that the witness is competent to testify and has personal knowledge of the facts recited in the affidavit. The affidavit should then set out the events and activities of which she has firsthand knowledge and show how she has acquired that knowledge. If the witness will qualify records, documents, electronically stored information, or other exhibits, the affidavit must set out the proper evidentiary foundation for each exhibit's admission in evidence, and the exhibit should be attached to the affidavit as an exhibit. Finally, the affidavit should be sworn to before a notary public, and a suitable attestation should be at the end of the affidavit.

Example:

AFFIDAVIT OF GLORIA PATTERSON IN SUPPORT OF MOTION FOR SUMMARY JUDGMENT

I, Gloria Patterson, having first been sworn, state under oath:

1. I am a resident of Tucson, Arizona, and have resided there since 2000.

2. Since January 1, 2002, I have been the president of Cross-Country Transportation, an Arizona corporation having its principal place of business in Tucson, Arizona. As president, I have the overall responsibility for its operations, including entering into contracts on behalf of Cross-Country Transportation.

3. On June 1, 2013, at approximately 10:00 A.M., I was in the office of Smith Corporation at 100 Main Street, Tucson, Arizona, for a meeting with John Smith, the president of Smith Corporation,

the defendant in this case. Also present was Adam York, the plaintiff in this case.

4. At that meeting, I saw John Smith sign his name to a contract, a copy of which is attached to this affidavit as Exhibit A. The signature at the bottom of page 5 of Exhibit A is that of John Smith, the defendant.

5. I have seen John Smith sign his name to various documents about 15 times over the past five years. Based on this previous experience, I recognize the signature on page 5 of Exhibit A as that of John Smith, the defendant.

I hereby declare, under the penalties of perjury, that the facts stated in this affidavit are personally known to me, and that they are true.

_____

Gloria Patterson

State of Arizona
County of Pima

Signed and sworn to before me on _____

_____

Notary Public

My commission expires on _____

Note that 28 U.S.C. §1746 sets forth a procedure for making and using unsworn declarations under penalty of perjury. It can be used for witness affidavits.

Expert witness affidavits, which should be prepared in the same way, involve one additional problem. Rule 56(c) (requiring personal knowledge) and FRE 703 (permitting expert opinion testimony without first admitting in evidence the facts or data the expert relied on to reach the opinion) seemingly conflict. Federal Rule of Evidence 703 should control. Experts rely on many sources that are not within their personal knowledge in evaluating problems and reaching opinions and conclusions, yet may, under FRE 703, base opinions and conclusions on such sources. Furthermore, Rule 56 did not intend to make affidavit requirements more stringent than the evidentiary rules applicable to trials.

The basic rule on expert witness affidavits is not to use one at all unless absolutely necessary. In most cases, one expert's affidavit will usually generate an opposing expert's affidavit, thereby probably defeating the summary judgment motion. An expert's affidavit is usually useful only when it contains principally facts and basic, indisputable matter that the other side cannot contest with an opposing expert's affidavit.

h. How does the summary judgment motion look when done?

Most effectively organized motions have several parts:

1. the motion itself, stating what relief is being sought
2. a memorandum of law, setting out the applicable law
3. a statement of facts, cross-referenced to discovery, exhibits, and witness affidavits
4. excerpts from discovery, marked and tabbed
5. exhibits, marked and tabbed
6. witness affidavits, marked and tabbed
7. a table of contents, if useful

Finally, your summary judgment motion should convey an overall impression of simplicity, clarity, and confidence. A verbose, complicated, and muddled motion has little chance of success. From your memorandum of law the judge must quickly understand the elements of the claims or defenses involved in the motion. Your statement of facts must convince the judge that it does indeed contain all the material facts necessary to decide the motion. Finally, from your supporting exhibits and witness affidavits the judge must be convinced that clear, sufficient, and admissible proof supports each of these material facts.

Example:

[Caption]

<u>MOTION FOR SUMMARY JUDGMENT</u>

Pursuant to Rule 56, defendant Albert Smith moves for an order entering summary judgment in his favor and against the plaintiff on:

1. Count I of the complaint;
2. Count II of the complaint on the issue of punitive damages only.

Defendant states that summary judgment is proper on these counts because there is no genuine issue as to any material fact in Count I, and no genuine issue as to punitive damages in Count II, and that defendant is entitled to summary judgment to the extent requested as a matter of law.

The following attachments support Defendant's motion:

1. memorandum of law
2. statement of facts
3. excerpts from interrogatories and interrogatory answers
4. excerpts from depositions
5. excerpts from requests to admit facts and responses
6. three witness affidavits

WHEREFORE, defendant Albert Smith requests the Court to enter an order granting summary judgment on Count I of the complaint, and on Count II on the issue of punitive damages.

_____
Attorney for Defendant

Not all summary judgment motions need to follow this itemized structure. Effective summary judgment motions are clear and simple, and the simplicity must be appropriate to the circumstances. For example, assume that defendant decides to move for summary judgment on the ground that plaintiff did not give the defendant, a municipal entity, proper notice of intent to sue within the required statutory period. The defendant's motion would only need to set forth the statutory notice requirement and cite the evidence, such as interrogatory answers or deposition transcripts, that shows that the plaintiff did not give proper notice within the required period. Its simplicity and brevity will make this summary judgment motion, requiring no more than two or three pages, particularly effective.

i.   Common problems

What are the common problems that arise when drafting summary judgment motions? Remember that a summary judgment motion takes time to do well and is expensive to the client. Therefore, the motion should not be made unless it has a realistic chance of success, is cost effective, and promotes the client's overall litigation strategy.

The most common drafting problem afflicting summary judgment motions is a lack of clarity and focus. Remember that the motion cannot be granted unless it demonstrates there is "no genuine issue as to any material fact and the movant is entitled to judgment as a matter of law." The motion must clearly set out both the applicable substantive law and the material facts that have relevance to the issues raised in the motion. Confusion, complexity, and verbosity are the enemies of successful summary judgment motions.

Another common mistake is to provide inadequate references to the factual proof contained in the motion's statement of facts. The statement of facts and its support are usually the most important part of the motion. Remember that the motion must establish what every necessary material fact is and show the admissible source of proof of each of those facts. If the motion alleges material facts without showing the source of proof or demonstrating that the source is admissible at trial, the judge can ignore the claimed facts and deny the motion on that basis. Each claimed material fact needs a citation to its sources of proof, much the way that a statement of facts in an appellate brief needs constant cross-references to the trial transcript, and a showing that the source of proof is admissible in evidence.

Finally, motions for summary judgment frequently contain defectively drafted witness affidavits. Remember that the judge will not consider any "facts" unless the motion affirmatively shows that the claimed facts are actually admissible at trial. Witness affidavits must demonstrate that the witness has firsthand knowledge of the facts recited in the affidavit and will be able to testify to those same facts if called at trial. Also, whenever the motion refers to an exhibit, such as a document, record, electronically stored information, photographs, diagrams, or summary charts, the judge cannot presume its admissibility. A witness affidavit from a competent witness must establish the evidentiary basis for the exhibit's proper admission in evidence at trial.

5. Opponent's responses

The opposing party can respond to a summary judgment motion in four basic ways. First, the nonmoving party can ask for a continuance under Rule 56(d) if her adversary brought the summary judgment motion early in the litigation. This rule permits the nonmoving party to "catch up" to the moving party as far as fact-gathering is concerned, so that she will not be unfairly disadvantaged when the motion is heard. The judge may order accelerated and focused discovery and defer hearing the motion for an appropriate period.

Second, the opponent should consider making a cross-motion for summary judgment. Provided the opponent can make this motion consistent with the requirements of Rule 11, it has the practical effect of opposing the original motion and making the judge inclined to deny both motions. This response is common in breach of contract cases.

Third, the opponent can actively respond to the motion. Of course, if the motion on its face fails to show that the movant is entitled to relief, the opposing party theoretically need not do anything. In practice, however, the opponent must look at the motion, determine if it is defective on its face, and pinpoint the defects in its memorandum in opposition to the motion. If the motion incorrectly sets forth the applicable law, point out the error. If the motion fails to state all the material facts necessary to decide the motion, point out the shortcomings. If the motion fails to cite to sources of proof for the material facts, point out the omissions. If the witness affidavits are improperly drafted, fail to show the witness's firsthand knowledge, fail to show the witness's qualifications, or fail to establish an evidentiary foundation for the admission of exhibits relied on in the motion, point out these failures. Review expert affidavits carefully. Look particularly for statements the expert would be expected to make but did not. These are the weaknesses in the expert's affidavit, and where your own expert's affidavit should focus. In short, meticulously analyze the motion, statement of law, statement of facts, and supporting affidavits and exhibits to make sure that they are complete and proper.

Fourth, if there are no defects in the motion itself, you will need to oppose the motion by presenting exhibits and witness affidavits that contradict the movant's exhibits and affidavits on some material facts. You thereby create factual disputes and issues of witness credibility. Since witness credibility issues and factual disputes over material matters can only be resolved at trial, the motion should be denied.

The response's organization differs according to the lawyers and issues. The important point, however, is that the response clearly and efficiently demonstrate that summary judgment is inappropriate under the circumstances, either because of a fatal defect in the motion or because your response demonstrates that material facts remain in dispute.

Example:

[Caption]

PLAINTIFF'S MEMORANDUM IN OPPOSITION TO DEFENDANT'S MOTION FOR SUMMARY JUDGMENT

Plaintiff Johnson submits this memorandum in opposition to Defendant Acme Corporation's motion for summary judgment on the claim for punitive damages. As demonstrated in this memorandum and supporting exhibits and affidavit, material facts remain in dispute. Defendant is therefore not entitled to summary judgment as a matter of law, and the motion should be denied.

Law

Defendant incorrectly states the applicable law . . .

Facts

The facts essential to the question of whether a genuine dispute over material facts remains are . . .

Argument

In this case, the parties dispute material facts . . .

Conclusion

Wherefore, Plaintiff Johnson requests that the court deny Defendant Acme Corporation's motion for partial summary judgment on the claim for punitive damages.

                                             _____
                                             Attorney for Defendant

6. Hearing on the motion

The court will usually schedule a hearing on the motion. How you prepare for the hearing and how you present your strongest points are much the same as for any hearing on an important motion. As the movant, keep in mind that simplicity and brevity are the key to a successful hearing. If you take a long time to demonstrate that you are entitled to summary judgment, the very length of your argument will help to defeat your motion. As the party opposing the motion, show how complex, convoluted, and contested the material facts are. The inevitable conclusion you want to establish is that the dispute can only be resolved through a trial. How to argue at a hearing on a motion is discussed further in §7.2.

The judge will take most summary judgment motions "under advisement" after the hearing and issue a written order sometime later.

§7.9. *Dismissals and defaults*[25]

Rule 41 governs dismissals. There are two types of dismissals, voluntary and involuntary. The rule applies to any claimant and therefore to any claim, counterclaim, cross-claim, or third-party claim. It permits dismissals of fewer than all claims against fewer than all parties.[26]

1. Voluntary dismissals

There are two ways to obtain a voluntary dismissal. First, if an answer or summary judgment motion has not yet been filed, a plaintiff can simply file a notice of dismissal with the clerk of the court. No court order is required. A plaintiff is permitted to withdraw a lawsuit that was ill considered or prematurely brought without incurring penalties.

Example:

[Caption]

NOTICE OF DISMISSAL

Please take notice that on June 15, 2013, plaintiff Wilbur Jackson filed this Notice of Dismissal to dismiss plaintiff's complaint without prejudice, pursuant to Rule 41, with the clerk of the Court.

_____

Attorney for Plaintiff

Second, if all parties who have appeared in the action agree on a dismissal, the plaintiff need only file with the clerk of the court a stipulation

---

25. Manual of Federal Practice §§7.5, 7.6, 7.63; Moore's Manual §§19.01–19.05; Wright & Miller §§2362–2376, 2681-2700; Moore's Federal Practice §§41.02–41.53, 55.02-55.84.

26. Rule 15, governing amendments of pleadings, and Rule 21, governing joinder, overlap Rule 41 and should always be checked. See Moore's Manual §19.23.

of dismissal signed by all parties. Again, no court order is required. This is the usual method for terminating a lawsuit following a settlement.

Example:

[Caption]

STIPULATION OF DISMISSAL

The parties, plaintiff Wilbur Jackson and defendant Frank Johnson, agreed on June 15, 2013, to dismiss the above-captioned action, with prejudice, and for each party to bear its costs of suit.

_____
Attorney for Plaintiff

_____
Attorney for Defendant

In all other circumstances, the plaintiff may obtain a voluntary dismissal only by court order. The court has power to impose terms and conditions that are appropriate under the circumstances. These may include the payment of costs, expenses, and attorney's fees to the defendant. Under ordinary circumstances the motion should be granted, unless the defendant can show that some actual legal prejudice would result from a second lawsuit.

As a tactical matter, the plaintiff should simply file and serve a motion for a voluntary dismissal of the action, stating reasons for granting the relief. If the court will only grant the motion upon terms that seem unduly harsh or expensive, the plaintiff should consider withdrawing the motion and continuing with the action.

Regardless of whether the voluntary dismissal is obtained through a notice of dismissal or court order, the dismissal is without prejudice unless otherwise stated.[27] If a plaintiff later files the same claim against the same defendant, Rule 41(d) permits the court to order the plaintiff to pay the costs of the previously dismissed action to the defendant. The court can order a stay of the new action until the plaintiff complies with the order for payment of costs.

Where the dismissal is made by notice of dismissal, the first one is without prejudice. To avoid abuse of this rule by repeated filings and dismissals of actions, Rule 41(a)(1) has a "two dismissal rule."[28] A notice of dismissal is with prejudice and constitutes a judgment on the merits if the second dismissal is based on the same claim previously dismissed in any federal or state court.

---

27. See Semtek International v. Lockheed Martin Corp., 531 U.S. 497 (2001), for a discussion of the meaning of dismissal "on the merits."
28. See Wright & Miller §2368.

The court ordinarily will not consider the plaintiff's motivation in seeking a voluntary dismissal. The only issues are whether a dismissal would create a legal prejudice to the defendant and what terms the order should include so that defendant's costs and expenses will be reasonably reimbursed. For instance, a plaintiff may dismiss an action that has been removed to federal court even if the only purpose of the dismissal is to defeat the removal and resulting federal jurisdiction, since a defendant has no absolute right to have a case tried in federal court.[29]

Under Rule 41(a)(2), the court will not allow a voluntary dismissal of a claim if a counterclaim has been pleaded before the plaintiff has served a motion for voluntary dismissal, if the counterclaim has no independent jurisdictional basis, or if the defendant objects to the dismissal. Having previously decided to sue, the plaintiff cannot now use a voluntary dismissal to avoid the counterclaim. If the defendant's counterclaim does have an independent basis for federal jurisdiction, the plaintiff may dismiss his complaint.

2. Involuntary dismissals

Involuntary dismissal permits the termination of a claim when a plaintiff has been guilty of misconduct. While the rule mentions only a defendant's motion to dismiss, the court may also dismiss on its own motion.[30] Several grounds support an involuntary dismissal.

First, a plaintiff's failure to prosecute a claim can result in dismissal. This conduct includes a plaintiff's lack of diligence in litigating, indicated by a failure to respond to motions, a failure to appear at hearings, and the use of other repeated dilatory behavior. Involuntary dismissal is a drastic remedy and will normally not be imposed unless other remedies are inadequate. The difficult cases often involve situations where the plaintiff's inaction is a result of his attorney's misconduct, but the plaintiff may have a valid claim. In these situations the court will usually do something short of involuntary dismissal.

Second, the court can involuntarily dismiss where the plaintiff fails to comply with rules of procedure or with court orders. Most failures to comply involve discovery. The Supreme Court has held that only the discovery rules control sanctions for discovery abuse.[31] Hence, Rule 41 will govern situations involving failures other than those related to discovery.

An involuntary dismissal is with prejudice unless otherwise ordered. Hence, it is a final and appealable order.

---

29. See Moore's Manual §19.20.
30. See Moore's Manual §§19.100-19.105.
31. See Societe Internationale v. Rogers, 357 U.S. 197 (1958).

3.   Defaults

Closely related to dismissals are defaults, which Rule 55 governs. This rule allows a plaintiff to obtain a default judgment against a party that fails to plead or take any steps to defend against the pending claim.

Defaults are allowed only when the claim seeks affirmative relief. If the claim is for a specific sum, or a sum that can be computed to a specific amount, a default judgment can be entered by the clerk of the court, provided the defendant is not a minor or incompetent. The plaintiff must present an affidavit to the clerk of the court setting out the facts showing default and the sum due. The affidavit should follow the same form as any notarized witness affidavit.[32]

In all other cases the claimant must make a motion for default at least seven days before the hearing. If the defaulting party has appeared in the case, you must serve a notice of motion on that party at least seven days before the hearing. You should serve a notice of motion eve on a defaulting party who has never appeared in the case. At the hearing the court will determine if the allegations of the claim are true and, if plaintiff is entitled to judgment, the proper amount of damages.

Example:

[Caption]

<u>MOTION FOR DEFAULT</u>

Plaintiff Joan Franklin moves for an order finding defendant Thomas Johnson in default, finding that the defendant owes plaintiff the sum of $84,246.80 plus costs, and for judgment against defendant in that amount. In support of her motion plaintiff states:

1. On March 1, 2013, defendant Thomas Johnson was personally served with the summons and the complaint, as shown by the affidavit of service on the summons.

2. Defendant has failed to answer the complaint, has failed to make an appearance, or in any way respond or defend, although over 90 days have passed since service upon him.

3. Defendant has not responded to three letters sent to him by plaintiff's attorneys. Copies of these letters are attached as Exhibits A, B, and C.

4. Plaintiff is prepared to testify to her reasonable damages, which total $84,246.80.

32. See §7.8.4(g).

WHEREFORE, plaintiff requests that the court find defendant Thomas Johnson in default, hold a hearing to determine the exact amount due plaintiff, and enter judgment for plaintiff and against defendant in that amount.

_____

Attorney for Plaintiff

Defaults are most commonly obtained in simple cases where a defendant who has been properly served fails to respond in any way to the lawsuit, and where enough time has passed so that the defendant obviously does not intend to defend against the claim.

If the sum due is clear, such as in a contract action for past due rent or in an action for an unpaid bill for purchased merchandise, an affidavit to the clerk of the court is appropriate. In many cases, however, the full damages can only be determined at a hearing. These cases require motions for default.

At the hearing on the motion, sometimes called a "prove-up," you should be prepared to show that service on the defaulting party was proper, and that the allegations of the complaint are true. Also, establish what the proper damages are. While judges vary on the formality of the prove-up hearing, you should have all your documentation available and any witnesses on hand who may be necessary to prove your case. For example, in an action on a contract, you should be able to prove proper service with the proof of service in the court file. If necessary, have the person who served the complaint and summons testify. You can prove the existence and execution of the contract by calling a witness who was present at its execution. Another witness along with exhibits can prove performance by the plaintiff, typically payment of the contract price. Other witnesses and records can show nonperformance by the defendant and the extent of the plaintiff's damages. Although the court may not require them, or permit witnesses to summarize what they know in a narrative fashion, it is always safer to have all your witnesses available and prepared to testify as if the proceeding were a trial.

A defaulting party can only have the default judgment set aside by establishing one of the reasons provided in Rule 60(b), principally excusable neglect.[33] For that reason, you should take certain steps to minimize the chances that a default will be vacated. First, serve the defendant by the most direct of the permitted service methods. Second, wait an appropriate period of time, at least 60 to 90 days, before seeking a default. Third, during this time you should send the defendant periodic letters asking

_____

33. What constitutes "excusable neglect" under Rule 60(b) is unclear, since the term is not defined in the rule, and the case law is hardly uniform. Some courts require a showing of culpable conduct or bad faith; others require only a showing of carelessness or negligence. The Supreme Court has not resolved the issue, although in Pioneer Investment Services Co. v. Brunswick Associates, 507 U.S 380, 388 (1993), it defined excusable neglect as "inadvertence, mistake, or carelessness" for the purposes of a bankruptcy rule. See Wright & Miller §2858.

for a response and spelling out the consequences of a default. Finally, send the defendant a notice of motion for the default motion, even though this is required only if the defendant has previously appeared in the case. Taking these steps now will support the motion itself and will make it less likely that the defaulted defendant will succeed in having the default judgment set aside later. The defendant will usually try to vacate the judgment only when you take steps to execute the judgment against the defendant's property, such as by garnishing a savings account.

Moving for a default judgment as soon as permitted under the rules often will stimulate action by the defendant. If you think the defendant really wants to defend, but is just dragging his feet, a quick motion for default is frequently an effective technique for getting the lawsuit going.

§7.10.   Consolidation and separate trials[34]

Under Rule 42 the court may consolidate separate cases for trial, or have parts of a single case tried separately.

1.   Consolidations

Rule 42(a) governs consolidation. It has several elements. First, actions can be consolidated only when all actions are "before the court." This means that the cases have all been filed and are presently pending in the same district. Second, the actions must have "common questions of law or fact." Typical are personal injury actions by several plaintiffs arising out of a single accident. Third, the court may decide to consolidate only certain issues for hearing or trial, such as the liability issues. Consolidation is a discretionary matter for the court.

2.   Separate trials

Rule 42(b) permits the court to order separate trials. It may do so where separation will create convenience, avoid prejudice, or permit a case to be tried more efficiently and economically. The court has broad authority to separate claims, counterclaims, cross-claims, and third-party claims; to separate issues in any claims; or to separate parties. The typical situation involves unrelated permissive counterclaims or third-party claims, where it makes sense to try unrelated claims later or spin off third-party actions to keep the trials simpler. Courts usually decide to order separate trials when discovery is complete and the case is on the trial calendar, often at the final pretrial conference.

---

34. Wright §97; Manual of Federal Practice §§7.3–7.4; Moore's Manual §§20.02-20.03; Wright & Miller §§2382–2392; Moore's Federal Practice §§42.10–42.24.

While the court has authority to separate issues, a problem often arises because the rule expressly reserves a party's rights to a jury trial. The case law is still unclear as to when a court may order separate trials of issues before different juries.[35] Separate trials on liability and damages issues can proceed before the same jury without a problem. But whether different juries can decide the separate issues is disputed.[36]

§7.11. Interlocutory appeal[37]

Motion practice can be a significant part of any litigation, and the trial court may rule on numerous motions — discovery and summary judgment motions, for example — as the litigation proceeds. Can the party that loses a motion immediately appeal the order, or must it wait until after the case ends and the trial court enters a final judgment?

A "final judgment" is a judgment order that decides the case on the merits and leaves nothing else for the trial court to do. While the distinction of what is final and what is not final is obvious in most cases, uncertainty can arise in some situations, usually involving complex litigation, because Rule 54 does not itself define what a final order is.[38] Merely designating an order as a "final order" is not determinative. Rule 54(b) does eliminate much of the uncertainty over what constitutes a final order by providing that the trial court may enter a final judgment as to fewer than all parties and claims, so long as the trial court expressly determines that there is no just reason for delay and expressly directs that judgment be entered.

As a general rule, parties can only appeal from a final judgment of the trial court. The benefits of the general rule are obvious: it prevents piecemeal appeals; it allows an appellate court to consider all appellate issues in the context of a complete trial record; and the trial court will be correct in its rulings most of the time. On the other hand, situations arise where an earlier appeal is sensible. Rules, statutes, and case law have allowed interlocutory appeals in several situations.

First, interlocutory appeals may be taken as of right under 28 U.S.C. §1292(a) if:

(1) the interlocutory order grants, continues, modifies or dissolves an injunction, or refuses to dissolve or modify an injunction;[39]

---

35. See Wright §97.

36. See Wright & Miller §2390.

37. Wright §§101–104; Wright & Miller §§3920–3930; James & Hazard §§12.10-12.12.

38. See, e.g., Ray Haluch Gravel Co. v. Central Pension Fund of the Int'l Union of Operating Engineers and Participating Employees, 134 S. Ct. 773 (2014).

39. An order granting or denying a preliminary injunction is appealable, but an order granting or denying a TRO is not. Wright §102.

(2) the interlocutory order appoints a receiver, refuses to wind up a receivership, or refuses to take steps to accomplish the purposes of a receivership;

(3) the interlocutory decree determines the rights and liabilities of parties in an admiralty case.

Second, interlocutory appeals are discretionary under §1292(b). This section, which is infrequently used, provides for interlocutory appeals if the trial court certifies in its order that the case "involves a controlling question of law as to which there is substantial ground for difference of opinion and that an immediate appeal from the order may materially advance the ultimate termination of the litigation." If the trial court issues such an order, the appropriate appellate court has discretion whether to permit the interlocutory appeal.

Third, courts have recognized decisions in an additional narrow class of special cases that may also be appealed immediately, although the principal litigation is not completed. These cases are covered by the so-called collateral orders doctrine.[40] They include situations where the trial court has decided one issue of a case that is entirely collateral of the main litigation but too important to deny review until the entire case is decided.[41] The issue must be independent of the principal action, the order must completely dispose of that issue, and it must be effectively unreviewable if an appeal is allowed only after final judgment. Qualifying situations are also infrequent and principally arise in complex litigation.

Fourth, the extraordinary writs of mandamus and prohibition may also be used to appeal the trial court's rulings in limited circumstances. For example, writs of mandamus are most commonly used to enforce a right to a jury trial where the trial court has improperly denied that right.

Fifth, decisions either to grant or deny class certification may be appealable. Rule 23(f) allows a party to ask the court of appeals to allow an interlocutory appeal from this order. Most of these requests are granted.

If you can properly take an interlocutory appeal, make sure you follow the applicable Federal Rules of Appellate Procedure, particularly Rule 5, which governs appeals by permission under 28 U.S.C. §1292(b).[42]

---

40. See Wright §101. In Mohawk Industries v. Carpenter, 558 U.S. 100 (2009), the Supreme Court held that a trial court's decision that no privilege existed cannot be reviewed through an interlocutory appeal. It can only be reviewed under 28 U.S.C. 1292(b), through mandamus, or by suffering contempt.

41. The leading case is Cohen v. Beneficial Industrial Loan Corp., 337 U.S. 541 (1949).

42. See Becker v. Montgomery, 532 U.S. 757 (2001), holding that failure to sign a notice of appeal is not a fatal jurisdictional defect, so long as the defect is promptly cured once the omission is called to the appellant's attention.

VIII

PRETRIAL CONFERENCES AND SETTLEMENTS

§8.1. Introduction

The vast majority of cases that survive dispositive motions or are not voluntarily dismissed settle before trial. The law encourages settlement, and clients often prefer settlement over the increased expenses and uncertainties of a trial. Small wonder, then, that lawyers settle most cases.

This chapter discusses the closely related topics of pretrial conferences and settlement. Judges often use pretrial conferences to facilitate or even force settlement discussions as a case nears trial. Although lawyers should and do discuss settlement at other times, settlement negotiations invariably occur after discovery has ended but before trial preparations have begun. Since pretrial conferences are commonly scheduled for this time, they and settlement are interrelated parts of the litigation process.

§8.2. Pretrial conferences[1]

1. Procedure

Rule 16 governs pretrial conferences. It gives the trial court broad authority to hold pretrial conferences on a wide spectrum of matters and to enter comprehensive pretrial orders. Rule 16 affords trial judges wide discretion, and many districts and individual judges have adopted local rules and instructions to regulate pretrial conferences and to specify the organization and contents of the pretrial memorandum. Hence, in preparing for a pretrial conference, you must comply not only with Rule 16, but also with applicable local and individual rules. Be aware of your judge's attitude toward pretrial conferences. Note that Rule 16(f) authorizes sanctions for failure to participate in good faith in pretrial conferences.

---

1. Wright §91; Hazard et al. §10.3; Moore's Manual §§18.01–18.06, 18.20-18.24; Manual of Federal Practice §§6.5–6.14; Moore's Federal Practice §§16.01–16.94; Wright & Miller §§1521–1530.

A pretrial conference serves three basic purposes. First, it is used early in the litigation process to develop a discovery plan. Second, a pretrial conference can be used to streamline the case for trial purposes. Third, it can be used to promote settlement of the case. This section discusses the second purpose, and §8.3 discusses settlement conferences.

Rule 16(e) authorizes the judge to hold a final pretrial conference. The stated purpose of these conferences is to prepare for trial, although they often include settlement negotiations that the judge facilitates. At the conference, the judge will force the parties to narrow the issues that will actually be tried, and she will work with them "to formulate a trial plan" that will streamline the presentation of evidence at trial. The plan will include stipulations, evidentiary rulings, and limitations on witnesses. Rule 16 requires that the conference "be held as close to the start of trial as is reasonable." For a complex case, the conference might occur several weeks before trial; for a routine case, it can happen only a few days before trial.

Judges vary widely in how they conduct pretrial conferences. Some will hold an informal meeting in chambers, without a court reporter, to discuss the general nature of the lawsuit. At the other end of the spectrum, some judges will hold a formal conference, sometimes in open court. They will conduct a detailed review of the pretrial memorandum, make all possible rulings, and detail them in an extensive pretrial order. Some judges actively encourage settlement, while others do not. Some judges are flexible and let the lawyers participate in deciding what type of conference would be most productive in a particular case. Learn how your judge conducts final pretrial conferences and prepare accordingly. If you do not know your judge's practice, ask around. The judge's law clerk is usually a good first person to ask.

2.   Pretrial disclosures and memorandum

Rule 26(a)(3) requires that each party must disclose to the other parties certain information that it "may present at trial other than solely for impeachment." The information must be disclosed at least 30 days before trial, unless the court directs otherwise. Required disclosures include:

1.   witnesses who are expected to testify at trial
2.   witnesses who may be called "if the need arises"
3.   witnesses who are expected to be presented through depositions (and a transcript of pertinent portions of the testimony)
4.   each exhibit expected to be offered at trial
5.   each exhibit that may be offered "if the need arises"

Parties receiving the pretrial disclosures can file objections to the designated deposition transcripts and the exhibits list within 14 days of receipt. All objections other than relevance are waived by failure to object.

These pretrial disclosures are usually made as part of a pretrial memorandum. How detailed to make the memorandum depends on local rules and the particular judge's procedures. Some judges and rules require only a short, general memorandum, while others expect a detailed review of the case. Sometimes the requirements vary, depending on the complexity of the case. Most require a pretrial memorandum that the parties prepare jointly. Keep in mind that many jurisdictions have local rules concerning the organization and contents of the memorandum, and individual judges have rules that further elaborate on these issues. These rules are frequently more extensive than what Rule 26(a)(3) requires. A pretrial memorandum ordinarily includes the following subjects, which the parties discuss at the final pretrial conference.

a.   Jurisdictional statement

Because federal courts are courts of limited jurisdiction, and because the plaintiff must affirmatively demonstrate the existence of subject matter jurisdiction, the jurisdictional basis for the case is usually the first item in the pretrial memorandum.

b.   Issues of law

A principal purpose of the pretrial conference is to reduce legal issues to those that will actually be tried. Pleadings often assert many possible claims and defenses against every possible party. In the pretrial memorandum the judge will usually require each party to state the claims and defenses that she will actually present at trial. The pretrial order, which reflects the pretrial memorandum, amends the pleadings. Therefore, if you decide to waive certain claims in the memorandum, they will be deemed waived for trial. At this time the judge may also permit amendments to the pleadings so that the pleadings accurately reflect the disputed trial issues.

As a strategic matter, you might consider pursuing only the strongest claims without presenting alternative theories of recovery, particularly if these theories are factually or legally inconsistent. Also, if the pursuit of multiple claims would pose a risk of confusion at trial, or would create the possibility of inefficiency, the judge has authority under Rule 42(b) to order separate trials to promote the orderly and efficient presentation of evidence.

c.   Uncontested and contested facts

To avoid unnecessary formal proof and to focus on disputed facts, the judge will usually require that each party state to which facts it agrees and which facts it contests. Parties may introduce agreed-upon facts at trial through stipulations. The judge has no authority to force the parties to stipulate to facts, but as a practical matter parties are often well advised to do so. If you do not admit a fact, your opponent can then serve a request to admit. If you do not admit the fact in your response to the request and your opponent later proves it at trial, Rule 37(c) enables the court to award costs and attorney's fees expended to prove the fact.

Some judges use the uncontested facts as an introduction to the case during jury selection. Therefore, a useful way to prepare the uncontested facts is to use storytelling to give a clear overview of the case, rather than merely to list them in some dry fashion.

d. Witness lists

The judge will usually require a list of lay and expert witnesses whom each party will call in its case in chief. Be safe. List all witnesses you may call at trial, including the adverse party and the adverse party's witnesses. You are not required to call all the witnesses you list, but you will be precluded from calling witnesses not listed. Judges also frequently require addresses, telephone numbers, and a summary of each witness's expected testimony and the qualifications of each side's experts. Under Rule 26(a)(3), this requirement does not extend to witnesses contemplated solely for impeachment. But the rule covers witnesses "whom the party may call if the need arises," which should include rebuttal witnesses. The judge may ask each party to state whether it intends to object to the subject matter of any witness's testimony or the qualifications of any expert. Also, the judge may eliminate cumulative or repetitive witnesses.

e. Exhibit lists

Judges will usually require parties to prepare lists of all exhibits they plan to introduce in evidence at trial. Rule 26(a)(3) extends this requirement to all exhibits the party expects to offer and exhibits the party "may call if the need arises." The party must also designate "those witnesses whose testimony the party expects to present by deposition." The usual procedure is to list and describe each exhibit, designate the sections of each deposition transcript by page and line number, and attach copies of the exhibits and the designated sections of each transcript to the memorandum. Judges may require opposing parties to state whether they object to any of the exhibits and, if so, to provide the legal basis for the objection. This requirement essentially operates as a motion in limine on objections to evidence. If no one objects to an exhibit, the judge will usually treat the exhibit as admitted in evidence. Where objections exist, the judge may be able to rule on them before trial. Keep in mind, however, that some objections, such as foundation objections, cannot be ruled on in advance of trial. However, the pretrial memorandum at least alerts the judge to the objections that will be raised at trial, thus enabling their more efficient resolution.

Again, be safe and err on the side of inclusion. You cannot introduce at trial an exhibit that you did not list in the pretrial memorandum.

f. Damages proof

In certain types of cases the judge may direct that evidence on damages issues be presented separately. Other parties will be required to state whether they object to the evidence or the amounts asserted. Parties often do not contest certain special damages, such as lost wages and medical bills, and these can be admitted at trial through stipulations.

g.   Jury instructions

The judge usually requires that each party submit proposed jury instructions, state whether it intends to object to the opponent's instructions, and, if so, provide the basis for each objection.[2] While the judge often cannot decide whether to give an instruction before a party presents evidence at trial, the judge can usually rule on the wording of proposed instructions. Since a review of proposed jury instructions can take a good deal of time, addressing this task at a pretrial conference can often avoid substantial delay at trial. If the case is one in which the parties will submit special interrogatories or verdict forms to the jury, the same procedure can be followed.

The usual practice is to put each instruction on a separate page, show at the bottom of each instruction its number, and identify which party requested it and the legal basis for the instruction. The court also gets a clean copy that contains only the instructions.

h.   Voir dire questions

Federal judges commonly ask all or most of the voir dire questions during jury selection. This practice is common in state courts as well. Where voir dire proceeds in this manner, the court may require the lawyers to submit proposed voir dire questions in the pretrial memorandum. The judge can then decide before trial whether to ask the questions during jury selection.

i.   Trial briefs

Most judges expect the parties to submit a trial brief discussing the applicable substantive law and likely evidentiary issues. Some judges want the parties to append their trial briefs to the pretrial memorandum. Others ask for trial briefs only if settlement negotiations have broken down and a trial looks likely. The trial brief alerts the judge and parties to anticipated procedural and evidentiary issues, it reviews applicable law, and it permits the judge to schedule hearings and make rulings. These briefs help enable each party to present its case in a smooth, uninterrupted way. Constant side bar conferences and recesses, taken to deal with legal problems and evidentiary objections, annoy jurors and prolong trial considerably. Trial briefs, coupled with pretrial motions and motions in limine, will minimize trial interruptions and benefit everyone.

The lawyers for both sides usually draft a simple joint pretrial memorandum. Each party contributes portions that reflect its own witnesses, exhibits, and objections to the other side's evidence. All of the necessary information thereby gets combined in one document. Because the pretrial memorandum is a joint project, always volunteer to do the final drafting work to make sure that it accurately contains all your material.

---

2. See Thomas A. Mauet, Trial Techniques and Trials §11.3 (9th ed. (2013).

Example:

[Caption]

<u>JOINT PRETRIAL MEMORANDUM</u>

Counsel for plaintiff Frances Johnson, defendant Robert Jones, and defendant Lisa Roberts submit the following Joint Pretrial Memorandum:

I   <u>Jurisdiction</u>

Jurisdiction is based on diversity of citizenship under 28 U.S.C. §1332. Plaintiff is a citizen of California, defendant Jones is a citizen of Arizona, and defendant Roberts is a citizen of Nevada. The amount in controversy exceeds the sum of $75,000, exclusive of interest and costs.

II   <u>Uncontested Facts</u>

The collision involving two cars occurred on June 1, 2013, at approximately 2:00 P.M. Plaintiff Frances Johnson was a passenger in a 2005 Honda Accord owned and driven by defendant Robert Jones. Jones was driving north on Kolb Road intending to turn left (west) on 22nd Street. As he was executing this turn, the defendant Lisa Roberts, who was driving her 2007 Buick Skylark southbound on Kolb Road, struck Jones' car.

Kolb Road has two lanes of traffic in each direction, a left turn lane at the intersection, and a median strip. Twenty-second Street has two lanes of traffic in each direction, a left-turn lane at the inter-section, and a median strip. The intersection of Kolb Road and 22nd Street is controlled by several traffic lights.

The weather on June 1, 2013, was sunny and clear. The road conditions were dry.

Plaintiff Frances Johnson was injured as a result of the collision. She was taken to St. Mary's Hospital emergency room for treatment and was admitted to the hospital for continued care. Plaintiff was discharged from St. Mary's Hospital on June 4, 2013. Plaintiff's hospital and physician bills for this period totaled $4,471.04.

Plaintiff was absent from work between June 1, 2013, and July 5, 2013, when she returned to her job as a bank teller at First National Bank.

III   <u>Contested Facts</u>

1. Which car had the right of way at the time of the collision?
2. What color were the traffic lights at the time of the collision?
3. What was the extent of plaintiff's injuries?

4. Does plaintiff have any permanent injuries or disabilities as a result of this collision?

5. Will plaintiff need further medical treatment in the future and, if so, what treatment?

6. What amount of money will reasonably compensate plaintiff for the damages incurred as a result of this collision?

IV   Contested Issues of Law

1. Was defendant Robert Jones negligent?
2. Was defendant Lisa Roberts negligent?
3. If both defendants were negligent, what is the relative degree of negligence of each defendant?

V   Exhibits

A. *Plaintiff Johnson's Exhibits:*   *Objections to Admissibility:*

1. Medical expenses totaling $4,471.04, as evidenced by vouchers in support of each expenditure contained in a blue brochure with a cover sheet listing the medical expenses. — None.
2. The Police Department official report of the accident. — Objected to by defendant Jones on hearsay grounds.
3. St. Mary's Hospital emergency room records of the plaintiff. — None.
4. Photographs of the plaintiff showing her shoulder deficit. — None.
5. X-rays taken of the plaintiff. — None.
6. Photographs and diagrams of the intersection involved. — None.

B. *Defendant Jones's Exhibits:*   *Objections to Admissibility:*
1. Plaintiff's hospital and medical records. — None.
2. X-rays. — None.
3. Plaintiff's employment records. — None.
4. Bills concerning property damage. — None.
5. Time sequence of signal lights. — None.
6. Photographs of the vehicles. — None.
7. The police report as far as it is admissible. — None.

C. *Defendant Roberts's Exhibits:*   *Objections to Admissibility:*

1. Police report of accident.   Objected to by plaintiff and by defendant Jones, for the reasons stated in the attached Memorandum of Law.

2. Photographs of vehicles involved.   None.

3. Plaintiff's medical records.   None.

VI   Witnesses

A. *Plaintiff Johnson's Witnesses:*

1. Plaintiff.
2. Elizabeth Martin, M.D.
3. Ernest Jackson, M.D.
4. Philip Wigmore, a bystander.
5. Bernie Sullivan, plaintiff's supervisor at First National Bank.
6. Investigating police officer Frank O'Malley.
7. Defendants.

B. *Defendant Jones's Witnesses:*

C. *Defendant Roberts's Witnesses:*

8. The parties to this action.
9. Doctors who have examined or treated plaintiff.
10. Richard Hollister, a bystander.
11. Officer Barbara Horn, Police Department.
12. Glenda Sylvester, accident reconstruction expert.

VII   Jury Instructions

Plaintiff and defendants' proposed jury instructions are attached.

Plaintiff Johnson objects to Jones's instructions numbers 4, 7, and 9, and objects to Roberts's instruction number 6 for the reasons stated in the attached Memorandum of Law.

Both defendants object to plaintiff Johnson's instructions numbers 6, 7, 8, and 13 for the reasons stated in the attached Memorandum of Law.

RESPECTFULLY SUBMITTED this 1st day of September 2014.

By _____
    Attorney for Plaintiff Johnson

By _____
    Attorney for Defendant Jones

By _____
    Attorney for Defendant Roberts

3.   Pretrial order

Rule 16(d) requires that the judge enter an order reciting the actions taken at the pretrial conference. Local rules frequently specify how and by whom the order will be drafted. Practices vary widely. Some judges prepare the order, either by reciting the results of the conference in open court so the court reporter will record it, or by issuing a written pretrial order. Other judges have the parties draft an agreed-upon proposed order, which the judge then reviews and signs. Some judges ask the parties to estimate the number of trial days necessary to try the case. For lengthy trials, judges may impose time limitations on the parties. The pretrial order then includes the estimated length of trial and any time limitations.

The content of the pretrial order is critical, since the order controls the trial. If the pretrial order incorrectly recites the disputed issues, witnesses, exhibits, or other matters, the parties must promptly correct it. The best time to do so, when possible, is while the order is in draft form, before the judge has signed it. Once entered, the order can be modified "only to prevent manifest injustice," as Rule 16(e) provides.

A simple pretrial order might look like the following.

Example:

[Caption]

<u>FINAL PRETRIAL ORDER</u>

The following are the results of pretrial proceedings in this cause held pursuant to Rule 16 and IT IS ORDERED:

I

This is an action for damages arising out of a collision involving vehicles driven by defendant Jones and defendant Roberts, which occurred on June 1, 2013, at the intersection of Kolb Road and 22nd Street.

II

Jurisdiction is based on diversity of citizenship under 28 U.S.C. §1332. Plaintiff is a citizen of California, defendant Jones is a citizen of Arizona, and defendant Roberts is a citizen of Nevada. The amount in controversy exceeds the sum of $75,000, exclusive of interest and costs. Jurisdiction is not disputed.

III

The following facts are admitted by the parties and require no proof:
1. The collision occurred on June 1, 2013, at the intersection of Kolb Road and 22nd Street.

2. Defendant Jones was the owner and operator of a 2005 Honda Accord that was involved in the collision.

3. Defendant Roberts was the owner and operator of a 2007 Buick Skylark that was involved in the collision.

4. Plaintiff Johnson was a passenger in defendant Jones' vehicle at the time of the collision.

5. The weather on June 1, 2013, was sunny and clear. The road conditions were dry.

6. The intersection of Kolb Road and 22nd Street is controlled by several traffic lights.

7. Plaintiff was absent from work from June 1, 2013, through July 5, 2013.

8. Plaintiff was admitted to St. Mary's Hospital emergency room on June 1, 2013, and was discharged from the hospital on June 4, 2013.

9. Plaintiff's hospital bill was $2,492.83.

10. Plaintiff's doctor bills to date total $1,978.21.

IV

The following are the issues of fact to be tried and determined upon trial:

1. Whether the defendants used due care in operating their vehicles?

Plaintiff contends that both defendants were speeding, not driving safely, and not keeping a proper lookout.

Defendant Jones contends that he was driving within the speed limit and operating his vehicle safely.

Defendant Roberts contends that she was driving within the speed limit and operating her vehicle safely, and that defendant Jones failed to yield the right of way.

V

The following are the issues of law to be tried and determined upon trial:

1. Whether the defendants, or either one of them, were negligent?

Plaintiff contends that both defendants were negligent and that their negligence jointly and directly caused plaintiff's injuries.

Defendant Jones contends that he was not negligent, and that his conduct caused no injuries to plaintiff.

Defendant Roberts contends that she was not negligent, that she did not violate any statutes, and that her conduct caused no injuries to plaintiff.

VI

1. The following exhibits are admissible in evidence in this case and may be marked in evidence by the Clerk:

      a. Plaintiff's exhibits: (see attached List number 1)

      b. Defendants' exhibits: (see attached Lists numbers 2 and 3)

    2. As to the following exhibits, the party against whom the same will be offered objects to their admission upon the grounds stated:

      a. Plaintiff's exhibits: (see attached List number 4)

      b. Defendants' exhibits (see attached Lists numbers 5 and 6)

    3. The parties will offer the following deposition testimony and have the following objections:

      a. Plaintiff deposition excerpts (see attached List number 7)

      b. Defendants' deposition excerpts (see attached List numbers 8 and 9)

VII

The parties will call the following witnesses at trial:

      a. On behalf of plaintiff: (see attached List number 10)

      b. On behalf of defendants: (see attached Lists numbers 11 and 12)

The parties will call the following expert witnesses at trial, with their areas of expertise and the subjects of their testimony:

      a. On behalf of plaintiff: (see attached List number 13)

      b. On behalf of defendants: (see attached Lists numbers 14 and 15)

VIII

The parties timely requested a jury trial. The parties anticipate that the case will require five trial days.

IX

Each side has submitted a set of proposed jury instructions and verdict forms:

      a. On behalf of plaintiff: (see attached Set number 16)

      b. On behalf of defendants: (see attached Sets numbers 17 and 18)

APPROVED AS TO FORM:

_____

Attorney for Plaintiff Johnson

_____

Attorney for Defendant Jones

_____

Attorney for Plaintiff Roberts

The foregoing constitutes the Final Pretrial Order in the above case. This Order supersedes all prior pleadings in the case. It shall not be amended except by consent of the parties and by order of this court.

_____
United States District Judge

The pretrial order bars parties from raising any claims or defenses not permitted by the order, and it restricts the witnesses, exhibits, objections, and any other matters to those contained in the order. While Rule 16(e) permits modification to prevent manifest injustice, a motion to modify the pretrial order comes within the court's discretion, and counsel must ordinarily present a persuasive reason for amending the order.

Since pretrial orders are not usually final orders, they cannot be appealed under 28 U.S.C. §1291 until the entry of final judgment.[3] However, an appeal following a final judgment can raise errors in the pretrial order.

§8.3.   Settlements[4]

Settling a case involves four basic steps: determining the case's settlement value, selling your assessment to the opposing side, having your client agree, and preparing and signing the settlement agreement. While the parties can settle their case at any time, they invariably explore settlement when a case nears the pretrial conference stage and a trial is just around the corner. Discovery will have ended, so sufficient information should exist for the parties to assess the case and likely outcomes accurately.[5] If settlement before or at a settlement conference does not occur, it can, and often does, occur just before or during trial. Settlement can happen just after jury selection, after opening statements, or after the plaintiff's testimony.

You should take stock of your case again when the final pretrial conference is first scheduled. Preparing the pretrial memorandum necessarily will involve a review of the pleadings, discovery, contested issues, witnesses, exhibits, and potential factual and legal problems. You might as well assess the case for its settlement potential in the same systematic way. The best way to prepare for settlement is to prepare for trial.

3. An interlocutory appeal may be permitted under special circumstances. See §7.11; 28 U.S.C. §1292; Moore's Manual §§27-03-27.04.

4. See, e.g., Spencer Punnett, Representing Clients in Mediation (2013); Charles B. Craver, Effective Legal Negotiation and Settlement (5th ed. 2005).

5. Obviously, settlement should be explored earlier as well. You should discuss settlement before filing suit, and then again just after doing so. Another moment for settlement negotiations is after the plaintiff's deposition. Settlement at these moments obviously can keep the costs of litigation low.

1.   Case evaluation

You need to evaluate the case in a systematic, progressive way so that you can accurately and realistically assess its strengths and weaknesses.[6] The sequence to use for your case evaluation should proceed in the following manner. It parallels your use of a litigation chart to structure your litigation plan.[7]

a.   List elements of proof

Look at the elements instructions for liability, special damages, general damages, and defenses for every claim you intend to pursue at trial. The elements instructions will itemize exactly what facts must be proved. This information should already be on your litigation chart.

b.   List sources of proof

List all lay and expert witnesses, with a summary of their testimony; all exhibits; and any other anticipated proof, such as stipulations and judicial notice. Include only evidence that you reasonably believe will be admissible at trial.

c.   Relate proof to elements

Now list the various witnesses and exhibits with the specific facts that must be proved for each claim and defense. Do this for your opponent's proof as well. This list will organize the evidence and show what evidence exists to prove and refute each element of the claims and defenses.

d.   Review credibility of the proof

Once you have organized the evidence and matched it to the elements of the claims and defenses, you must take the critical step. Realistically assess whether a jury will consider the evidence credible. How persuasive will the witnesses be? How probative are the exhibits?

Trial experience helps with this assessment, but you can get a "feel" for your case without it. Ask yourself: Do the witnesses have good personal, family, and employment backgrounds that will make them believable to a jury? Do they tell stories that make sense? What kind of impressions did they make at their depositions? Are their stories consistent with common life experience? Is witness testimony consistent? A good practice for any lawyer, regardless of experience, is to try out your case, giving an objective summary of your side's proof as well as the other side's proof. Do so before experienced trial lawyers, colleagues, friends, and spouses. Their reactions to the case and assessment of the case's strengths and weaknesses will

---

6. See James W. Jeans, Trial Advocacy ch. 20 (2d ed. 1993).
7. See §2.2.

usually be good indicators of how a real jury will view the proof you and your adversary will marshal at trial.

e.   Evaluate your case's jury appeal

Cases, of course, are not presented in a perfect, dispassionate world. A major consideration is whether your or your opponent's case has jury appeal. You must make this assessment whenever any party has made a jury demand. "Jury appeal" is an elusive concept, but it is extremely important to consider both before filing a demand for a jury trial with your initial pleading and before reviewing the case for settlement purposes. The basic components of jury appeal involve the claims, the parties, and the lawyers.

Whether the claims have jury appeal has much to do with whether a jury will be sympathetic to or offended by the conduct of either side. For the most part, juries sympathize with the unassuming individual who has been victimized. For example, a simple negligence case involving property damage or a routine contract action usually has little jury appeal. A negligence case against a drunk driver, however, or a contract action by a homeowner against a home builder charging faulty construction will have substantial appeal. Who the parties and witnesses are and how they testify can also influence jury appeal.[8] Finally, who the trial lawyer is will obviously have some impact. Experienced trial lawyers with a proven record for obtaining good verdicts in similar types of cases can be expected to get better verdicts than other lawyers. Accordingly, you should always investigate your opponent's jury trial experience and reputation as a trial lawyer and add this information to the overall analysis.

f.   Review jury verdict reporters

Most jurisdictions, particularly those with large metropolitan populations, have jury verdict reporter services that periodically report the facts of cases tried and the verdicts obtained.[9] By researching these services, not only for your jurisdiction but similar ones, you can learn the range of verdicts realistically attainable in similar cases. Keep in mind, however, that verdicts can vary widely depending on the jurisdiction, judge, lawyers, and facts — factors not readily reflected in the reports.

g.   Review the trial expenses

Trials are expensive, both emotionally and financially. The client must realize the emotional toll a trial can take and recognize the significant demands a trial will make on his time. These demands must take priority

---

8. See, e.g., Stanley L. Brodsky et al., The Witness Credibility Scale: An Outcome Measure for Expert Witness Research, 28 Behav. Sci. & L. 892 (2010); Geir Kaufman et al., The Importance of Being Earnest: Displayed Emotions and Witness Credibility, 17 Applied Cognitive Psychol. 21 (2013).

9. Frequently used national services include the ATLA Law Reporter and Jury Verdict Reports, which report the monetary range of successful plaintiff's verdicts.

over all other obligations. Give the client a projection of how much of his time you will need in order to prepare and try the case, and what he will be doing during those hours. If a client is unwilling to make the necessary commitment, or is unprepared to handle the emotional stresses and uncertainties of a trial, settlement is the obvious course.

The client should also be aware of the potentially substantial expenses that trial involves. You should review your litigation budget with your client.[10] If you are being compensated on an hourly basis, you should give the client a current estimate of the trial preparation and trial time involved. Experienced trial lawyers usually need at least one day of preparation for each day of trial, and often more. At hourly rates of $100 per hour, a five-day trial, requiring five preparation days, will cost a client over $10,000 in attorney's fees alone. If the case involves a cost-shifting statute, the losing side will bear even more substantial expense.

Witness fees, particularly for experts who must be compensated for their time and travel and housing expenses, can be substantial. Medical and other technical experts usually command hourly rates comparable to that of lawyers. For example, doctors usually insist on compensation that equals or exceeds the same hourly rate they would receive in their practice. Taking a doctor away from his practice for even half a day will cost at least a thousand dollars. Flying an expert in to testify at trial will obviously be substantially more expensive. Finally, do not overlook court costs and other expenses, including daily juror fees, since they can add up during a protracted jury trial.

h. Consider preparing a settlement brochure

Plaintiffs' personal injury lawyers frequently prepare so-called settlement brochures in major cases. These brochures essentially set out the plaintiff's background, along with the evidence showing liability and damages. Lawyers supplement these fact summaries with photographs and video recordings. They include documents as well, such as employment records; hospital and other medical records; bills; and medical and economic expert reports detailing the extent of injuries, the degree of permanent physical losses, and the plaintiff's economic future. Some lawyers believe that such a brochure presents the plaintiff's case most effectively before trial, and helps to obtain a favorable settlement. It can show graphically the nature and extent of the injuries, summarize the quality of the plaintiff's case, and demonstrate the plaintiff's jury appeal. Even if you decide not to prepare a settlement brochure, consider bringing graphic exhibits to the settlement conference to demonstrate your proof on liability and damages.

10. See §2.2.5.

i. Determine the settlement value

You have not completed your case evaluation until you have determined dollar figures and terms that represent the highs and lows of your settlement range. The high figure will reflect the "best result" you can realistically expect to receive after trial. The low figure will be the amount your client is willing to receive (as plaintiff) or pay (as defendant) rather than go to trial. How do you determine this settlement range?

Begin by determining the "best result," also called the "target point," that you can realistically expect to get if the case goes to trial. The target point is the most optimistic verdict estimate for your side. You will use this estimate as the basis to determine your first offer during the settlement negotiations. (Your first offer will typically be somewhat higher than your best result estimate.)

Next, determine the "worst result" if you go to trial and your case on liability and damages goes poorly. This is the most pessimistic verdict estimate for your side.

Once you have estimated your own best and worst results, you need to determine the client's bottom line. What are your client's needs and expectations? What dollar amount and terms will the client accept rather than go to trial? Obviously, to identify this bottom line, you need to discuss thoroughly with the client all the risks of going to trial, the financial and psychic costs of the trial itself, the "time value" benefit to the plaintiff of receiving the settlement money immediately, and the net amount that the client will actually receive (for plaintiffs, after deducting anticipated fees, costs, and amounts owed to lienholders). The client's bottom line, also called the "resistance point," will be the basis for determining your final offer during the settlement negotiations.

How do you estimate your best and worst results? First, you need to establish the dollar amount of a likely verdict if the plaintiff prevails on both liability and damages. In some cases, such as contract disputes, you may be able to identify a specific figure. The contract may have a liquidated damages clause or the claim may involve an unpaid debt. In most cases, such as personal injury cases, the better strategy is to determine a range bounded by your best and worst results. Some damages in personal injury cases, such as already incurred expenses for hospital and doctor bills, car repairs, and lost wages (sometimes called "special" or "out-of-pocket" damages), may be easy to determine. Other damages, such as future medical expenses, lost future income, and pain and suffering, may be harder to estimate. Thus, the range of possible damages may be substantial. For example, you may decide that the jury will award damages of $200,000 as a best result but only $40,000 as a worst result. Make the same kind of assessment of any counterclaims. The more ordinary the facts of the case are, the more accurately you should be able to determine the verdict range. Review jury verdict reporters for similar cases in your jurisdiction.

Second, determine the probability that the plaintiff will succeed on the issue of liability, expressed as percentages. As with damages, you should come up with a range that reflects both best and worst outcomes. For example, you may decide that, best case scenario, the plaintiff has a 75 percent likelihood of prevailing on liability. If things go badly, the plaintiff may have only a 25 percent chance of winning on liability. Make the same kind of assessment for any counterclaims. If a personal injury case involves comparative negligence, you need to determine the likelihood that the jury will find the plaintiff was also negligent, again expressed as percentages to reflect the best and worst results.

Third, analyze the additional costs the client will incur if the case goes to trial. These costs will include attorney's fees and other trial expenses, such as expert witness fees. If you are being paid on a contingency or flat fee basis, your client will not have to pay any additional attorney's fees. If you are being paid on an hourly basis, you should estimate the hours likely required to prepare and try the case, then multiply this time by your hourly rate. Make the same estimate for your opponent. These additional legal fees and trial expenses alter the net value of the case if it goes to trial and need to be factored into the settlement evaluation. (The fees and costs reduce the settlement value for plaintiffs and increase them for defendants.)

Fourth, you need to take into account the time value of money. Money received now is worth more than the same amount of money received at a later time. If you represent the plaintiff, you need to discount the value of the case to reflect the benefit of receiving an amount of money now rather than after a trial. (The defendant must do the opposite, since deferring payment is a benefit.) This discount, expressed as a percentage, depends on how much sooner the plaintiff will get the money and the increased value of getting it now. For example, if a case will not be tried for one year and the yield on a prudent investment or bank deposit is 5 percent, an amount received one year from now will be worth about 5 percent less than that amount received now.

Finally, determine if the defendant's insurance coverage or other ability to pay imposes a practical limit on what the plaintiff can realistically hope to recover. When insurance coverage is low and the defendant has no other substantial assets that could help satisfy a judgment, the policy limit may be the only amount the plaintiff can ever recover. In this situation, the defense may simply "tender the policy" to settle the case.

Example:

You represent the plaintiff in a personal injury case on a contingency fee basis. The applicable state's law is comparative negligence. Your settlement value analysis should proceed along the following lines:

1. Assuming liability, you assess the likely damages verdict at $100,000 as the best possible result and $50,000 as the worst possible result.

2. You assess the likelihood of obtaining a verdict finding the defendant negligent at 90 percent as the best possible result and 50 percent as the worst possible result. You assess the likelihood of a verdict finding the plaintiff also negligent at 0 percent as the best possible result and 50 percent as the worst possible result.

3. Since you represent the plaintiff on a contingency basis, the trial will not generate additional legal fees. However, you estimate that the plaintiff will have to pay $5,000 for trial expenses, principally expert witness fees and costs.

4. You estimate that the case will not be tried for one year, and the current rate of return for safe investments is 5 percent.

The settlement range of the case computes as follows:

1. Under the best possible result analysis, the $100,000 damages estimate must be reduced by 10 percent (the chance the jury will not find the defendant negligent), to $90,000, and by the trial expenses of $5,000, to $85,000, and by 5 percent (the time value of money), to $80,750. That figure, $80,750, is your estimate of the best possible result after trial. (This means that the net to your client is approximately $54,000 after your 33 percent contingency fee is deducted.)

2. Under the worst possible result analysis, the $50,000 damages estimate must be reduced by 50 percent, to $25,000, and by another 50 percent (the possibility the jury also will find the plaintiff contributorily negligent), to $12,500, and by the trial expenses, to $7,500, and by 5 percent, to $7,125. That figure, $7,125, is your estimate of the worst possible result after trial. (This means that the net to your client is approximately $4,775 after your contingency fee is deducted.)

This outcome range, between $80,750 and $7,125, is what you must then discuss with your client to determine the client's bottom figure. Assume that the client says he would rather go to trial than accept a settlement of less than $35,000 (which would net the client approximately $20,000 after fees and costs are deducted). Your first demand to the defense should be somewhat higher than $80,750 (perhaps $90,000); your last demand cannot go below $35,000. This will be your negotiation range during the settlement meeting.

The defendant, of course, should be making the same kind of analysis. However, because the defendant will usually be paying legal fees on an hourly basis and can expect to pay additional legal fees of perhaps $20,000 and costs of perhaps $5,000 if the case is tried, this $25,000 must be *added* to the defendant's settlement analysis. For example, the defendant may have assessed the best possible outcome at zero dollars (a complete defense win at trial) and the worst possible outcome as a $30,000 verdict for plaintiff. This means that any settlement for less than $25,000 will still be financially attractive to the defendant because even winning the case at trial will cost the defense that much. The defendant should be willing to settle the case anywhere between $25,000 and $55,000, and the defendant's bottom line should be $55,000.

Since the plaintiff is willing to settle for between $80,750 and $35,000, and the defendant should be willing to settle for between $55,000 and $25,000, the parties should reach a settlement somewhere in the $35,000 to $55,000 range.

During the past few years, litigation support firms have developed decision tree models to determine the settlement values of cases at various stages of the litigation process. A decision tree, a commonly used tool in the business world, divides the litigation process into its component parts and analyzes the risks that exist at each stage of the process. While assigning probabilities to each component of the process may be difficult — for example, what is the probability that summary judgment on plaintiff's punitive damages claim will be granted, or what effect will a ruling limiting expert testimony have on the trial? — this method does force you to analyze every possible influence on the settlement value of a case. Decision tree analysis is particularly common in large and complex litigation, where lawyers understand the need for thorough, systematic settlement estimates.

Settlements happen when both sides undertake reasonably objective case evaluations, identify reasonably justifiable estimates of verdict ranges and expenses if the case goes to trial, and bargain reasonably to achieve a compromise.

j.   Evaluate the tax consequences of settlement[11]

Finally, you must know the potential tax consequences of a settlement. The beginning point is 26 U.S.C. §104(a)(2), which excludes from income any damages received, through suit or settlement, for "personal physical injuries or physical sickness."[12] For example, a settlement of a negligence claim based on a vehicle collision in which the plaintiff received physical injuries will be excludable from plaintiff's income, even though part of the damages may reflect lost income. Section 104(a)(2) also provides that punitive damages received are taxable income, and that compensatory damages for nonphysical personal injury cases, such as defamation and wrongful discharge, are also taxable income.[13]

To fit within §104's exclusionary provision, the plaintiff at the complaint-drafting stage should bring tort, not contract, claims and allege damages for personal physical injuries whenever possible. At the settlement stage, the settlement agreement should state that the settlement is for the plaintiff's personal physical injury claims whenever possible. The settlement agreement should characterize the settlement amounts as compensatory, not punitive, damages. However, keep in mind that while the characterization in the settlement agreement may help, it is not dispositive. The IRS may challenge the characterization later.

11. See Robert W. Wood, Taxation of Damage Awards and Settlement Payments (4th ed. 2009); Robert W. Woods, *Tax Deductions for Damage Payments: What, Me Worry?*, 110 Tax Notes 243 (Jan. 16, 2006).

12. A 2012 amendment to an I.R.S. implementing regulation provides that the injury resulting in damages does not have to be "defined as a tort under state or common law." 26 C.F.R. 1.104-1(c)(2).

13. See, e.g., Murphy v. I.R.S., 493 F.3rd 170 (D.C. Cir. 2007), where the D.C. Circuit reversed a prior decision and held that nonphysical personal injury damages for emotional distress and injury to professional reputation are not excludable from gross income.

A defendant should not have a tax reason to resist characterizing a settlement as excludable under §104, since whether the defendant can deduct the settlement on his tax return (as a business expense, for example) does not depend on how the plaintiff treats the settlement on his return. However, the defendant does benefit by having any possible settlement treated as excludable under §104. If both sides agree that the settlement will be nontaxable to the plaintiff, the ultimate amount should be lower.

The foregoing is only a preliminary introduction to the tax complexities that settlements pose. In some instances, fees paid to lawyers in contingency fee cases are included in the client's taxable income. In some instances they are not, but they may qualify as an itemized deduction.[14] The complexities multiply in commercial litigation involving diverse claims, such as business torts, contract, antitrust, bad faith, and punitive damages, and in structured settlement agreement situations. You should never enter into a settlement unless you have determined the likely tax consequences to your client. You may need to receive the advice of an experienced tax specialist.

k.   Marshal your facts

During the settlement negotiations, you will need to support your positions on liability and damages with facts. If you take a position without having credible facts to support them, you are merely posturing. Your pitch will have no impact on the other side. Hence, you need to organize the facts that you will use to justify your positions and be ready to present them persuasively during the settlement meeting. Always ask: What are the strongest points of my case, and how can I most effectively present them?

Your opponent will be doing the same thing. Therefore, you need to assess what your opponent's likely positions are on liability and damages issues, as well as the factual arguments he can draw upon to support his positions. You must be prepared to rebut these arguments with credible facts. Always ask: What are the strongest points of my opponent's case, and how can I most effectively defuse them?

Finally, you need to determine how much factual information you will disclose during the negotiations and what facts you will "save" for trial. For example, you may have impeachment information that will seriously erode the credibility of your opponent's key eyewitness, and your opponent may know nothing about it. It is always possible that your opponent is only attending the settlement conference to try to pump you for additional information that has not been disclosed during discovery, or to learn your likely strategy if the case goes to trial. During settlement negotiations, each side constantly tries to glean more information from the other side than it discloses. You need to decide whether you are better off disclosing such facts now (because they may push the other side toward more

---

14. See Comm'r v. Banks, 543 U.S. 426 (2005); I.R.C. §62(a)(20); Richard Mason, New Rules, New Ruling, J. of Accountancy, Nov. 2006.

favorable settlement terms) or withholding such facts (because disclosure will give the other side an opportunity to obtain refuting evidence).

Remember Model Rule 4.1, which provides that, "[i]n the course of representing a client a lawyer shall not knowingly: (a) make a false statement of material fact or law to a third person." The comment to this rule states: "This rule refers to statements of fact. Whether a particular statement should be regarded as one of fact can depend on the circumstances. Under generally accepted conventions in negotiation, certain types of statements ordinarily are not taken as statements of material fact. Estimates of price or value placed on the subject of a transaction and a party's intentions as to an acceptable settlement of a claim are ordinarily in this category."

2. Negotiating a settlement with opposing counsel

The dynamics of negotiation have received a good deal of scrutiny in recent years. This attention has occurred in part because rising litigation and trial costs have made settlement more desirable, and also because lawyers now know that they can learn negotiation methods and thereby improve results. The literature on negotiation for lawyers has expanded rapidly, with a number of particularly useful books.[15] This text can provide only an introduction to this literature and these methods.

Settlements enable lawyers to eliminate the inherent risk of going to trial. The more you can minimize the risks that trial poses, the stronger a position you can take going into negotiations with your adversary. To do so, you should adequately prepare the case for trial. The more you know about the case, the fewer the uncertainties and unknown factors, and hence the less risk. Also, you should realistically evaluate the case for settlement purposes. If your adversary is more uncertain and unprepared—and thus if your adversary perceives more risk with trial than you do—the more flexible and compromising her position is likely to be. Factors that increase uncertainty for your adversary include your own thorough preparation, your willingness and ability to go to trial if necessary, and your client's preparedness for trial.

What negotiating approach should you use? Although negotiation styles are as varied as lawyers are numerous, two basic approaches predominate. The first is competitive: The lawyer makes an initial high offer, keeps the pressure on the opponent, and makes as few concessions as possible. The atmosphere is entirely adversarial, and the lawyer projects an attitude of strength. This approach is perhaps the traditional way in which settlement negotiations were conducted and has certain benefits. Most obviously, any settlement reached will probably be a good one for the client with the more competitive lawyer. But probably a lower percentage of cases

15. E.g., Charles B. Craver, Skills and Values: Legal Negotiating (2009); Charles B. Craver, Effective Legal Negotiation and Settlement (5th ed. 2005); R. Fisher & W. Ury, Getting to Yes (2d ed. 1991); W. Ury, Getting Past No (1991); S. Krieger et al., Essential Lawyering Skills (1999).

settle when lawyers pursue this tack. Perhaps you should take a competitive approach when you have a strong case and do not need to compromise.

The other approach, which is increasingly prevalent, is cooperative: The lawyer emphasizes the parties' shared interests, shows a willingness to make concessions, and makes a more realistic initial offer. The atmosphere is conciliatory, and egos remain sidelined. This approach probably produces more settlements. But the settlement may not be as good for your client, especially if the other side tries to take advantage of your attitude. This approach may make sense when both parties are equally strong. The key to the cooperative approach is to avoid taking rigid positions. Instead, the lawyers at the negotiation focus on the mutual interests of their clients, avoid personalizing the conflicts, and accept an expanded range of possible solutions. By avoiding personalities and rigid posturing, the cooperative approach leads to a joint effort to reach solutions.

Your settlement strategy includes more than a negotiation style. You also need to determine where and when the meeting will be held, who will make the first settlement overture and first offer, who will make the first concession, and the order in which the issues will be discussed.

Decide where and when the settlement meeting will take place. (Serious negotiations are usually conducted face-to-face.) Most lawyers, of course, prefer to have the meeting in their own offices on the theory that they will have the "home court" advantage. The other side may insist on a neutral site. Some lawyers like to start first thing in the morning; others like to start later and run late. These are all details, but they are important and need to be worked out in advance. Most lawyers do not bring their clients to the meeting; the client's presence is usually not conducive to the give-and-take atmosphere that productive negotiation requires. However, the lawyers know where their clients can be reached during the meeting in the event that they need to communicate with them.

Decide whether you should make the first settlement overture and the first actual offer. Lawyers traditionally have been reluctant to initiate settlement discussions or to make the actual first offer on the theory that starting the process will be taken as a sign of weakness. Recent years have witnessed a change, and more lawyers recognize that starting the process does not convey weakness if the lawyer has prepared properly and has made a reasonable offer. The more important question is: Is this first offer realistic? If so, it will encourage the negotiation process. If not, the other side will summarily reject it and the process may end before it really gets going.

The initial offer should be higher (if plaintiff) or lower (if defendant) than that party's best result assessment. Allow for the possibility that the other side has assessed the case differently and is willing to settle on the basis of that first offer. More commonly, this initial offer gives you leeway during the negotiation process, particularly since the other side will expect you to be flexible. For example, plaintiffs in personal injury cases will frequently demand an amount that is perhaps twice what they expect to recover if the case were to go to trial. (At least defense lawyers commonly believe that the plaintiff's initial settlement demand is based such a calculation.) An offer of this sort obviously leaves substantial room for negotiation.

Decide on the first concession and whether you should make it. Like the first offer, lawyers have traditionally been reluctant to make the first concession on the ground that it signals weakness and an eagerness to settle. But lawyers now realize that the concession itself does not convey a weakness, so long as the lawyer making it insists that the other side reciprocate with its own concessions. A negotiation is not really a negotiation if only one side is willing to make concessions.

Decide on the order in which you plan to take up the various issues that need to be negotiated. Most lawyers prefer to tackle the smaller issues first, with the larger or more difficult issues left for later. The idea is that if the parties can resolve the small issues, groundwork is set for cooperation and compromise on the more difficult issues.

Settlement negotiation meetings follow a predictable course, particularly if both lawyers genuinely cooperate to reach a compromise acceptable to both sides. The meeting usually starts off with the sort of polite talk that breaks the ice and establishes an appropriate atmosphere. Next comes the information-exchanging stage, during which the parties try to learn the other side's concerns, needs, and interests. After that comes the position-taking stage. The parties state their own positions and make their offers, justify their positions with supporting facts, and challenge the other side's positions with contradictory facts. At this point bartering really begins, with mutual concessions triggering further compromises until the lawyers reach an agreement. Remember that most concessions are made either at the beginning (usually the small concessions) or near the end (usually the major concessions) of the negotiations, as each party realizes that her adversary is starting to resist further concessions and the alternative is to try the case. During this bartering process, you should watch the other side and listen closely for verbal and nonverbal cues that reveal the opponent's true position and attitude, just as you might in a poker game.

Put an agreement in writing and review the details of the agreement before the meeting ends to avoid misunderstandings. Always volunteer to draft the actual settlement. If the other side insists, be sure to review the agreement carefully and change any language that does not accurately and fairly reflect the deal.

Finally, if the parties are unable to reach an agreement at the settlement meeting, the negotiation has not necessarily failed. It may have paved the way for future discussions, or for mediation or arbitration. The last offers by each side may be the basis for a high-low agreement if the case goes to trial. You might have gleaned some insight into how the other side intends to present its case at trial.

3.   Negotiating at a settlement conference

Under Rule 16(a), the court can direct that a conference be held to facilitate a settlement. The court may order the parties or representatives with settlement authority to attend the conference or be available by telephone.

With consent of each side, the court may engage in ex parte communications with the parties and their lawyers.

Courts most commonly hold settlement conferences after discovery ends but before final trial preparations begin. Settlement conferences may be held in conjunction with the final pretrial conference contemplated by Rule 16(e). A common practice is for a judge who will not try the case to preside over the conference.

Settlement conference practices vary widely. Some judges actively promote settlement, while others are more passive. Some will meet with the lawyers only, and others will insist that the clients be present. Some will meet with all of the lawyers or parties, while others will meet with each lawyer and party on an ex parte basis. Still others use both types of meetings. Ex parte discussions can be important, particularly for parties involved in emotionally charged cases, because they give parties a chance to express their feelings to the judge. Settlement may be much easier once a party gets his feelings off his chest. Some judges will review the court file before the conference, focusing on the pleadings and the joint pretrial memorandum, while others rely on the lawyers to tell them what the case is all about at the conference. Some judges require the parties to submit confidential settlement memoranda or letters containing the parties' positions on liability and damages, an assessment of their strongest and weakest facts, a justification of their settlement demands and offers, a history of their settlement negotiations, and their predictions of a likely verdict range if the case is tried.

Because practices vary widely, you must know the general procedures in your jurisdiction, as well as the specific practice of your particular settlement judge. If you don't know, ask the judge's clerk or secretary, or talk to lawyers familiar with the judge. Be prepared for the unexpected. The judge may ask a lawyer to cut her fees to facilitate settlement. The judge may ask the lawyer what the lawyer's fee is, or what the party's settlement authority is. The judge may want to talk to the client outside his lawyer's presence. The judge may propose settling the case using baseball arbitration rules. The important thing to keep in mind is that anything can happen at a settlement conference. Your job as the lawyer is to learn what you can expect from the particular settlement judge and to prepare yourself and your client appropriately.

The judge has two principal concerns at the settlement conference. First, the judge wants to know what the likely outcome of this case will be if it were tried before a jury. Second, the judge wants to learn which party is prepared and eager to try the case. These two concerns will shape the judge's attitude and recommendations during the conference.

As plaintiff, you will usually have the first opportunity during the conference to tell the judge what the case is all about. Be an advocate and project a winning attitude. Show that you are eager to try the case, yet remain willing to be reasonable. Decide how you would present your case to a jury and how you would justify the amount you are asking for, then argue your side to the settlement judge. Consider starting with proof of damages; use exhibits to reinforce them. For example, summarize your out-of-pocket expenses with supporting exhibits. In a personal injury case, those expenses exhibits would usually include all medical bills, photographs of the plaintiff, and expert reports. The judge will get a sense of how "big" the case is and what proportion of the damages sought are concrete, out-of-pocket expenses, as opposed to intangible damages such as pain and suffering. Next, summarize your proof on liability, again using supporting exhibits, such as police reports, photographs, and diagrams. Some plaintiffs' lawyers use a settlement brochure that summarizes the key damages and liability information and supporting exhibits. As defendant, your job is to show that plaintiff's alleged damages are over-inflated and will not convince a jury, that liability is questionable, and that your offer to settle is therefore reasonable.

Each side usually will have only a few minutes to present its best points on damages and liability. Your presentation will essentially be like a short closing argument in a bench trial, factually based and shorn of emotional rhetoric. Expect the judge to question your positions. After all, the judge will likely see her role as showing that the plaintiff's demand is unrealistically high, while the defendant's offer is unrealistically low. If the judge can get the plaintiff to come down and the defendant to come up, a settlement may be possible. Hence, your role as an advocate is to convey to the judge that you are prepared, that your figures are realistic and supportable, and that you and your client are ready and eager to try the case if the other side is unreasonable. While the expectation at the conference is that both sides will be flexible, your aim is to get the judge to adopt your position as the more prudent, realistic one and then pressure the other side to accept it.

If the judge recommends that the case be settled for a certain amount, what should you do? Keep in mind that the decision to settle or go to trial is the client's. While you can, and should, advise the client whether the recommended settlement is reasonable, the client makes the final decision, and you must live with it. Be prepared for an unusual or creative settlement suggestion. For example, if the stumbling block in a medical malpractice case is the extent of future medical expenses, the judge might suggest settling for a given dollar amount coupled with a reservation of right to sue if a future medical contingency occurs.

Who should be the negotiator at the settlement conference? While traditionally the lawyer trying the case has also been the negotiator, in recent years lawyers have increasingly brought in a negotiating lawyer for settlement discussions. By bringing in someone other than the lawyer who has been managing the litigation, so the logic goes, the chances for a settlement improve. This approach is increasingly common in large commercial cases. If a settlement conference is part of the final pretrial conference, however, Rule 16(e) requires that the lawyer trying the case attend the conference.

Finally, be patient. Experienced judges and litigators know that settlements often take time. A settlement may not be reached during the first settlement conference. The key is to get the parties talking about settlement. Once the ice is broken, most cases seek their own pace, and most eventually settle.

4.   Client authorization

Before you begin negotiations on behalf of a client, you must have authority to settle. In almost all jurisdictions, an agreement to represent a client does not confer authority to settle. Therefore, the client must expressly authorize his lawyer to settle.[16] A client cannot give a valid consent unless he is fully informed of the terms of the proposed settlement, understands the terms and the reasons for them, and expressly consents to them.

Involve the client in the decision-making and discuss the pros and cons of settlement options. Keep the client well informed throughout the litigation and up to date on the status of the case. Schedule a meeting with the client to discuss the upcoming settlement possibilities, give him your best present assessment of the case, and explain what you believe would be a reasonable settlement and the reasons for your evaluation. Listen to the client's questions and candidly address his concerns. If the client agrees to settle the case on the terms you have negotiated, obtain his written authorization for the settlement. The best way to do so is to send the client a letter that recites the terms of the settlement proposal. She should sign and return a copy of the letter acknowledging and approving its terms. When time is short, authorization by phone will suffice, but follow up with a letter reciting the details of the authorization, as in the example below.

Example:

Dear Mr. Johnson:

As we discussed yesterday, the defendant's lawyer in your case asked us to consider the possibility of settling your case without a trial. I write to make sure you understand what a settlement entails and to obtain your permission to reach a settlement with the defendant.

Trials involve risks, and I cannot predict with certainty how your case will look to a jury and what verdict the jury will return. Nevertheless, based on the present state of your case, I believe that, if a jury were to find the defendant liable, it would return a verdict in the $30,000 to $40,000 range. I feel, however, that the jury is equally likely to find no liability at all. In addition, the expenses of going to trial will be somewhere in the range of $2,000, a figure that primarily includes the costs of having the medical experts testify. Finally, keep in mind that my fee for representing you in your case is one-third of any recovery.

The "value" of your case for settlement purposes, then, is approximately as follows: a potential verdict of $30,000 to $40,000, discounted by 50 percent to reflect the possibility the jury will find that no liability exists, and reduced by the $2,000 trial expenses. This comes to a total in the $13,000 to $18,000 range.

16. E.g., *Magallanes v. Illinois Bell Tel. Co.*, 535 F.3d 582, 584 (7th Cir. 2008); Model Rules of Professional Conduct, Rule 1.2(a).

Of course, by settling the case, you will avoid having to pay the trial expenses.

Based on these considerations, I recommend that you settle your case for not less than the sum of $15,000, which, after deducting my fee, would result in an actual recovery of $10,000 for you. Each side will pay its own court costs, which for us have been approximately $150 to this date. Yesterday you told me to go ahead and try to settle your case for not less than $15,000. Of course, I will try to get a higher settlement from the defendant.

If you still authorize me to settle your case for not less than $15,000, please sign and date the copy of this letter in the spaces provided and return it to me as soon as possible. I will keep you fully informed of the settlement negotiations as they progress.

Sincerely,

_____

John Lawyer

Authorized:

_____

William Johnson

Date: _____

When representing a defendant covered by liability insurance, remember that your client is the party, not the insurance company. While insurance contracts customarily permit the insurer to select defense counsel and control the conduct of the defense, clients may have the right to authorize any settlement.[17] In short, you must represent the best interests of the insured, and the insurer usually cannot settle a case against the insured's wishes. If this occurs, the client can usually have the settlement set aside, since under these circumstances it is not binding.[18] Finally, keep in mind that when you represent more than one client, you have a professional responsibility to each client when making an aggregate settlement.[19]

17. See §8.3.5(h) on insurer good faith requirements. See also ABA Section on Litigation, *Ethical Guidelines for Settlement Negotiations*, Aug. 2002, at §3.7.

18. This conflict between a client and the client's insurer is a complex area of law and must be researched thoroughly. See, e.g., Couch on Insurance §203:8-203:10 (Supp. 2013); Allan D. Windt, Insurance Claims and Disputes §5:4 (6th ed. 2013); R. Keeton, Basic Text on Insurance Law ch. 7 (1971); R. Keeton & A. Widiss, Insurance Law (1988).

19. See Model Rules of Professional Conduct, Rule 1.8(g), governing aggregate settlement of claims.

5.   Settlement agreements

Since settlements are simply agreements between parties, general contract law principles apply. Good practice and some local rules require that the agreement be in writing and signed by each party.

Settlements are generally made with a release, a covenant not to sue, or a loan receipt. You must understand the differences among the various settlement methods. The choice of method depends upon the types of claims and number of parties involved, whether the settlement is intended to be complete or partial, the type of court action or approval that may be necessary, and the applicable law of contribution. You must know the law of the jurisdiction that governs the settlement agreement; statutes and case law concerning releases, covenants not to sue, and loan receipts vary among jurisdictions. Also, the agreement's drafting is important, since you need to ensure that the agreement is treated under the applicable law in the way you intend it, and that it has the effect you desire. This clarity is all the more crucial in cases with joint tortfeasors, where issues of contribution among them may arise.

a.   Releases, covenants not to sue, and loan receipts

A basic common law release operates as a discharge of all claims against the parties to the release as well as against any persons against whom the same claims are or could have been asserted. In short, a release is a complete discharge, or satisfaction, of an action. For this reason parties should use a release only when the settlement resolves the entire lawsuit, involving every claim and every party.

A covenant not to sue does not discharge any parties. It is simply a contract between two or more parties pursuant to which the plaintiff agrees not to sue or to pursue an existing claim against one or more defendants. A covenant not to sue is used for partial settlements that do not involve every party. The need for covenants not to sue lies in history. Since under the common law a release was a discharge of all joint tortfeasors, a plaintiff could not use a release when he wished to settle tort claims with fewer than all defendants. The covenant not to sue solved this problem. Today the common law release no longer has this effect in jurisdictions that have adopted the Uniform Contribution Among Tortfeasors Act.[20] However, state law is not uniform. A simple covenant not to sue does not prevent a nonsettling defendant from later bringing a contribution claim against the settling defendant after a final judgment, unless a statute (like the Uniform Contribution Among Tortfeasors Act) in the applicable jurisdiction prevents this result. Therefore, it is critical that you know how your jurisdiction deals with the question of contribution.

A third kind of partial settlement, the "loan receipt," or a "Mary Carter agreement,"[21] is sometimes used to generate some contribution

20. Dan B. Dobbs et al., The Law of Torts §491 (2d ed. 2011).
21. E.g., La Costa Beach Club Resort Condo Ass'n, Inc. v. Carioti, 37 So.3d 303 (Fla. Dist. Ct. App. 2010).

among joint tortfeasors. Under this settlement approach, one defendant agrees to "loan" a certain amount to the plaintiff. The plaintiff "settles" with that defendant, but that defendant remains in the case with his exposure limited to the loan amount. The defendant has a chance of recovering the loan amount if the plaintiff gets a recovery greater than a stated amount from the other defendants. The loan receipt approach enables a defendant to settle for a given amount, which might be recouped after trial. The plaintiff for her part gets an early partial recovery and a cooperative defendant. The legality of this basic settlement technique has been upheld in most jurisdictions over public policy objections, but courts have also generally required that the existence and terms of a loan receipt be disclosed to the remaining defendants. They can use the loan receipt to show the bias and interest of a witness associated with the settling defendant who testifies at trial.[22] For this reason, the loan receipt method is less common.

Any number of variations on the basic loan receipt formula are possible. The choices are numerous and depend upon the extent to which the details of such arrangements are admissible at trial, and whether the jurisdiction's law of contribution among joint tortfeasors affects any particular agreement's structure. Jurisdictions vary widely on the validity and enforceability of the numerous variations of Mary Carter agreements. Obviously, you should never enter into a loan receipt agreement unless you are familiar with the particular jurisdiction's applicable law.

b.   Drafting the agreement

Regardless of which method for settlement you decide to use, you obviously must take care in drafting the agreement to ensure that you tailor it specifically to the case involved. First, the agreement should clearly state whether it is a release, covenant not to sue, or loan receipt, and state what matters it does and does not resolve. Second, the agreement should describe the events involved in the case, since the discharge will only cover these events. Third, the agreement should recite the claims of liability and damages and the defendant's denial of them, since the compromise of these disputed claims constitutes the mutual consideration in the agreement. If the case involves personal injuries, draft the agreement to help the plaintiff to minimize the extent to which the proceeds qualify as taxable income. Fourth, the agreement should specify how the pending court case is to be terminated. Fifth, the agreement can contain a choice of law clause and specify the details of any contribution in a covenant not to sue, if appropriate and permitted under the applicable jurisdiction's law. Finally, if the terms of the settlement are to remain confidential, the agreement must expressly provide for confidentiality.

---

22. See Monti v. Wenkert, 947 A.2d 261, 272-277 (Conn. 2008); Goodwin v. White, 342 S.W.3d 282 (Ky. Ct. App. 2011). For a case pronouncing Mary Carter agreements as void as against public policy, see Magill v. Watson, 409 S.W.3d 673, 678 (Tex. App. 2013).

The following are simple examples of a release and covenant not to sue. They should be modified to fit the facts of any particular situation and the particular law of the applicable jurisdiction.

Example:

<u>SETTLEMENT AGREEMENT AND RELEASE OF ALL CLAIMS</u>

In consideration of the sum of $ _____, which Plaintiff acknowledges receiving, Plaintiff_____agrees to release Defendants_____and_____ and their heirs, survivors, agents, and personal representatives from all claims, suits, or actions in any form or on any basis, because of anything that was done or not done at any time, on account of the following:

All claims for personal injuries, property damage, physical disabilities, medical expenses, lost income, and all other claims that have been or could be brought, including all claims now known or which are presently unknown but in the future might become known, which arise out of an occurrence on or about ____*(date)*____, at ____*(location)*____, when Plaintiff claims to have been injured as a result of a collision between an automobile driven by Plaintiff and automobiles driven by the Defendants.

As a result of this collision, Plaintiff has brought suit against the Defendants for damages. The Defendants have denied both liability and the claimed extent of damages. This release is a compromise settlement between Plaintiff _____ and Defendant _____ and Defendant _____.

Plaintiff and Defendants expressly agree that this agreement is not an admission of liability or fault, but that this agreement and payment are made as a compromise to settle all claims arising out of this occurrence. The parties declare that they have voluntarily entered into this agreement in good faith, have read and understand it, and consider it to be a fair and reasonable settlement.

This agreement, which is a contract and not a mere recital, is a release and shall operate as a total discharge of any claims Plaintiff has or may in the future have arising out of the above occurrence against these Defendants and any other persons.

Plaintiff_____ and Defendant_____ _____ and Defendant _____ also expressly agree to terminate any actions that have been filed, particularly a claim by this Plaintiff against these Defendants currently filed as civil action no. _____ in the United States District Court for the District of _____, in _____. Plaintiff and these Defendants agree to execute a Stipulation of Dismissal, with prejudice, and file it with the Clerk of the above Court, thereby terminating that action in its entirety, within seven days of the execution of this agreement. The Stipulation of Dismissal shall provide that each party shall bear its own costs, attorney's fees, and filing fees.

Date: _____

_____
Plaintiff

_____
Defendant

_____
Defendant

Example:

COVENANT NOT TO SUE

In consideration of the sum of $ _____, which Plaintiff acknowledges receiving, Plaintiff _____ agrees not to institute, pursue, or continue any claim, suit, or action in any form or on any basis, because of anything that was done or not done at any time, against Defendant _____ and his heirs, survivors, agents, or personal representatives on account of the following:

Any claims against Defendant _____ for personal injuries, property damage, physical disabilities, medical expenses, lost income, and any other claims that have been or could be brought, including all claims now known or which in the future might become known, which arise out of an occurrence on or about ____*(date)*___, at ___*(location)*___, when Plaintiff claims to have been injured as a result of a collision between an automobile driven by Plaintiff and an automobile driven by Defendant.

As a result of this collision, Plaintiff has brought suit against Defendant for damages. Defendant has denied both liability and the claimed extent of damages. This covenant not to sue is a compromise settlement between Plaintiff _____ and Defendant _____.

This agreement is a covenant not to sue, and not a release or an accord and satisfaction. Nothing in this agreement shall operate as a discharge against any other persons, and Plaintiff _____ expressly reserves the right to pursue any claims against any other persons other than Defendant _____ and his heirs, survivors, agents, and personal representatives.

Plaintiff _____ and Defendant _____ also expressly agree to terminate any actions between them, particularly a claim by Plaintiff against this

Defendant currently filed as civil action no. _____ in the United States District Court for the District of _____, in _____. Plaintiff and Defendant agree to execute a Stipulation of Dismissal, with prejudice, and file it with the Clerk of the above Court, to terminate that action against this Defendant only, within seven days of the execution of this agreement.

Date: _____   _____
                                                 Plaintiff

                                                 _____
                                                 Defendant

You must keep the following issues in mind when drafting a settlement agreement. First, the common law rule that a release terminates all of the plaintiff's claims against all existing and potential defendants may or may not have been changed by statute, depending upon the jurisdiction. As a plaintiff, never agree to a release unless you fully understand the legal effect on all present and future litigation. Second, if the common law rule *is* still in effect, a covenant not to sue technically keeps the claims alive against the settling defendant since the plaintiff only agrees not to enforce claims against that defendant. As a result, a settling defendant is still exposed to contribution claims by the other defendants who remain in the lawsuit. As a defendant, never agree to a covenant not to sue unless you have adequate protection against later contribution claims, either by statute or by the settlement agreement. Third, remember that contribution among joint tortfeasors is not the same thing as indemnification. Contribution does not affect valid indemnification claims against any parties. Fourth, many states by statute protect a settling joint tortfeasor defendant by providing that any judgment against the non-settling tortfeasor be reduced either by the amount the settling defendant paid the plaintiff or by the percentage of fault subsequently attributed to the settling tortfeasor in a lawsuit against the non-settling defendants. These statutes also typically discharge the settling defendant from any later contribution claims by non-settling defendants and other joint tortfeasors. However, not all states have such statutes, so the settling defendant must know the applicable jurisdiction's law to assess his exposure to later contribution claims. Fifth, the settlement agreement can usually specify what jurisdiction's law will apply to the agreement. Such a choice of law clause can then result in the application of more favorable law to contribution issues. Sixth, jurisdictions vary in how they define a defendant's pro rata share of any judgment against joint tortfeasors.[23] If the jurisdiction does not protect a

---

23. The share may be the amount of money paid by the settling tortfeasor or calculated on a per capita or percentage of responsibility basis.

settling defendant from contribution claims, the defendant should make sure that the settlement agreement adopts the applicable jurisdiction's definition of a pro rata share. The defendant should insist that it get a "credit" for either the amount paid to the plaintiff to settle or a pro rata share, however defined, of any ultimate judgment plaintiff gets, whichever is greater. Finally, if the lawsuit involves both contract and tort claims, make sure you know how much of the settlement amount will be allocated to each type of claim. Contribution exists only in tort, not contract. Shifting the allocation of the settlement amount between the contract and tort claims will affect the amount of contribution to which the non-settling defendants may be entitled.

Settlement drafting can obviously be complex, particularly in situations involving joint tortfeasors. In general, every plaintiff wants a guaranteed dollar amount from the settling defendant, wants to keep claims alive against the non-settling defendants, and wants no relief from contribution for the settling defendant. Every settling defendant, by contrast, wants to get out of the case with a guaranteed dollar amount to cap his exposure, and the defendant wants adequate protection from later contribution claims, if a statute does not already provide it. A careful lawyer must know the legal effect and validity of these settlement devices and the contribution law that applies to the tort claims. The lawyer must prepare a carefully drafted instrument that fits the particulars of the case so that the final agreement achieves what the lawyer needs in order to adequately protect his client.

Faced with other plaintiffs having the same or similar claims, most defendants will insist on confidentiality as a condition for settling the case. Historically, courts routinely approved settlements that included confidentiality agreements. However, in recent years some courts have rejected confidentiality agreements, particularly when the lawsuit is of substantial public interest. If a confidentiality clause is desired and permitted, the following offers an example of what a settlement agreement might include:

Example:

> The parties agree not to disclose to or discuss with any person, entity, or public news media, directly or indirectly, in whole or in part, the terms, conditions, content, or nature of this settlement agreement or settlement negotiations, including but not limited to the settlement amount or whether the settlement was favorable or unfavorable. The parties also agree that any documents, electronically stored information, or things obtained from or produced by the defendant during this lawsuit shall be considered confidential information and will not be disclosed to any person, entity, or public news media, directly or indirectly, in whole or in part.

Consider submitting the settlement agreement to the court and asking the court to incorporate the settlement agreement in the order terminating the case and retaining jurisdiction over the settlement. Once the court approves a settlement agreement signed by the parties and incorporates it into the final order, the parties can enforce the agreement through the court and seek the court's contempt power to punish any violations of the agreement.

c.   Structured settlements

Structured settlements are common, particularly in personal injury cases involving serious and permanent injuries. A structured settlement is simply a settlement under which the plaintiff receives periodic payments rather than one lump sum or a combination of such payments. The plaintiff is assured of support over a period of years. The defendant's insurance companies also benefit, since they can reduce the true cost of a settlement by paying over a number of years. Structured settlements also can help ensure that the plaintiff will not become indigent and depend on the state for support. Under 26 U.S.C. §104(a)(2), periodic payments receive the same tax treatment as lump sum payments when properly designated. Some states have legislation regulating them, often based on the Uniform Periodic Payment of Judgments Act. The complexities of statutory regulation and tax laws counsel in favor of advice from someone experienced with structured settlements when drafting one.

Structured settlements most frequently provide for an initial lump sum, followed by a series of periodic payments. The lump sum is large enough to cover the plaintiff's attorney's fee, other legal expenses, and the plaintiff's unpaid bills. The periodic payments continue for either a fixed period of years or the plaintiff's lifetime. The periods are either annual or for a shorter time. If the payments extend over a number of years, they may be tied to the inflation rate by providing for increases based on the Consumer Price Index or some other measure. The defendant's insurer usually funds the periodic payments by purchasing an annuity from an established life insurance company that will automatically make the payments required under the agreement.

Example:

SETTLEMENT AGREEMENT

Plaintiff _____ and Defendant _____ are parties to a civil action, Case No. _____, presently pending in the United States District Court for the District of _____.

Plaintiff and defendant wish to avoid the burdens and expenses that will be incurred in further prosecuting and defending this action, and wish to resolve and settle all disputes in this action. By entering into this settlement agreement neither party admits to any fault or liability.

In consideration of the cash payments, mutual releases, and other obligations contained in this contract, the sufficiency of which both parties acknowledge, plaintiff and defendant agree to the following:

1. Plaintiff fully releases and discharges the defendant from all liabilities, losses, costs, and expenses related to the subject matter of this action.

2. Plaintiff will dismiss with prejudice its complaint in this action within 7 days of the execution of this agreement. However, the United States District Court before which this action is pending shall retain jurisdiction over this action to enforce the terms of, and resolve any disputes that may arise under, this agreement. The parties agree that the stipulation of dismissal shall contain the provision that the court shall retain jurisdiction over this action for the purpose of enforcing the terms of, and resolving any disputes arising under, this agreement, and that the court's order of dismissal shall incorporate the terms of this settlement agreement.

3. Plaintiff and defendant will bear their own costs and attorney's fees arising out of this action and settlement agreement.

4. Defendant will pay plaintiff the total sum of $500,000, to be paid by cashier's checks payable to plaintiff, according to the following schedule:

a. $200,000 to be paid at the time this agreement is executed by the parties.

b. $30,000 to be paid each year for a total of 10 years, beginning in 2014 and ending in 2023. The first payment shall be made on or before June 1, 2014, and each successive yearly payment shall be made on or before June 1 of that year.

5. The parties agree that the payments described above shall be without interest, provided that the payments are timely made.

6. The parties agree that in the event the defendant fails to make payment of any of the above amounts on or before the required dates, the remainder of all the payments shall immediately become due and owing, and the plaintiff has the right to immediately apply to the United States District Court for a judgment for the entire amount that remains due and owing. The parties agree that interest on the amount due and owing will bear an annual interest rate of 10 percent from the date of the breach of this agreement.

7. If any action is commenced between the parties to this agreement to enforce any provisions of the agreement, the prevailing party shall be entitled to recover reasonable costs and expenses, including attorney's fees.

8. This agreement shall be governed and interpreted in accordance with the laws of the state of _____.

Date: _____   _____

Plaintiff

_____

Defendant

The tax implications of structured settlements to both parties can be complex, particularly when annuities or contracts through insurance companies will fund future payments. You should never enter into such a settlement unless you have determined the likely tax consequences for your client and have received the advice of an experienced tax specialist.

d.   *High-low agreements*[24]

A high-low agreement is a contract between the plaintiff and the defendant that establishes the maximum and minimum recovery to the plaintiff and thereby eliminates the risk of either a complete win or loss at trial. Litigants frequently use these agreements in personal injury cases that involve large potential damages and contested issues of liability, as well as in commercial cases that threaten the defendant with punitive or treble damages.

Consider a personal injury case in which the plaintiff seeks damages in the millions, and the defendant contests both liability and damages. The plaintiff's principal fear is that the jury may return a defense verdict on damages. The defendant's principal fear is that the jury may return a verdict in favor of the plaintiff on liability and award several million in damages. Accordingly, the parties agree that the case will proceed to trial, and that, regardless of the jury's verdict, the plaintiff will not receive more than $2,000,000 and not less than $500,000. The $2,000,000 becomes the "high" and the $500,000 becomes the "low" in the high-low agreement. The agreement eliminates the possibility of a catastrophic verdict for either side.

Lawyers negotiate high-low agreements much like settlement agreements, but they are usually made just before or during trial. This is so because, as the trial progresses, the parties have a greater sense of urgency in avoiding a disastrous result. Also, both sides have a mutual interest in reducing risk and achieving finality by avoiding an appeal. The parties' last demand and offer before settlement talks collapsed are a good starting point for a high-low agreement, although the trial's progress will affect these numbers.

When negotiating such an agreement, be sure to consider all that the agreement ought to address. For example, will the agreement bar post-trial motions and any appeal? Will it bar an appeal of the verdict amount but not other issues? What happens in the event of a mistrial, caused either by events during the trial or by the jury's inability to reach a verdict on all or some counts? Who pays costs, and what are the included costs? Does the agreement cover prejudgment and post-judgment interest? When should the judge be informed that an agreement exists, since the existence of the agreement may influence how the judge conducts the trial? Must the judge approve the agreement?

In most cases, the lawyers will advise the judge of the agreement and its terms at the end of the trial, when the jury is ready to deliberate, and put on the record the terms of the agreement. When the jury returns its verdict, the judge later enters judgment consistent with the terms of the agreement and the jury's verdict. The jury, of course, is not told about the agreement.

---

24. See, e.g., Michael L. Forte, Admissibility of High-Low Agreements in Multi-Defendant Litigation, 87 Fla. B.J. 26 (2013).

e.   Terminating the suit

After the parties agree to settle, the lawsuit must be terminated. The standard method is to file a stipulation to dismiss with the clerk of the court. Rule 41 provides that a court order is not necessary.

Make sure the stipulation to dismiss is with prejudice as to the settling defendant, since this bars the plaintiff from refiling the claim later. If the settlement is only partial, as is the case with a covenant not to sue, the stipulation must indicate clearly which party is being dismissed and which parties remain in the case. The lawyers for the parties who have agreed to settle sign the stipulation.

Example (complete dismissal):

[Caption]

STIPULATION OF DISMISSAL

Plaintiff _____, Defendant _____, and Defendant _____ agree to dismiss this action with prejudice, and each party will bear its costs and attorney's fees.

Date: _____

_____
Attorney for Plaintiff

_____
Attorney for Defendant

_____
Attorney for Defendant

Example (partial dismissal):

[Caption]

STIPULATION OF DISMISSAL

Plaintiff _____ and Defendant _____ agree to dismiss this action with prejudice as to Defendant _____ only, and the action shall continue as to the remaining Defendants.

Date: _____

_____
Attorney for Plaintiff

_____
Attorney for Defendant

A simple stipulation of dismissal will be adequate when the case will not be dismissed until the parties have actually implemented the settlement. For example, in a personal injury case the parties typically file the stipulation of dismissal after the plaintiff has received and cashed the settlement check. This timing ensures that the defendant will not breach the settlement agreement.

If the settlement agreement requires future performance, the plaintiff will want the court to retain jurisdiction for the purpose of enforcing its terms. Such situations include instances when a settlement agreement requires the other party to make future periodic payments, or when it contains a noncompete clause. Have the agreement expressly provide for the court's ongoing jurisdiction, and ask the court to enter an order of dismissal expressly retaining jurisdiction. A district court retains jurisdiction over the case after a dismissal with prejudice only if the order of dismissal refers to and incorporates the settlement agreement and expressly reserves the court's jurisdiction to enforce the settlement agreement.[25] A party that violates the settlement agreement also violates the court order, and the district court will have jurisdiction to enforce it.

When you want the court to retain jurisdiction, make sure the settlement agreement has an appropriate clause.

Example:

> The parties agree that the court shall retain jurisdiction over this case and the parties for the purpose of enforcing the terms of the settlement agreement. The parties further agree that this case will be terminated only through an order of dismissal that expressly incorporates the terms of this agreement and expressly retains the court's jurisdiction over the case and the parties.

You will then need to prepare a draft order incorporating the agreement and retaining the court's jurisdiction and submit it to the court for signature.

In certain types of cases court approval is needed for any settlement. Examples include settlements in class actions and settlements involving decedents' estates or incapacitated parties like minors and incompetents. Check local statutes and rules to ensure compliance with the often technical requirements that such settlements trigger. The usual procedure is to present a petition to the court having jurisdiction over the party, usually a probate or family court, and to serve notice on all parties and other interested persons. The court then conducts a hearing on the proposed settlement and, if it approves, issues an appropriate court order authorizing the settlement.

---

25. Kokkonen v. Guardian Life Insurance Company of America, 511 U.S. 375 (1994).

f.   Offers of judgment

Rule 68 provides that a party defending a claim can serve an offer of judgment upon the opposing party more than 14 days before the trial. The purpose of Rule 68 is to encourage settlements when a party has made a reasonable offer to settle. It is a formidable weapon. If the plaintiff rejects a defendant's offer of judgment, and if a judgment following trial is the same or less favorable to the plaintiff than the offer of judgment, the plaintiff is responsible for the costs the defendant incurred from the time of the offer.[26] A party can make an offer of judgment on any "claim," including the plaintiff's claims against the defendant, the defendant's counterclaims against the plaintiff, cross-claims between defendants, or third-party claims against third-party defendants. The defendant's offer to settle must be reasonably certain in amount and must be unconditional, but the offer does not need to itemize the settlement and cost amounts.[27]

The principal difficulty with Rule 68's application involves the meaning of the term "costs." Costs an offeree might have to bear include court fees, witness fees, and court reporter fees.[28] The relationship of "costs" to attorney's fees is more complicated. Sometimes defendants can use Rule 68 offers of judgment to prevent a plaintiff from taking advantage of a fee-shifting statute. Rule 68 does not say anything about the costs a plaintiff, as the offeree, can recover. By implication, however, it denies plaintiffs the ability to recover costs when they obtain results less favorable than the defendant's offer. In Marek v. Chesney, 473 U.S. 1 (1985), a 42 U.S.C. §1983 civil rights action, §1988 allowed attorney's fees to the prevailing party, but defined such fees as "costs." The plaintiff prevailed, but the result was not as favorable as the defendant's offer of judgment. Accordingly, the plaintiff could not recover any attorney's fees incurred from the date of the defendant's offer, which included the attorney's fees for the entire trial. When fee-shifting statutes do not define fees as costs, however, the prevailing plaintiff may still be able to recover its fees, the offer of judgment notwithstanding. On the flip side, courts have generally rejected the notion that the offering party can recover post-offer attorney's fees if the outcome is less favorable than the offer, unless an applicable fee-shifting statute defines fees as costs and provides for fee-shifting for the sorts of outcome that the offering party obtains.[29] If a fee-shifting statute defines "costs" as including "fees," for instance, but only allows the award of "costs" to a "prevailing party," a party that makes an offer of judgment cannot obtain attorney's fees from the responding party if the responding party wins at trial. This is so even if the responding party wins less in damages than what the offer of judgment would have provided.

Rule 68's usefulness to defendants depends largely on whether "costs" include attorney's fees. Where they include only court costs and the like, these amounts are likely to be sufficiently small in most cases that they will

---

26. Delta Air Lines v. August, 450 U.S. 346 (1981).
27. Marek v. Chesney, 473 U.S. 1 (1985).
28. See 28 U.S.C. §§1920 et seq.
29. Crossman v. Marcoccio, 806 F.2d 329 (1st Cir. 1986); Wright & Miller §3006.2.

not exert much pressure on the plaintiff to settle. Where costs include attorney's fees because a statute expressly so provides, Rule 68 affords substantial leverage against a plaintiff, who risks forgoing attorney's fees from the date of the offer. As a defendant, always make sure the offer of judgment specifies whether attorney's fees are part of the offer, since courts differ over whether an accepted offer bars a plaintiff from obtaining additional statutory attorney's fees.

A defendant who wishes to make an offer of judgment to the plaintiff must do so more than 14 days before trial begins. Make sure the offer is actually delivered to the plaintiff's attorney within the permissible time, and that the offer has a reasonable time limit. Do not file the offer in court at this time, lest it influence the trial judge.

Defendants usually make settlement offers under Rule 68 when settlement negotiations have broken down and trial looms on the horizon. However, the offer can be made at any time, and you should consider making it earlier if you can realistically assess the case's value. The offer can be made in a letter, sent by registered mail or hand delivered, or in a formal offer with an attached proof of service.

Example:

[Caption]

<u>OFFER OF JUDGMENT</u>

To: <u>*(attorney for plaintiff)*</u>

Defendant Johnson Corporation offers to allow judgment to be entered against it, in favor of plaintiff Frank Jones, in the amount of fourteen thousand ($14,000) dollars, and costs of suit incurred to the date of this offer.

This offer is made under Rule 68 of the Federal Rules of Civil Procedure and Rule 408 of the Federal Rules of Evidence, is made as a settlement offer, and is not to be taken as an admission of, or any indication of, liability on the part of this defendant.

This offer shall remain open for ten days after service of the offer.

Date: _____   _____
                                 Attorney for Defendant
                                 Johnson Corporation

If the plaintiff elects to accept the offer of judgment, he simply sends written notice to the defendant that he accepts the offer. The plaintiff must accept an offer within 14 days of its service. Otherwise, the offer is considered withdrawn. Judgment can be entered on the accepted offer.

g. Evidence rules

Under FRE 408, compromises and offers of compromise are not admissible to prove liability or damages. Federal Rule of Evidence 408's broad terms bar settlement discussions from being introduced at trial on those issues. The rule, however, does not prevent admission of such evidence for other purposes, principally to expose bias and interest of a testifying witness. A party who has settled and later becomes a witness at the trial of the same case can be cross-examined on the settlement.[30]

h. Insurer good faith requirements

A defendant will often have some insurance coverage. The insurance contract normally has language pursuant to which the insurer reserves the right to manage the defense and negotiate a settlement. However, courts have usually imposed a duty on the insurer to deal fairly and in good faith to protect the interests of the insured. This duty is important because the interests of the insurer sometimes conflict with the insured's. The insured naturally wants the company to stand behind her and defend vigorously or, if a settlement is contemplated, to settle within the policy limits. The insurer also has an interest in defending vigorously, but it has no financial interest at stake above the policy limit. Hence, the insurer's and insured's interests come most sharply in conflict where there is a risk of exposure over the policy limit. In such situations, only the insured has additional exposure. Also, the insured may have noneconomic concerns with settlement, such as worries about reputational harm and the like, while such concerns matter little to the insurer. Because of such conflicts, the insurer has a good faith obligation to defend the case fairly and to adequately protect the insured's interests. In other words, the insurer has a duty to defend and must conduct the defense in the best interests of the insured as though no policy limits existed.[31]

Any settlement offer from the plaintiff should be communicated to the insured, since the insured is the actual party. Case law is not uniform on whether failure to notify the party of a settlement offer is a breach of good faith, but some courts have so held.[32] Obviously, you should notify your client of every settlement offer, regardless of how unrealistic it is. Where a duty to defend in good faith has been breached, the insurer is generally liable for the entire judgment, regardless of policy limits.[33]

The message for defense lawyers should be clear. The defense lawyer's client is the insured, and the lawyer's professional and ethical obligation is to serve the best interests of the client. The fact that the insurance company selected and pays the lawyer does not alter her professional obligations. The lawyer should keep both the insured and insurer apprised of the

---

30. Weems v. Tyson Foods, Inc., 665 F.3d 958 (8th Cir. 2011).
31. See Couch on Insurance §§198, 200 (Supp. 2013).
32. See Stephen S. Ashley, Bad Faith Actions: Liability & Damages §3:9 (2d ed. 1997).
33. See Stephen S. Ashley, Bad Faith Actions: Liability & Damages §8:3 (2d ed. 1997).

progress of settlement negotiations. Whenever possible, the insured and insurer should both agree in writing to any settlement. Since the lawyer serves the client, not the insurer, the lawyer must accept a reasonable settlement, even when it involves the policy limits, if it best serves the client's interests. When exposure above the policy limits is involved and you, as lawyer, cannot get both the insured and the insurer to agree to a settlement, you must research the status of the law in your jurisdiction to determine what the rights, duties, and liabilities of the insured and the insurer are.

i. Enforcing settlements[34]

A party may sometimes breach a settlement, although such breaches are uncommon. Since a settlement agreement is a contract, the adversary can always enforce it in a separate contract action, but this is not the preferred method. Under Rule 60(b), the wronged party can move to enforce the judgment, provided that, as discussed above, the order of dismissal previously entered expressly retained the court's jurisdiction for purposes of enforcing the settlement agreement. The motion must be made in the same court, preferably before the same judge to whom the case had been assigned, and must cite a permissible reason for obtaining relief from a final judgment. You may need to have the case restored to the court's active calendar before you make the motion. At the hearing on the motion, be prepared to prove up the breach of the settlement agreement.

j. Settlement statement

When a plaintiff's lawyer has received a settlement check from a defendant or defendant's insurer in accordance with a settlement agreement, the check must be deposited in the client's trust account. If the lawyer is to be paid under a contingency fee agreement, she should then prepare a written statement describing the outcome, the amount to be remitted to the client, and how she calculated that amount.[35] This statement, commonly called a settlement statement or sheet, shows the gross amount received in settlement, costs, attorney's fees, and the net disbursement to the client. The client needs to approve the accounting. Once he does so, the funds are disbursed from the client's trust account in accordance with the statement.

---

34. Wright & Miller §§2857-2866.
35. See Model Rules of Professional Conduct, Rule 1.5(c). Such a statement is required in every contingency fee case, whether the case is concluded by settlement, trial, or other means.

Example:

<u>SETTLEMENT STATEMENT</u>

June 1, 2013

Settlement amount	$100,000.00
Costs (per attached itemized list)	$10,000.00
Net amount (settlement amount minus costs)	$90,000.00
Attorney's fees (33 1/3 percent of net amount)	$30,000.00
Net amount to client	$60,000.00

ACCEPTED AND APPROVED:

_____

[client's signature]

Date: _____

k.   *Liens on settlements*

Lawyers also need to deal with liens on settlements in many personal injury cases. For instance, a hospital may place a lien on a settlement, to make sure that the bills the plaintiff incurred after the accident get paid. Federal and state statutes and contract provisions create these liens. Common sources of liens include Medicare, Medicaid, ERISA, Veterans Administration, and worker's compensation statutes; health and casualty insurance policies; and statutes establishing liens for health care providers. Model Rule 1.15(d) imposes specific ethical obligations on lawyers when receiving settlement funds on which a lien exists.

Determine first whether statutory or contractual liens exist and what third parties are claiming them. Second, determine if the liens are valid — if, for example, the lienholder has complied with the applicable statute, if care was necessary because of the acts of the third party, if care was medically necessary, and if the cost of care was reasonable. If the liens are indeed valid, the plaintiff's lawyer must pay the lien amount at the time of settlement. For some liens, such as worker's compensation liens, you may need to get approval from the lienholder before you can finalize the settlement. The amount paid to each lienholder is treated like any other expense. You should list the amount on the settlement statement, deduct it from the next amount the client receives, and indicate that the money is remitted to the lienholder.

As the plaintiff's lawyer, keep the required lienholders advised of the progress of the litigation and try to negotiate the lien amounts before the time of settlement. If the client will receive a settlement that is less than the full value of his damages, you may be able to convince the lienholder to reduce its lien proportionately. Also, a dispute may arise between the lienholder and your client as to the amount claimed. For instance, an uninsured plaintiff may argue that a hospital should bill him at the rate it would bill an insurance company for his treatment, not at the higher rate the hospital typically charges uninsured patients. When such a dispute exists, try to negotiate a compromise with the lien-holder before settling with the defendant.

If you have reached a settlement with the defendant, but a dispute with a lienholder persists, you must set aside an amount sufficient to pay the valid lien from the settlement. Keep these funds in your trust account until the dispute is resolved.

When you represent a party with complex lien issues, you might need to consult with an experienced lawyer. The law regarding liens is constantly evolving.

l. *Close the client's file*

When the case settles and the representation of the client terminates, remember that Model Rule 1.16 places certain obligations on lawyers to return the contents of the closed file to the client. In general, the client owns the file. The file contents the client is entitled to receive include everything the client sent to the lawyer during the course of the representation: pleadings, discovery, motions, documents, records and other exhibits, expert and other investigative reports, transcripts, drafts of documents, legal research, correspondence, billing records, probably the lawyer's work product, and perhaps even the lawyer's "notes." Ethics opinions regarding the lawyer's work product and notes are jurisdiction-specific and in conflict.

Make a paper or electronic copy of everything you return to the client, and put the copy in your closed file. (Do not charge the client for the copying expense.) Return the contents of the file with a cover letter to the client that recites the contents of the returned file, states that your representation of the client has ended, and confirms that the attorney-client relationship is over. Doing so will protect you from former clients thinking that you remain their lawyer.

APPENDIX

LITIGATION FILE: JONES v. SMITH

This appendix is part of the litigation file in Jones v. Smith, an automobile collision case. It illustrates each basic step in the pleadings, discovery, motions, and settlement stages of the litigation process.

FACTS

John Jones, a 23-year-old delivery truck driver, was involved in a collision with Susan Smith. The collision occurred on September 2, 2013, at the intersection of 40th Street and Thomas Road in Phoenix, Arizona. Jones injured his stomach, neck, back, a shoulder, and an ankle, and he was out of work for a month. His car was also damaged.

Jones filed suit in federal court in Phoenix, Arizona, on January 2, 2014. He claims that Smith negligently ran a red light at the intersection and crashed into his car (he was not operating a delivery truck at the time). Jones is a citizen of Arizona, and Smith is a citizen of Nevada.

UNITED STATES DISTRICT COURT
FOR THE DISTRICT OF ARIZONA

The "Caption" includes the Court, the parties, and the case number.

John Jones,
      Plaintiff,
v.
Susan Smith,
      Defendant
	No._____
	
	Civil Action
	
	**JURY TRIAL
	DEMANDED**

The court clerk will stamp the case number when the complaint is filed with the clerk. The jury demand is usually put in the caption as well as at the end of the complaint.

COMPLAINT

Plaintiff John Jones complains of defendant Susan Smith as follows:

1. This Court has jurisdiction over this matter pursuant to 28 U.S.C. §1332 based on diversity of citizenship. Plaintiff is a citizen of the State of Nevada. Defendant is a citizen of the State of Arizona. The amount in controversy exceeds the sum of seventy-five thousand ($75,000) dollars, exclusive of interest and costs.

This is the standard jurisdictional allegation in diversity cases. It should be the first paragraph of the complaint.

2. On September 2, 2013, at approximately 2:00 P.M., plaintiff John Jones ("Jones") was driving a vehicle northbound on 40th Street toward the intersection of 40th Street and Thomas Road in Phoenix, Arizona. Defendant Susan Smith ("Smith") was driving a vehicle eastbound on Thomas Road toward the same intersection.

3. Smith failed to stop for a red light at the intersection of 40th Street and Thomas Road, and negligently drove her vehicle into Jones' vehicle.

The liability allegations should be clear and factual. This makes it more likely that they will be either admitted or denied outright, making the pleadings easier to understand.

4. As a direct and proximate result of Smith's negligence, Jones injured his stomach, neck, back, shoulder, ankle, and other bodily parts, received other physical injuries, suffered physical and mental pain and suffering, incurred medical expenses, lost income, and will incur further medical expenses and lost income in the future.

The damages allegations are usually spelled out in some detail.

WHEREFORE, plaintiff John Jones demands judgment against defendant Susan Smith for the sum of $100,000, with interest and costs.

Many complaints simply ask for "a sum in excess of $75,000," the jurisdictional limit.

Dated: <u>January 2, 2014</u>

<u>*Anne Johnson*</u>
Anne Johnson
Attorney for Plaintiff
100 Congress Street
Phoenix, AZ 85001
johnson@gmail.com
882-1000

A generic damages
demand avoids
requesting unrealistic
damages. The danger
of exaggerated
damages is that, unless
amended, the
pleadings can be read
to the jury at trial,
making the plaintiff
look greedy.

<u>PLAINTIFF DEMANDS TRIAL BY JURY</u>

Most jurisdictions also
require submitting a
jury demand form and
paying a jury demand
fee to preserve the
right to a jury trial.

UNITED STATES DISTRICT COURT
FOR THE DISTRICT OF ARIZONA

John Jones,
          Plaintiff,
     v.   No._____
Susan Smith,
          Defendant

SUMMONS

TO THE ABOVE-NAMED DEFENDANT:
Susan Smith
200 Palmer Way
Las Vegas, Nevada

A lawsuit has been filed against you.

Within 21 days after service of this summons on you (not counting the day you received it), you must serve on the plaintiff an answer to the attached complaint or a motion under Rule 12 of the Federal Rules of Civil Procedure. The answer or motion must be served on plaintiff's attorney, Ann Johnson, whose address is 100 Congress Street, Phoenix, AZ 85001.

If you fail to do so, judgment will be entered against you for the relief demanded in the complaint. You must also file your answer or motion with the court.

Dated: January 2, 2014

Thomas Barber
Clerk of the Court

[Seal of U.S. District Court]

A good practice is to give the person who serves the complaint and summons any additional information about the defendant that may help make an effective service.

In this case service is made under the Arizona long-arm statute. Service could also be made using the mail and waiver of service provisions of Rule 4.

The person making the service must prepare an Affidavit of Service showing how service on the defendant was actually made.

The Affidavit of Service form is frequently attached to the summons form.

UNITED STATES DISTRICT COURT
FOR THE DISTRICT OF ARIZONA

John Jones,
      Plaintiff,

   v.   No. 14 C 1000

Susan Smith,
      Defendant

ANSWER

Defendant Susan Smith answers the complaint as follows:

    1. Admit
    2. Admit
    3. Deny
    4. Defendant denies plaintiff was injured as a result of any negligence by the defendant. She is without knowledge or information sufficient to form a belief as to the truth of all other allegations in Par. 4, and therefore denies them.

> Simple responses are more likely to be made since the complaint's allegations are correspondingly simple.

First Defense

Plaintiff's claimed injuries and damages were caused by plaintiff's own negligence, which was the sole proximate cause of any injuries and damages plaintiff may have received.

> Each defense should be set out separately.

WHEREFORE, defendant requests that plaintiff receive nothing, and that judgment be entered for the defendant, including costs of this action.

Dated: January 15, 2014

William Sharp

William Sharp
Attorney for Defendant
100 Broadway
Phoenix, AZ 85001
sharp@gmail.com
881-1000

AFFIDAVIT OF SERVICE

I, Helen Thompson, having been first duly sworn, state that I served a copy of defendant's Answer on plaintiff by personally delivering it to Anne Johnson, attorney for plaintiff, at 100 Congress Street, Phoenix, Arizona, on January 15, 2014.

Helen Thompson
_____
Helen Thompson

Signed and sworn to before me on January 15, 2014.

Mary Ryan
_____
Notary Public

My commission expires on December 31, 2014.

[Seal]

After the complaint has been served, every other court paper must be served on every other party in accordance with Rule 5. The usual service is personal delivery, mailing to the party's attorney of record, or e-filing the paper through the court's electronic case filing system.

An affidavit or certification of service should always be attached to every court paper showing how proper service was made, unless local rules provide otherwise when filing is done electronically.

All court papers except discovery documents must be filed with the court either before service or within a reasonable time after service.

In practice, court papers are usually filed with the court clerk the same day service is made.

UNITED STATES DISTRICT COURT
FOR THE DISTRICT OF ARIZONA

John Jones,
            Plaintiff,
        v.   No. 14 C 1000
Susan Smith,
            Defendant

PLAINTIFF'S INITIAL DISCLOSURES

Plaintiff John Jones makes the following initial disclosures to the defendant, pursuant to Rule 26(a)(1) of the Federal Rules of Civil Procedure:

(A) Individuals

The following individuals are likely to have discoverable information that plaintiff may use to support his claims:

1. John Jones, plaintiff
2. Susan Smith, defendant
3. Carol Brown (eyewitness to collision)
    42 East Cambridge Street
    Phoenix, AZ
    482-3737
4. Mary Porter (eyewitness to collision)
    42 East Cambridge Street
    Phoenix, AZ
    482-3737
5. Off. Steven Pitcher (officer at scene of
        collision)
    Phoenix Police Dept.
6. Lenore L. Lang, M.D. (treating
        physician)
    333 East Campbell Avenue
    Phoenix, AZ 85016
    482-6000
7. Frank Hoffman, M.D. (treating
        physician)
    222 West Thomas Road, Suite 100
    Phoenix, AZ 85013
    222-4000

8. J. Franks, D.C. (physical therapist)
   55 North 27th Avenue
   Phoenix, AZ 85007
   881-9876
9. Diane Devo (plaintiff's employer)
   Devo Wholesale Florist
   3731 40th Street
   Phoenix, AZ 85007
   434-1000
10. John Jones, Sr., and Mary Jones
    (plaintiff's parents)
    1020 N. 50th Street
    Phoenix, AZ 85013
    332-8571

Witnesses #1-5 are occurrence witnesses; witnesses #6-10 are medical and damages witnesses.

(B) Documents, ESI, and tangible things

The following documents and tangible things, which are attached, are in plaintiff's possession, custody, and control and may be used to support plaintiff's claims:

1. Devo Wholesale Florist employment records
2. Doctors Hospital medical records
3. Dr. Lang office records and bill
4. Dr. Hoffman office records and bill
5. Dr. Frank office records and bill
6. Walgreen's Pharmacy bills
7. Phoenix Police Dept. accident reports
8. X-rays
9. Photographs of accident scene

(C) Damages computation

The following is the computation of each category of damages claimed by plaintiff:

1. *Medical and related expenses:*
   Doctors Hospital bill $1,257.18
   Dr. Lang bill   339.70
   Dr. Hoffman bill   340.00
   Dr. Franks bill   697.80
   Walgreen's Pharmacy bills   83.13

2. *Lost wages:*
   Devo Wholesale Florist   700.00
3. Property damages:
   Toyota vehicle repair   1,213.00
4. *Other expenses:*
   Broken wristwatch   75.00
   College books   162.00
5. *Pain and suffering:*
   Past   over 40,000.00
   Future   over 30,000.00

The documentation of these damages is contained in the documents identified in section (B) above.

(D) Insurance

Rule 26(a)(1)(A)(iii) does not apply to the plaintiff since defendant has filed no counter-claims in this action.

Dated: January 20, 2014

Anne Johnson

Anne Johnson
Attorney for Plaintiff
100 Congress Street
Phoenix, AZ 85001
johnson@gmail.com
882-1000

UNITED STATES DISTRICT COURT
FOR THE DISTRICT OF ARIZONA

John Jones,
           Plaintiff,
           v.   No. 14 C 1000
Susan Smith,
           Defendant

DEFENDANT'S INTERROGATORIES TO PLAINTIFF

Pursuant to Rule 33 of the Federal Rules of Civil Procedure, defendant Smith requests that plaintiff Jones answer the following interrogatories under oath, and serve them on the defendant within 30 days:

1. Describe the personal injuries you received as a result of the occurrence described in the complaint (hereafter "this occurrence").

2. State the full names and present addresses of any physicians, osteopaths, chiropractors, and other medical personnel who treated you as a result of this occurrence, each such person's areas of specialty, the dates of each examination, consultation or appointment, the amount of each such person's bill, and whether each bill has been paid.

3. Were you confined to a hospital or clinic as a result of this occurrence? If so, state the name and address of each such hospital or clinic, the dates of your confinement at each facility, the amount of each such facility's bills, and whether each bill has been paid.

4. Have you incurred other medical expenses, other than these requested in Interrogatory Nos. 2 and 3, as a result of this occurrence? If so, state each expense incurred, the nature of each expense, when the expense was incurred, to whom it was incurred, and whether each expense has been paid.

5. Have you incurred any expenses as a result of this occurrence other than medical expenses? If so, state the nature of each expense,

Interrogatories will usually be the first discovery device the parties serve on each other.

In this example, the defendant served interrogatories on plaintiff two weeks after answering the complaint.

Note how each interrogatory deals with a separate, defined category and asks for all relevant data for the category. This approach will usually generate more complete answers. It also gives the answering party the opportunity of answering the interrogatory by producing the relevant records that contain the answers.

the date incurred, the amount of each expense, the reason for incurring each expense, and whether each expense has been paid.

6. Were you unable to work as a result of this occurrence? If so, state the dates during which you were unable to work, each employer during these dates, the type of work you were unable to do, and the amount of lost wages or income from each employer.

7. Have you recovered from the claimed injuries that resulted from this occurrence? If not, state the claimed injuries from which you have not recovered and any present disability.

8. During the 10 years preceding September 2, 2013, have you suffered any other personal injuries? If so, state when, where, and how you were injured and the name and address of each medical facility where, and physicians by whom, you were treated for these injuries.

9. During the 10 years preceding September 2, 2013, have you been hospitalized, treated, examined, or tested at any hospital, clinic, physician's office, or other medical facility for any conditions other than those requested in Interrogatory No. 8? If so, state the name and address of each such medical facility and physician and the dates of such services and the medical conditions involved.

10. State the full name and address of each person who witnessed, or claims to have witnessed, the collision between the vehicles involved in this occurrence.

11. State the full name and address of each person who has any knowledge of the facts of the collision other than those persons already identified in Interrogatory No. 10.

12. Describe your vehicle involved in this occurrence, any damages to your vehicle as a result of this occurrence, the name and address of any firm repairing your vehicle, the amount billed for repairs, when such repairs took place, and whether the repair bills have been paid. If your vehicle has not been repaired, state where it is presently located and its condition.

13. Identify, by date, description, and source, any medical records and any other records or documents of any kind in your or your attorney's possession or control that relate in any way to this occurrence and the injuries

The plaintiff's current condition and medical history are important areas that should be explored thoroughly. This can then be verified during the plaintiff's deposition.

Occurrence witnesses are obviously important in this kind of case. It's a good practice to break them up by category in appropriate cases.

Medical records are obviously critical in this kind of case. The descriptions you get will be used to send production requests to the plaintiff and subpoenas to third-party sources.

and damages you claim resulted from this occurrence.

Dated: February 1, 2014

William Sharp

William Sharp
Attorney for Defendant
100 Broadway
Phoenix, AZ 85001
881-1000

A proof of service must
be attached.

UNITED STATES DISTRICT COURT
FOR THE DISTRICT OF ARIZONA

John Jones,
             Plaintiff,
    v.   No. 14 C 1000
Susan Smith,
             Defendant

PLAINTIFF'S ANSWERS TO
INTERROGATORIES

Plaintiff John Jones answers Defendant's interrogatories as follows:

Interrogatory No. 1: Describe the personal injuries you received as a result of the occurrence described in the complaint (hereafter "this occurrence").

The usual way of answering interrogatories is to set out the questions and the answers, making it easy to correlate the two.

Answer: Cervical, dorsal and lumbar sprain and strain; cerebral concussion; multiple contraction headaches and concussion headaches; left hemiparesis with ataxia; ankle sprain; numbness; multiple contusions and abrasions.

Interrogatory No. 2: State in full the names and present addresses of any physicians, osteopaths, chiropractors, nurses, or other medical personnel who treated you as a result of this occurrence, each such person's areas of specialty, the dates of each examination, consultation, or appointment, the amount of each such person's bill, and whether each bill has been paid.

Answer:
Doctors Hospital
1947 East Thomas Road
Phoenix, Arizona 85016

Lenore L. Lang, M.D.
333 East Campbell Avenue
Phoenix, Arizona 85016

Frank Hoffman, M.D.
222 West Thomas Road
Suite 100
Phoenix, Arizona 85013

J. Franks, D.C.
55 North 27th Avenue
Phoenix, Arizona 85007

(See answer to interrogatory no. 4; answer may be supplemented as discovery and investigation continues.)

Interrogatory No. 3: Were you confined to a hospital or clinic as a result of this occurrence? If so, state the name and address of the hospital or clinic, the dates of your confinement at each facility, the amount of each facility's bills, and whether each bill has been paid.

Answer: No; treated, but not confined, at Doctors Hospital.

Interrogatory No. 4: Have you incurred other medical expenses, other than those requested in Interrogatory Nos. 2 and 3, as a result of this occurrence? If so, state each expense incurred, the nature of each expense, when the expense was incurred, to whom it was incurred, and whether each expense has been paid.

Answer:
Doctors Hospital	$1,257.18
Lenore L. Lang, M.D.	339.70
Frank Hoffman, M.D.	340.00
J. Franks, D.C.	697.80
Walgreen's Pharmacy	83.13

These bills have been paid.

(Answer may be supplemented as discovery and investigation continues.)

Interrogatory No. 5: Have you incurred any expenses as a result of this occurrence, other than medical expenses? If so, state the nature of each expense, the date incurred, the amount of each expense, the reason for incurring each expense, and whether each expense has been paid.

Answer:
Broken wristwatch	$ 75.00
College books	162.00

Wristwatch repair bill has been paid.

Here the plaintiff has prepared partial answers and acknowledges that further information will generate supplemental answers later. However, these partial answers were prepared within the 30-day requirement of Rule 33.

Interrogatory No. 6: Were you unable to work as a result of this occurrence? If so, state the dates during which you were unable to work, each employer during these dates, the type of work you were unable to do, and the amount of lost wages or income from each employer.

Answer: Yes, September 2, 2013, to October 1, 2013. Devo Wholesale Florist. Delivery truck driver. $700—one month's salary.

This is a typical interrogatory answer. It provides all the facts requested, does so efficiently, and does not volunteer anything not asked for.

Interrogatory No. 7: Have you recovered from the claimed injuries that resulted from this occurrence? If not, state the claimed injuries from which you have not recovered and any present disability.

Answer: Plaintiff still experiences headaches, neck pain, and lower back pain.

Interrogatory No. 8: During the 10 years preceding September 2, 2013, have you suffered any other personal injuries? If so, state when, where, and how you were injured, and the name and address of each medical facility where, and physicians by whom, you were treated for these injuries.

Answer: No.

Interrogatory No. 9: During the 10 years preceding September 2, 2013, have you been hospitalized, treated, examined, or tested at any hospital, clinic, physician's office or other medical facility for any conditions other than those requested in Interrogatory No. 8? If so, state the name and address of each such medical facility and physician, the dates of such services, and the medical conditions involved.

Answer: No.

Interrogatory No. 10: State the full name and address of each person who witnessed, or claims to have witnessed, the collision between the vehicles involved in this occurrence.

Answer:
John Jones, plaintiff
Susan Smith, defendant
Carol Brown, 42 East Cambridge Street,
  Phoenix, AZ

Mary Porter, 42 East Cambridge Street,
 Phoenix, AZ
Officer Steven Pitcher, Phoenix Police
 Department

(Answer may be supplemented as discovery and
investigation continues.)

Witness lists must
frequently be
supplemented over
time, since the
ongoing investigation
will often uncover
additional witnesses.

Interrogatory No. 11: State the full name and
address of each person who has any knowledge
of the facts of the collision, other than persons
already identified in Interrogatory No. 10.

Answer: See persons listed in answer to
Interrogatory No. 4; John Jones, Sr., and Mary
Jones, plaintiff's parents; Diane Devo, plaintiff's
employer.

(Answer may be supplemented as discovery and
investigation continues.)

Interrogatory No. 12: Describe your vehicle that
was involved in this occurrence, any damage to
your vehicle as a result of this occurrence, the
name and address of any firm repairing your
vehicle, the amount billed for repairs, when
such repairs took place, and whether the repair
bills have been paid. If your vehicle has not been
repaired, state where it is presently located and
its condition.

Answer: 2006 Toyota Corolla four-door sedan.
Extensive damage to left and front side of
car. Jack's Auto Repair, 2000 East Valley Road,
Phoenix. $1,213. Repair, completed about
September 30, 2013. Repair bill has been paid.

This is another typical
answer. It provides the
facts called for, yet
does not volunteer
anything.

Interrogatory No. 13: Identify, by date, description, and source, any medical records, and any
other records or documents of any kind in your
or your attorney's possession or control, that
relate in any way to this occurrence and injuries
and damages you claim resulted from this
occurrence.

Answer: Employment records of Devo Whole-
sale Florist
Doctors Hospital records
Dr. Lang's office records

Dr. Hoffman's office records
Dr. Franks' office records
Medical bills
X-rays taken by the above health care providers
Phoenix Police Department Accident Report
Photographs of the scene of the accident

(Answer may be supplemented as discovery and
investigation proceeds.)

Dated: February 25, 2014

John Jones
—————————————————
John Jones

State of Arizona
County of Maricopa | SS.

I, John Jones, being first duly sworn, state that:

I am the plaintiff in this case. I have made the foregoing Answers to Interrogatories and know the answers to be true to the best of my knowledge, information and belief.

The party making the interrogatory answers must sign them under oath.

John Jones
John Jones

Subscribed and sworn to before me this 25th day of February 2014, by John Jones, Plaintiff.

Mary Ryan
Mary Ryan, Notary Public

Like any court papers, the answers must be served on every party. A proof of service, showing how service was made, must be attached to the answer.

My commission expires on
    December 31, 2014.

[Seal]

UNITED STATES DISTRICT COURT
FOR THE DISTRICT OF ARIZONA

John Jones,
      Plaintiff,
    v.   No. 14 C 1000
Susan Smith,
      Defendant

REQUEST FOR PRODUCTION OF DOCUMENTS

Pursuant to Rule 34 of the Federal Rules of Civil Procedure, defendant requests that plaintiff produce within 30 days, in the law offices of William Sharp, 100 Broadway, Phoenix, AZ 85001, the following documents and electronically stored information for inspection and copying:

1. All medical reports, records, charts, X-ray reports, and all other records regarding any medical examinations and treatment received by plaintiff for the injuries claimed in the complaint. If any such reports, etc., exist in electronic form, those records are to be produced in the native format in which the reports, etc., were created and stored.

2. All U.S. Income Tax Returns filed by plaintiff for the years 2008 through 2013.

Dated: February 1, 2014

William Sharp

William Sharp
Attorney for Defendant
100 Broadway
Phoenix, AZ 85001
sharp@gmail.com
881-1000

Note that the defendant served this document request at the same time as the interrogatories.

Document requests usually depend on interrogatory answers to identify the relevant documents. Here, however, what the defendant wants is both simple and obvious, so the defendant decides to serve the requests with interrogatories.

A proof of service must be attached.

UNITED STATES DISTRICT COURT
FOR THE DISTRICT OF ARIZONA

John Jones,
         Plaintiff,
    v.   No. 14 C 1000
Susan Smith,
         Defendant

PLAINTIFF'S RESPONSE TO REQUEST FOR PRODUCTION OF DOCUMENTS

Plaintiff responds to defendant's Request for Production of Documents as follows:

1. Plaintiff will produce copies of all reports in plaintiff's possession regarding medical examinations and treatment of plaintiff for his injuries. These copies will be delivered to defendant's attorney on or before March 1, 2014.

2. Plaintiff herewith produces his U.S. Income Tax Returns for the years 2008 through 2012. The return for 2013 has not yet been prepared.

Dated: February 25, 2014

Anne Johnson

Anne Johnson
Attorney for Plaintiff
100 Congress Street
Phoenix, AZ 85001
johnson@gmail.com
882-1000

A response to a production request should be filed so there is a court record that shows how and when the request was complied with. If photocopying will be expensive, the requesting party will usually have to pay for the photocopying charges.

A proof of service must be attached.

UNITED STATES DISTRICT COURT
FOR THE DISTRICT OF ARIZONA

John Jones,
       Plaintiff,

    v.

Susan Smith,
       Defendant

No. 14 C 1000

SUBPOENA DUCES TECUM

TO: Diane Devo, President
       Devo Wholesale Florist
       3731 40th Street
       Phoenix, AZ 85010

YOU ARE HEREBY COMMANDED to appear and give testimony under oath at the law office of William Sharp, 100 Broadway, Phoenix, AZ 85001 on March 15, 2014, at 10:00 A.M. You are also commanded to bring the following:

    All records relating to the employment of John Jones at Devo Wholesale Florist, from the first day of employment through the present date, including but not limited to records showing wages received, hours worked, and the condition of John Jones' health.

Dated: <u>March 1, 2014</u>

[Seal]

Thomas Barber
<hr>
Clerk of the Court

A deposition subpoena that also requires the witness to bring specified records can be used to obtain records from nonparty witnesses. Under Rules 34(c) and 45, the records alone can be subpoenaed.

Make sure that you serve a Notice of Deposition on every other party, because other parties always have a right to attend any deposition and question the deponent.

UNITED STATES DISTRICT COURT
FOR THE DISTRICT OF ARIZONA

John Jones,
             Plaintiff,
        v.   No. 14 C 1000
Susan Smith,
             Defendant

NOTICE OF DEPOSITION

TO: PLAINTIFF JOHN JONES

Please take notice that the undersigned will take the deposition of John Jones, Plaintiff, on March 15, 2014, at 2:00 P.M. at 100 Broadway, Phoenix, AZ 85001. You are hereby notified that the plaintiff is to appear at that time and place of case and submit to a deposition under oath.

A subpoena is not necessary since the deponent is a party.

Dated: March 1, 2014

William Sharp

William Sharp
Attorney for Defendant
100 Broadway
Phoenix, AZ 85001
sharp@gmail.com
881-1000

Two weeks' notice is appropriate in this type of case.

The deposition will be recorded stenographically and by videotape.

A proof of service must be attached.

UNITED STATES DISTRICT COURT
FOR THE DISTRICT OF ARIZONA

John Jones,
            Plaintiff,
            v.   No. 14 C 1000
Susan Smith,
            Defendant

DEPOSITION OF JOHN JONES

DEPOSITION OF John Jones, taken at 2:13 P.M. on March 15, 2014, at the law offices of William Sharp, at 100 Broadway, Phoenix, AZ 85001, before Mary Ryan, a Notary Public in Maricopa County, Arizona.

Appearance for the plaintiff:

Anne Johnson
100 Congress Street
Phoenix, AZ 85001

Appearance for the defendant:

William Sharp
100 Broadway
Phoenix, AZ 85001

JOHN JONES

Called as a witness, having been first duly sworn, was examined and testified as follows:

EXAMINATION BY MR. SHARP:

Q. This is the deposition of the plaintiff, John Jones, being taken in the case of John Jones v. Susan Smith, Case No. 14 C 1000 in the United States District Court for the District of Arizona. It is being held at the law office of William Sharp, 100 Broadway, Phoenix, Arizona 85001. Today's date is March 15, 2014. Present in addition to Mr. Jones are myself, William Sharp, attorney for defendant

This is a standard introductory statement.

Under Rule 30(b)(5), the court reporter now makes this introductory statement.

Smith, Anne Johnson, attorney for plaintiff Jones, and Mary Ryan, a certified court reporter and notary public. Mr. Jones, you were just sworn to tell the truth by the court reporter, correct?

A. That's right.

Q. It's important that you understand the questions and give accurate answers. If there's anything you don't understand, or anything you don't know or aren't sure of, you let us know, all right?

A. Yes.

Q. Please tell us your full name.

A. John J. Jones.

Q. How old are you?

A. I'm 23.

Q. Are you married or single?

A. Single.

Q. Where do you live?

A. 1020 North 50th Street, Phoenix, Arizona.

Q. How far did you go in school?

A. I graduated from high school — Central High, 2008.

Q. What did you do after high school?

A. I joined the army.

Q. Tell us about your army experience.

A. After basic training, I was sent to an infantry division, and did most of my three years in Germany. I was a corporal when I received my honorable discharge. That was in August 2011.

Q. What did you do after that?

A. I came back to Phoenix, moved into my parents' house, and started working for Devo Wholesale Florist.

Q. Where is that located?

A. It's at 3731 40th Street, Phoenix.

Q. What kind of work do you do there?

A. I started as a sales clerk, then I became a driver on one of their trucks.

Q. What do you do as a driver?

A. I deliver flowers from the store to customers in the Phoenix area.

Q. What were your hours in August and September 2013?

A. It varied, but it was usually 6:00 A.M. to 2:00 P.M.

a. Personal background
Note the form of the questions and the tone of the examination. The principal purposes of this deposition are to acquire information and assess the plaintiff as a trial witness. Accordingly, the questions are usually open-ended, designed to elicit information and have the plaintiff do the talking. The questions are asked in a pleasant, friendly way.

b. Work experience

Q. Were those your hours the day of the accident?

A. Yes.

Q. Other than your job for Devo Florist, did you have any other jobs or activities in September 2013?

A. I didn't have any other job. I was a part-time student at Glendale Community College.

Q. Mr. Jones, were you ever involved in an automobile accident before September 2, 2013?

A. No.

Q. Did you ever have personal injuries of any kind before September 2, 2013?

A. No.

Q. During the past 10 years, other than for this accident, did you ever see a physician for any reason?

A. Well, our family doctor is Dr. Hoffman. I would see him from time to time for checkups, shots, and things like that. But I never had any serious injury or illness that I went to Dr. Hoffman for.

Q. Mr. Jones, tell me each injury you feel you've received as a result of the accident on September 2.

A. Okay. I hurt the left side of my neck, my lower back, my left ankle, my left shoulder, and my stomach.

Q. Let's start out with the left side of your neck. What injuries did you receive there?

A. I think I whipped my head to the side when the car crashed into me and I strained my neck. I had these shooting pains in my neck whenever I tried to move it.

Q. How long did that pain continue?

A. Well it was pretty severe about a week, and then it started getting better. I still get pains there from time to time.

Q. Tell me about the injuries to your lower back.

A. Well, that was sort of the same thing. I must have wrenched my back from the force of the collision. Just like my neck, it was stiff and hurt for a while. After about a week it started getting better, and today I only get the pain from time to time, especially toward the end of the work day.

c. Accident and health history must be explored, since preexisting injuries would affect the damages pictures.

d. Each claimed injury should be explored in detail.

The "tell me" form of questions are used to get the witness to disclose everything.

If the plaintiff at trial tries to claim additional injuries, he can hardly say he didn't mention all his injuries during the deposition because the lawyer didn't give him a chance to do so.

Since pain and suffering will probably be the largest single element of damages, these questions are important to "pin down" the witness and prevent later exaggeration at trial.

Q. Tell me about your left ankle.

A. I sprained my ankle during the accident. That was probably the worst injury. I had to stay off my feet for about two weeks, and I really couldn't start walking on it for three or four weeks. That's the injury that kept me out of work for a month.

Q. When did your ankle start getting better?

A. About a month after this happened it was well enough so I could start working, although I was still limping for quite a while. It probably took about four months before the ankle healed up completely.

Q. Tell me about the injury to your left shoulder.

A. I got some cuts and scratches and bruises on my left shoulder when I crashed into the dashboard of the car. That hurt for maybe two weeks, and then went away.

Q. Finally, tell me about the injuries to your stomach.

A. I guess I injured my stomach when I smashed against the steering wheel. It was just painful inside of my stomach. That went away after a few days.

Q. Other than these injuries to your neck, lower back, ankle, shoulder, and stomach, did you receive any other injuries?

A. Oh yeah. I received a concussion on the left side of my head. That's what the doctor told me.

The "any other injuries" question is always useful. Again, it prevents later exaggeration.

Q. Mr. Jones, let's talk about the medical treatment you received for these injuries following the accident. First, how did you get to Doctors Hospital?

A. An ambulance came to the intersection and they put me on a stretcher and drove me to the hospital.

e.   Medical treatment

Q. What happened when you arrived at Doctors Hospital?

A. The ambulance attendants took me into the emergency room, and some nurses checked me over, took my pulse and blood pressure, and stuff like that. After a while one of their doctors examined me. I think her name was Dr. Lang. I told Dr. Lang where I hurt and about the accident.

Note how this deposition is organized chronologically (with the exception of the accident itself). This is usually the best way to organize the questions, unless you have a specific reason for doing it another way.

Q. What kind of treatment did you receive at the hospital?

A. Well, they examined me, x-rayed, cleaned up some of the cuts on my shoulder and chest, and put my ankle in a cast. It wasn't one of those big plaster casts, it was a cast that went around the back of my ankle and foot and was surrounded with an elastic bandage. I must have been there a couple of hours, and by that time my parents had come to the hospital, and they took me home.

Q. Did you receive any medication prescription?

A. The doctor gave a prescription for Tylenol with codeine, which my mother picked up at the drug store. The doctor told me to follow instructions on the bottle and take the medication if I needed it for the pain.

Q. Mr. Jones, tell us about the month you spent before you went back to work.

A. Well, the first week I pretty much spent in bed. Sometimes I got up and lay on the couch and watched TV. At that time everything was aching, my neck hurt, my head hurt, my stomach hurt, my ankle was swollen up. I spent all my time with my foot up to keep the swelling down, and I was taking the medicine to keep the pain down.

f. Recovery period

Q. How long was it before you were able to move around the house?

A. I'd say the first week or 10 days I pretty much spent on my back. After that period of time the pain in my head, shoulder and stomach started going away, and the swelling in my ankle was starting to go down. I got a pair of crutches and started moving around the house a little bit. I couldn't stay on my feet very long before the foot would swell up if I stood up for any length of time.

Q. At the end of September 2013, what was your physical condition like?

A. The scratches and bruises had gone away. The pains in my neck, shoulder, stomach and leg, and back, had started to get better. The only places that really kept on hurting were my lower back and my ankle.

Q. Tell me about those.

A. Well my back would have these stabbing pains from time to time. It felt real stiff. My ankle was stiff. My ankle was still swollen, and I couldn't walk on it yet. Dr. Hoffman, my family doctor, had removed the cast about three weeks after the accident and I could start walking without crutches, but I was still limping and the ankle would get sore if I walked on it for any length of time.

Q. When did you see Dr. Hoffman?

A. My mom took me to Dr. Hoffman about three weeks after the accident. He checked me out, removed the soft cast from my ankle, and told me it was okay to start walking around without the crutches if I could stand it.

Q. When did you stop using the crutches?

A. I stopped using them when I went back to work at the beginning of October.

Q. What did you see Dr. Franks, the chiropractor, for?

A. Well, my mom thought that going to a chiropractor might help my back and ankle. My back still hurt, and my ankle was still sore. She thought that it might be a good idea to get some physical therapy to see if that might help. That's why I went to Dr. Franks.

Q. How many times did you see Dr. Franks?

A. I went to him for the first time around October 1st. I went to see him maybe twice a week for the next couple of months.

Q. What kind of treatment did Dr. Franks perform?

A. He would give me physical therapy. That involved bending my back, stretching it, applying heat treatments, things like that. The same thing was true for the ankle.

Q. Did it help?

A. Yes. About two months later, maybe by Christmas, most of the stiffness and pain had gone away.

Q. From December 2013 to the present day, describe your physical condition.

Since the defendant's purpose is to minimize the extent and length of the pain, these questions are important. Again, they prevent later exaggeration.

The history of the plaintiff's treatments is, of course, available from the medical records, which the defendant will have before the deposition. Nonetheless, these questions test the witness' recall and propensity to exaggerate.

A. It's better. I still have pain from time to time in my back and ankle.

Q. When do you get the pain there?

A. Well, it depends on how much or how hard I work. The more I work the more likely I am to get those pains.

Q. How often do you get those pains?

A. It's maybe once a week for an hour or two, usually at the end of the work day.

Q. When was the last time you took Tylenol with codeine?

A. I took that stuff for maybe six weeks.

Q. Did you ever take any painkillers other than Tylenol with codeine?

A. I sometimes take aspirin when I get these pains.

Q. Other than what you've told me about, do you have any other injuries or problems that you feel were caused by this accident?

A. No, you pretty much covered it.

Q. Mr. Jones, let's talk about some of the bills involved here. First the medical bills. Your interrogatory answers show that the bills from Doctors Hospital, Dr. Lang, Dr. Hoffman, and Dr. Franks have all been paid. Who paid those bills?

A. I'm not sure. I know they were paid by my health insurance. I think my mother paid the Walgreen pharmacy bill.

Q. Who paid for the wristwatch repair?

A. My mom paid that. I'm supposed to pay her back.

Q. You claim college books expenses in the amount of $162. Tell us about that.

A. Well, I was a part time student at Glendale Community College. I had already bought the books for the two courses I was taking. When I got injured, I couldn't take the courses I signed up for.

Q. Did you lose any tuition money?

A. No. The college said since I got hurt it wouldn't charge me for the courses I signed up for.

Q. How much income did you lose as a result of this accident?

A. I get paid $700 a month salary from Devo Florist. I went back to work October 1, 2013. The way I figure it, I lost one month's salary, or $700.

These questions effectively limit the damages.

g. Expenses and lost income

While the fact that most of the bills have been paid by insurance is not admissible at trial, it will have some effect on the settlement picture.

Q. The $700 is your gross income, isn't it?

A. Yes.

Q. What's your take-home pay?

A. We get paid on the first and fifteenth of the month. My take-home for half a month is about $270.

Q. Mr. Jones, let's talk about how this accident happened. Describe the vehicle you were driving.

A. It's a 2006 Toyota Corolla four-door. I bought it when I got out of the service. It was in really good shape, because I took good care of it.

Q. Is the title to that car in your name?

A. Yes.

Q. The accident happened around 2:00 P.M.?

A. Yes.

Q. At the time of the accident, where were you coming from?

A. I was coming from work at the flower shop.

Q. Where is that flower shop located?

A. On 40th Street and Thomas Road.

Q. 40th Street is the north-south street, correct?

A. Yes.

Q. Where is the flower shop in relation to the intersection?

A. It's not right at the corner. It's on 40th Street maybe 300 feet south of Thomas.

Q. Which side of 40th Street is the flower shop on?

A. It's on the east side.

Q. Tell me how you went from the flower shop north on 40th Street.

A. My car was parked in the lot next to the flower shop. When I got out of work, I pulled out of the lot and started going north on 40th Street.

Q. Describe what 40th Street looks like.

A. It's a pretty wide street. It has three lanes of traffic in each direction. In addition, it has left-turn lanes at the major intersections.

Q. There are traffic lights at the corner of 40th Street and Thomas, right?

A. Yes.

Q. Where are they located?

A. I think there's one at each corner and on the median strips.

h.   The accident

Note that here the questioner has saved the accident as the last topic. Some lawyers save the most important part of a deposition for the end, on the theory that the lawyer then has a better "feel" for the witness and the witness' guard will be down by that time.

These scene description questions are useful to see how effectively the plaintiff can describe the scene, and are good questions to see how effective a trial witness he will make.

Q. How many lights face the northbound traffic on 40th Street?

A. Probably around three.

Q. When you pulled onto 40th Street, which lane did you pull into?

A. I got into the inside lane, right next to the median strip.

Q. Mr. Jones, when was the first time you looked at the traffic lights at the corner of 40th Street and Thomas?

A. When I first pulled onto 40th Street and got in the inside lane.

Q. How far were you from the intersection at that time?

A. I guess around 100 feet.

Q. How fast were you going at that time?

A. Maybe 20 or 25 miles per hour.

Q. What was the color of the traffic lights at that point?

A. Green.

Q. What happened as you went northbound on 40th Street?

A. Well, it all happened really quickly. As I went north, the light turned yellow just before I got into the intersection. I was going through the intersection on the yellow light when suddenly I got smashed by another car from the driver's side.

Q. How long had the light been yellow at the time the other car collided with you?

A. It couldn't have been more than two or three seconds.

Q. How fast were you going when you were hit?

A. Maybe 25 or 30 miles per hour.

Q. Did you ever see the car that hit you before the impact?

A. Not really. I first saw it just before it was about to smash into me. It couldn't have been more than 10 or 15 feet from me. Before I could even put on my brakes, the car hit me.

Q. Tell us what happened from the moment the two cars hit?

A. Well, I remember putting on my brakes, I kind of skidded in the intersection, and the other car seemed to be stuck against the side of my car. I can remember getting bounced around inside the car and

This is a useful answer since he was only about three seconds from the intersection before he looked at the lights.

This answer is also useful since it suggests that the plaintiff was not paying much attention as he entered the intersection.

Note how the questions become more specific. The questioner's purpose now is to "pin down" the witness to specific facts.

smashing my head and chest against the inside of the car and the steering wheel.

Q. Were you wearing a seat belt at that time?

A. No.

Q. Did your car have seat belts?

A. Yes.

This is important, since in some jurisdictions this fact is admissible to show plaintiff's own negligence or failure to prevent damages.

Q. What happened when your car came to a stop?

A. I was pretty much numb. I can remember people coming up to me when I was in the car telling me not to move. I wasn't going to move anyway. I just hurt all over. I don't know how long it was, but after a while an ambulance came and they got me out of the car and put me on a stretcher.

Q. Mr. Jones, just before the impact, describe exactly what you were doing.

A. Well, I remember starting into the intersection. Since the light was yellow, I remember looking to the right to make sure that there weren't any cars taking a turn that might get in my way. I just looked to my right and then looked back up the road, then I saw the other car coming from my left just before it crashed into me.

Q. Did you ever put on your brakes before the impact?

A. No, I don't think so, there wasn't time to react.

Q. Mr. Jones, is there anything you remember about how this accident happened that you haven't told me about this afternoon?

A. No, nothing that comes to mind. I think I've pretty much told you everything.

Q. That's all the questions I have at this time. Do you have any questions, Ms. Johnson?

Ms. Johnson: No.

Mr. Sharp: Will you waive signature?

Ms. Johnson: No, we'll read and sign.

Some lawyers always ask this kind of question, since it's potential impeachment if the plaintiff "remembers" more at trial.

(The deposition was concluded at 3:06 P.M.)

The party deponent should not waive signature, since he should review the transcript for accuracy.

Note that the plaintiff's lawyer asked no questions. This is the usual practice, unless the party gave incorrect or confusing answers that need to be corrected or clarified.

Note also that the plaintiff's lawyer made no objections during the deposition. The questions were proper, so objections were unnecessary. The lawyer did not make objections for the purpose of coaching the plaintiff on desired responses, which is ethically questionable conduct in which some lawyers unfortunately engage.

The court reporter must arrange a meeting with the deponent so he can review the transcript, note any claimed inaccuracies, and sign the transcript. Any claimed inaccuracies are usually put on a separate sheet and attached to the transcript.

State of Arizona | SS.
Country of Maricopa |

    The foregoing deposition was taken before me, Mary Ryan, a Notary Public in the Country of Maricopa, State of Arizona. The witness was duly sworn by me to testify to the truth. The questions asked of the witness and the answers given by the witness were taken down by me in shorthand and reduced to typewriting under my direction. The deposition was submitted to the witness and read and signed. The foregoing pages are a true and accurate transcript of the entire proceedings taken during this deposition.

Dated: April 1, 2014

                Mary Ryan
                Notary Public

My commission expires on December 31, 2014.

UNITED STATES DISTRICT COURT
FOR THE DISTRICT OF ARIZONA

John Jones, 　　　　Plaintiff, 　　v. Susan Smith, 　　　　Defendant	No. 14 C 1000

NOTICE OF MOTION

TO:　Anne Johnson
　　　Attorney at Law
　　　100 Congress Street
　　　Phoenix, AZ 85001

PLEASE TAKE NOTICE that on June 10, 2014, at 9:00 A.M., or as soon as counsel can be heard, defendant in the above-captioned matter will present the attached Motion to Compel Discovery before the Hon. Joan Howe, Courtroom No. 4, United States Court House, Phoenix, Arizona.

As a professional courtesy, it's a good idea to call the opposing lawyer and let him know you're serving the motion.

Dated:　June 1, 2014

William Sharp

William Sharp
Attorney for Defendant
100 Broadway
Phoenix, AZ 85001
sharp@gmail.com
881-1000

UNITED STATES DISTRICT COURT
FOR THE DISTRICT OF ARIZONA

John Jones,
          Plaintiff,
          v.   No. 14 C 1000
Susan Smith,
          Defendant

MOTION TO COMPEL DISCOVERY

Pursuant to Rule 37 of the Federal Rules of Civil Procedure, Defendant moves for an order compelling plaintiff to answer in full interrogatories previously served on plaintiff. In support of her motion defendant states:

1. Defendant served interrogatories on plaintiff on February 1, 2014.

2. Plaintiff partially answered these interrogatories on February 25, 2014. Many of the answers are incomplete and do not provide the facts called for.

3. Plaintiff's answers to Interrogatory Nos. 2,4,10,11,13, and 14 stated that "answers may be supplemented as discovery and investigation continues."

4. To date plaintiff has neither supplemented his interrogatory answers nor advised defendant that no additional answers will be forthcoming, although defendant has requested, by telephone and letter, that plaintiff submit supplemental answers a letter sent to plaintiff's attorney is attached to this motion.

WHEREFORE, defendant requests the court to order plaintiff to serve supplemental interrogatory answers within 10 days and award reasonable expenses, including attorney's fees, incurred by defendant as a result of this motion.

Since over three months have passed since plaintiff served incomplete answers to interrogatories, this motion should be brought.

In many jurisdictions local rules require that a motion must be supplemented by a memorandum of points and authorities. In other jurisdictions this is done only for complicated or contested motions, such as for summary judgment. You should always show what efforts you have made to get compliance before filing the motion.

Rule 37(a)(1) requires a certification that the movant has in good faith conferred with the other party in an attempt to obtain the discovery.

Dated: <u>June 1, 2014</u>

<u>William Sharp</u>

William Sharp
Attorney for Defendant
100 Broadway
Phoenix, AZ 85001
sharp@gmail.com
881-1000

Note that Rule 37(a)(5) requires the court to award the reasonable costs incurred in being forced to bring this motion. This includes attorney's fees. Asking for perhaps $200-500 here would be reasonable.

AFFIDAVIT OF SERVICE

I, Helen Thompson, having been first duly sworn, state that I have served a copy of the attached Notice of Motion and Motion to Compel Discovery on plaintiff's attorney by mail at 100 Congress Street, Phoenix, Arizona 85001, on June 1, 2014.

<u>Helen Thompson</u>

Helen Thompson

Signed and sworn to before me on June 1, 2014.

<u>Mary Ryan</u>

Notary Public

My Commission expires on December 31, 2014.

[Seal]

UNITED STATES DISTRICT COURT
FOR THE DISTRICT OF ARIZONA

John Jones,
　　　　　Plaintiff,
　　v.　　　　　　　　　　No. 14 C 1000
Susan Smith,
　　　　　Defendant

REQUEST TO ADMIT FACTS
AND GENUINENESS OF DOCUMENTS

Pursuant to Rule 36 of the Federal Rules of Civil Procedure, Plaintiff requests Defendant to admit within 30 days after service the following facts and genuineness of documents:

1. Defendant was the owner of a 2009 Buick Skylark sedan on September 2, 2013.

2. Defendant was driving the 2009 Buick Skylark sedan when the collision occurred on September 2, 2013.

3. Defendant was a driver licensed by the State of Nevada at the time of collision.

4. Each of the following documents, attached as exhibits to this request, is genuine and a business record of the entity it purports to be from:

Exhibit No.	Description
1.	Phoenix Police Dept. accident report.
2.	Title and registration documents from Nevada Dept. of Transportation showing defendant to be the owner of a 2009 Buick Skylark sedan.
3.	Driver's license issued to defendant by the Nevada Dept. of Transportation.

Dated: June 1, 2014

Anne Johnson
Anne Johnson
Attorney for Plaintiff
100 Congress Street
Phoenix, AZ 85001
johnson@gmail.com
882-1000

If this case goes to trial, the plaintiff will need to establish basic facts. These requests cover facts that the defendant will probably not contest, and that will streamline the plaintiff's case during trial.

A proof of service must be attached.

UNITED STATES DISTRICT COURT
FOR THE DISTRICT OF ARIZONA

John Jones,
          Plaintiff,
          v.   No. 14 C 1000
Susan Smith,
          Defendant

DEFENDANT'S ANSWER TO PLAINTIFF'S REQUESTS TO ADMIT FACTS AND GENUINENESS OF DOCUMENTS

Defendant answers plaintiff's Requests for Admission of Facts and Genuineness of Documents as follows:

Request No. 1: Defendant was the owner of a 2009 Buick Skylark sedan on September 2, 2013.

Answer: Admits.

Request No. 2: Defendant was driving the 2009 Buick Skylark sedan when the collision occurred on September 2, 2013.

Answer: Admits.

Request No. 3: Defendant was a driver licensed by the State of Nevada at the time of the collision.

Answer: Admits.

Request No. 4: Each of the following documents, attached as exhibits to this request, is authentic and a business record of the entity it purports to be from:

Exhibit No.   *Description*

1.   Phoenix Police Dept. accident report.
2.   Title and registration documents from the Nevada Dept. of Transportation showing defendant to be the owner of 2009 Buick Skylark sedan.

Like interrogatories, the usual practice in answering is to set out both the request and the answer. This avoids confusion.

3.   Driver's license issued to defendant by the Nevada Dept. of Transportation.

<u>Answer:</u> Admits.

Dated: <u>June 20, 2014</u>

William Sharp

William Sharp
Attorney for Defendant
100 Broadway
Phoenix, AZ 85001
sharp@gmail.com
881-1000

A proof of service must
be attached.

UNITED STATES DISTRICT COURT
FOR THE DISTRICT OF ARIZONA

John Jones,
          Plaintiff,
     v.   No. 14 C 1000
Susan Smith,
          Defendant

OFFER OF JUDGMENT

Pursuant to Rule 68 of the Federal Rules of Civil Procedure, defendant offers to allow judgment to be taken against her in the amount of **THIRTY THOUSAND DOLLARS ($30,000.00)**, and costs of suit incurred to the date of this offer.

This offer is being made under Rule 68 of the Federal Rules of Civil Procedure and Rule 408 of the Federal Rules of Evidence.

By this time defendant has sufficient facts to assess the case's settlement value. The offer of judgment will put additional pressure on the plaintiff to consider a realistic settlement.

Dated: August 1, 2014

William Sharp

William Sharp
Attorney for Defendant
100 Broadway
Phoenix, AZ 85001
sharp@gmail.com
881-1000

A proof of service must be attached.

UNITED STATES DISTRICT COURT
FOR THE DISTRICT OF ARIZONA

John Jones,
            Plaintiff,
        v.   No. 14 C 1000
Susan Smith,
            Defendant

MOTION FOR ORDER TO COMPEL

Defendant moves under Rule 35 of the Federal Rules of Civil Procedure for an order compelling plaintiff to submit to a physical examination. In support of her motion defendant states:

1. Plaintiff's physical condition is genuinely in controversy since the complaint alleges a variety of physical injuries.

2. Plaintiff during his deposition stated that he still suffers from the consequences of the accident that is the basis for his complaint. These include periodic pain in his back and ankle.

3. There exists good cause, in light of the above, for a physical examination of the plaintiff to evaluate the plaintiff's current physical condition and prognosis.

4. Rudolf B. Anton, M.D., a board certified neurologist, has agreed to examine and evaluate the plaintiff at his medical office located at 4401 North Scottsdale Road, Scottsdale, Arizona, on September 15, 2014, at 5:00 P.M., or at another time, as directed by this court.

WHEREFORE, defendant requests that the court enter an order directing the plaintiff to be examined on the terms set forth above.

Dated: September 1, 2014

William Sharp

William Sharp
Attorney for Defendant
100 Broadway
Phoenix, AZ 85001
sharp@gmail.com
881-1000

Since plaintiff has not accepted the offer of judgment, defendant must continue her trial preparations. Getting a current evaluation of the plaintiff's medical condition and prognosis from a physician who has not previously seen the plaintiff is vital.

A proof of service must be attached.

UNITED STATES DISTRICT COURT
FOR THE DISTRICT OF ARIZONA

John Jones,
          Plaintiff,
          v.   No. 14 C 1000
Susan Smith,
          Defendant

JOINT PRETRIAL MEMORANDUM

Plaintiff and defendant submit the following joint pretrial memorandum:

Judges frequently have instructions on what the memorandum should contain and how it should be organized.

I   Jurisdiction

Jurisdiction of the court is based on diversity of citizenship under 28 U.S.C. §1332. Plaintiff is a citizen of Arizona. Defendant is a citizen of Nevada. The amount in controversy exceeds the sum of seventy-five thousand ($75,000) dollars, exclusive of interest and costs.

II   Uncontested Facts

Plaintiff Jones and defendant Smith were involved in a vehicle collision on September 2, 2013. The collision occurred at the intersection of 40th Street and Thomas Road in Phoenix, Arizona, at approximately 2:00 P.M. At the time of the collision Jones was driving his car, a 2006 Toyota Corolla four-door sedan, northbound on 40th Street; Smith was driving her car, a 2009 Buick Skylark sedan, eastbound on Thomas Road. The intersection is controlled by traffic lights.

On September 2, 2013, Jones was employed as a delivery driver by Devo Wholesale Florist and was being paid gross wages of $700 per month.

Jones received various physical injuries as a result of the collision. He missed one month's

These facts have all been admitted in the pleadings or during discovery.

work and wages from his job. His medical bills to date total $2,717.14. His vehicle repair costs totaled $1,213.00 His other out-of-pocket expenses totaled $237.00.

III   <u>Contested Issues of Fact and Law</u>

1. Did Smith run a red light?
2. Did Jones run a red light?
3. Was Smith negligent?
4. Was Jones negligent?
5. If both Smith and Jones were negligent, what is the degree of negligence of each of them?
6. What were the extent of Jones' injuries as a result of this collision?
7. What are Jones' reasonable damages?

IV   <u>Exhibits</u>

A. *Plaintiff Jones'*   *Objections, if any*
   Exhibits

1.	Doctors Hospital records	None.
2.	Dr. Lang's office records	None.
3.	Dr. Hoffman's office records	None.
4.	Dr. Franks' office records	None.
5.	All bills for above	None.
6.	X rays taken by above	None.
7.	Devo Wholesale Florist employment records	None.
8.	Phoenix Police Dept. reports	Objection, for reasons stated in attached memorandum.

If any evidence is objected to, the judge may rule on the objections, if possible to do so, during the pretrial conference.

9. Accident scene photographs	None.	If objections are made, the objecting party
10. Jack's Auto Repair records and bill	None.	should state the basis for the objection, with
11. Watch repair bill	None.	supporting citations if
12. Glendale Community College bills	None.	necessary.
13. Walgreen's pharmacy bill	None.	
14. Accident scene diagrams	None.	

B. *Defendant Smith's*   *Objections, if any*
    Exhibits

1. Plaintiff's hospital and
   medical records   None.
2. Rudolf Anton, M.D.,
   medical records   None.
3. Accident scene
   photographs   None.
4. Accident scene   Objection,
   diagrams   misleading.
5. Phoenix Police Dept.
   reports to extent
   admissible   None.

V Witnesses

A. *Plaintiff Jones' Witnesses*
    1. Plaintiff
    2. Carol Brown, 42 East Cambridge
       Street, Phoenix
    3. Mary Porter, 42 East Cambridge
       Street, Phoenix
    4. Dr. Lang
    5. Dr. Hoffman
    6. Dr. Franks
    7. Diane Devo, Devo Wholesale Florist
    8. John Jones, Sr., and Mary Jones,
       plaintiff's parents
    9. Officer Steven Pitcher, Phoenix
       Police Dept.
    10. Defendant
    11. Personnel from Jack's Auto Repair,
        to qualify exhibits
    12. Personnel from above hospitals and
        physicians, to qualify exhibits

B. *Defendant Smith's Witnesses:*
1. All of plaintiff's witnesses
2. Dr. Rudolf Anton

VI   Jury Instructions

Plaintiff's and defendant's proposed jury instructions are attached.

    1. Plaintiff objects to defendant instruction nos. 6, 7, and 9, for the reasons stated in plaintiff's attached memorandum.

    2. Defendant objects to plaintiff instruction nos. 2, 3, 4, and 6, for the reasons stated in defendant's attached memorandum.

RESPECTFULLY SUBMITTED,

Date: <u>November 1, 2014</u>

Pretrial memoranda frequently also contain a memorandum of law from each party that discusses any legal issues that the judge will need to resolve before or during trial.

Anne Johnson

Anne Johnson
Attorney for Plaintiff

William Sharp

William Sharp
Attorney for Defendant

The judge's final pretrial order will usually track the language and organization of the memorandum and contain all rulings on admissibility issues that were made at the conference.

RELEASE

In consideration of the sum of thirty-six thousand dollars ($36,000), which plaintiff acknowledges receiving, Plaintiff John Jones agrees to release Defendant Susan Smith and her heirs, survivors, agents, and personal representatives from all claims, suits, or actions in any form or on any basis, because of anything that was done or not done at any time, on account of the following:

All claims for personal injuries, property damage, physical disabilities, medical expenses, lost income, and all other claims that have been or could be brought, including all claims now known or that in the future might be known, which arise out of an occurrence on or about September 2, 2013, at 40th Street and Thomas Road, in Phoenix, Arizona, when plaintiff claims to have sustained injuries as a result of a collision between an automobile driven by plaintiff and an automobile driven by defendant.

As a result of this collision plaintiff has brought suit against defendant for damages. Defendant has denied both liability and the claimed extent of damages. This release is a compromise settlement between Plaintiff John Jones and Defendant Susan Smith.

This agreement is a release and shall operate as a total discharge of any claims plaintiff has or may have, arising out the above occurrence, against this defendant and any other persons.

Plaintiff John Jones and Defendant Susan Smith also agree to terminate any actions that have been filed, particularly a claim by this plaintiff against this defendant currently filed as civil action No. 14 C 1000 in the United States District Court for the District of Arizona, in Phoenix, Arizona. Plaintiff and defendant agree to execute a Stipulation of Dismissal, with prejudice, and file it with the Clerk of the above Court, thereby terminating that action in

A release would be the standard way of settling this case, since it is a complete settlement by all the parties.

its entirety, within five days of the execution of this agreement.

Date: <u>December 1, 2014</u>

<u>John Jones</u>
John Jones

The parties, not their lawyers, must sign the release.

<u>Susan Smith</u>
Susan Smith, Defendant

UNITED STATES DISTRICT COURT
FOR THE DISTRICT OF ARIZONA

John Jones,
          Plaintiff,
          v.   No. 14 C 1000
Susan Smith,
          Defendant

STIPULATION OF DISMISSAL

Plaintiff John Jones and Defendant Susan Smith agree to dismiss this action with prejudice, and each party will bear its costs and attorney's fees.

The stipulation of dismissal terminates the lawsuit. No court order is necessary.

Dated: December 2, 2014

Anne Johnson
Anne Johnson
Attorney for Plaintiff

William Sharp
William Sharp
Attorney for Defendant

INDEX